FRANCES ABINGTON as Thalia, the Comic Muse by Reynolds

# A BIOGRAPHICAL DICTIONARY

OF

ACTORS, ACTRESSES, MUSICIANS, DANCERS, MANAGERS & OTHER STAGE PERSONNEL IN LONDON, 1660 - 1800

*Volume* 1: Abaco *to* Belfille

*by*

PHILIP H. HIGHFILL, JR., KALMAN A. BURNIM

*and*

EDWARD A. LANGHANS

SOUTHERN ILLINOIS UNIVERSITY PRESS

CARBONDALE AND EDWARDSVILLE

FOR

MOLLY
VERNA
FRANCES

# *Preface*

THE PURPOSE of these volumes is to provide brief biographical notices of all persons who were members of theatrical companies or occasional performers or were patentees or servants of the patent theatres, opera houses, amphitheatres, pleasure gardens, theatrical taverns, music rooms, fair booths, and other places of public entertainment in London and its immediate environs from the Restoration of Charles II in 1660 until the end of the season 1799–1800.

The authors recognize the impossibility of achieving this end. No one knows precisely how many people were engaged in entertaining the London public during these 140 years. We have found at least some information on probably more than 8,500 individuals. We hope that this information will be augmented when our entries are seen by specialists in eighteenth-century theatre and drama; but it is not likely that the number of persons now known surely or conjectured fairly to have been connected with theatrical enterprises in this period will ever be increased considerably.

We have included actors and actresses, dancers, singers, instrumental musicians, scene painters, machinists, management officials, prompters, acrobats, contortionists, pyrotechnists, magicians, dwarfs, freaks, animal trainers, strong men, public orators, mimics, dressers, callers, concessionaires, and also members of certain trades operating on salary and within the physical confines of the theatres—such employees as tailors, carpenters, and barbers.

Our definition excludes the hordes of amateur actors stricken with the *cacoethes ludendi*, declaiming in the "spouting clubs" and posturing in private theatricals (though we record the involvement of professionals in these entertainments). Neither have we admitted the many dramatic authors who, for pelf and publicity, acted in their own plays, unless they were at some time *bona fide* actors in addition to being playwrights. (Non-acting authors as a theatrical class have been denied admission for reasons obvious to anyone who will consider the bibliographical and critical implications of their inclusion.) Finally, we have excluded a few amateurs who were allowed to play prominent roles at benefits given them in compassion to some distress—being widowed, orphaned, or threatened with debtors' gaol, rendered destitute by acts of God, or being physically disabled. It will suffice to give one rather striking example, that of "Dr. Clancy, who is *Blind*," as the playbill announced, and who played Tiresias, the blind prophet in *Oedipus, King of Thebes* at Drury Lane on 2 April 1744:

This Gentleman being deprived of the Advantages of following his profession, and as the writing he had produced for the stage could not be brought out this season, the Master of the Playhouse has been so kind as to favour him with a Benefit Night: It is therefore hoped, that as this will be the first instance of any person laboring under so heavy a deprivation, performing on the stage, the *Novelty,* as well as the *Unhappyness of his case,* will engage the favour and protection of a BRITISH AUDIENCE.

There were also professionals among the dancers and musicians who were very closely related to the life of the theatres but who are not represented because they never performed. Principally these were teachers. A good example would be "Mr. Cavellier [Caverley], Master of the Boarding-School in Queen Square" when he died in October 1745 at age 104. He had taught generations of stage dancers, including Kellom Tomlinson, but he never was on stage.

We have provided information about several hundred Restoration Court musicians, most of whom are not recorded in *Grove's Dictionary of Music and Musicians*.[1] There is ample proof that some of these people also performed, usually with (but occasionally without) royal permission, at public concerts and theatres; but for many we find no certain evidence of performances away from the Court. Rather than consign these partially documented musicians to oblivion, we have included them, hoping that future research will bear out our conjecture that most Court employees, because their wages were so often in arrears, sought supplementary employment.

Though we have recorded equestrians at the amphitheatres, sporting figures such as pugilists and swordsmen are not listed unless they appeared onstage in some regular dramatic performance or as a subsidiary part of a bill which was predominantly dramatic or musical in nature. We have allowed entry to a few animals which performed, like the monkey General Jackoo, Moustache the Marvelous Poodle, and Nippotate the Tame Hedgehog. But we have excluded anonymous *fauna* like Costello's dogs. We have excluded "sleeping partners" —people who provided financial backing but were neuters so far as the active direction of production was concerned (like Congreve at the Queen's Theatre) —as well as financial partners who briefly attempted more active management of affairs but who were prevented from interfering by their professional partners (Rutherford, Dagge, Leake, and Mrs Powell, for example, in the early troubled years of Colman's management at Covent Garden).

Selection of matter for inclusion in each entry has been difficult, and we have followed no rules more invariable than those imposed by the general principles of accuracy, usefulness, and interest. There are hundreds of people about whom we know very little. For some of these almost every fact that we have found has been set down in the hope that later identification may be assisted. From these virtual anonyms on up to the celebrities about whom far more is known than is convenient to include in a compendium, each of our individuals required a different treatment.

The ideal entry should perhaps contain: date and place of births, christening, marriages, death, and burial, and inclusive dates and places of residences and of careers; information about spouses and children; first and last appearance; involvement in notable occurrences onstage; habitual "lines" of character; assessments of professional worth from respectable contemporary reviews; salaries; pseudonyms; theatrical offices; associations and liaisons; clubs; honors; other occupations; and creative contributions, including writing, painting, choreography, and musical composition. For very few of our subjects, of course, can information in even a majority of the applicable categories be provided. An effort has been made to follow many British performers to foreign engagements and into the nineteenth century, but we do not claim exhaustive treatment for foreign performers or for those whose careers were principally outside our terminal dates.

We hope that we have been restrained in our employment of anecdotes, which are abundant and, often, apocryphal. It has sometimes been necessary to report a good but fictitious story of widespread currency in order to impeach it. Separating an actor from his legends is, after all, a delicate and painful operation not only because some excellent stories may be true but because most are at least illustrative of traits of character and thus possess some inner truthfulness. Fortunately or not, this matter has usually been decided for us by our policy of writing entries as brief as has seemed compatible with thorough treatment.

The authors have combed every source that ingenuity could suggest. We have canvassed the many repositories cited in the expressions of gratitude near the end of these remarks. The titles which relate to our period in the revised Lowe's *Bibliography*[2] have been investigated. The indispensable *London Stage, 1660–1800*[3] has been sifted for actors' roles and comment. Published biographies and diaries of dozens of non-theatrical people have been read. We have scaled mountains of manuscripts: letters, memoirs, diaries, theatrical account books, parish registers, wills, and Lord Chamberlain's records. We have inspected numerous collections of London, provincial British, American, and continental playbills and newspaper notices of performances, and numbers of annotated scrapbooks, extra-illustrated volumes, original paintings, and engravings. We have made levy also on local histories, official surveys, maps, contemporaneous poetry, periodical essays, sales catalogues, plays, critical works, genealogies, rate books, and ships' lists.

The names in our files have been filtered through the published registers of parishes contiguous to the London and Westminster theatrical districts, and those of Westminster Abbey, St Paul's Cathedral, St George,

Hanover Square, St Marylebone, and Bath Abbey. Many individuals and families have been sought through manuscript registers in London, and in Dublin, Edinburgh, and provincial English towns. The search through parish registers is far from complete, even for London, but it cannot be brought nearer completeness without the indexing and publication of a great many more registers.

We have found wills and official administrations of property for many hundreds of our subjects. Vital information has come from the unpublished archives of various professional societies and guilds and from the records, both published and unpublished, of British and Irish colleges, universities, and clubs. Selfless scholars have given us the results of their own investigations.

For reasons besides expense we have decided not to include either bibliographies appended to the entries or a cumulative bibliography. Individual lists would be foolishly repetitive because of the constant citation of certain sources (for example *The London Stage*, the *Public Advertiser*, the *Monthly Mirror*, the parish registers published by the Harleian Society), and they would be of little help because some of the sources are so large and amorphous (the Burney newspaper clippings, the Winston and Kemble jottings). In most entries we have provided in the text itself as much citation as has seemed necessary. So far as printed theatrical sources are concerned, a cumulative bibliography would have been an expensive redundancy indeed so soon after the publication of the revised Lowe.

Like all biographers and historians, we have placed greatest reliance on firsthand factual evidence, particularly from any legal or quasi-legal *locus*: sworn courtroom testimony, legal depositions, wills, parish registers, and theatrical account books. Nearly as credible are diaries, letters, and annotated playbills. Epitaphs are fairly trustworthy and so is necrology published in periodicals soon after the event (though

---

1. Edited by Eric Blom (9 vols; London: MacMillan and Co., Ltd., 1954; with a Supplementary Volume edited by Eric Blom and Denis Stevens, 1961).

2. James Fullerton Arnott and John William Robinson, eds., *English Theatrical Literature 1559–1900 a Bibliography, incorporating Robert W. Lowe's A Bibliographical Account of English Theatrical Literature published in 1888* (London: The Society for Theatre Research, 1970).

3. Pt I: 1660–1700 ed. William VanLennep; Pt II: 1700–1729 ed. Emmett Avery; Pt III: 1729–1747 ed. Arthur H. Scouten; Pt IV: 1747–1776 ed. George Winchester Stone, Jr; Pt V: 1776–1800 ed. Charles Beecher Hogan (Carbondale: Southern Illinois University Press, 1961–70).

occasionally we find actors indignantly correcting reports of their deaths). Somewhat murkier are the memoirs. In employing these we have had to make a careful analysis of motive and wide allowance for the vagaries of aging memory before granting credence. In every critique of performance the possibility of bias has been considered, particularly if the criticism was current — for, if encomiastic, it may have been a puff written or inspired by an interested manager or, if pejorative, a libel paid for by a jealous rival. Yet criticism has to be current to be meaningful, for as Dr William Mavor observed in *The British Nepos* (1798), "the transient beauties of dramatic acting have no 'local habitation'; they blaze, and expire in an instant. The spectator can scarcely fix them in his memory; and posterity can form no idea of them, except from the effects they are recorded to have produced." The observation is of course as valid for most dancers and musicians.

We hope that we have brought enough imaginative skepticism to our task to discriminate fact from attractive myth. We have tried to keep the constant temptation to conjecture within reasonable bounds; and we have stated as true only those details which are verifiable.

It is no part of the authors' intention to serve as more than general or occasional critics of those numerous creative contributions which our people made — their music, painting, choreography, and dramatic and other literary works — and which survive for inspection. For not only do we lack special competency in some of the arts which our subjects practised, but to examine attentively more than occasional representative examples would swell our work to dropsical proportions and extend our labours inordinately.

Yet, for each of the performers who wrote we have attempted a complete listing of *oeuvres*, drawing on the *Cambridge Bibliography of English Literature*, the check-lists in Allardyce Nicoll's *A History of English Drama, 1660–1900*,[4] the late Father Carl Stratman's *Bibliography of English Printed Tragedy, 1565–1900*,[5] and many and various specialized bibliographies. In addition, however, we have made fresh contributions from hundreds of obscure sources, and we have corrected information previously printed and have called attention to manuscripts unpublished.

Several specialized works, devoted to the examination of one or another class of theatrical persons, have given us vital assistance. Yet we have been able to supplement technical information provided by each of them as well as to give new and significant biographical detail. We may cite as prominent examples the notes on theatrical scenery and painters by Miss Sybil Rosenfeld and Mr Edward Croft-Murray,[6] to which we have gone gratefully and often, and the admirable census of British puppeteers by Mr George Speaight.[7]

We have found it difficult to decide what kinds of data to include about the more prominent musicians. Many gifted composers, both British and continental, were also performers in London at one time or another: Abel, Arne, Arnold, J. C. Bach, Boyce, Clementi, Handel, Haydn, Mozart, Pepusch, the Purcells — to name a few of the better-known. We are not musicologists, nor are we critical bibliographers of music. Some of the more famous musicians have been the beneficiaries of excellent recent full-length studies, with appended bibliographies; and many of the better-known ones are treated with admirable thoroughness in the excellent fifth edition of *Grove's Dictionary of Music and Musicians*, to which we are thankfully beholden. (Our readers should always go to Grove for technical information and that musical bibliography which we do not furnish.) Furthermore, many foreign-born musicians came to London late in their careers and many stayed there for short periods only. We have decided, in view of these facts, to provide for each of the figures who appear in Grove a full life-sketch, but one which emphasizes theatrical and musical activity in London, with whatever additions and corrections to both canon and life we have been able to verify. We may say, however, that our inspections of early biographical dictionaries and manuscripts and especially our searches in parish registers, wills, the Sainsbury correspondence in Glasgow, and the hitherto largely unexploited records of the Royal Society of Musicians and the London Guild of Musicians, have given us massive amounts of fresh information about quite important secondary musical figures and about the corps of journeymen instrumentalists and singers in the places of public entertainment whose activities are nowhere else recorded.

The iconography may prove a useful feature. We have gone beyond embellishment of the text (which involves the publication of some 1400 likenesses through our projected 12 volumes—at least one picture of each of our subjects for whom a portrait exists) to attempt to list all original portraits any knowledge of which is now recoverable. We have tried to ascertain the present location of portraits in every medium by either visiting or writing to many hundreds of galleries and collections or by recourse to catalogues. We claim for our efforts in this direction neither completeness nor much authority, for not only has the yield from correspondence been meager but we have not been able to examine many of the pictures reported to us. Thus we must cautiously qualify the information kindly furnished about identification and provenance by those of our correspondents who replied affirmatively. A variety of catalogues (such as those of J. F. Kerslake [8] and Lillian A. Hall [9]) have assisted us in our efforts to find portraits.

We have used two criteria to select engravings for reproduction: faithfulness to the original (when this was ascertainable) and interest of pose, role, or dress. There were some excellent engravers during the period who limned actors and dramatists for the popular periodicals with skill, but there were some poor ones, too. The poetess and critic Anna Seward, for instance, wrote her fellow author Edward Jerningham in the late 1790's about the shortcomings of the illustrations to a prominent journal of theatrical biography:

> I am glad you do not like that vulgar insensible Block in the Monthly Mirror, who stares upon the page, & calls itself *me*, tho' it has not even the lineaments of my face, & features. Shewn to my Servants, with the name concealed, not one of them cou'd guess for whom it was designed.[10]

Many actors, managers, dancers, and musicians could have voiced the same complaint. Still, inferior engravings are sometimes all that survive to suggest the features of popular performers. We have tried to collect for reproduction in our volumes as many faithful reflections as we could.

Diligence alone will not produce any work of scope and complexity. We have had the extreme good fortune to be the beneficiaries of the generosity of the very people and institutions who could contribute most usefully to our cause. We have been assisted in our long adventure by more

4. Fourth edition (Cambridge: at the University Press, 1955–59).

5. (Carbondale: Southern Illinois University Press, 1966).

6. "A Checklist of Scene Painters Working in Great Britain and Ireland in the 18th Century," *Theatre Notebook,* XIX, XX (1964, 1965).

7. *The History of the English Puppet Theatre* (London: George G. Harrap and Co., Ltd., 1955).

8. *Catalogue of Theatrical Portraits in London Public Collections* (London: Society for Theatre Research, 1961).

9. *Catalogue of Dramatic Portraits in the Theatre Collection of the Harvard College Library.* 4 vols. (Cambridge, Massachusetts: Harvard University Press, 1930).

10. Huntington Library MS JE 768.

smiling faces and helping hands than we can acknowledge by name.

Of the many who have sustained us with encouragement, advice, friendship, and information, none stand further forward in our affectionate remembrance than our teachers, especially Professor Dougald MacMillan and Professor Alois Nagler, who set our feet firmly on this path.

The authors are deeply grateful to Dr Louis B. Wright, Director Emeritus of the Folger Shakespeare Library. He threw open to us the immense resources of the Library, on which we have drawn through every phase of the investigation and writing, and he provided for seventeen years secure storage for our massive records. We also thank Dr Wright for kindness in his capacity as Chairman of the Committee of Selection of the Guggenheim Foundation and for his decisive testimony in our behalf to other sources of assistance. But we are chiefly thankful for the support of his friendship and advice for over twenty years. For the innumerable courtesies of Dr O. B. Hardison, the present Director of the Folger Library, and of the Associate Director and sometime Acting Director Dr Philip Knachel, we also make warm acknowledgment.

To Miss Helen Willard, Curator Emeritus of the Harvard Theatre Collection, we owe a great debt for the patience and courtesy with which over many years we have been received at that splendid treasury. We are especially grateful for permission to photograph some hundreds of pictures.

To Mr George W. Nash, Curator of the Enthoven Collection in the Victoria and Albert Museum, we give hearty thanks for guidance in the use of that rich repository and for his personal interest and thoughtfulness in advancing our project.

We are deeply indebted to Mr James Cunningham, Mr W. Henry Chace, and other officials of the Genealogical Society of the Church of Jesus Christ of Latter-Day Saints in Salt Lake City, and to the Church itself, for access to the magnificent collection of filmed British manuscript records in the Society's archives, particularly the wills. We express thanks also to the President of the Court of the Admiralty and the officials of the Principal Probate Register and of the Literary Room, Somerset House, London, where we worked and from which the wills in Salt Lake City also proceeded.

Our especial thanks go also to the Secretary of the Royal Society of Musicians for permission to draw extensively upon the Society's records.

To the Trustees of the British Museum and to Sir Frank Francis, its Director Emeritus, we owe our gratitude for the fruits of our many visits to that unparalleled institution.

We are much indebted to the Trustees of the Garrick Club and to Sir Julian Hall, the Secretary, for the use of various documents and pictures in the possession of the Club.

The unselfish cooperation of our colleagues in theatrical scholarship has saved us many months of work. From the beginning of our study, the editors of *The London Stage, 1660–1800* gave unstinted assistance and valuable advice. Like all students of the period, we are vastly indebted to their published discoveries. But, in addition, long before publication of their several volumes, Professor George Winchester Stone and Professor Arthur H. Scouten donated an extensive initial list of names from their notes; the late Professor Emmett L. Avery provided us with copies of an extensive index he was undertaking; Mr Charles Beecher Hogan astonished us by graciously providing for our use his card file of biographical data on great numbers of London and provincial performers.

We make grateful acknowledgment to Professor Ben R. Schneider, Jr., Director of *The London Stage* Information Bank, for making available to us computer printouts of many performers' roles.

Professor John Harold Wilson turned

over to us his notebooks, the distillation of years of his careful scholarship. Miss Sybil Rosenfeld allowed us to take data from her manuscript on the York theatre. Miss Kathleen M. A. Barker provided us with extensive and invaluable information about London actors in Bristol. Professor Hubert Heffner gave us valuable data on early American actors. Professor George Tuttle opened to us his files on the Royal Circus. Professor George Kahrl turned over to us, long before publication of his edition of the Garrick letters, the manuscript of that work.

This project has enjoyed large financial support. Without the generous contributions of the following foundations and institutions, our bark would have foundered early in the voyage:

We express our deep gratitude to the Trustees of the John Simon Guggenheim Foundation and to its successive Directors, Mr Henry Allen Moe and Mr Gordon N. Ray, for fellowships awarded Mr Highfill and Mr Burnim. To the Trustees and successive Directors of the Folger Shakespeare Library, Dr Louis B. Wright and Dr O. B. Hardison, we are indebted for several summer fellowships and grants-in-aid. In addition, Mr Highfill wishes to express his gratitude for a lengthy half-time appointment as Consultant in Literature and for a Senior Fellowship at the Library.

We are extremely grateful to the Trustees and officers of the National Foundation for the Arts and Humanities for two munificent grants to the partnership, providing for time and travel.

We thank the *Washington Evening Star* for a generous fellowship grant to Mr Highfill.

We are obliged to the Trustees and to the Director Emeritus of the Henry E. Huntington Library, Dr John Pomfret, for a summer grant to Mr Highfill.

We thank the American Council of Learned Societies for a generous grant to Mr Burnim.

Finally, we are indebted to the Trustees,

Presidents, and faculty research funds of the George Washington University, the University of Rochester, Tufts University, and the University of Hawaii for many and large grants over the years and for several sabbatical leaves and leaves of absence.

For valuable assistance with books and manuscripts at various times over the years we owe thanks to the following: Mr John Alden of the Boston Public Library; Miss Dorothy Bridgewater of the Yale University Library; Miss Beth Browne of the University of Edinburgh Library; Mr Alan Cohn of the Southern Illinois University Library; Mr Earle E. Coleman of the Princeton University Library; Mr Robert O. Dougan, Librarian, Henry E. Huntington Library; Mons Y. Duhamel of the Bibliothèque Municipale de Douai; Miss Mary Isabel Frye of the Henry E. Huntington Library; Miss Helen O. Hardy of the Claremont College Library; Mr John F. E. Hippel of the Edwin Forrest Home; Mr Anthony Latham of the Enthoven Collection, Victoria and Albert Museum; Miss Harriet C. Jameson of the University of Michigan Library; Mrs E. V. Lewis, Reference Librarian, Finsbury Public Library; Miss Macdougall of the Edinburgh Public Library; Mr John Russell Mason, Librarian Emeritus, Lisner Library, George Washington University; Miss R. N. Waveney Payne, Librarian of the Shakespeare Collection, Birmingham Public Library; Miss Jeanne Newlin of the Harvard Theatre Collection; Mr James Ritchie, Deputy Keeper of Manuscripts, the National Library of Scotland; Mr John R. Russell, Librarian Emeritus of the Rush Rees Library, University of Rochester; Mr R. A. Sayce of the Worcester College Library; Miss Neda M. Westlake of the Van Pelt Library, University of Pennsylvania; Miss M. Y. Williams of the Minet Library, Lambeth Public Library, the Rev G. C. Taylor, Rector, and Mr P. H. Wheatland, Verger, St Giles in the Fields. Mr J. C. Morgan, Mr J. Ballantyne, and Miss M. Swarbrick, Westminster Public Library.

By far the greatest number of the portraits which we reproduce in these volumes comes from the prints and engravings in the Harvard Theatre Collection. For gracious permissions to reproduce original paintings in their possessions, or for important information or other assistance relating to pictures, we render thanks to the following persons: Her Majesty the Queen; Mr Keith R. Andrews, Keeper of Prints and Drawings, National Gallery of Scotland; the Earl of Bradford; Major A. S. C. Browne, D.L.; Mr T. E. Callander, Chief Librarian, Croydon Library; Mr Richard E. O. Cavendish; Mr M. Cormack, Fitzwilliam Museum, Cambridge; Mr Alec M. Cotman, Castle Museum, Norwich; Mr Perry B. Cott, Chief Curator, National Gallery of Art, Washington; Sir Francis Dashwood, Bart.; Mr F. G. Emmison, M. B. E., Essex County Archivist; the Marquess of Exeter; Mr David Gerard, Librarian, Nottingham Libraries; Mrs Stephen R. Gray, Pennsylvania Academy of Fine Arts; Lord Gretton; the Earl of Haddo; Mr Henry Hartland, Assistant Keeper, Birmingham Museum; Miss D. Beatrice Harris, Secretary, Petworth House; Mr J. T. Hayes, Assistant Keeper, London Museum; Miss Ursula Hoff, Curator of Prints and Drawings, National Gallery of Victoria; Mr John Ingamells, Curator, City of York Art Gallery; Miss Elizabeth Johnson, Keeper of Paintings, Manchester Art Gallery; Mr Edward S. King, Walters Gallery, Baltimore; Colonel the Lord Langford, O.B.E.; Mr William R. LeFanu; M Andre Veinstein, Curator, Rondel Collection, Bibliothèque de l'Arsenal; Miss Laura C. Luckey, Boston Museum of Fine Arts; Mr Michael H. Parkinson, Keeper of Decorative Art, City of Manchester Art Gallery; Earl Spencer; Mr M. P. Statham, Suffolk County Archivist; Mr J. F. W. Sherwood, Librarian, Hereford Library; Mr Stuart Smith, Director, Beaverbrook Art Gallery, Frederickton, New Brunswick; Mr Daniel Thomas, Curator, Art Gallery of New South Wales; Mr Duncan Thomson, Assistant Keeper, Scottish National Portrait Gallery; Mr. Gordon Thomson, Deputy Director, National Gallery of Victoria; Mr Robert Wark, Curator, Henry E. Huntington Art Gallery; Mr William Wells, Keeper, Burrell Collection, Glasgow Art Gallery; Mr Geoffrey Wilding, Curator, Shugborough, Great Hayward, Staffordshire; Mr K. K. Yung, Curator, Johnson Birthplace Museum, Lichfield.

Our sincere thanks are due also for much gracious assistance from the librarians, keepers, or curators, and from the staffs of the following institutions, as well as from many staff members in the institutions named above: Houghton Library, Harvard University; Massachusetts Historical Society; New York Public Library (especially its Theatre Collection, Lincoln Center); Bodleian Library, Oxford University; University of London Library; the Library of Congress; Manchester Public Library; Lilly Library, Indiana University; University of Hawaii Library; John Rylands Library; London Guildhall; the Public Record Office, London; Middlesex Guildhall; Tufts University Library; Sir John Soane's Museum; Clark Library of the University of California at Los Angeles; Bibliothèque Nationale; Newberry Library; Bristol Public Library; Bedford Settled Estates; University of Chicago Library; Toneel Museum, Amsterdam; University of North Carolina Library, Chapel Hill; Greater London Council; the Sterling and Beinecke Libraries, Yale University; the Elizabethan Club, Yale University; Westminster Public Library; Marylebone Public Library; Bibliothèque de l'Opéra; Trinity College Library, Dublin; the National Library of Ireland; Ohio State University Library; William Rockhill Nelson Gallery of Art; Connecticut Historical Society; Richmond, Surrey, Public Library; Bath Public Library; West Indies Reference Library, Kingston, Jamaica; Public Record Office, Spanish Town, Jamaica; the Holburne of Menstrie

Museum, Bath; Bernard Quaritch, Ltd; Messrs Martin Secker and Warburg, Ltd. We also thank those hundreds of people who had to answer negatively our letters of inquiry.

For kindnesses too numerous and varied to specify, we express our warm gratitude also to these friends: Professor Kathrine Koller, Dean Calvin D. Linton, Dr James B. MacManaway, Dr Giles E. Dawson, Miss Dorothy Mason, Dean Arthur Burns, Professor Bernard Schilling, Provost Harold Bright, Professor Lewis Beck, the late Reverend Carl Stratman, C.S.V., Professor E. E. Folk, Professor Alfred L. Nelson, Dean Charles W. Cole, Professor John P. Reesing, the late Professor Alan W. Downer, Professor Leo Hughes, Professor Aline Taylor, Professor Lucyle Hook, Mr Richard Stoddard, Mrs Letitia Yeandle, Miss Lily Stone, Mrs Mary Nash, Mrs Elaine Fowler, Miss Megan Lloyd, Mrs Sandra Powers, the late Dr Allen Stevenson, the late Professor William S. Clark, Professor Marvin Rosenberg, Mrs Barbara Kemple, Professor Gwynne B. Evans, Professor Ralph Allen, Miss Margarethe Cox, Professor Carol Carlyle, Professor Wood Gray, Professor John Latimer, Professor Chester Burgess, Mr Peter Vaughn Davies, Mr P. Svengaard, Professor Harry M. Ritchie, Mr Leonard Rapport, Mr Michael Papantonio, Mr. K. E. Butler, Professor Douglas J. Nigh, Miss Selma Jeanne Cohen, Mr John Boyt, Mrs Marjorie Gleed, Mr Allerton Hickmott, and Mrs Irene Rickabaugh.

We acknowledge gratefully the intelligent diligence of our sometime student assistants in the complicated and often sensitive housekeeping necessary for so large a work: Professor Robert Wright, Dr Joan Lidoff, Mr Daniel Atwood, Professor Michael Malkin, Mrs Pauline Kilbride, Mrs Carol Bannerman Bridgman, Mrs Nancy Wilson Schick, Mrs Margaret Beckman, Miss Darcy Pulliam, Mrs Jo Bierlein, Mme Yves Ducenne, Mrs Shirley Hafezi, Mrs Pamela Berger, Miss Susan Akau, Mrs Kate Setti, Miss Marcia Kipnees, Mrs Diana Del Vecchio, Mrs Catherine Bahl, and Miss Michele Billy.

Without the wise patience and unfailing helpfulness of Mr Vernon Sternberg, Director of the Southern Illinois University Press, these volumes could never have been published.

Far the greatest debt of all is owed our families. They lent us to the task when they had better claims on our time and energies; and on many occasions they actually joined the enterprise. Special tributes are due Mrs Highfill and Mrs Burnim, who many times unselfishly sacrificed their other concerns to keep our apparatus from smothering us. They efficiently filed and transcribed, summer after summer. Mrs Highfill read all copy. Both wives patiently listened for decades to the peculiar woes of the mass biographer. We thank them as well for their forbearance and love as for the active assistance with which they have helped us to this conclusion.

P. H. H., *Jr.*

K. A. B.

E. A. L.

# List of Illustrations

## MAPS AND VIEWS OF LONDON AND THEATRE SITES

*Volume 1*

Abaco *to* Belfille

# = A =

**Abaco, Giuseppe Marie Clément.** *See* DALL' ABACO.

**Abbé.** *See* L'ABBÉ.

**Abbington.** *See* ABINGTON.

**Abbot, John** *d. 1744, singer.*

The Reverend John Abbot was a clerk and lecturer of the parish of St Andrew, Holborn, a member of the Chapel Royal, and one of the Canons, both of St Paul's and of Westminster Abbey. He was a bass, and in 1743 he was probably the Abbot in Handel's company who sang the Attendant on Athalia in a revival of that oratorio. The bass solos in the Dettingen *Te Deum* were composed especially for him. He wrote his will on 18 December 1723, and it was proved on 9 February 1724 by his widow Sarah, to whom he left all his estate.

**Abbott, Mr** [*fl. 1718–19*], *numberer.*

An Abbot was a numberer at Lincoln's Inn Fields Theatre during the 1718–19 season. He shared a benefit with Burrell on 19 May 1719.

**Abbott, Mr** [*fl. 1799*], *instrumentalist.*

A Mr Abbott was in the band for the Covent Garden oratorios of 8 February to 15 March 1799.

**Abbott, Anthony Duke** [*fl. 1795–1799*], *musician.*

Anthony Duke Abbott, "son of Anthony Abbott, late of Gracechurch St London Vintner deceased" was on 11 July 1795 bound apprentice to "John Betts citizen and musician to learn the art of playing the violin tenor and bass harpsichord and organ with the knowledge of buying and selling Musical Instruments for seven years in cons[ideration] of £150," according to the apprentice register of the Worshipful Company of Musicians. He may have been the instrumentalist named Abbott who was concerned in the oratorios at Covent Garden Theatre in 1799.

**Abbott, George** [*fl. 1740*], *musician.*

George Abbott was bound apprentice to the musician George Hindmarsh on 3 July 1740, according to the records of the Worshipful Company of Musicians. There is no notice of a performance by him.

**Abbott, Henry** [*fl. 1762–1784*], *stage doorkeeper.*

Henry Abbott was employed at Covent Garden Theatre as a stage door keeper in the seasons 1762–63, 1767–68, and 1770–71, and continuously from 1777–80, 1781–84. He gave a deposition at the beginning of the lawsuit between Colman and Harris in 1768. He may have been the Abbot who was important among the house servants at the Liverpool theatre in the summers of 1776, 1777, and 1778, where he provided various services and recruited supernumeraries.

Abbott's wife, Ann, was buried on 26 May 1765 in St Paul, Covent Garden churchyard.

**Abbott, T.** [*fl. 1788?–1821?*], *actor, singer.*

There was an Abbott in the bills of the summer company at the Haymarket Theatre in 1788, appearing infrequently in trivial roles and seldom speaking. He returned there in 1789 and slightly widened his repertoire, achieving parts like Selim in *A Mogul Tale* and Ben Budge in *The Beggar's Opera*, which obliged him to sing and perhaps to dance also. But he was usually confined to walk-ons like one of the Cries in *Ut Pictura Poesis* or the Mercer in *The Miser*. Occasionally during the winter of 1789–90 he joined in specially-licensed performances at the Haymarket. From 15 June to 15 September 1790 he was once more with the regular summer company, and he returned during the next 10 seasons without fail. He was there again in 1804 and 1805, and probably he was the "Abbott" on the list in 1810.

There is no doubt that the subject of this notice was the player who signed "T. Abbott" to a payment receipt (for £47 15*s.*, 191 nights) at Covent Garden Theatre in 1798, and who, every season from 1793–94 through 1803–4, served Covent Garden in the winters as faithfully and humbly as he served the Haymarket in the summers. His first appearance at Covent Garden was as a Planter in *Inkle and Yarico* on 13 June 1793. His singing voice was an asset which insured him regular employment at £1 5*s.* per week (until 1796–97; after that £1 10*s.*), and he sang in the strange choruses which were attached to *Macbeth* and *Hamlet* in this era, in the "Solemn Dirge" which accompanied Juliet to her tomb, as a "Musical Character" in *The Mountaineers*, and in minor roles in ballad operas. He was also worked hard as Scaramouch in the pantomimes, in Irish and Jewish dialect characters, and as peasants, servants and shepherds. Among his very few named parts were: Rifle in *Love and War*, Shopman in *The Way to Get Married*, John in *Heir at Law*, Ned in *The Flitch of Bacon*, Jacob in *The Road to Ruin*, William in *The Deaf Lover*, Ali Beg in *The Mountaineers*, Gregory in *Laugh When You Can*, and Capucius in *King Henry VIII*. The *Authentic Mem-*

*oirs of the Green Room* already was stigmatizing him in 1799 as being "so insignificant that the bare mention of his name will be sufficient. Though of theatrical parentage, he seldom does more than help to increase a mob, be an attendant, or deliver a message." Though records of his nineteenth-century efforts are incomplete, it is much to be feared that the description remained apt.

This Abbott was probably the one in the cast of *Richard III* at the opening of the New Theatre Royal, Bath, on 12 October 1805. In the summer season of 1809 an Abbott who was a veteran of London conducted with Mallinson a momentarily successful theatrical venture at Tenby. Possibly T. Abbott was also the one at Covent Garden in 1812–13, and at Edinburgh in 1815–16, 1818, 1819, and 1821, who was said to have had the permission of the manager Harris at Covent Garden to play in Scotland. He may have been the *Thomas Abbott* who witnessed the will of the musician Thomas Shrubsole on 30 December 1799.

**Abeé.** *See* **L'ABBÉ.**

**Abegg, Mrs** *[fl. 1758–1763]*, *actress, singer.*

Mrs Abegg first came to the notice of the London public singing in *Acis and Galatea*, performed for her benefit in the Great Room in Dean Street, Soho, on 31 March 1758. The performance had been announced for 27 March but had been postponed because of her illness.

She made her first attempt in a patent house ("a Gentlewoman who never appeared before") on 23 November 1758, as Zaida in *The Sultan*, a role which she played again on 3 January 1759. She first sang the role of Polly in *The Beggar's Opera*, on 29 January, and repeated the part on 5 February and 20 March. On 24 and 27 March she was in a chorus of shepherdesses in Garrick's rewriting of *The Winter's Tale* called

*Florizel and Perdita* but was promoted to the part of Dorcas in the same piece by 2 May. Thereafter during her first season she was employed but sparingly, usually in secondary singing roles like Juno in *The Judgment of Paris*.

Mrs Abegg was on the Covent Garden company list in the 1759–60 season, but there is no clue in the bills as to her activities beyond the fact that she was among the "Vocal Parts" in the *Macbeth* produced 17 April 1760. In 1760–61 she was earning five shillings per night, the lowest salary among the four women singers constantly employed. She occupied roughly the same position in the 1760–61 season, her only notable role being Laura in *The Chaplet* on 6 April 1761, when she shared an unsatisfactory benefit with Miss Fielding and Miss Lee. She played only occasionally for Rich during the 1761–62 season, when her salary totalled approximately £70. However, this year saw her as Jessica in *The Merchant of Venice*, the second (and last) Shakespearean role of her London career, and in this part she sang several songs. The last season in which she appeared on the Covent Garden roster, or in London, was 1762–63, when she was confined chiefly to singing in the choruses.

## Abel, Karl Friedrich *1723–1787, instrumentalist, composer.*

Karl Friedrich Abel was born into a distinguished musical family in Cöthen, Anhalt, Germany, on 22 December 1723. He was the son of Christian Ferdinand Abel (b. c. 1695), violist and violoncellist; grandson of Clamor Heinrich Abel (b. 1665), violist; and brother of Leopold August Abel (1718–94), violinist, conductor, and composer at various German courts. His brother Christian's sons, August Christian Andreas Abel and Friedrich Ludwig Aemilius Abel, were to add further luster to the name. Johann Sebastian Bach was godfather to his elder sister Sophie Charlotte (b. 1720).

The exact circumstances of Karl Friedrich's musical education are not known, but there was enough talent in his immediate family to ensure competent early tutelage. From 1748, his twenty-fifth year, until 1759 he played under Hasse in the court band of the electoral King of Poland at Dresden. He is supposed to have quitted Dresden impulsively, "with three thalers in his pocket and six symphonies in his bag." By the early spring of 1759 he was in London and on 5 April began a series of concerts at the Great Room in Dean Street, Soho, where he played with great charm and expertise not only his chief instrument, the *viola da gamba*, but also on a variety of other instruments, including harpsichord, horn, and pentachord. For these performances he hired such singers as Signora Passerini, Quilici, Tedeschino, Tenducci, and Mrs Storer; and his instrumentalists were of the caliber of Pinto, Tacet, Barbandt, and Paxton.

Abel quickly attracted a fashionable following and the patronage of the Duke of York and was appointed chamber musician to Queen Charlotte (to whom he later dedicated several compositions), with an annual emolument of £200.

On the arrival at London of Johann Christian ("English") Bach in the fall of 1762, Abel left his lodgings at Mr Herve's, watch-maker, in Greek Street, Soho, and moved with Bach into a house at No 9, Dean Street. The first of their many joint concerts was held at Spring Garden on 29 February 1764; they performed Bach's serenata *Galatea*. From 23 January 1765 and for several years afterward, Bach and Abel jointly conducted at Carlisle House the Soho Square subscription concerts sponsored by the notorious singer and entrepreneur Mrs Theresa Cornelys. By 1772 Mrs Cornelys was bankrupt, but on 1 February 1775 Abel and Bach were concerned in the first of the series of concerts at the Hanover Square Rooms, later shifted to Almack's Rooms. The *European Magazine* com-

*Harvard Theatre Collection*

CHARLES FREDERICK ABEL

by Gardiner

1772 Abel was among twenty musicians who by special authority performed Metastasio's serenata *Endymion* and several concerts at the Little Theatre in the Haymarket; and in the winter of 1772–73 he played in the band and performed *viola da gamba* solos in special performances at the Haymarket. In 1772 Bach and Abel welcomed to London Wilhelm Cramer, the brilliant young violinist, and introduced him to the English public in a benefit concert at Hickford's Rooms.

Abel played with growing critical success at public concerts and in private gatherings of musicians and the *cognoscenti* in London, and on 20 May 1776, along with Cramer and the singer Signora Sales, he began a long series of recitals at the Music Room in Oxford. No other professional travels in England outside London are recorded for

mented on the continuing series "known by the name of Bach and Abel's Concerts" that "To this musical assembly (composed of the most capital musicians in London) was added yearly every solo performer of note that visited the kingdom." But the partners were equally desirous of maintaining the quality of music played by their *virtuosi*, and introduced much new music to their patronage. Haydn's works were played for the first time in England at these concerts.

In 1766–67 and probably in later seasons, Abel was a member of the band of music at the King's Theatre, and he was intimately concerned with the musical life of the capital generally. He and Bach were subpoenaed to testify before Sir John Fielding in Bow Court in February 1771 on a matter relative to Gaetano Guadagna's unauthorized performance of *Artaserse* at Mrs Cornelys's house. In March and April

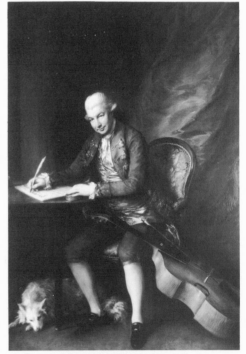

*By Permission of the Huntington Library*

CHARLES FREDERICK ABEL

by Gainsborough

Abel, but he is supposed to have visited Paris in 1772, and in 1783 he played at that city on his return from a visit to his brother Leopold August Abel in Germany. At Berlin and Ludwigslust he was triumphantly successful as a soloist, and King Frederick Wilhelm, then Prince Royal of Prussia, presented him with a jewel-encrusted snuff box and a hundred pieces of gold.

Back in London by 1785, Abel again plunged vigorously into the musical life of the city, playing at the new Professional Concerts and in the subscription affairs arranged by Salomon and Madame Mara in the Pantheon. But by 1786 his professional activities were greatly diminished, probably because of the onset of the disease of which he died. We have no record of his performing after 21 May 1787, when he appeared at a benefit for his old friend the singer Mrs Elizabeth Billington.

Abel was stubbornly loyal to the six-stringed *viola da gamba*, an instrument which by his day was already regarded by many musicians as obsolescent. Despite his versatility he hardly ever performed on any other instrument after 1765. Famous for the exactness, clarity, and emotion of his execution, especially of slow movements, he was vain of his playing to the point of megalomania. When Richards, the leader of the Drury Lane Theatre's band, issued a challenge to him to play he exclaimed, "What, challenge Abel! No, no, there is but one God and one Abel."

Through his association with the Queen and with the Earl of Abington and "Sir John" Gallini, who backed his subscription concerts, and with all the fashionables who attended them, Abel moved freely and widely in London society. He thus attracted many pupils among the nobility and gentry and, more importantly, among aspiring musicians. F. H. Barthélemon, J. H. Schroeter, George Leopold Jacob Griesbach, Brigitta Banti, John Crosdill, and Giacomo Cervetto the younger all studied with him. Though Abel's manner was irascible and overbearing to those whom he disliked, he

was capable of great kindness and staunch friendship. He seems to have earned the devotion of his pupils. One of them, the great J. B. Cramer, long after, in 1820, published a selection of adagios from his quartets "as a tribute of respect to his memory."

Abel's many compositions were much played in his time and they included nearly every kind of musical expression from songs and sonatas, to trios and quartets, to concertos and symphonies. The best of these works evince, according to E. van der Straeten, "a high degree of taste, little musical imagination, and unlimited command over the peculiar resources" of the *viola da gamba*. His contemporary, Dr Burney, summed up his compositions and performance in this way:

His compositions were easy and elegantly simple, for he used to say, "I do not choose to be always struggling with difficulties and playing with all my might. I make my pieces difficult whenever I please, according to my disposition and that of my audience." — Yet in nothing was he so superior to . . . other musicians, as in writing and playing *adagios*; in which the most pleasing, yet learned modulation, the richest harmony, and the most elegant and polished melody, were all expressed with such feeling, taste, and science, that no musical production or performance with which I was then acquainted seemed to approach nearer perfection. The knowledge Abel had acquired in Germany of every part of musical science, rendered him umpire of all musical controversies, and caused him to be consulted on many different points . . . The taste and science of Abel were rather greater than his invention, so that some of his latter productions, compared with those of younger composers, appeared somewhat languid and monotonous; yet he preserved a high reputation in the profession till his death.

Abel was the portraitist Thomas Gainsborough's dearest friend. Writing on the day of the musician's death, Gainsborough thought that he should thenceforth ceaselessly gaze up to heaven "in the hopes of getting one more glance of the man I loved from the moment I heard him touch the string." Abel died peacefully at his house in Marylebone parish on 20 June 1787 after lying in a coma for three days. His death was said to have been hastened by his notorious devotion to drink in good company.

An administration of his property dated 25 September 1787 gave an unspecified sum to his brother Ernst Heinrich Abel for the benefit of a nephew, Ernst Heinrich Abel of Hamburg.

Abel was a large man of dignified mien and port, so pompous in bearing as to lend himself easily to caricature. There is in the British Museum collection an anonymous 1773 engraving of "Seignor Catgutaneo," a man playing a humanoid *viola da gamba* the upper part of which is a carved head resembling Abel's rubicund face. In 1787 J. Nixon published a slightly caricatured print by W. N. Gardner, "A Solo on the Viola da Gamba Mr Abel." Abel was painted several times by Gainsborough. A large oil portrait by that artist is at the Henry E. Huntington Art Gallery, San Marino, California. A small oil partial copy of this work was owned in 1936 by the Dowager Lady Hillingdon and was loaned to the Sassoon Gainsborough Exhibition and identified as of "J. C. Bach." An unfinished "Mr Abel" was in Mrs Gainsborough's sale of 1797. An oil portrait by Robineau is at Hampton Court. Another by an anonymous painter is in the Music School at Oxford. Abel is also one of 39 eighteenth-century composers depicted in a large commemorative engraving by Luigi Scotti between 1801 and 1807.

**Abel, John** *1650?–1724? singer, instrumentalist.*

The birthdate of John Abell was probably about 1650, though some sources suggest 1660. He was a Scotsman and, according to Sir Samuel Forbes, writing in 1716–17, a native of Aberdeenshire "and his kin-

dred are known by the name of Eball; and, it is said, there are others of his family as good as he." Yet when Abell sang in Aberdeen in later years he made no mention of it as his home.

The earliest government references to Abell are equally confusing: on a livery grant of £16 2s. 3d. dated Michaelmas 1675 his name was listed beside Alphonso Marsh's, which was deleted, but this could be an addition made in 1681 when Abell did indeed replace the deceased Marsh. If Abell began his royal service as early as 1675, a birthdate of about 1650 would be reasonable, but his connection with the King's musical establishment probably did not begin until 1 May 1679, when he was sworn a Gentleman of the Chapel Royal extraordinary—that is, without pay until a position became vacant; on 10 January 1680 at the death of singer Burges Howes, Abell was admitted in ordinary. Shortly after joining the Chapel Royal, Abell was appointed on 31 May 1679 to replace the deceased musician Anthony Roberts in the King's private music at £40 annually, the patent for this second position being issued on 5 June following.

Within the private music Abell was granted a double position: on 20 December 1681 he was appointed to replace Alphonso Marsh the elder, deceased, as singer and lutenist, and Richard Dorney the younger, deceased, as violinist. In addition to the favor he had obviously gained within the two chief musical organizations Abell must have attracted the attention of the King himself, for soon after these appointments Charles II sent him to Italy—to study, according to some sources, but, say others, to show the Italians that England also had good singers. He was newly returned from his trip on 27 January 1682 when Evelyn heard him sing at Sir Stephen Fox's and wrote, "indeede I never heard a more excellent voice, one would have sworne it had ben a Womans it was so high, & so well & skillfully manag'd." The diarist called Abell a "Trebble" but he was, more correctly, a countertenor or *alto*. The King continued his favors by sending the singer to Scotland, probably in February, for Abell was paid £20 for the charges of his journey on 9 March 1682.

In December 1685 or January 1686 the singer married Frances Knollys, sister of the titular Earl of Banbury, but when Banbury heard the news, despite Abell's apparent good standing at court, he turned his sister out of his house. Though the Earl's motives were not stated, Abell's quixotic behavior in later years suggests that perhaps Banbury found the singer's character, as well as his profession, unsuitable. Of Abell's wife nothing more is known, and possibly the marriage did not last.

Since Abell was a Catholic, he continued to flourish at court during the reign of James II, and by 1688 the gifts and bounty payments to him from Charles and James totalled at least £740. His salary in the Chapel Royal by this time was £60 annually, according to a Treasury Book warrant dated 5 July 1687, and during this year he was the only member of the Chapel Royal who also held a position in the King's private music. To show his appreciation and patriotism, Abell produced a lavish entertainment for the King on 18 June 1688; the performance took place on the Thames before Whitehall with 130 vocal and instrumental participants. "On Monday night a great performance was upon the water of Vocal and Instrumental Musique in a Barge borrowed from one of the Companies of London stuck round with lighted fflambeaux, and many of the Nobility and Gentry invited thereto." After the entertainment the

Nobility and company that was upon the water gave three shouts to express their joy and satisfaction [presumably with the King]; and all the gentlemen of the musick went to Mr Abell's house, which was nobly illuminated and honoured with the presence of a great Company of the nobility. . . . The entertainment lasted till three of the clock the next morning, the music playing and the trumpets sounding all the while.

Though Abell's Catholic persuasion put him in a less favorable position under William and Mary, he was still listed as a member of the King's Musick on 25 March 1689 at a salary of £30 annually. Shortly after this, however, he must have received his dismissal, for his name does not appear in the accounts pertaining to the royal service after this date.

For the next decade Abell travelled on the Continent extensively, sometimes with full equipage and sometimes on foot, as his fortunes permitted. He went to Holland, France, and Germany, singing in public to gain an income, but spending improvidently. His wanderings finally took him to Warsaw where, if the story is true, he almost ended up as bear bait. Shortly after his arrival there the King summoned him to court to sing and, for some reason, Abell refused; the next day the command was repeated and this time the singer came to court. Upon arrival he was ushered to the middle of the hall, and as soon as he was seated, his chair was hauled high in the air as some wild bears were loosed beneath him. Appearing in a gallery facing Abell, the King asked the singer whether he would now prefer to sing or to be lowered to the floor. Abell naturally chose the former alternative and, according to him, never sang better in his life.

There are a number of allusions to Abell's continental years in Tom Brown's *Letters from the Dead to the Living* (1703) which suggest that the singer was not only a vagabond but a rascal and child of misfortune. "You have met . . . with but small Encouragement in the main," the letter states, "and made but a slender Fortune in comparison of what might have been reasonably expected from your Talents. The most civiliz'd Quarter of the

World has been your Audience and Admirer; and you have left every where a
Name that cannot die but with Musick." As
evidence Brown noted that Abell received a
diamond from the King of France as admiring payment for his singing, only to
have it stolen by some Irishman—a misfortune for a Scotsman surely; but Brown also
scolded Abell for having run off with
money given him by the Elector of Bavaria, apparently for services not rendered:
" 'twas no better than robbing him to run
away with his Money, and especially before
you had done any thing for it. However this
may be your Consolation, that the Duke
[presumably the Elector] can't say you
cheated him to some tune."

A calendar of some of Abell's activities
in 1695 was kept in a letter written at Zell
by a Mr J Cresset to a friend in Holland:

1695, July 12. Abel the musician who is
very poor and comes to sing and beg in these
courts is gone to Hanover to offer his services . . . July 15. Abel diverts [or awaits?]
the Princesses at Hanover . . . Sept. 3. Abel
has been at Berlin, but is come back as far as
Brunswick and will be here in a few days. So
soon as he comes, I will be sure to tell him
how favourable you are to him, and if I obtain by your kindness the permission of coming to Loo myself, I believe he will be glad
to have a Cart so far on his way with me,
though he is tempted to stay the carnival at
Hanover, and is offered a considerable sum
. . . 6th. Abel is now with me, and his Cath-
olicity does not hinder him from singing
Victoria for us . . . Abel with Cresset to Loo
in Holland on the rejoicings for the taking of
Namur . . . Oct. 9. The Harmonious Vagabond Abel is now here. He tells me he will
hasten to England, but I think his crochets
make it uncertain. He maintains the character
of the Vertuose Canaglia.

Abell did not return to England at this time,
however, for in 1698 and 1699 he was the
Intendant at Cassel—one of the few permanent posts he seems to have held while
on the Continent.

Near the end of the century he finally received permission from William III to return to England; his *Collection of Songs in
Several Languages* (1701) was dedicated
to the King and thanked him for permitting
the wanderer to return home. His *Collection of Songs in English* was published in
1701 and contained an introductory poem
saying, "After a twelve years' industry and
toil, / Abell, at last has reached his native
soil."

Once home in early 1700 Abell busied
himself with concerts. On about 20 January Alice Hatton wrote a letter in which
she said "Mr Abel is to have a fine musicke
meeting tomorrow, and y^e tickets are guineas a piece, w^ch is a little to much for me to
throw away; so I shall not be there, and I
find so many y^t can afford it better of my
mind, y^t I fancy, if he had had lower rates,
he would have got more." The singer was
soon off again, however, this time, judging
from the puzzling pieces of evidence, to
Ireland. A petition to the Duke of Ormonde, undated but possibly submitted
about 1700, was from Robert Abell, father
of John, asking that his son be allowed to
bargain with any playhouse; the petition explained John's need to be able "himselfe to
pay his debts and to discharge yo^r. Peti-
tioner for his Baile for severall considerable Summes of Money Wherein he stands
Bound for his Son." A petition sent to Ormonde would presumably have concerned
Ireland, not England, and later letters suggest that the Irish knew of Abell; yet the
letter may have referred to another, younger
John Abell, for it seems most peculiar that
the singer, now about 50, would be using
his father to petition for him. But John
Abell was in fact preparing for a stage career about this time, already had a checkered financial career, and may well have
spent some time in Ireland in 1700 and,
typically, may have run himself into debt.
By December he was in England again, for
on 10 December 1700 Congreve, writing
from London to his friend Keally, said,

"Abell is here; has a cold at present, and is always whimsical; so that when he will sing, or whether he wil sing or not upon the stage, are things very disputable: but he certainly sings beyond all creatures upon the earth; and I have heard him very often both abroad and since he came over."

The singer's stage career did not begin on schedule; on 15 January 1701 Congreve wrote John Drummond that "Mr: Abell tho' he has receivd 300 li of the money belonging to the new Play-house [presumably Lincoln's Inn Fields] has not yet sung and is full of nothing but lies and shifting tricks. His character I suppose is not new to you." Instead of fulfilling his obligations to the theatre during 1701 and 1702, Abell sang concerts in a variety of places around London: at Stationer's Hall, Chelsea College (for Queen Anne's coronation), Richmond, Hampstead, and Dorset Garden. In addition, he set himself up as a teacher. The *Post Boy* of 22 November 1701 ran an advertisement by Abell in which he invited any person of quality who would like to hear him sing selections from Part II of *Orpheus Britannicus* (the book of songs) to inquire at his house in Bond Street, Picadilly, where he would also teach singing. By 29 October 1702 he was advertising that he would teach two days a week in London and two in Westminster. Finally, on 29 December 1702 he sang Paris in *The Judgment of Paris* at Drury Lane, his first and apparently his last theatrical engagement.

Abell gave a few concerts during the 1702–3 season in London and then, perhaps, began travelling again. By 1705 he was in his native land: on 26 October 1705 he advertised in the *Edinburgh Courant* that "Whereas Mr Abel hath had the Honour to pay his Humble Duty to the Nobility and Gentry, in several Parts of the Kingdom of Scotland, and four several Voyages from Forreign Parts; Does intend with the Help of God, to be at Aberdeen on Saturday the Third of November 1705." Curiously he made no mention of Aberdeenshire being his birthplace, and one would certainly expect him to have mentioned it in this puff if he was, indeed, born there. The reference to four different voyages suggests that perhaps in 1704, when he was apparently not active in London, he may have made another continental trip.

After his Scottish tour there seems to be no record of him for ten years. On 30 June 1715 he sang a recital at Stationer's Hall, billed as lately returned from Italy and prepared to present music from 14 countries. But he may not have been abroad during all of the ten preceding years, for Hawkins reported that Abell was in Cambridge at the latter end of the reign of Queen Anne; his Italian trip may have come after Cambridge and before the Stationer's Hall concert in London.

Information about Abell's death is as obscure as that about his birth. Although he supposedly had discovered a secret that helped him preserve his voice in his later years, he died in poverty—in Cambridge in 1724 say some sources, in Canterbury that year say others, and in 1716 say still others. Grove accepts Cambridge, 1724. A John Abell of St Botolph's parish was buried on 16 January 1724, and another John Abell's estate was administered on 29 January 1722 and again on 24 September 1724—but there are no clues to help identify these Abells with the singer, and the name was a fairly common one at the time.

**Abell brothers**  [fl. 1726–1727], *house servants?*

In the Lincoln's Inn Fields theatre accounts for 1726–27 an Abell and his brother appeared on the free lists; they seem to have been house servants connected with the issuing of tickets authorized by the managers.

**Aberdein.** *See also* ABERDEEN, ABERDIEN.

**Aberdein, Mr**  [fl. 1782–1796], *actor, singer.*

A Mr Aberdein, who hung about the outskirts of theatrical activity in London off and on over a span of nearly 15 years, was a representative of an unfortunate class of actors who never quite achieved a steady living in London, but who kept trying.

By several indications besides his name, he was of Scots origin and was probably nearly related to the Aberdiens (or Aberdeens) who were dressers and scenemen at Drury Lane and the Haymarket at various times late in the eighteenth century.

Aberdein was first noticed in nameless walk-on roles in several performances by down-at-heels actors given by special permission of the Lord Chamberlain at the Haymarket Theatre in the winter of 1782 and spring of 1783. He was similarly desultorily engaged in 1783–84. He was first named in a specific character in a Haymarket playbill of 9 February 1784 when he played the sentimental part of Sir William Worthy in *The Gentle Shepherd* "By Authority of the Lord Chamberlain. At the request of several of the Scotch Nobility. Benefit of Raeburn." Most of the principals of this performance appeared to have been Scottish irregulars looking for London theatrical billets: M'Donald, Cockburn, Murray, and Raeburn.

Aberdein was back at the Haymarket for more small efforts the next winter but seems to have grown discouraged and perhaps to have retreated to Scotland, to the English provinces, or to other pursuits.

On 22 October 1792 Aberdein bobbed up again at the Haymarket as Sir William Worthy, the only major part he seems to have mastered, or anyway was allowed to play. He was absent again for over a year until, again at the Haymarket, and in an out-of-season pantomime called *Harlequin Peasant*, he was one of several watchmen on 26 December 1793 and 27, 28, and 30 January 1794.

Aberdein was in a "Chorus of Guards" in *The Mountaineers*, but this time at Drury Lane, on 31 October 1794. This piece was repeated on 27 October 1795 and on 11 January 1796. It was as if Aberdein had spent all his vital efforts scaling the heights of the foremost patent theatre, for after these three performances his name dropped permanently from the record.

**Aberdein, Mr** [*fl. 1783–1819*], *dresser, scene man?*

An Aberdein was among those delivering tickets for benefit performances at Drury Lane Theatre on 31 May 1783, 22 May 1784, 20 May 1785, 29 May 1786, and 1 June 1787. He may have been the "Aberdien" who worked as scene man at the Little Theatre in the Haymarket in the summer of 1804. He was probably also the "Aberdeen" who repaid a loan to Drury Lane Theatre in June 1789, and who was listed as a men's dresser in 1801, at 9s. per week. An Aberdeen was in charge of payments to the Drury Lane dressers in September 1802, and probably the same person received the nine-shilling payment in the seasons of 1815–16, 1816–17, and 1818–19. In 1812–13 there was also an "Aberdeen, Jr" in that function. These persons were perhaps related to the actor Aberdein.

**Abington, James** *d. 1806, trumpeter, singer.*

James Abington was one of the King's trumpeters. The first known public notice of him was his performance of a concerto for the trumpet at a benefit for Ridley Dorman at the Long Room at Hampstead, 5 August 1752. He sang in performances at Drury Lane in February and March 1756 in the role of Ventoso in Garrick's "operatic" alteration of *The Tempest*, with music by John Christopher Smith.

Sometime between 19 June and 27 September 1759, he married the actress Frances Barton. The Abingtons departed for an engagement in Ireland in November. The marriage very quickly failed and a separation ensued. Frances Abington quickly became one of the most accomplished and

May the 5<sup>th</sup> 1774

It is agreed this day between M<sup>rs</sup> Abington & M<sup>r</sup> Garrick that the former shall be Engag'd to him & M<sup>r</sup> Lacy patentees of the Theatre Royal in Drury-Lane for three years, from this date or three Acting Seasons at the Sum of twelve pounds a week with a Benefit and Sixty pounds for Cloaths — The above Agreement to be put into Articles according to the usual form.

Frances Abington

D. Garrick
for M<sup>r</sup> Lacy & himself

Articles of Agreement between Garrick and Mrs Abington, 5 May 1774

celebrated English actresses of the eighteenth century and Abington proved an embarrassment to her. She paid him a fixed yearly sum to live apart from her.

Abington sang at the Handel Memorial Concerts at Westminster Abbey on 26, 27, and 29 May and at the Pantheon on 3 and 5 June 1784. He died in July 1806.

### Abington, Mrs James, Frances, née Barton 1737–1815, actress.

Frances Abington was born to very humble circumstances, as Frances Barton. Her father, upon discharge from service with a Guards regiment, opened a cobbler's stall in Vinegar Yard, Windmill Street, not far from Drury Lane Theatre. Of her mother nothing is known except that she died when Fanny was only 14. An early account says that for a time thereafter the child was cared for by a relation of her father's who lived in Sherrard Street, Golden Square. Fanny's brother was a hostler at an inn situated in Hanway Yard. Thus an aristocratic pedigree discovered for Mrs Abington after her theatrical fame was established cannot be believed without question since it cannot now be confirmed. The story that her paternal grandfather was the son of one Christopher Barton, Esq, a gentleman of land and dignities of Norton, Derbyshire, may be correct, nevertheless.

Many colorful tales have been told about Fanny Barton's rise from the grinding poverty of her origins to the luxury and social distinction which accompanied her success. None of them can be endorsed with much confidence. Perhaps the least credible is Arthur Murphy's account of the small slum girl's recitations from the works of the dramatic poets from atop the tables of Covent Garden taverns. But the outlines of Fanny's early life can be discerned. There seems little doubt that she both sold flowers and sang in the streets around the Piazza in Covent Garden at the age of fourteen, earning the sobriquet of "Nosegay Fan"; and that she was, successively, assistant to a

French milliner in Cockspur Street, a ballad singer, and a cookmaid in a kitchen presided over by Robert Baddeley, later a famous comedian who was perhaps at that time cooking for Samuel Foote, an even more famous one. We must notice but reject as unproved the innuendoes about her early "promenading" in St James's Park and Leicester Fields. More circumstantially convincing are the details of her stay with a certain Mrs Parker, who, in the words of the *Manager's Notebook*, took Fanny "into her house, in Spring Gardens, where [Mrs Parker] was living under the protection of Mr Byron, a rich West Indian. He was so pleased with Miss Barton's manners that he engaged masters to instruct her; while Mrs Parker . . . gave Fanny good clothes, and, in fact, made her her companion." The denouement is obvious. Mr Byron's interest in Fanny—and Mrs Parker's jealousy—grew, and she became again a girl of the streets.

At some time early in Fanny's life there must have been instruction in French and Italian, for she could converse in both and by her maturity showed some acquaintance with many foreign authors. She seems to have retained an unusual determination to own some part of the elegance and gentility which she glimpsed at the theatres during her Covent Garden childhood. At seventeen she was a local character already very well known to the actors at the nearby patent houses. By the summer of 1755, when Theophilus Cibber secured authority to pull together for ten performances at the Haymarket a company composed of young novices, under the banner of "Bayes's New-rais'd Company of Comedians," Frances Barton was among them. For her first recorded appearance on the stage she was announced only as a "young gentlewoman" in the character of Miranda in Mrs Centlivre's *The Busy Body* on August 21. She followed her debut, on 25 August and still anonymously, as Kitty Pry in *The Provok'd Husband*. That part she repeated on 1 September, on a night when she first saw her name in the bills, and also played Desdemona: "Miss Barton, first time in a Tragedy." On 9 September, Fanny passed one of the obligatory tests of comediennes when she played Sylvia in *The Recruiting Officer*, advertised as "Miss Barton, her first appearance in boys' clothes." The playbills are not fully descriptive, and not all survive, so Fanny doubtless acted other parts before the short season ended. The comic genius Edward Shuter attended several of her performances, and finally he came behind the scenes and engaged her for the Bath company. After one season in minor roles at Bath, Fanny was again recruited by Shuter, this time for the summer theatre at Richmond. There Garrick's co-adjutor Lacy went to corroborate Shuter's poetic reports of her abilities, and by the fall of 1756 Fanny was a member of the Drury Lane company, having also had Samuel Foote's unqualified recommendation.

Frances Barton's salary at Drury Lane

FRANCES ABINGTON, as Estifania

on a delftware tile
after James Roberts

was at first fixed at a decent 30 shillings a week, and her first part, on 29 October 1756, was a good one, Lady Pliant in *The Double Dealer*. The prompter Cross noted in his diary that she "did Lady Pliant pretty well"; and she repeated the part on 1 November and many times during succeeding seasons.

But Fanny was now in one of the world's finest theatres, and she had her apprenticeship to serve. During her first season, 1756–57, she was allotted only a few notable secondary roles, like Miss Lucy in *The Wonder* and Arabella in *The Modern Fine Gentleman*. She was employed sparingly, no doubt because there was an abundance of talented actresses in her general line of pert servants and secondary ingenues at Drury Lane. But she ended the season on 19 June as Lucy in *The Beggar's Opera*. In the following two seasons she repeated Kitty Pry, assisted in several pantomimes, and was Inis in *The Wonder*, Lucy in *The Virgin Unmasked*, Dorcas in *The Mock Doctor*, Rhodamintha in *Zara*, and Harriot in *The Heiress*.

At some date between her last appearance of the 1758–59 season, which was 19 June, and her first appearance of the next, 27 September, she was married to James Abington, King's Trumpeter and minor player, who was by some accounts also her music master. Some disagreement with management made her desert Drury Lane after 31 October 1759. She and her husband departed London on 5 November to join Brown's Dublin company.

Mrs Abington's success in Ireland was immediate and profound, socially and professionally, from her first appearance at Smock Alley on 11 December 1759, as Mrs Sullen in *The Beaux' Stratagem*. Her marriage, however, very soon began breaking apart in consequence of her new prominence, whether from her husband's jealousy of her importance onstage or the constant importunate (and sometimes favorably considered) entreaties she received from the crowds of emotional Irish gentlemen she found at her feet. Her portrayal and her dress as Kitty in *High Life Below Stairs* were the talk of the town. Her "Abington Cap" became the rage among the female half of the Irish nation. Wilkinson reported that not a milliner's shop window in Dublin but displayed it, with the large letters "ABINGTON." With this success began her reputation as *arbitrix elegantiarum* which was to remain with her and grow until her retirement.

Fanny's new and powerful friends soon interested themselves in transferring her talents from Smock Alley to the Crow Street Theatre, and her first appearance at the latter house was on 22 May 1760, when she played both Lady Townley in *The Provok'd Husband* and Lucinda in *The Englishman in Paris*. She performed several nights and was rewarded with a clear benefit, which was fashionably and excellently patronised.

When Crow Street reopened in the autumn of 1760, now under Henry Woodward's management, Mrs Abington rejoined the company. During the next four years she alternated from Crow Street to Smock Alley, cleverly keeping afloat and on course in the swirling currents of Dublin's changing theatrical tides.

Early in her Irish sojourn she had met the wealthy Mr Needham, Irish M.P. for Newry, County Down, and had become his mistress. When in 1765 he was called to England on business she accompanied him. He died that summer at Bath. Mrs Abington nursed him devotedly through the last stages of his illness and is supposed to have been rewarded not only with the provision in his will of a handsome competence but also with the kindness and countenance of his family.

At David Garrick's earnest solicitation Fanny Abington rejoined the company at Drury Lane, with a salary of £5 per week. Her first appearance in London after her pleasant exile of six years was on 27 No-

*Harvard Theatre Collection*

FRANCES ABINGTON, as Scrub
by J. Sayer

vember 1765, as the Widow Belmour in Arthur Murphy's comedy *The Way to Keep Him*. Her performance drew from Murphy a warmly flattering letter and, later, a dedication in a new edition. During the next 17 seasons she remained at Drury Lane. Her temperament and sense of her own growing importance threw her into conflict with Garrick, and they quarrelled with mounting frequency and bitterness in the latter years of his management. Parts of a lengthy correspondence between them survive to document their essential incompatibility. There was pride and pettiness on both sides, but Garrick seems nevertheless to have been sorely tried by her whims. She became convinced that he discriminated in Jane Pope's favor in assigning roles. Garrick became convinced that she, Francis

Gentleman, and others had formed a cabal to ruin him. Garrick denounced her unfairly as "the worst of bad women," but was frequently called upon to swallow his pride and spleen because he did not care to discharge an excellent box-office attraction. She clung to her contract because it was profitable. She was earning £8 per week in 1773, more than any other woman except Miss Pope, and she was also receiving a regular allowance of £2 per week for clothes. On 5 May 1775 she and Garrick signed a pact which granted her £12 a week salary and continued her £60 per year for clothing. In the spring of Garrick's own final withdrawal from the stage, 1776, Fanny pretended to him that she, too, would renounce acting at the end of that season. She bedevilled the poor exhausted Roscius into playing for the last time his Archer to her Mrs Sullen in *The Beaux' Stratagem,* for her benefit, and gave out her intention to move to seclusion in Wales for the rest of her life. But in the fall she had gone back to her old station at Drury Lane.

When in 1776–77 Sheridan took over the management of Garrick's company Fanny was given a salary of £12 a week, plus £200 "in lieu of her benefit," and her clothing allowance was doubled. But it was not long before her general dissatisfaction with Drury Lane became acute, and she began a flirtation with the other house, though it took her six years more to decide to make a permanent transfer.

On 29 November 1782 Fanny made her first appearance at Covent Garden, as Lady Flutter in *The Discovery*, a play never before acted there, and was thunderously received by the audience when she came forward to make the expected complimentary address. She earned that year £600 and a liberal sum on her benefit night. Absent from the boards altogether during the fall of 1783, she earned £30 a night at Covent Garden from 23 January to 2 June 1784. She remained there through the next two seasons, went to Dublin in the summer and

stayed through the fall of 1786, and was back at Covent Garden from 26 January to 7 May 1787. She played steadily at Covent Garden from 17 October to 9 June 1787–88. She did not play in London at all in 1788–89, but she came back on 5 November 1789 and performed steadily until 12 February 1790, when she suddenly retired, this time with an honest intention to forsake the boards forever. Whimsical to the last, she left the theatre after 12 February 1790 without even a farewell benefit. (Her relationship with her managers at Covent Garden had not been a smooth one either, for there survives a "Memorial" of 1787 from Fanny to "the Right Hon. Henry Dundas" supporting the project then afoot to solicit the authority of Parliament for a license to enact plays in a theatre near Wellclose Square. In it she speaks of the "cruelty" and "tyranny" of the regime under which she labours; and accompanying the memorial is a note begging Dundas to keep her sentiments secret from her manager, Harris.)

Fanny had bought the lease on a house at Hammersmith-hope, near the Thames (which she later sold to Sophia Baddeley: £250 for the furniture "and the lease to be paid for besides"); and she apparently settled down there in the expectation of a quiet life. She kept away from the stage — except for some few appearances in Limerick, Ireland, in July of 1793 — for the next seven years. When in 1797 a benefit performance was planned at Covent Garden for the widows and orphans of men killed in the Earl of St Vincent's victory over the Spanish fleet, she wrote the Duke of Leeds, a trustee of the charity, and offered her services; and on 14 June 1797 spoke an Epilogue to the performance. She was immediately pressed to resume her old situation, for the recent retirement of Miss Wallis and the death of Mrs Pope had left a gap, particularly in her own line of the comic.

Mrs Abington bowed to the pressure of

her friends (and a promise of £40 per night) and came back to Covent Garden on 6 October 1797 to play Beatrice in *Much Ado About Nothing* to the Benedick of Lewis, welcomed home by a flattering prologue written by George Colman.

But time had passed, and though the audience which had idolized her had not substantially diminished, few could pretend that her Beatrice had gained anything but weight. Boaden's judicious word is usually taken for the collective memory of those worshippers who witnessed her return:

Her person had become full, and her elegance somewhat unfashionable; but she still gave to Shakespeare's Beatrice what no other actress in my time has ever conceived; and her old admirers were still willing to fancy her as unimpaired as the character itself.

But Boaden was writing years later, peering through the mists of time and sentiment. *The Monthly Visitor* of October 1797 was more harshly realistic:

Her former Beatrice was a chaste, animated, unaffected and captivating performance; but her Beatrice of this night was, for the greater part, languid and unattractive. Her deportment, however, is easy and graceful; but her person is too big and heavy to give any effect to the more gay and sprightly scenes. We conceive it to be the height of folly and imprudence in her to come forward in the present advanced period of her existence; and that, too, with a person so ill calculated for the department, and attempt characters which demand all the vigour and activity of youth.

Mrs Abington played a few more times that season, did Mrs Oakly in *The Jealous Wife* for Lacy's benefit out-of-season at the Haymarket on 17 December 1798 and made her absolutely last appearance, for Pope's benefit, at Covent Garden on 12 April 1799, when she played Lady Racket in the farce *Three Weeks After Marriage*.

Again, one of her gallant companions of

*Harvard Theatre Collection*

FRANCES ABINGTON, as Lady Betty Modish

by Cosway

the stage, John Bernard, testified that in this role:

The perpetuated evidence of youth was in character with her person and her powers; the slimness of her figure, the fulness of her voice, the freshness of her spirits, the sparkle of the eye, and the elasticity of her limbs, savoured alike of a juvenility that puzzled the mind, whilst it pleased it: of her it was justly said that "she had been on the stage thirty years; she was one-and-twenty when she came, and one-and-twenty when she went."

It was a nice conceit, but it was in Bernard's *Retrospections*, and its date was 1830.

Francis Abington acted in what appears at first glance to have been a fairly restricted line, but it was one in which there was much opportunity to experiment and "create." Though at the beginning of her career she quickly settled down to a succession of young women in comedies, there is ample evidence that she could have succeeded in tragedy as well had it paid as handsomely.

In 1777, Richard Brinsley Butler Sheridan brought to Drury Lane Theatre the greatest British comedy to be written between Congreve and Wilde, *The School for Scandal,* creating his characters almost exactly from the personality traits of those actors who he knew would assume the principal parts. Lady Teazle was as much Mrs Abington as Mrs Abington was Lady Teazle. It was her most famously successful part, as it has been for a long succession of leading ladies. General "Gentleman Johnny" Burgoyne wrote expressly for her the part of Lady Bab Lardoon in his slight but pleasant *Maid of the Oaks,* gallantly furnishing her with a line which she pronounced with gay irony and which procured her much applause: "You shall see what an excellent actress I should have made, if fortune had not unluckily brought me into the world an Earl's daughter."

Other roles in which Frances Abington excelled included: Letitia in *The Old Bachelor,* Miss Prue in *Love for Love,* Phillis in *The Conscious Lovers,* Miss Hoyden in *The Trip to Scarborough,* Lydia Languish in *The Rivals,* Biddy Tipkin in *The Tender Husband,* Lappet in *The Miser,* Lady Froth in *The Double Dealer,* Penelope in *The Gamesters,* Miss Walsingham in *The School for Wives,* Charlotte Rusport in *The West Indian,* Second Constantia in *The Chances,* Narcissa in *The Widowed Wife,* Fatima in *Cymon,* Lady Fanciful in *The Provoked Wife,* both Charlotte and Maria in *The Hypocrite,* Belinda in *All in the Wrong,* Lady Harriet in *The Funeral,* Lady Lace in *The Lottery,* Mrs Vintage in *No Wit Like a Woman's,* Mrs Sullen in *The Beaux' Stratagem,* Mrs Oakly in *The Jealous Wife,* the title role in *The Capricious Lady,* Lady Sadlife in *The Double Gallant,* Lady

Betty Modish in *The Careless Husband,* Estifania in *Rule a Wife and Have a Wife,* Millamant in *The Way of the World,* Aurelia in *The Twin Rivals,* Miss Notable in *The Lady's Last Stake,* Ruth in *The Committee,* Arabella in *The Fair Quaker of Deal,* and Clarinda in *The Suspicious Husband.* Her Shakespearean parts were, though successful, strangely few and included only Mrs Ford in *The Merry Wives of Windsor,* Portia in *The Merchant of Venice,* Maria in *Twelfth Night* (in which she sang "a French air"), and her famous Beatrice.

Mrs Abington's acting abilities were praised as often if not quite as highly as were those of her adversary Garrick. It would be easy to compile an extensive collection of encomiums, but perhaps it will suffice to accept the judgment of the actor-author Tom Davies, who had seen Woffington and Pritchard and myriads more, when he says of her portrayal of Charlotte Rusport in *The West Indian*:

It is impossible to conceive that more gaiety, ease, humour, elegance, and grace, could have been assumed by any actress than by Mrs Abington in this part; her ideas of it were entirely her own, for she had seen no pattern. . . . Her person is formed with great elegance, her address is graceful, her look animated and expressive. To the goodness of her understanding, and the superiority of her taste she is indebted principally for her power of pleasing; the tones of her voice are not naturally charming to the ear, but her incomparable skill in modulation renders them perfectly agreeable: her articulation is so exact, that every syllable she utters is conveyed distinctly and even harmoniously.

To all this evident excellence, Mrs Abington added professional discretion. She kept to one fairly narrow band of the wide spectrum of parts she might have played, and was nearly always to be found in comedy of manners and the less lachrymose sentimental comedies. Her essays at tragedy were few, and they ceased after she saw that they were not successful. Her taste failed her only once, when, on 10 February 1786, contrary to the advice of her friends, she played for her benefit the comic servant Scrub, in *The Beaux' Stratagem*. For this aberration she was roundly abused in the papers, and several satirical prints showing her as Scrub were published.

The truth was that the public found Mrs Abington delicious and did not want her degraded. Everything she did or said was remarked, especially by women when clothes were concerned. What she dictated, duchesses and dairy maids adopted. When she made her tall figure taller by piling her hair into a ziggurat, all did so. But the *Gazeteer* of 14 October 1778, informs that:

The ponderous, towering head-dress, which has been for some time a great weight upon female shoulders, is now lessening almost to its natural size. Mrs Abington has been one of the first to begin this happy reformation in dress, as she made her first appearance this season in the School for Scandal with her hair *remarkably low,* which exhibited such evident marks of propriety that all the high heads in the house looked more like caricatures upon dress than real fashion.

Male writers might rail at her for falling "into the absurdity of wearing *red* powder" and advise, since "her influence on the *ton* is too well known — let her at once deviate from this unnatural French custom, or, if she is determined to continue a *red head*, let her frizeur throw a little brick-dust on her arches [eyebrows]"; but she powdered red as long as she liked, and the town followed.

The German visitor W. D. Archenholtz noted that she

has invented for herself an occupation quite particular. As she possesses the most exquisite taste, she spends a good part of the day in running about London, to give advice on the dresses and new fashions. She is consulted like a Physician and fee'd in the handsomest manner. There is no marriage celebrated, and no entertainment given, where her assistance in regulating the decorations is not requested. In this way she is said to make *annually* nearly fifteen hundred pounds a year. It is quite sufficient in London to say "Mrs Abington has worn this" to stop the mouths of all Fathers and Husbands.

Though Fanny Burney placed her fastidiously among "the frail ones," her early connection with Mr Needham, and her subsequent acceptance of the "protection" of the Marquis of Lansdowne, which is supposed to have gained her a settlement of £500 on the marriage of that nobleman, did her no noticeable harm in the opinion of the *haut monde*. She is said to have lived a life of circumspection after the Lansdowne episode. But she entertained lavishly, was welcomed to the greatest houses, and conversed on terms of intellectual parity — in several languages — with persons of dignity as different as Horace Walpole, the Duke of Dorset, General Paoli, and Dr Johnson. Johnson, indeed, was her staunch admirer, and after supping with her on one occasion irritated Mrs Thrale, his next hostess, by remarking "Mrs Abington's jelly, my dear. lady, was better than yours." Having been wheedled into attending her benefit in 1775, he sat so distant from the stage that he could not see and could scarcely hear. "Why then did you go?" asked the incautious Boswell. "Because, Sir, Mrs Abington is a favourite of the public," replied Johnson, "and when the public cares a thousandth part for you that it does for her I will go to your benefit too." Nor was the aging philosopher oblivious to her physical attractions. He again provoked Mrs Thrale in a letter of 12 May 1775: "Yesterday I had I know not how much kiss of Mrs Abington."

Late in Fanny's life J. P. Collier "saw her twice at Serjeant Rough's parties in Bedford Row. She was shrunken by age into a small woman, but was very sprightly, and, in spite of her wrinkles, attractive." Henry Crabb Robinson also saw her at Rough's, and though he did not find her physically prepossessing, was surprised at her social presence:

Mrs Abington would not have led me to suppose she had been on the stage by either her manner or the substance of her conversation. She speaks with the ease of a person used to good company, rather than with the assurance of one whose business it was to imitate that ease. Her language was now and then incorrect as to grammar, but her whole deportment in other respects [was] unexceptionable.

Frances Abington's life, wherever she travelled in the Three Kingdoms, was a round of high social enjoyments, and her surviving letters teem, without any suggestion of name-dropping, with the learned, fashionable, highly-placed, and amusing people with whom she consorted: Mrs Edward Wheler, Lady Cecelia Johnston, Lady Ailesberry, General Conway, Edward Jerningham, Sir Henry and Lady Cavendish, Oliver Goldsmith, Maurice Morgan, Isaac Reed, and many others.

Her estranged husband James died in 1806, and the monetary settlement which she had made to him apparently reverted to her. By 1807 she had moved from her long-time residence in Piccadilly and was living at No 9, Eaton Square.

Frances Abington died at her Pall Mall apartment on 4 March 1815 and was buried in St James's, Piccadilly. The talk of the town toward the end of her life was that she was in much straitened circumstances. John Taylor remembered having seen her looking, he thought, like the wife of an inferior tradesman, in a common red cloak. But she was certainly not destitute, as her will, proved 21 March 1815, shows. It left an estate, untotalled, for the execution of her solicitor Joseph Garman, Esq of Jermyn Street, St James. The actor Henry John-

stone's widow, Jane, of Wimpole Street, was left £200. Other bequests were: to Hanley Miller, son of William Miller, Esq of Hertfordshire, £50 "for books"; William Barton, Cook Street, Cork, bookseller, £100; Henry Favre of Pall Mall, watchmaker, £50, and his sister £10; William Cook, barrister of Piccadilly, £50 for a funeral ring; Mrs Elizabeth Morris, her "honest servant," £20 and her wearing apparel. The Theatrical Funds of Drury Lane and Covent Garden each received £50. Joseph Garman was to receive £100 immediately and the residue of the estate after bequests, debts, and funeral expenses were settled.

As might be expected, Frances Abington was painted by a great many of the best portraitists (and some of the worst) of her era. Sir Joshua Reynolds was her staunch admirer, and in 1772 took twelve tickets for her benefit. He matched his famous picture of "Mrs Siddons as the Tragic Muse" with "Mrs Abington as the Comic Muse." This portrait hangs now at Waddesden Manor, Aylesbury, Buckinghamshire, as a part of the James A. de Rothschild bequest to the National Trust. Cosway also painted her as "Thalia," and this portrait was engraved by Bartolozzi. An anonymous artist of c. 1785 portrayed her as "Comedy" in the same picture in which he pictured Mary Ann Yates as "Tragedy"; and an anonymous artist of c. 1783 also saw her as "Thalia," and Walker engraved this representation.

Sir Joshua Reynolds also painted her formal portrait in white domino as Miss Prue in *Love for Love*, and again as Roxalana in *The Sultan*, and both were much copied and engraved.

J. Roberts did several portraits of her in water color on vellum, which are reproduced in Bell's *British Theatre* and Bell's *Shakespeare*. There are other portraits of her in character by Samuel De Wilde, J. H. Ramberg, R. West, T. Cook, D. Dodd, C. R. Ryley, R. Cosway, DeFesch, I. Taylor,

E. F. Burney, J. Sayer, T. Hickey, and by many anonymous artists. She is even one of several actresses pictured in Delftware wall tile (examples in the City of Manchester Art Gallery).

Mrs Abington was linked suggestively with Lord Shelburne (as "Malagrida") in one of the *Town and Country Magazine*'s satirical engravings in 1777, but she remained otherwise uncaricatured, except for the several satirical prints which gibed at her ill-starred attempt in Scrub.

A painting by Joseph Highmore, showing a man and a woman seated in a castle hall, possibly a scene from *Cymon* as played by Robt Bensley and Mrs Abington, is apparently the property of Mr Frank T. Sabin, of London.

**Abington, Joseph** *d. 1774, violinist.*

At some time during the 1710–11 season a benefit concert was given for Joseph Abington at the Greyhound Tavern in the Strand. He received the benefit of other concerts, at Hickford's Rooms, on 4 March 1720 and 9 March 1722, though there was no indication that he performed on these occasions.

By 1738 he must have been a leader of his profession, for he was listed as one of the founding Governors of the Royal Society of Musicians of Great Britain and one of the original subscribers to the Society, in the Declaration of Trust establishing the organization, dated 28 August 1739. At this time he was living in the parish of St James, Westminster.

A Joseph Abington played the violin at performances of the *Messiah* in the Chapel of the Foundling Hospital in May 1754 and April 1758, being paid 10s. on each occasion.

By 1763 Mortimer's *London Directory* lists both a Joseph Abington, "One of his Majesty's Band of Music. Beauford-buildings," and a Joseph Abington, Jr who was "Performer on the Trumpet and Harpsichord. Compton-street," probably the son of the subject of this entry. Joseph Abington, Jr was trumpeter at a concert in Hampstead on 30 August 1754.

The will of Joseph Abington "late Musician in Ord$^{ny}$ to the King" was proved on 23 December 1774, and administration of his property was granted to William Abington, his son, though Joseph's relict, Sarah, was named executrix. Sarah "Died without taking upon her the Execution of the s$^d$ will." Perhaps the younger Joseph was dead by this time.

**Abington, Joseph** ₍fl. 1763₎, *trumpeter, harpsichordist.* See **ABINGTON, JOSEPH** d. 1774.

**Abington, Leonard** *d. 1767, violinist, trumpeter, composer, singer?*

Between 1740 and 1767 many slight pastoral songs were produced by Leonard Abington and published as sung by popular singers at Marylebone Gardens. Abington may have been a member of the band at the pleasure gardens. He is said by Mortimer's *London Directory* to have been a performer on the violin and the trumpet and to have lived in 1763 in Great Pultney Street, Golden Square. He apparently died in the early summer of 1767, and administration of an unspecified property was granted to his widow Elizabeth, of the Parish of St Marylebone on 28 November 1767.

**Abington, Leonard Joseph** ₍fl. 1794₎, *singer.*

Leonard Joseph Abington was listed by Doane's *Musical Directory* (1794) as a bass singer, a member of the Long Acre Society and Surrey Chapel Society, and a subscriber to the Choral Fund. He lived in 1794 at No 6, Gilbert Street, Bloomsbury. Abington was granted £5 for medical relief on 7 September 1817 by the Royal Society of Musicians because of a recent accident. On 3 March 1822 the Royal Society of Musicians granted a Mrs Abington £6 for being above 70 years old; and on 6 April 1823 it granted £8 for her funeral expenses to her daughter Jane. (These references may, however, refer to William Abington, the composer.)

**Abington, William**  [fl. 1774–1794], *composer, instrumentalist.*

William Abington the composer very probably performed in public instrumental concerts in London. He was almost assuredly that William who was mentioned as a son in the will of Joseph Abington the violinist (d. 1774).

Abington published at London at least three works for instrumental performance: *Six Favorite Canzonets for the Piano Forte, with an Accompaniment for a Violin* [?1790]; *The Royal East India Quick March, for a Trumpet, Horns, Clarinets, and Bassoons, also adapted for the Piano Forte* [1796]; *The Royal East India Slow March* . . . [1797]; and a song, *The Jew* [?1796].

**Able.** *See* ABEL *and* ABELL.

**Aborie, L'.** *See* L'ABORIE.

**Abrahall, Mr**  [fl. 1700], *musician.*
On 3 June 1700 a Mr Abrahall replaced the deceased William Hall in the King's Musick.

**Abraham, Mr**  [fl. 1793].
A Mr Abraham presented an entertainment entitled "The Siege of Valenciennes" at a booth at Bartholomew Fair in 1793.

**Abraham, John**  [fl. 1688], *instrumentalist.*
John Abraham was appointed bowmaster in the King's Musick on 8 December 1688, replacing the deceased Thomas Farmer; he was probably, like Farmer, a violinist.

**Abraham, John**  *1777–1856.* *See* BRAHAM, JOHN.

**Abrahams, David Bramah**  *1775–1837, violist, violinist, singer.*

David Bramah Abrahams was born on 12 August 1775 in the parish of St James's, Duke's Place, London, according to a sworn deposition his mother, the widowed Esther Abrahams of Wellclose Square, signed with her mark at the Police Offices in Lambeth Street, White Chapel, on 12 October 1798. (He was probably the son of John Abrahams and his wife Esther Lyon and brother of the singer John Braham, of the six singing Abrams sisters, Harriet, Miss G., Eliza, Flora, Theodosia, and Jane, and of Charles and William Abrams.) The deposition was preparatory to his recommendation on 4 November 1798 by the violinist James Sanderson, the leader of the band at the Royal Circus and Ranelagh, to membership in the Royal Society of Musicians. At that time he was said to have

practised music for a living upwards of seven years, and was also articled to Mr Griffiths for five years preceding. He is engaged at the Royal Circus, Ranelagh, and has other engagements and [teaches] private scholars. He is a Married Man but without children, aged twentythree performs on the Violin and Tenor.

On 3 February 1799, Abrahams was unanimously elected to the Society, at which time Sanderson paid his subscription; Abrahams formally attended and signed the registry on 7 April 1799.

Our subject was doubtless the "D. Abrahams" of No 5, Ratcliff Highway who is listed in Doane's *Musical Directory* (1794) as "canto, violin" and a member of the Handelian Society and of the "Royal theater" (which probably means the band at the Royalty Theatre). He had been a part of the "grand performances [in celebration of Handel] at Westminster Abbey."

Abrahams was appointed by the Governors of the Royal Society of Musicians to the lists of those who played for the annual May benefit concerts for the clergy of St

Paul's Cathedral in 1799, 1800, 1803, and 1806. He was on the list in 1804 simply as "Bramah," and for some reason seems to have appeared, both in public and in the records of the Society from 1806 onward as "David Bramah." A New Royal Circus bill of October 1806 for a night on which he shared a benefit with Mrs Cross, wife of the equestrian proprietor of that establishment, calls him "Bramah" and "Leader of the Band." He answered to the same appellation on 3 December 1815 as a member of the Committee of Accounts of the Royal Society of Music.

Nothing more was recorded about Abrahams in the Society's records until 1 July 1827, when he was granted sick relief of £5 5s., he having deposed on 4 March that for nine years previously he had been suffering a paralytic affliction. He proposed on that date that the Society accept two houses which he owned at Islington and grant him an annuity in exchange. Evidently this scheme was unacceptable to the Governors. On 7 February 1830 he was permitted to make affidavit under a magistrate in Chancery inasmuch as he was lame. On 2 January 1831 his sick allowance was reduced to £3 (probably monthly), but on 1 January 1832 his "full allowance" was restored. On 3 January 1836 he sent thanks to the Society for a special donation sent to him. On 5 March 1837 his widow, Jane, was granted the "usual allowance" of £2 12s. 6d. The Minute Book recorded her death on 2 December 1838.

### Abrahams, John   [fl. 1775–1779], house servant?

By Garrick's order several payments of £20 were made to a Mr Abrahams from the treasury of the Drury Lane Theatre during the 1775–76 season. He may have been a house servant, but, since he is identified at least once as the father of Harriet Abrams, he is also the father not only of her sisters Miss G., Eliza, Flora, Theodosia, and Jane, but probably also of the celebrated singer

John Braham and perhaps as well of Charles and William Abrams and David Bramah Abrahams. (His wife was Esther Lyon, sister of Meyer Lyon [Michael Leoni] the singer, and the first name of the mother of David Bramah Abrahams is known to have been Esther.)

John Abrahams received and signed for the salaries of Harriet and Miss G. Abrams at various times up until 1779.

### Abrams, Charles   [fl. 1794], violoncellist.

Charles Abrams was listed by Doane's *Musical Directory* (1794) as a participant in the concerts of the Academy of Ancient Music, a player in the Oratorios at Covent Garden, a performer in the Handelian celebrations at Westminster Abbey and the Pantheon, and an employee of the Opera House.

He lived in 1794 at No 73, Charlotte Street, Rathbone Place, and thus was connected with Eliza, Miss G., Flora, Harriet, Jane, Theodosia, Charles and William Abrams, with David Bramah Abrahams, and with John Braham the singer. It is probable that they were his siblings and that, therefore, John Abrahams (fl. 1775–79) was his father.

### Abrams, Eliza   b. 1763?, singer.

Eliza Abrams sang in company with some of her five sisters at the Ladies' Catch and Glee Concerts and perhaps at other concerts and the theatres. Her sisters were Harriet, Miss G., Flora, Jane, and Theodosia. She appears also to have been related, probably also as sister, to Charles and William Abrams, David Bramah Abrahams, and John Braham. Her father was John Abrahams (fl. 1775–79).

### Abrams, Flora   [fl. 1778], singer.

Flora Abrams's benefit concert at the Panton Street Rooms was announced for 12 May 1778. She was undoubtedly a sister of the other Abrams girls (Harriet, Jane, Miss

G., Eliza, and Theodosia) who were at this time singers and probably also of Charles and William Abrams, David Bramah Abrahams and John Braham. Her father was John Abrahams (fl. 1775–79).

**Abrams, Miss G.** [*fl. 1778–1780*], *singer, actress.*

Miss G. Abrams first appeared in the Drury Lane bills in a singing part in Sheridan's new pantomime *The Wonders of Derbyshire* at its introduction on 8 January 1779. She presumably sang in at least 24 performances of the popular piece that season, until 15 April 1780. That she was a juvenile performer at this time is indicated by the fact that she was one of the children in *Medea*, 25 March 1779, and was young Lord William in *The Countess of Salisbury* on 16 March 1779. She was present in the theatre with her older sister Harriet on 30 September 1779 and sang on that date and later in *The Wonders*. She played "First Genii" in the afterpiece *The Genii* on 5 May and repeated the part on 17 May 1780. Unlike Harriet, she shared in no benefit. Her other sisters were Flora, Jane, Theodosia, and Eliza. She appears to have been related also (probably as sister) to Charles and William Abrams, David Bramah Abrahams, and John Braham. Her father was John Abrahams (fl. 1775–79).

**Abrams, Harriet** *1760–1825? singer, composer.*

Harriet was the most celebrated of the daughters of John Abrahams, the singing Abrams sisters, and the most often employed. She was a prize pupil of Dr Thomas Augustine Arne, and as such was the object of great care when she was brought before the public at Drury Lane under David Garrick's sponsorship.

Garrick wrote to George Colman in October 1775, "I am somewhat puzzled about introducing my little jew Girl—she is surprizing! I want to introduce her as the little Gipsy with 3 or 4 exquisite songs."

*Harvard Theatre Collection*

HARRIET ABRAMS, as Sylvia

artist unknown

Garrick had written his afterpiece *May Day; or, the Little Gipsy* and Arne had furnished new music, expressly for the debut of the winsome 15-year-old girl on 28 October 1775, under the conventional anonymity of "A Young Lady, first appearance on any Stage." William Hopkins told his diary: "This Musical Farce of one Act was wrote by Mr G on purpose to introduce Miss Abrams (a Jew) about 17 Years old. She is very small, a Swarthy Complexion, has a very sweet Voice and a fine Shake, but not quite power enough yet—both the Piece and the Young Lady were receiv'd with Great Applause." One London newspaper confidently identified her: "It is said the Little Gipsy is a Jewess, and her name Handler. The number of Jews at the Theatre is incredible." Another paper came somewhat nearer her name, calling her "Miss Adams."

Harriet repeated her debut part several times before her next attempt, which was Leonora in *The Padlock*, on 7 December 1775 ("The Young Lady who performed the Little Gipsy"), and the prompter Hopkins pronounced only "So, so" in his diary.

In the season of 1776–77 Harriet was paid £2 10*s.* per week, opening as Little Gipsy in September and closing as Leonora in June. She was heard with her sister Theodosia at the opening of the Concerts of Ancient Music under Joah Bates's organization in 1776, and they returned to sing there for many seasons. A surviving account of money paid to singers by the Academy of Ancient Music in the 1787–88 season shows that the Misses Abrams, "Principal Singers" (probably Harriet and Miss G.), received £63.

Until the spring of 1780 Harriet each season sang occasional leads, or secondary roles like Gillian in *The Quaker*, at Drury Lane but mostly assisted in the choruses there. Until at least 1779 her father John received her salary, as well as that of one of her sisters, Miss G. Abrams.

Harriet sang as soloist at the Oxford Music Room on 23 November 1782 and is listed as a "treble" singer in the Handel Memorial Concerts at Westminster Abbey on 26, 27 and 29 May and the Pantheon on 3 and 5 June 1784. She was also probably the Miss Abrams who sang at Astley's Amphitheatre on 27 September 1787. In 1794 she and her sister Theodosia were both living at No 73, Charlotte Street, Rathbone Place, which fact establishes a relationship with William Abrams, Charles Abrams and thus with John Braham. A British Museum manuscript of the later eighteenth century calls her "Braham's sister." Her other sisters were Jane, Flora, and Eliza.

Harriet Abrams was a composer of popular songs of a sentimental tendency, and there are 16 of her works listed in the British Museum catalogue of printed music,

with such titles as "A Smile and a Tear," "The Friend of My Heart," "The Orphan's Prayer." Her most engaging song, sung over and over at the theatres for years, was "Crazy Jane."

An engraving of her playing a part in the masque of *Cymon* was published by J. Bew in 1778. She is the subject of a satirical print of 1788 "by S. W. Forrest Satirist," an alteration of a plate which had before depicted the demi-rep Miss Martha Ray with her lover, John Montagu, Fourth Earl of Sandwich, the notorious "Jemmy Twitcher." The alteration shows instead two figures identified in the British Museum copy as "Miss Abrams's." No connection is known other than the fact that Sandwich was a director of the Ancient Music Concerts.

**Abrams, Jane**   (*fl.* 1799),   *singer?*

John Philip Kemble noted in a memorandum of 19 April 1799: "Dined with Harriet, Jane, Theodosia & Eliza Abrams." Jane is not named in any records of performance, but she is probably concealed in the numerous notations of "the Miss Abrams." She was the sister of the singers Kemble named, as well as of Flora and Miss G. Abrams, and very probably also of Charles Abrams, David Bramah Abrahams, William Abrams, and John Braham. Her father was John Abrahams (fl. 1775–79).

**Abrams, Theodosia, later Mrs Thomas Fisher, Mrs Joseph Garrow**   *c. 1761–1849, singer.*

Theodosia Abrams is first noticed as singing, at about age 15, with her sister Harriet, at the opening of the Concerts of Ancient Music in 1776. Her voice was contralto in pitch. She sang at the Handel Memorial Concerts at Westminster Abbey and the Pantheon in May and June of 1784, and as soloist at the Oxford Music Room on 5 April 1788. Her aria, "Thou shalt bring him in," in the second act of *The Israelites in Egypt,* sung at the Tottenham Street

Concert House, 22 February 1788, brought her critical credit. She apparently lived with her numerous family at No 73, Charlotte Street, Rathbone Place, in 1794. (Her father, John Abrahams, apparently had these other musical children: Eliza, Flora, Miss G., Harriet, Jane, Charles and William Abrams, and David Bramah Abrahams and John Braham.) She retired toward the end of the eighteenth century. She was married first to Captain Thomas Fisher, and then, in April 1812, to Joseph Garrow, and died at Braddons, Torquay, on 4 November 1849.

**Abrams, William**  *[fl. 1794], violinist, violist.*

William Abrams is said by Doane's *Musical Directory* (1794) to have played in the band at the Concerts of Ancient Music. His residence at No 73, Charlotte Street, Rathbone Place, connects him (probably as their brother) with the female singers Harriet, Miss G., Jane, Eliza, Flora, and Theodosia Abrams, with John Braham, and with Charles Abrams and David Bramah Abrahams, all musicians. Their father was apparently John Abrahams (fl. 1775–79).

**Achmet, Mrs, stage name of MRS WILLIAM CAIRNS, CATHERINE ANN, née EGAN**  *b. 1766, actress.*

Mrs Achmet, as she called herself for the duration of her brief theatrical career, was born Catherine Ann Egan in 1766. According to the *Hibernian Magazine* her father was a surgeon of Kilkenny and her mother a Miss O'Neill from Dublin. Egan is supposed to have died in 1777 after gambling away his wife's dowry, leaving his family dependent upon relatives.

By 1784 Catherine was bearing the name Achmet. *The Secret History of the Green Rooms* (1790) though wishing kindly "to veil the early foibles of those whose subsequent conduct inclines to virtue" nevertheless hinted broadly that she was "of an easy and obliging temper," and "the debauchees of Dublin celebrated her beauty." The same source declares that she lived unmarried with "Mr Achmet" for less than a year before "becoming pregnant." Feigning labor and sending Achmet one night for a midwife, she eloped with an officer. Achmet pursued and retook her and then married her.

W. J. Lawrence, more charitably, believed that she was in 1784 already legally entitled to the real name of her husband, which was Cairns. Though Lawrence himself discovered a license for William Cairns and Catherine Egan to marry, which specified St Thomas's Church of the Church of Ireland, in Dublin, as the place for the ceremony, he nevertheless believed that they probably had been wed previously by a Roman Catholic priest. Lawrence explained that, under the laws which obtained at the time, Mrs Cairns probably had to make her recantation of Roman Catholicism and remarry in the Church of England to make the union legal.

Much of the career of her husband up to that point of their association is equally murky. According to the highly colored anecdotes told of him by Sir Jonah Barrington, he was really one Patrick Joyce, out of Kilkenny, though he went by the name of Cairns up to his assumption of the *nom de guerre* Dr Achmet or Achmet Borumborad. How this came about is detailed scrupulously, but variously, in a number of sources. He was apparently engaged in his apothecary's trade in Dublin when his restive disposition impelled him to sign on board a privateer fighting the French. Taken prisoner, he voluntarily enlisted in the squadron of the adventurer Thurot, who was terrorizing the Irish coast. At some opportunity, Cairns deserted, went to London, and took employment as an attendant at some public "Turkish" baths, where he made certain technical improvements. He then went to Dublin where, because of the persuasiveness of his arguments to the medical faculty that public steam baths would improve the health of the populace, he secured the backing of 26 medical men. He took on the name and style of Dr Achmet and a terrifying black beard to enhance his credibility. An even odder variant has him acquiring his name and baleological expertise in a trip to Constantinople.

Certainly Achmet did establish the "Royal Patent Baths at No 40, Bachelor's Quay" and prospered hugely under the patronage of Dublin physicians and the elite. He was tall and impressive in manner, and only a few of his fellow Hibernians at first questioned his Ottoman origins, but growing numbers of doubters took the edge from his exoticism, and after his property was condemned and he had to move to another quarter of the city custom declined and he abandoned his project.

Mrs Achmet first appeared at Smock Alley Theatre in Dublin on 8 November 1784 for six nights, as Indiana in *The Conscious Lovers,* and she returned for six more nights on the same contract in 1785. She was advertised by Atkins to open his season at Belfast on 3 October 1786 as "the celebrated Mrs. Achmet the first female ornament of the Irish stage," and on 23 October she played as Estifania in *Rule a Wife and Have a Wife.* The Belfast *Newsletter* reported "For her debut, Mr. Whyte, the celebrated poetical schoolmaster of Dublin (whose pupil she was) wrote an excellent special prologue." She speedily won over the difficult Belfast audiences in a series of characters: Euphrasia in *The Grecian Daughter,* Polly in *The Beggar's Opera,* Juliet in *Romeo and Juliet,* Sigismunda in *Tancred and Sigismunda,* Calista in *The Fair Penitent,* Monimia in *The Orphan,* and in the "breeches part" of Sir Harry Wildair in *The Constant Couple.* From this encounter apparently dated Lee Lewes's professional interest in her, for he is said to have coached her in acting at Belfast.

In 1786 and 1787 she played successively at Belfast, Cork, Waterford and Limerick, before coming to a season of 100 nights at Crow Street, Dublin, in 1787, her first regular engagement on salary.

Mrs Achmet brought her exquisite figure, lovely face, and growing abilities to London in 1789, having been assiduously "puffed" preparatory to her first appearance at Covent Garden on 14 September. She was given the considerable compliment of being invited to appear as Juliet to open the season opposite Joseph George Holman, who had been absent from London for two years. Most reviews were decidedly favorable, especially to her action in Act IV when she drank the potion without following it with the usual "phrenzy." One journal, however, deplored the "preposterous ornaments" with which she decorated her head, "which made her resemble the figure of Queen Esther in a Puppet Shew." The *Biographical and Imperial Magazine,* though praising her person, believed that "The greatest defect is a want of variety, her features appear to have little expression, except that of a settled sorrow." Though she repeated Juliet on 21 September and 9 November she was replaced 7 December and subsequently by Miss Anne Brunton. She "had the pleasure of sporting a smart leg before a crowded auditory" as Sir Harry Wildair on 30 September and 30 October. On 16 November, "for the first time," and to Holman's Hamlet, she was Ophelia. Only occasionally during the rest of Covent Garden's 1789–90 season was she named in the bills: as Julia Montfort in *The Force of Fashion,* and another breeches part, Jessamy in *Lionel and Clarissa.* She earned £6 per week.

In early 1790 Mrs Achmet went to Limerick and Ennis. She played at least once again in Limerick in 1791. But *The Morning Post* of 29 November 1790 reported that "Mrs. Achmet is sporting her gig in Ireland with a Theatrical Baronet of Limerick who has an amiable wife and family and the public have interfered and will not let her act."

An unascribed manuscript note in the Folger Library, dated 15 April 1791, gives us our latest news of her: "Mrs Achmet formerly of C. G. Theat. has eloped fr her Husbd & is adverd by him in the Dub. Papers." John Jackson recalled having seen her at Shrewsbury for awhile during the same year, and she was also on the York bills.

Mrs Achmet was blessed with beauty, a natural elegance, and, many critics thought, considerable talent. The *European Magazine* believed that she "formed herself on Mrs. Crawford," certainly no bad model. Yet like many young adventurers of early promise, she failed to find a permanent place in the theatrical capital. It seems likely that the Miss Achmet who appeared briefly in London was her daughter.

**Achmet, Miss** ₍*fl. 1794*₎, *actress.*

A Miss Achmet played in London once only, as Miss Mortimer in *The Chapter of Accidents* at an out-of-season benefit performance at the Haymarket on 2 June 1794.

**Achurch, Miss.** *See* **MAHON, MRS ROBERT.**

**Achurch, Sarah.** *See* **WARD, MRS HENRY.**

**Achurch, Thomas** *d. 1771, actor.*

Thomas Achurch is probably that Achurch who was first noticed as a "page" in *Fatal Love* at the New Haymarket on 21 January 1730 and then played Jack in *The Author's Farce* on 30 March and at least 35 times until 1 July. He acted Selim in *Amurath the Great* and Noodle in *Tom Thumb* in Penkethman's booth at Southwark Fair the following September. He is not known to have been in London again until 3 April 1749 when he took the part of Sharp in *The Lying Valet* at Covent Garden, for the benefit of his daughter Sarah, Mrs Henry Ward. He was noticed in the bill as "from York," and, indeed, had

been with the York company at that time for eight years.

Achurch was at York a total of 30 years, always in possession of key supporting roles in both comedy and tragedy, including Gloucester, Mercutio, Jaques, Banquo, and Peachum in *The Beggar's Opera.* He was a mighty favorite with the York audiences, and Tate Wilkinson, attempting there Major Sturgeon in *The Author,* was hissed and pelted with oranges for his presumption in assuming one of Tom Achurch's parts.

One of Achurch's daughters, Sarah, became Mrs Henry Ward, and another, whose first name is not known, married Robert Mahon. (There seems no foundation for Isaac Reed's assertion that she was later married to Robert Palmer, comptroller of the Post Office.) Achurch probably had at least two other daughters: A Miss Henrietta Achurch was acting at York in 1763. She and a Miss Anne Achurch were subscribers to Henry Ward's *Works,* published in 1746.

Thomas Achurch died at Leeds on 30 August 1771.

**Achurch, Mrs [Thomas?]** ₍*fl. 1734*₎, *actress.*

The Mrs Achurch who is recorded only as Harriet in *The Miser* at the tennis court on James Street, 31 May 1734, was probably the wife of the actor Thomas Achurch.

**Ackerill, Mr** ₍*fl. 1793–1795*₎, *slackwire dancer, equestrian, tumbler.*

Mr Ackerill was a dancer on the slack wire in Handy's New Circus company at the Lyceum Theatre in 1793, 1794, and 1795. He also performed feats of tumbling and horsemanship and played very minor dramatic roles.

**Ackerill, Master** ₍*fl. 1793–1795*₎, *slackwire dancer, violinist.*

Master Ackerill was probably the son of the Mr Ackerill who offered the same sorts of entertainment in the minor theatres and circuses as did the younger performer. The boy (as "Ackerhill") did "Chironomical Performances" on a high wire, usually with young Miss Riccardini, at Hughes's Royal Circus in St George's Fields in 1793, "In the course of which," boasted the bills, he would "play a Tune on the violin, the wire in full swing, and he standing on his head." In 1795 he was featured in slackwire dancing in Handy's New Circus, at the Lyceum, where the elder Ackerill also performed.

**Ackery, Mr** ₁*fl. 1787*₁, *actor.*

Toward the ends of the seasons of 1782–83, 1783–84 and 1785–86, Ackery (or Sickery) was among a dozen people, many of them identifiable as dancers and musicians, delivering tickets at Covent Garden Theatre for a benefit performance.

*Permission of the Birmingham Museum and Art Gallery*

DAVID GARRICK as Lord Chalkstone, ELLIS ACKMAN as Bowman, and ASTLEY BRANSBY as Aesop

in *Lethe*

by Zoffany

**Ackman, Ellis**  *d. 1774, actor.*

Ellis Ackman was a useful actor at Drury Lane Theatre, where he remained a member of the company for nearly 25 winter seasons.

Ackman's first recorded appearance was as Lennox in *Macbeth* on 23 April 1750, an auspicious date for a Shakespearean debut, and in Ackman's case an augury. This part was the beginning of his long service in the minor, secondary, and supporting Shakespearean roles which became the meat of his personal repertory during the burgeoning midcentury revival of Shakespeare's plays on the London stage: Alexas in *Antony and Cleopatra,* Antonio and Borachio in *Much Ado about Nothing,* Balthazar, Benvolio, and Tybalt in *Romeo and Juliet,* Caliban and the Shipmaster in *The Tempest,* Caphis in *Timon of Athens,* the Captain and a Gentleman in *Cymbeline,* the Captain in *King Lear,* Duke Senior and LeBeau in *As You Like It,* a Gentleman in *All's Well that Ends Well,* Guildenstern and Marcellus in *Hamlet,* Hastings in *2 Henry IV,* the Herald in *Henry V,* the Lord Mayor and Tressel in *Richard III,* Lovell in *Henry VIII,* a Messenger in *Othello,* the First Outlaw in *The Two Gentlemen of Verona,* Oxford in *Richard III,* Peter in *The Taming of the Shrew* (in Garrick's alteration *Catherine and Petruchio*), Pistol in *The Merry Wives of Windsor,* a Roman in *Coriolanus,* Seyton in *Macbeth,* Snout in both original *A Midsummer Night's Dream* and as altered to *A Fairy Tale* by George Colman the elder, and Westmoreland in *1 Henry IV.*

Aside from Shakespeare's plays, Ackman's roles were meagre and infrequent, never ascending much above such as Sergius in *The Siege of Damascus,* Thomas in *The Miser,* Lord Lurewell in *The Miller of Mansfield,* or Bowman in *Lethe,* and frequently, to oblige David Garrick his manager, descending to anonymous slaves, servants, soldiers, sailors, tavern drawers, and country fellows. He was kept on for general utility and apparently did odd chores about the playhouse. In at least one season (1749–50) he served the theatre also as a copyist of voice parts. In 1766 he lived near the theatre, "next door to the Fountain, Catherine-street." By 1772 he was even nearer, "at Mr Pitt's in the Piazza, Covent Garden."

Ackman seems to have been faithful and dependable and a steadying influence on his colleagues. When the actors' committee met on 18 May 1774 to set up the Drury Lane retirement fund, he was a member. He was also popular with the public (except in 1763, when he was briefly under its displeasure during the half-price riots), and his benefits, always shared except in his final year, were well attended. By 1765 he was making £1 10s., which placed him in the respectable fifth rank of performers so far as remuneration was concerned, and in this relative position he seems to have ended his active days. His last recorded performance was as Tom in *The Jealous Wife* on 18 May 1774, at Drury Lane.

Ackman acted at Richmond and Twickenham in the summers of 1752 and 1753 and in the summers of 1765 and 1766 both at Richmond and with Foote at the Haymarket; and he was occasionally at the Haymarket again in the season of 1770–71 for benefit performances.

Hugh Kelly in his *Thespis* (1766) praised the strict propriety and care with which this "tolerable player" prepared his small roles and also commended his punctuality in performance. The *Rational Rosciad* (1767) disagreed:

*Immodest Ackman, in the simplest parts,*
*From Nature and his author's sense, departs;*
*His round of characters indeed are small,*
*But then he blunders largely in them all.*

Ellis Ackman was found dead outside his lodgings in Gray's Inn early on the morning of 1 October 1774.

The celebrated large oil painting by Johann Zoffany of David Garrick as Chalkstone, Astley Bransby as Aesop, and Ellis Ackman as Bowman in the 1776 revival of Garrick's *Lethe* hangs in the City Museum and Art Gallery, Birmingham.

**Ackman, Mrs** ₍fl. 1779₎, *house servant?*

A Mrs Ackman was one of several members of the Covent Garden house delivering benefit tickets for that theatre on 21 May 1779. She may have been Ellis Ackman's widow, but no connection has been established.

**Ackroyde.** *See* AKEROYDE.

**Acqua, dé.** *See* DEL'ACQUA.

**Acres, Miss Ann.** *See* MURRAY, MRS CHARLES.

**Acroyd.** *See* AKEROYDE.

**Actime.** *See* ARTIMA.

**Adamberger, Valentin** 1743–1804, *singer.*

Valentin Adamberger was born in Munich on 6 July 1743. He was placed early in his youth with the great singer-teacher Johann Evangelist Wallishauser, known as Valesi, and at his urging travelled to Italy. There he took the name of Adamonti, and sang with considerable success in several of the principal cities.

By 1777 Adamberger had come to London and in the next two seasons at the King's Theatre he starred in at least sixty-two performances to great critical approval and popular acclaim. His roles there were, successively, in 1777–78: Creso in *Creso,* Learco in *Erifile,* Scipione in *La clemenza di Scipione,* and Alessandro in *Il re pastore.* In 1778–79 he sang Demofoonte in the *pasticcio Demofoonte,* Artabano in *Arta-*serse, Latino in *Enea e Lavinia,* and Megacle in *L'Olimpiade.*

His success in London reached the Emperor Joseph who called him to Vienna where he appeared at the Hof-und-National Theater from 21 August 1780.

Adamberger was a successful concert singer and a famous teacher. W. A. Mozart was his close friend.

He was married in 1782 to the actress Maria Anna Jacquet. He died in Vienna 24 August 1804. His wife also died in 1804.

**Adamonti.** *See* ADAMBERGER, VALENTIN.

**Adams, Mr** ₍fl. 1669–1673₎, *actor.*

A minor member of the Duke's Company at Lincoln's Inn Fields from about 1669 to 1670, Mr Adams also played with the King's troupe in 1673 during their stay at the same theatre. Specific references to him are rare, but on 11 or 12 August 1670 he was ordered to be apprehended for absenting himself from the playhouse, and he is known to have played Draxanes in *The Women's Conquest* in December 1670 and the second Witch in the burlesque *Macbeth* epilogue to Duffett's *The Empress of Morocco* in December 1673. He may have been the Jack Adams, clown, who seems to have been active about 1667.

**Adams, Mr** ₍fl. 1728₎, *actor.*

An Adams played at the Haymarket theatre from July through December 1728 with a mixed company of amateurs and professionals, but the performances were sporadic. His roles were important ones, however: the title role in *Tamerlane,* Torrismond in *The Spanish Friar,* Young Traffick in *The Metamorphosis,* Freeman in *The Lottery,* and Carlos in *Don Carlos.* After the end of 1728 his name disappeared from the bills, and presently the troupe dissolved.

**Adams, Mr** ₁*fl. 1736–1748*₁, *dancer, actor.*

It is probable that the Adams who was first noticed in the character of James, in *The Female Rake,* in Charlotte Charke's company of casuals at the New Haymarket Theatre on 26 April 1736 was the dancer Adams who had executed a hornpipe in the same theatre on 16 February. He is presumably the same actor-dancer who was recorded in scattered bills for the next four years: in the summer of 1741 at Yates's booth at West Smithfield; in August 1741 and August 1743 with Yates at Bury Fair; in March 1743 at the James Street Theatre; in August 1743 at Hippisley and Chapman's booth at Bury Fair (though the existence also that month of "Godwin and Adam's Booth" at Bury Fair may probably argue the presence of two of this name); in May 1744 at Hallam's "New Theatre, Mayfair"; on 11 July 1745 at Shepherd's Market; dancing his *Jockey Dance* on 25 August 1746 at Yeates, Sr and Bennet's booth "facing the Hospital Gate"; at Yeates and Lee's Great Tiled Booth at Southwark Fair September 1747; and in August 1748 at Yeates and Lee's booth at Bury Fair.

Adams again did his *Jockey Dance* when he took a benefit with the minor actor Scudamore at the Haymarket on 30 April 1748. At least one Adams, a dancer, was at Lee and Yeates's Booth at Southwark Fair in September 1748, and on 4 July 1748 a Mrs Adams had received a benefit there. Adams performed his *Jockey Dance* at New Wells, Shepherd's Market on 29 December 1748; and at the Old Theatre, Bowling Green, Southwark on 13 February 1749, where he was listed as a harlequin. An Adam or Adams, dancer, appeared for the first and apparently the last time at Drury Lane on 21 February 1749 in the masque *Triumph of Peace.*

**Adams, Mr** ₁*fl. 1763–1770?*₁, *singer.*
Both the *Royal Magazine* and the *Lady's Magazine* in 1763 published a dialogue song *Lads and Lassies blithe and gay,* as sung by Master Adams and Miss Carli at Finch's Grotto Gardens. The male singer was *"Mr Adams"* when in c. 1770 another dialogue song, *Sylvan and Cynthia,* was published, as sung at the same resort by the same singers.

**Adams, Mr** ₁*fl. 1782–1800*₁, *bird imitator, tumbler, equestrian.*

A Mr Adams first came to public notice as a featured performer on the stage of Astley's Amphitheatre when, from 17 October 1782, he filled in between equestrian acts seven times as an imitator of songbirds. On the bill of 4 November he was distinguished as "the English Rossignol." (*See* ROSSIGNOL, Sieur Gaetano à la).

Adams reappeared at Astley's in August, September, and October of 1785, his imitations "Accompanied by a Full Band of Music," taking his benefit on 27 September. Two bills of 1786—12 May and 9 October—survive carrying Adams's name. Four years later, on 6 April 1790, he whistled for the last time at Astley's.

By 23 June 1800 Adams was to be found at the "New Splendid Equestrian Pantomime" at Davis's New Royal Circus in St George's Fields "warbling and chirping," according to the bill.

The Royal Circus playbill of 24 September 1800 advertised the "Benefit of Mr and Mrs Adams." Except for some horsemanship by Saunders this performance was strictly an affair of the family:

For that Night only, the Miss ADAM's will dance a Grand MINUET and GAVOTTE (in Character).

At the particular request of several Friends, and for that Night only, Mr Adams will perform (in sight, on the Stage) his IMITA-TIONS of VARIOUS BIRDS, viz. the Thrush, Sky-Lark, Whitethroat, Lapwing, Quail, Robbin, and Nightingale; and will accompany, to a Full Band of Music (which, for that Night, will be considerably augmented), a GRAND OVERTURE A-LA-ROSSIGNOL, composed by Signor Gossee, in a surprizing manner, and in a style of precision, execution, and tone, peculiar to himself, which has been the admiration of the Musical Amateurs and Cognoscenti.

An entire New PANTOMIMIC BALLET, in which the Miss Adams's will dance Lady Charlotte Campbell's favourite Strathspey and Reel.

The whole to conclude with
A GRAND SPECTACLE;
Particulars of which, and the other Amusements, will be expressed in future Bills.

Tickets that night were to be had of Mrs Adams, who, from perhaps before 1798 to after 1800, was box-office keeper and treasury assistant at the Circus.

We know nothing of Mr and Mrs Adams after about 1800. But the Misses Adams danced and sang, singly or together, fairly regularly in the Royal Circus company from September 1800 until 1803. There were never more than three of them dancing at a time during this period, and they are at various times severally distinguished as the Misses E., H., and S. Adams. They are surely "the three Miss Adams" making their "first appearance" at Covent Garden on 27 May 1800, executing "A New Dance (By Permission of the Proprietors of the Royal Circus)." There was also a fourth Miss Adams. Mr C. B. Hogan calls our attention to a notice in the *Hibernian Magazine* of December 1803 of a Miss Anna Matilda Adams, aged 18, who had been at the Crow Street Theatre, Dublin, for four years, chiefly as a dancer. She may have been the fourth of "The four sisters Adam" who were dancing in ballet divertissements at Brighton in the summer of 1808. A Miss Adams had acted in Edinburgh in 1804–5, and another was seen at Drury Lane in 1807–8, and "3 Adams," not distinguished by sex, were on the Covent Garden roster temporarily on 2 January 1808.

The "Infant Rossignol," who was to imitate "the Notes of various Birds, and also accompany the band on a Dumb Violin," at Astley's on 27 July 1795, may have been the son of the Adams of this entry.

**Adams, Mr** [*fl. 1788*], *actor.*
A Mr Adams performed six nights at the Crow Street Theatre, Dublin, on and after 28 February 1788. He appeared at the Haymarket Theatre as Scrub, in *The Beaux' Stratagem,* being introduced as "A Gentleman," on 24 July 1788. Nothing more is known of him.

**Adams, Mrs** [*fl. 1731*], *actress.*
A Mrs Adams played Favourite in *The Gamester* at Lincoln's Inn Fields Theatre on 1 April 1731.

**Adams, Mrs** [*fl. 1748*], *dancer or actress. See* ADAMS, MR [*fl. 1736–1748*].

**Adams, Mrs** [*fl. 1750*], *actress, singer.*
Mrs Adams played the part of Manon l'Effrontee in *L'Opera du gueux,* a translation of *The Beggar's Opera* into French which was performed by an organized group of actors at the Haymarket on 16 and 21 February 1750.

**Adams, Mrs** [*fl. 1798–1800*], *box-office keeper. See* ADAMS, MR [*fl. 1783–1800*].

**Adams, Master** [*fl. 1763–1766*], *singer.*
Master Adams was singing at Finch's Grotto Gardens in 1763 and again (or still) in 1766. In both years he performed duets with Miss Carli.

**Adams, Master** [*fl. 1795*], *bird imitator. See* ADAMS, MR [*fl. 1782–1800*].

**Adams, Miss.** *See* ABRAMS, HARRIET.

**Adams, Anna Matilda** [*fl. 1800?–1808?*], *dancer, actress? See* ADAMS, MR [*fl. 1782–1800*].

**Adams, Charles** [*fl. c. 1745–1751*], *actor.*

Charles Adams was an established player at Leicester when he and his wife Elizabeth came to London in December 1748. He bore with him the hearty recommendation of Garrick's friend, the dramatist and poet John Gilbert-Cooper (1723–1769). But, as a long correspondence published by Alan D. Guest has shown, the recommendation was fruitless. Garrick wrote Gilbert-Cooper on 19 November 1748 revealing that he had already been angered by Adams's delay in answering a letter: "When I have heard him speak I shall be able to judge if I can do him any Service, if not, I will either recommend him Elsewhere or give him ye best advice. Your Judgment goes a great Way with me, but in ye Country, where Actors are judg'd by Comparison, the best Critick may be mistaken."

In a report from London to Gilbert-Cooper at Leicester dated 3 January 1748 (N.S. 1749), Adams complained colorfully and convincingly of Garrick's reneging his promise to give him the part of Tressel in *Richard III* on the excuse that his manners were insufficiently urbane: "he inform'd me he did it out of pure Tenderness, to prevent my being pelted off the Stage, for I had so much of the Country Way of Speaking 'twould not do." But though Adams stood up to Garrick, informing the manager that none but he and Barry in that theatre could teach him much about acting, "The Prompter gave me a little Part in the Emperor of the Moon (a Farce) but so trivial 'twas impossible to be taken any Notice of in it."

Garrick refused either to provide better parts or to raise Adams's pay above 20 shillings a week, which the actor regarded as near the starvation line. Moreover, by 17 January 1749 his wife had fallen "prodigious ill." Attempts by Lord Stamford to introduce his friend Adams into the Covent Garden company list also failed.

The baffled performer had already received an "Invitation from the York Company with a Proffer of Seventy Pounds a Year certain for my Self & Wife—exclusive of my chance in benefits," and he apparently concluded that this was his best recourse. In 1749–50 and 1750–51 he appeared on the bills of Joseph Baker's York company. After that season he seems to have abandoned the stage.

**Adams, Miss E.** [*fl. 1800–1808*], *dancer, singer.* See **ADAMS, MR** [*fl. 1782–1800*].

**Adams, George** *1777–1810, instrumental musician.*

George Adams was born the son of Thomas and Esther Adams in London on 24 April 1777 and baptized in August at St Martin-in-the-Fields. He seems to have been related also to the Thomas Adams who was born in 1783, and to James and James Blake Adams and John Adams (fl. 1794).

When he was proposed for membership in the Royal Society of Musicians 5 August 1798, by J[ames] B[lake] Adams, it was affirmed that "he has studied music for a livelihood upwards of seven years, performs on the violin, viola, and violoncello, French Horn and Trumpet, has many engagements [and] a considerable number of scholars on the Pianoforte and also the Harp. Was Twentyone years of age on the 24$^{th}$ April last, is married and has two children, is sober and attentive to his business." He was unanimously elected on 4 November 1798 and on 2 December attended the meeting and signed the membership book.

Adams was appointed by the Society's Board of Governors to play at the annual benefit for the clergy at St Paul's Cathedral in May 1802 but was granted the privilege of sending a deputy then and again in 1803 and 1804. He played for the occasion on the violin in 1799 and on the trumpet in 1800. Probably he was the Adams elected a Governor of the Society in January 1804. He died in 1810.

From 2 December 1810 until October 1816 the Minute Books of the Royal Society of Musicians reflect the concern of the Society's Governors over the well-being of two young orphans of a deceased member Adams who was probably George. One of the boys, Grosvenor, was boarded and educated at Deal and applied in October 1814 for £5 to enable him to accompany a Captain Jones to the East Indies as steward.

**Adams, Miss H.**  [fl. 1800-1808], *dancer, singer. See* ADAMS, MR  [fl. 1782–1800].

**Adams, Jack**  [fl. 1667?], *clown.*
Jack Adams may have flourished before rather than after 1660; Evelyn mentioned him in his *Numismata* (1667) along with such other early fair performers as The Turk and Proteus Clark, but he failed to give the clown's period of activity. Francis Kirkman's preface to *The Wits* (1673), speaking of Adams without specifying his dates, identified him simply as "that well known Natural Jack Adams of Clarkenwel." He may have been the Mr Adams who acted with the patent companies in the 1670's.

**Adams, James**  b. c. *1771, violinist, organist.*
The James Adams who was listed in Doane's *Musical Directory* (1794) as organist at both Brompton Chapel and Hampstead Church was probably the elder of the two children of James Blake Adams. He was said to be 13 years of age in 1784. He played violoncello at the Concerts of Ancient Music and perhaps presided at the Brompton Chapel organ in succession to James Blake Adams, who we believe was his father. He was probably also related to John Adams (fl. 1794), to George Adams, and to the two Thomas Adamses.

**Adams, James Blake**  b. c. *1749, organist, violoncellist, violinist.*

When James Blake Adams was recommended by Francis Hackwood for membership in the Royal Society of Musicians on 1 February 1784, he had "studied & practis'd upwards of seven years." He was a proficient "on the Violin, Tenor & Violoncello, about thirty five years of Age [and] Organist of Brompton Chapel." He had "a Wife & two Children, the Eldest thirteen Years." He was probably the father of James Adams (b. c. 1771), and related also to John Adams (fl. 1794) and to George and the two Thomas Adamses.

J. B. Adams was admitted to the Royal Society in 1784. He was concerned as violoncellist in the Handelian Memorial Concerts in Westminster Abbey and the Pantheon in June, 1784; was paid £4 10s. as violoncellist in the band employed in the 1787–88 season by the Academy of Ancient Music; and was most likely also the Adams, violoncellist, who was listed to play at the annual May concerts for the relief of the clergy of St Paul's Cathedral in 1785, 1789, 1790, 1793, and 1795. Nothing was recorded about his performances after that date.

J. B. Adams published a number of songs and airs for voice and harpsichord, of which 18 are in the British Museum collection: "L'Adieu," "Ode to May," "L'Amour Timide," "Lovely Seems the Moon's Fair Lustre," "Invocation to the Nightingale," "The Power of Music," "The Death of Daphne" (words from Pope's *Pastorals*), "The Bacchanalian," "The Request," "The Invocation," "A Definition of Love," "Come Gentle God of Soft Repose," "Daphne," "Maria," "Myrtilla," "Phyllida, a Pastoral," "The Jealous Lover," and "The Disaster."

**Adams, John**  [fl. 1739], *musician.*
"John Adams, Sen[ior]" is listed as one of the original subscribers, "being musicians," to the Royal Society of Musicians of Great Britain, in the Declaration of Trust establishing the Society, on 28 August 1739.

**Adams, John**  ₍fl. 1739₎,  *musician.*
"John Adams, Jun[ior]" is listed as one of the original subscribers, "being musicians," to the Royal Society of Musicians, in the Declaration of Trust establishing the Society, on 28 August 1739.

**Adams, John**  ₍fl. 1794₎,  *horn player, organist.*
John Adams was a tenor horn player and organist who performed at the Cecilian Society concerts and with the Surrey Chapel Society. In 1794 he lived at No 11, Oakley Street, Lambeth. He was probably related to George, James, James Blake, and the two Thomas Adamses.

**Adams, Miss S.**  ₍fl. 1800–1808₎, *dancer, singer. See* **ADAMS, MR**  ₍fl. 1782–1800₎.

**Adams, Thomas**  *b. 1783, oboist, organist.*
Thomas Adams was born on 5 September 1783, according to a letter written by him in 1823. He testified that he had begun his musical studies under Dr Thomas Busby "at about 11 years of age."

It seems that the Thomas Adams who was proposed in 1807 by Benjamin Jacobs for membership in the Royal Society of Musicians was a member of the family of musicians which included James Blake Adams, James Adams, John Adams (fl. 1794), George Adams, and George's father, Thomas. It is also probable that he was playing publicly before 1801.

Thomas was not accepted by the Society in 1807, his name being withdrawn on 7 June for "not living within the limits." But he was admitted, again on Jacobs's motion, on 4 September 1808.

In 1802 Adams had been appointed organist of Carlisle Chapel, Lambeth, remaining in that office until March 1814 when he was chosen by competition in performance from among 29 candidates to be organist of St Paul's, Deptford, a position he still held in 1823. He superintended the evening performances of the Apollonicon from their commencement until at least 1823.

Thomas was probably the Adams, oboist, who was listed to play at the Society's annual May concert for the clergy of St Paul's Cathedral in 1811, 1812, and 1815, and his first name is furnished in 1813.

Thomas Adams was married in 1806 to the eldest daughter of Charles Triquet, Esq, of the Bank of England, herself a singer in private gatherings. She bore him nine children.

Adams published six voluntaries in 1812 and six *Grand Organ Pieces* in 1824.

**Adamson, Owen**  *d. 1672, singer.*
Owen Adamson, probably a relative of the singer Richard Adamson, was one of the choristers of Westminster who sang at the funeral of James I; he continued his service with the church under Charles II, being mentioned in Dr Busby's 1664 accounts as a member of the Westminster Abbey choir. He was buried in the East Cloister of the Abbey on 24 February 1672.

**Adamson, Richard**  ₍fl. 1661₎,  *singer.*
On 16 February 1661, along with Henry Purcell the elder and others, Richard Adamson was installed as a singing man in the Chapel Royal. He was cited again on 30 March 1661 for a 7s. 4d. gift from Princess Mary, the King's eldest sister. He was probably related in some way to the singer Owen Adamson.

**Adcock, Mr**  ₍fl. 1794?–1803?₎,  *actor, singer? manager?*
A Master Adcock sang among the Windsor choristers in 1794. He may have been the Mr Adcock who was listed as playing one of the peasants in *Love and Madness* which was given for Waldron's benefit at an out-of-season performance at the Haymarket on 21 September 1795.

Adcock next played the Earl of Southampton in *The Earl of Essex*, in another specially licensed performance ("Benefit for a Widow") at the Haymarket on 27 April 1796. He almost certainly was the Adcock who made his York debut on 22 February 1800; and he may have been the man referred to by J. Robertson in a letter of early 1803 to James Winston. Robertson, the proprietor-manager of the Halifax theatre, told Winston "The half of the [property in the] company you speak of is dispos'd of to a Mr Adcock who joins me in March."

**Adcock, Miss** ₁fl. 1782–1783₁, *singer.*

A Miss Adcock was listed as a chorus singer at Covent Garden Theatre during the season of 1782–83. Her salary was £1 10s. per week.

**Adcock, Abraham** *d. 1773, trumpeter, organist, violinist, organ builder.*

The first notice of Abraham Adcock was by his last name only in a Drury Lane bill of 21 May 1740 when he played a "Trumpet Piece" between the acts. "Adcock" was listed among the trumpeters playing in the band for the performance of the *Messiah* at the Foundling Hospital in May 1754 and May 1758, each time earning 10s. 6d. The Covent Garden music list carried him at 5s. *per diem* in 1757 and at 5s. 10d. in 1766. When George Colman took over Covent Garden Theatre's direction in 1767 and threw Adcock with others out of employment, the musician said that he had been connected with the theatre for 28 years, sometimes as organist, sometimes as trumpeter.

For some three years after his discharge from Covent Garden, Adcock was employed in the Birmingham Theatre. By the summer of 1770 he was back in London, and David Garrick wrote to his brother George on 30 August: "Have you spoke to Richards [leader of the Drury Lane Theatre band] about Adcock ye Trumpet who begs to be restor'd." He was hired at Drury Lane and may have remained there

until his death on 28 December 1773. In 1763 Mortimer's *London Directory* gave Abraham Adcock's address as "the Corner of Orange-street, in Castle-street, near the Mews," where he was established as an organ builder, and in 1768 the *Theatrical Monitor* called him "greatly eminent in his profession of an organ-builder and ever was, and is esteemed as one of the best trumpets in England."

Adcock's will, dated from the parish of St Martin-in-the-Fields, 15 December 1774, and proved 7 January 1774, leaves

unto Rebecca Sarah my well beloved wife all my plate Jewells Money Goods Chattels and personal Estate whatsoever.

I make this Request to her from my Confidence in her Compliance and the uprightness of her Mind that she will do all in her Power for my Nephew Abraham Adcock towards bringing him up and placing him in the World.

The boy was the son of John Adcock, Abraham's brother, and at the time of the signing of the will was living with his uncle. On 3 May 1795 the Governors of the Royal Society of Musicians ordered £5 paid to John White for the funeral expenses of Mrs Sarah Adcock, presumably the relict of Abraham.

**Adcock, Sarah Maria.** *See* WESTON, MRS THOMAS.

**Adcock, William** ₁fl. 1752–1772₁, *actor.*

William Adcock may have been with William Hallam's company at New Wells, Lemon Street, in 1751–1752 or earlier. The playbills for those dates do not reflect the presence of every member of the company. He was certainly with the Hallam company when it went to America in 1752, and he played the role of Mercury in *Lethe* at Williamsburg, Virginia, on 5 September 1752. His later parts there included

Friendly in *Flora*, Young Gerald in *The Anatomist*, Aimwell in *The Beaux' Stratagem*, Paris, Albany, and Catesby. He also sang the role of Macheath in *The Beggar's Opera*.

At some point early in his American career William married Mary Palmer, said to be the daughter of one of the London actors of that name. She had also come over with the Hallam company. She was being called Mrs Adcock in the Philadelphia bills by 15 April 1754. She performed Lady Anne in *Richard III*, the Nurse in *Romeo and Juliet*, Regan in *King Lear*, and Mrs Peachum in *The Beggar's Opera*, a variety illustrative not so much of her versatility as of the meager resources of the company.

From 15 April to 24 June 1754 the Adcocks were at Philadelphia, he playing Rossano in *The Fair Penitent*, Captain Loveit in *Miss in Her Teens*, and, for his benefit, the Prince of Tanaris in *Tamerlane*.

After performing in Charleston, South Carolina, in January 1755, the company departed for Jamaica. It is not known how long the Adcocks remained on the island, but on 12 January 1758 William turned up at the Haymarket playing Don Philip, in *She Wou'd and She Wou'd Not* and billed as for the "first time on any stage"; and on 18 January, Mary played Belvidera in *Venice Preserved*, more honestly described as being for the "first time in that part on that stage." These casual performances in pickup companies at the Haymarket, which was usually dark in winter, apparently failed to interest either of the patent companies in the talents of the young couple, and they were next heard of in 1760 at the Crow Street Theatre, Dublin, where they played until 1763, making also several excursions to Cork.

On 12 November 1764 William made his Drury Lane debut as Aimwell to the Archer of one of the Palmers in *The Beaux' Stratagem*. His salary was established at £2 per week. His wife came on as the Nurse in *Romeo and Juliet* on 16 May 1765 for a benefit shared by her husband with three other underlings.

The Adcocks do not seem to have acted in London again, and after the 1764–65 season they probably took their talents back to the Irish provinces. An Adcock, presumably William, was at Edinburgh during some parts of the 1771–72 season. It is hardly likely that the Adcock who was in the Edinburgh bills from 1813–14 through 1815–16 was our subject, though it is not known when William Adcock died.

Mary Palmer Adcock died on 13 February 1773 and was buried next day in St Margaret's Church at King's Lynn, Norfolk. The Adcocks had one child on the stage. She was Sarah Maria, later successively the common-law wife of the actors Thomas Weston and Richard Wilson.

**Adcock, Mrs William, Mary, née Palmer** *d. 1773. See* **ADCOCK, WILLIAM.**

**Addison, Mrs** [*fl.* 1747–1752], *dancer.*

Mrs Addison was first noticed at Drury Lane Theatre on 2 November 1747, dancing *ensemble* with others in a "Polish Dance." She assisted in *Comus* on 13 November 1747 and 26 December 1748. She danced in *The Beggar's Opera* on 15 October 1748 and appeared as a "follower of Pomona" in the Grand Ballet *Vertumnus and Pomona* on 27 October 1748, as a shepherdess in *The Triumph of Peace* on 21 February 1749, and a nymph in *Emperor of the Moon* on 11 October 1749. She was still in the regular corps of dancers at Drury Lane from 1750–51 through 1755–56 and was there again in 1757–58, but she was rarely a featured performer, though on a few occasions she danced *en paire* with the celebrated Noverre.

**Addison, John** *c. 1766–1844, double bass player, violoncellist, composer.*

John Addison was born about 1766 in

London, the younger of two sons of a clever inventor who was three times invited to demonstrate his ingenious mechanisms to George III. He, with his brother Robert, was educated under the Reverend Mr Heathfield at the school at Northaw, Hertfordshire.

John learned at school to play the flageolet and quickly proceeded to the flute, bassoon, and violin. A Miss Willems, a niece of Frederick Charles Reinhold, the great bass singer, had become a ward of the Addison family. She possessed a fine voice and an attractive person, and young Addison was soon captivated by both. He settled on music as a profession and married Miss Willems at St Giles, Camberwell, on 16 February 1791.

In the beginning of their joint career Addison was somewhat eclipsed by his wife, who appeared at Vauxhall Gardens in 1791 with great popular success in sentimental ballads. (However, one anonymous critic censured her for her "extravagant cadences" as she sang her favorite song, the title of which was "With Heaving Breast and Downcast Eye.") She proceeded to an engagement in the oratorios at Covent Garden Theatre from 24 February to 30 March 1792, and it is possible that her husband played bassoon on these occasions.

Mrs Addison was again singing at Vauxhall in the summer of 1792. On 8 July was published *A Roundelay Sung at Vaux Hall by Mrs. Addison; Written by Mr. A. Set by Mr. Hook*; and Hook's *The Beauty of the Mind*, as sung by her at Vauxhall, was published in 1792. Her husband again had written the words. Hook's *The Warning*, as sung by her, was published in 1793.

Apparently after Vauxhall closed in the summer of 1791 Mrs Addison engaged to sing with Francis Aickin's company at Liverpool. Shortly after the arrival of the Addisons, the double bass player at the theatre became ill, and Hime, the leader, induced Addison to substitute, although his training had been on the cello only. From this period he performed almost exclusively on the double bass.

The couple proceeded next to Dublin, to the private theatre in Fishamble Street conducted by the Earl of Westmeath and Frederick Edward Jones, Esq. Here Mrs Addison sang principal roles; and although Addison, unlike his wife, had sought no engagement, he speedily found himself director and superintendent of an orchestra composed of amateurs, including the Earl of Westmeath, Counsellor Curran, and Colonel Lambert Walpole. He embarked on a study of counterpoint and was soon arranging instrumental accompaniments for performances.

On 17 September 1796 Mrs Addison made her London theatrical debut at Covent Garden as Rosetta in *Love in a Village*. She earned £4 per week and stayed with the company only through 27 December, playing again as Victoria in *The Castle of Andalusia* on 21 October and making her first appearance as Polly in *The Beggar's Opera* on the last night of her appearance at Covent Garden.

The couple joined Macready at Birmingham in June 1797, she appearing there from 30 June, while he played in the band. Addison gained credit and experience as a singing-master in noblemen's families. Among his pupils was Lady Charlotte Packenham, later Duchess of Wellington. The Addisons summered and spent the autumn in Bath, where Addison placed his wife under the tutelage of Rauzzini. They were at Crow Street Theatre, Dublin, by 1 February 1798 where she played, advertised as "from Covent Garden," and according to Sainsbury she received a three-year contract. But on 18 September 1798 they were at Cork, and on 1 October at Limerick, despite powerful opposition from Miss Poole and Mrs Second. Cork and Limerick saw them again in August and September of 1799, and they were again in Cork on 15 August 1800. When in 1800 Addison's close friend Thomas Ludford Bellamy became joint proprietor with Ward of the theatre at Manchester, the couple joined that company, also playing and singing at concerts in Liverpool. After some months Addison forsook his profession to enter the booming cotton trade at Manchester, but the resumption of the war pushed him near bankruptcy. His creditors divided his stock and extricated him, and he returned to London.

At London, Addison was persuaded by Michael Kelly to join him in his music shop at the corner of Market Lane in Pall Mall, which opened on 1 January 1802. He was also engaged to play the double bass at the Italian opera, in the Concerts of Ancient Music, and at the Vocal Concerts, at all of which he continued to perform for many years.

W. D. Adams asserted that, after Mrs Addison's Covent Garden appearances, she "sang in the English provinces and in Ireland (as 'Mrs. Nun')," but this appears to be erroneous.

Teaching singing was Addison's principal occupation from about 1810 onward, and he was the master of such well-known singers as Pyne, Pearman, Millar, Dean, Mrs Rennett, Beaumont, Witham, Healey and Leoni Lee. (On 23 May 1812 the Drury Lane company at the Lyceum paid him £25 for instruction of a Master Lee at the theatre.) Addison was a member of the Royal Society of Musicians from before February 1798. He was a member of the Committee in 1801. He subscribed 13s. to the Fund in 1806 but was delinquent in 1807. He was a member at least until 11 April 1813, when he was named in the Minutes.

In 1824 he helped John Baptist Cramer and Cramer's pupil John Beale to found the music firm of Cramer, Addison, and Beale. At his death this versatile man was evidently in business as a globe-maker, also.

The date of death of Elizabeth Addison is not known, but apparently it was before that of her husband, who expired on 30 January 1844.

The will of John Addison, of No 13, Camden Cottages, Camden Town, professor of music, was dated 13 May 1839 and proved 6 March 1844. It left the bulk of his properties to his grandniece Susanna Ann Addison, the younger daughter of his late nephew Robert Addison. The property included both his household goods (furniture, books, and musical instruments) and his leasehold messuage at No 116, Regent Street. The proceeds of two insurance policies totalling £410 went to Susanna Ann, the widow of Robert; and one of several codicils gave to his nephew John "of Tottenham Court Road Globe maker" all his copper plate and other apparatus for manufacturing 36-inch globes.

**Addison, Mrs John, Elizabeth, née Willems** [fl. 1785?–1840]. See ADDISON, JOHN c. 1766–1844.

**Addison, John** d. 1799, musician.
John Addison first appeared obscurely as "Mr Addison" in the minute books of the Royal Society of Musicians in late December 1784 and in the following January. Under date of 6 September 1789, it was noted that Mr Addison had made application for an allowance from the Society's funds (perhaps for temporary relief from disability). But he had claimed as a married man, and, "when it appearing that he had married only six weeks prior to his claiming, . . . it was resolved that he receive no increase, and that his conduct merited the severest censure of this society."

Addison sent a letter on 3 July 1791 once more requesting an increase in his allowance, "which on a reference to the minutes of 6 September 1789 was rejected."

On 3 February 1799 Anna Addison informed the governors that her husband John Addison had died on 3 January 1799, whereupon they ordered a five-guinea monthly payment to her and provided for his funeral expenses.

No relationship to the better known John Addison (d. 1844) can be traced.

**Adeane, Mr** [fl. 1786], *dancer?*
Mr Adeane was one of the characters in an unnamed new pantomime given at the Royal Circus on 28 October 1786; he was very likely a dancer.

**Adelaide, Mlle** [fl. 1788–1789], *dancer.*
Mlle Adelaide was among a number of French dancers imported to the King's Theatre from the Opera in Paris in the winter of 1788–89. For a short season she was given £400, a benefit free of the charges of the house, and the expenses of her journey.

The first English appearance of Mlle Adelaide was on 10 January, the opening night of the new season, when she danced with nine others in a "New Divertissement" and in *L'embarquement pour Cythère*, a ballet by Didelot. The *Biographical and Imperial Magazine* thought her "inferior to [Mlle] Hilligsberg, whose place she is meant to supply."

Mlle Adelaide was apparently unfortunate in being among the first few dancers procured by Gallini to build up the greatly deteriorated *corps de ballet* at the English Opera. He was frantically working to entice better dancers from abroad to supplement his few stars like the Simonets; but the newcomers were not yet arrived in sufficient force at the beginning of the season to appease critics and audiences. On 31 January there was a fresh disturbance at the house, and the *World* commented: "The [new] Dance, if such it can be called, was like the movements of heavy Cavalry. It was hissed very abundantly. Gallini has the excuse of not having been able to get better dancers." On 7 February, the dancers were driven from the stage by the rioting audience, who demolished the interior of the theatre. Mlle Adelaide was among the spurned dancers on this occasion.

Mlle Adelaide danced in several other productions until the end of the season, then returned to Paris.

**Adriani, Mr** [fl. 1765–1767], *dancer.*
Adriani was a minor member of the corps of dancers at the King's Opera in the Haymarket in the seasons of 1765–66 and 1766–67. He did not appear in London thereafter.

**Adridge.** *See* **ALDRIDGE.**

**"Aesopus."** *See* **QUIN, JAMES.**

**"African, The"** [fl. 1793–1795], *equestrian, tumbler.*
"The African" was to be seen in 1793 at Philip Astley's Amphitheatre in "his astonishing Stage and Equestrian Performances" in *La Force de Hercules: Or, the Ruins of Troy*, and also engaging in "Tilts and Tournaments" and "Military Exercises."

In the late winter and early spring of 1795, he was in Benjamin Handy's troupe of horsemen and wire-dancers at the Lyceum in the Strand, where he went "through several wonderful feats of Activity never attempted by any other man in the Kingdom," unfortunately left undescribed. He was at the New Royal Circus in April and May of 1795.

His real name, and whether or not he was actually "African," are facts unknown. He did not again appear in London, at least under this *nom de guerre*.

**Agas.** *See* **AGGAS.**

**Agata, dell'.** *See* **DEL' AGATA.**

**Aggas, Robert** [fl. 1662–1679], *drummer.*
On 7 April 1662 Robert Aggas (or Aggis) was granted livery as a drummer to the Duke of Ormonde, and on the tenth his appointment with the Duke was confirmed. He very likely spent the ensuing

years in Ireland, but on 22 January 1679 he was admitted as a drummer in ordinary without fee in the King's Musick in London. His fee was to be granted when the next position became vacant, but there is no record of his permanent appointment.

**Aggas, Robert**  *d. 1679, scene painter.*
Robert Aggas (or Angus) was probably the son of Samuel Aggas, a citizen painter-stainer of London from Stratford Langthorne parish of West Ham, Essex. Samuel Aggas died in April 1669, and in his will, dated 8 January 1668 and proved 10 May 1669, he left £20 to a son, Robert. Another son, Samuel Jr, received all of his father's painting materials and money to make him a freeman of London, the implication being that Samuel Jr was still a youth and that Robert was the eldest son and already established. Their mother's name was Dorothy, and she was bequeathed all of her husband's land and buildings in Buckinghamshire.

Though Robert Aggas flourished as a landscape painter from 1656 on, he was apparently not employed by the players until 1677. He and Samuel Towers collaborated on some scenery for the King's Company but had to petition the Lord Chamberlain on 8 August 1677 for the £40 owed them. The players were immediately ordered to pay the painters, but the warrant was ineffective: on 22 April 1678 actors Mohun, Hart, Cartwright, and Kynaston were ordered to appear before the Lord Chamberlain in connection with the debt. The records of the case after this date are misleading. Aggas supposedly died in 1679; yet he and Towers were named in a new petition on 2 December 1682 for payment of £32 owed them for scenery painted for the United Company. There may be an error in this date, or the debt could have been the remainder owed the painters; King's Company debts would have been carried over to the United Company, just as Ag-

gas's name, even after his death, might still appear in connection with the case. It is probable that Aggas died without ever receiving his full payment.

**Agile, L'.** *See* **L'Agile.**

**Aglyffe.** *See* **AYLIFF.**

**Agnetta, Signora**  [*fl. 1747–1751*], *singer.*
A Signora Agnetta sang, accompanied by "an Extraordinary Band of Musick," at Yates's Great Theatrical Booth at Bartholomew Fair, 24–27 August 1748, this "being the first Time[s] of her Performing since her Arrival," presumably from Italy. She was probably the Miss Agnetta who sang the lead part of Flora in *Hob in the Well* at Hallam's small theatre at New Wells, Lemon Street, on 27 March 1749. Miss Agnetta sang again at the New Wells, Shepherd's Market, for Stephens's benefit on 20 August and at Phillips's booth at Southwark Fair on 7 September 1750, after which time she did not appear again.

**Aguiari, Lucrezia,** later MME GIUSEPPE COLLA *1743–1783, singer.*
Lucrezia Aguiari was born at Ferrara, reputedly the illegitimate daughter of an Italian nobleman. Her name consequently appeared often in continental notices as La Bastardini or La Bastardella.

Lucrezia studied singing under an Abbate Lambertini and after her Florentine debut in 1764 toured with great acclaim to Rome, Pisa, and other cities in Italy. Mozart, who heard her sing at Parma in 1770, praised her astonishing range and flexibility and preferred her performances to those of Madame Mara. Sainsbury reports Sacchini as saying "he had heard her go up to B flat in altissimo."

At the Milan Carnival of 1774 Aguiari received enthusiastic praise for her singing in Giuseppe Colla's opera *Tolomeo*. In

1775 Aguiari accompanied Colla to London and engaged at once at the Pantheon in Oxford Street, where her success was enormous. She received £100 a night for singing only two songs but delighted the management nevertheless by always filling the auditorium. Fanny Burney, whose letters and diaries are filled with the most fulsome admiration for the singer, thought she had "all the powers of thunder and lightning in her."

At some time in 1775 Aguiari, who in her turn greatly admired Fanny's father, the music historian Dr Burney, spent an evening at the Burney house in London. Fanny fascinatedly picked up and later recounted one of the legends with which the singer was surrounded and which she never discouraged:

She was accompanied by Signor Colla, . . . and the Reverend Mr Penneck. She is of the middle stature, and has the misfortune to be lame; owing perhaps (if there is any truth in the story), to her being mauled when an infant by a pig, in consequence of which she is reported to have a silver side. Her face is handsome, and expressive of all her words. She has the character of being immensely proud. She was, however, all civility here, though her excessive *vanity* was perpetually self-betrayed. Signor Colla, to whom she is reported to be married, is a lively,—I might almost say, *fiery* Italian. She sings no songs but of his composition, and he is her constant attendant.

In a conversation with one of the Burney girls later the same evening, Aguiari denied being Colla's wife, and apparently they were not married until 1780, though their personal and professional relationship remained close while she sang at the Pantheon.

Aguiari and the Burneys got along famously, and Fanny's "singer of singers" came to tea with them on 11 June 1775. Though she had a cold, she sang for them, accompanied by Colla, and astonished the company with a "song, which was taken from Metastasio's opera of Didone, set by Colla: *Non hai ragione, ingrato*."

As this is what is called an *Arria parlante,* she was desirous that we should all understand the words, before we heard the music; and in a voice softly melodious she repeated the song through, before she sang it, and then translated its sense into French. . . . She was *sublime*: I can use no other word, without degrading her . . . [she] has vocal talents, that almost surpass *belief* to those who have not heard her. Her voice reaches from the middle of the harpsichord to two notes above it, yet it is never husky when low, or shrill when high. . . . I could not forbear regretting to her, that she should perform in a place where her talents were half obscured, as she seems so much formed to grace a Theatre, from her excellent ideas of action. She made faces at the name of The Pantheon and took herself off when standing there—*"Comme une statue!—comme une petite Ecolière!*

To display her various powers to my father, she sung in all styles, the Bravura, the Arria Parlante, the Cantabile, Church-Music, Recitative, and Rondeau, though she laughed at herself in the latter, saying, "Ah! je hais ces misères là; ils me fout guignon!"

Dr Burney himself assessed her very highly in his *History of Music*:

Lucrezia Agujari was a truly wonderful performer. The lower part of her voice was full, round, of an excellent quality, and its compass, after she quitted its natural register, which it was to be wished she had never done, beyond any one we had then heard. . . . Though the pathetic and tender were not what her manner or figure promised, yet she had expressions sometimes that were truly touching, and she would have been capable of exciting universal pleasure as admiration, if she had been a little less violent in the delivery of her passages, and if her looks had been more tempered by female softness and timidity.

Lucrezia Aguiari sang at the Pantheon until the fall of 1777. She died at Parma on 18 May 1783.

Giuseppe Colla, her husband, was an accomplished musician and an industrious and productive second-rank composer of operas and other works. He was born in Parma on 4 August 1731 and died there on 16 March 1806. The puzzling denial that he accompanied Aguiari to London, contained in his entry in *Grove's Dictionary,* goes plainly against Fanny Burney's testimony. There is, however, no record of his having performed publicly in England.

Antonio Fedi painted Aguiari as one of a large group of eighteenth-century singers in 1801.

**Aguilar.** *See* G IRELLI A GUILAR, Signora.

**Agus, Joseph** [*fl.* 1763?], *violinist, composer? See* A GUS, J OSEPH *1749–1803?, violinist, composer?*

**Agus, Joseph** *1749–1803?, violinist, composer?*

A Joseph Agus of St Alban's Street was listed by Mortimer's *London Directory* of 1763 as a performer on the violin. A violinist identified only as Agus, Jr and a "scholar of Nardini lately arriv'd from Italy" played a solo on the violin after a performance of the *Messiah* at the Haymarket on 26 February 1773 and another solo at the "Concerto Spirituale" given at the Haymarket on 3 March 1773. It seems likely that these two were father and son. It is difficult, however, to report their lives separately (if, indeed, they were different persons) because of their identity of name and professional specialty.

Marie Louise Pereyra, writing in *Grove's Dictionary* (5th ed.), cites Constant Pierre's work *Le conservatoire national de musique et de déclamation* (1900) to the effect that a Joseph Agus (1749–May 1798) was professor of *solfège* at the Conservatoire as of 22 November 1795; but she says also that Fétis in his *Biographie universelle des musiciens* and Eitner in his *Quellen-Lexikon*

apply these dates to Henri Agus, who "may be the same man."

The British Museum's *Catalogue of Printed Music* lists a number of compositions which it attributes to "Giuseppe" Agus. From several indications, Joseph Agus "Junr." was the composer of some and may have been composer of others; but if he arrived in London only in or near 1773, as he is said to have done, then he cannot have been responsible for all. At least one other Agus (Joseph the elder or Henri) must have composed several:

*The allemands danced at the King's Theatre . . . by Mr. Slingsby & Sig^{ra} Radicate . . . set for the German Flute . . .* published by Welcker in London, without date but tentatively dated 1767 by the *Catalogue,* must actually have been published after the return of Slingsby to the theatre, after a two-year absence, in the season of 1772–73. The publication would have waited upon the completion of the season, during which Slingsby danced often with Signora Radicatti at the opera. Joseph Agus the younger could thus have been the composer.

If the British Museum's placing and dating are more accurate in the case of *Six Duetts for two Violins . . .* [separate parts], *London* [1780?]; *Sei trii per due violini e violoncello, opera III* [separate parts] [London 1775], with a dedication in Italian to Sir William Hamilton, and the second edition in 1780; and *Six Italian Duetts for Two Voices, with a Thorough Bass for the Piano-Forte . . . Op. 9,* J. Dale: London [1795?], then the younger Joseph Agus *could* have composed these. He is certainly named, along with 15 other composers, from Bach and Purcell to Paxton and his own master Nardini in the title page to Fentum's *Choice Collection of Catches and Glees; Adapted for a Violin and Violoncello . . .* [1790].

If we hold to sometime late in 1772 or early in 1773 for the implied date of the younger Joseph Agus's arrival in London, then *The Opera Dances both Serious and*

*Comic, Danced at the King's Theatre . . .
1771 for the German Flute, violin or Harpsichord. Book III* [which necessarily posits
two earlier "Books"], and *A Second Book
of Opera Dances for 1776, including the
favourite Ballet "La fête du village" . . .
Composed and adapted for the Piano Forte,
German Flute & Violin,* Welcker: London
[1776], can hardly have been his productions. The Agus named with a dozen other
composers as contributing music to the
*pasticcio* opera by Isaac Bickerstaff, *Love
in a Village,* which was introduced at Covent Garden on 8 December 1762, must
have been the Joseph Agus of 1763.
We may likewise attribute to him (or to
"Henri") *Sonate a violino solo e basso*
[London, 1760?]; *Six Solos for a Violin
with a Thorough Bass for the Harpsichord,* printed for John Johnson: London
[1765?]; and, with the same title, *Opera
Seconda,* from the same publisher [1765?].

It seems entirely out of question, in any
case, that the Joseph Agus who continued
active as an instrumentalist in London and
on the rolls of the British Royal Society of
Musicians from 1 July 1781 through 1803
was the professor at Paris. If we assume the
professor to have been Henri, then it is he
who was named on the title page of the
*Solfèges pour servir a l'étude dans le Con-
servatoire de Musique à Paris par les ci-
toyens Agus, Catel, Chérubini, Gossec, Lan-
glé, Le Sueur, Martini, Méhul et Rey . . .*
Leipzig [1795?].

The Joseph Agus who was admitted to
the Royal Society of Musicians in 1781 was
almost certainly the younger Joseph. But
unfortunately his recommendation papers,
which would have told us not only his
sponsor but also his age and professional
specialties, are missing from the Society's
files. (His name is often spelled "Augus"
in these records.)

An Agus is on the list of musicians for
the opera at the King's Theatre in 1783,
and an Agus played among the first violins
at the Handel Memorial Concerts at West-

minster Abbey and the Pantheon in May
and June of 1784. The name is on the
roster of musicians at the King's Theatre in
1784–85 and of second violins with the
King's opera company performing at the
Pantheon in 1791. In 1794 Joseph Agus
was reported by Doane's *Musical Directory*
as a violinist, residing in Windmill Street,
Haymarket, who belonged to the Royal
Society of Musicians, the Academy of Ancient Music, and the band of the opera.

On 2 September 1798 it was reported to
the meeting of the Royal Society that
"Joseph Augus" was in extreme distress as
the result of his dismissal from the Little
Theatre in the Haymarket in mid-season,
and a benefaction of five guineas was voted.
He made fresh representations of distress on
7 October, when he was granted 10 guineas,
and on 3 November when he was given five
more. On 5 October 1800 he reported his
wife was ill and received three guineas for
treatment, and on 2 November he was himself in an "infirm state" and was given six
guineas. On 4 January 1801 he reported
an injury to his wife which prevented her
attention to her family, and he petitioned
the Society again on 1 March, the difficulties of both husband and wife continuing. From 5 April through 2 August he
was granted a regular monthly allowance
of £6 6s. On 6 September he was again
allowed six guineas for extraordinary assistance for the continuing illness of his
wife and himself, and on 4 October 1801
his regular allowance was renewed. He
stated on 4 July 1802 that his wife "laboured under much indisposition" and
prayed that the Society continue an allowance to his children "during Mr Coleman's
season," and this was done.

Agus died sometime between that application and May 1803, probably in April,
since on 1 May Mrs Agus informed the
Society of the death of her husband and
sought the continuation of the usual allowance plus funeral expenses. On a motion by Condell, seconded by Waterhouse,

she was granted a continuing allowance of £2 12s. 6d. per month for herself, and £2 2s. for her children. She was also to have £7 7s. for medical assistance and £8 for her husband's funeral expenses. On 2 October 1803 school bills for "Mrs Augus's" two children were ordered paid. On 5 October 1806 Mrs Agus affirmed that her daughter June (or Jane) would be 14 the following December, and the girl was on 1 February 1807 formally apprenticed, with the approval of her guardians in the Society, to Mrs Jesse Croft "Dressden & Fancy worker of great Pulteney St." On 6 September 1807 Charles Ashley informed the Board that Mr Coombe of the Admiralty had undertaken to provide a situation in the sea service for Mrs Agus's son, and on 6 December the boy had been placed with Mr Foster, captain of a coaster out of Hull, and his allowance had ceased. By 3 January 1808 Mrs Agus was reporting that her son had been returned by Captain Foster as unfit for service. His allowance was renewed. On 5 February formal thanks were offered by the Board to a Mr Mackintosh for services rendered in the attempt to place young Agus, and reimbursement was made of £5 expenses. On the application of "Agus' daughter," for clothing necessary to "going into service" she was given £11 on 3 February 1811. Evidently Mrs Agus was employed by the Society as a cleaning woman or housekeeper from before 2 August 1812, when she received an unexplained payment of 4s., until 7 February 1813 when "because of improper neglect" the Board discharged her and appointed Mrs Roost "to take care of the room." Mrs Agus was granted medical expenses of £1 on two occasions, 2 April 1820 and 1 July 1821, and of £4 on 5 August 1821. She died in August, and on 2 September the Society set aside £8 for her funeral expenses.

**Aickery.** *See* **ACKERY.**

**AICKIN.** *See also* **AITKIN.**

**Aickin, Francis** *d. 1805, actor.*

Francis Aickin was born in Dublin. His father was a weaver, and Francis was apprenticed to the trade. Nothing is known of his schooling. His younger brother James having early left the family to join a touring company in Ireland, Francis in 1754 forsook his father's business and joined the provincial Irish company of Philip Lewis, uncle of the well-known London actor William Thomas Lewis. His first part is said to have been the title role in *George Barnwell.*

After two seasons as an itinerant player at Tralee, Belfast, and other Irish towns, Aickin obtained an engagement at Smock Alley Theatre in Dublin in the season of 1756–57. He was probably at Edinburgh in the summer of 1757 but was back in Ireland, advertised as among the Drogheda

*Harvard Theatre Collection*

FRANCIS AICKIN, as Bolingbroke
by R. Dighton

comedians at "The Vaults" in Belfast on 6 February. The company was at Cork by 13 February 1758, and remained there until June.

At some time before the first appearance of her name in the Belfast bills, on 6 February 1758, Francis married the first of his two wives. The Deputy Keeper of Public Records, Dublin, in a report dated 1794, cited a marriage between a Francis Aickin and a Catherine Tipper. Lysons's *Environs* gives a first name of Mary. Yet the clerk of St Paul, Covent Garden, parish entered her name twice as Margaret. She was later described as a "lady of family and fortune," of a "different religion" than Aickin's. A romantic tale was circulated of Aickin's assembling "a party of armed friends" to effect an elopement. The first Mrs Aickin never acted in London, and nothing is known of her abilities. She was evidently singing with the "Belfast Opera" at the Canongate Playhouse in Edinburgh on 22 February 1762, as was Francis.

In the spring of 1765 Aickin left Ireland for London. He was enthusiastically seized by Garrick after his first appearance ("Aickin from Dublin") at Drury Lane as Dick, in *The Confederacy*, on 17 May 1765. His rapid rise to a respectable level at London's chief house was due to the qualities assigned to him by Hugh Kelly in *Thespis* (1766): a handsome person, inborn ease, manly accent, ready memory, and happy ear.

Aickin remained under Garrick's management until near the end of the season 1773–74, when he was dismissed for wearing his hat behind the scenes, according to an incredible story told by Aickin. Garrick in a series of letters in August 1774 suggests other reasons but refuses to state them.

Aickin was immediately taken on at Covent Garden where the £7 per week which Garrick had paid him had by 1778–79 increased to £8 10*s*. and in 1783–84 was £10. He was constantly at Covent Garden during the winter seasons until the fall of 1792, although his utility seems to have lessened in the final years, and in 1789–90 his salary was reduced to £8. His last appearance in London was as Jaques in *As You Like It* on 9 November 1792.

Aickin also played during the summers of 1774, 1775, and 1781 at the Haymarket; was at Richmond in the summers of 1769 and 1775; at Bristol in the summer of 1778; and returned to Cork in the summers of 1780, 1781, 1783, and 1785. He appeared at Liverpool for the first time on 11 September 1786. In 1787 he undertook the management of the summer theatre there, and in 1789 he and John Philip Kemble obtained from the owners a seven-year lease of the house. Boaden "heard at the time that the consideration they were to give was £1,200 down and a rent of £350 per annum." The lease was renewed for seven years to Aickin alone on 1 January 1796.

During his early years as proprietor and manager at Liverpool, Aicken was a model of brisk efficiency, raising the roof of the house to provide better acoustics and more room, building a colonnade over the entrances in Williamson Square, acting and directing in his own person, and attracting the best-known London players—Mrs Siddons, Munden, Lee Lewes, the younger Bannister, Incledon, Farley, Stephen Kemble, and many others. But he had fractious and sometimes violently obstreperous audiences, particularly the sailors and their doxies who inhabited the upper galleries, and gradually the condition of the house deteriorated to the point at which respectable playgoers refused to buy tickets and the better actors avoided engagements. The October 1799 issue of *The Monthly Mirror* scolded Aickin for the slovenly state of the auditorium, the tattered condition of the scenery, the filth in the lobbies, and the decline in quality of visiting players. As he grew older, Aicken, in the absence of effective competition, grew ever more lax. When his lease expired in January 1803, his application to renew it was refused, even though he offered £100 more than the £1500 by which William Thomas Lewis and Thomas Knight finally secured the new contract.

Aickin had already entered into a partnership with John Jackson to take over the management at Edinburgh, relinquished by Stephen Kemble in 1800, and at the beginning of the 1801–2 season he was in the Scottish capital. One "Candidus," in a pamphlet of 1802, voiced disappointment in the physical condition of the Edinburgh theatre and on the assignment of characters, but the company seems nevertheless to have been an improvement over Kemble's troupe.

Francis Aickin's first wife, Margaret, had died on 25 September 1786 at the age of 37 and had been buried at Paddington. He had then closed down a hosier's shop in which she had assisted and where he had secured the patronage of some members of the Royal family. In March 1788 he espoused Mrs Lowe, a widow who brought him £800 a year. She was not an actress.

Aickin was a diligent, not brilliant, performer whose 90 or more characters embraced a wide range both in comedy and tragedy over his entire career. As time went on, however, he concentrated more and more on characters of a forthright, blunt, harsh, and finally villainous tendency, until at his retirement he was known as "Tyrant Aickin."

A listing of his Shakespearean characters will illustrate a remarkable variety of attempts, however: Antigonus, Antonio, Banquo, Belarius, Brabantio, Buckingham, Capulet, Dauphin, Douglas, Duke Senior, Edmund, Falstaff (1 Henry IV), Ford, Ghost (Hamlet), Guiderius, Henry IV (both parts), and Henry VI (Cibber's Richard III), Henry VIII, Hubert, Jaques, Don John, Kent, Laertes, Leonato, Macbeth, Macduff, Montano, Pembroke, Polixenes, Richmond, Rosencrantz, Ross, Sergeant (Macbeth), Tybalt, Prince of Wales. He had a striking portfolio of stage Irishmen,

of course, among them O'Flaherty in The West Indian, Connolly in The School for Wives, Foigard in The Beaux' Stratagem, O'Trigger in The Rivals, and O'Donovan in The Toy. Selected other parts in which he seems to have excelled were: Stockwell in The West Indian, Narbas in Merope, Mr Bromley in The Times, Sir John Melville in The Clandestine Marriage, Sciolto in The Fair Penitent, Pierre in Venice Preserved, Marcian in Theodosius, Zanga in The Revenge, Dionysius in The Grecian Daughter, Sealand in The Conscious Lovers, Alwin in The Countess of Salisbury, and Tamerlane in Tamerlane.

Francis Gentleman, the actor-critic, was often severe with Francis Aiken in The Dramatic Censor (1770), nor was he kinder in his doggerel critique called The Theatres (1772):

> Who has not seen, upon rejoicing night
> Squibs sputter, fret and bounce by partial light?
> So elder Aickin shatters tragic strains,
> And fritters Nature with uncommon pains;
> Struts, foams and roars; good lack! what noise he makes,
> While sense and harmony condemn his breaks;
> Most cracker-like he moves, a short-liv'd joke,
> Shines with false fire, and soon concludes with smoke

Gentleman thought that as Manly in The Plain Dealer Aickin was "a lamentable falling off from both Holland and Quin," as Leonato "he fails extremely in attempting to describe the force and delicacy of paternal feelings," and Marcian, in Theodosius: "Mr Aickin, mounted on Lee's fiery, hard-mouthed Pegasus, sits in a very ticklish, tottering situation."

William Hawkins in 1775 thought that Aickin's "forte seems to lie mostly in the impassioned declamatory parts of tragedy, in which he without doubt deserves notice," but that "he wants that natural ease and vivacity . . . necessary for the comedian, though there are a few parts wherein he makes a tolerable and decent appearance." "Anthony Pasquin" in 1788 flayed Aickin for vulgarity and over-emphasis and disliked his Irish accent:

> But whoe'er sees his PIERRE, and with-
>     holds applause,
> Must be envious of Merit, or dead to the
>     cause

F. G. Waldron, who acted with him, thought in 1795 that "His person is rather too short and bulky" but "The honest sentiment that flows pure and sincere from the heart he always delivers well, and we never wish to see the trusty faithful Steward, the tender and affectionate Parent, better delineated."

John Taylor disagreed and wrote to Edward Jerningham, also in 1795, in reference to Jerningham's comedy *The Welsh Heiress*, "I would advise you to cut out that solemn canting Aickin whose melancholy utterance was a wet blanket. Indeed I do not think the Steward's part is necessary."

James Boaden remembered him in his latter days as "a sensible speaker, firm, articulate, and impressive, without the tenderness of his brother James, and with little or no variety."

Aickin seems to have had little taste in stage dress, and Waldron thought that when he attempted "the performance of a foreign monarch . . . with all the cumbersome load of fancied habiliments, the addition to his bulk make him appear not unlike a bear placed upon his hind legs."

A popular man, both among his fellow actors and with his audiences, Frank Aickin was gentlemanly and gregarious. He and David Garrick were godfathers to Thomas John Dibdin and fast friends until their mysterious quarrel. Aickin belonged to the society called the School of Garrick, formed soon after the great actor-manager's death by those who had been associated with him in London.

Aickin had at least five children by his first wife: Sophia, who was baptized at St Paul, Covent Garden, on 2 May 1779 and was buried there ("Aged 50"!) on 8 December 1846, was probably the Miss Aickin who was on the Drury Lane company list in the season of 1805–6. She lived at the time of her death in Brook Street off Bond Street. Jonathan was baptized 5 September 1784 and perhaps died in infancy. Graves, the actor, who is noticed separately in this work, died 23 February 1799. Francis, an army officer, married Mary Anne Winifred Heneage of St Giles Parish at St George, Hanover Square, on 9 December 1797. He fought a bloodless duel with an Ensign Armstrong at Horsham in May.

Francis Aickin died at Edgeware, aged 76, on 8 November 1812 and was buried at Stanmore Church. His will, made 25 April 1811 and proved on the day of his death, is characteristically simple:

Having at present no will by me and my age and infirmities making my situation rather hazardous I think it proper to put down on this humble bit of paper the way in which I wish my little property may be disposed of in case of death ffirst I bequeath to my son Captain ffrancis Aickin of the 5th Dragoon Guards two hundred pounds to be paid in two months after my death together with my gold watch Chain and Seals and my gold Sleeve Buttons. To my daughter Sophia Aickin I bequeath all else I die possessed of money in the ffunds bond[s] debts household furniture plate books ec ec.

A codicil of 11 February 1812 adds: "Since I wrote the within it pleased God to add two hundred a year to my Income on the Edinburgh Theatre which I leave to be divided equally between my son . . . and my daughter."

Aickin's successive London addresses were: in 1782, No 6, York Street; in 1785,

No 5, York Street; in 1786, No 9, Paddington Green; in 1787, No 26, Great Tichfield Street; in 1788–90, No 5, Gower Street, Bedford Square.

There is in the British Museum an India-ink drawing tinted with water colours, by Robert Dighton, of Francis Aickin as Bolingbroke in *Richard II*. It was engraved by Charles Grignion for Bell's acting edition of Shakespeare's plays in 1776. Dodd painted Aickin as Phocion, and Walker engraved the likeness in 1777. In the Folger Shakespeare Library there is a water color by W. Loftis of Aickin as Henry IV. In the Harvard Theatre Collection are an undated engraving by James Heath of a bust painted by A. Davis and an undated and anonymously drawn and engraved portrait of Aickin as Zanga in *The Revenge*.

### Aickin, Graves  d. 1799, actor.

Graves Aickin was a son of Francis Aickin the actor and his first wife Margaret. Graves made his London debut at the Haymarket Theatre on 18 September 1797 as Moody in *The Country Girl* and Puff in the afterpiece *Miss in Her Teens*. On the same night, his wife played Alithea in the mainpiece. Neither he nor his wife appeared again in London.

Aickin died at Cheltenham on 23 February 1799. The *Monthly Mirror* reported the accident "from the bursting of a blood vessel, during his performance of Osmond, in the Castle Spectre."

His widow was married to Henry Robert Bowles, the provincial manager, on 11 February 1806. She died in 1814 and was buried in Yarmouth Chapel, aged 44.

### Aickin, Mrs Graves  1770–1814, actress. See AICKEN, GRAVES.

### Aickin, James  c. 1735–1803, actor.

James Aickin, younger brother of the actor Francis Aickin, was born in Dublin about 1735. He decamped from his father's weaving establishment at an early age and joined a strolling company in Ireland. An Aicken, certainly not Francis and probably James, was with James Love's company at Tralee in the spring of 1756 and was with the Smock Alley company in Dublin the following season. He was probably in the winter company at Dublin from 1756–57 through 1758–59.

By 23 June 1759 James was with a summer company in Edinburgh. James Boswell, in a critical commentary, noted: "Mr Aickin, a young Actor, made his first appearance here, in Horatio, in which he gave pretty general satisfaction." Boswell commended him as Frederick in *The Miser*, found him "not bad" as Scandal in *Love for Love*, but thought his Pyrrhus in *Orestes* "on every account . . . bad." His Hotspur was "too cool" and he performed the Fine Gentleman in *Lethe* "scurvily."

Aickin's art was sufficient, however, to gain him a prominent place in the second-rate company under the management of James Dawson and David Beat at the Canongate Theatre until the winter season of 1766–67. He played such parts as Peachum in *The Beggar's Opera*, Lord Randolph in *Douglas*, and Polydore in *The Orphan*. Samuel Foote, a better judge of acting than Boswell, saw him there and pronounced him to be excellent. Aickin's wife, whom he probably met in Edinburgh, acted with him at the Canongate from her debut on 25 June 1759 until her death, which seems to have occurred after the end of the 1762–63 season.

In January 1767 the failure of the managers to re-engage George Stayley, a popular favorite, occasioned a riot which destroyed the interior of the Edinburgh house. Troops from the Castle put down the riot, but when the law students who were responsible were threatened with legal action, they in turn sought to bring the proprietors under certain statutes of Anne and George II providing for the whipping of owners of unlicensed theatres at the cart's tail. Several

JAMES AICKIN, as Phocion
by D. Dodd

tober 1768 and as the Earl of Pembroke in *The Earl of Warwick* on 9 November 1768 —he was hissed for being imperfect and was replaced in the parts. But gradually he grew in public favor and his manager's esteem until he was settled in a busy line of secondary characters which did not extend his good but limited abilities.

James Aickin remained as an active player at Drury Lane through the beginning of the season of 1799–1800. In 1798 when Richard Wroughton retired as acting manager, Aickin assumed the place. His health was not good. From 31 January through May 1771 others took his usual roles and he did not play on his benefit night on 31 May, evidently being ill through the entire spring. In 1789 he was often laid up with gout. In June 1799 it was reported that he had "been much hurt in resisting some villains who attempted to rob him." He was seriously ill in the winter of 1799–1800 and could not play for several weeks. Thomas Dutton reported on 7 January 1800:

We were extremely gratified at seeing the universally esteemed and respected Manager . . . Mr AICKIN, resume his professional functions, after a serious indisposition which gave general concern to every person acquainted with his worthy and amiable character, [playing Obadiah in *Bold Stroke for a Wife*] with his wonted accuracy and chasteness.

But he had evidently suffered a mild stroke. He played for the last time on 14 February 1800, as Las Casas in *Pizarro*. A more serious stroke occurred in February, leaving him paralyzed. He lingered on until 17 March 1803, when he died in his sixty-ninth year. He was buried at St Anne's, Soho, attended by the performers of Drury Lane.

Aickin had begun at Drury Lane at £5 per week, and his acting never earned him more than £7. But from 1798 he was paid in addition £5 weekly for his executive duties, and his Haymarket earnings pro-

of the proprietors of the Edinburgh theatre were judges of the Supreme Court of Judiciary of Scotland. The actions against the students were not pressed. But Aickin had signed a manifesto of the managers against Stayley and he probably anticipated further trouble from the students, for he left the Canongate at the end of this violently truncated season and went down to London for the summer of 1767.

Aickin came to the Drury Lane house as Young Belmont in *The Foundling* on 6 November 1767, billed only as "A Gentleman." He was at Drury Lane for the rest of his career, playing at the Haymarket also almost every summer. He did not at first fare as well in the English metropolis as he had in Scotland and Ireland. On two occasions—as Carlos in *The Revenge* on 14 Oc-

vided a tidy supplement in the summers. He always took £60 in lieu of a yearly benefit from 1783 on.

He played in several related lines of blunt men, "honest" men, elderly men, Irishmen, and eccentrics. They were usually roles of some importance, though as late as 1789 a newspaper critic wished "that Mr Aickin, whose style of playing is certainly deserving of a better part than that of the principal Witch, be dismissed from attending on the duties of the Cauldron" in *Macbeth*. Yet the excellent comedians Moody and Burton helped him stir the cauldron.

Aickin's Shakespearean characters were many besides Principal Witch, and a listing will demonstrate their range: Adam, Albany, Antigonus, Antonio, Belarius, Brabantio, Buckingham (*Richard III*), Caesar, Camillo, Capulet, Casca, Cassio, Cominius, Cranmer, Duke Frederick, Duke Senior, Duncan, Edgar, Escalus (*Measure for Measure*), Exeter, Ghost, Gloucester, Gonzalo, Henry IV (*1 Henry IV*), Henry VI (Cibber's version of *Richard III*), Horatio, Hotspur, Don John, Kent, Laertes, Lafeu, Friar Laurence, Leonato, Lord Chief Justice, Macduff, Montano, King Philip, Poins, Richmond, Rosencrantz, Ross, Salarino, Senator (*Timon*), Sergeant (*Macbeth*), Siward, Stanley, Surrey, Tybalt, and Worcester.

Aside from Shakespeare, a selection of his more popular characters might include: Colonel Blunt in *The Committee*, Major O'Flaherty in *The West Indian*, Subtle in *The Alchemist*, Sir William in *Love in a Village*, Sealand in *The Conscious Lovers*, Lord Randolph in *Douglas*, Solerno in *The Regent*, Sir William Cecil in *Mary Queen of Scots*, Pounce in *The Tender Husband*, Rightly in *The Heiress*, Old Mirable in *The Inconstant*, Sterling in *The Clandestine Marriage*, Sir Oliver in *The School for Scandal*, and Old Wilding in *The Liar*. He was the original Rowley in the memorable first cast of *The School for Scandal* in 1777.

Many of the characters James Aickin played were in the same line with, or even the same characters as, those his brother Francis played, but his style was different, being in tragedy more flexible and in comedy less sentimental.

"Anthony Pasquin" in his *Children of Thespis* (1786) declared that "Few Actors have e'er better known Nature's laws, / And, learning her dictates, have got less applause" which was probably an extreme statement each way.

The actor-critic Francis Gentleman (1770), though unfriendly to his brother Francis, thought James "natural" and "modest," and possessing "ease," and believed that he should have better parts and "more pounds per week":

The force and feeling which [Aickin] gave to the amiable character of Stedfast [in *The Heir at Law*]—a character, indeed, strongly resembling his own for manly bearing, probity and truth—must, we are persuaded, [make] a strong, indelible impression on the minds of all as have had an opportunity of witnessing his performance of that part.

Gentleman judged his Southampton in *The Earl of Essex* to be "modest, sensible, feeling, and within the lines of nature, but rather faint for a large audience: if this gentleman could rouze up a little more expression, there is a degree of propriety about him which few reach."

Like his brother, James appears to have been well thought of generally. When he was appointed acting manager at Drury Lane, the *Monthly Mirror* praised him as "in every respect fitted for this arduous situation: he has independence, integrity, good sense, gentlemanly manners, the esteem of his principals, the confidence of his brethren, and the regard of the public." He was one of the committee of actors appointed in 1776 to set up the Drury Lane Actors' Fund. His only publicized difficulty with one of his fellows came in 1792 when some difference over management made him call out John Philip Kemble to a duel. But Aickin missed Kemble and Kemble did not fire, and they smoothed over the difference, resuming a close personal and professional relationship.

Aickin's physique earned him late in life the nickname of "Belly," alluding to a corpulence which is apparent in some of his portraits.

Robert Dighton painted James Aickin as King Henry VI, and the picture was engraved by Walker for Bell's edition of Shakespeare in 1776. An anonymous portrait, said to be of Aickin and sometimes attributed to Samuel DeWilde, hangs in the Garrick Club. The Club owns another anonymous picture, a so-called "School of Garrick" portrait of Aickin. D. Dodd drew him as Horatio in *The Fair Penitent,* and this likeness was engraved by W. Walker in 1776. The same artists rendered him as Phocion in *The Grecian Daughter* for the *New English Theatre* in 1777. I. Wenman published an anonymously-drawn picture of him as Young Bevil in *The Conscious Lovers* in 1778. In 1789 W. Loftis executed a water-color of him which is now in the Folger Library, as Guyomar in *Sir Walter Raleigh.* A. Devis drew and J. Heath engraved a formal portrait of him in 1800, and there are anonymous and undated engravings of him as Lusignan in *Zara,* as Essex in the *Earl of Essex,* and as Cato in *Cato.*

**Ailsworth.** *See* AYLEWORTH.

**Aimé, Mlle** [*fl.* 1791], *dancer.*
Mlle Aimé was featured in a dance called *La Capricieuse* in two special "Entertainments of Music and Dancing" at the King's Theatre on 6 and 7 June 1791. She may have been in the *corps de ballet* earlier in the season but was at no other time named in the bills.

**Aingel.** *See* ANGEL.

**Ainsworth, Mr** [*fl.* 1788–1790], *house servant.*
Ainsworth was a minor employee of

Drury Lane Theatre in the seasons of 1788–89 and 1789–90. In the latter season his salary was 15 shillings a week.

**Aire, James** [*fl.* 1794], *singer.*
James Aire was a tenor singer who participated in London concerts. He sang in the Handelian performances in Westminster Abbey in 1784. He was said by Doane's *Musical Directory* of 1794 to live in King's Court, St George's Fields and to be connected with the Chapel Royal Choir. It is probable that he was Master of the Children of the Chapel Royal, for a letter of uncertain date signed by him, now in the Public Record Office, petitions the Lord Chamberlain for an allowance of clothing for the children.

**Airs.** *See* AYRES.

**Aitkin.** *See also* AICKIN.

**Aitkin, John** [*fl.* 1764–1774], *singer.*
John Aitkin sang at London's pleasure gardens, including Ranelagh and Finch's Grotto Gardens, St George's Fields, Southwark, in 1764 and occasionally until 1771. He may have been the Aitkin who sang on eight occasions at the concerts of the Musical Society of Edinburgh from 5 February through 22 April 1768.

Aitkin sang once at the Haymarket, in January 1770. By October 1771 he was advertising as a watchmaker in Dublin, but Isaac Reed heard him at the Grotto Gardens again on 13 August 1772 (he played the Father in *The Ephesian Matron*, and, according to the bill, was to "sing in character the favourite song O that my Wife wo'd drink Hooley and Fairly"). The last time he is traceable in records is to 17 September 1774 when he sang a "Scotch song" at the Haymarket, advertised incorrectly as being his "First appearance on that Stage."

**Akeroyde, Samuel** *b. c. 1650, composer, instrumentalist.*
Samuel Akeroyde is said to have been

born about 1650 in Yorkshire. He seems to have first appeared on the musical scene as a composer, and among his earliest works were songs for plays. He composed for the United Company productions of *Sir Courtly Nice* (9 May 1685), *The Commonwealth of Women* (mid-August 1685), *The Banditti* (January 1686), and *The Beggar's Bush* (1 December 1686) before service for the King reduced his availability for theatre work. On 25 April 1687 Akeroyde was appointed to replace John Twist in the King's Musick—apparently as a violinist—and he continued active for the following three years. When William and Mary came to the throne, he was reappointed at £30 annually and was scheduled to go to Holland with the king at the beginning of 1691. At this point, however, references to him in the Lord Chamberlain's accounts cease, so he may have left the royal service and reduced his performing activities.

Songs by Akeroyde were published regularly in the early 1690's and, starting in 1693, he began again to compose for the theatre. For the United Company at Drury Lane and Dorset Garden he wrote songs for *The Maid's Last Prayer* (end of February 1693), *The Prophetess* (May 1693), and *3 Don Quixote* (November 1695). After the break-up of the United troupe he composed both for Betterton at Lincoln's Inn Fields and Rich at Drury Lane: *Love's a Jest* (June 1696 at Lincoln's Inn Fields), *Love's a Lottery* (March 1699 at Lincoln's Inn Fields), *Massaniello* (May 1699 at Drury Lane), *The Bath* (31 May 1701 at Drury Lane), and *Wonders in the Sun* (8 April 1706 at the new Queen's Theatre in the Haymarket, for Betterton's group). Well into the eighteenth century his songs were published in collections—such as the popular *Wit and Mirth*—but though he was clearly one of the most successful composers of his day, he never wrote music of any great distinction.

Near the end of the 1690's Akeroyde returned to performing. The *Post Boy* of 18–21 June 1698 reported a dispute of the previous year at Tunbridge Wells between two companies of musicians, an old group and a new one headed by Akeroyde. By June 1698 the rivalry had been settled, not in Akeroyde's favor, and the old company was granted exclusive performing rights.

Akeroyde's death date is not known; it was certainly after 1706 and possibly much later, but the bulk of his composing seems to have been done in the early years of the 1680's and 1690's, with periods of performing activity at the ends of each of these decades. He was probably the Samuel Akeroyde whose wife Mary had a daughter Ann, baptized on 16 July 1686 at St Giles in the Fields.

**Akery, Mr** [*fl.* 1767–1788], *house servant?*

A Mr Akery was among minor members of the Covent Garden Theatre house staff distributing benefit tickets at the ends of the seasons 1782–83, 1783–84, 1785–86, and 1787–88. He may possibly be the Akery who was employed in some capacity at the Bristol Theatre Royal in 1767.

**Akin.** *See* AICKIN *and* AITKIN.

**Alard.** *See* ALLARD.

**Albergotti, Vittoria** [*fl.* 1713], *singer.*

Billed as newly arrived from Italy, Signora Albergotti made her first appearance in England at the Queen's Theatre in the Haymarket on 26 February 1713 as Edwige in the premiere of *Ernelinda*. On 9 April of the same year a concert of vocal and instrumental music was given for her benefit at Hickford's Great Room.

**Albertarelli, Francesco** [*fl.* 1788–1792], *singer.*

Francesco Albertarelli was an Italian tenor who had sung in Milan and Vienna before coming to London in 1791. At Vienna, in 1788, he had been Mozart's Don Giovanni. In 1790–91, he was involved in a series of 41 concerts of vocal and instrumental music presented at the King's Theatre between 26 March and 9 July, although he may not have appeared after 7 June. His songs included a "Hunting Song" composed by Philador and a comic duet with Sga Sestini. In 1792, he appeared for a while on Tuesdays and Saturdays at Ranelagh, under the music direction of Federici Morelli. Doane's *Musical Directory* listed him as living at No 15, Fluyder Street, Westminster, in 1794, and as belonging to the Opera, but his name is not found in any opera bills.

**Albone, James** ₁*fl. 1740*₁, *singer.*
James Albone sang at the New Wells, Goodman's Fields, on 17 October 1740.

**Albrici, Bartolomeo** *b. c. 1630, instrumentalist, singer, composer.*
Bartolomeo Albrici (or Albrigi, Albrei, Albreis) was born in Rome about 1630. With his brother Vincenzo he worked in Sweden in the 1650's and then moved to Dresden where he held a post as organist at the Saxon court church. With their sister Leonora the brothers left Dresden in order to find better places—or so Bartolomeo's passport stated—and before the end of 1662 they had arrived in England and become members of the King's Italian Musick, though some sources have them arriving in London two years later. From 1664 to 1667 the brothers shared responsibilities as composers to Charles II and on 5 May 1668 gold medals were awarded them for their services.

Vincenzo returned to Dresden in 1671, probably with his sister, but Bartolomeo remained in England and became part of London musical life, earning his living composing, teaching, and playing the harpsichord. In the last great English court masque, John Crowne's *Calisto* on 15 February 1675, a Mr Bartleme—probably Bartolomeo—played lute and "harpsicall." The Popish Plot of 1678 made life difficult for

Roman Catholics in England, and on 18 November 1679 Albrici and three other Italians submitted a petition reciting how they had left foreign posts to come to England at the King's request but were now ill-treated, four years behind in their salaries, and forced to leave the country. But Albrici and at least two of his countrymen stayed in England and, especially after the accession of James II, found royal favor again.

By 1682 Bartolomeo was teaching music to John Evelyn's talented daughter Mary, and when James II opened his Catholic chapel near the end of 1686 Bartolomeo was one of the Gregorians, his yearly salary being £40. His duties occasionally included going with the King and Queen on their trips out of London. After William and Mary assumed the throne, the Catholic chapel was disbanded, and records of Albrici, who would then have been nearing 60, cease.

Though his brother Vincenzo seems to have been more successful, Bartolomeo Albrici was clearly a man of varied talents who was held in considerable esteem. Evelyn, upon hearing Bartolomeo and other members of the King's Italian Musick perform on 24 January 1667 in Charles's private chambers, found them "rare *Italian* voices," and after he heard Bartolomeo play harpsichord at Mr Slingsby's he wrote on 20 November 1679 of the music being "exquisitely performed by four of the most renowned masters." Albrici did some composing, and two of his cantatas have been preserved at the Dresden Museum.

**Albrici, Leonora** ₁*fl. 1662–1671*₁, *singer.*
Leonora, the sister of Bartolomeo and Vincenzo Albrici, apparently came to England with her brothers about 1662 and became a part of the Italian Musick of Charles II. She was certainly a part of this establishment in 1667 when Evelyn praised the "rare *Italian* voices," and was esteemed enough to be awarded a gold medal and chain by the

King on 5 May 1668. Since there seem to be no records of her in England after this, she may have returned to the continent with her brother Vincenzo in 1671.

### Albrici, Vincenzo  *1631–1696, instrumentalist, singer, composer.*

Vincenzo Albrici was born in Rome on 26 June 1631. He was the brother of Don Bartolomeo and Leonora Albrici, and of the three the most successful. Most of his activity was outside England. He studied under Carissimi, and in 1650 Queen Christina of Sweden brought him to Stralsund where he directed her Italian opera house until her abdication in 1654. With his brother he then moved to Dresden as one of the members of the private music of the Crown Prince of Saxony. In 1662 he was made Capellmeister to the Saxon court and colleague of Heinrich Schütz, but by the end of the year he apparently resigned his post, for King Charles's Italian Musick was established in 1662 and the three Albricis were apparently members, having been recruited for Charles II by the theatre manager Thomas Killigrew.

By 1667 Evelyn described the Albrici trio as "rare *Italian* voices," but Vincenzo's major duty under Charles II was composition. On 12 February 1667 Pepys, naming him "Vinnecotio," said he was the chief composer among the Italians in the King's employ, and on 16 February the diarist heard the group at Lord Brouncker's:

. . . and by and by the musique, that is to say, Signor Vincentio, who is the master-composer, and six more, whereof two eunuches . . . They sent two harpsicons before; and by and by, after tuning them, they begun; and, I confess, very good musique they made; that is, the composition exceeding good, but yet not at all more pleasing to me than what I have heard in English . . . [T]heir justness in keeping time by practice much before any that we have, unless it be a good band of practised fiddlers.

Pepys, always patriotic when it came to music, was somewhat grudging in his praise, but the King, by a warrant dated 5 May 1668, expressed his pleasure in the Albricis' work by presenting all three with gold medals and chains.

Vincenzo, probably with his sister, left England in 1671 to resume his position at Dresden. Ten years later he was appointed organist at St Thomas's Church in Leipzig, to qualify for which position he became a Protestant; a year later he moved to Prague and became the director of music at St Augustine's Church. He had a son who, upon the recommendation of John Blow, applied for the position of organist to the Earl of Rutland in 1693, offering to work for £20, but of this son nothing more seems to be known. Vincenzo Albrici died at Prague on 8 August 1696. Many of his compositions were destroyed in 1760 when Dresden was bombarded, but much of his early work done in Sweden is preserved in the Upsala University Library, and manuscripts of a variety of other works, including three *Te Deums,* masses, cantatas, and instrumental music still exist. Two of his songs were printed in Godbid and Playford's *Scelta di canzonette* in 1679.

### Albuzio, Mr  [*fl. 1753–1754*],  *singer.*

A Mr Albuzio was a principal singer at the King's Opera under the management of Vaneschi during the season 1753–54. He sang Artabanes in *Artaserse* on 29 January 1754 and eight times thereafter and probably sang in the several other operas which were performed that season.

### Alchorne, Mrs  *1683–1787, strong woman.*

Mrs Alchorne (sometimes Aleborne) performed astonishing feats of strength and endurance in the middle of the eighteenth century at public rooms in Drury Lane, at Bartholomew Fair (1752), and at May Fair. Billed as the "Strong Woman," she was exhibited by her husband. In a letter to the *Gentleman's Magazine,* dated 6 March 1816, and thus written many years in retrospect, a correspondent described her husband as a Frenchman and her as a foreigner.

Mrs Alchorne was reported as being short, beautifully and delicately formed, and of lovely countenance. She had light auburn hair, reaching to her knees, which length she used to advantage in her exhibitions. Twisting her hair around the projecting part of an anvil, she would lift the ponderous weight, "with seeming ease," some inches from the floor. Then reclining on her back on a bed, she would have the anvil placed upon her uncovered bosom, whereupon three blacksmiths would forge a horse-shoe "with the same might and indifference as when in the shop at their constant labour." Mrs Alchorne appeared to endure with great composure, talking and singing until she cast the anvil from her body and jumped up "with extreme gaiety, and without the least discompose of her dress or person." She then concluded her performance by applying a red-hot salamander to her naked feet.

According to an obituary notice in the *Scots Magazine,* Mrs Alchorne died in London on 7 November 1787, in her one-hundred-and-fourth year.

**Alcidor, real name PHILIPPE TOU-BEL** [*fl.* 1662–1668], *actor.*

On 25 August 1663 an unnamed French troupe, possibly that headed by Alcidor and Lavoy, was granted permission to bring stage decorations to England. They had performed in Brussels on 20 May 1662, billing themselves as *"les comédiens du roi d'Angleterre à Bruxelles,"* and they played also at the Hague that year. Alcidor was apparently with the troupe for only a brief period, and in succeeding years he changed companies frequently. In 1666 he was a member of the Beauchamps troupe; in 1672 he formed a company of his own; in 1676 he was listed among the *"comédiens de la Reine"* at Charleville; two years later

he was part of *"le troupe de Mademoiselle"* at Amiens; in 1679 he was playing at the Hague in the Prince of Orange's company; by 1685 he was in the Longchamps troupe; and in 1686 he formed another group of his own, only to become part of the Dauphine company in 1688.

**Alcock, Mr** [*fl.* 1714], *actor.*

Mr and Mrs Alcock were members of the Duke of Southampton and Cleveland's Servants at Richmond in the summer of 1714. On 1 November of this year at the King's Arms Tavern in Southwark the same troupe, probably, performed *Injured Virtue,* with Mr Alcock playing the British Slave and his wife the role of Hellena.

**Alcock, Mrs** [*fl.* 1714], *actress. See* **ALCOCK, MR.**

**Alday, Paul** 1764–1835?, *violinist, composer.*

Paul Alday was born into a French family of musicians at Paris in 1764. His father was a mandolin player from Perpignan. His brother (born 1763) was also a mandolin player and a violinist who, after appearing at the Concert Spirituel in Paris, established a music business at Lyon about 1795. Paul Alday, more talented than his brother, was taught by Viotti. He became celebrated as a violinist at the Concert Spirituel, playing there frequently from 1783 until 1791, when he came to Britain. There is no record of any concert activity in London, if any, other than his playing a concerto on the violin, his first performances in the kingdom, in the oratorios at the Haymarket on 8, 15, and 22 March 1793. He soon moved to Oxford, where it was announced on 25 May 1793, that "Mons Alday, who was the celebrated Performer on the Violin in Paris, and whose musical talents have met with such general Approbation in the Metropolis here," was engaged to lead the band at the Oxford Music Room, with

Philip Hayes conducting. Alday's wife played the harp in these concerts.

In 1806, Alday settled in Edinburgh as a director and teacher of music. He moved to Dublin in 1809, opened a music business in Rhames Street in 1811, began a music academy in 1812, and by 1820 had established himself as a professor of the violin in that city. The Minute Books of the Governors of the Irish Musical Fund, of which he was a member, indicate he was appointed to lead the annual Handelian Commemoration Concerts in Dublin in 1818 and 1828. Alday composed a number of concertos, trios, quartets, duets, and variations. Several trios for two violins and a brass were published in London by Lavenue. His violin concerto in D minor (published in Paris, 1780), according to Mendel-Reissmann, "was a favourite of all virtuosos and advanced violinists of that time and is distinguished by fine artistic traits." Grove suggests that Alday died at Dublin in 1835.

**Aldridge, Mr**  *d. 1768, performer?*
According to the *Public Advertiser* of 12 August 1768, a Mr Aldridge of Covent Garden Theatre had died "lately" at Bristol. The only person by this name certainly known to have been in the Covent Garden company at this time was Robert Aldridge the dancer, who was indeed performing at Bristol in the summer of 1768 but did not die until 1793.

**Aldridge, Mr**  [*fl. 1790*], *performer?*
A Mr Aldridge paid 4s. on 6 September 1790 for a license to perform a medley entertainment at Bartholomew Fair.

**Aldridge, Mary.** *See* LEE, MARY ALDRIDGE, LADY SLINGSBY.

**Aldridge, Robert**  *d. 1793, dancer, ballet master.*
Robert Aldridge was a principal dancer on the London stage for 20 years between 1762 and 1782. His origins seem to have been Irish, and before coming to London he performed at Kilkenny (1755), Dublin (1758), Drogheda (1757–58) and Cork (1760 and 1761). On 8 October 1760 he arranged some special dances for a production of Woodward's *The Fairies* at the new Theatre Royal at Cork.

Aldridge made his debut on the London stage on 23 October 1762 at Drury Lane in a new dance called *The Irish Lilt,* with Miss Baker, who later often appeared with him. He remained at Drury Lane through 1765–66 at £4 per week (and probably through 1766–67, although his name is not found in the bills) and then moved over to Covent Garden at the beginning of 1767–68, making his first appearance there, again in *The Irish Lilt,* on 21 September 1767. His performance several weeks later on 9 October in a new dance called *The Merry Sailors* drew extravagant praise from a correspondent to the *Theatrical Monitor* (21 November 1767): "his stature, strength, agility, and swiftness are beyond anything I ever saw on Covent Garden theatre: he stands tip-toe on the pinnacle of perfection, and gives us an idea of Homer's pyrrick dance delineated on the shield of Achilles."

Aldridge was regularly engaged at Covent Garden from 1767–68 through 1781–82. His articles of employment dated 31 August 1768 were for five years at £3 per year plus 13s. per night for the first year, 16s. 4d. per night for the second and third, and 19s. per night for the fourth and fifth. In subsequent articles at that theatre he was paid £6 per week in 1776–77 and 1777–78 and £7 per week in 1780–81 and 1781–82. Aldridge seems to have been out of London in 1778–79 and 1779–80, for on 20 September 1780 he was announced in *The Frolick* at Covent Garden, his "first appearance here these 2 years."

On 27 April 1782 he was billed as ballet-master. He worked regularly as a dancer in the repertory and his name is found in the bills for a number of dances, many of which he choreographed, such as

*All in the Downs,* the *Bacchanals' Dance* in *The Tempest* and a celebrated *Tambourine Dance.* Aldridge also once played a straight acting role when he performed Macheath ("for that night only") on 28 April 1779. While ballet-master he trained a number of young dancers including the Masters Harris, Jackson, Langrish and Lyon, and the Misses Lings, Nicolls, and Parish.

Robert Aldridge married Mary Gilbert at St Paul, Covent Garden, on 17 September 1763. They were listed in the marriage register as bachelor and spinster, both of the parish. (There is no record that his wife ever performed either as Miss Gilbert or Mrs Aldridge.) Their daughter Catherine was christened at the same church on 10 March 1770. The Aldridges were living at No 2, Great Maddox Street, Hanover Square, in 1777, at the Carpet Warehouse in the Piazza of Covent Garden in 1778 and 1779, and at Rumler's, Clare Court, Drury Lane, in 1782.

During summers Aldridge usually was a member of the *corps de ballet* at the Bristol theatre; he was there from 1765 to 1770, in 1773, 1777, and 1778. He also returned to Ireland at least once, in the summer of 1775, to seek local patronage in a benefit at Cork, where he had been a performer before going to London. He appealed to the town for he had "no emolument whatever for dancing [except] such as may arise from his benefit." Aldridge also performed at Cambridge in 1779 in Joseph Glassinger's company; perhaps he was the Aldridge who had a benefit at the York theatre on 1 February 1780.

Aldridge left Covent Garden at the end of the 1781–82 season to engage with Jackson at Edinburgh, where he seems to have performed for several years and where he was also a dancing master. A person named Aldridge paid 4s. on 6 September 1790 for a license to perform a medley entertainment at Bartholomew Fair. The *European Magazine* stated that Robert Aldridge died at Edinburgh on 3 June 1793; the *Scots Magazine* gave his death-date as 27 May.

**Aldwin, Mr** [*fl.* 1741], *singer.*

Mr Aldwin was a countertenor in the chorus for the productions of Handel's *Acis and Galatea* at Lincoln's Inn Fields on 28 February and 11 March 1741.

**Aleborne.** *See* ALCHORNE, MRS.

**Aledore** [*fl.* 1711], *singer?*

The name Aledore is put down for £5 in a document ascribed to manager Owen Swiney, listing payments to various individuals, mostly singers, for the period 6 March to 2 May 1711. Most of the other payments are considerably larger, suggesting that Aledore's function must have been minor. The name itself may be in error, for Aledore is otherwise unknown.

**Aleworth.** *See also* AYLEWORTH.

**Aleworth, Jeoffry** *d.* 1687, *instrumentalist, singer.*

In 1674 Jeoffry Aleworth received the standard £16 2s. 6d. livery fee as one of the King's musicians, replacing Humphrey Madge. Aleworth seems to have been both a violinist and a sackbut player, and his participation in the production of the court masque *Calisto* on 15 February 1675 as one of the regular band of 24 violins suggests that he was an accomplished musician. In March of this same year he attended the King on a trip to Newmarket, and he was appointed on 4 September to fill John Strong's vacated position among the wind players at a wage of 1s. 8d. per day plus the usual livery fee. By 13 December 1679 his salary as a member of the wind music was £46 10s. 10 d. annually, and he still held a position among the violins, probably at an additional fee.

On 22 November 1681 he and three other members of the King's Musick were suspended because they "neglected their duty in attending at y^e play acted before his Ma^te at Whitehall" on 15 November. Whether Aleworth ever played at the public theatres or not is not known.

He was also a singer, for a warrant dated 31 August 1685 listed him among a group of countertenors in the private music of James II. Under James, as under Charles, he was regularly chosen to attend the King on trips out of London. The last document listing him as active is dated 9 November 1686; he was authorized 3s. per day while attending the King at Windsor. By 17 July 1687 he was dead, for on that date (Richard?) Lewis was appointed to replace the deceased Aleworth in the private music; on 3 August Charles Powell was appointed to fill one of the other vacancies left by Aleworth's death.

The parish registers of St Clement Danes contain several entries for a Jeffery Aylworth (both names variously spelled) and his wife Margarett; the dates fit with the years of Aleworth's activity, and the name of one son, Pelham (after the musician Pelham Humphrey?) may not be coincidental. A daughter Jane was baptized on 2 February 1669; a son William was baptized on 26 August 1671 and buried on 8 March 1674; a son Pelham was baptized on 6 November 1673 and buried the following 3 December; a son Jonathan was baptized on 4 April 1675; a son John was baptized on 1 August 1676. Margarett Ayleworth, probably Jeoffrey's wife, was buried on 9 January 1684.

References to a Joseph Aleworth in *The King's Musick* seem to be errors for Jeoffrey.

## Aleworth, William [fl. 1662–1669], violinist.

William Aleworth, possibly a relative of the musician Jeoffrey, was a violinist appointed as a musician in ordinary without fee in the King's Musick on 27 October 1662. When Henry Comer's place became vacant on 31 March 1669, Aleworth was

his replacement at an annual salary of £23, which was to be deducted from Comer's income. A petition of Alexander Clerke, surgeon, against William Aleworth, musician, dated 22 July 1669, commanded the musician to appear before the Lord Chamberlain, but the details of the case are not known. A song, "A Dialogue betwixt Philander and Sylvia" by a William Aylworth —probably the violinist—was published in the fourth book of Playford's *Theater of Music* in 1687.

## "Alexander." See GOODMAN, CARDELL, or VERBRUGGEN, JOHN.

## Alexander, Mr [fl. 1666–1667], actor.

In Flecknoe's intended cast for his *Damoiselles à la Mode,* published in 1667, a Mr Alexander was listed as Sganarelle. There seems to be no evidence that when the play was done in the 1666–67 and 1668–69 seasons by the King's Company at the Bridges Street Theatre that a Mr Alexander played the role, and since he is otherwise unknown, perhaps Flecknoe erred or possibly this was a nickname for some other member of the troupe. If a Mr Alexander did act in the 1660's, he was probably not the "Alexander" of later in the century, a name used by John Verbruggen and applied to Cardell Goodman.

## Alexander, Master [fl. 1759], actor.

Master Alexander appeared as Siffroy in a performance of *Cleone* by children at the Haymarket on 10 May 1759. The performance was given "By Authority" and for his benefit.

## Alexander, Benjamin [fl. 1794–1795], violinist.

Benjamin Alexander was listed in Doane's *Musical Directory* (1794) as a violinist, a member of the Cecilian Society, and then living at No 24, Bethnal Green. He was one of the instrumental performers who played in *The Thespian Panorama,* a musical, rhetorical, and imitative entertainment given at the Haymarket on 4 March and repeated on 11, 13, 18, and 20 March 1795.

**Alexis, Mr** [*fl. 1794*], *violinist.*

Mr Alexis was listed in Doane's *Musical Directory* (1794) as a violinist and a player in the grand Handelian performances in Westminster Abbey. He was then "with West's Company," which could be a reference to any of several provincial companies headed respectively by James West (in America), by Thomas West (in the south of England), or by William West.

**Alfred, Edward** *d. 1793, actor, house servant, singer.*

Edward Alfred was first noticed as an actor in off-season performances given sporadically at the Haymarket in 1777–78, with his name first appearing in the bills for an unspecified role in *The True-Born Irishman* on 9 October 1777. It is doubtful, however, that this was his first appearance, since such debuts are particularly specified in this set of Haymarket bills. He also appeared in *The Students* on 13 October 1777. In 1781–82 he was back at the Haymarket appearing in *The Fashionable Wife* on 6 May and as King Henry in *Richard III* on 4 March, the latter being the first role for which he was specifically identified. Few such important roles were to come to him again. During his subsequent eleven-year engagement at Drury Lane, which began in the season 1782–83, he played very minor servant roles, such as the drawer in *The Gamester*, the postboy in *The First Floor*, the coachman in *High Life Below Stairs,* the servant in *No Song No Supper*, Hounslow in *The Stratagem*, and Antonio's Boy in *The Chances*. During 1792–93, his last season with the Drury Lane company (which was then playing at the King's and the Haymarket while its new theatre was being built), he was still playing similar

roles. He also took on unspecified characters in the pantomimes and sang bass in the general chorus. Perhaps he was the same Mr Alfred who danced at the Birmingham theatre on 28 July 1791.

Alfred shared in some benefits but most years he was allotted a number of tickets with other lowly actors and house servants. When not performing, he seems to have functioned as a ticket-taker. On 27 September 1788 his salary was increased by 1*s*. 8*d*. per day from an unspecified sum. He was earning £1 10*s*. per week in 1789–90. In June 1786 he was living at No 2, Middle Temple Lane.

Edward Alfred's full name is found in Winston's Drury Lane Fundbook, where he subscribed 10*s*. 6*d*. in 1782–83. He claimed against the fund in September 1793, apparently ill and no longer able to work. A month later, in October 1793, he died.

**Aliff.** *See* **AYLIFF.**

**Alison.** *See* **ALLISON.**

**Allaby, William** [*fl. 1641–1662*], *musician.*

William Allaby (or Anlaby), a musician extraordinary (that is, without fee) and stringer of lutes in the musical establishment of Charles I in 1641, was appointed a musician in ordinary under Charles II on 13 August 1660 as lute-maker, a new place having been created for him. He was listed again as a member of the King's Musick in 1662 but not thereafter.

**Allanson, Charles** [*fl. 1691–1696*], *singer.*

In April 1685 Charles Allanson was one of the boys who sang in the Chapel Royal. By warrants dated August 1691, Michaelmas 1692, and 7 January 1696, he was granted livery as a former chapel boy who had left the choir after his voice changed.

## Allard, Sieur [fl. 1702], dancer.

The Sieur Allard (or Elard) who appeared in England about 1700–1702 may have been either Charles or Pierre Allard, both of whom were French dancers active at the Saint-Germain fair as early as 1678; if the performer in England was not one of these, he was very likely related.

The author of *A Comparison Between the Two Stages* (1702) had little good to say of Allard and his "sons"—probably Joseph Sorin and Richard Baxter:

SULL[EN].   And the Sieur Allard ——.

CRI[TIC].   Ay, the *Sieur* with a pox to him —and the two *Monsieurs* his Sons—Rogues that show at *Paris* for a Groat a piece, and here they were an entertainment for the Court and his late Majesty.

RAMB[LE].   Oh—*Harlequin* and *Scaramouch.*

CRI.   Ay; What a rout here was with a Night piece of *Harlequin* and *Scaramouch?* with the Guittar and the Bladder! What jumping over Tables and Joint-Stools! What ridiculous Postures and Grimaces! and what an exquisite Trick 'twas to straddle before the Audience, making a thousand damn'd *French* Faces, and seeming in labour with a monstrous Birth, at last my counterfeit Male Lady is delivered of her two Puppies *Harlequin* and *Scaramouch.*

SULL.   And yet the Town was so fond of this, that these Rascals brought the greatest Houses that ever were known: 'Sdeath I am scandaliz'd at these little things; I am asham'd to own my self of a Country where the Spirit of Poetry is dwindled into vile Farce and Foppery.

When John Weaver published his *History of the Mimes and Pantomimes* in 1728, he spoke of "the Night Scene of the Sieur Allard and his two Sons, performed on the Stage in *Drury-Lane* about seven or eight and twenty Years ago" as being the remains of ancient pantomimes "but sunk and degenerated into Pleasantry and ludicrous Representations of *Harlequin, Scaramouch, Columbine, Pierot,* &c." When one consid-

ers Allard's apparent popularity it is odd that no specific performance records or other information concerning his stay in England have come to light. An Alard, probably the same person, presented a *Grand troupe allemande, anglaise et écossaise* at the St Laurent fair in 1719–20.

## Allard's Sons. *See* BAXTER, RICHARD, and SORIN, JOSEPH.

## Allden, Mr S. [fl 1794], violinist.

Mr S. Allden was listed in Doane's *Musical Directory* (1794) as a violinist living at Buckingham House and a member of the King's Band.

## Allegranti, Teresa Maddalena, later MRS HARRISON *c. 1750–c. 1802, singer.*

Born about 1750 in Florence, the soprano Signora Teresa Maddalena Allegranti made her debut in 1770 at Venice singing secondary roles. In the following year she went to Mannheim to study under the excellent maestro Holzbauer. Burney heard her at Schwetzingen in 1772 and thought she had a "pretty unaffected manner." After performing in Germany until about 1778, she returned to Venice to sing at the Teatro San Giovanni Grisostomo in 1779 and at the Teatro San Samuele in 1780–81.

In 1781–82 Signora Allegranti was engaged at the King's Opera in London, where on 11 December 1781 she made her debut singing the role of Bettina in Anfossi's comic opera *Il viaggiatori felici.* The piece was repeated many times that season through 29 June. Horace Walpole heard her in it on 8 January 1782 and wrote that he approved her and that she was "almost as much in fashion as Vestris the dancer was last year: the applause to her is rather much greater." That season she also sang Sandrina in Sacchini's comic opera *La contadina in corte.* According to her benefit

TERESA MADDALENA ALLEGRANTI
by R. Cosway

bill on 18 April 1782 she lived at No 23, Queen Street, Golden Square.

She returned to the King's Theatre in the following season on 2 November 1782 to sing the burletta role of Alfonsina in *Il convito*, in which the *Public Advertiser* (4 November) reported "Allegranti displayed unusual powers—a most brilliant shake, which she does not always favour us with, a *sostenuto* of prodigious extent, and above all, what she never fails to favour us with: exquisite grace, taste and feeling." She also sang Giannina in *Il trionfo della costanza,* Zemira in *Zemira e Azore,* and Vitosa in *Il vecchi burlati.* She now lived at No 232, Piccadilly.

After her final performance of the season on 13 May 1783, as Vitosa, Signora Allegranti left London to engage at Dresden as *prima donna buffa* at a salary of one thousand ducats per year. After staying there for many years, she sang again at Venice in

1798 and then returned to London in the spring of 1799. She was announced for Carolina in *Il matrimonio segreto* at the King's Theatre on 6 April 1799 but became so seriously ill as, "in the opinion of Sir George Baker, to render her immediate appearance extremely dangerous." She did sing the role, however, three days later on 9 April, but in a very disappointing manner, perhaps caused by her illness but more likely by her decline. The Earl of Mount-Edgcumbe wrote that "Never was there a more pitiable attempt: she had scarcely a thread of voice remaining, nor the power to sing a note in tune: her figure and acting were equally altered for the worse." After three more attempts at the role on 13, 18, and 20 April, she retired from the company and never performed again. It was reported that she married an Englishman named Harrison and moved to Ireland, where she died about 1802.

When Signora Allegranti first sang in London in 1781 she possessed a rich, clear, and powerful soprano voice "of extensive compass, blended with taste and expression," according to W. T. Parke's *Musical Memoirs.* Although she employed no *vibrato* in her voice, she otherwise sang so elegantly and effectively that this ornament of voice was not missed. By the end of her first London season she did, however, introduce "a shake the most liquid, brilliant, and perfect imaginable." According to Burney "her voice was very sweet and flexible, though not very powerful." A portrait of her was engraved by Bartolozzi after Cosway.

**Allen.** *See also* **ALLEYN, ALLYN.**

**Allen, Mr** [*fl.* *1732–1733*], *actor.*

A Mr Allen played Serainger in *The Miseries of Love,* performed by some minor actors at the Haymarket on 29 November 1732. Perhaps he was the Mr Allen (fl. 1733–1734) who had a benefit as treasurer the following season, or Thomas

Allen (1696?–1738), Drury Lane numberer, who may have tried his hand at acting on this occasion at the Haymarket, on a night when, incidentally, Drury Lane was dark.

## Allen, Mr  [fl. 1733–1734], treasurer.

A Mr Allen was treasurer at the Haymarket in the summer of 1734, after the seceders had returned to Drury Lane on 10 April. He had a benefit on 10 August 1734. He could have been Thomas Allen (1696?–1738), who was numberer and door keeper at Drury Lane during the regular season, or Mr Allen (fl. 1732–1733), actor.

## Allen, Mr  [fl. 1737–1740], house servant.

A minor house servant at Drury Lane named Allen shared tickets on 30 May 1737 and shared benefits in the seasons 1737–38, 1738–39, and 1739–40. He was not Thomas Allen who was at this theatre during the same period.

## Allen, Mr  [fl. 1746–1757], actor.

An actor, or actors, named Allen appeared at the London fairs and theatres in the middle of the eighteenth century. The name was in the bills for the roles of the father in *The Schemes of Harlequin*, at Hussey's booth in George Inn Yard, Smithfield, on 23 August 1746; the first witch in *The Universal Parents*, a droll, at Lee and Yeates's great booth at Bartholomew Fair, 24 August 1748; Didymo in *Jeptha's Rash Vow*, at Yeates and Warner's great booth, Southwark Fair, 7 September 1750; and Brittle in *The Happy Gallant*, at Bence's Room, Swan Tavern, West Smithfield, 6 September 1755. A minor actor named Allen was at Drury Lane in 1752–53 and 1757–58. He was first billed as Nym in *The Merry Wives of Windsor* on 18 May 1753, and his next and last billing was as a character in *The Rehearsal* on 29 September 1757. Probably he acted other minor roles and he may have been a house

servant as well. (There had also been an Allen at Norwich in 1744–46, along with a Mrs Allen.)

One of these persons could have been Adam Allyn, who was a member of the original David Douglass company. Allyn arrived in New York with his wife in 1758. He made his American debut in Philadelphia's South Street Theatre on 20 July 1759 in *The Recruiting Officer*. He also played in New York, making his first appearance there at the Beekman Street Theatre in November 1761, and in Newport in 1762. Adam Allyn died in New York City on 15 February 1768, and a tombstone was placed by his fellow actors in Trinity Churchyard there, the inscription of which reads: "Sacred / to     the / Memory / of / Adam Allyn.  Comedian./ Who / Departed  this Life / February 15th: 1768./  This Stone was Erected / By the American Company / As a / Testimony of their / Unfeigned Regard./ He Posesed / Many Good Qualitys / But as he was a Man / He / Had the Frailties / Common to Man's Nature." A drawing of this tombstone in the Harvard Theatre Collection provides an incorrect variant to the last lines: "But as he was a Man / He / Had the Frailties of a / Man."

## Allen, Mr  [fl. 1761–1774?], house servant?

A Mr Allen was entered on the pay list at Covent Garden in 1761 as 15s. per week with no position specified. He was probably the same Mr Allen found in the pay lists of the same theatre from 1766–67 through 1773–74 at £1 per week.

## Allen, Mr  [fl. 1764–1765], dresser.

A men's dresser named Allen was at Drury Lane during 1764–65, being paid 12s. per week.

## Allen, Mr  [fl. 1793], dancer.

A male dancer named Allen performed at Covent Garden Theatre in the spring of 1793. He danced the role of a Creolian insurgent in a new musical afterpiece, *The Governor*, on 11 March and again on 16 March, 1 April, and 23 April 1793. Possibly he was the Allen who was in the Margate company in the summer of 1797 or Edward Allen, the music teacher and dancing master.

**Allen, Mrs** ₁*fl. 1789–1792*₁. *See* **HAGLEY, MISS.**

**Allen, Mrs** ₁*fl. 1746–1767*₁, *house servant?*

The name of a Mrs Allen was entered intermittently in the Covent Garden pay list between 1746–47 and 1766–67. In 1746–47 she was paid 2s. per day; in 1748–49, 2s. 6d. per day; in 1756–57, £1 per week; and in 1766–67, 19s. 8d. per week. Perhaps she was the same person as Miss Ann Allen (fl. 1742–1769).

**Allen, Ann** ₁*fl. 1742–1769*₁, *actress, house servant?*

An actress by the name of Miss Ann Allen was at Covent Garden, according to *The London Stage*, every season between 1742–43 and 1768–69. She also played at Richmond, Surrey, in September 1744. Although she was employed in the theatre for at least 26 years, her name almost never appeared on the bills. She played such roles as Patience in *Henry VIII* (4 May 1749 and 16 April 1751), the maid in *The Inconstant* (11 October 1764), and Mrs Trippet in *The Lying Valet* (15 December 1775). Miss Allen shared tickets fairly regularly with other minor house personnel. In 1746–47 she was on the payroll at 7s. 6d. per week and in 1767–68 at 19s. per week. The valuation of her stage wardrobe at £13 given in an inventory in July 1769 (the last mention of her name) indicates how very minor her roles were. Her first name is found in a letter to Colman signed by the Covent Garden performers. An Ann Allen was buried at St Paul, Covent Garden, on 29 March 1795.

**Allen, Bab** or **Barbara.** *See* **KNEPP, MARY.**

**Allen, James** ₁*fl. 1732*₁, *singer.*

James Allen appeared in the role of the Persian Officer in Handel's oratorio *Esther*, performed privately at the Crown and Anchor Tavern, 23 February 1732, by a cast of professionals and amateurs.

**Allen, John** *d. 1722, violinist.*

John Allen was mentioned twice in the parish registers of St Giles, Cripplegate: "Robert son of John Allen Musishan and Elizabeth" was born 7 March and died 23 April 1721 and on 4 November 1722 was buried "John Allin Fidler Consumption."

**Allen, John** ₁*fl. 1761*₁, *musician?*

John Allen was bound by the Worshipful Company of Musicians as an apprentice to the musician John Ward on 8 October 1761. There is no record of his having become a freeman.

**Allen, Thomas** *1696?–1738, house servant, pugilist.*

A Thomas Allen was christened at St Paul, Covent Garden, on 17 July 1696, the son of Thomas Allen and Isabella Allen (née Carter), who had been married in the same church on 14 July 1695. This Thomas Allen was very likely the theatrical employee and pugilist. His sister Rachel was also christened at St Paul, Covent Garden, on 24 November 1698.

Thomas Allen was a complex but obscure personality. He may have been the Allen who acted at the Haymarket in 1723–24, or the Allen who acted at the same theatre in 1732–33, or both. It is likely that he was the Allen who was treasurer at the Haymarket in the summer of 1734. In 1731–32, Thomas Allen was first noted as a numberer and gallery boxkeeper at Drury Lane, positions he retained at least through 1736–37 and probably in 1737–38. (He should not be confused with an-

*Harvard Theatre Collection*

THOMAS ALLEN, with Lady Morgan
artist unknown

other Mr Allen who was a servant in that house in 1736–37; this person shared in tickets with other servants on 30 May 1737, while Thomas Allen received his usual benefit on 27 May 1737).

Thomas Allen was also a pugilist at Jack Broughton's Amphitheatre. He was buried at St Paul, Covent Garden, on 5 May 1738, his pall supported by Broughton and five other boxers. An obituary reported that he was commonly called "Pipes" and that he was particularly famous for his art and bravery in boxing. His funeral, "which was extraordinarily decent," was paid for by the management of Drury Lane. An Anne Allen, wife of Thomas Allen from St. Andrew Holborn, was buried at St Paul, Covent Garden, on 15 January 1734, and another Anne Allen, daughter of Thomas Allen, was buried there on 16 June 1733. The former may have been the pugilist's wife and the latter his daughter or sister.

**Allen, Thomas** *[fl. 1791], dwarf.*

A dwarf named Thomas Allen was exhibited at the Lyceum in the Strand in December 1791 along with another dwarf named Lady Morgan, the "Windsor Fairy." The pair evidently became a general topic of conversation among the nobility and gentry, and they were visited by the Dukes of Clarence and York, who conversed with the Lilliputians "in the most affable and engaging manner." A newspaper of the day described Thomas Allen as being in his twenty-fourth year and "of beautiful symmetry." An engraving from the *Wonderful Magazine,* November 1803, which pictured the two dwarfs, stated that Thomas was 35 in 1792.

**Allen, Thomas** *[fl. 1794], musician.*

Thomas Allen was listed by Doane's *Musical Directory,* 1794, as a tenor violinist who played at the grand performances in Westminster Abbey and at the Portland Chapel Society. Possibly he was the Allen who was later entered in the Drury Lane account books as a member of the band between 1812–13 and 1816–17.

**Allen, W.** *[fl. 1794], musician.*

W. Allen was listed by Doane's *Musical Directory,* 1794, as a player on the bass, the violoncello, and bassoon, and a performer at the grand performances in Westminster Abbey. Then living at Bexley, Kent, he was possibly the Allen who was later entered in the Drury Lane account books as a member of the band between 1812–13 and 1816–17.

**Allenson.** *See also* **ALLANSON** *and* **ALLISON.**

**Allenson, Mr** [*fl. 1669–1670*], *actor?*
Mr Allenson was a member of the Duke's Company during the 1669–70 season at the Lincoln's Inn Fields playhouse, but his function is not known. About 12 August 1670 he was ordered to be apprehended for absenting himself from the troupe.

**Allers, Mr** [*fl. 1793*], *equestrian.*
Mr Allers was an equestrian performer at the Royal Circus in 1793. Perhaps he was the George William Allers, bachelor, who married Catherine Warren, spinster, at St George, Hanover Square, on 20 February 1806.

**Alleyn, Mr** [*fl. 1723–1724*], *actor.*
A Mr Alleyn acted several roles at the Haymarket in 1723–24: among them Sir Zealwou'd Fainall in *The Female Fop* on 12 December and Testimony in *Sir Courtly Nicely* on 5 February.

**Allingham, Mr** [*fl. 1798*], *house servant?*
A Mr Allingham (sometimes Hillingham) performed some minor function, perhaps that of house servant, at Drury Lane in the seasons 1797–98 and 1798–99. On 13 January 1798 his salary was raised 10*d*. per day, and on 27 October 1798 it was raised 4*s*. 2*d*. per day. He may have been related to the actress Maria Allingham and her brother, John Till Allingham, the dramatist.

**Allingham, Maria Caroline, later MRS SAMUEL RICKETTS** *d. 1811, actress.*
Maria Caroline Allingham was the daughter of a wine merchant in the City of London and the sister of the dramatist John Till Allingham (fl. 1799–1810). According to *Authentic Memoirs of the Green Room* (1799), she engaged in amateur theatricals in London for some time previous to her professional debut at Covent Garden in the role of Palmira in *Mahomet* on 13 October 1796. Reputedly she received £100 for her engagement, which lasted only half the season, and in which she performed but five times. In addition to another performance of Palmira (18 October), she played Juliet (27 October), Bellario in *Philaster* (24 November), and Hermione in *The Distrest Mother*. Although she had beauty and a sweet voice, she did not impress her auditory. She was musical in the "familiar" or quieter portions of her roles, but her tendency toward rant and declamation was found by the critic of *How Do You Do* (22 October 1796) to be a trap for her inexperience. As Palmira, she exaggerated her high tones and passions and did not always manage her figure gracefully. Her Juliet showed no spontaneity—"it is all cold, stiff, and mechanical" (*Monthly Mirror* November 1796)—but rather suggested her attempts to imitate Mrs Siddons in grandeur of action and Mrs Esten in hollowness of voice. She pumped out the intonations of Juliet's lines, frequently becoming inaudible for the greater part of the sentence in order to emphasize some closing word. *The Monthly Mirror* found her to be an actress of some promise, but by no means prepared for the first line of tragic roles in which she made her opening attempts. The prediction of John Williams (*A Pin Basket to the Children of Thespis*, 1797) was that "she'll but strut out her year and no more, / Then be cast in the gutter to seek Ruin's shore."

By January of 1797, she was out of Covent Garden and on her way to Manchester (where a reporter to *The Monthly Mirror*, March 1797, claimed she had formerly lived). Beginning on 30 January with Juliet, in the course of a week she performed Rosalind, Hermione, and Beatrice. For her well-attended benefit on 6 February she played Belvidera in *Venice Preserv'd* and then left for Dublin. She returned to England by 7 November 1797 to join the company at the Orchard Street Theatre, Bath. She played also at Bristol in both that and the following season, after which she retired from the stage in consequence of her marriage to Samuel Ricketts of Clare Street, Bristol, at St Stephen's Church, in that city, on 18 April 1799. Later she accompanied her husband to Surinam, South America, where he became a planter. According to *The Gentleman's Magazine* (July 1811), she died there on 9 April 1811.

**Allinson, Mrs** ⌊fl. 1699⌋, *singer.*

"Songs in the new Comedy call'd Love & a Bottle. Sung by Mrs Allinson" appear in *A Collection of the Choicest Songs & Dialogues Composed by the most Eminent MASTERS of the Age* which John Walsh, musical instrument-maker in ordinary to King William published around the beginning of the eighteenth century. Mrs Allinson is not otherwise recorded as a public performer.

**Allison, Mr** ⌊fl. 1735⌋, *actor.*

A Mr Allison appeared as Bullock in *The Recruiting Officer* and Hob in *Flora*, performed at the Great Booth on the Bowling Green, Southwark Fair, on 7 April 1735.

**Allison, Mr** ⌊fl. 1788–1792⌋, *dancer.*

A Mr Allison danced occasionally at the Haymarket, out-of-season, from 1788 to 1792. On 9 April 1788, he performed a hornpipe at the end of Act I of *The Irish Widow.* He danced again, with his pupils, on 26 September 1791 and performed *The Dance in Fetters* on 12 December 1791. His final recorded appearance, again with his pupils, was in a new dance, *The Caledonian Cottagers*, on 22 October 1792.

**Allison, Mrs** ⌊fl. 1703–1705⌋, *actress.*

A Mrs Allison, who may have been the same as Betty or Maria Allison, played Urania in *The Fickle Shepherdess* in March 1703 at Lincoln's Inn Fields and acted at the same theatre in November. On 1 July 1704 she shared a benefit at Drury Lane when *The Squire of Alsatia* was performed. Her last recorded appearance was on 1 August 1705 when she played Lucinda in *The Cares of Love,* this time back at Lincoln's Inn Fields.

**Allison, Betty** ⌊fl. 1693–1697⌋, *actress.*

As a member of the United Company in late February 1693, Miss Betty Allison (sometimes Allenson) made her first appearance at Drury Lane as the page Jano in *The Maid's Last Prayer.* She stayed with Christopher Rich's company at this theatre when the troupe split, but the records show only one role for her in September 1695 and three appearances during the 1696–97 season. Her last recorded appearance was as "A very young Beau" in *A Plot and No Plot* at Drury Lane on 8 May 1697, unless one of the roles assigned below to Maria Allison actually belong to (her sister?) Betty. Betty Allison seems to have been used chiefly for little-boy roles or as a speaker of prologues and epilogues.

**Allison, Maria** ⌊fl. 1698–1699⌋, *actress, singer.*

A Miss Allison, probably Maria, played Leanthe and sang "When Cupid from his Mother fled" in *Love and a Bottle* in December 1698 and Edward, Prince of Wales, in the Cibber version of *Richard III* in late December 1699 at Drury Lane, though one or both of these roles may have been played by (her sister?) Betty Allison.

**Allison, Ralph** ⌊fl. 1690's⌋, *singer.*

Ralph Allison's voice broke and he left the choir of the Children of the Chapel Royal at some period before 4 December 1693. On that date he was granted £20 annually plus clothes. He was last referred to in a warrant dated 31 March 1697 when, as a former Chapel boy, he was to be provided with material for a suit.

**Allouette** or **Alouette.** *See* **L'ALLOU-ETTE.**

**"Allweight."** *See* **QUIN, JAMES.**

**Allyn, Adam** *d. 1768, actor. See* **ALLEN, MR** [*fl. 1746–1757*].

**Alsedger, Mr** [*fl. 1794*], *bassoonist.*
Mr Alsedger was listed in Doane's *Musical Directory* (1794) as a bassoonist, then living at Birmingham, and as a player in the grand Handelian performances in Westminster Abbey.

**Alyfe** or **Alyff.** *See* **AYLIFF.**

**Amadei, Alexander** [*fl. 1684*], *mountebank.*
Alexander Amadei claimed to be a "florentine, an hebrew by the grace of God turned Christian" and, among other abilities, he said he could teach "the hebrew, Chaldick, Rabinith, Talmudi, Strick, Italian, spanish and portugese tongues." He was active as a mountebank around London for some years, but the chief record of him is in connection with the trial of actor Cardell Goodman in the fall of 1684. Some of Goodman's enemies, apparently, contrived to have Amadei confess to the Principal Secretary of State, the Earl of Sutherland, that Goodman had tried to hire him to poison two of the sons of Charles II and the Duchess of Cleveland, Goodman's mistress. Amadei's testimony brought Goodman to trial.

**Amadei, Filippo** *b. c. 1683, instrumentalist, composer.*
Filippo Amadei, sometimes incorrectly named Filippo Mattei, and affectionately known by Londoners as "Pepo," "Piepo," or "Pippo," was born in Reggio about 1683. He served Cardinal Pietro Ottoboni in 1711

and participated in performances of the oratorio *Santa Cassilda* and the opera *Teodosio il giovane*, the latter designed by Filippo Juvara. He arrived in London sometime before November 1718, when *entr'acte* music composed by Amadei and Clodio was played at a production of *A Woman's Revenge* at the Lincoln's Inn Fields Theatre. On 23 December 1718 he played the cello at a Stationer's Hall concert, and at Hickford's rooms the following 13 February he performed on the violin. This was the beginning of a series of concerts at various halls, often given in conjunction with the Drury Lane violinist Carbonelli. On 29 April 1719 "a Scholar of Pipo, who never sung in publick before" performed at Merchant Taylor's Hall, so Amadei, in addition to being a versatile string player, was a voice teacher as well.

It was as a violoncellist that he joined Handel's orchestra at the Royal Academy of Music when it was organized in 1720, and for that society he adapted Orlandini's opera *Amore e maestà* in February 1721, calling it *Arsace* and supplying fourteen new airs of his own; the production opened on 1 February at the King's Theatre in the Haymarket. In 1721 Amadei composed the first act of the Royal Academy's next production, *Muzio Scevola,* done on 15 April 1721, for which Bononcini wrote the second and Handel the third act. Amadei's work on the opening act was wrongly attributed by Burney and Hawkins to Ariosto, an error which, though long ago corrected, still appears in some current works. The opera was received with huzzas, but Amadei and Bononcini were no match for Handel, and his act triumphed.

A year later, on 14 March 1722 at Drury Lane, "Signior Pippo" played a concerto of his own composition on the bass viol at a benefit for his colleague Carbonelli, and on 20 March 1723—the last record of his activity—he played a concerto by Corelli at Drury Lane. He must still have been popular in London in May 1724, however, for he was given a stanza in *The Session of Musicians* which was published that month:

> As he [Dieupart] walk'd off, who
>    stepp'd into his Place,
> But Signor P[ip]po with his four-
>    string'd Bass:
> How far his Merit reach'd, the God
>    [Apollo] did know,
> And bow'd to him and's Bass prodigious
>    low;
> Vowing to him alone the Bays he'd
>    grant,
> Could the Orchestre but his Presence
>    want;
> Since that was Time and Reputation
>    losing,
> Keep to your playing, and leave off
>    composing.

**Amand** or **Amant.** *See* ST AMAND.

**Amantini, Signor** [fl. 1778], *singer.*
Signor Amantini sang several songs at a concert of vocal and instrumental music given for the benefit of Cervetto and directed by J. C. Bach and Abel, at the New Rooms in Tottenham Street, Charlotte Street, Rathbone Place, on 24 April 1788.

**Amber, Norton** [fl. 1744–1754], *patentee, banker, pit-doorkeeper.*
Norton Amber was a banker in the Strand, who, with his partner Richard Green, advanced the money to James Lacy for purchasing the patent and effects of Drury Lane Theatre from Charles Fleetwood in December 1744. As security for the mortgage of £2250, plus interest, Amber and Green held two equal third-parts of the patent, scenes, wardrobes, and house lease, along with a covenant for sharing any new patent that should be obtained. Amber and Green failed as bankers in December of the following year, 1745, a circumstance which encouraged David Garrick to think he might be able to negotiate with Lacy for the patent of Drury Lane. When Garrick

and Lacy finally entered into partnership in that theatre on 9 April 1747, the agreement indicated that the two bankers still held their mortgage and covenant, and they were paid £4000 to release the encumbrances.

Amber obviously fell on hard times soon after these transactions, for he became a minor employee of the theater which he had once owned in part. On 17 December 1751, he was given a benefit at Drury Lane, the bill for which described him as "formerly a Patentee, & Banker, now Pit Doorkeeper." Amber cleared about £160 for the night, and on the following day he thanked the public, in the *Public Advertiser,* for their "generous appearance." Several years later, on 21 December 1753, he was given a benefit at the other house, Covent Garden.

**Ambler, Mr** [fl. 1661], *singer.*
In the Westminster Abbey Muniments Precentor's Book under the date of 30 March 1661, Mr Ambler, one of the Gentlemen of the Chapel Royal, received 7s. 4d. for singing at the funeral of Princess Mary, the King's eldest sister. He may have been identical with Ralph Amner.

**Ambroise, Antonio** [fl. 1752–1778], *puppet-showman.*
Antonio Ambroise (sometimes Ambrosia, Ambrosiano, Signor Antonio, or Signor Salt-Box), who apparently was an Italian originally called Ambrogio, first appeared on the London stage at the Haymarket on 29 February 1752 in an entertainment called *The Old Woman's Oratory,* given for his benefit. He delivered a song in the character of a lion and played "the Cremona Staccato, vulgarly call'd the Salt-Box." Throughout the next season, 1752–53, he gave similar entertainments at the Haymarket. (A singer by name of Signora Antonia Ambrosini, who may have been his wife, performed in the comic opera *L'amour costante* at Covent Garden during February 1754.) Presumably he was the same Ambroise who worked about this time as a

street-entertainer and puppet-show operator in the Paris fairs.

After some years of absence, he returned to London on 5 November 1755 to announce that he and Mr Brunn were establishing an *Ombres Chinoises* repertory at the Great Room in Panton Street. The spectacle was promised as entirely new, the same one which had been presented to Louis XVI and his court on 27 February 1775. The season, which lasted five months (December through April), was apparently very successful. The shadow plays, consisting of short episodes and sketches with musical accompaniment, included such pieces as *The Metamorphosis of a Magician, African Lion Hunt, Storm at Sea,* and *Escape of a Highwayman from Prison.* The following winter, 1776–77, Ambroise and Brunn returned to Panton Street, now billing themselves as the *Original Ombres Chinoises,* to distinguish them from a rival company which Braville and Meniucci had opened in St Albans Street, off Pall Mall. This second season lasted through July 1777. The next January, Ambroise (now Antonio) was back at Panton Street, with Gabriel and Ballarini as partners, until May. He also took his shadow plays to Dublin in 1778. Presumably he then returned to Paris.

**Ambrose, Mr** ₁*fl. 1735–1736*₁, *house servant.*

Latreille noted two persons by the name of Ambrose at Covent Garden in 1735–36: a boxkeeper at 2*s.* per night and a box office keeper at 2*s. 6d.* per night. The latter, called "Mr," may have been Latreille's misreading of a *Mrs* Ambrose who was listed by another British Museum manuscript as being on the payroll that season at 2*s. 6d.* Perhaps they were the William and Elizabeth Ambrose, parents of William Ambrose who was baptized at St. Paul, Covent Garden, on 24 June 1739.

**Ambrose, Mrs, later Mrs Jona.** See **AMBROSE, MISS** ₁*fl. c. 1739–1813*₁.

**Ambrose, Mrs** ₁*fl. 1735–1736*₁, *house servant?*

A Mrs Ambrose was paid for 143 nights at Covent Garden from 18 October 1735 to 15 May 1736, at 2*s. 6d.,* or a total of £17 17*s. 6d.,* and "left the company the week following to go into the country by leave of Mr. J. Rich," according to a British Museum manuscript. She may have been the wife of the Ambrose who was a box office keeper at the same theatre that season.

**Ambrose, Mrs, née Mahon** ₁*fl. 1770–1789*₁, *singer.*

Mrs Ambrose was a member of the Mahon family which was connected with music at Oxford during the last three decades of the eighteenth century. This musical family included her three brothers John, James, and William, and three sisters, M. Mahon (later Mrs Warton), Sarah (later Mrs Second), and another girl (later Mrs Munday, who became the mother of the celebrated soprano Eliza Salmon).

Mrs Ambrose was a favorite soprano at Oxford and in the festivals at Birmingham, Salisbury, and Winchester in the 1770's and 1780's. Along with Madame Mara and Mrs Billington, she was one of the principals at the Westminster Abbey grand performances in 1786 and again with Mara in the following year. She also sang at the Three Choirs Festival at Worcester in 1788. Her first appearance in a London theatre was on 5 February 1788, when she sang the song "Sweet Echo," accompanied on the oboe by W. Parke, in the masque of *Comus* at Covent Garden. According to one newspaper critic she possessed a "great sweetness of voice." Her only other theatre appearances were for the oratorios at Covent Garden from 27 February through 3 April 1789, in which she was a featured singer of the songs of Handel and Arne.

Prior to her London appearance early in 1788, the *Public Advertiser* (11 January 1788) had announced her as Mrs Ambrose, the late Miss Mahon. Her husband perhaps was John Ambrose, the instrumentalist and composer. If so, then she had three sons by him, the earliest, John, in 1786, then Charles in 1790, and Robert in 1791. This young family could explain why her professional career ceased in 1789. According to John Ambrose's application for membership in the Royal Society of Musicians, dated 3 November 1793, he was a widower, so if the soprano Mrs Ambrose was his wife, she had died by this date.

### Ambrose, Miss  [fl. 1731–1732], dancer.

Miss Ambrose was a minor dancer listed in the Drury Lane bills of 1731–32 as a bridesmaid in *Perseus and Andromeda* (25 November and many times thereafter) and in the ensemble of a dance called *Le Chasseur Royal* (22 February and several times thereafter).

### Ambrose, Miss, later Mrs Kelf and then Mrs Egerton  [fl. 1739–1813], actress.

Miss Ambrose was born at Gibraltar "a few years previous to the breaking out of the Spanish war in the year 1739." The story of her life is bizarre and is one which the author of the *Theatrical Biography* (1772) cautioned may be told "too largely in poetical prose." If most of the colorful events were true, then she had indeed undergone a "variety" which was "liberal and unbounded."

The father of Miss Ambrose was a Portuguese Jew, a sutler to the British forces on Gibraltar, who had assumed the name of Ambrose, and her mother was a native of Britain. A few years after her birth, the father was convicted of being a spy and was hanged, leaving behind him "a young handsome widow, with two blooming daughters, unpossessed of everything, but their beauty and misfortunes." The English officers took up a charitable subscription which allowed the three women to pay their debts and go to London, where they took a small house in Westminster.

The mother remarried in London to Mr Jona, a master of language, a prompter at the Opera, and a house servant at Covent Garden. Jona either had three of his own children by a previous marriage or three by Mrs Ambrose after their marriage. He died in October 1756, and at Covent Garden on 8 December 1756 a benefit was given for his widow and her five children, for which it was announced that tickets were available of Mrs Jona in Little Warrick Street, Charing Cross. She received another benefit at that theatre on 21 December 1758. The two original Ambrose sisters never assumed the name of their step-father. Nothing is known of the other three children.

The author of *Theatrical Biography* claimed that the Ambrose sisters went to Ireland to take up their theatrical careers. Wilkinson played with them, and also with their mother, at Smock Alley, Dublin, in 1760, and at Winchester in July of that year. "Miss Ambrose," wrote Wilkinson, "was a most agreeable young lady, as also was her sister; we used to have frequent parties, and have been from that time on a most friendly intimacy."

The Ambrose sisters made their first appearances at London on 15 June 1761 in unspecified roles in *All in the Wrong* at Drury Lane, which was under the summer rental of Arthur Murphy and Samuel Foote. Miss Ambrose next appeared as a fairy in the harlequinade *The Wishes* on 27 July, a production which was severely criticized for the hanging of Harlequin in full view of the audience.

That fall the sisters engaged with Mossop at Smock Alley, Dublin. Miss Ambrose played Dorinda in *The Stratagem* there on 19 October 1761 (her sister played Cherry). When the play was performed again on 23 November, she was billed as Mrs Kelf. According to *Theatrical Biography*, she had married the bailiff of a London sponging house, where the family had been held for a debt of £100. He paid the debt, prevailed upon the mother to give him Miss Ambrose's hand, and then became an engraver. She wearied of him and went off to Ireland. The story is doubtless apochryphal. Her change of name at Smock Alley suggests that she married in Ireland. *The Morning Post* of 29 April 1800 described Mr Kelf as a hatter, but that she left him soon after marriage seems true. Again, *Theatrical Biography* claims he gave her up, for a financial settlement, to an Irish baronet, Henry E——h——n, who had become infatuated with her. But Sir Harry's inconstancy soon turned him to her sister and then to her mother. Despondent, Miss Ambrose fell into the arms of another Irish noble, but she soon fell out.

The Ambrose family remained in Ireland until 1770. Billed as Mrs Kelf, the elder Ambrose sister played at Cork in October and November 1762 and at Drogheda in August 1765. While at the latter place she and her sister supposedly lived in a rented house with two gentlemen (Major B——h and Colonel B——e), with the mother as *gouvernante*. Mrs Kelf now fell into an earnest profligacy, it is reported, by taking up with a French lady, Madame B——, with whom she reportedly set out to live in Paris for over a year, but not before playing again at Cork in August and September of 1766.

In the fall of 1770, she engaged with Garrick, assuming for unknown reasons a new stage name. Advertised as Mrs Egerton from the Theatre Royal in Dublin, she made her appearance at Drury Lane on 16 October 1770 in the role of Lady Townley in *The Provok'd Husband*. The prompter Hopkins wrote in his diary that she had a "smart figure," though she was "not much of the Gentlewoman." *Theatrical Biography* thought the role too difficult for her on the whole, yet it gave her "an opportunity of shewing such excellencies . . . as to stamp her an agreeable and useful ac-

tress." She next appeared as Mrs Oakley in *The Jealous Wife* on 6 November 1770 and as Mrs Kitely in *Every Man in his Humour* on 16 November. On 19 January 1771 she created the role of Mrs Fulmer in Cumberland's *The West Indian*, a play which, as Hopkins predicted on opening night, would have "a great run."

In March 1771 William Dawson, the Dublin manager, asked Charles Macklin to try to engage Mrs Egerton for the Capel Street Theatre, but she remained at Drury Lane for the next two seasons, 1771–72 and 1772–73. She also played for Foote at the Haymarket in the summer of 1772. At Drury Lane she acted such roles as Regan in *King Lear*, Maria in *Twelfth Night*, Emilia in *Othello*, and the Queen in *Hamlet*, along with the other leading roles of Alithea in *The Country Girl*, Mrs Strickland in *The Suspicious Husband*, Lady Lurewell in *The Constant Couple* and Olivia in *The Plain Dealer*. In April of 1772 she lived at King Square Court, Dean Street, Soho. For reasons now unknown, she left the Drury Lane company at the end of the season 1772–73 but engaged again with Foote at the Haymarket in the summer of that year. Then at the age of about 36 she left the London stage entirely, according to William Hawkins (*Miscellanies in Prose and Verse*, 1775), for "love and enjoyment." She did make several more acting appearances, at Cork on 2 August 1785 and at Limerick on 16 August in the same summer, when at the age of 48 or more she played Juliet to Joseph Holman's Romeo. From that time little is known of her whereabouts or activities. Some years later, on 29 April 1800, the *Morning Post* reported that she had reconciled with the man she had left when she had first gone upon the stage (presumably Mr Kelf) and that she had remarried him. The *European Magazine* of January 1813 reported her still to be alive.

Although never a threat to first rank actresses like Mrs Abington, she was a very useful and pleasing performer who showed considerable merit, especially in such comic parts as Lady Townley, and Mrs Cadwallader in *The Author*. Her highest praise came as Mademoiselle in *The Provok'd Husband*. Garrick, who played Sir John Brute regularly in the same cast, apparently thought her performance in that role was as perfect and finished as could be.

### Ambrose, Miss E. [*fl. 1756–1787*], actress.

Miss E. Ambrose was the younger sister of Miss Ambrose (later Mrs Kelf and then Mrs Egerton), under whose entry the story of her parentage and early years is traced. Miss E. Ambrose made her first appearance in London on 15 June 1761 as a member of the Murphy-Foote summer company at Drury Lane in an unspecified role in *All in the Wrong*. She next appeared in *The Citizen* on 2 July and as the maid in the harlequinade *The Wishes* on 27 July. That fall she accompanied her mother and sister to Ireland, making her debut at Smock Alley on 19 October 1761 as Cherry in *The Stratagem*. During her engagement there apparently she received some acting instruction from Charles Macklin. Little more is known of her stay in Ireland beyond the colorful stories of her amorous escapades carried out in league with her sister.

She returned to London with her sister in 1770, and made her first appearance at the Haymarket on 5 June 1771 as Lady Brute in *The Provok'd Wife*. When her sister assumed the stage name of Mrs Egerton, Miss E. Ambrose dropped her first initial and was billed only as Miss Ambrose. She also played Emily in *The Deuce Is in Him* (8 July), and Juno in *Dido* (24 July). In the fall of 1771, she engaged at Drury Lane, along with her sister who had joined that theatre in the previous season. Miss Ambrose made her debut there on 3 October 1771, as Nerissa in *The Merchant of Venice*, a role she played regularly throughout her career. That season she also played Arabella in *The Committee* (26 December), Isabella in *The Wonder* (31 December), Phebe in *As You Like It* (17 December), and Mrs Page in *The Merry Wives of Windsor* (15 January). Miss Ambrose engaged again with Foote at the Haymarket for the summer of 1772, and for the next season, 1772–73, at Drury Lane, but then seems to have been absent from a winter theatre royal for the next few seasons, although she was with Foote at the Haymarket every summer from 1773 through 1776. She also appeared in a winter company at the Haymarket in 1774–1775, which gave ten performances "by permission." By now she had also played a variety of roles including Celia in *As You Like It* (17 November 1772), Lady Macduff (3 May 1773), Arabella in *The Author* (3 June 1774), Lucy in *The Bankrupt* (21 July 1773) and Lucy in *The Minor* (1 May 1773).

Absent from Drury Lane for two seasons, she hoped to return for 1775–76. On 20 June 1775 the Marquis of Hertford solicited Garrick for a position on her behalf, or rather in behalf of a friend with an interest in Miss Ambrose. "All I have any title to say is, that I should be glad to contribute to her being placed under your countenance at Drury Lane Theatre, in any situation you may think her fit for." But Garrick was not responsive. Perhaps the managers of Covent Garden received a similar appeal, for she was engaged there instead, where she was to work regularly through 1781–82, at a salary of £2 2s. per week, raised in 1779–80 to £2 10s., and in 1780–81 to £3. Her first role at Covent Garden was as the maid in *The Refusal* on 24 October 1775, followed by Erixene in *The Grecian Daughter* (25 October) and Charlotte in *Love-a-la-Mode* (27 October). Other roles that season included Anne Bullen in *Henry VIII* (9 November) and Regan in *King Lear* (22 February), the latter role becoming one played regularly through her career.

Miss Ambrose left Covent Garden in May 1782. She played Clarissa in *The Temple Beau* at the Haymarket several months later on 21 September 1782 and then seems to have retired. Five years later, however, she made one final appearance when the Covent Garden managers asked her to substitute for the ill Mrs Norton on 5 May 1787 as Charlotte in the afterpiece *Love-a-la-Mode.* "Long disuse to it had made her timid," reported *The World* on 7 May 1787, "but she was well received by the public, and performed well." She was not heard from again.

While she sometimes ventured into more serious roles like Lady Macduff or Regan, in the main Miss E. Ambrose played a line of secondary and tertiary younger and ingenuous women. In addition to the roles already indicated, among her other roles at Covent Garden were Melinda in *The Recruiting Officer* (23 September 1776 and often), Emily in *Cross Purposes* (27 September 1776), Lucinda in *The Conscious Lovers* (8 October 1777), Megra in *Philaster* (3 October 1780), and Clarinda in *The Double Gallant* (28 October 1781). During her career between 1761 and 1783 she seems to have stirred little critical or enthusiastic comment. At the time of her first season at Drury Lane in 1771–72, Gentleman wrote of her and her sister in *The Theatres,* "Ambrose and Egerton, a dismal pair, / Not worth the critic's, or the poet's care."

### Ambrose, John *b. 1763, instrumentalist, composer.*

Baptized 31 January 1763 at St. Nicholas, Deptford, John Ambrose was the son of Samuel Ambrose, who lived on the Green there. Dr Arnold proposed him for membership in the Royal Society of Musicians on 3 November 1793 (elected 5 yeas, 2 nays, 2 February 1794), when it was attested that he had studied and practiced music for a livelihood for upwards of seven years, was organist of St Anne, Limehouse, at a

salary of £20 *per annum,* and was also a teacher of the harpsichord. John Ambrose's first wife may have been the soprano, Mrs Ambrose (née Mahon), whose professional career ceased in 1789. At the time of his application to the Royal Society of Musicians in November 1793, he stated that he was a widower with three children: John, aged seven; Charles, three and a half; and Robert, two.

According to Doane's *Musical Directory,* Ambrose still held the post of organist of St Anne, Limehouse, in 1794 and was living at No 78, Three Colt Street, in that parish. By this time, he was also known as a composer. He participated as a violinist in the annual benefit concerts for the clergy at St Paul's Cathedral regularly from 1794 to 1798. The Ambrose who was on these same concert lists from 1799 through 1804, variously as playing the kettle drum, trumpet, or bassoon, was probably the same man. When John Ambrose died is not known, but a Mrs Ambrose, who perhaps was his second wife, sent thanks to the Royal Society of Musicians on 3 June 1821 for a £5 benefaction.

### Ambrosia or Ambrosiano. *See* AMBROISE.

### Ambrosini, Antonia *[fl. 1754], singer.*

A singer by the name of Antonia Ambrosini performed the role of Celindo in the comic opera, *L'amour costante,* given in Italian and French at Covent Garden five times from 11 to 20 February 1754. Perhaps she was related to Antonio Ambroise.

### "American Farren, The." *See* JOHNSON, MRS JOHN, ELIZABETH.

### "American Woman, The" *[fl. 1781], dwarf?*

At Astley's Amphitheatre starting 10 December 1781 "The American woman in miniature will make her appearance for a few evenings." Perhaps she was a dwarf, though the bill is not specific, either as to that or as to what were her accomplishments.

**Amicis.** *See* DE AMICIS, ANNA LUCIA.

**Amiconi, Jacopo**   *c.   1675–1752,*
*scene painter.*

Jacopo Amiconi (or Amigoni) was born in 1675, according to *Bryan's Dictionary of Painters* and the *Cyclopedia of Painters and Painting,* and in 1682, according to the *New International Illustrated Encyclopedia of Art.* His birthplace was either Venice or Naples. He studied at Venice and Düsseldorf and was influenced in the rococo style by Francesco Solimena and Sebastiano Ricci.

Among his first works at Venice were two altarpieces in the Church of the Fathers of the Oratorio and a picture of St Catherine and St Andrew for the Church of St Eustache. After achieving some reputation in Italy, he entered the service of the Elector of Bavaria, for whom he frescoed many ceilings in the castle at Schleissheim and did oil paintings for the church and court between 1717 and 1727.

Amiconi came to England in 1729 and obtained a position as a scene painter at the King's Theatre. Although notices of Amiconi's scene designs are not extant, according to Angelo "nothing had been seen equally splendid and imposing with this department of stage effect, in England, before this epoch." For Rich's new Covent Garden Theatre, which opened on 7 December

*Courtesy of the National Gallery of Victoria, Melbourne*

JACOPO AMICONI (2nd on right) with Pietro Metastasio, TERESA CASTELLINI, and CARLO BROSCHI ("FARINELLI")
by Amiconi

1732, Amiconi designed and painted the ceiling, in which were represented Apollo and an assembly of Muses "dignifying Shakespeare with the Laurel." He also worked with Harvey on the decorations of the proscenium and subsequently with George Lambert on painting scenery for the new stage. While in England during this period he found a number of patrons for whom he did frescoes and portraits. He received £200 for painting classical motifs on the staircase at Ossulston House in Charles Street, for the second Earl of Tankerville. He also designed a *plafond* to a magnificent staircase at Buckingham Palace which has since been removed in alterations. His other works in England include a painting of "Boys playing with a Lanet," at Hampton Court; portraits of Anne, Princess of Orange, at Windsor Castle; and an altarpiece for Emmanuel College, Cambridge. Of his decorative works, only the four paintings of the "Story of Io," painted for Moor Park in 1732, survive.

Amiconi left London about 1739, worked in Paris and at the Court of St Petersburg for a while, and returned to Venice a wealthy man. In 1741 he was back in London as scene painter for the Opera under the management of Lord Middlesex, but he apparently soon went back to Venice. In 1747 he became a court painter at Madrid, where he died in 1752.

The National Gallery of Victoria in Melbourne, Australia, has a portrait group done by Amiconi about 1750 showing Farinelli, Teresa Castellini, and the Abate Metastasio, together with a self-portrait.

### Amner, Ralph  *d. 1664, singer.*

Since the first record of Ralph Amner is his election as a lay clerk at Ely Cathedral in 1604, it is likely that he was born not very long before 1584. He was related to John Amner, Ely organist and composer who died in 1641, but the relationship is unclear. Ralph Amner surrendered his clerk's position in 1609 to Michael East (or

Este) and was probably admitted to holy orders about that time and consequently styled Vicar.

Sometime during the next twelve years he went to London; he was certainly there by 1621, for he was paid 20s. for his attendance, perhaps as a deputy, at the Chapel Royal. He did not succeed to a position in the Chapel until 16 December 1623 when, as "Ralph Amn[er], a base from Winsor," he replaced John Amery—apparently no relation—who had died on 18 July of that year. In May 1633 he was one of several musicians who accompanied the King on a trip to Scotland. During the Commonwealth the Chapel Royal was disbanded, but when it was reinstituted at the Restoration, Amner was again a member. He was apparently active through 1663, but in his old age he spent little time in London. He died at Windsor on 3 March 1664, and Dr William Child wrote a "Catch instead of an Epitaph upon Mr. Ralph Amner of Windsor, commonly called the Bull Speaker."

### Amoretti, Giustina  [fl. 1748–1749], *singer.*

Sga Amoretti was a member of a small company of Italian singers who performed seven comic operas, a "New Serenade," and an "Entertainment of Music," under the direction of Dr Francis Croza at the King's Theatre in 1748–49. They opened on 8 November 1748 with Rinaldo da Capua's burletta *La comedia in comedia*, libretto by Francesco Vanneschi, announced as "Being the first of this Species of Musical Drama ever exhibited in England." Despite Croza's constant financial troubles and poor public relations, the troupe was moderately successful, playing some forty-three times during the season until 20 May 1749. Sga Amoretti sang Vespino in *La comedia in comedia* and probably roles in the other comic operas for which no casts were listed. When Dr Croza took his company to the Haymarket the following season, Sga Amoretti was not with him.

**Amorevoli, Angelo** *1716–1798, singer.*

Angelo Amorevoli, an Italian tenor, was born in Venice on 16 September 1716. After enjoying great success at the principal opera houses in Italy, including the one in his native city in 1730, he was engaged at the King's Opera at London in 1741, by now sufficiently celebrated to command 850 guineas for the season. Amorevoli was listed by Burney as singing the tenor part in *Alexander in Persia*, which opened at the King's Theatre on 31 October 1741 and sustained twelve performances, but according to Horace Walpole his first appearance in London was on 10 November 1741, at the second performance of the piece. That season he also sang Polimnestor in *Polidoro*, Asdrubale in *Scipione in Cartagine*, and unspecified roles in *Penelope, Meraspe o L'Olimpiade*, and *Cefalo e Procri*. The following season, 1742–43, he sang the title roles in *Gianguir* and in *Temistocles*, an unspecified role in *Enrico*, Dorimaspes in *Mandane*, and Rosbales in *Sirbace*, making his final London appearance in the last on 17 May 1743.

Celebrated for the perfection of his shake, Amorevoli was an admirable tenor. While Burney had heard better voices of his pitch, none on the stage had "more taste and expression." In the first performance of Fielding's *Miss Lucy in Town* at Drury Lane on 6 May 1742, John Beard, in the role of Signor Cantileno, mimicked Amorevoli "intolerably," yet the opera singer was well-enough known to have the burlesque delight the audience. Little is known about Amorevoli's private life. While in London, supposedly he kept "some low English woman," according to Horace Walpole, but she married Vanneschi, the opera manager and librettist. After leaving London, Amorevoli was engaged at the Court Theatre at Dresden, where he spent most of the rest of his life, dying there on 15 November 1798. A list of his roles on the Continent is found in the *Enciclopedia dello Spetta-colo*. He was pictured in a painting by Antonio Fedi of a large group of musicians, an engraving of which was printed between 1801 and 1807.

**"Amphi-Philip."** *See* ASTLEY, PHILIP.

**Analeau, Mr** [fl. 1687–1688], *singer?*

On 5 July 1687 a Mr Analeau (or Anatean?) was a member of the Chapel Royal, receiving a yearly salary of £60; in the Treasury Books his name was grouped with those of Abell and Pordage, both singers of considerable eminence, and all three were separated from the lesser paid Gregorians and instrumentalists. On 19 December 1687 and again on 20 October 1688 one Anatean—who was probably the same person and was again grouped with Abell and Pordage—was paid for accompanying the King to Windsor. He was a foreigner and perhaps stayed in England only a short time.

**Ancell.** *See* ANSELL.

**Anderson, Mr** *d. 1767, actor.*

A Mr Anderson was an actor in London for at least twenty-nine consecutive years, possibly thirty-five, yet little is known about him except the many roles he portrayed. Perhaps he was the Mr Anderson who was announced for his first appearance on the stage in the role of Castalio in *The Orphan*, at the Haymarket on 8 May 1732. He did not repeat the performance and no actor by that name is found in the bills until six years later. On 13 March 1738, Mr Anderson appeared as Basset in *1 Henry VI*, at Covent Garden. In the following season, 1739–40, he was a regular member of the Covent Garden company, playing the minor roles (James in *The Mock Doctor*, the Captain in *The Island Princess*, the Duke in *Othello*, and Coleville in *2 Henry IV*) the likes of which were to be his lot throughout his long career. He remained at Covent Garden until his death in 1767, except for a few months at the beginning of the 1743–44 season when he was alternating between there and Drury Lane. An actor by the name of Anderson was also listed in the account books as a member of the Jacob's Well Theatre at Bristol, in the summers of 1741, 1743, 1748, and 1749. An Anderson was at Richmond, Surrey, in 1740, and in the Liverpool summer company in the early 1760's.

Mr Anderson was one of those innumerable actors who labored in virtual anonymity almost every night in the London theatre, never after his debut rising above the rank of third or fourth-grade roles. He played regularly at least seventy different roles in the repertory, including some thirty-six Shakespearean characters, and never once was seen in a major leading role, except that single portrayal of Castalio at his very first appearance. In 1740–41, he was paid 3s. 4d. daily and by 1761 a bit less than 6s. daily. His annual benefits were always shared with several other minor actors and house servants. A sampling of his roles indicates that the company relied on him mostly for dull servants, solid citizens, older statesmen, and foolish older characters, with little significant relationship to his own age at any particular time, except perhaps in his later years. They include, in addition to those mentioned above, and among many others: Gayless in *The Lying Valet*, Buckram in *Love for Love*, Alonzo in *The Mourning Bride*, Hotman in *Oroonoko*, Blunt in *London Merchant*, Sir Charles and Boniface in *The Stratagem*, Thessalus in *The Rival Queens*, a boor in *The Royal Merchant*, Guildenstern in *Hamlet*, Ratcliff and Stanley in *Richard III*, Paris in *Romeo and Juliet*, Trebonius in *Julius Caesar*, Catesby in *Jane Shore*, Humphrey in *The Conscious Lovers*, Peregrine in *Volpone*, and Vainlove in *The Old Batchelor*. On 3 May 1765, while coming from Chelsea to town about three o'clock in the afternoon, his chaise was overturned. Despite the fact that several of his ribs were broken and he was "very much bruised," the accident did not keep him long from work. His usual role of the governor in *Love Makes a Man* was omitted on 10 May, but on 15 May he was again on the boards as Daran in *The Siege of Damascus*.

In his last season at Covent Garden, 1766–67, he played the Duke in *The Merchant of Venice* on 6 April and the Player in *The Beggar's Opera* on 7 April, the latter proving to be his last performance. He died suddenly on 15 April 1767, and the tickets delivered out by him for his scheduled shared benefit on 8 May were declared invalid.

The several extant critical comments on his acting suggest an uninspired talent. *The Rosciad of C-v-nt G-rd-n* (1762) reported: "In ev'ry scene, in ev'ry word, we find / The symptoms of a dull unfeeling mind; / Whether in poor Rodolpho's peaceful part, / His *stupid* words flow from his *stupid* heart; / . . . Or, when enrag'd at Pistol's swagg'ring speech, / His angry foot salutes the boaster's breech." John Hill suggested in *The Actor* (1750) that if the manager would cast him in the role of Abel Drugger, "the folly of the part might hang . . . naturally" about him.

**Anderson, Mr** [fl. 1794], *musician*.

A Mr Anderson, tenor violinist, was listed in Doane's *Musical Directory* (1794) as living at No 11, Great Distaff Lane, Friday Street, and as a player in the Cecilian Society concerts. One Mr Anderson was on the Drury Lane pay list at £2 per week between 1812–13 and 1816–17 as a member of the band and in the Haymarket band in 1816–17. Perhaps he was connected with Mr G. F. Anderson who was elected to the Royal Society of Musicians on 5 March 1815 and was still serving that organization as a member of the Court of Assistants in January 1839. A George Anderson witnessed the will of the musician Charles James Griesbach on 14 February 1853.

**Anderson, Mrs** [fl. 1724–1734]. See **HILL, MRS** [fl. 1724–1734].

79

**Anderson, Mrs** ₍fl. 1743?–1750₎, *actress.*

A Mrs Anderson sang Dorothee Cour de Nuit in *L'Opéra du gueux* in a performance given by a set of English performers at the Haymarket Theatre on 29 April 1749. The piece was a translation into French of an excerpt from *The Beggar's Opera.* It was performed eight other times through 31 May and twice more the following season on 16 and 21 February 1750. *The London Stage* lists a Mrs Anderson, actress, at Drury Lane in 1743–44, but her name does not appear in the bills.

**Anderson, Miss** ₍fl. 1733–1737₎, *dancer.*

Miss Anderson (often billed as Mrs Anderson but the same person) was a minor chorus dancer at Drury Lane from 1733 to 1737. Her first noticed appearance was as one of the ladies of pleasure in *The Harlot's Progress* on 24 October 1733, which was repeated frequently during the season. She danced regularly during her four years at Drury Lane as a milkmaid in *The Country Revels,* a siren in *Cephalus and Procris,* and a nymph in *Cupid and Psyche.* She also appeared in specialty dances such as a *Grand Ballet, Tit for Tat, La Badine, The Shepherd's Mount,* and a *Grand Polenese Ballet.* She danced in *The Tempest* on 10 February and 29 April 1737. On 1 April 1734, she danced for Lally's benefit at Lincoln's-Inn-Fields. Miss Anderson's last performance of record was in a minuet at Drury Lane on 9 May 1737.

**Anderson, Miss** ₍fl. 1782₎, *actress.*

A Miss Anderson played in a single performance of *Love at a Venture* (cast unlisted) at the Haymarket on 21 April 1782, with the principal characters by performers "engaged from different theatres." No other London performance by her is recorded.

**André** or **Andree, St.** *See* ST ANDRÉ.

**Andre, Mary Anne.** *See* ANDREAS.

**Andrea, Sieur** ₍fl. 1781₎, *whistler.*

The Sieur Andrea whistled "the Notes in a surprising Manner" at a performance given by the conjuror Breslaw at Green-Wood's Room, Haymarket, in 1781.

**Andreas, Miss** ₍fl. 1779–1780₎, *dancer.*

Miss Andreas was a dancer at the King's Theatre in 1779–80, first mentioned in the bills on 14 December 1779 in a new pantomime, *Il desertore,* which was repeated frequently throughout the season. She also danced in a *Pastoral Ballet* on 2 May and 6 May. Miss Andreas may have been the dancer, Miss Mary Anne Andre, who performed at Smock Alley, Dublin, in the season 1785–86.

**Andreoni, Mr** ₍fl. 1739–1742₎, *singer.*

Although he may have appeared in concerts earlier, the Italian castrato soprano Andreoni made his first billed appearance in London as Selinunte, in *Meride e Selinunte,* on 22 January 1740, as a member of Lord Middlesex's company at the Haymarket. He then sang Oberto in *Olimpia in Ebuda* and Anubi in *Busiri, overo, il trionfo d'amore,* which opened on 15 March and 10 May, respectively. The three operas were repeated frequently that season. In the following season, 1740–41, Andreoni joined Handel's company at Lincoln's Inn Fields for occasional singing in opera and recitals. Engaged as the first man, for Handel he sang in *L'allegro, Acis and Galatea, Saul, Imeneo,* and probably in *Il Parnasso in festa.* He created the role of Ulisse in Handel's new opera, *Deidamia,* which opened on 10 January 1741 but lasted only three performances. Because Andreoni could not, or would not, sing in English, he had to be supplied with Italian airs even in *L'allegro* and *Saul.* He also sang in a series of twenty weekly concerts, with Cecilia Arne, at Hickford's Room, which commenced on 5 December 1740 and was completed in May 1741. Burney ranked Andreoni as a singer "of the second class," the position in which he was placed the following season, 1741–42, when he joined the company at the King's Opera. There he sang in *Alexander in Persia*, Deiphilus in *Polidoro*, and Bomilcare in *Scipione in Cartagine*.

**Andrews, Mr** ‹*fl. 1752*›, *actor.*

On 19 September 1752, the *General Advertiser* published a little poem "To Mr Andrews the Comedian—by a Gentleman who saw him mending his Cart the other day at Cobham in Surrey." There is, however, no other record of a Mr Andrews on the London stage at this time.

**Andrews, Mr** ‹*fl. 1792–1799?*›, *dresser, house servant.*

On 15 February 1792, a Mr Andrews was added to the pay list of Drury Lane, as a dresser, at 1*s.* 6*d.* per day. He shared tickets on 15 June 1792. He was also in the house as a minor servant or performer in 1792–93 and 1794–95. He may have been the same Mr Andrews, of George Street, Richmond, Surrey, who on 9 April 1799 applied for the position of checktaker of the box door at the Richmond theatre, at one shilling per night.

**Andrews, Mr** ‹*fl. 1794*›, *music porter.*

A Mr Andrews, music porter, was listed by Doane's *Musical Directory* (1794) as belonging to the Haymarket Theatre and Salomon's Concerts and living at No 20, Noel Street, Soho.

**Andrews, Mr** ‹*fl. 1794*›, *singer.*

A Mr Andrews, bass singer, was listed by Doane's *Musical Directory* (1794) as belonging to the Madrigal Society and living at Somerset House. Perhaps he was related to the Mr Andrews who was listed in the Haymarket company in 1816, at a salary of £1 10*s.* per week, and in the "English Opera" at the Lyceum in 1818. Children of a

Kenwick Andrews, musician, of No 5, Mary Street, New Road, St Pancras, husband of Hannah, were christened at St Giles in the Fields in 1814 and 1817.

**Andrews, Mrs** ‹*fl. 1696–1697*›, *actress.*

As a member of Christopher Rich's company at Drury Lane and Dorset Garden, Mrs Andrews played three roles that were recorded: Eugenia in *The Cornish Comedy* in June 1696 at Dorset Garden, Mrs Susan in *The World in the Moon* at the same playhouse in June 1697, and Serena in *Imposture Defeated* at Drury Lane in September 1697. She may have been related to the Mr Andrews who was active in Dublin from about 1675 to 1680 but who apparently never played in London.

**Andrews, Miss** ‹*fl. 1796–1798*›, *singer, actress.*

A pupil of Dr Samuel Arnold, Miss Andrews made her debut at Drury Lane on 13 May 1796, billed as "A Young Lady" in the role of Louisa in *No Song No Supper*, her only appearance that season. She was the replacement for Miss Leak at the Haymarket the next summer (1797), when she performed Laura in *The Agreeable Surprise*, Caroline in *The Dead Alive*, Rosina in *Rosina*, and Eliza in *The Flitch of Bacon*. *The Monthly Mirror* of July 1797 reported that she possessed a voice more sweet than powerful, and, although she sang with some taste, her recitation was extremely imperfect and her manner awkward. Despite that critic's belief that practice would "no doubt, greatly improve her talents," she performed only one more time in London, as one of the principal vocalists in the *Messiah*, at the Haymarket on 15 January 1798.

**Andrews, Mr E.** ‹*fl. 1760–1770?*›, *singer.*

Mr Andrews made his first appearance on the London stage with a song in the character of an English officer in *The Siege* of *Quebec* at Covent Garden on 14 May 1760. Apparently he never again performed in a patent house. Occasionally during the sixties he offered comic impersonations and songs at Sadler's Wells. In 1762, he sang "What Monarch in Europe for Grandeur can stand," in the character of a soldier; "Wonderful Age," in the character of a ballad singer in *Harlequin Quack*; and "Tis the Genius of Britain, ye Britons, that calls." Other songs included "Hark the sound of ye drum," in the entertainment of *The Tempest* (1764), "To yonder Beeches friendly Shade" (1765?), "The whistling Plowman hails ye blushing Dawn," a hunting song (1770?), and "Come bind my Brows, ye Wood Nymphs fair," a bacchanalian song (1770?). In 1760, a song *By the force of our ships* was published as "Sung by Mr E. Andrews," providing a first initial, which never again appeared. He may have been related to the John Andrews who brought Sadler's Wells diversions to Cambridge in 1779. (A James Andrews subscribed to the Irish Musical Fund from 1787 to 1790 and was expelled 1 May 1791 for non-payment.)

**Andrews, Robert C.** [*fl. 1789–1819*], *scene painter, proprietor.*

The first notice of Robert C. Andrews was in 1789, when he decorated Mrs Baker's new theatre at Canterbury and supplied new scenery for its stage. In 1794 he went to work at Sadler's Wells with the elder Greenwood, a scene painter whose pupil he was. Andrews became in time a principal painter at Sadler's Wells, which in 1800 came under the management of the younger Charles Dibdin, until 1818. In his *Memoirs*, Dibdin remarked on the rapidity with which Andrews worked, motivated by the fact that he often was paid by the piece. He designed and executed numerous scenes for Dibdin's pantomimes and aquadramas. Many of his original sketches of scenes are found in an album now in the Garrick Club and described in detail by Sybil Rosen-

feld in *Theatre Notebook*, XV (1960). They include a scene of "Burning Moscow" for a production of *Iwanowna* (13 May 1816), which Dibdin claimed had produced "an electrical effect upon the audience."

As chief painter for Dibdin, Andrews was empowered "to call in whatever assistance he might deem necessary" in order to exhibit "as beautiful displays of scenery as *any Theatre in London*." The rival painter at Covent Garden, John Richards, reportedly said to Dibdin one day about Andrews, who was a short man, "Little Bob, Sir, is a Giant in the Art." According to Dibdin, writing about 1830, Andrews's "professional eminence has never been surpassed;" but such high opinions were not shared by Charles Lamb, who laughed at the scenes for *Edward and Susan* (1803): "a prodigious fine view of the vale of Buttermere—mountains very like large haycocks, and a lake like nothing at all."

In 1802 Andrews bought five shares in the proprietorship of Sadler's Wells, which he sold at the end of the 1811–12 season. He continued there, however, as scene painter, assisted by Luke Clint and John H. Grieve, until 1818, when Dibdin terminated his management. In 1819 Andrews joined Drury Lane at a salary of £4 12s. 6d. per week.

Robert Andrews died probably about 1825. Charles Dibdin, speaking of him in his memoirs written about 1830, stated that "he died a very few years since." Andrews's nontheatrical painting includes a work entitled "England's Glory" and a picture entitled "The Glorious First of June," after the De Loutherbourg painting which is at the National Maritime Museum at Greenwich. He was also the creator of a well-known print which shows the exterior and environs of the New Theatre in Sadler's Wells in 1813.

In the summer season of 1814 at the Surrey Theatre, a Mr Andrews had been announced on the bills as a principal scene painter, but this person may have been Robert's son, Thomas Andrews, who later was employed at Drury Lane and was reportedly a painter superior to his father. Thomas Andrews became "very dissipated" and died near the end of a sea passage to America.

**Andrioni.** *See* ANDREONI.

**Anereau, John** [*fl.* 1794–1797], *singer*.

Anereau was a chorus singer at Drury Lane between May 1794 and May 1797. The Drury Lane account book for 1795–96 listed him as a countertenor, and Doane's *Musical Directory* (1794) described him as an alto. In 1794, he lived at No 13, Norton Falgate, and was a member of the Choral Fund and the Handelian Society.

**Anfossi, Pasquale** *1727–1797, composer, music director*.

Born at Taggia, Italy, on 25 April 1727,

*Gabinetto Nazionale dei Disegni e delle Stampe, Rome*

PASQUALE ANFOSSI
after L. Scotti

Pasquale Anfossi studied violin at the Conservatorio di Santa Maria di Loreto at nearby Naples under Piccinni and Sacchini. His first opera, *La serva spiritosa*, was played at Rome in 1763. His first lasting success was in 1773 with *L'incognita perseguitata*, a piece which brought him a reputation as a foremost opera composer.

Anfossi's opera *Il trionfo della costanza* (with a libretto by Carlo Francesco Badini) was written expressly for a performance given at the King's Theatre in London on 19 December 1782 before the composer's arrival. Anfossi himself came to London in the fall of 1783 to take up his post as composer to the Opera. *Silla*, a *pasticcio* opera to which he contributed some music, was performed at the King's with "the Music under the Direction of Anfossi" on 29 November 1783. In his first season there he also composed a new serious opera *Il trionfo d'Arianna* (17 January 1784), another new serious opera *Issipile* (8 May 1784), and a new comic opera *Le gemelle* (12 June 1784). Anfossi continued as composer and director of music in the next season 1784–85, in which he presented for the first time in London (but played previously in Italy) *Il curioso indiscreto* (18 December 1784) and *Nitteti* (26 March 1784). He contributed to the *pasticcio*, *Didone abbandonata*, on 14 February 1786 and offered the entirely new *L'Inglese in Italia* on 20 May 1786. Carlo Badini's libretto to the last piece received praise in the *General Advertiser* of 22 May, but Anfossi's music was criticized as laboring "under a tedious monotony." During the season, Anfossi received three payments from the theatre treasury in amounts of £370, £170, and £200.

After departing London in the summer of 1786, Anfossi settled in Rome as *maestro di capella* of San Giovanni in Laterano. He continued to write for the stage and many of his subsequent operas were successful at Rome, Venice, and Weimar. He died at Rome in February 1797.

In addition to more than 70 operas, Anfossi wrote church music and 12 oratorios. Although his music was not popular in the nineteenth century and is almost forgotten today, it was much admired in his own time. A list of his works and an account of his continental career are found in the *Enciclopedia dello Spettacolo*. An engraving of Anfossi, after L. Scotti, is in the Gabinetto Nazionale dei Disegni e delle Stampe, Rome.

(A Signor Anfossi, perhaps a descendent, was a double-bass player at the King's Theatre in 1817 and 1818. By his will in 1846, Domenico Dragonetti bequeathed a double bass to Signor Anfossi, a performer on that instrument who was residing at No 54, Poland Street.)

**Anfoy.** *See* D'ANFOY.

**Angel, Mr** ₁*fl. 1720–1732*₁, *harper.*
On 27 February 1720 at the Lincoln's Inn Fields Theatre there was "An Entertainment on the German Harp by Mr Angel [Angelo?], who never perform'd on the Stage before," with a performance of *A Devil of a Wife*. On 25 February 1732 a Mr Angel and a Mr Cook shared a benefit concert at the same playhouse; this was probably the same Mr Angel, and possibly he was one of the theatre's staff musicians.

**Angel, Edward** *d. 1673, actor.*
Edward Angel (or Aingel), "best of Mimiques," was a member of John Rhodes's troupe at the Cockpit in Drury Lane in 1659–60. He acted female parts, among which was the title role in *The Maid in the Mill*, which veteran James Nokes had previously played—suggesting that Angel was already fairly experienced and may have been trained as a boy actor in the Caroline theatre. His first recorded role after the Restoration was Pyropus in *Ignoramus*, done at court by the Duke's Company on 1 November 1662. From this point on he played regularly with the troupe at Lincoln's Inn Fields and, starting in 1671, at Dorset Garden.

Angel's specialty was low comedy—such roles as Friskin in *The Unfortunate Lovers*, Dufoy in *The Comical Revenge*, and Fribble in *Epsom Wells*—but during the 1660's he appeared in most of the Earl of Orrery's tragedies and tragi-comedies as well. By the 1667–68 season his line and his popularity, especially with the courtly circle, seem to have been firmly established. In the Davenant-Dryden version of *The Tempest*, which opened on 7 November 1667 at Lincoln's Inn Fields and was performed frequently over the course of the next year, Angel played Stephano; on 20 February 1668 he acted Trincalo in *Albumazar*, which Pepys saw two days later, and commented, "It is said to have been the ground of B. Jonson's 'Alchymist': but, saving the ridiculousnesse of Angell's part, which is called Trinkilo, I do not see any thing extraordinary in it, but was indeed weary of it before it was done. The King here, and, indeed, all of us, pretty merry at the mimique tricks of Trinkilo."

Dryden, in the Prologue to *The Conquest of Granada*, referred to Angel and James Nokes as "the best Comedians of the Age," and they seem, indeed, to have worked extraordinarily well as a farcical team, famous for off-color jokes and foolery. In the spring of 1671 Aphra Behn commented in the Prologue to *The Amorous Prince* on the jaded tastes of audiences

*Who swear they'd rather hear a smutty Jest*
*Spoken by Nokes or Angel, than a Scene*
*Of the admir'd and well penn'd Cataline . . .*

Playwrights began to create special parts for these actors. For example, Edward Howard wrote a special prologue to *The Women's Conquest*, in which Angel, Nokes, and the droll Cave Underhill appeared as themselves.

Wycherley, in *The Gentleman Dancing*

*Master,* performed at Dorset Garden on 6 February 1672 with Nokes as Monsieur de Paris, wrote a passage comparing Nokes, Angel, and Tiberio Fiorelli, the famous Scaramouch:

MONS[IEUR]. Ay, ay, the *French* Education make us propre à tout; beside, Cousin, you know to play the Fool is the Science in *France,* and I diddè go to the *Italian* Academy at *Paris* thrice a week to learn to play de Fool of Signior *Scaramouchè,* who is the most excellent Personage in the World for dat Noble Science. *Angel* is a dam *English* Fool to him.

HIPP[OLITA]. Methinks now *Angel* is a very good Fool.

MONS. Nauh, nauh, *Nokes* is a better Fool, but indeed the *Englis'* are not fit to be Fools; here are vèr few good Fools.

. . . . . . . . . . .

HIPP. But is it a Science in *France,* Cousin? and is there an Academy for Fooling: sure none go to it but Players.

MONS. Dey are Comedians dát are de Matrès, but all the beaux monde go to learn, as they do here of *Angel* and *Nokes;* for if you did go abroad into Company, you wou'd find the best almost of de Nation conning in all places the Lessons which dey have learnt of the Fools, dere Matrès, *Nokes* and *Angel.*

Angel sometimes went too far, if Aphra Behn's Epistle to the Reader which prefaces *The Dutch Lover* (1673) refers to him; though the cast is not known, it seems likely that Angel played Haunce, the title role. She complained that

this Play was hugely injur'd in the Acting, for 'twas done so imperfectly as never any was before, which did more harm to this than it could have done to any other sort; the Plot being busie (though I think not intricate) and so requiring a continual attention, which being interrupted by the intolerable negligence of some that acted in it, must needs much spoil the beauty on't. My Dutch Lover spoke but little of what I intended for him, but supplied it with a great deal of idle stuff, which I was wholly unacquainted with

until I heard it first from him; so that Jackpudding ever us'd to do: which though I knew before, I gave him yet the Part, because I knew him so acceptable to most o'th' lighter Periwigs about the Town, and he indeed did vex me so, I could almost be angry: Yet, but Reader, you remember, I suppose, a fusty piece of Latine that has past from hand to hand this thousand years they say (and how much longer I can't tell) in favour of the dead. I intended him a habit much more notably ridiculous, which if it ever be important was so here, for many of the Scenes in the three last Acts depended upon the mistakes of the Colonel for Haunce, which the ill-favour'd likeness of their Habits is suppos'd to cause.

Mrs Behn's reluctance to speak ill of the dead (after just having done so) was no jest. Angel played DeBoastado in *The Careless Lovers* on 12 March 1673 at Dorset Garden, and after this date there are no further records of his acting. The Edward Angell of Peters Street who was buried at St Clement Danes on 26 April 1673 was probably the actor, though the prompter John Downes in his list of actors lost to the troupe about 1673 made no mention of Angel's death.

An undated *Elegy* by C. B. (c. 1673) was written "Upon that Incomparable *Comedian, Mr* EDWARD ANGELL":

> Hang the Stage all in black; this
>     sable night
> Hath brought a deluge, caus'd an
>     Angels flight.
> Before Creation, Heav'n lost an Angel
>     thence;
> Our Stage's Angel hath made his Exit
>     hence.
> His pregnant Actions of Transcendant
>     Wit,
> Rung Peals of Mirth, in Gallery, Box,
>     and Pit.
> He was the best of mimiques, and
>     took's Degree
> Master of Art, in every Comedy.
> To hear his Mimick voyce, which did
>     dispense

Divertisement to all Spectators sense.
It fill'd 'em with amazement to behold,
What actions sprung from his cor-
    poreal mold.
His loss is felt at Court, where it
    does move
The Great Ones there, like the true
    Soul of Love.
The City too bewails: And now in lieu
Of former Mirth, from them drop
    showers of Dew.
He was the Poets Darling, not one
    but wears
Clouds on his brow, his eyes flow
    seas of tears.
The Actors all, at Fate's so swift
    command,
Are turn'd some Ghosts; others like
    Statues stand.
Who shall play Stephano now? your
    Tempest's gone,
To raise new Storms i'th'hearts of
    every one.
Farewell Dufoy; That Comical revenge,
That always pleasing Play, is now
    unhing'd.
Adieu, dear Friskin: Unfort'nate
    Lovers weep,
Your mirth is fled, and now i'th'Grave
    must sleep.
No more to Epsom; Physicians try
    your skills,
Since Frible now has ta'n his leave
    o'th'Wells.
His parts too numerous were for Elegy,
And Scenes too Comical to be express'd
    by me:
Let best of Poets do't, it shall suffice
I on thy Grave this Epitaph Incize:
    EPITAPH.
Here lies Ned Angel, who rul'd as
    he thought fit,
The English Stage of Comic,
    Mimick Wit.

## Angelelli, Augusta, stage name of Mrs Vittorio Correr, née Wynne

[fl. 1798], singer.

Using the stage name of Signora Angelelli, Mrs Augusta Correr made her debut on the London stage singing the role of Donna Ciprigna in La scola dei maritati at the King's Theatre on 23 January 1798. The next morning, the Morning Chronicle described her as a young and elegant woman with a thin and feeble voice. She repeated the role on 27 January. The same opera was announced for 31 January, but, Signora Angelelli being indisposed, Nina was put in its place. Signora Angelelli recovered sufficiently to sing Donna Ciprigna again on 10 February and then three more times on 10 and 17 February and 6 March. Her other roles that season included Eurilla in La cifra (10 March and twice more), Giannina in Il consiglio imprudente (10 and 13 April), Fiordispina Coribanti in Il capriccio drammatico (10 April and five more times), Carolina in Il matrimonio segreto (21 April and six more times) and a principal role in Il barbiere di Siviglia (5 June and four more times).

Signora Angelelli was the cousin of Elizabeth Wynne, who recorded in her diary her reaction when she was in the audience at the singer's debut: "to my no small surprise and vexation I find this woman to be Augusta Correr! She sings with taste but her voice is too small for so large a theatre. She lives with a German and has been lately brought to bed." Elizabeth Wynne returned to hear her sing on 27 January, despite the fact that in her diary she had written "I would give the world that she had not chose London to expose herself." Back stage, Signora Angelelli mentioned to Elizabeth that she had seen her uncle, Richard Wynne, and Elizabeth's father, at Verona, but then her German friend put a damper on the conversation by whispering in her ear. The singer then changed language and said in Italian that she was a little in disgrace with her family. "How pleasant it is for me to have such a woman for my cousin?" wrote Elizabeth that night in her diary.

Signora Angelelli was probably related to the singer Cassandra Frederick, who married Thomas Wynne and who was the sister-in-law of the musician Joseph Mazzinghi.

**Angeli, Francesco**  [*fl. 1678–1679*], *actor.*

Possibly to be identified with Francesco delli Angioli, Francesco Angeli was a member of the Duke of Modena's Italian troupe which came to England in November 1678, performed six times, and left on or about 13 February 1679, when a departure pass was issued to them. They were apparently caught in the middle of anti-Catholic sentiment created by the Titus Oates plot and had a most unsatisfactory stay. Angeli was apparently one of the *zanni* in the troupe, though his role is not clear; Antonio Riccoboni was the *Pantalone*, Giovan Antonio Lolli the *Dottore*, and several members of the noted Constantini family were in the company.

**Angelica, Mrs**  [*fl. 1785*], *singer.*

Mrs Angelica (possibly a stage name) played a principal character in the burletta *The Milk-Maid's Disaster* on 21 October 1785 at the Royal Circus.

**Angell, George**  [*fl. 1736–1739*], *musician.*

One of the original subscribing members of the Royal Society of Musicians, founded in 1739, George Angell participated in London concerts during the 1730's. He played the cello at the Cannons Concerts, for which he was at one time receiving £7 10s. per quarter. Angell took a benefit concert at the Crown and Anchor Tavern on 4 February 1736. Possibly he was related to Benjamin Angell, one of the five musicians who played at a reception in Jamaica given to the new governor, Robert Hunter, sometime between 1727 and 1730. Descendants of Benjamin Angell were to be found in Jamaica as late as 1875.

**"Angelo."** *See* ZANONI, ANGELO.

**Angelo, Signor**  *d. c. 1663, musician.*

Henry Purcell the elder, father of the famous composer, was appointed to the King's private music on 21 December 1663, succeeding Signor Angelo. Angelo was probably the same musician who received an allowance in 1612 for mourning the death of Prince Henry of Wales.

**Angelo, Signor**  [*fl. 1723–1724*], *scene painter?*

The *Daily Journal* of 6 November 1723, noting the production of Aaron Hill's *Henry V* at Drury Lane, stated that "the scenes are reported to be designed by Signior Angelo, an Italian." Though this may have been true, there is the possibility that the reporter confused *scena per angolo*, a perspective technique probably employed in the scenery for this production, with the name of the scene painter. John De Voto was a scene painter at Drury Lane at this time and introduced *scena per angolo* to the English stage; if there was a painter named Angelo at the theatre working with De Voto, it would be an amusing coincidence.

**Angelo, Signora**  [*fl. 1714–1715*], *singer?*

Signora Angelo's name was included in a list of performers to be paid unspecified amounts for their services; the document apparently dates from 1714–15, though it has been dated c. 1711, and the impresario Heidegger probably wrote it. Though no Signora Angelo was in the opera company at the Queen's Theatre under Heidegger that season, Angelo Zanino, sometimes called "Angelo" was, so perhaps the Signora was his wife and a minor singer in the troupe.

**Angier, Mr**  [*fl. 1784–1785*], *singer.*

Mr Angier made his first appearance singing a principal part in the oratorio *Judith* at the Haymarket on 3 March 1784, under the direction of Barthelemon. He sang the next oratorio season at the Haymarket with Arrowsmith, Mrs Arne, and Mrs Kennedy in *Judas Maccabaeus* on 23 February 1785 and again in *Judith* on 16

March 1785. Perhaps he had some connection with Charles Angier, married to Elizabeth Angier, whose daughters Mary and Anne were christened at St Paul, Covent Garden, on 3 November 1740 and 27 February 1741, respectively.

**Angioli.** *See* ANGELI.

**Angiolini.** *See* PITROT.

**Angler, Mr** [*fl. 1786*], *performer.*
A Mr Angler was one of the performers in *A Sale of English Beauties at Grand Cairo* on 17 September 1786 at Astley's Amphitheatre.

**Angus.** *See* AGGAS.

**Anlaby.** *See* ALLABY.

**Anna, Signora** [*fl. 1703*], *singer.*
Signora Anna sang at a concert in York Buildings on 5 March 1703 for the benefit of Signor Francisco; she was billed as lately arrived from Rome and making her first public appearance in England. It is possible, perhaps probable, that Anna was her first, not her last name.

**Annereau.** *See* ANEREAU.

**Annesley.** *See also* ANSLEY.

**Annesley, Mr** [*fl. 1800*], *manager?*
In 1800, a Mr Annesley procured a license, for an unspecified period, for a play and entertainment at the Haymarket Theatre.

**Annesley, Mrs** [*fl. 1744–1749*], *dancer.*
Mrs Annesley (or Ansley) made her first appearance of record at Drury Lane on 2 October 1744 in a *Grand Turkish Dance.* She was at this theatre throughout 1744–45 and during 1746–47 and 1748–49. She apparently was the Mrs Ansley who was

billed in the role of Liberty in the masque afterpiece, *The Triumph of Peace*, on 21 February 1749. In August of that year she appeared at Cross and Bridge's Booth during Bartholomew Fair and probably had similar minor engagements during her brief career in London. Always a member of the dancing ensemble, she never attained any prominence or solo billing.

**Annibale.** *See also* FABRI, ANNIBALE PIO.

**Annibali, Domenico** *1705–1779?* *singer.*
Domenico Annibali, sometimes "Annibalino" (but not to be confused with his contemporary Annibale Pio Fabri), was born probably at Macerata in the Marches sometime between 1700 and 1705. He was first noted as singing at Rome in 1725 and then at Venice in 1729. He then settled for

*Brera Gallery, Milan*

DOMENICO ANNIBALI

by Mengs

his principal engagement at Dresden between 1729 and 1736, where he achieved prominence in singing in almost all of the operas of Hasse and in those of other composers. On 18 June 1736, the *London Daily Post* announced that "Sig Dominichino, one of the best singers now in Italy," had been engaged by Handel for the ensuing opera season at Covent Garden. Annibali arrived in London that autumn and on 5 October was called to Kensington to sing several songs before the Queen and Princesses. His first appearance at Covent Garden was on 8 December 1736, when he sang Handel's *Porus*. That season he sang two other Handelian title-roles: in *Arminius* and in *Justin*, as well as the lead parts Ahasuerus in *Esther* and Demetrio in the new opera *Berenice*. For the revival of the ode, *Alexander's Feast*, on 16 March 1737, Handel arranged part of an additional cantata, "Cecilia Volga," for him.

After this single season in London, Annibali returned to the court at Dresden to spend the major period of his career. In 1740, he sang Regolo, a role written especially for him by Metastasio, in *Attilio Regolo*, set by Hasse. He left Dresden in 1764 with a pension of 1200 thalers a year to retire in Rome. Known to be alive in 1779, he probably died in that year or soon thereafter.

According to Grove and Angus Heriot, Annibali was a soprano, with an exceptionally high voice which was capable of attaining *F in alt.*, but Winton Dean contends that the parts which Handel wrote for him prove that he was a low alto. He made no great impression during his one season in London, and Burney never remembered his name "to have been mentioned by those who constantly attended the operas at those times." Perhaps he was too much overshadowed by Farinelli's sensational engagement that season in Porpora's competing opera company at the King's Theatre. Mrs Pendarves wrote, however, that Annibali had "the best part of Senesino's voice and

Carestini's, with a prodigious fine taste and good action."

There is a fine portrait of Annibali, in the Berea Gallery in Milan, which was painted by Anton Raphael Mengs, apparently as a token of gratitude to the musician. As a child, the painter had been tyrannized by his father, who kept his children in a state of terror and weakness. When invited by Mengs's father to sing at his house, Annibali became aware of their treatment and subsequently brought their plight to the attention of the Elector himself, who relieved their condition and eventually sent the young Anton Raphael Mengs to study painting in Italy. A list of Annibali's roles on the Continent may be found in the *Enciclopedia dello spettacolo*.

**Ansani, Giovanni** *1744–1826, singer, composer.*

Giovanni Ansani was born at Rome in 1744. He sang at Copenhagen in 1770, at Venice in 1774, and at Naples in 1777–78. He made his first appearance in London at the King's Theatre on 2 December 1780,

*Instituti di Storia e D'Arte, Milan*

GIOVANNI ANSANI
by Bicci

singing Rodoaldo in *Ricimero*, and immediately incurred the animosity of Francesco Roncaglia, who resented sharing the public's applause that night. Despite the appeal of the *Public Advertiser* (4 December) to lay aside "petty Prejudice," the two rivals developed an irreconcilable antipathy. Ansani made several other appearances, but his peevish and quarrelsome temperament was unable to contend with that of the saucy and conceited Roncaglia, so he terminated his engagement in mid-season, much to the inconvenience of the management. His last performance that season was as Ubaldo in *Rinaldo* on 16 January 1781. He returned to the King's Theatre for the following season, probably having gone to Italy in the interim, and sang Massino in *Ezio* on 17 November 1781. His other roles in 1781–82 included *Junius Brutus*, Lucio Papiro in *Quinto Fabio*, and Leango in *L'eroe cinese*. He gave his last London performance on 25 May 1782 as Agamennone in *Ifigenia in Aulide*.

Ansani's wife, the singer Sga Giuseppa Macchierini, who had accompanied him when he returned to London for the season 1781–82 and had made her London debut at the King's Theatre on 12 January 1782, was an indifferent singer with a disposition rivaling that of her husband. Later in their careers in Italy, it was said that if both happened to be engaged at the same theatre, when one received greater applause, the other employed an opposition claque to hiss.

Ansani sang in Florence and Rome in 1784 and subsequently elsewhere in Italy. A list of his roles in Italy may be found in the *Enciclopedia dello spettacolo*. He retired to Naples in 1794, where he spent his later years teaching singing, apparently until his death in Florence on 15 July 1826. His finely toned, full, and commanding voice impressed Burney enough for him to call it one of the sweetest, yet most powerful tenors he had ever heard. Ansani also composed duets and trios for soprano and bass, with a *basso continuo*. An opera entitled *La vendetta de Nino*, performed at Florence in 1791, has been attributed to him by Gerber, but Grove states it was by Prati, although Ansani may have sung in it.

He was pictured in a painting by Antonio Fedi of a large group of musicians, an engraving of which was printed between 1801 and 1807. Other engraved portraits of Ansani, which are at the Instituti di Storia e D'Arte, Milan, include those by Eridi (1792); by Lasinio, after Antonio Bicci; by Antonio Viviani, after Eugenia Bosa; and a mezzotint bust portrait by an anonymous engraver.

**Ansani, Signora Giovanni, Giuseppa.** *See* MACCHIERINI, SIGNORA.

**Anselin.** *See* ASSELIN.

**Ansell, Mr** [*fl.* 1785], *dancer.*
An Ansell Junior made a single appearance on 28 May 1785, dancing a *Minuet de la cour and gavot* with Miss Rowson at Covent Garden. He probably was Thomas Ansell (1763–1820), or William Ansell (b. 1777), both sons of Thomas Ansell, house servant, but he could have been the son of either John or William Ansell, also of Covent Garden.

**Ansell, Mrs** [*fl.* 1788–1791], *house servant?*
A Mrs Ansell shared tickets at Covent Garden on 31 May 1788 and a Widow Ansell shared tickets on 2 June 1791. She was probably the wife of John, William, or Thomas Ansell, house servants.

**Ansell, Miss** [*fl.* 1787–1788], *house servant?*
A Miss Ansell shared tickets at Covent Garden on 27 May 1788. She may have been Sarah Ansell, baptized 2 January 1770, daughter of Thomas Ansell, boxkeeper. One Elizabeth Ancell, of Downing Street, married the composer and singer Luffman Atterbury in September 1790, and she too

may have been connected with the Ansell family of servants at Covent Garden.

## Ansell, Mrs Francis Hutchings, Sarah. *See* YATES, MRS THOMAS.

## Ansell, John [*fl. 1761–1788*], *boxkeeper.*

John Ansell, boxkeeper at Covent Garden, shared benefits, usually with Green, another boxkeeper, regularly between 1761–62 and 1787–88. From 1776–77 through 1782–83, he was on the account books for a salary of 12*s*. per week. His address during most of his career was Davies Street, Berkeley Square. No doubt he was related to William and Thomas Ansell, also house servants.

## Ansell, Thomas *d. 1788, house servant.*

Thomas Ansell was employed as a house servant at Covent Garden, beginning at least in the season of 1770–71. From 1776 through 1784, he was paid 15*s*. per week. He shared regularly in tickets through 1783–84 but presumably remained at the theatre until his death in 1788. There were a number of Ansells employed at Covent Garden during the last quarter of the eighteenth century, and Thomas must have been related to them. (Perhaps he was the brother of the boxkeeper, John Ansell, and the bill-sticker, William Ansell.)

On 2 April 1763, Thomas Ansell, bachelor, of St Paul, Covent Garden, married Mary Blackmore of the same parish, the daughter of the tailor at Covent Garden Theatre. They had at least six children: Thomas, christened 6 November 1763, buried 18 September 1820; Sarah, christened 2 January 1770; Mary, buried 15 July 1771; Elizabeth, christened 11 October 1772, buried 5 February 1775; Frederick John, christened 30 January 1775, buried 17 November 1776; and William christened 21 December 1777.

Thomas Ansell was buried at St Paul,

Covent Garden, on 15 June 1788. His wife may have been the Widow Ansell who shared tickets at Covent Garden on 2 June 1791. A Mary Ansell, aged 73, was buried at St Paul, Covent Garden, on 9 February 1814. This woman could have been Thomas's wife, or the wife, also named Mary, of the boxkeeper, William Ansell.

## Ansell, William [*fl. 1762–1790*], *house servant, bill-sticker.*

William Ansell was a minor servant and bill-sticker at Covent Garden, sharing in benefits and tickets regularly from at least 1774–75 through 1789–90. From 1776 through 1784 he was paid 12*s*. per week, and on 28 February 1788 he was paid £26 4*s*. "for painting Mr Lewis's house." His full name was given in *The World*, '14 January 1788, when he was a witness at the Royalty Theatre trial. He probably was brother to John Ansell and Thomas Ansell, house servants at the same theatre during this period.

A William Ansell married Mary Ansell (a cousin?) at St George, Hanover Square, on 25 April 1762. One Mary Ansell was buried at St Paul, Covent Garden, on 9 February 1814, probably his wife or that of Thomas Ansell. A Mrs Ansell shared tickets with William on 31 May 1788, and a Widow Ansell received tickets on 2 June 1791.

## Anselmo, Mr [*fl. 1786–1803*], *house servant.*

Mr Anselmo served as a minor house servant at Covent Garden for at least 17 years between 1786 and 1803. His name first appeared as a sharer of tickets with other servants on 2 June 1787. In the seasons 1793–94 and 1794–95 he was paid 12*s*. per week, a salary he was still on the account books for in 1802–3. His wife, Mrs Anselmo, was a dresser at the same theatre, at least between 1794–95, and 1803–4, also at 12*s*. per week. She was probably the Martha Anselmo who lived in Brownlow

Street, Drury Lane, St Giles in the Fields, the administration of whose will was granted on 2 November 1812 to "John Hill the natural and lawful brother and one of the next of kin of the said deceased."

**Anselmo, Mrs** ⟨*fl.* 1794–1804⟩, *dresser. See* ANSELMO, MR.

**Ansley.** *See also* ANNESLEY.

**Ansley, Abraham** *d. 1662, trumpeter.*
Abraham Ansley was identified as a trumpeter of Trinity Minories in his will, which was proved 16 December 1662 by his wife Joanne.

**Anslow.** *See* ONSLOW.

**Answorth.** *See* AINSWORTH.

**Anthony, Mr** ⟨*fl.* 1733⟩, *French horn player.*
The Mr Anthony who played in a concert at Hickford's music room on 20 April 1733 may have been related to the Restoration trumpeter Peter Anthony.

**Anthony, Joseph.** *See* GANTHONY, JOSEPH.

**Anthony, Peter** ⟨*fl.* 1672–1673⟩, *trumpeter.*
On 22 February 1673 Peter Anthony was granted a lifetime pension of 16d. per day, but he did not go into retirement; on 13 March he was paid £50 for his extra expenses while attending Prince Rupert at sea, and on 1 December he received £36 5s. for the same service from 23 April 1672 to 14 September 1673. He may have been related to Anthony the horn player of 1733.

**Antinori, Luigi** ⟨*fl.* 1726⟩, *singer.*
An Italian tenor in the King's Theatre company for at least half of the 1725–26 season, Luigi Antinori sang Marzio in *Elisa*

(15 January 1726), C. Lelius in the premier of *Scipione* (12 March), and Leonato in the premier of *Alessandro* (5 May). In the last he sang with Faustina, Cuzzoni, and Senesino, this being the first time that great trio performed together in London.

**Antonia, Marie.** *See* MARCHESINI, MARIA ANTONIA.

**Antonie, Mons** *d. 1732, actor, acrobat.*
Monsieur Antonie was the Pierrot in Francisque Moylin's French company when it played at Lincoln's Inn Fields at the invitation of John Rich during the first half of the 1718–19 season. On 13 January 1719 he was billed as playing Madame Pernelle in *Tartuffe*. The troupe proved so popular that after their engagement at Rich's playhouse they transferred, on 11 February, to the King's Theatre in the Haymarket, where Antonie's acrobatic skill was displayed. On 2 March the feature was a leap over 12 hoops by Antonie and Octave, and at the company's last performance on 19 March the bill said that at Octave's challenge Antonie would perform a leap through a cask stopped at both ends. In addition to his acting and acrobatic talents, Antonie was also a rope dancer. He died in France in 1732.

**Antonio.** *See* AMBROISE, ANTONIO.

**Anunciati, Signora** ⟨*fl.* 1766–1767⟩, *singer.*
On 6 August 1766, the *Public Advertiser* announced that Signora Anunciati had been engaged as first woman for the Opera at the King's Theatre and was expected to arrive in that month with "the best company that could be got in Italy." A surviving cast list for one of the six operas produced in 1766–67 did not include her name, nor was she mentioned in any reviews or other notices. If she did come to London as announced she probably made her first appearance in *Gli stravaganti* on 21 October 1766.

**"Ap Arthur, Jeffrey"** [*fl. 1759*], *dancer.*

On 21 September 1759, a hornpipe was performed at the Haymarket by Jeffrey Ap Arthur, who was announced as "not exceeding five years, just arrived from Monmouth." The dance took place after the mainpiece, entitled *Galligantus*, which was also announced as a new English burletta, "taken from the Memoirs of Jeffrey Ap Arthur." The name is a pseudonym for one of the performers in Christopher Smart's company, possibly a child of John Arthur.

**"Ap-Leek."** *See* HIPPISLEY, JOHN.

**"Ap-Shinkin, David."** *See* CARNEY, MR; HIPPISLEY, JOHN; YATES, RICHARD.

**Appleby, Mr** [*fl. 1696–1699*], *acrobat.*

With Edward Barnes, Mr Appleby performed at Bartholomew and Southwark fairs in the late summers of 1696 through 1699. The *Post Man* for 5–8 September 1696 described Appleby's specialty at Southwark Fair: "Likewise you will see the famous Mr Appleby, who is the only Tumbler in all Europe, fling himself over 16 mens heads, through 12 hoops, over 14 Halbards, over a Man on Horseback, and a Boy standing upright on his Shoulders"—not all at once, supposedly, but in sequence. In 1698 Barnes took Appleby on as his partner, and this arrangement continued in 1699. In the latter year Ned Ward recorded his impressions of the Barnes-Appleby booth in *The London Spy*; it was probably Appleby he was admiring in the following passage: ". . . it was very admirable to think that use should so strengthen the springs of motion, and give that flexibility and pliableness to the joints, nerves, sinews, and muscles, as to make a man capable of exerting himself after so miraculous a manner." How long Appleby continued his career after this is not known; after the turn of the century Barnes operated his booth alone, and the advertisements do not mention "the famous Mr Appleby."

**Appleby, Mr** [*fl. 1792*], *puppet-show man.*

An Appleby presented puppet-shows at Bartholomew Fair in 1792.

**Appleby, Master** [*fl. 1798–1819*], *dancer. See* APPLEBY, WILLIAM.

**Appleby, William** [*fl. 1787–1818*], *messenger, porter.*

William Appleby served Drury Lane Theatre as a messenger for at least 31 years. The first account book payment to him was on 25 September 1787, in the amount of 6s. 9d. for a "Messenger's Bill." Similar small payments continue regularly, averaging about 18s. per week until 1808–9, when his salary seems to have been set at £1 5s. per week. Usually he was given the opportunity to share tickets with other minor house servants at the end of each season. On 3 March 1795, the management gave him £1 2s. 6d. "to pay his surgeon."

In addition to carrying messages, Appleby also was a music porter in the theatre. In 1794, according to Doane's *Musical Directory*, he lived in Princess Street, Drury Lane. Appleby probably was a house "character." In his *Reminiscences*, Thomas J. Dibdin speaks of "poor little Appleby, well known to fame at Drury-Lane Theatre as a half-crazy messenger." A Mrs Appleby, doubtless his wife, also worked occasionally at Drury Lane as a cleaning woman and dresser; on 14 September 1805 she was paid £1 7s. and on 17 June 1807, 14s. for such services. (She may have been the Mary Appleby, of King Street, who was buried at St Paul, Covent Garden, on 31 December 1821, at the age of seventy-seven.) Their son first appeared on the stage as Master

Appleby, playing one of the children in the afterpiece *The Eleventh of June* on 5 June 1798 at Drury Lane. By 1808–9, as Appleby Junior, he was receiving £1 5s. per week as a dancer, and was at that salary at Drury Lane at least through 1818–19.

**Appleton, Master** [*fl.* *1790–1793?*], *musician.*

In March of 1790, when he was little more than four years old, Master Appleton, a musical prodigy, was brought to London by his father, a maltster from near Birmingham. The elder Appleton was anxious to find able instruction in music for the boy. The *Scots Magazine* reported that in May 1789, the lad, who had previously been vexed to tears by hearing music played, suddenly became "passionately enamoured" of it. His father gave him grounding in the principles of keys and chords, and by the time of the boy's arrival in London he could play on the *pianoforte* and organ—"in perfect time, and fine taste"—several of Corelli's and Handel's difficult fugues. Clementi and other musical professors who had heard him play reputedly regarded Master Appleton as the most extraordinary musical prodigy in their experience. Musical children were not uncommon on the London stage at this time. Young Appleton may have been the six-year-old "musical child" who played a violin solo and conducted a concerto at Astley's Amphitheatre on 3 April and 24 October 1793.

**Aquilanti, Chiaretta** [*fl.* *1742–1763*], *dancer*

Sga Chiaretta Aquilanti first appeared in London, so far as the bills show, dancing with Checo Torinese at Drury Lane Theatre on 8 November 1742. She appeared again several times that season, alone, with Torinese, and with Signor Boromeo, on 22 November in *A New Comic Ballet; call'd Les Moisoneurs de la Styrie*, on 10 December in a "New Comic Dance," *La Recue des houssars,* on 31 January in *The Italian*

*Gardeners* and *The Neapolitan Punch*, and on 10 March in *A New Sicilian Peasant Dance*. On the latter date she was, according to James Winston's notation, the recipient of "A poor Benefit."

Nothing more was recorded of Signora Aquilanti's activities in London, and she may have soon gone back to Italy. A long letter printed in the *Theatrical Review* in 1763, dated from London on 18 March 1763, and purportedly a "Translation of a letter from Signor Bimolle (a Florentine fiddler) in London, to the Signora Chiara Aquilante (the famous Opera Broker) at Naples" and signed "Arcangelo Bimolle," is replete with gossip about London musicians and *impresarii*, but gives us no further information about Chiaretta Aquilanti.

**Aragoni.** *See* **ARRIGONI.**

**Archell, Mr** [*fl.* *1794*], *trumpeter.*

A Mr Archell was listed in Doane's *Musical Directory*, 1794, as a trumpeter living in Lower Grosvenor Street and belonging to the New Musical Fund.

**Archer, Mr** [*fl.* *1735–1742*], *actor.*

An obscure actor named Mr Archer played Sir Tunbelly in *The Relapse* at York Buildings on 17 July 1735. He or someone else by the same name played Slap in *The Indian Merchant* at Phillips and Yeats's booth opposite the hospital gate, West Smithfield, on 25 August 1742, at the time of Bartholomew Fair.

**Archer, Alexander** *1757?–1817, actor.*

First appearing on the stage as Master Archer, at Cork on 7 October 1782, Alexander Archer spent most of his life as a provincial actor. As Mr Archer he made his debut at Dublin in 1786 and then joined the company at Edinburgh from 1786 to 1792, playing mainly juvenile roles and young walking gentlemen. He also acted at York (1790, 1791, 1795, 1796), Belfast

(1794, 1795)—where he played leading roles, including Beverly in *The Gamester*—Dublin (1795), Liverpool, and Exeter. At Brighton in 1796 he was regarded as an actor of considerable merit who played his namesake Archer in *The Beaux' Stratagem* with "great spirit."

After passing some 12 years in the provinces, Archer made his debut at Drury Lane in the role of Shylock on 13 December 1798. According to the *Monthly Mirror* (January 1798), Archer played the role in a traditional manner, aiming at no particular novelty of interpretation. His voice was powerful, but not melodious, and he was said to be in full control of his emotions and powers, managing both "with great judgment." Archer received "the most flattering encouragement" from the audience. As the *Monthly Mirror* observed, he had no claim to the first characters of a London theatre, yet he was worthy of a respectable engagement. Although he played no other roles in that 1797–98 season, he was engaged at Drury Lane for the following three seasons at £3 per week. He made his second appearance on the London stage as Antonio in *The Merchant of Venice* on 13 November 1798. Other parts at Drury Lane included a principal role in *Feudal Times*, Frank in *The Secret*, Lord Brumptom in *The Funeral*, Doricourt in *The Belle's Stratagem*, and Prince Lupanski in *Lodoiska*. When Packer suddenly became ill on 19 September 1799, Archer at the last minute played Claudius in *Hamlet*, suggesting that he was familiar with it from provincial experience. It was reported that the robes of majesty, in this instance, "seemed to sit sufficiently upon him," although no other role of such significance, except Antonio in *The Merchant of Venice*, was ever to be his lot in a winter theatre at London. On 11 June 1800 he replaced Aickin, who was ill, in the character of Rogue in *The Mountaineers*, apparently his last performance at Drury Lane.

In the summers of 1799 and 1800, Archer was co-lessee of the Brighton theatre with Blogg, but after the second season they disagreed and Archer gave up the enterprise. He was a member of the summer companies at the Haymarket in 1803 and 1804, playing a line primarily of older nobles or gentlemen: Henry in *1 Henry IV*, Alphonso in *The Voice of Nature*, King Edward in *The Surrender of Calais*, Rawbold in *The Iron Chest*, St Francis in *The Point of Honour*, Buckingham in *Richard III*, Schedoni in *The Italian Monk*, the Duke in *As You Like It*, Lt Worthington in *The Poor Gentleman*, and Lord Glenmore in *The Chapter of Accidents*.

On 28 December 1801, Archer played Shylock at Wolverhampton, where he had gone for the season. His performance, according to the *Monthly Mirror*, "gave much satisfaction to the amateurs of the drama; he possesses some versatility of talent, and may, with certainty, be pronounced the best tragedian that has visited Wolverhampton these several seasons." Having also played at Worcester in 1803–4, Archer returned to Edinburgh in 1805–6, from which time he was a regular member of that company through 1814–15. His wife Elizabeth, née Jefferie, was found as Mrs Archer in the Edinburgh bills by 1789–90. Presumably she accompanied her husband's early provincial wanderings, and she played in the same company with him at York, Wakefield, Hull, Pontefract, and Leeds in 1790–91, at York in 1791, at Dublin and Belfast in 1795, and at Edinburgh again in 1805 through 1807–8. Apparently she never acted on the London stage.

Alexander Archer died in Edinburgh on 1 July 1817, at the age of 60, according to the inscription on his monument in Greyfriars Churchyard. His wife, also memorialized on the monument, predeceased him on 6 December 1814.

**Archer, Elisha** *1760–1800, violinist.*

Born in 1760 or 1761, probably in London, Elisha Archer spent most of his professional life as an instrumentalist in the theatre bands and playing at important concerts. An Elisha Archer of St Martin-in-the-Fields who was buried at St Paul, Covent Garden, on 3 November 1776, was probably his father.

William Dance recommended the younger Elisha Archer for membership in the Royal Society of Musicians on 1 August 1784 (admitted 5 September 1784), at which time Archer was said to be engaged at the Haymarket, had been in the profession for at least seven years, was single, "23 or 24 Years of Age," and played the tenor violin and violoncello. During the 1790's he had engagements at the patent houses as a member of the regular band and for the oratorios. He was at Drury Lane 1790–91 (when his salary was raised by 1s. 8d. on 18 February) and 1791–92 and also played at the opening of the new Drury Lane in the spring of 1794. From 1795–96 through 1798–99, he was at Covent Garden, where on 17 November 1799 his salary was 10s. per day.

In addition to his work at the theatres Archer was a regular participant in the concert life of the town. His name is found as violinist on the list for the annual concert for the clergy at St Paul's Cathedral in May 1785 and on subsequent lists every year between 1789 and 1798. He also played at the grand performances in Westminster Abbey in memory of Handel.

In 1794, Archer lived at No 44, Greek Street, Soho. His wife, whom he married after 1784, apparently died before he did. He died late in 1800 and on 4 January 1801, Miss Archer, his daughter, was granted £8 from the Fund of the Royal Society of Musicians for his funeral expenses.

**Archeveque, Mr**  [fl. 1773–1774], *box office keeper.*

Mr Archeveque was box office keeper at Drury Lane for one season, 1773–74.

**Archey, Mr**  [fl. 1708], *house servant.*

On 8 March 1708 a Mr Archey was listed for a salary of 3s. 4d. per day as part of the wardrobe staff at the Queen's Theatre in the Haymarket.

**Argentina, Signora.** *See* VITTORA, SIGNORA.

**"Ariell, Little Miss."** *See* BRACEGIRDLE, ANNE.

**Arigoni.** *See* ARRIGONI.

**Ariosti, Attilio Malachia**  *b. 1666, composer, violist.*

Attilio Ariosti (or Ariosto), was born in Bologna, Italy, on 5 November 1666. He became a Servite monk in 1688, taking the name Ottavio. He left the monastery, however, and in 1693–1694 was serving as organist at Santa Maria de' Servi in his native city. He entered the service of the Duke of Mantua in 1696 but left a year later for an appointment as composer to Sophia Charlotta, Electress of Brandenburg. Before leaving this Berlin post he became acquainted with Handel. He also met and collaborated with Giovanni Bononcini, with whom he was to work again during his London years. By 1703, when he left for Vienna, Ariosti had composed a number of

*Munich Theater Museum*

ATTILIO ARIOSTI

by Grignion

operas, now lost, and had written at least one libretto. After serving Joseph I in Vienna from 1703 to 1711, he returned to Bologna.

Sometime during the next five years he journeyed to London, for 12 July 1716 at the King's Theatre in the Haymarket he played a solo on the *viola d'amore*—a novel instrument to the English then—between the acts of Handel's *Amadigi di Gaula*. He remained in London for the next season at least, and if, as Grove supposes, the opera *Tito Manlio* is his work, he may have composed it there.

The next record of Ariosti is again in London in 1722 when he had just returned—perhaps from Italy. With Bononcini he took part in the direction of the Royal Academy of Music and for it wrote seven operas during the next five years: *Cajo Marzio Coriolano* (1723), *Vespasiano* (1724), *Aquilio consolo* (1724), *Arta-serse* (1724), *Dario* (1725), *Lucio vero* (1727) and *Teuzzone* (1727)—all performed at the King's Theatre in the Haymarket. Ariosti did not, as some sources still state, compose a portion of *Muzio scevola*; it was the work of Handel, Bononcini, and Amadei.

When the satirical poem *The Session of Musicians* was published in May 1724, Ariosti, along with many other musicians active in London, came in for a roasting. The poem describes a mock trial held by Apollo to determine which musician was the greatest. When it came Ariosti's turn to be judged, others having been found wanting, he felt his chances were good:

> Pleas'd with their Doom, and hopeful
>    of Success,
> At[ti]l[i]o *forward to the Bar did press:*
> *The God perceiv'd the Don the Crowd*
>    *divide,*
> *And, e'er he spoke, stopp'd short his*
>    *tow'ring Pride,*
> *Saying——the Bays for him I ne'er*
>    *design,*
> *Who, 'stead of mounting, always does*
>    *decline;*
> *Of* Ti[tu]s Ma[nli]us *you may justly*
>    *boast,*
> *But dull* Ves[pasi]an *all that Honour*
>    *lost.*

One by one the contenders fell, and Handel, of course, won the day.

Ariosti was still in London in 1728 and published a volume of cantatas and *viola d'amore* lessons; after that year he returned to the Continent.

An engraving of Ariosti by Grignion was reproduced by Hawkins in his *History*. E. Seeman, Jr, painted Ariosti in 1719, and J. Simon made an engraving of his work.

*By Permission of the Trustees of the British Museum*

ATTILIO ARIOSTI
by E. Seeman, Jr.

"Arlequin." *See* **Moylin, Francisque.**

**Armalena, Mr** [*fl. 1777*], *musician?*
One Armalena was a member of an Ital-

ian company that toured the English provinces in the fall of 1776. The troupe played at London in Cockspur Street during February 1777, and in late March, when they announced some new acts, Armalena's name was first mentioned. He, Galmeena, and the whistler Nicola performed a new droll piece called *Musica Arabatia,* and from the title one may guess that Armalena was possibly some kind of musician. The troupe performed with the famous conjurer Breslaw. Whether or not Armalena remained with the company when it moved to the Great Room in Panton Street from 19 June to 15 July 1777 is not certain, though he probably did.

**Armistead, Mrs.** *See* **ARMSTEAD.**

**Armoir** or **Armoy.** *See* **HAMOIR.**

**Armstead, Mrs, stage name of Elizabeth Bridget Blane, later Mrs Charles James Fox** *1750–1842, actress.*
Mrs Armstead was the stage name of Elizabeth Bridget Blane, who was born at Greenwich in 1750. She is described in *Lodge's Peerage* as having been, before her marriage to Charles James Fox, "Elizabeth Blane, otherwise Armstead." The *Public Advertiser,* 29 June 1781, gave her maiden name as Elizabeth Bridget Cane. Little is known of her early life except that she was supposedly a woman of good manners and education who had been at one time a waiting woman to the actress Frances Abington.

Mrs Armstead was said to have made her way to the stage under the patronage of a "noble lord," who may instead have been General Richard Smith. The *Town and Country Magazine,* July 1776, published a gossipy memoir of "Sir Matthew Mite," usually believed to be General Smith, whom Foote had caricatured as Sir Matthew Mite in *The Nabob* (though Foote denied it), and Mrs. A——st——d, "that celebrated Thais . . . who for some time has been the reigning toast in that line upon the *haut*

ELIZABETH ARMSTEAD
artist unknown

*ton.*" Here Smith is painted as a dissolute son of a cheese-and-bacon vendor who rose to some prominence in fashionable drinking societies and Mrs Armstead as a woman not of high pedigree who enjoyed a series of advantageous conquests, eventually becoming Smith's mistress. If we may believe the gossip, which is highly suspect, of course, Mrs Armstead had been born in a cellar, of a father who "though no statesman, has borne very heavy burthens," and of a mother who "addicted herself to the culling and vending of simples." An early lover installed Elizabeth in lodgings in the "polite part" of town, and she was known thereafter to have had a number of admirers who accompanied her to Ranelagh and other public places, among them a "Levite" who was most lavish in his presents.

She made her first appearance in London as Indiana in *The Conscious Lovers,* at Covent Garden on 7 October 1774, billed as a young lady never before on any stage but identified by manuscript notes of the Drury Lane prompter Hopkins as Mrs Armstead. Playing several other roles that season, including Perdita in *The Winter's Tale* ("with the Sheep Shearing Song") and Miranda in *The Busy Body,* she continued to be billed as "The Lady who performs Indiana." The *Westminster Magazine* (October 1774) reported that although her figure and sensibility promised much, her stage fright had subdued her expression; the critic described her as of "lusty" person, in profile and plaintive voice "very much resembling the late Mrs. Cibber."

There is no record of her in the bills for 1775–76, but the following season she was acting at the Haymarket from 15 May through 27 June 1777. Her roles were Emily in *The Deuce is in Him* and Amelia in *The English Merchant.* Of her performance in the latter, the *Morning Chronicle* (16 May 1777) identified her by name and observed that she still suffered stage-fright but that the candid applause of the audience greatly dissipated her fears; "she spoke the pathetic speeches with remarkable sensibility." With this performance, however, Mrs Armstead's theatrical career ended, without her name ever actually appearing on a bill. (A Mrs Armstead was holder of a box at the Opera in 1783.)

Soon after, perhaps in 1778, Mrs Armstead formed a connection with the famous Whig statesman, Charles James Fox (1749–1806). She lived with him at St Anne's Hill, a house with thirty acres of land well situated near Chertsey in Surrey, which she had bought apparently with the assistance of her paramour. When he could take time to escape the pressures of high politics, Fox could there indulge his taste for literature and gardening in the company of a woman to whom he was sincerely attached and who seems to have been most

dedicated to him. In the summer of 1787, they journeyed abroad, staying longer than expected after Mrs Armstead sprained her ankle in Italy and returning on 24 November 1787. Seven years later, on 28 September 1795, Fox married his mistress in a private ceremony conducted by Rev J. Pery, the Rector of Wynton, near Huntingdon. The marriage register gives her name as Elizabeth Blane ("of this parish"); one of Fox's memoirs states she was a widow at the time. Despite Fox's concern that she be treated with appropriate deference and honor at the great houses which customarily entertained the powerful, he did not announce this marriage until 1802. By all reports, she was an exemplary wife, who managed his rural estate with diligence and skill and was pleasing and gentlewomanly. Together they were known to enjoy a felicitous domesticity, living without ostentation. On his birthday, 24 January 1799, Fox presented her with the following lines:

*Of years I now have half a century pass'd,*
*And none of the fifty so bless'd as the last:*
*How it happens my troubles thus daily*
*    should cease,*
*And my happiness thus with my years*
*    should increase;*
*This defiance of nature's more general*
*    laws,*
*You alone can explain, who alone are*
*    the cause.*

Fox died peacefully on 13 September 1806 and was buried in Westminster Abbey. His wife continued to live for many years at St Anne's Hill, where she died on 8 July 1842, at the age of 92. Her funeral was intended to be private, but a number of people were anxious to show their respects because of her urbanity and charity; the procession included about thirty of the local tradesmen and some members of Parliament and of the nobility. She was buried in a vault at the northeast end of the churchyard at Chertsey, in a coffin bearing the simple inscription, "The Hon. Elizabeth Bridget Fox, *obit*, July 8th, *aetat*. 92 years."

Of Mrs Armstead's marriage with Charles James Fox there was no issue, although Fox had children otherwise. Fox's entry in the *Dictionary of National Biography* states that he had an illegitimate son, who was deaf and dumb and who died at the age of fifteen. Farington writes in his *Diaries* (5 November 1793) of Fox's "little girl, at this time 7 or 8," who was not the child of Mrs Armstead.

A small bust engraving of Mrs Armstead, in oval frame, was published in *Town and Country Magazine* in July 1776.

**Armstrong, Mr**  [*fl. 1717–1719*], *singer*.

A singer at the Lincoln's Inn Fields Theatre, Mr Armstrong's first recorded appearance was Metius in *Camilla* on 2 January 1717 and his last as the singer of a *cantata* on 3 April 1719, accompanied on the harpsichord by Babel. He was presumably active during the intervening years.

**Armstrong, Mr**  [*fl. 1722*], *dancer*.

A Mr Armstrong danced at Walker's booth at Southwark Fair on 25 September 1722.

**Armstrong, Mr**  [*fl. 1726*], *trumpeter*.

With a production of *The Orphan* at the Haymarket Theatre on 24 February 1726, a Mr Armstrong played Henry Purcell's trumpet song, "Sound Fame."

**Armstrong, Elizabeth, stage name of Kitty Ann Worlock, later Mrs John Moody the second**  *1763–1846, dancer*.

Kitty Ann Worlock, known on the stage also as Elizabeth Armstrong, was born at London on 20 April 1763, the daughter of Simeon and Elizabeth Worlock, and was baptized at St James's, Clerkenwell, on 10 May 1763. Presumably her mother was separated later from Simeon Worlock and

resumed her maiden name of Elizabeth Armstrong, which Kitty Ann took for her stage name.

By the age of six, Kitty Ann was a student of the dancer Peter D'Egville. On 19 October 1769, D'Egville, who was at the time ballet master at Drury Lane Theatre, entered into an agreement with the manager of Sadler's Wells, Thomas King, in behalf of himself and his five pupils, namely John Holland, Harriet Medlicot, Mary Ross, Richard Scriven, and Elizabeth Armstrong. The children were to receive jointly £175 for dancing "as often as required" at Sadler's Wells and were not to dance anywhere else without King's consent, except at the theatres royal in London. By this agreement, Miss Armstrong appeared in specialty dances at Sadler's Wells in 1769–70 and at Drury Lane in 1770–71. Apparently absent from the stage in 1771–72 (but possibly dancing in D'Egville's ballets without billing), she was again at Drury Lane by 1 April 1773 for occasional appearances.

D'Egville left Drury Lane in 1773–74, taking his scholars with him, and Miss Armstrong next appeared at the King's Theatre on 28 April 1774 in a minuet and allemande with Master Holland. For the seasons 1774–75 and 1775–76 she was at Covent Garden but returned to Drury Lane in 1776–77, where she was engaged through 1781–82 at a salary of £50 per season until her last two years when she received £100 per season. For the most part she was assigned ensemble dancing roles but occasionally appeared in specialty numbers, minuets, and allemandes, usually with D'Egville and for his benefit. On 7 November 1776 she danced in *The Triumph of Love* with Signora Crespi, Mlle Dupré, Gallet, and Helme. Under the direction of the senior Vestris, she appeared in the new ballets to the opera *L'omaggio* at the King's on 5 June 1781.

Miss Armstrong's name did not appear in the bills after May 1782. She claimed against the Drury Lane Fund in March 1792, at which time Winston noted in the Fund Book that she had retired from the stage.

On 22 May 1806, Kitty Ann Worlock became the second wife of the actor John Moody (1727?–1812) at St Dionis Backchurch; she was described in the register as a spinster, he as a widower. A few days later, in June 1806, she "was struck off the List" of the Drury Lane Fund Book and described as Mrs Moody, "late Miss Armstrong." They lived for a time at Lawn Place, Shepherd's Bush, Hammersmith; and when Moody died on 28 December 1812 he left her some unspecified amounts in public funds, all the household goods, and a house at Barnes, Surrey.

Kitty Ann's mother, Elizabeth Armstrong, was still alive in 1813, also residing at Shepherd's Bush. She had been named principal residuary legatee of Kitty Ann's will, which was drawn on 28 May 1813, but a codicil of 24 February 1833 indicates she had died since. Kitty Ann Moody died on 29 October 1846 at the age of 83. She was placed in a tomb in Barnes churchyard with the remains of John Moody and his first wife, Anne. Her will, proved in London on 13 November 1846, suggests that she had been modestly well-off. She bequeathed £100 in three percent annuities to the Drury Lane Fund. She left her house at Barnes to Mary Amelia Layton (née Miller), the wife of her executor, Edward Layton of Hans Place, Chelsea.

**Armstrong, John** [fl. 1769], *proprietor.*

In June 1769 the proprietor of Pancras Wells, John Armstrong, advertised the virtues of the waters at that London pleasure garden. Although his name was a common one, possibly this vendor of health waters was Dr John Armstrong (d. 1779) who lived in Russel Street, Covent Garden, and was physician to actors. Dr Armstrong was also an amateur musician and author of medical treatises, travel books, and some essays on dramatic criticism.

**Armstrong, Mr W.** [fl. 1708–1713], *violist.*

A document at Harvard ascribed to the impresario Heidegger and dating c. 1708 lists a W. Armstrong as playing the tenor violin (i.e. viola) in the Queen's Theatre band; Armstrong had petitioned for the job and asked one shilling nightly. Another document of c. 1710 in this same group, however, shows him receiving 10s. daily, so the one-shilling bid may be an error for one pound. Armstrong's first initial appears on a receipt dated 24 June 1712, and he was still listed as one of the gentlemen in the music room at the Queen's about 1713. After this date there seem to be no certain references to him, but a Widow Armstrong was given a benefit concert at Stationer's Hall on 27 March 1717, and if she was W. Armstrong's relict, perhaps he died shortly before this date.

**Arnauld.** *See also* **ARNOLD** and **ARNOULD.**

**Arnauld, Mons** [fl. 1764–1770], *dancer.*

Monsieur Arnauld made his first appearance on the English stage at Covent Garden on 3 October 1764 in a new comic ballet, *Blind-Man's Buff.* The following evening he danced in a new grand pantomime ballet, *La femme maîtresse.* He was a regular member of the dance company at Covent Garden every year from then through 1769–70. Arnauld also danced in the summer of 1766, alternating in Spranger Barry's company at the King's Theatre and then in Foote's company at the Haymarket. Although he achieved no great reputation, he was often a featured dancer in pantomimes and comic ballets.

**Arnault.** *See* **ARNULL.**

**Arne, Master.** *See* ARNE, RICHARD and ARNE, MICHAEL.

**Arne, Michael** *c. 1740–1786, composer, singer, musician.*

It is often asserted that Michael Arne, the son of Thomas Augustine Arne, was born in 1740 or 1741. According to Burney, Michael was Thomas A. Arne's bastard son. But possibly the natural son referred to by Burney was really Charles Arne, who was christened at St Paul, Covent Garden ("son of Thomas Arne") on 9 January 1734, before Thomas A. Arne was married to Cecilia Young. Michael's name does not appear at all on the St Paul, Covent Garden, register of christenings, where most of the Arne family are to be found.

Michael Arne made his stage debut when very young as the page in *The Orphan,* a role for which his aunt, Mrs Susanna Cibber, had prepared him. He may well have been the "Master Cornel" who performed the page ("with a new song") in a production of that play at Drury Lane on 12 April 1746. If he was, and if he was born in 1740 or 1741, he was a mere four or five years of age, very precocious for this particular role. On that night, indeed, Mrs Cibber played Monimia, Mrs Arne sang several specialty songs, and the program was for the benefit of Thomas A. Arne. "Master Cornel" may have been a pseudonym. It may even have reflected the name of his mother if he was, as Burny said, the child of one of his father's indiscretions.

In any event, his father turned Michael toward music. Grove states that he made his debut at Galli's concert at the Haymarket on 2 April 1750. He took a benefit performance at the same theatre ten months later on 5 February 1751, in a bill which demonstrated his extraordinary versatility for one so young. Now billed as "Master Arne," he sang one of the vocal parts in a *pasticcio,* played a new concerto by his father on the organ, and sang the role of Paris to Mrs Arne's Juno in his father's setting of

*The Judgment of Paris* (tickets "at Mr. Arne's in Beaufort Buildings in the Strand"). On 30 April 1751 he sang in a concert at Hickford's Great Room in Brewer Street, when another musical prodigy, Miss David ("a child of Seven"), made her first appearance singing and playing on the harpsichord and flute. Several days later, at Covent Garden on 3 May 1751, for the benefit of Mrs Arne, he played the title role in *Tom Thumb,* a burlesque opera his father had written in 1733 as *The Opera of Operas,* and in which at that time his uncle, Richard Arne, had made his debut also billed as "Master Arne." He also sang at Marylebone Gardens that summer of 1751.

Michael sang the next season at Covent Garden, where Mrs Arne was engaged, but his real talent did not rest in his voice. Even at his tender age he was already able to rival most senior musicians at the harpsichord. He executed Scarlatti's *Lessons* with "wonderful correctness and rapidity," and his facility in executing "double shakes" was acclaimed. During the seasons 1754–55, 1756–57, and 1758–59, he gave occasional concerts on the organ at Drury Lane. By this last season he was living independently from his parents at his chambers in No 4, Garden Court, the Temple.

Michael Arne's main reputation, however, was to be won, as was his father's, as a composer of music for the theatre and of popular songs. Among his earliest compositions for the theatre, written at the age of about nine or ten, was a song "The Highland Lad," which, according to the bills, Master Arne set for Master Mattocks to sing at Drury Lane on 28 April 1750. He also wrote a "New Sheep-Shearing Song," which Mrs Cibber sang in *The Winter's Tale* at Drury Lane on 21 January 1756. Published that year, it was to be heard in most productions of this play for many years thereafter. In the early years he began to write for the pleasure gardens as well, and about 1755 was published *The Flow'ret, A New Collection of English Songs sung at the*

*Publick Gardens, Composed by Master Arne,* followed in 1758 with another *Collection of English Songs, Sung . . . at the Publick Gardens and both Theatres.*

Also like his father, Michael became engaged as composer to Drury Lane. With Boyce and Aylward, he wrote music for *Harlequin's Invasion,* 31 December 1759; he also provided music for *Edgar and Emmeline,* 31 January 1761, and three numbers for the Garrick-Colman alteration of *A Midsummer Night's Dream,* 23 November 1763. (For the latter, he contributed five numbers when it appeared as the reduced *A Fairy Tale* at the Haymarket, 18 July 1777.) The following season, 1764–65, he collaborated with Jonathan Battishill on a setting of a new serious English opera, *Almena,* by Rolt, which opened at Drury Lane on 2 November 1764 and was performed but six nights to thin houses. At this time he was living at No 14, Crown Court, Russell Street, Covent Garden. He was elected to the Madrigal Society on 20 March 1765; in the following year his membership ceased and he was re-elected on 16 December 1767.

On 5 November 1766 Arne married Elizabeth Wright, the Drury Lane singer, at St Mary's, Lambeth, and the register reveals that Arne was at the time a widower. Nothing is known of his first wife. (It was known by Garrick on 15 July of that year that Miss Wright, then 15 or 16 years old, would marry Arne; the manager expected her to retire, but she returned to Drury Lane. For his honeymoon, Arne had to borrow £50 from the Drury Lane treasury. He paid back the sum on 22 May 1767.)

Arne's next important work after his marriage was the extravaganza *Cymon,* produced by Garrick on 2 January 1767, with Elizabeth Arne in a singing role. In an arrangement unusual for composers (especially as Garrick himself was author of this piece), Arne received, "one third part of the Profits of the first three Nights which the author shall take for his own benefits" (the third, sixth, and ninth performances). Their

agreement, dated 22 August 1766, carries the further notation that on 15 January 1767, Arne received of Garrick £119 17s. 10d., being one third of the receipts for the author's benefit nights. (Garrick took for himself slightly over £240 for writing *Cymon.*) Several months later, Arne collaborated again with Garrick on *Linco's Travels,* brought out at Drury Lane on 6 April 1767, with music also by Joseph Vernon.

Garrick hoped to retain Arne for the following season, according to a letter to Garrick's brother George dated 23 April 1767, but the composer turned his attention strongly towards the study of chemistry, or more correctly alchemy, in an absurd pursuit of the philosopher's stone. He had been living at Mr O'Keeffe's at the Golden Unicorn, near Hanover Street, Long Acre, but he built an expensive laboratory at Chelsea, in which to carry out his experiments. The venture ruined him, and by necessity and the return of good sense he resumed his profession. His wife Elizabeth Arne died very young on 1 May 1769, reportedly done to death by the heavy schedule of professional appearances demanded by her husband. In 1770, while living as a widower again, at Mr Doron's, facing the Vine Tavern near Vauxhall, Arne published several volumes of songs which his wife had introduced for him at Vauxhall Gardens.

Arne travelled in Germany in 1771 and 1772. In Hamburg he conducted Handel's *Alexander's Feast* on 23 November 1771 and the first performance in Germany of the *Messiah* on 15 April 1772. The soprano music was sung by Miss Ann Venables, one of his pupils and next-wife-to-be, who had accompanied him on the journey. Back in London, he played the organ occasionally during the 1772–73 season at Covent Garden. He was married for the third time on 1 May 1773, at St Giles in the Fields, to Ann Venables, whom he had also recently introduced as a singer at Drury Lane on 12 November 1772. About Christmas time 1776 he went to Dublin, having been engaged by Thomas Ryder to present *Cymon* at the Smock Alley Theatre. Arne was lured back to his research for gold while in Ireland and took a house near Clontarf to set up shop for his experiments. But the story that he was so reduced by this venture as to be thrown into a Dublin sponging house in the summer of 1777, where he composed the music for Fielding's *The Fathers,* is doubtless apocryphal. The production of *The Fathers* at Drury Lane was not until some fifteen months later, on 30 November 1778, and Arne contributed but one song. Moreover, in August of 1777, he and his third wife were at Cork, offering for the first time in that city a series of operatic productions, beginning with *Cymon.* The venture failed and the composer admitted publicly on the first of September that the receipts had "fallen considerably short of the expenses for the House."

After Ireland, Arne took up work again at Drury Lane. On 31 January 1778 he was paid £21 for some more music to *Cymon,* and on 2 June he was given £15 15s., his moiety of receipts due his late father from that theatre. (Thomas A. Arne, who had died 5 March 1778, had left him a share in a ruined but once excellent organ and half the profits to accrue from any future productions of the elder Arne's works in manuscript or copyright.) He was granted co-administration of his father's will on 21 March 1778. That spring Michael wrote a new song, "The Cottage on the Lawn," introduced by Mrs Farrell at Covent Garden on 11 May 1778. He also wrote a song for a production of *The Conscious Lovers* at Covent Garden on 27 September 1779, a song and minuet for the revival of *The Belle's Stratagem* at Covent Garden on 22 February 1780, and the music for *The Artifice* at Drury Lane on 14 April 1780.

After another engagement at Dublin with Ryder in 1779, Arne was engaged as composer at Covent Garden for several years, at a salary of £8 6s. per week in 1781–82 and £8 10s. per week in 1782–83. His compositions during this time included

*The Choice of Harlequin,* 26 December 1781; *Vertumnus and Pomona,* 21 February 1782; *The Positive Man* (with William Shield), 16 March 1782; *The Capricious Lady,* 17 January 1783; and *Tristram Shandy,* 26 April 1783. When the famous Alsatian designer De Loutherbourg opened his spectacular picture show, *The Eidophusikon,* in April 1781 at Leicester Street, Leicester Square, Arne composed the music and accompanied the display. He also had charge of some Lenten oratorios at the Haymarket in 1784 and 1785, for which he played the organ.

According to Burney, Arne "was always in debt, and often in prison." He died on 14 January 1786 at South Lambeth, leaving his third wife, Ann Venables Arne, as Burney reported, in "absolute beggary." He also left a daughter named Sarah (but by which wife is not clear), whose health had been worn down in caring for him in his last illness. She recovered and had some success as a singer at the end of the century and at the beginning of the next, first as Miss Arne and later as Mrs Gardiner, and died in 1808. Thomas A. Arne had left ten guineas in his will to a grand-daughter, Jemima, for her kindness, identifying her as Michael's daughter. Perhaps she and Sarah were the same person.

Michael Arne's works did not have the happy simplicity of his father's, but Sainsbury thought, nevertheless, that his merits "very justly entitled him to a high and distinguished rank among English composers." Smith's *Catalogue of Printed Music . . . in the British Museum* lists about 80 different publications of his works, many of them incidental songs for the gardens and theatres. According to Grove, a fine portrait of Michael Arne was painted by Zoffany and was at one time in the possession of Alfred H. Littleton.

**Arne, Mrs Michael the second, Elizabeth, née Wright,** *1751?–1769, singer.*

Mrs Elizabeth Arne was born in 1751 or

1752, if Thomas Davies's assertion that she was only in her seventeenth or eighteenth year at the time of her death is accurate. She was born Elizabeth Wright, probably of a theatrical family. There were numerous Wrights performing in the Three Kingdoms during the century, and a Mrs Wright was being paid 9s. a week at Drury Lane as a women's dresser in 1764–65 while Elizabeth was engaged as a singer there.

Elizabeth made her first appearance at the age of nine or ten in the suitable part of a fairy in *Edgar and Emmeline,* at Drury Lane on 31 January 1761, although the advance bills had indicated Miss Marten for the role. Music for the production was provided by her future husband, Michael Arne, then about 20 years old. She appeared again as a fairy in *Queen Mab* at the same theatre on 23 October 1761. She sang at Ranelagh Gardens in 1763 and in the oratorio of *Judith,* set by her future father-in-law Thomas A. Arne, at the Chapel of the Lock Hospital on 29 February 1764. The next winter season she was back at Drury Lane, earning £4 per week. On 2 November 1764 she sang in a new serious English opera, *Almena,* on the music for which Arne had collaborated with Jonathan Battishill. After a summer of singing such songs as "Through the Wood Laddie" and "The British Fair" at Vauxhall, she appeared in Bickerstaffe's *Daphne and Amintor* at Drury Lane on 8 October 1765, in the role of Daphne, which had been written, according to the *Universal Museum* (October 1765), for the purpose of introducing her as an actress in "a new department, with some degree of eclat." The critic found her appearance "not perfectly advantageous" but put blame on the character itself, which required an air of awkwardness, and described her as a "pleasing little warbler." In the following season on 14 April 1766, she made her first attempt as Polly in *The Beggar's Opera.* Throughout 1765 and 1766 a number of songs were published in the magazines as sung by her at the gardens or theatres.

Elizabeth Wright became the second wife of Michael Arne on 5 November 1766 at St Mary's, Lambeth. She was perhaps 15 years old. In announcing the marriage the London *Evening Post* referred to her as a "celebrated singer" of Drury Lane. Despite David Garrick's fears, expressed in a letter to his brother on 15 July 1766, that she would retire, she continued her career and remained engaged at Drury Lane for the next three seasons, 1766–69. She was billed as Mrs Arne when she played Ariel for the first time on 4 April 1767, singing additional songs composed by Dr Arne. Neville thought her "the prettiest performer at the house" and was taken by her "sweet little voice." Those qualities of girlish beauty and delicate voice endeared her to London audiences who demanded that she perform constantly; overwork seems to have contributed greatly to her premature death. Her performance as Sylvia in her husband's setting of the spectacular *Cymon* on 2 January 1767 was highly praised, but one critic censured her for "singing at the top of her voice," a deficiency which her teacher-husband was called upon to correct.

In the summer of 1767 Elizabeth sang at Ranelagh. She created the role of Leonora in the enormously successful comic opera *The Padlock* on 3 October 1768, the role in which she also made her last appearance on the stage on 16 February 1769. For the next performance on 18 February she was replaced by Miss Radley. Her health was too fragile to continue playing. Burney said that her husband had sung her to death. She was known to be "very ill at Bristol" on 16 March, and it is probable that she died there on 1 May 1769 at age 17 or 18. (Perhaps she died giving birth to either Sarah or Jemima Arne. Both were daughters of Michael Arne, but by which wife is unknown.) The actress Jane Pope called her death "the unspeakable loss of all her admirers, for she was a sweet Syren." Sturtz wrote to Garrick on 5 August 1769 of his dismay at the death of "poor little Mrs

Arne" who was "so young and so blooming." She had been termed the "nightingale of the stage" (according to Davies), whose melody, fullness, and flexibility of tone were without equal among her contemporaries.

### Arne, Mrs Michael the third, Ann, née Venables [*fl. 1772–1820*], *singer*.

The third wife of Michael Arne was born Ann Venables, conjecturally of theatrical parents and probably in the middle of the 1750's. (In that decade an actor by the name of Venables was working at several London theatres, and a Mr Venables was at the Haymarket as late as 1781–82. A Mr and Mrs Venables were in Roger Kemble's company at Worcester in 1767, and on 20 January 1759 at St Paul, Covent Garden, the dramatist Dr Thomas Francklin married Miss Mary Venables, the daughter of a wine merchant.)

A pupil of Michael Arne, Ann Venables made her first appearance on the London stage as Philadel in *King Arthur* at Drury Lane on 12 November 1772. In his manuscript diary, the prompter William Hopkins noted, "She is very Short, & has a mean appearance a tolerable Voice—but little applause." The reviewer of *Town and Country Magazine* wrote of her debut that she exhibited but very moderate talents for the stage, but he was confident she would improve "under so good a master" and when she gained "a greater share of maturity"—a comment which suggests her youthfulness. Before her London appearance, Arne had taken her on a trip to Germany, where she sang the soprano music in the first performance of the *Messiah* in that country, conducted by Arne in Hamburg on 15 April 1772.

She did not have a very active professional career. At Covent Garden on 19 March 1773 she sang a new song composed by Arne and was a principal singer of his "Thunder Ode," descriptive of "Hurricanes of the West Indies." She became Arne's third wife on 1 May 1773 at St Giles in the Fields, and thereafter the records of her appearances are sparse, though it probably can be assumed she was to be found working in some capacity wherever her husband was engaged. In 1774 she accompanied him to Ireland, where she played at Smock Alley. She acted again in 1776–77 at Dublin and at Cork, and was again at Cork in October 1779. One of her roles in Ireland was Sylvia in *Cymon,* which she had first played on 7 April 1778 at Drury Lane. When she made her first appearance at Covent Garden on 4 May 1780, as Polly in *The Beggar's Opera,* she was announced as from the Crow Street Theatre, Dublin. She also played Rosetta (for the first time) in *Love in a Village.* For this engagement, which lasted through 25 May, she was paid £4 4s. per night. She later sang in the oratorios under her husband's direction at the Haymarket in 1784 and 1785, including *Judith* (3 March 1784), *Samson* (10 March 1784), *Eliza* (17 March 1784), and *Judas Maccabaeus* (23 February 1785).

Ann Arne's career was closely allied to performances which her husband produced or for which he wrote music. She achieved no distinction whatever as a performer. When he died on 14 January 1786, her career seems to have ended. According to Burney, he had left her in "absolute beggary." The Minute Books of the Royal Society of Musicians show that from 1801 to 1820, a Mrs Arne (and she was the only surviving Mrs Arne) received annual benefactions in amounts of five or ten guineas by order of the general meeting, which she usually acknowledged with a letter of gratitude. The last such letter is recorded in the minutes of 2 January 1820, and it may be presumed she died soon thereafter, although no entry to that effect has been found. She may have been the mother of Michael's daughter, Sarah Arne Gardiner, singer, who died in 1808.

### Arne, Richard *b. 1719, singer, actor.*

Richard Arne was the seventh child of

Thomas and Mary Arne to be christened at St Paul, Covent Garden. He was baptized there on 15 February 1719. No doubt Richard was the Master Arne who was listed in the bills between 1734 and 1736. When his older brother Thomas Augustine Arne, at the beginning of a distinguished career, set the music for the revival of Addison's opera *Rosamond* at Lincoln's Inn Fields Theatre on 7 March 1733, Master Arne, "who never yet appeared in public," played the page, a principal role. His sister, Susanna Maria Arne, later Mrs Cibber, sang the title heroine. Shortly thereafter, on 31 May 1733, Master Arne appeared at the Haymarket as Tom Thumb in his brother's *The Opera of Operas.*

In the following season, 1733–34, Master Arne and his sister frequently sang duets in Italian at the Haymarket. She played Venus and he played Cupid in the *Impromptu Revel Masque, on the Joyous Occasion of the Royal Nuptials*, presented there on 24 November. Earlier, on 10 October 1733, Michael Arne acted Francis in *1 Henry IV,* "being his first attempt in that way." When the performers at the Haymarket who were seceders from Drury Lane returned to the latter theatre in the spring, the three Arnes joined them. Richard Arne made his first appearance at Drury Lane on 21 March 1734, singing his brother's songs in the role of Mercury in *Love and Glory.* They shared a benefit on 29 April 1734, with tickets announced to be had of Mr Arne in King Street, the address of their father's upholstery shop. On 27 June 1734 Master Arne sang at Richmond, and later that summer on 24 August he performed Cupid in *Fair Rosamond* at the Bullock-Hallam-Hippisley booth at Bartholomew Fair. He continued to sing and act at Drury Lane during the following two seasons, 1734–35 and 1735–36. He played Estifania in *Trick for Trick* on 10 May 1735 (the night that Charles Macklin killed Thomas Hallam backstage) and Almanzor in *The Man of Taste* on 9 September 1735.

"Master Arne" disappeared from the bills after 1735–36, not to reappear until the 1750's, when this designation applied to Michael Arne, the son of Thomas A. Arne. If Richard was alive, it is surprising that he did not continue in a profession in which he already had a good start and in which his brother and sister were now achieving some fame. The death of Richard himself is not noted in the register of the family church, St Paul, Covent Garden.

**Arne, Sarah.** *See* GARDINER, SARAH.

**Arne, Susanna Maria.** *See* CIBBER, MRS THEOPHILUS the second.

**Arne, Thomas** *1682–1736, box-numberer, manager?*

Thomas Arne, the Drury Lane house servant and patriarch of one of the most important musical-theatrical families in England during the eighteenth century, was christened on 30 December 1682 at St Paul, Covent Garden, the "actors' church," in the registers of which are found many entries concerning his numerous family. His father, also named Thomas Arne, obtained a marriage license there on 4 February 1681 (being at that time a bachelor and upwards of 27 years of age) to marry Mary Thursfield, spinster, age 20, of the parish of St Martin-in-the-Fields. They were married, however, at St Mary Woolnoth on 10 February 1681.

Thomas Arne, the box-numberer, was the eldest of at least six children. The others (all listed in the registers of St Paul, Covent Garden) were: Richard, christened 19 August 1684, who probably died in infancy; John, christened 2 August 1688; Susan, christened 16 June 1690; another Richard, christened 30 March 1693 and buried 13 July 1699; and Phillip, twin of the second Richard, also christened 30 March 1693. Their mother, Mary Arne, apparently died in giving birth to the twins and was buried on 4 April 1693. The father remarried, and another child by his second wife, Margaret, was christened Mary Arne on 9 November 1697; but, as with so many of the children of the Arne family, she died in infancy and was buried one month later, on 10 December 1697. The family apparently fell on hard times and moved about successively to the parishes of St Mary, Islington, and St George, Southwark. The father died in Marshalsea debtors' prison and was buried at St Paul, Covent Garden, on 24 December 1713. The administration of his estate was granted to his widow Margaret on 14 April 1714.

The theatre servant and upholsterer Thomas Arne (subject of this entry) married one Mary Sharpe at some time in advance of the christening of their daughter Mary at St Paul, Covent Garden, on 22 February 1703. The mother was buried at the same church on 20 August 1703, and Thomas was granted administration of her independent property on 3 November of that year. The child Mary was buried on 3 November 1704.

Thomas Arne's second marriage, to Anne Wheeler at the Mercers' Chapel in April 1707, produced at least seven children. Four never survived infancy: Elizabeth, christened 11 April and buried 12 May 1703; Marah, christened 22 June and buried 5 July 1712; Anne, christened 2 July and buried 9 July 1715; and a second Anne, buried 3 December 1716.

Fortunately for musical history and the audiences of London, two other children did survive to maturity: Thomas Augustine Arne, christened 28 May 1710, the eminent composer, and Susanna Maria, christened 28 February 1713, the great tragic actress known to fame as Mrs Theophilus Cibber. The youngest child, Richard Arne, who was christened on 15 February 1719, also appeared on the stage as Master Arne but died young.

Thomas Arne was by trade an upholsterer and reputedly also a coffin-maker, with shops in the heart of the theatrical district. Probably in his earlier years he was associated in business with his father. In 1698 he

moved his shop from the George and White Lion in the Covent Garden Piazza a short distance to the George in Bedford Court near Bedford Street. Before 1710 he moved again, to King Street in Covent Garden, now No 34, but then known as the Crown and Cushion, the place where Thomas Augustine and Susanna Maria were born. There he seems to have managed his business more successfully than his father had done and prospered at his trade at least sufficiently to enable him to send Thomas Augustine to Eton and to offer both the boy and Susanna Maria excellent early education in music.

Arne is said to have been the upholsterer with whom the visiting North American Indian kings lodged during Queen Anne's reign, as chronicled in *Spectator* No 50 and *Tatler*, No 171. Biographers have also identified him as the original Political Upholsterer of *Tatler* No 155, who in his great concern for the affairs of Europe neglected his business and put his family in poverty. Here he is probably confused with an Edward Arne, also an upholsterer and perhaps a cousin, who according to a colorful story appeared as a ghost to relate the gruesome tale of his death by torture and neglect in the Fleet prison while awaiting trial for murder. Edward Arne, "from Fleet Prison," was buried at St Paul, Covent Garden, on 23 October 1725, and on 14 May 1729 a report which was read to the House of Commons, and which set forth atrocious penal conditions, alluded to his unfortunate case.

Thomas Arne may have provided some coffins for actors, but the only record of his business with the theatrical profession before he became a house servant was on 14 October 1715, when the Drury Lane managers paid him £4 17s. 3d. for upholstery and for stuffing and tacking some seats in the theatre. At some point later he became a house servant there, perhaps by the influence of his son Thomas Augustine, who was engaged at Drury Lane by 1734. Testifying in 1735 at the trial of Charles Macklin for the killing of Thomas Hallam,

Arne identified himself by name as "the numberer of the boxes, of Drury Lane playhouse," and on 3 June 1735, he shared a benefit with Mr Allen, another numberer. Perhaps by then, a year before his death, he was unable to carry on his upholstery trade. At that time he was no longer living in Covent Garden but in the neighboring parish of St Giles in the Fields, where his son the composer also lived.

The contention that Thomas Arne was the impresario of some "English Operas" at the Haymarket Theatre in 1732, in association with Henry Carey and J. F. Lampe, is suspect, and his actual connection with these performances is tenuous. Scholars have credited "Thomas Arne, Senior" with arranging a pirated dramatic version of Handel's *Acis and Galatea* at the Haymarket on 17 and 19 May 1732 (announced "With all the Grand Chorus's, Scenes, Machines, and other Decorations; being the first time it was ever produced in a Theatrical Way") and have also suggested that he had organized a production of Lampe's opera, *Amelia*, earlier, in March 1732. But there is little substantive evidence that the upholsterer, who perhaps by 1732 was also a lowly numberer at Drury Lane, was ever actively involved in these performances, much less their co-producer.

His daughter, Susanna Maria, did sing Galatea. It has been asserted that his son, Thomas Augustine, conducted the music, but there is no evidence for this supposition either. Burney and the bills mentioned Susanna Maria but did not mention the father or the son. This misunderstanding of Arne's role in the project results from an advertisement that subscriptions for the English Operas were to be "only taken in by *Mr. Arne*, at the Crown and Cushion, King's Street, Covent-garden." So it seems that Thomas Arne senior provided a convenient place for Lampe and Carey to distribute subscriptions for an enterprise in which two young Arnes were also adventurers.

Thomas Arne was buried at St Paul, Covent Garden, on 17 June 1736, at the age of 53. His second wife, Anne Wheeler Arne, died in 1757.

## Arne, Thomas Augustine 1710–1778, *composer, musician.*

Thomas Augustine Arne was born on 12 March 1710 in a house in King Street, Covent Garden, in the heart of the area where he was to rise as his period's most gifted and prolific English composer of theatrical music. He was christened at St Paul, Covent Garden, on 28 May 1710, the son of Thomas Arne, the upholsterer and Drury Lane box-numberer, and Anne Wheeler Arne. He, his sister Susanna Maria (later the second wife of Theophilus Cibber), and his brother Richard were the only three children of his father's family to survive beyond infancy (see above, ARNE, Thomas, for his forebears and siblings). Although Arne had been baptized in the Church of England with only the Christian name of Thomas, he apparently adopted the second name of Augustine at the influence of his mother, Anne Wheeler Arne, whom Burney described as a bigoted Catholic.

Young Thomas was sent to Eton by his father, who intended him for the law. Burney was told by several of Arne's former school-mates that his developing passion for music, released on a miserable cracked flute, tormented them day and night. After leaving Eton, he was articled by his father to an attorney for three years, but he also continued to practice his music surreptitiously. A creature of Covent Garden, young Thomas often borrowed livery from servants in order to take advantage of the free admission to the upper gallery, which was granted to domestics by the management of the Opera.

The belief that his father strongly opposed his preference for a career in music is doubtless overstated in the romantic story that Thomas privately contrived to get a spinet into his room and, by muffling the

*Harvard Theatre Collection*

THOMAS AUGUSTINE ARNE
after F. Bartolozzi

strings with a handkerchief, practiced undetected during the night. (The same story was told of Handel.) Another story is that Arne's father, upon visiting a gentleman's house on some business, found his son playing first fiddle with an amateur band and had to be mollified by the company, so irate did he become. The fact that all three of the senior Arne's surviving children demonstrated extraordinary musical talents at an early age and followed their inclinations to celebrated careers points to the contrary likelihood that their father encouraged their efforts actively.

In any event, Thomas gave up the pursuit of the law after his three years of apprenticeship, took violin lessons from Michael Festing, and, as the story goes, charmed his entire family by his violin

playing at home. Discovering a sweet-toned voice in his sister, he also introduced her to musical instruction. It is difficult to accept the story that both were mere novices in 1732 when, at her brother's arrangement, Miss Arne began her professional career in a London theatre, singing in J. F. Lampe's opera *Amelia*. Thomas had had some experience in music by then and some acquaintance with or connections with Lampe and Henry Carey. He may have conducted the music for the so-called "pirated" production of *Acis and Galatea* at the Haymarket on 17 and 19 May 1732, but the first definite record of his connection with the theatre came in a newspaper clipping dated 4 November 1732: "We hear that Mr. Arne, jun. has taken the Theatre-Royal in Lincoln's-Inn-Fields of Mr. Rich to represent English Opera's after the Italian manner, on Mondays and Thursdays during the Winter season . . . and that he will open with a new English Opera on Monday the 20th of this Instant." The opera proved to be Henry Carey's *Terminta*, set to music by John Christopher Smith, with Miss Arne in the title role.

On 7 March 1733, Arne offered his own setting of Addison's opera, *Rosamond*, again with his sister in the title role, and with his brother Richard making his first appearance in public in the principal role of the page. The cast also included Leveridge, Corse, Mrs Barbier, Miss Chambers, and Miss Jones. *Rosamond* was his first composition of some importance, from which only six songs and a duet survive. It played a total of seven times that spring (not the successive ten nights claimed by the *Dictionary of National Biography*) with the last performance on 30 April designated for Arne's benefit. He seems not to have been connected with a production of *Ulysses* at the same theatre on 16 April; however, Miss Cecilia Young sang Penelope in that piece, so probably by this time he had met his future wife.

Having succeeded at serious opera, Arne

next tried his hand at burletta. At the Haymarket on 31 May 1733 he brought out his adaptation from Fielding, a musical burlesque called *The Opera of Operas*, with Master Richard Arne as Tom Thumb. Honored with three different royal visits, the piece was acted eleven times, with a twelfth performance deferred by excessive heat. By the end of this season of 1732–33, Arne, now just 23 years old, was a decided success as a theatrical composer. At the same theatre in the following season, on 12 January 1734, he provided new music to a revival of Barton Booth's masque, *Dido and Aeneas*, in which again his brother and sister sang. It, too, was enormously successful, attaining seventeen performances. Shortly thereafter, the three young Arnes were engaged at Drury Lane, when the seceders to the Haymarket returned there. Thomas wrote music for his brother and sister to sing as Mercury and Venus in *Love and Glory*, 21 March 1734, on the occasion of the royal nuptials. In 1736 he furnished music for Hill's *Zara*, the play in which his sister, now Mrs Cibber, first appeared as an actress, and for the *Fall of Phaeton*, a dramatic masque invented by Pritchard, on 28 February 1736. By now identified as "Composer to the Theatre Royal in Drury Lane," he was residing in a house in Great Queen Street near Lincoln's Inn Fields.

On 15 March 1737, at Lincoln's Inn Chapel, Arne married the singer Cecilia Young, daughter of Charles Young, the organist of All Hallows Church, Barking. Her father disapproved of the marriage on religious grounds and never forgave his daughter for converting to Catholicism, the faith Arne practiced and which supposedly prevented him from receiving many professional appointments later on in his career. On the authority of Burney, Thomas A. Arne's only child was Michael Arne, born about 1741, supposedly a bastard. Michael's name is not found in the register of christenings at St Paul, Covent Garden,

where most of the Arne family are recorded. However, a Charles Arne, "son of Thomas Arne from St Martin's in the Fields," was buried at that church on 9 January 1734, probably in infancy, and he, more likely than Michael, was the so-called natural son of the composer whom Burney reported. There seems to have been also another child, Henry Peter Arne, "son of Thomas Arne" of St Giles in the Fields, who was buried at St Paul, Covent Garden, on 17 December 1740.

In 1739 Thomas A. Arne became one of the original member subscribers and organizers of the Royal Society of Musicians. By the end of the 1730's he was clearly a candidate for theatrical and musical fame. He had earned his credentials as a lyric composer with the charming and delicate music he created for Dalton's adaptation of Milton's *Comus*, at Drury Lane, 4 March 1738. Here he introduced a fresh originality, wholly different from the styles of Purcell and Handel, which set the direction for a peculiarly English style, one, as Sainsbury wrote, so easy, natural, and agreeable to the whole kingdom "that it would have lasting effect on national taste." Of the melodious music to *Comus*, Hubert Langley has written that

Arne had found himself, and fixed a standard by which we can judge the whole of the rest of his work; for, although at times it is reminiscent of Handel, yet it has its own very decided individuality and spontaneous expression. There is freshness and natural grace in all the airs, no striving after effect to please the ears of the groundlings, no sacrifice of taste in order to indulge in mere vocal display. It became the model for what was to be recognized for nearly a hundred years as typical English music, and English song deteriorated in proportion as it fell away from this level.

Arne's next important works were also settings of masques, Congreve's *The Judgment of Paris* and Thomson and Mallet's *Alfred*. Both were performed on 1 and 2

August 1740 on an outdoor stage at Clivedon House near Maidenhead, residence of Frederick, Prince of Wales, for a *fête* commemorating the accession of George I (1714) and the birthday of Princess Augusta. The event is memorable for Arne's introduction in *Alfred* of his majestic national song, "Rule Britannia," sung for the first time by Thomas Lowe, whom Burney asserted to be the finest tenor he had ever heard. For Wagner this song expressed the entire English character in the first 10 notes. By some chance the composer's name was omitted in the newspaper report of the first performance; for some time confusion existed as to the song's real author, and by some it was attributed to Handel. It was first published by Henry Waylett, appended to the music of *The Judgment of Paris*, under a copyright privilege dated 29 January 1741 which Arne had received for fourteen years, by royal grant. *Alfred* was altered to an opera by Arne and performed at Smock Alley, Dublin, on 10 March 1744. "Rule Britannia" was not heard in London until 20 March 1745, when *Alfred* played for the first time at Drury Lane. In this year of the Jacobite rebellion, the song became very popular; Handel was moved to adapt some of his words from his *Occasional Oratorio* (1746) —"War shall cease, welcome Peace"—to the opening bars of Arne's anthem.

The other Clivedon masque, *The Judgment of Paris*, was brought out earlier at Drury Lane, on 12 March 1742, at advanced prices for which Arne hoped the Town would not be offended, for he had stood an extraordinary expense "for copying all the Music, building the stage, additional instrumental performers, chorus singers, and erecting an Organ." The performance was for Arne's benefit; so great was the attendance that not all the tickets put out could be accommodated and some had to be accepted at the next performance, on 19 March.

About this time Arne wrote some beautiful songs for Shakespearean productions at Drury Lane. On 20 December 1740 his melodious settings of "Under the greenwood tree," "Blow, blow, thou winter wind," and "When daisies pied," were first heard in a revival of *As You Like It*. He wrote two songs for the performance of *Twelfth Night*, 15 January 1741, and two songs for that of *The Merchant of Venice*, 15 February 1741 (the night Macklin first played Shylock). For a revival of *The Tempest* on 31 January 1746 he composed new music for the masque and the lovely song, "Where the Bee sucks." Arne's Shakespearean songs have worn well, retaining a plaintive poignancy of times past, expressive of the green pastures and shady trees of the peaceful English countryside, in contrast to the uncompromising, determined strains of "Rule Britannia."

In March of 1742, Arne and his wife were living at No 17, Craven Buildings, near Drury Lane. That June they left for Dublin. There they found Handel, who in the previous April had offered the world the *Messiah* in a glorious performance at the Great Room in Fishamble Street, with Arne's sister, Mrs Cibber, in the contralto part. That season also brought the young David Garrick to Dublin, but unfortunately we do not know whether or not the dazzling quartet of talents were in close association there. At the Great Room in Fishamble Street, however, on 21 July 1742, the Arnes were given a benefit concert consisting of songs from the selected works of Arne and Handel, sung by Mrs Arne and Mrs Cibber. In a production of *Comus* at the Aungier Street Theatre on 25 April 1743, Arne conducted and also played on the harpsichord—the first record of his performing on an instrument in public. In collaboration with Dubourg he offered six Handelian oratorios by subscription during 1743–44. He also added another string to his artistic bow by acting Prince Hal in *2 Henry IV,* at Aungier Street on 28 January 1744.

The Arnes remained in Ireland until the autumn of 1744. They returned to London on 30 September to take up quarters next door to the Crown in Great Queen Street. Arne was re-engaged as composer at Drury Lane and produced the comic opera *The Temple of Darkness* on 17 January 1745 (revived as *Caprochino and Dorinna*, at Marylebone Gardens, 28 July 1768). When Gordon died, Arne succeeded him as leader of the band. In the same year of "the '45" Arne re-arranged an old English tune of "God Save our Noble Lord," which was sung on the stage of Drury Lane on 28 September by Mrs Cibber, Beard, and Reinhold, accompanied by horns, violins, tenor, and bass. The rival theatre, Covent Garden, got up another arrangement of the anthem, this by Charles Burney, then Arne's pupil. Until the end of the Jacobite Uprising, the anthems were sung on both stages each night, thereby establishing the impetus for what would later evolve, after more changes by other composers, as the national hymn of "God Save the King."

While continuing in his positions at the theatre, Arne also engaged in the summer of 1745 with Jonathan Tyers, who had decided to add vocal music to his concerts at Vauxhall Gardens. Arne composed many songs for Mrs Arne, Thomas Lowe, and the elder Reinhold, among others, to sing at Vauxhall. This engagement proved to be a most important move in Arne's career. He held the position for many years and also composed for Ranelagh and Marylebone gardens. The success of his songs made him very popular throughout London. Eventually Arne published over 200 songs which he had written for the gardens. Some 20 books of songs were circulated throughout the kingdoms in such collections as *Summer Amusement*, *Vocal Melody*, and *The Vocal Grove*. Twenty-nine examples of his glees and catches were printed in Warren's collections. According to a manuscript in the British Museum, Arne was paid about 20 guineas for every collection of eight or

nine such songs he wrote for the pleasure gardens. The introduction of vocal music at Vauxhall had given impetus to a revival of popular English song in the eighteenth century.

By mid-century Arne's reputation was fully established. On 6 July 1759 Oxford conferred on him the degree of Doctor of Music. In the 1750's, in addition to many songs, he wrote music for at least nine more comic operas and masques which were played at Covent Garden, the Haymarket, Sadler's Wells, and Smock Alley, as well as at Drury Lane. He produced his first London oratorio, *Abel* (a work he had offered at Smock Alley on 18 February 1744 as *The Death of Abel*), at Drury Lane on 12 March 1755 and another oratorio, *Judith*, at the same theatre on 21 February 1761. (The latter was given also at the Chapel of the Lock Hospital, Pimlico, on 29 February 1764.) Neither achieved much success, possibly because of the inadequacies of the performers. In connection with the *Abel* he was accused of exhibiting his oratorio in direct opposition to those of Handel, "a malicious insinuation" which he contradicted in the press: "This is to assure the Publick that Mr. Arne (so far from meaning the least offence to that Gentleman for whose merit he has the utmost veneration) has for many Years declined Performances in that branch of his Profession merely in deference to Mr. Handel's undeniable abilities," yet since he had thought it his duty to respond to the encouragement of the Town to "produce something new," he had decided upon this honest endeavor "to support himself and his Family."

On another visit with his wife to Dublin in 1755–56, Arne's domestic problems surfaced. Perhaps Mrs Arne's frequent illnesses, which often kept her off the stage, contributed to the breach. She had to some degree contributed to his great success and had introduced many of his songs and ballads at Vauxhall, thereby increasing both their reputations, but she seems to have given up her singing career at about the same time that Arne attracted to his tutelage Miss Charlotte Brent, who had accompanied them to Dublin. Arne's probity was not equal to his talents, and apparently he had been chronically unfaithful and had abused Cecilia Arne with indignities beyond infidelity. Charlotte Brent, who first appeared in Dublin singing in his *Eliza* on 29 November 1755, no doubt had been instrumental in contributing to the marital rift. After Mrs Arne stopped singing in public, it was for Miss Brent that he composed a great number of his more florid airs. When Arne left Dublin in 1756, never to return, he also left his wife there. The couple remained estranged until their reconciliation in 1777, the year before he died.

Before this visit to Ireland, Arne had occupied a fine house at No 66, Great Queen Street, which at different times previously had been occupied by the Countess of Essex and Wortley Montague. The rate books cite him as living there in 1748. But by February 1751 he was living in Beaufort Buildings in the Strand; he was at Mr West's, a frame maker in Duke Street near Lincoln's Inn Fields by 1752, and then in lodgings near the Roe Buck in Bow Street, Covent Garden (1753–54), and in Chelsea Street, Covent Garden (1754–55). Upon his return from Dublin he lodged first "next door to the passage in Charles Street, Covent Garden," eventually moving to the Little Piazza (by 1763), then to his house in West Street, which he occupied until about 1777, and finally to Bow Street again. He was frequently to be found in a suit of velvet—even in the dog-days—visiting the Bedford Coffee House, on the northeast corner of the Piazza across from the entrance to Covent Garden Theatre. He was a professional member of the Noblemen and Gentlemen's Catch Club and for a brief time also a member of the Madrigal Society. But despite these respites of leisure, Arne was becoming severely overworked.

*Harvard Theatre Collection*

THOMAS AUGUSTINE ARNE
after Dunkarton

He had disagreements with Garrick which had caused him to transfer his talents to the other house in 1760–61. But even before that year, Arne had been writing for Covent Garden more and for Drury Lane less. His last major efforts for Garrick had been the score for Henry Woodward's pantomime *Mercury Harlequin* on 27 December 1756 and some incidental music for Garrick's alteration of *Isabella* on 2 December 1757.

At Covent Garden on 28 November 1760, his setting of Bickerstaffe's *Thomas and Sally* was performed with Beard, Mattocks, and Miss Brent in the chief roles. *Thomas and Sally* became one of the most popular musical stage pieces of the century and served as a model for similar secondary plays up to the mid-nineteenth century. According to Langley, it was in this work that the clarinet made its appearance for the first time in England. During the 1760's, Arne composed music for at least nine more comic operas or pantomimes, includ-

ing *The Birth of Hercules*. This was rehearsed in 1763 but never played, on account of the Fitzpatrick half-price riots. He
wrote the music which accompanied Bon-
nell Thornton's burlesque *Ode on Saint
Cecilia's Day* for a famous concert at Ranelagh on 10 June 1763.

His setting of Metastasio's *Artaserse* on
2 February 1762, the liberetto of which he
translated into English, proved successful
enough to hold the stage for many years.
Arne sold the copyright for 60 guineas. He
had set this opera in the artificial, florid
recitative, after the Italian manner, and provided another novelty to English ears used
to spoken dialogue. In order to display
Miss Brent's talents, he "crowded the airs"
with difficult Italian divisions. The role of
Mandane became a challenge which only
the most able of soprano singers could
meet. His other setting of a Metastasio text,
*L'Olimpiade*, brought out at the King's
Theatre on 27 April 1764, was unsuccessful. Arne contributed some songs to the
popular *pasticcio*, Bickerstaffe's *Love in a
Village*, at Covent Garden on 8 December
1762. One of the more interesting of his
contributions was the medley given in this
piece to Margery the housemaid, which was
a sophisticated rendering of the familiar
"Here we go round the Mulberry Bush." It
is the same catch called "Nancy Dawson"
for which he had been paid £3 3*s*. by Jonathan Tyers at Vauxhall, the number by
which the celebrated Nancy Dawson horn-
piped her way into theatrical history. The
tune became part of the popular repertory
and is still sung in the nursery.

David Garrick had never been on close
terms with Arne. He was upset with the
musician for not sending him Charlotte
Brent, he was offended that Arne had
raised the prices for the Drury Lane oratorios against Garrick's better judgment,
and there had been a misunderstanding between them about allegations that Arne
had hissed Thomas Norris at his debut on
26 October 1762. (In a letter to Garrick,

Arne denied having hissed, and Garrick
replied that he had never charged him with
doing so.) But when in 1769 Garrick
needed help on the Stratford Jubilee, he
turned to Arne for the musical directorship.
Arne wrote incidental music, some songs,
and the setting of Garrick's impressive *Jubilee Ode*. His oratorio, *Judith*, was also performed—somewhat incongruously in memory of Shakespeare—at Trinity Church.
Garrick paid him 60 guineas in full "for
the sole property of the music . . . com-
pos'd to the Commemoration Ode" and
then made a small fortune with his performances of it at Drury Lane the next
season.

From 1769 until 1778, Arne wrote for
the managers of both patent houses as well
as for the Haymarket. His series of light
operas and incidental music—for such
pieces as Garrick's garbled version of *King
Arthur* (Drury Lane, 13 December 1770)
and Colman's *The Fairy Prince* (Covent
Garden, 12 November 1771)—were slight
and inconsequential compared to his earlier
compositions. But he was paid well for his
work. For the music to *The Fairy Prince* he
received £121 11*s*. 6*d*. from Covent Garden. In the next season that theatre paid
him £90 for music he wrote for Mason's
*Elfrida*, which opened on 21 November
1772. Among his last efforts was the incidental music to Mason's *Caractacus*, played
at Covent Garden on 6 December 1776.
Mason referred to Arne as "that old fum-
bler," but Samuel Arnold believed that the
score contained "some of the brightest and
most vigorous emanations of Dr. Arne's
genius." *Caractacus* was published with a
preface and introduction in which with
stilted but insightful language Arne discussed the relationship between dramatic
poetry and music. He also gave minute directions concerning the constitution of the
orchestra which presage similar annotations
of nineteenth century composers.

The statement by Charles Dibdin, his
contemporary, that Arne had a cheerful and

even temper which allowed him to endure "a precarious pittance" is hardly borne out by other evidence. Never a man of easy temperament, his career seems to have been marked by little bickerings which revealed his sensitive nature and demeaned his dignity. He was, according to Burney (who had been his articled pupil), an erratic teacher, with no head for business, absentminded, and often quarrelsome. At one time he had sufficiently alienated James Worsdale, the painter and actor, for him to comment in his will (8 October 1764, proved 2 June 1767): "unto Dr. Arne I bequeath my honesty of heart but I fear his heart is too case harden'd to harbour any social virtue; I have try'd, and prov'd him unworthy of any man's friendship." Worsdale left £20 to Mrs Arne, "independent of her cruel and unworthy husband" who he said had treated her "most inhumanly." In August 1775 Arne accused Garrick in a letter of an irresistible "apathy" toward him, to which Garrick replied in a few days, "I suppose you mean *Antipathy*, my dear Doctor," and politely assured him of his respects. In the same year Garrick sent a more pithy note, "I have read your play and rode your horse, and do not approve of either," endorsing his own copy, "Designed for Dr. Arne, who sold me a horse, a very dull one, and sent me a comic opera, ditto."

In 1777 Dr Arne became ill of a "spasmodic complaint." After some temporary improvement in his health, he suffered a relapse and died of a "spasm in his lungs" about eight o'clock in the evening of 5 March 1778, a week before his sixty-eighth birthday, in a house which he rented from Mrs Woodeville in Bow Street, Covent Garden, not far from where he had been born. There are two different accounts of his last hours. The first has it that, recalling his instruction in the principles of the Catholic Church, he had sent for a priest. About an hour before his death, he had risen in his bed to sing a Hallelujah,

as if preparing to enter on his hoped-for reward. According to Mrs Barthélemon, he was a practicing Catholic. He had been known to attend services at the Sardinian Chapel in Oxford Road, where reportedly he had also "for several years" been organist. So the account is not too unlikely and does not necessarily conflict with the testimony of Joseph Vernon, the singer, who was at his death bed, that Arne took his last exhausted breath attempting to illustrate in a feeble voice part of an air, "during which he became progressively more faint until he breathed his last." Devout Roman Catholic or not, he was buried in the Anglican church of St Paul, Covent Garden, on 15 March 1778.

In his will, dated 6 December 1777 and proved 16 March 1778 by oath of his wife Cecilia, to whom administration was granted (and also reserved for his son Michael), he left a small personal estate of goods and effects. To his wife and "only son" he gave the sad remains of a once-excellent organ, now "Mangled and trod to pieces by and through the Villiany of wicked Servants," as well as his books and plate. He ordered that any profits still to be had from his musical books and manuscripts were to be equally shared by wife and son. The books were to remain her property, and she was to retain "an unquestionable right to be Satisfied As to the Probability of Success in the undertaking and an equal right to employ a Trustee or Treasurer to sit in the Treasurer's Office all and every Night Whereon any of my Works are Performed." (Several months later, on 2 June 1778, Michael and Mrs Arne were paid £15 15s. each by Drury Lane for money due the late composer.) To his grand-daughter Jemima, Michael's child, he bequeathed ten guineas (from Michael's share) "as a present . . . for her Love and Kindness." Most of his manuscripts were destroyed in the Covent Garden Theatre fire of 1808.

Thomas Augustine Arne, William

Boyce, and George Frederick Handel were the foremost composers in England during the Georgian Age. As such their professional activities were often linked by time and circumstance. Boyce and Arne, both Londoners, were born in 1710, the same year that Handel came to England. One cannot argue with Burney's assessment that the measurement of Arne's accomplishment against Handel's mighty genius was the contention of an infant with a giant. Certainly no English musician could escape the German's shadow, and all British achievement from Purcell onwards must be measured against him. But while Arne did not possess the original grandeur of thought and style of a truly great composer, he surpassed his other contemporaries in ease and variety. As Burney pointed out, no candidate for musical fame was admired by the nation at large more than Arne was during the 46 years of his career. Nevertheless, he spent most of his time, it would seem, frittering away his talents as a musical hack for theatrical managers.

Arne was, as Langley points out, the musician *par excellence* of Covent Garden as Purcell had been of Westminster. There he was born and buried, passing most of the days of his life working and living in the parish and its immediate environs. But his direct influence on the development of English music and song was greater even than Handel's. He held, by most reports, a reverence for Handel and a respect for the science of Pepusch and Geminiani. His own talents pointed in another direction: from oratorios and festival compositions toward the quick parts for the many different performers who toiled nightly in the theatres and pleasure gardens for the approbation of many different kinds of listeners. In that sense, certainly, Arne was a modern, who feared not to "set the more polished Burney's teeth on edge" with such irreverences as editing Purcell's music for *King Arthur*. His was a talent of more daily use in the numerous stage masques,

comic and ballad operas, trifling burlesques and pantomimes, and in the dozens of songs he churned out for the popular singers of his day. (See lists in Grove, Nicoll, and the *Catalogue of Printed Music in the British Museum*.) Even when most apt to embellish his compositions with Italianate decorations, as in *Artaserse* and *L'Olimpiade*—a tendency criticized by Burney—he managed to incorporate them into his own property. At his best he wrote in a simpler form, in songs like those he gave to Shakespeare's plays earlier in his life, typical theatre music for solo voice and small orchestra. One of his most charming and successful songs, "Thou soft-flowing Avon"—his setting for Garrick's *Jubilee Ode*—was exquisite elegy. There is much theatrical wisdom in Sainsbury's judgment that "Excellent and attractive indeed must the airs be, that can atone to English sentiments, and habits for the recitative and consequent destruction of all interest in the language, the incidents, and the plot." In combining simplicity of expression with technical and theatrical artfulness, Arne made a strong impact on his own generation, and many of his works are still attractive today.

According to the *Dictionary of National Biography*, a fine oil painting of Arne by Zoffany was in the possession of Henry Littleton, Esq, in the nineteenth century, but it is not listed by Lady Manners in her *John Zoffany*. An engraving of him, done by Rhodes after R. Dunkarton, was published in the *Biographical Magazine* in 1794. A well-known print of him by F. Bartolozzi from his original sketch was published by W. Humphrey on 10 May 1782. Something of a caricature, it depicts Arne in bag-wig, his sword protruding from the back of his coat, standing in profile and playing on his harpsichord. The exaggerated figure, the elongated and melancholy face, confirm that he was of very slender physique, with hollow cheeks and aquiline nose, not a handsome man. The element of caricature is more pronounced in a copy engraved by W. N. Gardiner. Arne was not, as sometimes stated, the subject of Hogarth's design for "The Enraged Musician," that person having been John Festing. Arne's full-length figure is sculpted on the south-east angle of the frieze of the Albert Memorial.

Charles Dibdin claimed that he once tried to organize an Arne commemoration similar to the homage bestowed upon Handel, but that he had had to give up the project for lack of interest. In 1910, on the bicentenary of Arne's birth, a memorial tablet was placed in St Paul, Covent Garden, after a more ambitious plan to erect a memorial window failed to gain financial support. A small street turning out of Long Acre is named after him.

**Arne, Mrs Thomas Augustine, Cecilia, née Young** *1711–1789, singer.*

Mrs Thomas Augustine Arne was born Cecilia Young in 1711, the eldest daughter of Charles Young, organist of All Hallows (Barking by the Tower). Three of Charles Young's daughters—Cecilia, Isabella, and Esther (and possibly a fourth, Mary Esther)—all appeared on the stage at some time in their lives as "Miss Young," thereby making it often difficult to discriminate among their respective careers. In addition, their brother Charles Young, an organist and Treasury official, also had two daughters who performed publicly. Cecilia was to become the most celebrated of her generation of Youngs.

Cecilia was a pupil of Geminiani, who taught pure *bel canto*, a technique aimed at making the voice "as flexible and obedient as any instrument." From him she acquired her "Italian style." She also inherited English singing traditions going back to Purcell's time, and even earlier, through Dr Anthony Young (her grandfather or uncle), who had been a member of the Chapel Royal. Geminiani brought her out in public at Drury Lane on 4 March 1730 in *A Concert of Vocal and Instrumental Music*, which was announced as for her benefit. Ticket prices were advanced: pit and boxes at half a guinea, first gallery 5s, and upper gallery 2s. A year to the day later, on 4 March 1731, she made her second appearance, in a concert given for her benefit at Stationers' Hall. Her first appearance in a singing theatrical role was as Britannia in J. F. Lampe's opera of that name on 16 November 1732 at the Haymarket Theatre. The fledgling soon became temperamental. Engaged to perform the title role in *Judith*, De Fesch's oratorio, at Lincoln's Inn Fields on 9 February 1733, she caused a postponement until 16 February, at which time the composer explained to the town that the company had been victimized by "the misconduct and pretended sickness of Cecilia Young." She was replaced by Miss Chambers. On 16 April 1733 a Miss Young, very likely Cecilia, sang the title role in *Ulysses* at Lincoln's Inn Fields. In a production of *The Tempest* at Drury Lane on 26 November 1733, the singing role of Amphitrite was billed as for "Miss Young, who never appeared on any stage before," and in view of Cecilia's several known earlier appearances, this neophyte perhaps was her sister Isabella Young.

While engaged in singing at the theatres, Cecilia Young continued her appearances at the various concert halls of the town with some frequency. She sang again at Stationers' Hall on 22 February 1733 for her benefit, and then the next month on 8 March at York Buildings for the benefit of her father. Her other concerts included: Devil's Tavern on 22 March 1734; York Buildings on 8 March 1734 and 29 April 1736 (benefit of Young, organist of St Clement Danes and presumably Anthony Young); Stationers' Hall on 28 March 1734; Hickford's on 10 July 1734; Mercers' Hall on 13 December 1734 and 11 February 1736, both with her sister Isabella and both for the benefit of their father; and Swan Tavern on 26 November 1736, again with her sister ("songs and duets"). During this period she also sang in several of Handel's oratorios at Covent Garden in 1734–35: *Ariodante* on 8 January, *Deborah* on 28 March, *Alcina* on 16 April. She sang Athalia in the first performance of that oratorio on 1 April 1735 and the contralto part in *The Feast of Alexander* on 19 February 1736.

On 15 March 1737 Cecilia Young married Thomas Augustine Arne at Lincoln's Inn Chapel in a Roman Catholic ceremony, which displeased her father, who never forgave her. The marriage was not to be a successful one. Michael Arne, the son of Thomas Augustine, born about 1741, was reputedly illegitimate, but perhaps the natural child referred to by Burney was really Charles Arne, "son of Thomas Arne," christened at St Paul, Covent Garden, on 9 January 1734. If Michael Arne was not Cecilia's child, they nevertheless apparently had a close relationship, and as a youngster he appeared frequently at her benefits. Thomas and Cecilia probably had a child, who died in infancy: a Henry Peter Arne, "son of Thomas Arne," was buried at St Paul, Covent Garden, on 17 December 1740.

Several weeks after her marriage Cecilia sang at Hickford's Rooms on 1 April 1737 as "Mrs Arne, late Miss Cecilia Young," in a concert for the benefit of her husband. The Arnes were now living in Great Queen Street. In 1737–38 and 1738–39 she played intermittently at Drury Lane, Covent Garden, and the King's Theatre, sometimes still billed as Miss C. Young. She then engaged at Drury Lane for three years (1739–42) singing in such productions as *The Tempest, Comus* and *Rosamond*. She was performing in one of the masques, *The Contending Dieties*, at the Clivedon House *fête* on 1 and 2 August 1740 when her husband's anthem "Rule Britannia" was first sung in *Alfred.* Together with Andreoni and Reinhold she sang in a weekly subscription series of 20 musical performances at Hickford's

Rooms which began on 5 December 1740 and concluded in May 1741.

By 1742 the Arnes were in lodgings at No 17, Craven Buildings, near Drury Lane. When Mrs Arne left this address in June of that year to accompany her husband to Ireland (with the infant Michael presumably?), she was in the high tide of her career, and her partnership with Thomas A. Arne had at least nourished their professional lives. At the Aungier Street Theatre in Dublin she sang in the six subscription oratorios sponsored by her husband in 1743–44 and in her husband's settings of *Comus* on 25 April 1743 and *Rosamond* on 7 May 1743. Here, on 9 January 1744, she made her first attempt at straight acting, in the comic character of Marge in *The Dragon of Wantley.* Also in the cast was James Worsdale, who later was to remember her in his will.

Returning with her husband in September 1744 to London, where they took up lodgings next door to the Crown in Great Queen Street, Mrs Arne accepted frequent specialty singing engagements at Drury Lane and elsewhere. At Drury Lane on 14 January 1745 she made her "1st appearance in England for three years" as the Nymph and Sabrina in *Comus.* Her introduction of her husband's many songs at Vauxhall and at the other pleasure gardens during these years did much to increase their popularity. In 1748–49 she returned to Dublin, without her husband but accompanied by her sister Isabella (now Mrs J. F. Lampe). While there she suffered from a nagging illness which prevented her singing in the early part of the season, but later she performed in a number of Handel's oratorios, including *Esther, Solomon,* and *Acis and Galatea.* In the last one she shared a benefit with her sister on 7 February 1749.

Upon her return to London she was engaged at Covent Garden for the seasons 1750–51 and 1751–52. At a benefit for Master Michael Arne at the Haymarket on 5 February 1751 she sang on a program dominated by the family: she and Master Michael sang a *pasticcio,* Michael played his father's new concerto on the organ, and finally she and Michael performed in *The Judgment of Paris.* Also at the Haymarket she sang the part of Britannia in the first performance of her husband's *Eliza* on 29 May 1754.

The Arnes were again in Dublin for the season 1755–56, having taken with them her sister Esther Young and her nieces Elizabeth and Polly Young. Also in the party was Miss Charlotte Brent, Arne's pupil, who made her first theatrical appearance there on 29 November 1755, singing in his *Eliza,* and who was soon to become the darling of London.

It was at Dublin that Mrs Arne's health and marriage began to deteriorate seriously. Arne had not been a model husband. He was a man of erratic and sometimes mean temperament; and no doubt his wife's recurring illnesses, which often kept her from work and delayed his business, did not support his patience in domestic crises. He had some reputation as well for being unfaithful, and certainly the presence of Charlotte Brent could have been no solace to Mrs Arne. Biographers of the Arnes have usually made Cecilia a waning innocent victim of her husband's indignities, yet in fairness to him it must be said that he was not wholly the villain. According to Letitia Pilkington's young son James, who had been an apprentice in the Arne household, Cecilia Arne was "prodigiously fond of gin" to the extent that "she used to take so much of it that she seldom knew what she did." One time the boy saw her strike her husband— whom Pilkington said was "really a good natured man"—over some dispute about missing music books, and then she made such a fuss she persuaded Arne to beat James in order to extract a confession that he had stolen them. (The horsewhip was provided by Thomas Lowe, the singer who introduced Arne's "Rule Britannia" and who was a frequent visitor to the house.)

Poor James Pilkington wrote his mother that the only reason he could think of for Mrs Arne's ill treatment of him was the fact that he once saw her and Lowe "toying on the bed together."

When Arne returned to London he left his wife behind at Dublin and turned his attention to writing his pleasure-garden songs and leading comic-opera roles for Charlotte Brent. Too broken in health and spirits to continue with professional singing, Cecilia Arne fell into poor circumstances. She took on singing pupils to support herself and her niece Polly Young (later the celebrated Mrs Barthélemon), who had remained with her. (Polly's apprenticeship to the Arnes had been another cause of their marital disputes. She was just a child at this time and seems to have been raised almost entirely by Mrs Arne.) In August of 1758 Mrs Delany met Mrs Arne living in service as singing teacher to the daughter of the Bayley family in County Down and wrote of her as an "object of compassion" who looked much humbled. "She has been severely used by a bad husband, and suffered to starve, if she had not met with charitable people." Mrs Delany heard her sing to the accompaniment of nine-year-old Polly on the harpsichord. That voice which Burney so highly praised "had lost its flower," but she still sang well enough to give evidence of her training and previous charm. She and Polly were back in London by 1762, but her continuing poor health retired her from public life. The painter and sometime actor James Worsdale, alluding to the "case harden'd" heart of Dr Arne, had left her £20 in his will (written 8 October 1764, proved 2 June 1767), "independent of her cruel and unworthy husband." In 1770 she appealed to her husband through a lawyer to bring current her small allowance "which fell greatly short of supplying her with common necessaries." Arne did not respond with the dignity or charity his position would have made possible.

On 16 May 1774 she came out of retirement for one night, according to Grove "for the first time for twenty years," to sing for the benefit of Mr Barthélemon and her niece, now Mrs Barthélemon, with whom she lived her last years. It has been said that she also sang Mandane (a role which her husband wrote for Charlotte Brent) in *Artaserses* at a performance in 1769, but the only performance of this opera to be found in the *London Stage* calendars which could be remotely close was at the King's Theatre on 1 June 1769 when Mrs Barthélemon sang Mandane. (Grove suggests some confusion with Cecilia's daughter-in-law Elizabeth, Mrs Michael Arne, but Elizabeth died on 1 May 1769 after a long illness, and Michael did not remarry until 1773.)

After a separation of more than 20 years Cecilia Arne was reunited with her husband, "through the accidental agency of their great-niece, a little girl of ten," as Langley re-tells the story:

The child's mother, Mary Barthélemon . . . used to visit her uncle to receive from him her aunt's separate maintenance money, and on one occasion her daughter accompanied her. The mother declared, on leaving, that she was tired of coming continually for the same purpose and suggested that Arne should be reconciled to his wife. . . . Arne flew into a passion and became violent, whereupon the child, who was sitting on his knee, burst into tears. The old man, who was very fond of her, was so affected that a few days later he wrote to say that "if his dear old wife would be reconciled he would be happy to see her, and her nephew and niece with their dear child, at dinner on Sunday."

They enjoyed some several months of happiness together living in a house rented of Mrs Woodeville in Bow Street, Covent Garden, until he died on 5 March 1778. Perhaps in contrition, Arne left her a small estate of goods and effects, a "mangled" organ, and any profits from his musical books and manuscripts to be shared equally with

son Michael Arne. He named her as executrix of his will, to which she was granted co-administration on 16 March 1788. He also gave her the right to determine the "Probability of Success" of any future productions of his music, directing her to appoint a representative to sit in the treasurer's office to protect her interests when they should be performed. On 31 January 1778 the Drury Lane treasury paid her £15 15s. for her share of the money due to her late husband for writing new music to *Cymon*.

Mrs Arne's circumstances could not have much improved. In the spring of each season from 1778–79 through 1787–88, the managers of Covent Garden allowed her to share with their minor house servants the delivery of some tickets. Her son Michael Arne died in 1786. She died on 6 October 1789 in the house of her niece Polly Barthélemon, at Vauxhall, in her seventy-eighth year, and was buried in the vaults of St Martin-in-the-Fields. She had remained a strict and pious Catholic and, according to Langley, she died in that faith.

Between 1735 and 1750, Cecilia Arne had been one of the most pleasing singers of her day. Charles Burney, to whose morals and conduct she had given careful "parental attention" when he was apprenticed to the Arnes, said she possessed "a good natural voice and a fine shake"; she had been so well taught that in her prime years "her style of singing was infinitely superior to that of any other English woman of her time."

**Arnold.** *See also* **ARNAULD** and **AR-NOULD.**

**Arnold, Mr** [*fl. 1696–1702*], *actor.*

Mr Arnold was a minor member of Betterton's company at Lincoln's Inn Fields and may possibly have been the Michael Arnold who filed a petition with the Lord Chamberlain's office on 23 March 1664. His first recorded role was Mr Ventre in *The City Bride* in March 1696. Among other roles, he acted Alonzo in the premier of *The Mourning Bride* (probably 20 February 1697), Dowglas in the Betterton revision of *Henry IV* (9 January 1700), and the Duke of Savoy in Gildon's version of *Measure for Measure* (February 1700). His last recorded role was Lord Euphenes in the premiere of *The Stolen Heiress* on 31 December 1702. His specialties appear to have been heavy and elderly parts.

**Arnold, Mr** ₁*fl. 1771–1785?*₁, *proprietor.*

Sometime before June 1771, a Mr Arnold, goldsmith and jeweler, paid Samuel Rosomon £2500 for a fourth interest in Sadler's Wells. By 1772 Thomas King and Mr Serjeant had bought the remaining shares from Rosomon and were co-owners with Arnold. Arnold's role there, if it extended beyond that of share-holding, is not known. About 1785 Arnold and the actor Richard Wroughton bought out the interests held by King and Serjeant for £12,000.

At some point his son, "Arnold jun," inherited his interest in Sadler's Wells. He was certainly the T. Arnold listed by Charles Dibdin in his *Memoirs* as the holder of 10 shares in 1799. The remaining shares were owned then by Richard Hughes (10), William Siddons (10), Richard Wroughton (five) and William Coates (five). By 1802 T. Arnold had disposed of his shares. A Mr T. Arnold was granted a license to perform plays and entertainments at the Haymarket on 27 April 1807 and for concerts at the Pantheon from 26 May to 31 September 1809.

**Arnold, Miss** ₁*fl. 1794–1796*₁, *actress.*

A Miss Arnold played only once in London, as Rosina in the musical piece of that name at Covent Garden on 3 June 1794, billed as "Mrs Clendining's Sister (1st appearance on any stage)." A "Young Lady," also billed as Mrs Clendining's sister, played Edwin in *Robin Hood* at the Bir-

mingham theatre on 3 August 1796. Both performances were for the benefit of Mrs Elizabeth Clendining who was the daughter of a musician named Arnold from Stourhead in Wiltshire.

**Arnold, Anne.** *See* **BELFILLE, ANNE.**

**Arnold, Elizabeth** *1768–1799. See* **CLENDINING, MRS WILLIAM.**

**Arnold, Mrs Henry, Elizabeth, née Smith, later Mrs Charles Tubbs** ₁*fl. 1784–c. 1799*₁, *actress, singer.*

Presumably before she went upon the stage, Miss Elizabeth Smith married Henry Arnold at St George, Hanover Square, on 18 May 1784. There is no record of Henry Arnold's involvement in the theatrical profession at London, although he may have been the Mr Arnold who played at Cork on 29 August 1786. Perhaps he was with the Covent Garden company with his wife in 1790–91, but account book entries suggest salary payments to her only. It is believed that he died about 1790.

Mrs Arnold was first noticed in London in a chorus role in the very popular comic opera *The Woodman*, which opened at Covent Garden on 26 February 1791 and played 27 more times that season. She had, however, been placed on the pay list on 25 December 1790 at £1 5s. per week. She remained at Covent Garden through 1794–95, receiving £3 per week in her last two seasons. While there she never rose above chorus or supernumerary roles except in the instance of playing Theodosia in *Maid of the Mill* on 13 June 1795, the last time of her performing in London. Her assignments were for filling general musical chorus parts in pieces like *Zelma, Orpheus and Eurydice, Oscar and Malvina, Blue Beard, The Mysteries of the Castle,* and *Comus.* She played such specified roles as Laura in *A Bold Stroke for a Husband* on 29 May 1795 and Catalina in *The Castle of Andalusia* on 3 October 1794. Frequently she sang in the solemn dirge of the musical procession which accompanied the burial of Juliet, and once she sang in *Macbeth*, on 22 September 1794.

Mrs Arnold and her young child Elizabeth Arnold (c. 1788–1811) played at Birmingham in 1795 and then set off for North America, where their chief claims to reputation, as the grandmother and mother of Edgar Allan Poe, would be established. With her daughter, Mrs Arnold arrived at Boston on the *Outram* on 3 January 1796, and on 12 February 1796 Mrs Arnold made her debut at the Federal Street Theatre as Rosetta in Bickerstaffe's comic opera *Love in a Village*. Her daughter, Elizabeth, now about eight years old, made her debut at the same theatre on 15 April 1796 when she sang "The Market Lass" between acts of *The Mysteries of the Castle*. At Boston, Mrs Arnold played a wide variety of roles before the season ended on 16 May 1796, after which she and Elizabeth toured New England with Joseph Harper's company. They played Providence, Portsmouth, and Portland; at this last city Miss Arnold again sang in a concert on 1 June 1796.

About this time Mrs Arnold married Charles Tubbs, an actor who perhaps had been in the Boston company and on tour with her. At Portland he had advertised himself as "late of London." Mrs Arnold, now Mrs Tubbs, continued to tour with husband and daughter along the eastern seaboard. They were at Newport in the spring of 1797, and in New York that summer with John Sollée's company at the John Street Theatre. In October of that year they accompanied Sollée to Charleston. After the Charleston company closed its season on 2 May 1798, we hear no more of Mr and Mrs Tubbs. It has been suggested by some historians of the American theatre that they were victims of yellow fever.

Elizabeth Arnold continued to act in Virginia and joined the Philadelphia company for four years, 1799–1803. In July of 1802 at Philadelphia she married a young comedian named C. D. Hopkins. They continued to play in Philadelphia, Virginia, and Washington. Hopkins died on 26 October 1805. Within a month Elizabeth married another member of the Virginia Players, David Poe. As Mrs Poe, she had a varied career in Philadelphia, Boston, and New York. Her second husband either deserted her or died in 1810, leaving her with two children, one of whom was Edgar Allan Poe. Mrs Poe died at Richmond, destitute, on 8 December 1811.

**Arnold, Samuel** *1740–1802, composer, conductor, manager, organist, musical editor.*

Samuel Arnold was born in London on 10 August 1740, the son of Thomas Arnold. He became one of the most eminent musicians of the eighteenth century. Through the patronage of the Princesses Amelia and Sophia he was educated in music at the Chapel Royal by Bernard Gates (who left Arnold a small sum in his will) and Nares. He was also noticed and advised by Handel.

By the age of 23, Arnold was engaged by Beard as composer to Covent Garden Theatre. His first important success, and one which decided his close connection with the stage over the next 37 years, was on 31 January 1765 with Isaac Bickerstaffe's *The Maid of the Mill*, for which Arnold compiled and arranged a *pasticcio* of the music of about 20 other composers, including J. C. Bach, Galuppi and Jommelli, with four numbers of his own. According to *Grove's Dictionary*, "The work was one of the first, since the time of Purcell, in which concerted music was employed to carry on the business of the stage, and it was used by Arnold with great cleverness." *The Maid of the Mill* proved to be a most reliable stage piece for many years. On 6 December 1765, in the next season, Arnold provided six numbers to another *pasticcio*, Cumberland's *The Summer's Tale*, which was later revived at Drury Lane on 14 December 1771, in a revised version, as *Amelia*.

Continuing as composer to Covent Garden through 1768–69, Arnold provided music for Woodward's very successful *Harlequin Doctor Faustus* on 18 November 1766, *Rosamond* on 21 April 1767, Bickerstaffe's *The Royal Garland* on 10 October 1768, and Joseph Reed's *pasticcio Tom Jones* (after Fielding) on 14 January 1769. In May of 1769 he was paid a total of £118 18s. by Covent Garden "for composing music." On 2 June 1770 he was paid another £61 19s. as composer.

In 1769 Arnold took a lease of Marylebone Gardens, the popular out-door summer entertainment resort. For opening of the 1769 season he advertised the "very effectual drains" that had been newly arranged in the Gardens, "so that they become very dry and pleasant in a short time after heavy rains." He engaged, among other vocalists, Mrs Pinto (the former Charlotte Brent), Bannister, Mrs Barthélemon, Reinhold, and Master Brown, along with Hook as organist and music director, and Barthélemon as leader. For the Gardens on 16 June 1770 he added music to Pergolesi's *The Servant Mistress* (translated by Stephen Storace from *La serva padrona*) and on 28 August 1770 he arranged another *pasticcio, The Mad Man*. It seems that Arnold did not provide music, as sometimes stated, for Thomas Chatterton's burlettas *The Revenge* and *The Woman of Spirit*, which, although written by Chatterton for Marylebone Gardens in 1770, were in fact never produced. Arnold composed, however, for other burlettas there, including *The Magnet* on 27 June 1771 and *Don Quixote* on 30 June 1774.

In the summer of 1772 Arnold engaged the Italian pyrotechnist Morel Torré, who on 4 June arranged the fireworks in celebration of the King's birthday. Fireworks became an important feature of entertainments at Marylebone, but soon the residents of the neighborhood complained and Ar-

*Harvard Theatre Collection*

SAMUEL ARNOLD

after Russell

nold was summoned to magistrate Fielding "to shew cause why he should not pay the penalty of £5 which is inflicted by the Act of Parliament on those who cause fireworks to be made." Justice Kynaston recommended that the proprietor of Marylebone Gardens be indicted as a nuisance, but when the case came before the Bow Street Court on 1 July 1772, the matter was dismissed. Despite the fact that under his management Marylebone Gardens offered a greater variety of quality entertainment than at any other period, Arnold lost a reputed £10,000 and in 1774 was obliged to give up his lease.

During this same period, he had also turned to the composing of oratorio music. He set Brown's ode, "The Cure of Saul," for an oratorio at the Haymarket on 19 February 1768. This work, which achieved some success, was followed by *Abimelech*, *The Resurrection*, and *The Prodigal Son*, which were performed during Lent in 1768,

1773, and 1777 at Covent Garden and the Haymarket. In 1773 the University of Oxford asked his permission to perform *The Prodigal Son* at the installation of Lord North as chancellor and also offered the honorary degree of Doctor of Music to the composer. Arnold granted the request for his oratorio but declined the honorary degree, preferring to take it in the ordinary prescribed manner. When he sent his composition exercise to the Oxford professor of music, Dr Hayes, the latter supposedly returned it to him unopened, remarking, "Sir, it is quite unnecessary to scrutinize an exercise written by the composer of *The Prodigal Son*." The degree of Doctor of Music was conferred upon Arnold on 5 July 1773.

In 1774–75 and 1775–76, Arnold again composed for Covent Garden's musical productions, including Sheridan's *St Patrick's Day* on 2 May 1775. About this time the elder George Colman purchased the Haymarket Theatre from Samuel Foote, and, determined to include a great variety of musical pieces in his repertory, he hired Arnold in 1777 as his house composer and music director. For the Haymarket, under the Colmans, Arnold composed almost 100 operas, musical afterpieces, and pantomimes over the next 25 years, up to his death in 1802. Lists of his theatrical works are in Grove and Nicoll; and those published, including his many incidental songs, airs, and overtures, are listed in *The Catalogue of Printed Music in the British Museum.* The theatrical pieces included many texts by O'Keeffe (*The Positive Man, The Birthday, The Agreeable Surprise*), by the younger Colman (*Two to One, Inkle and Yarico, The Surrender of Calais, The Mountaineers*), and by his own son Samuel James Arnold (*Auld Robin Gray, Who Pays the Reckoning?, The Irish Legacy, The Shipwreck*). Others, such as Morton's *The Children in the Wood* and Boaden's *The Italian Monk*, were among the most popular pieces in the repertory.

Samuel Arnold held numerous other musical positions during his later years and was an active participant in the important concert life of the town. Arnold became a member of the Royal Society of Musicians on 4 March 1764, and in 1785 he served as a Governor, and in 1797 as a member of the Court of Assistants, of the Society. On 14 April 1773 he conducted the music which he wrote for a performance of *The Jesuit* at the Crown and Anchor. He was the conductor of the Pantheon concerts in January 1774, and he played the organ for the performances of the *Messiah* and *Ruth* at the Chapel of the Foundling Hospital on 26 and 30 March of that year. In 1776 he bought some puppets which Charles Dibdin had employed in *The Comic Mirror*, but he seems not to have put them to any use. Arnold succeeded Nares as organist and composer to the Chapel Royal in 1783 and he wrote several services and anthems in these offices. He was an assistant director of the Handel Memorial Concerts at Westminster Abbey and the Pantheon in May and June 1784. From the organ he conducted the performance of the *Messiah* at Drury Lane on 3 March 1786.

With James Wall Callcott, Arnold was associated with the founding of the Glee Club in 1787, the first meeting of which was held on 22 December at the Newcastle Coffee House. When changes in the constitution of the Academy of Ancient Music caused Benjamin Cooke to resign his conductorship in that organization, Arnold succeeded him in 1789. So strongly did Cooke feel about his treatment that he refused to belong to a small musical club called "Graduates' Meeting" which had been founded on 24 November 1790 at a meeting in Arnold's house at No 485, the Strand. Arnold was still the conductor of the Academy of Ancient Music when it closed in 1792. He was also a member of the Anacreontic Society.

At the death of Stanley, Arnold became the director of the oratorios at Drury Lane, which were performed in 1790 in opposition to those under the direction of Ashley and Harrison at Covent Garden. Adhering to a more classical line, Arnold's oratorios did not compete successfully with the more novel light compositions at the rival theatre. He directed oratorios again at Drury Lane in 1793. On 14 February he was paid by that theatre the sum of £58 16s. for "the Use of Books and Selections" for the oratorios. On 15 January 1798 he conducted oratorios at the Haymarket, and at the same theatre in the following year he conducted the *Messiah* on 24 January 1799 and *The Prophecy* on 29 March, the latter, by Thomas Busby, being a new oratorio based on Pope's *Messiah*—"the only one composed in this Country, nearly these 30 years."

Despite the financial disaster he had experienced at Marylebone Gardens some years previously, in 1794 Arnold seemed determined to put his hand back into theatrical management. From Mr Lingham he leased the Lyceum, a structure near Exeter Exchange whose rooms were used in the 1770's by the Society of Artists for exhibitions, and afterwards for occasional concerts, lectures, and dances. Intent upon musical productions, Arnold pulled out nearly the whole interior and replaced it with a combination playhouse and circus. But unable to retain a license, probably because of pressures brought on the authorities by the patent houses, Arnold was obliged to give up his scheme and return the lease to Lingham.

At the King's Theatre on 7 February 1795, Arnold directed the choruses for a revival of Bianchi's *Semiramide*. Several months later on 8 April he conducted the choir at the wedding of the Prince of Wales. In 1797 he conducted the annual concert given by members of the Royal Society of Musicians at St Paul's for the benefit of the clergy. In 1801 he was granted a license for 11 nights of oratorios at the Haymarket, on Wednesdays and Fridays between 17 February and 28 March. He re-

ceived a similar license for oratorios at the Haymarket in 1802.

Among Arnold's last works for the theatre were the overture and music for a new romantic ballet, *Corsair, or, The Italian Nuptials* on 29 July 1801, and the music for *The Sixty-Third Letter* on 18 July 1802 and *The Fairies' Revels* on 14 August 1802, all at the Haymarket. After his death some of his unperformed music was arranged by G. T. Smart for a production of Samuel James Arnold's *Foul Deeds Will Rise* at the Haymarket on 18 July 1804.

In 1793 Dr Arnold had succeeded Cooke as organist at Westminster Abbey. A few years later, coming down the steps of his library there, he fell and broke a tendon of his leg, suffering also internal injuries which eventually led to his death. He expired in

*Harvard Theatre Collection*

SAMUEL ARNOLD
by Dance

his house at No 22, Duke Street, Westminster, on 22 October 1802, at the age of 62. He was buried on 29 October 1802 in the north aisle of Westminster Abbey next to the grave of Purcell and near those of Blow and Croft. An anthem, "I heard a Voice from Heaven," written by Callcott, was sung at the funeral.

Samuel Arnold was survived by his wife Mary Ann Napier, the daughter of Dr Archibald Napier, whom he had married in 1771. His son, Samuel James Arnold (1774–1852), for whom he had a "blind affection," became a prolific dramatist and well-known London manager in the nineteenth century. Dr Arnold's elder daughter, Caroline Mary Arnold, died on 13 December 1795, at the age of 17, and was buried in the West Cloister of the Abbey. Another daughter, Marianne, married William Ayrton, the second son of the musical Dr Edmund Ayrton, on 17 May 1803. Their daughter, Charlotte, was buried at the age of nine months in the North Cloister of the Abbey on 11 March 1807.

Samuel Arnold died intestate. The administration of his goods and chattels, estimated in value at less than £2000, was granted to his widow on 6 December 1802. Further letters of administration were granted on 31 December 1812 to his son Samuel James Arnold, Mrs Arnold being then dead.

In addition to many editions of his music for the theatres, Samuel Arnold published three collections of Vauxhall songs, six eight-part overtures, and some sets of sonatas, lessons, and minuets for the harpsichord. In 1785 he published an *Ode for the Anniversary of the London Hospital*, and in 1790 a continuation of Boyce's *Cathedral Music*, in four volumes—"being a collection in score, of the most valuable & useful Compositions for that Service by the several English masters of the last Two Hundred Years." In 1786, at the request of George III, he began a uniform edition of Handel's works, eventually publishing 180

numbers in 40 volumes, but the subscription was insufficient to encourage him to complete the plan. The inaccuracies of Arnold's editing were responsible for many misreadings of Handel, until the publication of the German Handel Society's edition. In collaboration with Thomas Busby in 1786 he began to bring out a *Musical Dictionary*, of which 197 numbers were published but which was then apparently abandoned. Arnold also wrote some political squibs for Tory newspapers.

As a composer, Arnold was eminent in his day but inferior to many of his contemporaries. His dramatic music is seldom revived. Among his fellows he was apparently regarded as a generous and good-natured man. The organist Redmond Simpson by his will in 1787 left all his manuscripts and printed music to Arnold to dispose of to the best bidder "for the benefit of the Creditors of the late Edward Tams Esquire to whom I was joint Executor." Arnold was also remembered with a remainder of £50 in the will of the musician Thomas Sanders Dupuis. Among Arnold's pupils were William Henry Cutler, the singer Miss Andrews, the singer Caroline Dickons, and Benjamin Carr, who later became a composer and music publisher in America.

A pencil sketch of Samuel Arnold by George Dance, dated 25 January 1795, is in the National Portrait Gallery and was published in an engraving by William Daniell in 1812. An engraving of him from an original picture by J. Russell was published by Bellamy and Roberts in 1790. A portrait of him by his son, S. J. Arnold, engraved by W. Ridley, was published as a plate to the *Monthly Mirror* in 1803. An engraving of him was done by the artist T. Hardy.

**Arnold, Mrs Stewart, Mary.** *See* **JAMESON, MARY.**

**Arnold, T.** [*fl. 1799*], *proprietor. See* **ARNOLD, MR** [*fl. 1772–1785*].

**Arnould.** *See also* **ARNAULD** and **AR-NOLD.**

**Arnould, Mr** [*fl. 1687–1688*], *singer.*
One Arnould was listed on 5 July 1687 in the Calendar of Treasury Books for a yearly salary of £50 as a Gregorian in the Chapel Royal. The last mention of him seems to be on 20 October 1688 when he was paid for accompanying the King to Windsor.

**Arnull, Mr** [*fl. 1784–1817*], *musician.*
A Mr Arnull was listed by Doane's *Musical Directory* (1794) as an oboist, a member of the New Musical Fund, and living at No 104, Bank Buildings, Cornhill. He was doubtless the oboist who was listed variously as Arnault and Arnult among the instrumental performers in the Handel Memorial Concerts at Westminster Abbey and the Pantheon in May and June of 1784. There were two members of the Drury Lane band, one entered as Arnull, the other as G. Arnull, on the pay lists from 1812–13 through 1816–17 at £2 10s. per week; probably they were father and son.

**Aron, Robert** [*fl. 1702*], *mountebank.*
Robert Aron was one of many strollers cited as mountebanks and required to pay town constables 2s. a day, according to a notice in the *Post Man* of 8 September 1702. It is not clear whether or not he was active in London.

**Arrigoni, Carlo** *b. 1697, composer, band leader, lutenist.*
Carlo Arrigoni was born in Florence on 5 December 1697, and little is known of his early years or education. He was already thirty-one years old by the time of his first professional notice, in December 1728, when his oratorio, *Il pentimento d'Accaba*, was performed at Brussels. Sev-

eral years later, on 30 November 1731, the Dublin Academy of Music opened its new hall "for the practice of Italian Musick" under his direction, so his reputation seems to have been well established by then, and perhaps he was already a familiar figure in the Irish musical world.

Sometime in 1732 Arrigoni went to London and published his "cantata de camera." Along with several other Italian musicians, including St Martini and Pasqualino, he participated in Thursday concerts at Hickford's Room during April of 1733, at which he played his own concerto for the lute. On 7 May 1733 he played in a benefit concert for Lancetti at the disused Lincoln's Inn Fields Theatre. Apparently Arrigoni remained moderately active in the opera and concert life of London until 1736. In the figure of the "King of Arragon" he was noted as one of Handel's adversaries in Arbuthnot's satire, *Harmony in an Uproar* (1733). The Opera of the Nobility gave four performances of his opera *Fernando* (wrongly attributed by Burney to Porpora) in 1733–34. Arrigoni played the harpsichord at three evening concerts given by the Earl of Egmont at his home on 15 February and 8 and 22 March 1734. At the last of these concerts Arrigoni also sang with the Earl's daughters. There was a concert for Arrigoni's benefit at Hickford's Rooms on 27 March 1735 and another there on 5 March 1736, at which he played a solo on the lute. He performed again three days later on 8 March, for the benefit of John Clegg, at Lincoln's Inn Fields.

Leaving London about this time, Arrigoni went to Vienna, where he produced several of his cantatas and an oratorio, *Ester*, in 1737 and 1738. He returned then to Florence, his native city. In 1739, his operas *Sibace* and *Scipione nelle Spagne* were performed there during *carnavale* season.

According to early biographers, Carlo Arrigoni died in Florence on 19 August 1744, at the age of 46. However, a musician named Arrigoni, perhaps his kin, conducted concerts at Dublin from April 1758 to 1762, and when the first foreign company appeared at Edinburgh, under the directorship of Gurrini, on 21 June 1763, performing the burletta *La serva padrona*, it was reported that "Signor Arrigoni conducted the band." Gurrini's company continued its summer tour, playing in Newcastle, York, and Durham, supposedly on its way to a winter engagement at the Haymarket, but there is no record of any subsequent appearance in London. Joseph Reinagle, born in 1762, was instructed on the violin by a Mr Arrigoni.

**Arrowsmith, Daniel** ₍*fl. 1783–1794*₎, *singer, composer.*

Daniel Arrowsmith was a tenor singer in the oratorios and at the public gardens in the 1780's. In his *Reminiscences*, Henry Angelo provides a colorful memoir of Arrowsmith, claiming that the singer sponsored a benefit ball and concert for himself at the Paul's Head Tavern about 1780, in which he performed Purcell's cantata of "Mad Tom," rushing out from the closet in tattered blanket, with straw sceptre and crown, rattling his chains, much to the fright of the ladies. At the same time Arrowsmith was reputedly butler to John Poney, sword-bearer to the Lord Mayor. His master patronized his musical talent and set him up as a teacher of music. According to Angelo, he next became "a public actor on Drury Lane stage," but there is no corroborating evidence in the bills or elsewhere to this effect, although he did sing in occasional oratorios at that theatre.

Arrowsmith lived in his indulgent master's house in Took's Court, Chancery Lane, where as a teacher of singing he was "eminently clever," following the precepts of Dr Arne by insisting on proper emphasis and pathos in the expression of the words as well as the music. He was a gifted mimic and was "famed" at convivial parties for caricaturing the principal singers of the day. He was learned in the best authors, and no one, according to Angelo, could

read Milton aloud so well, except perhaps his friend Barthélemon, the singer.

Arrowsmith first sang at Vauxhall on 14 April 1783. He was received, according to a contemporary clipping, "with uncommon applause," and was encored in his two songs, probably "The top sails shiver in the wind," and "A truant tar the world I've rang'd," both written by Michael Arne, whose pupil he was. Possessed with a voice of great power and sweetness, Arrowsmith, because of his energetic and spirited manner of singing, was favorably compared to the late Vernon. Arrowsmith also composed several songs which he introduced at Vauxhall (published about 1785): "The British Sailor," "Charming Sue," and "The Heart of Oak." Other Vauxhall songs, not of his composition, included Samuel Arnold's "The Royal British Tar" (words by M. P. Andrews, 1783), Jonathan Battishill's "At Eve with the Woodlark I rest" (1785?), "The Cryer" (1784), "A Word to Wives" (1785?), and "Ode to the return of Peace" (1783), the latter three by James Hook.

Arrowsmith was one of the vocal performers in the Handel Memorial Concerts at Westminster Abbey and the Pantheon in May and June 1784, and he frequently sang the music of Arne and Handel in the spring oratorios at the Haymarket in 1784, 1785, and 1788. In the spring of 1786 he was a principal performer in the oratorios at Drury Lane under the direction of Samuel Arnold; he sang in *Messiah* (3 March) and *Redemption* (10 April). Several weeks later, on 25 April 1786, he sang Acis in *Acis and Galatea* at the Pantheon. He was a member of the company at the Royalty in 1787–88, where he sang principal roles in Carter's *The Birthday* and in the *pasticcio, Apollo turn'd Stroller*, by John Oldmixon. He also sang there on 29 September 1788, the evening of the first exhibition of Monsieur Diller's much admired Philosophical Fireworks. After this year, he seems to have left the stage.

Doane's *Musical Directory* listed Arrowsmith in 1794 as a member of the New Musical Fund, living at the Jack of Newbury, in Newbury, bearing out Angelo's statement that after quitting the stage he took an inn at his native town. It is probable that he tried his hand at theatrical management in his late years. When James Winston was gathering materials about the theatre at Newbury for his *Theatric Tourist,* he received a letter dated 10 January 1803 from a G. H. Arrowsmith there, who regretted he could provide him with no information and advised that his father, to whom Winston had addressed his inquiry, had been dead "nearly four months." The late manager, of course, may have been a relative of the musician. But if he was Daniel Arrowsmith, we can credit him with at least one son and date his death about September 1802.

**Arthur, John**  *1708?–1772, actor, machinist, manager.*

John Arthur was perhaps the John, son of Thomas and Mary Arthur, who was christened at St Paul, Covent Garden, on 23 April 1708. His early years were obscure ones. A performer by the name of Arthur appeared as a forester in *Harlequin's Contrivance* at Penkethman's Booth on 9 September 1730. Perhaps this was John Arthur's first London appearance. On 18 September 1735 a production of *The Fair Penitent* was given at York Buildings for benefit of "Mr Arthur." John Arthur's career as a harlequin was to be advanced by John Rich, under whose professional training he came in 1737–38, when he began a three-year engagement at Covent Garden. His roles that first season included Clodpole in *The Amorous Widow,* Pate in *The Northern Lass,* Johnson in *The Prodigal Reform'd,* Scroop in *Henry V,* Sir William in *Henry VI,* Antonio in *Measure for Measure,* Johnson in *The Nest of Plays,* Hearty in *The Contrivances,* and Lyrick in *Love in a Bottle.* A ballad opera of Arthur's authorship, *The Lucky Discovery; or, the Tanner of York,* was performed on 24 April 1738 and was subsequently published in that year at York. The piece became popular enough to remain in the repertory for several seasons.

In the following season Arthur added the following roles to his repertory: Seyton in *Macbeth,* Alphonso in *The Spanish Fryar,* Essex in *King John,* Scale in *The Recruiting Officer,* Trapland in *Love for Love,* and at least seven others, including Shylock. Arthur's playing of Shylock in Granville's *The Jew of Venice* at Covent Garden on 23 January 1739 proved to be the last performance of that version at a patent house. He was apparently the only actor to play the character in both the Granville version and the Shakespeare original. (He performed the latter some years later at Covent Garden 11 times between 6 April 1754 and 6 December 1757, when Macklin was absent from that theatre.) Known as a master in portraying cunning and folly, Arthur interpreted Shylock according to the comical tradition which prevailed for that role prior to Macklin.

By the end of his first four years at Covent Garden, Arthur had played at least 55 different roles in the repertory. In these early years, Arthur often played in summer at the various theatrical booths at Bartholomew Fair (1739, 1740, and 1741, when he was billed as "Arthurini") and at Southwark Fair (1741 and 1743). He was also involved with the young David Garrick in a curious invention of some kind prior to that actor's famous debut at Goodman's Fields. Garrick wrote to his brother Peter Garrick on 11 July 1741 that he was busy with Jack Arthur "upon our Catapult-Project," which he failed to elaborate upon but expressed doubts that it would turn to good account. Arthur had fitted up a shop and waited to hear from Peter Garrick on the price of a set of tools. Garrick also mentioned that Mrs Arthur had been "brought to bed," thereby providing the first notice of the obscure woman who was Arthur's first wife. She was probably the actress of that name who played later at

Bath under the management of Palmer. Apparently she never performed in London. (In 1760, a Mary Arthur was left £50 and wearing apparel in the will of the actress Margaret Woffington, whose servant she had been.) The first Mrs Arthur died at Bath on 6 August 1768. In her obituary notice, the *Bath Journal* described her as "a Woman of nice Chastity, and possess'd of the amiable wifely Qualities that render Marriage happy." It is not known if the child who brought her to bed in July 1741 survived.

Leaving Covent Garden and his salary of 6s. 8d. per day at the end of the 1740–41 season, Arthur was engaged at Drury Lane for three years. In 1744–45 he returned to Rich's employ for three more years. He rejoined Drury Lane when Garrick became manager in 1747–48 but stayed only for that season and a few performances at the beginning of the next. On 26 September 1748 he played Peachum at Covent Garden, where he was to be engaged every season from then through 1757–58. In April of 1750 he was living in Duke's Court, and by 1756 he may have been the proprietor of an establishment known as Arthur's Coffee House, which was located near the theatres. His salary at Covent Garden in 1757–58 was £8 per week. During this period he acted in the summers at Twickenham in 1749 and at Bristol in 1754 and 1756.

Arthur had a head turned to mechanics. He contrived many machines, properties, figures, and other theatrical devices which were needed by Rich in the pantomimes. Garrick, recalling their earlier venture with the "Catapult-Project," paid him £1 1s. in September 1744 for some "Faces, Asps, &c." in connection with private theatricals given by the Duke of Bedford at Woburn. No doubt he supplied Garrick with devices while employed at Drury Lane. Arthur once constructed an ass's head for a mock procession of strange figures in a dung cart, which Paul Whitehead and Carey the surgeon used to affront the Free Masons. In

*Harvard Theatre Collection*

JOHN ARTHUR
artist unknown

the 1750's, involved with William Pritchard in a premature scheme for a home and fund for infirm actors, he drew up a plan for a large building with a chapel in it, on the model of Dulwich College, but the undertaking proved too expensive and ambitious for the subscribers.

After ten years at Covent Garden, Arthur went in 1758 to act for Woodward and Barry at the new Crow Street Theatre in Dublin. Probably he was back in England by the fall of 1759, when he may have been performing in Christopher Smart's company at the Haymarket. (A five-year-old child, billed as Jeffrey Ap Arthur, possibly his son, performed a hornpipe there 21 September 1759.) At this point in his long career, Arthur turned to the more venturesome pursuits of theatrical management. He also put his hand to designing theatres, applying his years of experience in lieu of any formal training as an architect. Becoming manager, about 1760, of the Orchard Street Theatre at Bath, under the proprietorship of the elder John Palmer (d. 1788), he remodeled that building.

While at Bath he projected the building of a theatre at Portsmouth to his specifications, which, after much difficulty in finishing, he opened on 20 July 1761. Winston tells a colorful story in *The Theatric Tourist* of the stage still being waist deep in builder's shavings on noon of the opening day. Arthur surmounted his problem by "extraordinary talents and determined will." As the crowd milled outside impatient for the doors to open, the manager suddenly appeared among them "decorated with an old flapped hat, and woman's apron, grasping a broom, and peeping from a visage as black and greasy as any barn Othello in the dog days," and beguiled them with harangues and appeals until the doors opened at seven, the theatre ready to play.

But Arthur also had a knack for incurring public wrath and at Bath was frequently accused of treating his auditory with contempt. He also frequently quarrelled with Samuel Derrick, master of ceremonies at Bath. One such dispute became matter for the public press in April 1763, when Arthur refused to provide a few of his band of music to play at Anne Catley's concert for Derrick's benefit. He also tried the patience of his old friend and manager Garrick in 1766. Garrick was trying to come to terms with the young actress, Ann Reynolds, of the Bath Theatre, and Arthur, trying to dissuade her, painted so dismal a picture of London life and expenses that she drove a very hard bargain, obliging Garrick to bid higher than he wished. Garrick wrote of him to Colman, 6 March 1766, "Arthur is an old Acquaintance, but has a peculiarity in him that will not give way ev'n to his own interests."

During his tenure at Bath, he also became involved in the stage at Bristol. He played at the Jacob's Wells Theatre there in 1763 and 1764; and, in partnership with William Powell, Matthew Clark, and John

Palmer, he opened a new theatre in 1766. The building was constructed to Arthur's plans and was esteemed "in fancy, elegance, and construction" inferior to none in Europe. (In time it proved inconvenient. The dome, which was so prominent a part of Arthur's design, seriously hindered sight and hearing and had to be altered in 1778.) Garrick, who had seen the theatre rising during a visit to Bristol in the spring of 1766, supplied the prologue and the epilogue which were spoken by Powell and Arthur respectively at the opening performance on 30 May 1766. The epilogue, which Garrick had sent to Arthur with a letter of instructions on how to speak it, was published in the *Jesters Magazine*, July 1766. Arthur's connection at Bristol, however, was to be short-lived. His "insolence and tyranny" met with so much public and professional resentment that he was driven from the management. From a letter by William Powell to Garrick at the beginning of September 1766, it appears that Powell and Clark had suffered from his "repeated ill treatment" and from his "very great inattention to our success in his department." The lease of the theatre was rewritten, with Charles Holland nominated in Arthur's place.

For a time between 18 September 1767 and 31 May 1768, Arthur was acting at Bath in a strolling company managed by Roger Kemble, apparently at a locale other than the theatre in Orchard Street which he himself managed. His first wife, as noted above, died at Bath on 6 August 1768, and within a few months he married a young actress then in the Bath company, Miss Grace Read, at Bath Abbey on 29 October 1768. With his new wife, he soon was engaged in Foote's summer company at London. They appeared on the Haymarket stage on 15 May 1769 in *The Devil upon Two Sticks* and then played in many of the comic and farcical pieces presented that summer.

Arthur died at Bath on 8 April 1772,

two days after making his will, which was proved at London on 22 August 1772. He left certain tenements and messuages in trust with some Bath tradesmen for his wife Grace. She was remarried in October 1774 to the Reverend Daniel Williams at Marylebone.

In some 42 years on the stage, John Arthur played dozens of secondary roles in the eighteenth-century repertory. He was hard at work almost every night when engaged in the London theatres. He rose to no great reputation as an artist, but his abilities as a performer of old men and country squires, a line he began early in his career, and as a diverting pantomime clown were generally admired, even by his detractors at Bath and Bristol. In addition to those already cited, some of his regular roles included Couple in *The Relapse*, Foresight in *Love for Love*, Dashwell in *The London Cuckold*, Sir Politick in *Volpone*, Fernando in *The Fatal Marriage*, Don Lopez in *The Wonder*, Fondlewife in *The Old Batchelor*, Scrub in *The Stratagem*, Fluellen, Touchstone, Polonius, and Justice Shallow. In such roles as Sir Gilbert Wrangle in *The Refusal* and Trappanti in *She Would and She Would Not*, according to the critic of *The Theatrical Examiner* (1757), he had more of the spirit of pantomime about him than any person he had ever seen. The critic of *A Letter to a Certain Patentee* (1748) found him an inferior actor who had a "comical Screw of his Face," while others commented that his merit diminished when he began to speak. The most complete assessment of his abilities is found in the *Theatrical Review* of 1757–58, where it is claimed that his merit was greater than his reputation. Here he is described as an actor without false ambitions to sacrifice sense for applause, who could skillfully balance the knavery and folly of the characters he portrayed by the odd cast of his eyes, which could be very expressive of both qualities separately or at the same time. He had a face adaptable to a variety of ludicrous expressions which made laughter irresistible.

The Garrick Club has a small pencil drawing of Arthur, by an unknown artist. A small portrait of him by "T.W.," published on 2 September 1803 by S. Harding, depicts him as shrewd-looking, but not handsome, with a humorous mouth and a large nose. Davies characterized him as "a man of understanding and good observation, but the particularity of his humor often led him in whimsical distresses." Oddly enough, although a popular player for many years, he was never, so far as we know, the subject of a contemporary biographical notice or green-room memoir.

### Arthur, Mrs John the second, Grace, née Read, later Mrs Daniel Williams *[fl. 1760–1774], actress, singer.*

Grace Read (sometimes Reed), who later became the second wife of John Arthur, was likely the daughter of a theatrical family, for while she was acting under her maiden name at Bristol in 1766 and later as Mrs Arthur at the Haymarket in 1769, a Mrs Read, probably her mother, was on the same bills. Grace was doubtless the Miss Reed who made her first appearance on the London stage as Isabel in *Double Disappointment* at Drury Lane on 27 November 1760. In her first season she also played in *Agis* (23 January 1761) and created the role of Maria in *The Register Office* (25 April 1761). She shared a benefit on 29 May, at which time she played a servant in *High Life Below Stairs*. Reengaged at Drury Lane for the next two seasons, 1761–62 and 1762–63, she seldom rose to billed roles, but she did perform Arethusa in *The Contrivances*, for the first time, on 13 May 1762. Foote engaged her for his summer company at the Haymarket in 1763, where she played young ladies such as Maria in *The Citizen* and Lucinda in *The Englishman Return'd from Paris*.

Soon after, she went to play at Bath under the management of John Arthur.

When she married him at Bath Abbey on 29 October 1768, the *London Evening Post* (2 November 1768) reported she had been acting in the Bath Company for several years. Earlier that year, on 6 February 1768, she received a benefit as a member of Roger Kemble's strolling company when it visited that city. With her new husband she returned to London to play again for Foote's Haymarket summer company, making her appearance, now billed as Mrs Arthur, on 15 May 1769 in *The Devil Upon Two Sticks*. (A singer named Mrs Read, who probably was her mother, made her first appearance at that theatre as Lucy in *The Virgin Unmasked* on that same date.) That summer, Mrs Arthur also performed Sally in *Thomas and Sally*, Nell in *The Devil to Pay,* and Kitty Carrott in *The What D'Ye Call It.*

Presumably she returned to Bath with her husband, where he died on 8 August 1772, leaving in trust for her by his will certain tenements and messuages. On 8 October 1774, *Bonner & Middleton's Bristol Journal* announced that "a few days since" Mrs Arthur, the widow of John Arthur and herself formerly of the Theatre Royal, Bath, had married the Reverend Daniel Williams at Marylebone, London. This marriage is not, however, found in the Marylebone Registers. Apparently with her second marriage she gave up the stage.

**Arthur, Roger** [fl. 1669], *musician.*
On 17 December 1669 Roger Arthur and four other musicians were listed in an arrest warrant for performing without licenses.

**"Arthurini."** *See* ARTHUR, JOHN.

**Artima, Baldassare** [fl. 1669–1671], *scenekeeper.*
Baldassare Artima (sometimes Actime) worked for the King's Company at the Bridges Street Theatre in 1669–70 and probably other seasons before and after this. On 9 September 1671 he petitioned against his fellow scenekeeper Diancinto Corcy (or Jacinto Concie) for a debt.

**Asbridge, John** 1725–1800, *kettle drummer, bassoonist, piper.*
John Asbridge (sometimes Ashbridge) was a member of the Drury Lane band from at least 1771 to 1798. His name first appeared on the extant account books on 11 November 1771 when he was paid £4 4s. for "exchanging Kettle Drum banners." In 1778–79 he was paid £1 5s. per week for playing the bassoon and pipe, but all other entries, which are frequent and regular, list him as playing on the kettle drum. By 1789–90 he was raised to £1 10s. per week, and by 1797–98 he was receiving from £8 to £10 per month. Like most minor musicians, he also appeared in other concerts throughout the town. In 1783 he worked at the King's Theatre, and he played the double kettle drums in the famous Handel Memorial Concerts at Westminster Abbey and the Pantheon in May and June 1784. By this year he was a member of the Royal Society of Musicians, serving as one of the Court of Assistants at their meetings. He was also on the Society's list of those directed to play at the annual benefit concert for the clergy, at St Paul's from 1789 to 1793. He was paid £12 12s. as one of the players employed for the 1787–88 season by the Academy of Ancient Music, and he also played at Drury Lane oratorios. Doane's *Musical Directory* in 1794 gave his address as No 18, Stangate Street, Lambeth. In *Ode upon Ode* (1787), Peter Pindar (John Wolcot) called him "a Kettle-Drummer of great Celebrity."

Asbridge retired from Drury Lane at the end of 1797–98 (his last payment was £10 on 10 January 1799 for an "Old Debt," or salary arrears), probably because of illness or old age. On 13 December 1798, he had made his will, describing himself as "late of Stangate Street in the parish of St Mary

Lambeth but now of Ipswich, Suffolk, Gentleman." He died, probably in late March 1800, at Ipswich at the age of 75. Administration of his will, which was proved at London on 7 April 1800, was granted to Mary Asbridge, his widow and residuary legatee. To her he left his leasehold dwelling house in Stangate Street, Lambeth, along with the furniture, plate, china, wearing apparel, and other effects. He made bequests from a bond of £760 (dated 15 March 1784) due him from Joseph Liddell of Moor House, Cumberland, as follows: £10 to his eldest daughter, Mary Martin, wife of John Martin of Southwell, Nottingham, yeoman; all his musical instruments, goods, and implements to his son-in-law Robert William Foster (probably the theatrical musician William Foster who died in 1811); £50 to his daughter Elizabeth Sibina Porter, late of Wigton, Cumberland, but then of Maryport, of the same county, the widow of Robert Porter; £5 to John Wharton of Cockermouth, Cumberland, cooper; the residue of the £760 and interest to his wife. Executors of his will were Samuel Atkinson of Carlisle, gentleman, William Dalston of Haymarket, London, grocer, and William Bond of Tottenham Place, Tottenham Court Road, London, gentleman.

**Ash, Joe** [*fl. 1680's?*], *boxkeeper.*

Joe Ash was apparently a boxkeeper at Drury Lane and a friend of the second Duke of Buckingham. He was referred to in a letter from Buckingham to Lord Berkeley in which the Duke asked Berkeley to tell a certain lady he had resolved to swear by no other than Joe Ash, "and if that be a sin, it is as odd a one as ever she heard of." Ash may have been well off and perhaps loaned Buckingham some money.

**Ashberry.** *See* **ASHBURY.**

**Ashbridge.** *See* **ASBRIDGE, JOHN.**

**Ashbuny, Mr** [*fl. 1689*], *house servant?*

The Lord Chamberlain's accounts contain a warrant dated 15 October 1689 pertaining to a complaint by the actor Joseph Haines against several members of the United Company, including Bray the dancing master, the bookkeeper (probably John Downes), the property maker, "Ashbuny" (or Ashbury?), and Trefusis. Ashbuny may have been a house servant at Drury Lane or, like Joseph Trefusis, a minor actor.

**Ashbury, Mr** [*fl. 1767–1769*], *house servant?*

The Covent Garden accounts list a Mr Ashbury, function unknown but possibly a house servant, for the period 1767–69.

**Ashbury, John** [*fl. 1690–1700*], *fifer.*

On 12 April 1690 John Ashbury was appointed fifer in the King's Musick, replacing the deceased Clement Newth. By 1699 his yearly salary was £24, not quite half what most of the regular instrumentalists were paid and apparently the lowest salary scale in the entire group. Though there is no proof, it is possible that this John Ashbury was the same as the one who made three-keyed bassoons about 1700, no specimens of which have survived.

**Ashe, Andrew** *c. 1759–1838, musician.*

Andrew Ashe was born in Lisburn, in the north of Ireland, about 1759. His biography in Sainsbury's *Dictionary of Musicians* was taken almost *verbatim* from an autobiographical account provided by the musician himself, the holograph manuscript of which is now in the Glasgow University Library. Before he was nine years old, his parents sent him for schooling to an academy near Woolwich in England, where he developed his early great interest in music and received lessons on the violin from the master of an artillery band nearby. When he was twelve, as the result of a lawsuit which was settled unfavorably against his grandfather, his parents could no longer support his attendance at the school.

As Ashe told the story, while he was sobbing at the prospect of having to leave Woolwich, he was approached by a nobleman, Count Bentinck, a relation of the Portland family and a colonel in the British army, who arranged with the headmaster and his parents to take the lad under his patronage. Bentinck took Andrew to Minorca, where his regiment was stationed, and provided him with instruction on the violin by "an eminent Italian master." At Minorca, and in his travels with the count throughout Spain, Portugal, France, Germany, and Holland, young Ashe made extraordinary advances as a musical prodigy. While at the Hague he was introduced to a new kind of flute, with six keys, owned by the musician Sieur Vanhall, brother of the celebrated composer. To Vanhall, the keys were still only ornamental but it was said that Ashe, upon trying the instrument, found he could produce "all the half notes as full and round as the tones natural to the instrument in its unkeyed state." Ashe bought the flute at a considerable cost and, giving up the violin, devoted his practice to it. At this time, about 1774, Ashe was not yet sixteen years of age.

"Anxious to launch into the world from under the roof which had so long sheltered him," Ashe soon left Bentinck to enter the service of Lord Torrington and subsequently of Lord Dillon, both at Brussels, where in 1778 he also secured the position of first flute at the opera house. By this time Ashe accounted himself also "a general linguist, in addition to his flute playing." After a few years in Brussels, he intended to join a Mr Whyte, an Irishman and "great amateur of music," for a grand continental tour. But Whyte instead was called to Dublin. Ashe accompanied him

and by 1782 he was engaged for the Rotunda concerts there. The minute books of the Irish Musical Fund indicate that he subscribed to that society in the amount of 13s. per year from 1 January 1787 to 1 January 1791 but that on 4 April 1793 he was expelled for non-payment, a circumstance explained by the fact that in 1791 he went to London.

In 1791, Salomon brought the great composer Haydn to London and was anxious to assemble a suitable orchestra for his works. Having heard Ashe play at the Rotunda in the previous summer, he gave him "a very liberal engagement" in the concerts at the Hanover Square Rooms. Ashe made his first public appearance in London at Salomon's second concert on 24 February 1792, when he played a concerto of his own composition "which was replete with such novelty as to excite very considerable admiration." He soon became a reigning first flutist in London musical life. On 25 April 1792 he played for the oratorio at Covent Garden and in the following season, between 12 March and 12 April 1793, he played for the Drury Lane oratorios at a salary of £21 for the engagement. His other duties at the theatres included accompaniments to Mrs Crouch's renditions of "Hush Ev'ry Breeze" and Handel's "Sweet Bird" at Covent Garden on 25 April 1793, a performance which he repeated at the opening of the new Drury Lane Theatre on 12 March 1794. He also played at the Covent Garden oratorio concert on 15 April 1796.

In 1794, Ashe was living at No 28, Air Street, Piccadilly. He married a Miss Comer of Bath on 23 September 1799 in a ceremony performed at Cheltenham. A pupil of Rauzzini, as Mrs Ashe she became a principal singer at the Bath concerts, but there is no evidence that she ever performed at London. They had a numerous family, of which, in Ashe's own odd phrase in his autobiography, "nine or ten" were alive in 1823. The eldest daughter became a talented harpist and married a gentleman

# ASHLEY

of property in the West Indies. His second daughter, about 19 in 1823, was an accomplished singer and player on the *pianoforte*.

Upon the resignation of Monzani, Ashe became the principal flute at the opera, a position he held for several years during the first decade of the nineteenth century. He and his wife also performed many times at the Oxford Music Room in these years. When Rauzzini died in 1810, Ashe was unanimously elected director of the Bath and Bristol concerts, which he conducted for twelve years. In the last four years of his directorship—"the times being unpropitious for public undertakings"—he reportedly lost a considerable sum of money and relinquished his position in the winter of 1821–22. In a letter to Sainsbury written from Bath on 7 December 1823, Ashe indicated he was moving his family from that city. At the time he continued "in full possession of his powers" and "in robust health." He died at Dublin in 1838.

### Ashley, Charles Jane  c. 1773–1843, violoncellist.

Charles Jane Ashley was the son of John Ashley, the bassoonist. He was born about 1773, for he was certified to be "a single man aged twentyone years" when his father John proposed him for membership in the Royal Society of Musicians on 1 January 1794.

At the time of this proposal he was "engaged at Ranelagh, Oratorios, Covent Garden, and several concerts" and had "several scholars on the violoncello." He was elected to the Royal Society on 6 April 1794, and he attended to sign the membership book on 4 May 1794. In the years 1794 through 1799 he was a Governor of the Society. He was elected Secretary on 2 May 1811, a position he held for several years; and he was also that year a member of the Court of Assistants. "C. Ashley" was named by the Governors to play at the Society's annual May benefit concerts for the clergy of St Paul's Cathedral in 1791 and

from 1794 through 1804, but in 1803 and 1804 he requested a deputy to attend. His father left him all his musical instruments, music, and books, as well as the residue of an estate after certain annuities were paid, apparently no great sum remaining.

Ashley was one of the original members of the Philharmonic Society and a founder of the Glee Club. His address in 1794 and 1797 was No 4, Pimlico Terrace, the same as for his father John.

C. J. Ashley was a surpassingly fine performer on the cello, and he performed all over England with his father and brothers. He was repeatedly featured in the Concerts of Ancient Music. He was violoncellist for the Covent Garden oratorios every year from 1793 until at least 1805. After the death of his father in 1805 he and his brother General Christopher Ashley carried on the oratorio series. In 1817 he was a violoncellist in the band at the King's Theatre. His reputation as a cellist approached that of the great Robert Lindley himself.

Ashley was imprisoned for debt in the King's Bench Prison for 19 years. As a consequence, during his later years his health broke down. The Minute Books of the Royal Society of Musicians show payments to him for medical assistance of £10 in 1835, £26 5s. in 1836, and £4 4s. in 1840.

During the final year or so of his life he assumed the proprietorship of the Tivoli Gardens, Margate. He died on 29 August 1843 at Margate. The Administration Books of the Prerogative Court of Canterbury show a property worth some £300 granted to a creditor, one Sarah Elizabeth Oakes, his cousin John Hedgely, next of kin, failing to appear.

### Ashley, General Christopher  1767–1818, violinist.

General Christopher Ashley was born 9 November 1769 and christened that odd name at St George, Hanover Square, on 29 November, the son of John Ashley the bassoonist and Mary his wife. Very early he studied violin under both Giardini and Bar-thélemon.

The boy was bound apprentice to his fa-ther for the usual seven years on 22 Octo-ber 1784, according to the records of the Worshipful Company of Musicians. In June of 1784 he had taken part, with his father and brothers, in the Handelian com-memorative concerts at Westminster Ab-bey and the Pantheon, playing the violin. He was certainly also one of the three Mas-ters Ashley who sang "treeble" in the cho-ruses at the concerts.

When his father recommended him "as a proper person to be a member" of the Royal Society of Musicians on 3 January 1791 he was "a single man aged twenty-one years," had ended his apprenticeship, and was "employed at Ranelagh, and private concerts on the violin." He was elected to the Society on 3 April 1791, and his legal signature when he signed the Admission Book was "General Christopher Ashley."

By 1792 he was violinist and leader of the band in the Covent Garden Oratorios supervised by his father John Ashley and Samuel Harrison. He continued in this ca-pacity and as soloist until he and his brother Charles assumed the direction of the entire enterprise on the death of their father in 1805. G. C. Ashley played under the direction of Viotti in the latter's "Sym-phones Spirituales," at the Concerts of An-cient Music, and at Ranelagh. In 1794 he lived at No 4, Pimlico Terrace, the address of his father. In 1792, 1793, 1799, and 1800 he was among the musicians ap-pointed by the Governors of the Royal So-ciety to play at the May benefit concerts for the clergy at St Paul's. In 1795 he was a Governor of the Society. On 8 October 1800 he was made free of the Worshipful Company of Musicians and admitted to the livery on 6 April 1803. He seems also to have been a teacher, for the nineteenth-century musician Neville B. Challoner de-clared himself his pupil. In his father's will signed in 1804, of which with his brother

Charles he was an executor, he received only the right to moneys unspecified al-ready advanced to him.

General Christopher Ashley died in Lon-don on 21 August 1818. He was then of King's Row, Pimlico, but formerly of James Street, Westminster. His will, signed on 10 March 1817 and proved in September 1818, left the bulk of his unspecified prop-erty to his wife Sarah. Trustees and resid-uary legatees were two of his brothers, Charles and Richard Godfrey Ashley.

(Both the *Dictionary of National Biog-raphy* and *Grove's Dictionary of Music and Musicians* have furnished a nonexistent "General Charles Ashley" to whom have been assigned the few facts their writers knew about General Christopher Ashley. Documentary evidence has now relieved John Ashley of the imputed eccentricity of naming two of his sons General and two of them Charles. Another son of John the elder, Richard Godfrey Ashley, has also now been identified.)

**Ashley, Jane**  *1740–1809, bassoonist?*
Edward F. Rimbault, writing in *Grove's Dictionary*, lists a male musician, Jane Ash-ley, who was born in London in 1740 and died there 5 April 1809 and says he played the bassoon. He is called the brother of John Ashley the bassoonist. There are no records, however, of public performances by a musician of this name nor does Rim-bault give his authority for this Ashley's dates, which we have not found.

**Ashley, John**  *1734–1805, bassoonist, oratorio manager.*
The origins of John Ashley are un-known. Though he became the best bas-soonist in Britain, as well as a notable entrepreneur, and was the progenitor of a remarkable family of performing musi-cians, the names of his teachers are not known.

It is certain that the John Ashley, bache-lor, who married Mary Jane, spinster, at

St George, Hanover Square on 14 February 1769 was the musician, in view of the facts that the baptismal certifications of their sons baptized in a regular progression at the same church from 10 months after the wedding give Mary as their mother's name, and that John Ashley's will speaks of "Richard Jane, the brother of my wife."

Ashley was assistant to Joah Bates in conducting the first Handel Memorial Concerts at Westminster Abbey and the Pantheon on 26, 27, and 29 May and on 3 and 5 June 1784. On these occasions also he personally reintroduced the contra bassoon, which had been abandoned in England after Handel's use in 1749. All four of Ashley's talented sons, General Christopher (1769–1818), John James (1771–1815), Charles Jane (c. 1773–1843), and Richard Godfrey (1774–1836) were present at these festivals, performing on instruments, and three of them sang. (The boys also seem to have attracted attention by nailing the coattails of an Italian musician to his chair and filling his viol with pennies, precipitating a disturbance which caused King George III to send an equerry to inquire into its cause.)

John Ashley was a prominent member of the bands at the Concerts of Ancient Music, and at Ranelagh Gardens. He was also the first bassoon in the band at Covent Garden Theatre. A payment-roster of the Academy of Ancient Music for the 1787–88 season bears the notation: "Bassoon (£6), Violin (£6), Violoncello (£4 / 4), Tenor (£4 / 4), Violin (£4 / 4) – John Ashley, for Self & sons." For many years he and his sons were especially identified with the Lenten Oratorios at Covent Garden Theatre. John Ashley assisted Samuel Harrison in their management from 1791, and from 1795 until his death in 1805 he took over their entire direction. On 28 March 1800 he stole a march on his rival, John Peter Salomon, who had urged Franz Joseph Haydn to attempt his first oratorio, *The Creation,* by producing that work at Covent Garden before Salomon could prepare a production. Salomon struck back by alleging in the newspapers that only he had been given an early copy and had been "favoured by [Haydn] exclusively with particular directions on the style and manner in which it must be executed," to which allegation John Ashley defensively detailed the provenance of his copy and instructions.

Ashley was also in demand outside London, playing solos at the second Chester Musical Festival held in September 1783 and at the Three Choirs Festival at Worcester in 1788. He was made free of the Worshipful Company of Musicians 28 October 1771 and admitted to livery on 24 December 1792. The minutes of the Royal Society of Musicians show him to have been a member of its Court of Assistants in 1785 and from 1794 through 1800, and he was a Governor of the Society in 1796. (They also reflect but do not explain a quarrel he had with J. B. Cramer in 1789.)

Ashley was a competent teacher of instruments and of singing. Among his pupils were the virtuoso John White, whom he taught singing, thoroughbass, and organ, and the notable Eliza Salmon, whom he introduced to the public at one of his oratorios in 1803. By the terms of John Ashley's will, dated 6 July 1804, with a codicil 19 January 1805, he asked his executors, his sons Charles and General Ashley, to administer an annuity arising from the sale of properties at Chepstow belonging to his wife's brother Richard Jane (evidently an incompetent) for the benefit of the brother and of John's wife Mary. Mary also received his gold watch. Other bequests were directed to his sons John, Charles, General, and Richard Godfrey Ashley (as detailed in their entries).

On 19 May 1765 at St Paul, Covent Garden, "John Ashley of this Parish, *Widower,* and Sarah Collins of this Parish, Spinster," were married. A Charles Ashley witnessed. Who this John Ashley was is beyond verification, but it is at least possible that he was the father of the John Ashley of this entry.

John Ashley is sometimes confused with the Bath, Bristol, (and perhaps London) musicians, John and his brother Josiah Ashley, and in view of this fact, it may be well to give a biographical note on John Ashley of Bath, who was also a bassoonist: In a letter to the musical biographer Sainsbury, he described himself as having, in 1823, performed "on the Bassoon at the Bath Concerts and Theatre nearly half a century." He said he was also a vocalist at the concerts, Harmonic Society, and Vauxhall Gardens in that city. He boasted that he had published "more Ballads and Songs, serious and comic" sung by singers like Braham, Chatterly, Bannister, and Mathews "than any English man now living."

**Ashley, John James** *1771–1815, organist, violist, drummer, pianist, composer.*

John James Ashley, son of John and Mary Ashley, was born in London on 6 March and baptized on 15 March 1771 at St George, Hanover Square. He was first a pupil of Johann Schröeter and then was bound apprentice for seven years to his father, the bassoonist, on 15 October 1787.

When his father proposed him for membership in the Royal Society of Musicians on 1 April 1792, he was single, sang tenor, performed "on the organ, violin, and tenor," and was "employed at Ranelagh, the oratorios in Covent Gardens and at private concerts." He was at that time organist of Tavistock Chapel and was teaching "some scholars on the piano forte."

John James performed with his father and brothers in the Handelian memorial concerts at Westminster Abbey and the Pantheon in June 1784. He played kettle drum in the Concerts of Ancient Music for several years and was for some time organist at Covent Garden Theatre. He was associated as organist with his brothers, under the direction of his father, at the

oratorios there from 1792 until after the end of the century. He was named a Governor of the Royal Society in 1795. From 1793 to 1804 he was on the list of those appointed to play in the Society's May concerts for the benefit of the clergy of St Paul's Cathedral. He was a good teacher of singing, and his pupils included Miss Capper, Mrs Vaughan, Mrs Salmon (also taught by his father), the glee composer Elliot, and Charles Smith.

John James Ashley was married to Charlotte Sophia Lockley at St George, Hanover Square, on 5 November 1793. He was left an annuity of £80 by his father's will of 1804. He died in London on 5 January 1815.

**Ashley, Richard Godfrey** *1774–1836, violist, kettle drummer, violinist, organist.*

Richard Godfrey Ashley, son of John Ashley the bassoonist and Mary his wife, was born in the parish of St George, Hanover Square, Middlesex, on 8 September 1774 and baptized at that church two days later.

He was listed by Doane's *Directory* as living in 1794 at No 4, Pimlico Terrace (the address of his father) and was said to be a performer on viola and drums. At nine years of age he had participated in the Handelian memorial performances at Westminster Abbey and the Pantheon in May and June of 1784 (no doubt he was one of the three Masters Ashley whom Burney lists as "treeble" singers). In 1794 he was engaged, as drummer, in the Covent Garden Oratorios with the rest of the family. In 1794 he was appointed by the Governors of the Royal Society of Musicians to the list of musicians who played in the annual May benefit concert for the clergy of St Paul's Cathedral, even though he was not yet a member of the Society. From 1795 through 1805 he played on that occasion either viola, violin, or drums. In 1806 he was allowed to send a deputy.

Richard was proposed for membership in the Society by his father John on 5 December 1795 and was elected on 6 March 1796. His father's proposal certified him to be single and a performer on organ, violin, viola, and kettle drums "at Covent Garden Theatre and other places."

His father John's will forgave £800 for which he was indebted to the estate and spoke of his having been placed "in a better situation than either of his Brothers are placed in."

In 1810 he was elected a member of the Society's Court of Assistants, and he was still or again one of that body in 1812, 1813, and 1819. He had become a freeman of the Worshipful Company of Musicians on 8 October 1800 and was admitted to the livery on 7 July 1802.

Richard Ashley had a long orchestral and solo concert career. He was in 1798 and afterward at Ranelagh Gardens, where his father was influential, and played also under the elder John's leadership for many years at the Oratorios, apparently continuing there after his brother assumed the directorship. He was on the roster of the King's Theatre band in 1817.

He was still called "bachelor" when at 42 he married Elizabeth Palmer, spinster, at St George, Hanover Square, on 1 April 1816. He died in London between 10 October 1836, when he signed his will, and 21 October, when it went to probate. At the time of his death he lived at Park Place, Chelsea. He left all his furniture, stocks, rents, funds, and securities to his wife, minus an annuity of £80 to Harriet Plowman, probably a daughter. The executor of this estate was to have been Francis Godwith, surgeon. But the Minute Books of the Royal Society reveal that in 1837 his possessions were sold to satisfy partially a debt of £1000 or more. On 5 March 1837 his widow Elizabeth, who was epileptic, was granted £5 for medical aid by the Society. A widow's allowance of £2 12s. 6d. was granted Mrs Richard Ashley on 5 February 1837 and on 6 January 1839 £8 was voted for the funeral of the "widow of the late Richard Ashley," although for some reason her first name is there entered as Jane.

**Ashley, William** [*fl. 1672*], *musician.*
William Ashley and sixteen others were apprehended by an order dated 2 October 1672 for playing music without a license.

**Ashmore, Frances.** *See* SPARKS, MRS RICHARD.

**Ashmore, Joseph** [*fl. 1794*], *singer.*
Joseph Ashmore was a tenor singer who sang at occasional concerts of the Cecilian Society. He also belonged to the Surrey Chapel Society. He lived at No 15, Snowhill, London, in 1794.

**Ashpey.** *See* ASPEY.

**Ashton.** *See also* ASTON.

**Ashton, Mr** [*fl. 1698*], *actor.*
In December 1698 a Mr Ashton played Nimblewrist in *Love and a Bottle* at Drury Lane; this notice may have been an error for Anthony Aston, for Aston was probably acting at Drury Lane during 1697–98 and may have started the 1698–99 season there before going to Dublin.

**Ashton, Robert** [*fl. 1675–1679*], *violinist.*
Robert Ashton was a member of the King's Musick, playing violin under Nicholas Staggins at least between 1675 and 1679 and perhaps before and after. He was probably the Ashton who was added to the regular 24 violins for the production of the court masque *Calisto* on 15 February 1675. In 1679 he was among the musicians chosen to accompany the King to Windsor from 30 June to 26 September and to Newmarket from then until 13 October. He may have been related to the other musical Ashtons of the Restoration and eighteenth century.

### Ashton, Thomas [fl. 1673], musician.

Thomas Ashton was one of the musicians playing at the Nursery, the training company of players operated by the patent houses; on 15 April 1673 he was apprehended on an unspecified charge and four days later he was discharged. He may have been related to the other musical Ashtons of the Restoration and eighteenth century.

### Ashton, Thomas [fl. 1737–1758], musician.

Thomas Ashton of Snow Hill became a Freeman of the Worshipful Company of Musicians on 31 January 1737, was admitted to livery on 17 May 1753, and was still alive in 1758. He may have been related to the musical Ashtons of the Restoration.

### Ashwin, Mr [fl. 1795–1813?], tailor, actor, dancer?

A Mr Ashwin is identified in 1795 in the accounts of the Covent Garden Theatre as the house tailor. He may also have been employed as an actor, for a Mr Ashwin is named in the bills, as a domestic in the pantomime *Raymond and Agnes* at Covent Garden on 17 February 1800, repeated 24 March and 1 May. On the roster at this time was also a dancer named Ashwin.

Some Ashwin received 12s. per week in the season of 1800–1801 and 15s. the next season. An Ashwin was again (or still) at Covent Garden in some capacity unspecified during the 1812–13 season. There was an Ashwin acting at Edinburgh's Theatre Royal in 1818–19.

Probably the scene painter named Ashwin (fl. 1793) was related to these Ashwins.

### Asker, Mrs [fl. 1782–1784], actress, equestrienne?

Mrs Asker performed with Hughes and Dibdin's Circus between about 1782 and 1784. Along with John Decastro, she left

MᴿASKINS,
*The Celebrated VENTRILOQUIST,*
*now performing with universal applause at*
SADLERS WELLS.

*By permission of the Trustees of the British Museum*

MR ASKINS

artist unknown

to join the equestrian troupe of Philip Astley in 1784. Mrs Asker acted and perhaps rode also. She was said to have had a good "breeches figure."

### Askey, Mr [fl. 1794], singer.

Mr Askey (so listed in Doane's *Musical Directory*) was an alto singer who in 1794 lived at No 4, Old Round Court in the Strand. He belonged to the Portland Chapel Society, sang at Bermondsey Spa and in the Oratorios, and subscribed to the Choral Fund.

### Askins, Mr [fl. 1796], ventriloquist.

Mr Askins, a one-legged ventriloquist from Staffordshire, performed "with universal applause" at Sadler's Wells in 1796, raising admiration by conversing with "little Tommy," his invisible interlocutor.

N. Andrews published on 1 August 1796 a coloured print depicting Askins, with a wooden leg strapped to the stump of his left thigh, attired in a long blue frock coat, buff trousers, and a black stove-pipe hat.

**Askwin, Mr** [fl. 1793], *scene painter.*
Askwin was an assistant scene painter working under the direction of Lupino at Covent Garden in September 1793.

**Aspey, Mr** [fl. 1742–1744], *singer, actor.*
Mr Aspey first appeared in a benefit performance for himself, singing three *entr'-acte* songs at Godman's Fields Theatre on 2 February 1742. The bills record only this performance and his appearance as a singing sailor in the musical play *The Queen of Spain* at the Haymarket Theatre on 19 January 1744.

**Aspine, Aspino.** *See* **Di Aspino.**

**Asselin, Mr** [fl. 1772–1775], *dancer.*
Mr Asselin was a foreign dancer who was announced as making "his first appearance in this Kingdom" in a *New Ballet* at Covent Garden on 5 November 1772. He danced again in the same piece on 10 November. On 17 November he was paid £10 10s., presumably for these two appearances. Several weeks later, on 1 December 1772, he appeared in a *New Serious Ballet* at the King's Theatre, which was repeated 8 December and periodically throughout the winter. Asselin continued to dance at the King's Theatre, in opera, during the following two seasons, 1773–74 and 1774–75. He may have been related to the Mlle Asselin who danced at London in the 1760's.

**Asselin, Mlle** [fl. 1759–1766], *dancer.*
Mlle Asselin (sometimes Anselin) ap-

peared on 10 March 1760 at the King's Theatre in a new dance of her own devising, with her pupil, "Miss Polly," a child of seven (probably Polly Capitani). Soon after, on 27 March, Mlle Asselin was announced to dance in men's clothes at the Haymarket with Sga Provenzale in *New Grand Dances*, but she sprained her ankle and Gallini took her place. Having sufficiently recovered to perform again at the King's on 12 and 14 April, she then danced a minuet with the great Noverre at the Haymarket on 5 June. It was announced on 25 August 1760 that she had been engaged for the coming season as the first woman dancer in Sga Mattei's opera company. She continued to dance at the King's opera for the next three seasons, 1760–63, and in 1765–66.

Probably she was the Asselin, "so long on our English stage," whom Elizabeth Percy, first Duchess of Northumberland, had seen as the fourth dancer in the King's Salle at Paris in May 1770. She also may have been related to Mr Asselin who danced in London between 1772 and 1775.

**Astley, Miss** [fl. 1773], *equestrienne, actress?*
Miss Astley, daughter of Edward Astley and sister of Philip Astley the equestrian and manager, rode for the latter at his circus near Westminster Bridge in 1773 and perhaps a little earlier and later. She may have been the married sister, Elizabeth Harding of Newcastle-under-Lyme, to whom Astley left £30 in his will signed in 1814.

**Astley, Edward** [fl. 1782–1793], *doorkeeper, bill-sticker, hostler.*
Edward Astley was the father of Philip Astley, the equestrian and showman. He was a native of Newcastle-under-Lyme. His primary trade was cabinet-making and veneer-cutting, but with his son's success in the hippotheatre he gravitated to the theatrical world.

Edward Astley and his son Philip were in frequent conflict and Philip left home as a boy. He was later reconciled to his father and took the older man into his London house. But on 24 December 1782 Edward Astley deposed under oath to the Lord Mayor that his son had beaten him, cast him out, and, as he wrote to a newspaper, "used him with such unbecoming abuse and scurrilous language, that the Deponent cannot, without impropriety, state the same in a public paper." He asked the public to contribute to his support by leaving donations at Astley's Punch-House on Ludgate Hill and at No 3, Reeve's Mews.

Philip Astley explained his treatment of his father by complaining that Edward had taken a place "as a doorkeeper to a place of public amusement" and would not hearken to his son's objections. The elder Astley was thereafter employed as a billsticker by his son's bitter professional rival, Charles Hughes. In 1793 he was sent by Hughes to Russia as hostler to accompany horses bought for Catherine the Great.

## Astley, John Philip Conway 1767–1821, *equestrian, actor, manager, playwright.*

John Philip Conway Astley is in some accounts called John and in others Philip, Jr. This uncertainty has made for confusion and has led even to the occasional mistaken supposition that his father, Philip Astley the equestrian, had two sons.

John grew up under his father's tutelage and learned all the techniques of equestrian manage, acrobatics, and showmanship. He was sturdy and quick and was certainly riding in the ring by 17 August 1772 when he was for the first time featured as "the greatest performer that ever appeared . . . and as a horseman, stands unparalleled by all nations." The hyperbole was justified to the public on the grounds that he was only five, so he must have been large for his age. Even allowing for the exaggeration of the playbill text, his performance seems

rather precocious. In a "most amazing equilibrium, whilst his horse is on a gallop," he vaulted, danced, and, simultaneously, played the violin.

John remained one of the chief attractions of the Astley enterprise in all the various locations—London, Dublin, Paris, and elsewhere—described below in the entry on his father. He trained horses, performed, and helped with the management. In October 1782 he was advertized as performing "A Comic Dance, called the FRENCH FARMER," in which he changed costume on his horse at full speed and then did "a Hornpipe and a Comic Flag Dance, called the GRACES." Occasionally also he devised a spectacle and directed its production. He attracted royal attention in Paris in 1783, by dancing a minuet on three galloping horses, and was inferentially twinned in artistry with the great ballet dancer Vestris (the "French Rose") by Marie Antoinette, who dubbed him the "English Rose" and presented him with a diamond-encrusted medallion. Horace Walpole wrote of him at the same period that "Mercury did not tread the air with more sovereign agility."

After about 1784 John was entrusted with the management of the Astley amphitheatre in Lambeth while his father toured in England and Scotland. Here the younger Astley presented himself as a broadsword performer, one who could vault 21 feet, and dance, fiddle, and stand on his head on horses at full speed. He rounded out his program with Signor Rossignol the bird imitator, a mandolin player, pretty equestriennes, part-singing, pantomime, and tumbling.

He had a reputation for gallantry and the *Review* of 20 June 1786 felt constrained to warn him. He "seems every night to become more and more the favourite of the town . . . We would, however, caution him against admiring the ladies too much, lest he should be thrown off the saddle." John performed in Dublin

JOHN ASTLEY, as Count Staffo
by W. Heath

pensive estate near Weybridge, Surrey, where he spent much time. He associated himself in a partnership with John Parker and William Davis, but while they throve financially John spent more than his share of the proceeds of the Royal Amphitheatre performances. Aparently exhausted by indulgence, he fell ill of a liver complaint in 1820. He died at Paris in his father's house and in the same bed in which his parent had expired, on 19 October 1821. He was buried close to his father in Père Lachaise cemetery under the inscription "The Once Rose of Paris."

J. P. C. Astley's will left everything he owned to his wife, but apparently his debts amounted to £8000, and his only real assets were the license and the Astley name. His widow nevertheless carried on his theatrical concerns for some years.

John Philip Conway Astley seems to have been handsome, witty, amiable, and vain, with a streak of indolence and one of coarseness. He was evidently talented in dancing and music and had a fecund

at Astley's Amphitheatre in Peter Street, and in January 1801 he married one of the leading dancers and equestriennes there, Miss Hannah Waldo Smith (identified erroneously by *The Monthly Mirror* as "granddaughter of the celebrated author of the *Wealth of Nations*").

On 4 May 1794 John Astley "of Hercules Hall, Lambeth," was proposed for honorary membership in the Royal Society of Musicians on the same day as his father.

Philip Astley's will left his enterprises to John in 1814, but the son did not prosecute them with vigor. Whereas his father had been not only energetic but thrifty to the point of parsimony, John let the business of the ring languish in favor of going into society. He sold the family house in London, Hercules Hall, and acquired an ex-

JOHN ASTLEY, at Versailles
artist unknown

imagination which helped him in devising pantomimes, spectacles, and equestrian dramas. He was credited with: *The Pirate*, 1800; *The Daemon's Tribunal*, 1801; *The Iron Tower, or, The Cell of Mystery*, 1801; *British Glory in Egypt*, 1801; *The Death of Abercromby*, 1801; *The Phoenix, or, Harlequin and Lillipo*, 1802; *The Silver Star, or, The Mirror of Witchcraft*, 1803; *The Man in the Moon, or, The Witches' Rout*, 1808; *The Honest Criminal, or the False Evidence*, 1808; *The Magic Pagoda, or, Harlequin's Travels*, 1808. In 1810, Astley and William Davis re-staged George Colman's *Blue Beard* as an equestrian melodrama at Covent Garden.

In 1812 W. Heath drew and engraved a portrait of John Astley as Count Staffo in *The Brave Cossack*. A colored engraving of him at Versailles, standing on the back of a running horse, is in the Sidney Bernstein collection.

### Astley, Mrs John Philip Conway, Hannah Waldo, née Smith [*fl.* 1791–1834], *equestrienne, actress, manager.*

Hannah Waldo Smith was first noticed in 1791, riding and performing in Philip Astley's Dublin company. She and John Astley, the proprietor's son, were married in January 1801. (There is no basis for the assertion published at the time of their marriage that she was the granddaughter of Adam Smith, the economist.) It is likely that she performed in London as well as in Dublin before 1801, but this is not certain. On 2 September 1803 her mother, the old actress then known as Mrs Woodham, perished in the fire which consumed Astley's Amphitheatre.

Hannah's wish to be a dramatic actress like her mother was evidently largely responsible for the introduction of the regular melodrama which was performed at Astley's after the destruction of the Royal Circus. John wrote several of his spectacle-melodramas for his wife as the heroine and

HANNAH ASTLEY, as Joanna
artist unknown

himself as the dashing mounted swain.

When Philip Astley had made his will before his death in 1814, he had stipulated that his son John was to have all the profit of the Royal Amphitheatre, but that business affairs, including rentals, should be left in the hands of the three nieces who had lived in his house, Sophia, Louisa, and Amelia Gill. He directed that, should his son die without issue (and this was the eventuality), the ownership was to be divided into sixteen shares, only two of which were allotted to Hannah Astley. Personal debts of some £8000 left by John also complicated Hannah's attempt to carry on theatrical affairs for the family. William Davis, an old associate, tried loyally to help, but a squabble over the change of name from "Astley's" to "Davis's" Royal Amphitheatre set Hannah and the Gills against him. In 1822 the antagonists engaged in costly litigation over the license without which the property was useless. Hannah and the Gills prevailed and Davis had to share the license with them.

In 1824 Davis was ousted and Andrew Ducrow and James West joined Hannah and the Gills as licensees. Ducrow put fresh spirit into Astley's, and a new era began under his management. As late as 1834 Ducrow, West, Hannah Astley, and two of the Gill sisters were still obtaining licenses for their equestrian performances.

In 1828 W. West published in the "penny plain" series an engraving of Hannah Waldo Astley, seated on horseback, as Joanna, in *Ferdinand of Spain.*

### Astley, Philip *1742–1814, equestrian, manager.*

Philip Astley was born in Newcastle-under-Lyme on 8 January 1742, the son of a cabinet-maker and veneer-cutter to whom he was apprenticed when he was nine years of age. At 17 he ran away from home after a dispute with his father and joined Colonel Elliott's newly raised regiment of light horse, the 15th Dragoons. Already in love with horses, and a good rider, he was quickly made corporal in charge of breaking new mounts and was sent to Lord Pembroke's estate at Wilton. There Domenico Angelo was instructing in horsemanship. Angelo described Philip's abilities at trick riding as astonishing even at that date.

At 19, Astley embarked with his regiment to serve with the forces of King Frederick of Prussia. He was made sergeant as a reward for putting his phenomenal swimming ability to use by saving a horse which had fallen from the deck of a transport at Hamburg. At the battle of Emsdorf he distinguished himself by capturing a French regimental standard. Again, at Warburg, he commanded a detachment which boldly pierced the enemy lines to rescue the Duke of Brunswick. For that feat Astley was promoted regimental sergeant-major. When the regiment was recalled to London,

he laid the captured standard at the feet of King George III at a review in Hyde Park and received the monarch's thanks, an episode which he recalled with pride for the rest of his life.

Astley obtained his discharge at Derby on 21 June 1766 and rode off to London on a white charger, "Gibraltar," given him by General Elliott. He was in 1766 said to be married and was perhaps the "Philip Astley, of Egham, Co Surry, B[achelor]" who married Patty Jones of the parish of St George, Hanover Square, at that church on 8 July 1765.

Astley opened an exhibition of horsemanship between Blackfriars and Westminster bridges, by some accounts as early as 1766; he was the only performer and the white horse Gibraltar was his only mount.

*Harvard Theatre Collection*

PHILIP ASTLEY

artist unknown

But he soon acquired a couple of horses at Smithfield beast market. One of them was "Billy," later known to fame as the "Little Learned Military Horse," or "Spanish Horse," who could compute, feign death, fire a pistol, do mind-reading tricks (with the aid of a human confederate), dance, and spell out "ASTLEY" by marking with his hoof in the tanbark. By 1768 Astley was a well-known entertainer and a familiar figure in London, riding his white charger through the streets distributing handbills for his performances.

At this time he exhibited both at his riding-school at Halfpenny Hatch and at New Spring Gardens, Chelsea. His wife assisted him until late summer of 1768 when the performances were closed down for the birth of his son John. In the fall Astley took a small company on a northern tour.

In 1769 Astley obtained a mortgage to the site on Westminster Bridge Road on which in 1770 rose his wooden theatre, with sheltered seats but an unroofed riding ring, which he called "Astley's Riding School." He is supposed by legend to have found on Westminster Bridge a ring worth £60, which paid for the boards in his fences. He is also said to have quieted the rearing horse of the King as a royal procession crossed Westminster Bridge and to have earned thereby a command benefit performance.

Astley had now collected a more numerous company, consisting not only of trick riders but also of Fortunelle the clown on the slack rope, acrobats like Signor Colpi, Breslau the conjurer, and some tumblers who formed the "Egyptian Pyramids; or La Force D'Herculi." Astley's wife had become a proficient in riding standing on two or three horses; and the Little Learned Horse amazed audiences with his mathematical ability. But the center of the ring continued to be dominated by Astley himself, daring disaster as he vaulted over two or three horses, rode standing with one leg

poised behind him "like Mercury flying," and took high jumps standing balanced on several horses in parallel.

Philip Astley had evidently been joined early in his success by elements of his family from Newcastle, and in 1773 there was "a young Lady (Sister to Mr Astley)" riding in the circus along with Griffin, Costetomepolitan, Huntly, and others. The bills also promised that "Between the different Exhibitions Mrs Astley, so well known for her surprizing Command over the BEES, will perform with that useful Insect really astonishing [sic]." She calmly circled the arena on horseback with swarms of bees covering her hands and arms like a muff. All of this excitement was offered for one shilling in the Riding School or two in the Gallery, a refurbished barn.

But these exhibitions were always in summer. Having equipped himself with neither license nor shelter in London for the seasons after September, Astley began to travel farther and farther from the metropolis. On 17 December 1773 the "celebrated Mr Astley and his pupils" were to be seen "at the New Circular Riding School on the Inn's Quay," Dublin. Admission was two British shillings. Performance was in the open and since cover was provided for the nobility no notice was to be taken of brief showers.

Astley was a sensation in Dublin, not only giving daily exhibitions but attracting more pupils to his equitation lessons than he could handle. Dawson engaged him and his Learned Horse to appear at Capel Street Theatre, and the horse alone was hired at Smock Alley Theatre to do a brief act with a dwarf called the Corsican Fairy.

The Astleys remained in Dublin through 9 June 1774, when Master John Astley took a benefit. They returned year after year, and in 1789 Philip erected his Royal Amphitheatre in Peter Street under a Royal Letter Patent of 23 April 1788, granted for a period of seven years thereafter, which allowed him to play between 29 October and the succeeding 29 January. He was given a monopoly of circus performances but expressly forbidden to trespass upon the prerogative of the Crow Street Theatre Royal to present regular plays.

Astley's practice of touring much of England, Scotland, and Ireland in the autumns and during the winter seasons made him from about 1773 until near his death in 1814 perhaps the most familiar theatrical figure in the three kingdoms, and he was also very well known on the Continent. His habit of erecting temporary amphitheatres (he built some 20 of them) earned him the derisory nickname "Amphi-Philip." He often remained for many weeks in the larger cities, like Edinburgh, where he usually played at Green Gardens, a sort of Vauxhall establishment. But his companies were always the authentic and full London ones. For instance, at Birmingham, one of his shorter stands, "for five nights only," on 27 to 31 December 1776 he offered tumbling by Richer, Humby, Porter, Robinson, and Phillips; slack rope dancing by Dawson and Jones the clown; and ladder and rope dancing by Caratta Ali and the Young Turk Ali and Signors Dubia and Ferzi. There was also a "Roman Battle," a pantomime, and "The Egyptian Pyramid" by 18 other performers.

As Astley travelled through the countryside *en caravane*, with his performers riding the show horses and his wagons loaded with costumes and equipment, he excited as much attention as a royal progress. But, although Charles Dibdin says that as late as 1787 Astley cleared nearly £2000 after expenses in a campaign through Liverpool, Birmingham, and Manchester, London continued to be his main bastion and chief source of supply. There he early weathered the defection of his best horseman, Charles Hughes (who went into competition from 1772 to 1775 and after 1782); and despite reverses Astley's London career was a long chain of successes.

Astley had been arrested for "illegally performing" on 14 July 1773, and his theatre had been closed for most of the summer; in October 1777 he was tried but acquitted at Kingston assize "for performing, contrary to Act 25 Geo. II, various feats of horsemanship accompanied with music." In 1778–79, determined to test this Act which limited theatrical patents to two "legitimate" theatres and the Opera, Astley put a roof on his arena. This enabled him in 1780 to advertise "Winter Evening Amusements" by candlelight, at which he displayed *Ombres Chinoises* (shadow figures he had first introduced at his Great Room at No 22, Piccadilly) along with his usual athletic melange of horsemanship, vaulting, slackrope and tight-rope dancing, and animals audacious and sagacious. From 27 December 1782 to 14 January 1783 Astley was committed to prison for defying laws regulating theatricals. He was released at the intervention of the Lord Chancellor, Thurlow, whose daughters he had served as riding master, and subsequently he encountered little trouble in renewing year after year the license granted him by the magistrates in 1784, or in playing generally what he wished. After his victory Astley celebrated by painting the interior walls of his theatre with vines and trees and renaming it the Royal Grove.

Astley had travelled on the Continent in 1782, to Brussels, Paris, and as far east as Belgrade. At Versailles Mr and Mrs Astley performed seven times in a two-week stay, gaining from the King a royal patent for exclusive performance at Paris for eight years and clearing 4,650 louis d'ors. Sir Robert Murray Keith introduced him to the Emperor at Vienna, and his exhibit of dressage and his forthright personality procured for him an invitation to the Palace. When later that year he returned to London, the King granted him a 14-year monopoly on the breaking and training of cavalry horses and hunters "in a peculiar manner, to stand the noise of drums, trumpets, music, explosion of ordnance and small arms."

In the fall of 1783 Astley had realized a long-standing wish by finally establishing a permanent base in Paris, the *circque* which survived until the nineteenth century as Franconi's. Astley answered the colors again when war broke out in 1792, re-enlisting in his beloved 15th Light Dragoons. He once more found himself the hero of an action when, at Ribecourt on 7 August 1793, he recaptured a gun which the French had taken. Presented by the Duke of York with the horses which had drawn the gun carriage, Astley auctioned them off and bought wine for his comrades.

On 16 August 1794 Astley's Amphitheatre in London burned, with all the scenery and properties, including "three excellent wigs" once the property of David Garrick. Astley obtained leave from the Duke and returned to London as the escort of Prince Ernest. He at once set about rebuilding the theatre even though Mrs Astley seems to have died only a few days after the fire. By Easter Monday of 1795 Astley was again purveying his spectacles, in "Astley's New Amphitheatre of the Arts," to a public to whom he had become a legend and an institution.

He had opened a new amphitheatre in Dublin in January 1789, and he continued to send expeditions across St George's Channel, to the growing towns of the North of England, and to Scotland. Philip suffered a dangerous burn from fireworks in 1789. He turned over the London management to his son John in 1797 and after the Peace of Amiens went to Paris to ask compensation for his Amphitheatre, which had been commandeered for quartering Revolutionary troops. War was resumed while he was in France, and English subjects were ordered interned, but he escaped by way of Germany and Holland.

In 1803 the rebuilt London amphitheatre again burned, and this time Astley was insufficiently insured and lost over £25,000. He immediately began a new building to house 2,500 spectators, which was finished in time to open on Easter Monday 1804. It had lavish interiors splendidly painted by John Henderson Grieve, the scene painter at Covent Garden. This year, also, he personally designed a fireworks display on the Thames in honor of the King's birthday. It was fired by the pyrotechnicists "Messrs Cabanell and Son, who," it was advertized, "will let [the rockets] off on the Thames this evening at different signals from Astley, Sen., who will be mounted on the Gibraltar Charger, placed on a Barge, in the Front line of the Fireworks."

In 1805 Philip Astley obtained a license, through the influence of Queen Charlotte, for the erection of his Olympic Pavilion in Wych Street, on the Westminster side of the Thames. He is supposed to have lost another £10,000 in this venture. He sold the Pavilion to Robert William Elliston in 1812 for £2800 and a small annuity, of which there was but a single payment, for Philip died in his house in the Rue de Fauxbourg du Temple on 20 October 1814. Upcott cites "gout in his stomach" as the cause of death. He was buried in the cemetery of Père la Chaise.

By the terms of his will, signed 18 April 1814, Astley instructed his trustees to sell to the best advantage his estate in France, the "Amphitheatre of Menage and Equitation" with its extensive shops and buildings in the parish of St Laurent, Paris, and to deliver the proceeds to his son John Philip Conway Astley. To John also were to go the property and profits of the Amphitheatre at St Mary Lambeth. John survived his father only seven years. At his death the much-diminished property then passed, by the entailment terms of Philip's will, to the several shareholders: Philip's nieces, Sophia Elizabeth, Louisa, and Amelia Ann Gill, who had lived with him for many years, received eight shares; another niece, Harriet Renaud Lavenu ("wife of John Baptist Lavenu") two shares (with her children Elizabeth and John as residuary legatees of all shares); Philip's nephew Robert Gill

PHILIP ASTLEY
by J. Smith

of London, one share; nephew Robert Hall of Newcastle-under-Lynne, one share; Philip's married sister, Elizabeth Harding of Newcastle, two shares; and Hannah Waldo Astley, John's wife, only two shares. The Gill sisters were made trustees, each with a yearly compensation of £32 for the duty. They also received Astley's furnishings from his mansion, Hercules Hall. Other bequests were to: Elizabeth Harding £30; Robert Gill £20; nephew Philip Taylor £10; Robert Hall £20; and Harriet Lavenu £30.

Philip Astley was a tall, well-made, and very handsome man with manners which could unpredictably change from charming to brutal, but he was generally affable, if forceful. His most prominent characteristic was courage, which he displayed impressively in all the crises of his life, on the battlefield and in the show ring, and also in the dogged combat with adversity after the fires and financial reverses which periodically threatened to overwhelm his later life. Astley was a natural leader, and had he

been born into a higher sphere he might have been a field marshal. Indeed, by 1799, the *Monthly Mirror* was referring to him as "The General." He was compensated for his lack of formal education by a natural cunning, and he was not without wit. He was well aware of his habitual malapropism and may have exaggerated it for comic effect, but he did not like people to take liberties; he was fined £5 for assaulting Rees, a mimic who "took him off" on the stage.

Astley had a stentorian voice which stood him in equal stead as a sergeant-major and a ring-master and was valuable also when he wished to overbear conversational adversaries. For four hours on Christmas Day 1788, Charles Dibdin shared a coach with Philip, who he says bawled out in a "curious rant" *ex cathedra* opinions the whole length of the journey: "he was so kind to oblige me with his idea of improving the theatres, the courts, the parliament and the nation . . . [with] new rules for making music, writing, singing, playing, and speaking English." But his blunt integrity was as unquestioned as his energy, and though he clashed with his father and treated him with disrespect and even violence, the older man seems to have been much at fault. His performers, with the single exception of Charles Hughes, apparently regarded him with amused affection mixed with awe.

Astley wrote the following works: *Astley's Method of Riding, a Preventative of Accidents on Horseback*, c. 1773; *The Modern Riding Master*, 1774, 1775; *A System of Equestrian Education*, 1801, 5 edns. to 1802; *Astley's Projects in his Management of the Horse. An Abridgement of his Book of Equestrian Education*, 1804; *Natural Magic, or Physical Amusements Revealed*, 1785; *A Description and Historical Account of the Places now the Theatre of War in the Low Countries*, 1794; *Remarks on the Profession and Duty of a Soldier*, 1794.

J. Smith drew a profile silhouette of Philip Astley, which accompanied the 1802 edition of his *A System of Equestrian Education*; and there is in the Harvard Theatre Collection an undated engraving of him seated in a conveyance, holding a horse's reins.

## Astley, Mrs Philip, Patty, née Jones
*d. 1794, equestrienne. See* ASTLEY, PHILIP.

## Aston. *See also* ASHTON.

## Aston, Anthony *c. 1682-c. 1753, actor, singer, dancer, manager, author, composer.*

Anthony Aston, alias "Mat Medley" and affectionately known as Tony, had one of the most colorfully checkered careers of any performer of his time; he dabbled in numerous trades, travelled widely, wrote wittily, hoodwinked unmercifully, performed before Parliament, and wrote delightful biographies of performers of his day—including a semi-facetious sketch of his own life which he attached to his *The Fool's Opera* in 1731 and upon which much of our knowledge of his early years must be based.

He was probably born about 1682 in the town where he was first schooled, Tamworth in Staffordshire, the son of "*Richard Aston*, Esq; Principal of *Furnivals-Inn*, and Secondary of the *King's-Bench* Office; of *Staffordshire* Extraction, [who] liv'd in *Brooke's Market*." Of the two Richard Astons in Staffordshire, the father of the actor was probably the Richard who was the third son in Edward and Dorothy Aston's family of seven children. Anthony's grandfather was the brother of Sir Edward Aston, father of Sir Walter, first Lord Aston. The actor identified his mother only as the daughter of Colonel Cope of Drumully Castle in the country of Armagh, Ireland. Aston claimed to be related to actress Anne Bracegirdle who, according to Anthony's

*Harvard Theatre Collection*
ANTHONY ASTON
artist unknown

father, came from Walsal or Wolverhampton in Staffordshire. The pedigree of the Staffordshire branch of the Bracegirdle family does show a connection with the Astons through the Chetwynds, but Anne Bracegirdle seems almost certainly to have come from the Northampton branch of the family, so any connection with the Astons would have been very distant. Anthony may, on the other hand, have been lying about his birth. Was he instead the Anthony Aston, son of Richard and Abigall, who was born in High Holborn "next Rose Ally" and baptized on 7 July 1678 at St Andrew, Holborn? He confessed to being the black sheep in an otherwise respectable family: "As for my Relations every where, I don't care a Groat for 'em, which is just the Price they set on me."

Aston's own version of his early schooling is confusing, but he probably received his "Grammatical Education" at Tamworth where, according to him, he wrote his first verses at the age of seven, after which his father moved the family to London. There the Astons lived in Brooke Market, near Furnival's Inn where the elder Aston studied and then practiced law; wishing his son to enter the legal profession, he put him to school with one Ramsay, "who first innoculated the Itch, and also good Latin." In time young Anthony became "an unworthy, idle unlucky Clerk, first to Mr. *Randal* of the Six-Clerks-Office; after that transplanted to that incomparable Man Mr. Paul Jodrel." But Aston had little interest in his duties and spent his time "making Verses, reading Plays; and, instead of going to proper Offices, I went to see *Dogget* make comical Faces in the two last Acts; This you must think gave me a Taste of the Girls, and which I am afraid I shall never leave off." Stage-struck at about 14, he left the law and embarked on his theatrical career.

Aston seems to have joined the Duke of Norfolk's company of players about 1696 when John Coysh was leading it and just before Thomas Doggett became the manager. Though his own chronology differs, it seems probable that with the strolling troupe he gained his first acting experience, that he may have played at Drury Lane during 1697–98, that when Doggett went to Ireland in 1698 Aston accompanied him, and that upon their return he performed again in London—perhaps at the Lincoln's Inn Fields playhouse where Doggett acted with Betterton's company in 1699–1700. Aston claimed to have acted at "the *Old Play-House*, and succeeded in many Characters."

It was probably after his initial fling at acting that Aston became for a brief time a soldier; he enjoyed playing the role of a rich man's son in uniform and picked up during his spell in the service some useful training which aided him in his foreign travels later. He tried his hand at other jobs too, but when and where is uncertain: as a sailor, an exciseman, a corn-cutter, and a tavern-keeper; it is likely that most of these

experiences would have come when he was a bit older.

In late 1701 he boarded the brigantine *Diligence* and sailed for Jamaica. The captain, named Walters, put Aston in irons for misbehaving with a wealthy passenger: "one *Betty Green* (who went by the Name of *Pritchard*, and was married to a Gentleman of *Lincolns-Inn*, and had a Thousand Pounds given her to quit him) would not remember or take Notice of me, because she had a great Cargo on board . . ." How much of the eleven-week trip Aston spent in confinement he failed to report.

He arrived at Kingston early in 1702 apparently, set himself up as a lawyer, and "got Money, kept my Horse, liv'd gay, boarded at my Widows, pay'd all off." Governor Selwyn invited Aston to join his regiment and assured him of the first vacant commission, but Selwyn died shortly thereafter, and his successor, Colonel Thomas Handasyde, who took office in 1703, did not show such favor to Aston. The commission did not materialize and Aston set sail for South Carolina.

His ship, again the *Diligence*, ran aground on the sands of Port Royal and was saved by a sloop from Bermuda; and though Aston was plundered by his rescuers, he finally arrived in Charleston "full of Lice, Shame, Poverty, Nakedness and Hunger." He "turn'd *Player* and *Poet*, and wrote one Play on the Subject of the Country"—which has not survived, if, indeed, it was actually written. His chief activity in Charleston, however, was in the military: he was made a Lieutenant of the Guard in one of Governor Sir Nathaniel Johnson's companies but took umbrage at the way his captain treated him and sailed away to the north.

He took a sloop to North Carolina, hoping to find passage back to England from there, but his ship encountered a storm so furious that Aston was "lash'd to the Helm to steer for twelve Hours" before the vessel was knocked to pieces and Tony was washed ashore. He returned briefly to Charleston, but in November of 1703 he sailed for New York, only to be blown ashore in Virginia and forced to travel to his destination by horse. During the winter of 1703–4 in New York he found friends and spent his time "acting, writing, courting, fighting," and then he tried for England again. This time, though his route took him back to Virginia where he was handsomely treated by Governor Nicholson, he managed to make it back home. His passage and provisions had been given to him, but when his ship anchored in the Downs on 7 August 1704, Aston was penniless, his knack for talking anyone into anything having again been exceeded only by his ability to lose whatever he gained.

He went to London and "marry'd a *Bartholomew*-Fair Lady" who acted with him for some years thereafter. Aston tried to get a commission in Colonel Salisbury's expedition to Portugal, but this never materialized—nor, apparently, did a journey to "*Hispaniola*" which Aston claimed to have made but never described. Disappointed, Aston turned again to acting "up and down in *England, Scotland, Ireland* . . . 'till I set up my *MEDLEY*—sometimes increasing, sometimes decreasing in Circumstance."

About 1706, when Aston was near 24, his son Walter was born, but this new responsibility failed to diminish the actor's wanderlust. In 1709 he took his family to Ireland, where a play by him, *Love in a Hurry*, was produced at the Smock Alley Theatre in Dublin; Aston played the role of Melanctio. According to Chetwood, the production was not successful. A second Aston play was performed and published in the same year, *The Coy Shepherdess*, a pastoral in which Mrs Aston played Pastora. Perhaps it was while the Astons were still in Ireland that Tony created his famous "Medley"—a hodge-podge of scenes from standard plays, songs, dances, monologues, and the like. He seems to have started performing his potpourri about 1710, and, with constantly changing ingredients, it was his specialty in and out of London for many years to come. He was continuing the tradition of the "drolls" of Commonwealth times and should perhaps be considered a link between these and the variety bills that became increasingly popular in the regular playhouses later in the eighteenth century.

By January 1712 Aston was apparently back in London and may have worked in Richard Estcourt's Bumper Tavern in James Street where, according to Estcourt's advertisement, the best wines from Brook and Hellier would be delivered by "trusty Anthony." In his autobiography Aston did, in fact, mention having "kept an elegant Tavern on the Parade at Portsmouth" at some unspecified point in his life, so it would hardly be surprising if he worked for a spell in a London tavern for fellow Irishman and ex-actor Estcourt. During 1712 and the year or two following there are no records of any theatrical work by Aston, though his *The Coy Shepherdess* was given an English printing this year and was performed by the Duke of Richmond's Servants at Tunbridge Wells.

By 1715 Aston was again acting in Dublin, his license to do so having been signed on 10 September of that year:

By the Lord Mayor of the City of Dublin, I do hereby give Liberty and License to Anthony Aston, gentleman, with his wife and son, and musick to exhibit and represent, within this City and the Liberties thereoff, such lawful Diversions as may tend to the innocent Recreation of all those who are willing to see the same, they behaving themselves faithfully and honestly, as becomes his Majesty's Subjects.

Aston's stay in Dublin was not long, however, for he was back in England the following year.

His return to London was by way of Bath; after performing his Medley there he came to London and advertised in the *Daily Courant* of 27 December 1716:

Tony Aston's Medley From Bath. Begins to Morrow, being Friday the 28th Instant, at the Globe and Marlborough's Head in Fleetstreet. He gives his humble Duty to the Quality, and Service to his Friends and Acquaintances, hoping they then grace his first Night, at 6 a-Clock, Price 1s. That Night's Entertainment will be, *1.* A new Prologue. *2.* Riot and Arabella. *3.* Woodcock Squib and Hilaria. *4.* Serjeant Kite and Mob. *5.* Ben and Miss Prue. *6.* Fondlewife and Laetitia. *7.* Teague. *8.* Jerry Blackacre and Widow. *9.* The Drunken Man. *10.* A new Epilogue. With Dances, and new Comical Songs. NB. All this is perform'd by Mr. Anthony Aston, his wife, and son of 10 Years only, and will continue Nightly, Bills being stuck up of the whole Entertainment, which varies each Night.

For this fairly typical bill Aston not only served as producer and actor but also wrote the music and lyrics for most of the songs, sang and danced himself, and adapted the scenes from standard plays. This particular London engagement was fairly ambitious and, by Astonian standards, remarkably permanent: the Astons stayed in the city for four months. They set up a schedule of performances every other day throughout January and February of 1717. By 14 February, perhaps because of sagging attendance, Aston found it necessary to advertise a benefit for "A Gentleman in Distress"—very likely Aston himself, whether he was in distress or not. He announced that this would be his next to last performance "at this part of the Town," but it was not; he and his family continued playing for the rest of the month, apparently to good crowds. His advertisement had worked.

By the beginning of March, Aston was encouraged enough to try a full production of *The Spanish Friar*; with an augmented company he opened at the Globe and Marlborough's Head on 2 March 1717. He ap-

parently closed after one performance, perhaps because he was encountering resistance from the patent houses; there followed a week of silence and then, on 11 March 1717, Tony advertised his Medley again. At the next performance, he announced, the audience could "hear that Surprising Musick without Wind or String"—whatever that may have been—and since Aston was going "to divert his Friends Gratis" he would have "Toothpickers to sell at 1s. each." He was obviously getting around the patent houses and the law by charging no admission and yet still getting an income; the ruse must have worked, for the Astons gave regular performances three days a week through the rest of March and April.

After April 1717 Aston must have taken to the road again; the next London notice was in December 1718 and typically quaint:

Tony Aston, from Bath:—Most humbly gives notice to the Quality and Gentry. That he hath brought to Town from Wales, an admirable Curiosity Viz.: A Mock Voice, never heard in London before. He imitates with his Voice Domestic Animals, as Cocks. Hens. Ducks, Turkey-Cocks, and Turkey Hens, Swine, Horses, Dogs. Also Ravens, Lap-wings, Sea Fowl, Sheep, Lambs. Bulls, Cows, Cats, &c. and that too after a comical manner. following them through their different passions; as Surprize; Fear, Anger, etc.; in their Eating, Walking, Converse, etc. To be heard at the Globe and Duke of Marlboroughs Head Tavern in Fleet Street at a minutes warning from 9 in the morning to 9 at night. Any Person of Quality or others may command him to their House &c by sending word to the place above. Note: Tony Aston's Medley consisting of select parts of Comedies, new Songs. Prologues. Epilogues, &c Mr Purcell's and other comical English Dialogues, is performed every Monday, Wednesday, and Friday at the place above. beginning at 6 o'clock. Pit 1s 6d being new each night.

This latest courageous stand in London did not last long: Aston performed on 3 and 26 December 1718 but not again. The next four years in his life are a blank. Perhaps he toured again, or perhaps during this period he engaged in some of the other trades he mentioned in his life sketch.

In 1722 he was in London again and at what was for him a most unlikely address: the Lincoln's Inn Fields Theatre, as a member of John Rich's patent company. On 13 January 1722 he played Fondlewife in *The Old Bachelor*, being billed as "Aston, who never appear'd upon this Stage before." On 22 January he took over Christopher Bullock's old role of Scrub in *The Beaux' Stratagem*—called then simply *The Stratagem*—and he continued acting regularly with the troupe until the middle of May. In February he scored a great success singing "The South Sea Ballad" as an added entertainment in *Harlequin Director*, and on 5 March he played Teague in *The Committee* "after the Manner of the late Mr. Estcourt" and spoke a new epilogue "in the Character of Teague riding on an Ass." For his benefit on 17 May he chose Gomes in *The Spanish Friar* and concocted a typical Astonian bill:

Amicus curiae in Re incerta cernitur. This being the last day of Term, Mr Anthony Aston of the Parish of St Andrews, Holborn. now Comedian but, olim Clerie in Cane, and Son of Richard Aston Esq. Secondary in Banco Regis, most humbly moves the two fold learned and judicious body of the Law in behalf of his Benefit Play, the Spanish Fryar with comical appurtenances to the same, more or less which are to be performed on Thursday the seventeenth instant at the Theatre Royal in Lincoln's Inn Fields, where all non appearance will thereafter be debarred contemplating his Phiz, for that bona fide he acteth there no more. NB. He also desireth the quality and gentry to whom he hath the honour to be known to accept this Advertisement in his favour, not forgetting all his acquaintance in England and Ireland, and West Indies whom he invites to prick at his Lottery Book. Tickets to be had at Belcher's Coffee House, in Brooks Market [near his father's home].

Neither all this blarney, nor a new song "representing a Hyde Park Grenadier," nor a new prologue and epilogue which he wrote and spoke managed to drum up much business: the receipts were a pitifully small £17 1s. in door money and £37 6s. in tickets.

True to his word, Aston did not return to Lincoln's Inn Fields the following season but performed his Medley at various taverns around the town from October 1723 through December 1724. His tavern-hopping suggests that he may have been staying a step ahead of the authorities, as a typical sequence of performances in December 1723 shows: on the fourth he was at the King's Arms Tavern near Temple Bar, on the tenth at the Castle Tavern without Cripplegate, on the twenty-third at the Bull Head next to Clifford's Inn, Holborn, and on the thirty-first at the Anchor and Vine in Chancery Lane. In March, as a variation, he and his family played a benefit for themselves at Rousseau's Dancing School on the fourth, were at the Blue Posts Tavern on the eleventh, the Horseshoe Tavern in Queen's Street by Little Tower Hill on the thirteenth, back at the Blue Posts on the eighteenth, and back at the Horseshoe on the twentieth. The repeat engagements suggest that the Medley was popular, but the frantic changes of place look like a clever manager baffling the bailiffs. In August 1724 Aston played at Lee's booth at Bartholomew Fair and during the fall he returned to tavern playing, but without quite the vigor of the previous season.

After a 2 December 1724 engagement at the Dog Tavern in Ludgate Street, Aston and his family packed up and headed for Edinburgh. By 10 December the *Caledonian Mercury* reported that "last night a company of comedians came to the Canongate from London"; this was probably Aston's little band, for he would just have had time to get there. After spending the winter in Edinburgh, Aston toured England; but in 1726 he returned to Edinburgh, apparently at the express invitation of the city magistrates. For his opening this year his friend Allan Ramsay wrote a special prologue in which he had Aston say

*'Tis I, dear Caledonians, blythsome Tony,*
*That oft, last winter, pleas'd the brave*
*    and bonny,*
*With medley, merry song, and comic*
*    scene:*
*Your kindness then has brought me here*
*    again*
*After a circuit round the queen of isles,*
*To gain your friendship and approving*
*    smiles.*
*Experience bids me hope: — Th[o]' south*
*    the Tweed,*
*The dastards said, 'He never will suc-*
*    ceed! . . .'*

In 1727 Ramsay also published *Some Hints in defence of Dramatic Entertainments* in which he defended Aston handsomely. After noting that Aston had a company of eleven, high expenses, and precious little profit, Ramsay praised the actors' behavior: "Mr Aston and his family live themselves, to my certain knowledge, with sobriety, justice, and discretion, he pays his debts without being dunn'd; is of a charitable disposition and avoids the intoxicating bottle." There must have been concern among some of the Scots that the players would depart with their profits, but Ramsay assured his readers that "Mr Aston is resolved to live and die in the place" — something Tony might well have told Ramsay in an expansive moment but hardly a vow such a wanderer could keep.

During the 1726–27 season Aston apparently performed unmolested, aided by Ramsay's friendship, the patronage of the Earl of Lauderdale, Lord Somerville, and Lord Belhaven, and the complacency of the obliging city magistrates. He was away between seasons, and when he returned in the fall of 1727 he found the personnel of the magistracy changed and playing prohibited.

He performed *Love for Love* anyway and was prepared to mount his next production when the "magistrates imposed a moderate fine for his contempt, discharg'd [that is, prohibited] him thereafter to act any play, farce or comedy within the liberties and caused affix a padlock upon the door of the Skinner's Hall, which he had hired and prepared for that purpose." Aston took the matter to court and finally won his right to perform, but resistance came from another quarter when, on 1 December 1727, Lady Morrison, who lived below the Skinner's Hall, petitioned the magistrates to forbid Aston's playing because the audiences on the floor above her "bended" her roof and "her house was in danger of being destroyed by the fall of the floor." Her fears of having a theatre drop in her lap were well founded: the city hired tradesmen to check the building and they reported that it was, indeed, unsafe. Aston complained, but in the end he lost his battle.

How many performances he managed to offer during these events is not known, but he certainly gave some, and he was still in Edinburgh in April when the *Caledonian Mercury* of 15 April 1728 reported another Aston incident: "We are well informed that the marriage of Mr Walter Aston with Mrs Jean Ker has been mutually declared. *Nota.* Mr Aston and his father were incarcerate [in Tolbooth] last week, as supposed to have enticed away that young gentlewoman." Shortly after this, Aston and his newly augmented family were apparently forced to leave town.

After the Edinburgh years Aston's activity outside London decreased. His son Walter was now married and soon embarked on an acting career of his own; by 1728 Anthony was nearing 50, and though his wanderlust never left him, his activity over the next 20 years was less frantic than before.

In November and December 1729 Aston was in charge of a troupe playing thrice-weekly at the "Front Long Room" next to the opera house in the Haymarket. His son Walter was in the troupe, as were the Griffins, Norris, and Mrs Spiller. On 29 November 1729 Aston played Woodcock in *Tunbridge Walks* and on 1 December Bonniface in *The Stratagem*. The troupe advertised that for four guineas they would hire out their show on alternate nights to any gentlemen interested.

In 1730–31 Aston took some time off to write *The Fool's Opera* and the life sketch attached to it, published in 1731. It was during this season that Walter Aston began his own acting career, contributing to some confusion in the bills as to whether the father or the son—or possibly even a third Aston—was referred to. On 28 May 1731, for example, an Aston shared a benefit with two others at Lincoln's Inn Fields, sang some songs, and did his "Drunken Man." This certainly sounds like Tony, yet his son Walter grew up learning the same entertainments and could have used them. Only when the bills make a distinction, as they did on 28 January 1732 when Tony played Teague and Walter played Story in *The Committee* at Covent Garden, is it possible to be certain. On 8 March 1732 the elder Aston played Yeoman in *Tunbridge Walks* at the Haymarket, clearly billed as Aston Sr, making his first appearance on that stage and coming from Lincoln's Inn Fields. It is probable that he was not permanently affiliated with any troupe. In August 1732 he acted at the Miller-Mills-Oates booth at Bartholomew Fair, and the next season he was off again doing his Medley.

By this time he was nicknamed Mat Medley, and on Fridays in December 1732, apparently in his own rooms in St Patrick's Close, he performed his potpourri. The following July he may have toured to Edinburgh again, but by August 1733 he was back, co-managing with Paget a booth at the Horn's Inn in Pye-Corner at Bartholomew Fair while his son was acting at the Lee-Harper booth. In January 1734 he was offering his Medley in taverns again, and

in July he appeared briefly at the Haymarket.

Aston was busy with a very different matter in 1735. Sir John Barnard had introduced in Parliament this year a Playhouse Bill, supposedly aimed at the theatre in Goodman's Fields but actually designed to strengthen the monopoly of the patent houses. Theophilus Cibber's *Dissertations on Theatrical Subjects* (1756) described what happened:

But when it was plainly perceived, this Bill was chiefly calculated to serve the Managers of two Theatres—it began to be treated with less respect, than it was at its first Appearance; 'till, at length, even Tony Aston (a strolling Player of Interludes) of drole Memory, was introduced to the Bar, where he pleaded his Cause, in *Forma Pauperis*, before the Honorable Ch—m—n of the C—m—te; —and, operating on the risible Muscles of the Gay, and Good-Natured, he fairly laughed it out of the House.

Aston's speech, duly published in 1735, opened with a typically jaunty introduction of himself as "their most Grave, Facetious, Profound, Whimsical, Humourous, Serious, Open and Occult Humble Servant." He then went on to report that he was in Leeds, Yorkshire, on 28 January 1735 and had an urge to come to London; on the trip he had a nightmare in which he saw a "prodigious motly Vulture with Ninety Wings and Seventy Four Claws" showing him a "Terrible BILL" and screaming "in Quakerlike Agony, 'Regulation! destruction! Acting inconsistent with Christianity! Down with the Players!'" Upon understanding that such a bill was actually before Parliament, Tony sped to the rescue. To the Lords and Commons he said, "The Joy which I conceive in this your exuberant Condescention, pumps from my Heart a Deluge of Gratitude; but I humbly hope, that the Lacrymatic Issue of the Ocular Effusion will be totally absorb'd by the Sunshine of your Goodness." Then he defended acting, remarking that it was especially useful as a device to teach clergymen and lawyers "beautiful Position, decent Action and Face, Cadence of Voice, and force of Energy." He argued that though some regulation was needed, the present bill would not help, and poor strollers like himself would be hurt by it. If "all Country Actors must promiscuously suffer by this Act," he cried, "I question if there is Wood enough in *England* to hang them all on." He claimed he was "esteem'd through the Kingdom as a top Proficient" yet the London patentees refused him work; if the bill should pass he would starve. Then he impudently threw in a puff for his Medley which he had been performing for the past 25 years and concluded by ironically begging for an exclusive patent so that "I only, and none else, may be allow'd to exhibit a Medley throughout Great Britain." Aston's mockery, plus other attacks on the bill, helped to defeat it on 30 April 1735, though the Licensing Act was passed two years later.

Aston may have gone to Ireland after his Parliamentary performance; he was there, at any rate, on 23 March 1736, doing his Medley at the music room in Crow Street, Dublin. Performances by an Aston in and around London in 1735 and 1736 must surely refer to Walter, for Anthony's relations with the patent houses and their players would have been particularly strained at this time; the assumption, for example, that Tony played Shylock at Covent Garden on 18 February 1735 must certainly be an error for his son (who was a member of the company and regularly played elderly Shakespearean roles), and since the actors at the Southwark Fair booths in August and September 1736 were from the patent houses, it is likely that the Aston playing there was, again, Walter.

In 1737–38, still advertising himself as from Bath, Aston the elder played at the George Tavern at Charing Cross on 1 May 1738, but this time it was not his famous Medley but rather "his most Learned, Serious, Comical and Whimsical Extra-Rhapsodical Declamation" for a shilling. He was apparently performing solo and added a quaint footnote: "Come this night or not at all When disput$^{ns}$ will be maintained ag$^t$ any or all who are—whimsical enough to oppose *him* in y$^e$ premises." Perhaps by this time his wife was dead; there are no further records of the Medley, which had always been a family affair, being performed.

Sometime before 14 March 1740 his son Walter died, for on that date at Mr Rainton's Crown and Cushion in Russell Street, Covent Garden, Aston exhibited his "serious and comic Oratory on the Face & Head with nine Songs all of his own making with his Drunken Man," for the benefit of the widow and three children of Walter Aston. In April Tony performed at Ashley's Punch House, Ludgate, and at the Leg Tavern, apparently with a similar entertainment.

On 26 December 1743, apparently still playing alone, Aston gave his "learned comic demonstrative Oratory on the Face, with English, Irish, Scotch and Negrie Songs, in proper Habits" at the Temple Punch House, billing himself as "Tony Aston, the oldest approv'd actor in the three Kingdoms, being deni'd his bread in both Theatres . . . He is under Misfortunes, and desires the Company of the Ingenious and Humorous." Though 61 at this time, Aston performed frequently, as though making a serious comeback, and by 22 March he had augmented his entertainment by adding Widow Motteux, an actress who had performed with his troupe in 1731 in *The Fool's Opera*. He may have intended a revival of something like his old Medley, but whether he succeeded or not is unknown, for performance records of him cease after the 1743–44 season.

In 1748 Aston published, as an addition to Cibber's *Apology*, the useful notes called *A Brief Supplement to Colley Cibber*—an attempt to augment the list of performers discussed by Cibber and describe some of their faults. It was a work written in his usual style, amusing and candid, but less fragmentary and nervous than the *Sketch* of his own life done in 1731, and not in his facetious vein. It is unfortunate that he did not at this point go back and write a fuller story of his own career and the theatrical life of his time, just as it is lamentable that so lively a performer should disappear so quietly from history. Chetwood, writing in 1749, said "I believe he is Travelling still, and is as well known in every Town as the Post-Horse that carries the Mail." Though 1753 is usually given as the year of Aston's death, precisely when and where he died is still a mystery.

One of Aston's characteristics was an engaging manner which made people forgive his faults. The *Craftsman* of 14 August 1731, for instance, cited Aston while criticizing Walpole's monopoly of governmental powers:

Tony Aston is a Monopolizer of this Kind; he plays all Characters; he fills none; he is the whole Comedy in his single Person; he receives, indeed, the Salary of Proper Actors, and this is poor *Tony's* only View; for his Plea is Necessity; he confesses his Inability to sustain so many Parts, and picks your Pocket of half a Crown, with some Appearance of Modesty; but if he should enter with the Air of a *Drawcansir*, and swear that He alone was fit to represent every Character, that He alone was fit to receive all the Pay, and that he would never permit any one else to tread the Stage, I think he would be hiss'd by the People.

And yet Aston often did try to put down all competition, but he apparently used art, not craft, and hence made few enemies. Chetwood, who apparently knew him well, wrote that on tour Aston

. . . pretended a Right to every Town he entered, and if a Company came to any Place where he exhibited his Compositions, he would use all his Art to evacuate the Place of these Interlopers . . . If he met with a sightly house, when he was Itinerant, he would

soon find the Name, Title, and Circumstances of the Family, curry them over with his humorous verse, and by this means get something to bear his Charges to the next Station.

Though Aston was frequently but a step ahead of the authorities, whatever was dishonest in his behavior often did, indeed, spring from necessity, and, when possible, he tried to rectify his wrongs. One of Chetwood's anecdotes about him is typical: Tony had stayed at the Black-Boy Inn in Chelmsford, Essex, and, unable to pay, he left his fine stage clothing in a trunk as security; unbeknownst to the landlord, the trunk had a false bottom, and Aston stole back his clothes before he left, replaced them with bricks and cabbages, and fled. But he returned later and paid his bill.

Chetwood summed up Aston's colorful career neatly: "He play'd in all the Theatres in London, but never continued long in any; his way of living was peculiar to himself and Family, resorting to the principal Cities and Towns in England with his Medley . . ." in which "between every Scene, a Song or Dialogue of his own Composition, fill'd up the Chinks of the slender Meal."

The frontispiece to *The Fool's Opera* (1731) provides the only pictures extant of Anthony Aston: in a scene from the work he is shown with a fool's cap on his head, and an oval inset, somewhat larger, gives a closeup of his lean, droll face.

### Aston, Mrs Anthony [*fl.* 1704–1735?], actress.

Anthony Aston's wife acted with her husband for three decades and toured the three kingdoms as much as he, though very little is known about her. The pair met after August 1704, she having been a "*Bartholomew*-Fair Lady" according to Aston— so perhaps she had done some performing before they met. In about 1706 she and Anthony had a son Walter who, before he was ten, joined his parents in performances of Aston's Medley, a mixture of scenes, songs, dances, and monologues that the family performed all over Great Britain for 25 years or more. About 1709 Mrs Aston was in Dublin with her son and husband and there acted Pastora in Aston's *The Coy Shepherdess* at Smock Alley. Her career presumably paralleled her husband's to about 1735, but her name was rarely mentioned in advertisements. The last specific listing of her was on 8 March 1732 when she played Lucy in *Tunbridge Walks* to her husband's Yeoman — unless this could refer to their son Walter's wife. After January 1734 Aston stopped performing his famous Medley and by the 1737–38 season the bills sound as though he was performing alone. Perhaps by this time Mrs Aston was dead.

### Aston, Walter   *c. 1706-c. 1739,* actor.

Walter Aston, usually identified in sources simply as Aston Junior or Young Aston, was born about 1706, the son of the quixotic Anthony Aston and his "*Bartholomew*-Fair Lady" wife. Walter's first appearance on stage was probably in Dublin in 1715 when the authorities gave his father a license to perform with his wife and son. His London debut was probably on 28 December 1716 at the Globe and Marlborough's Head in Fleet Street when he was advertised as ten years old. In both Dublin and London he appeared as part of his father's Medley, probably playing minor roles in scenes and possibly doing some singing or dancing. The first recorded role for him was on 26 February 1717 when he played Quicquid, "a Comical Servant" in the *Way of the Town.* For the next 15 years Walter probably barnstormed with his parents, playing chiefly in taverns or makeshift theatres all over Great Britain, though only occasionally do the bills specifically mention anyone but the elder Aston.

The family was in Edinburgh in 1728,

and on 15 April the *Caledonian Mercury,* mentioning the younger Aston by name for the first time, said, "We are well informed that the marriage of Mr Walter Aston with Mrs Jean Ker has been mutually declared. *Nota.* — Mr Aston and his father were incarcerate last week, as supposed to have enticed away that young gentlewoman." The Edinburgh *Daily Courant* of 8 April has described the affair this way: "Tony Aston the elder, and the younger, were committed to the Tolbooth, charged with carrying off a young Lady, intended as a wife to Mr Aston Jun$^r$." This new responsibility probably encouraged Walter to leave the itinerant life in a few years and embark on a career of his own.

The next year, in London, Walter was playing in a company led by his father at the Front Long Room next to the Haymarket opera house; here he acted Reynard in *Tunbridge Walks* on 29 November 1729 and Archer in *The Stratagem* on 1 December. This may have been Walter's first opportunity to make useful contacts with actors from the London patent theatres, for in the troupe were Green, the Griffins, Norris, Peters, Mrs Rhodes, and Mrs Spiller. Though Walter played in his father's *The Fool's Opera* sometime before 1731 when the work was published, by the time the new Covent Garden Theatre opened in December 1732 he had become a member of John Rich's patent company and began what was to be a fairly successful stage career of his own. Precisely when Walter made his first appearance with Rich's troupe is difficult to determine, for the bills for 1730–31 and 1731–32 do not distinguish between Walter and his father, who also appeared with the patent company. It was probably Walter who played Cogdie in *The Gamester* at Lincoln's Inn Fields on 10 January 1732, and it was certainly he who played Story in *The Committee* there on 28 January when Anthony Aston acted Teague. After this the two Astons are easier to distinguish, except for summer activity at the fairs, for Walter performed regularly at Lincoln's Inn Fields and then Covent Garden through the end of the 1737–38 season, while Anthony was at odds with the patent houses and apparently never played at them again.

Walter Aston's first important assignment was on 11 April 1732 when he played Damon in the afterpiece *Damon and Phillida*, though he may have been substituting for someone else, since he played the smaller role of Arcas on 9 May. He seems to have been used chiefly in afterpieces at first, though he occasionally played minor roles in major works: he was Blunt in *The London Merchant* on 22 May 1732, Stratocles in *Tamerlane* on 4 November, Rigadoon in *Love and a Bottle* on 30 March 1733, Renault in *Venice Preserv'd* on 12 April, and the Gentleman Usher in *King Lear* on 21 April. Though he occasionally took roles requiring singing and dancing ability, or parts in farces, he seems not to have had the musical and comic flair his father had.

As time went on, Walter Aston settled into medium-sized roles, many of them Shakespearean and many of them elderly types. By the end of the 1737–38 season at Covent Garden he had played Page in *The Merry Wives of Windsor*, Worcester in *1 Henry IV*, Stanley in *Richard III*, Brabantio in *Othello*, Scroop in *Richard II*, and Cornwall in *King Lear*. He tried two large Shakespeare roles, Shylock (in the Granville adaptation, *The Jew of Venice*) on 11 February 1735, and, at Lincoln's Inn Fields, Hamlet on 16 April 1736. Both were single performances, the attempt at Hamlet being for his benefit. His Shylock has sometimes incorrectly been assigned to his father.

Some of his non-Shakespearean roles during these years, mostly at Covent Garden but occasionally at Lincoln's Inn Fields, included Ulysses in Dryden's *Troilus and Cressida*, Cheatly in *The Squire of Alsatia*, Stanmore in *Oroonoko,* Acasto in *The Or-*

*phan*, Lucius in *Cato*, Scale in *The Recruiting Officer*, Peachum in *The Beggar's Opera*, Tiresias in *Oedipus*, and Sealand in *The Conscious Lovers*.

When he played Hamlet on 16 April at Lincoln's Inn Fields, the afterpiece was *Cleora; or, The Amorous Old Shepherdess*, "A new Pastoral. Written by Mr Aston." This might have been Anthony Aston's *The Coy Shepherdess* in a new dress, though the bill makes it look like Walter's work.

After the 1737–38 season at Covent Garden, Walter Aston's name disappeared from the bills, and he may have died sometime during the next season, for on 12 March 1740 at Mr Rainton's Crown and Cushion in Russell Street, Covent Garden, Anthony Aston performed his "Oratory" for the benefit of Walter's widow and three children.

**Atcheson, Mr** [*fl.* 1722], *actor.*

A Mr Atcheson played Dumont in *Jane Shore* on 28 June 1722 at the Haymarket with a group billed earlier as persons who had never appeared on stage before.

**Atchmet, Mrs.** *See* ACHMET, MRS.

**Atherton, Miss** [*fl.* 1732–1744], *dancer, singer, actress.*

Miss Atherton was first seen in London in the part of Flora in *The Lover's Opera* at Drury Lane on 1 May 1732. In a summer performance at Drury Lane of *The Beggar's Opera* she sang the role of Lucy and doubled as Jenny on 1 August 1732. On 17 August, also at Drury Lane, she played Prudentia in *The Devil of a Duke*. She was next noticed as a member of the company of the Fielding-Hippisley booth at the George Inn, West Smithfield, during Bartholomew Fair time, in late August. She joined the Drury Lane company as a dancer at some time before her appearance on 17 November 1732 as a milkmaid in *The Country Revels*. She repeated the role of Lucy on 18 December and sang, danced, and acted in 10 other productions during the season.

In 1733 Miss Atherton was again at Bartholomew Fair, dancing at the Cibber-Griffin-Bullock-Hallam booth. She danced as a member of the "loyal" Drury Lane company until 10 March 1734, and the next month saw her at the New Haymarket where she also performed in the following summer.

When Miss Atherton played Nell in *The Devil to Pay* at a benefit performance at Lincoln's Inn Fields Theatre on 19 June 1735, she was said, erroneously, not to have acted for two years previously. She was advertised as one "who has not appeared these three years" when she joined Charlotte Charke's Haymarket company as Melinda in *The Recruiting Officer* on 13 December 1735. On 17 December she was Lamorce in *The Inconstant* and on 19 and 20 January 1736 was both Leonora in *The Revenge* and Sukey Ogle in *The Rival Milliners*. From 23 through 26 August of that year she was at Bartholomew Fair once again, acting in the Hallam-Chapman booth. Nothing more was seen of her in London, so far as the bills show, until August of 1740, when she turned up at the Lee-Phillips booth at Tottenham Court Fair. Absent from both the winter theatres and fair booths for the next few seasons, she may have gone strolling in the country. In August 1743 she performed for Pinchbeck and Fawkes in their Great Booth at Bartholomew Fair. She is almost certainly to be identified with the actress billed as Mrs Atherton who played Polly in *The Beggar's Opera* at the James Street Theatre on 2 March 1744 and Lady Bountiful in *The Beaux' Stratagem* at Mrs Charke's booth at May Fair in June.

Most of the time she was what a later century would call an ingenue, but other parts ranged from malapert sewing girls through ladies of the town to innocent but seductive young women of high fashion. A representative list might run: Milkmaid in *Country Revels*, a country lass in *Betty*, Caelia in *The Imaginary Cuckolds*, Lady of Pleasure in *The Harlot's Progress*, Scentwell in *The Busy Body*, Harriet in *The Miser*, a Masquerader in *Ridotto al' fresco*, Doll Common in *Sir John Falstaff*, Phillis in *The Livery Rake*, Kissinda in *The Covent Garden Tragedy*, Dorothea in *Don Quixote*, and Miss Grey Goose in *The Modern Pimp*.

**Atherton, Miss** [*fl.* 1790–1791], actress.

Miss Atherton played Miranda in *The Busy Body* for a special benefit for Lee Lewes at the Haymarket Theatre on 7 March 1791. She does not seem to have appeared again on the London stage.

**Atherton, Joshua** [*fl.* 1745–1794?], musician.

A Joshua Atherton was apprenticed to the musician Miles Nightingale in London on 20 September 1745, according to the records of the Worshipful Company of Musicians in London Guildhall. Though there is no notice there of his having become a freeman of the company, he may have played professionally in London.

Joshua may possibly be the Atherton carried on the account books of the Liverpool Theatre as a musician at 15s. weekly in 1776 and 1777, summer and winter. A Mr Atherton, violinist, is listed as living in Liverpool and playing occasionally at the Manchester Music Meeting in 1794, and there was an Atherton, music seller, possibly the same, also at Liverpool that year. Joshua is less likely to be the Atherton who shared a benefit with a singer named Solomon at Harmony Hall in Charleston, South Carolina, in 1788.

**Atkins.** *See also* ATKINSON, ATKYNS.

**Atkins, Mr** *d.* 1725?, pit doorkeeper.
Probably the husband of Mrs Atkins the boxkeeper, Mr Atkins served as pit door-

keeper at Lincoln's Inn Fields during the 1723–24 season and shared a benefit on 22 May 1724. He was referred to in the theatre accounts again on 31 December 1724, but the following spring Mrs Atkins switched from the Haymarket to Lincoln's Inn Fields and styled herself Widow Atkins in the bills for her benefit on 7 May 1725; thus Atkins probably died in early 1725.

**Atkins, Mr** [*fl. 1783–1792*], *house servant.*

Atkins was a minor employee of Covent Garden Theatre from the 1783–84 season through June 1792. He is among identifiable people belonging to the house who were delivering benefit tickets at the end of each of these seasons. He was taken onto the house pay list ("replaces Crosby") on 2 December 1786, at a salary of 12*s.* per six-day week.

**Atkins, Mrs** [*fl. 1722?–1739*], *box-keeper.*

There may have been two different women named Atkins working in the 1720's at the theatres, but it seems likely that the Mrs Atkins who had benefits at the Haymarket on 28 June 1722 and 6 March 1723—with no indication on the bills of her participation or position—was the Mrs Atkins, sometimes called Widow Atkins, who served as a boxkeeper at Lincoln's Inn Fields and then at Covent Garden from 1724–25 through 1738–39. During the 1723–24 season, which is unaccounted for in the above sequences, a Mr Atkins, probably her husband, served as pit doorkeeper at Lincoln's Inn Fields. He apparently died in early 1725 and it seems probable that his widow left her job at the Haymarket and took his place, though not his particular position, at Lincoln's Inn Fields. Though the records are not complete, she appears to have had benefits

throughout the years of her affiliation with John Rich's company.

**Atkins, Charles**   *d. 1775, dancer, singer, actor.*

A Mr Atkins was on the company list at Covent Garden Theatre as a dancer in the seasons 1748–49 through 1750–51. He earned 15*s.* per week in 1749–50. He danced as "from Covent Garden" at Southwark on 18 September 1749 and performed "equilibres" on the slack rope at New Wells, Shepherd's Market, on 10 May 1750. On 3 May 1751 he appeared at Covent Garden as Doodle in *Tom Thumb*, and by 26 December 1751 presumably the same Atkins was dancing in *Harlequin Ranger* at Drury Lane. An Atkins remained on the Drury Lane payroll as an actor through the season 1760–61 and essayed many minor roles, chiefly comic. He sang and danced from time to time at Sadler's Wells from 1753 to 1755. He played for the benefit of distressed actors at Richmond on 19 June 1760.

After the season of 1760–61 this Atkins was absent from the regular Drury Lane company until his appearance on 6 December 1769 in "a New Dance call'd The English Gardeners," though he is doubtless the same Atkins who is identified as a figure dancer "not on list" by a Drury Lane account book notation of 25 October 1766. In the summers of 1767 and 1769 an Atkins danced at the Richmond Theatre and in 1771 with the Bath and Bristol company. An Atkins, probably the same, was also principal dancer at Sadler's Wells in 1772 when he lived at No 8, Martlet Court, Covent Garden. *The Miller's Song, Sung by Mr Atkins at Sadler's Wells* and *Would You Obtain the Gentle Fair* were published in 1750, as sung by him at Sadler's Wells, as was *A Term full as Long as the Siege of Old Troy* in 1760, and *The Plumber* in 1765. In 1774–75 Atkins was back at Drury Lane dancing and singing for £3 per week.

A Charles Atkins was a subscriber to the Drury Lane Fund; and a notation in the Winston transcript of the Fund Book—"d. July 1775"—connects him with the "Mr Atkins dancer" of Drury Lane who (Isaac Reed says) died on 29 July 1775.

Charles Atkins "of Marlets Court Bow Street Covent Garden . . . Dancing Master" signed his will on 29 July 1775 (if Reed is correct, the day of his death). Except for his "Topaz Ring set Round with Diamonds," and £6 for mourning dress to his brother Michael, he left his entire property, worth unspecified, to another dancer, his "Dear ffriend Catherine Valois of Covent Garden Theatre Spinster" and named her his executrix. The will was proved on 3 August 1775 when administration was granted to Miss Valois.

### Atkins, James [fl. 1794], singer.

James Atkins, bass singer living at No 8, Change Alley, Lombard Street, in 1794, must have been the brother of William Atkins, bass singer of that address. Like his brother, James belonged to the Choral Fund and had sung in both the Handelian concerts at Westminster Abbey and in the Covent Garden oratorios. He was the bass singer taken on as a chorus extra at Drury Lane from time to time between 1794 and 1799.

"A male stillborn of James Atkings" was buried in St Paul, Covent Garden, churchyard on 10 December 1794.

### Atkins, John d. 1671, composer, violinist.

John Atkins (or Atkinson) was one of the regular band of 24 violinists in the private music of Charles II and seems to have played from the very beginning of the Restoration period, receiving New Year's gifts and livery annually. His career was uneventful except for one incident: on 2 December 1661 he and five other musicians were assured that their complaints against Nicholas Lanier, the Master of the King's Musick, had been heard; Lanier had apparently prevented them from rehearsing in the violin practice room with the other members of the band, and they had complained to the Lord Chamberlain. In 1665 Atkins, along with Benjamin Brockwell, tried for a spare-time position outside the royal musical establishment and was restrained, though other members of the group were permitted such employment. Since the few songs of Atkins which have survived (in manuscript, at the British Museum and the New York Public Library) suggest possible theatrical origins, Atkins and Brockwell may have tried working at one of the playhouses.

On 15 February 1671 Thomas Finell was appointed as a replacement for Atkins, who had apparently died quite recently. On 23 June 1673 an order was issued to assure Atkins's arrears in salary going to his executors; Finell was to receive his own first year's salary in full, but after that Atkins's executors were to receive half of Finell's salary until the arrears were paid. Atkins's will has not been located, so the details of what seems to have been some litigation are not known.

### Atkins, Michael [fl. 1755–1775], singer, actor.

The Atkins who sang Demetrius in the operatic version of *A Midsummer Night's Dream* called *The Fairies* at Drury Lane theatre on 3 February 1755 was probably the senior Michael Atkins. This Atkins remained in the company through the season of 1760–61. He was also, it seems, singing in the pleasure gardens, for in 1758 was published a song *Huzza! for the tars of Old England*, as "Sung by Mr Atkins." It is possible that he was the Atkins who was an extra in Bristol in 1767, but his name does not occur in any bill of the metropolis after 1761.

The elder Michael Atkins was left a ring and a sum to purchase mourning by the will of his brother Charles Atkins the dancer, in 1775. The better-known Michael Atkins (1747–1812), the Belfast manager, was the son of this subject.

**Atkins, Michael** *c. 1747–1812, actor, manager, scene painter, dancer, composer, singer.*

The second Michael Atkins was more versatile, talented, and durable than his father Michael the singer (fl. 1755–1775). His London acting engagements, however, seem to have been confined to his early youth. He made his career virtually wholly in Ireland, and principally as manager at Belfast and its satellite theatres of Newry and Derry.

Michael Atkins the younger is almost certain to have been that Master Atkins who appeared for the first time as Flash in *Miss In Her Teens* in an all-juvenile performance at Drury Lane on 5 April 1759. The Atkins, singer and actor, who appeared at Drury Lane from 1755 through 1760–61 was his father, and it is likely that the young Michael remained at Drury Lane during a good part of the period. Cape Everard places him at that theatre in the early 1760's. But a master and a Miss Atkins were at Jacob's Wells Theatre, Bristol, in the summers of 1761 and 1762.

In 1761 young Michael played at Kilkenny several times from January to June. By 1762 he was at Smock Alley Theatre, Dublin, making his debut as Sir John Loverule and, according to Hitchcock, "Being a painter, machinist and harlequin, he that winter brought out a pantomime entertainment called *Harlequin's Funeral*, which was liked and brought some money."

There is a gap in our knowledge of Atkins until 1768 when he turned up in James Parker's company at Belfast, singing, and acting young blades like Mirabel in *The Inconstant*. He returned to Dublin's Ranelagh Gardens during the summer of 1771 to perform in the burlettas but was

again with Parker at Newry by 2 August.

In 1771–72 Atkins was lodging at Mr Lee's house in Hercules Lane, Belfast, and was on the rolls of the Belfast company of comedians. W. J. Lawrence traced many of his subsequent activities from bills and notices in the Belfast *Newsletter* and believed that his abilities as harlequin and machinist account for the epidemic of pantomimes which broke out in the Belfast theatre this season. But Michael also played a wide variety of prominent "straight" roles, including tragedy parts like Orestes in *The Distrest Mother*. On his benefit night he even danced a hornpipe. And on 2 January 1772 the Belfast physician-author Thomas Marryat brought out a comic opera the title of which has been forgotten, the music "entirely new and composed by Mr Atkins."

In the season of 1773–74 Atkins assembled a company at the Mill Gate Theatre which included Mr and Mrs Kenna from Smock Alley, Mrs Knipe, Mr and Mrs Waker, Messrs Pye and Hamilton, and Farrel, a dancer, and the Misses Farrel, his daughters. Atkins was actor and manager, living nearby with his wife at "Mrs Mountfort's, High Street." Substantially the same company was under his captaincy until 1777–78, when it was freshly augmented by Mrs Pero, the Widow Villars, Mrs Booth, and R. C. Rowe. Atkins was this year resident "at Mr Dawson's."

Atkins was at the Crow Street Theatre, Dublin, during parts of the season 1778–79 and 1779–80 but was advertised to be in his old capacity of manager at Mill Gate by 20 March 1781, when he was living "at Mr Gelston's on Hanover Quay." He was also operative there in the seasons 1781–82 and 1782–83, though the records are scarce. In 1783–84 recruiting was brisk, for Atkins not only brought in William Macready the elder and acquired Mrs and Miss Hoskins from Crow Street, Kennedy from Drury Lane, and "the celebrated Miss Jameson (confessedly the first public singer in Ireland)," but the inimitable Andrew Cherry, within a few years to reach high fame in Dublin and London as a comic actor. In 1783 when his company went on the usual tour to Derry and Sligo under his deputy John Bernard, Atkins was busy in Belfast supervising the building of a more commodious theatre.

The new house in Rosemary Lane opened in the spring of 1784. Whether it was the strength of the opposition under Myrton Hamilton, who at once enlarged his Ann Street playhouse or some other cause, the Rosemary Lane Theatre seems to have been dark in 1784 except for a performance or two in August, and Atkins himself was performing in Lisburn during part of the season.

On 3 October 1786 Atkins advertised that he had secured Mrs Achmet "the first female ornament of the Irish stage," Lee Lewes from Covent Garden, Jemmy Fotteral from Smock Alley, and Mr and Mrs Freeman from York; and he retained several of the old hands like Rowe, Tyrrel, and Mrs Collins. This fine company played until June 1787. In August Atkins added the young star Anne Brunton from Dublin, for the new season.

From 1788–89 through 1790–91 Atkins continued to strengthen his company with solid second-rate players, leavened with as many occasional London and Dublin names as he could afford: Miss Hughes, J. G. Holman, the Chalmerses, Mrs Melmoth.

After a survey determined that structural defects in the Rosemary Lane house were irreparable, Atkins once more canvassed the town for support and laid the foundation stone of the Arthur Street Theatre on 7 September 1791. It opened on 22 February 1793 but proved also to be very flimsily built: On 7 October 1794 the press of people at "Little Cherry's" benefit was so great that the floor of the pit gave way, but no one was hurt and the damage was repaired in a few days.

In 1794–95 and 1795–96 Atkins had successful seasons. But he apparently encountered financial difficulty in 1796 and was said to be acting in a barn in Dundalk in April 1797. In December 1798 he was promoting concerts at Arthur Street, but there is no record of plays there.

Out of the doldrums by 1800–1801, Atkins introduced Montague Talbot to the stage, brought in Holman, Lewis, and Mansell from Covent Garden and Hammerton from Dublin, and took the sensational singer Incledon off tour for an extended engagement. In the fall of 1802 he secured Mrs Siddons to play opposite Talbot for 14 nights.

Atkins gave William Henry West Betty, the "Young Roscius," his first professional engagement of four nights in August 1803. (Betty had been discovered by Hough the Belfast prompter, who resigned in September to accompany the prodigy on tour.)

At the end of the 1803–4 season, when Atkins advertised his benefit, he rather pitifully appealed for relief to the public, as their servant of 35 years' standing. The "heavy losses" he spoke of had been sustained partly through his efforts to obtain the best players he could find. Lawrence cites a letter from George Frederick Cooke, offering to play in Belfast for 10 nights for 300 guineas, an offer which the manager not only accepted but to which he added 100 guineas to provide for three nights at Londonderry.

In February 1805 Atkins went to London to beat up for recruits, and on 21 March came back with a dozen, including Ryley, F. G. Waldron, E. H. Ayliffe, and a thin and morose young actor named Edmund Kean, then only 18 years old. This year Atkins again indulged his strange appetite for juvenile tragedians by introducing a "Female Infant Roscius"—little Miss Mudie, six years of age—as Young Norval in Home's Douglas. The year was more seriously signalised by the last appearance in Belfast of Sarah Siddons, in a whole range of her most famous characters, and by the retirement as manager of Atkins after some 32 years in that capacity. But he did not cease from acting; and when at the end of the season he sold his theatrical rights to the singer Thomas Ludford Bellamy, he stipulated that he should remain a member of the company. His household effects at Castle Lane were sold by auction and he moved into rented rooms over McKee's confectionary shop in Ann Street. He died on 15 April 1812.

The registers of Old Parish Church, High Street, Belfast, record Michael Atkins's marriage in 1771 to Catherine Hutton, of Belfast. She was then an actress, or later became one, and performed at Belfast, Cork, and Derry until 1798. She died aged 58 on 1 October 1808. Michael and Catherine Atkins had two daughters and a son:

Miss Atkins, the elder daughter, was one of the "principal singers" at a "grand Instrumental and vocal concert" at the Belfast Theatre on 3 December 1798 and appeared from time to time in Michael Atkins's company at Belfast and Derry until about April of 1799 when a Mrs Boucheron was added, who played until 1803. The *Hibernian Magazine,* in reporting the death of Mrs Boucheron at Newry in August 1807, indentified her as the "daughter of M. Atkins."

Mary Anne Atkins, a second daughter, acted with her father in her childhood. She married William Murphy in 1808.

A son, Charles Atkins, like Michael both actor and painter, began work with his father about 1800. He was afterwards connected with the Glasgow, Aberdeen, and Bristol theatres. His daughter Katherine married the celebrated actor William Charles Macready. Charles Atkins and his son were drowned off the Welsh coast when the Liverpool packet *Alert* foundered on 26 March 1823.

### Atkins, William  *1763–1831, singer, actor.*

William Atkins, the bass singer, was born about 1763. The whereabouts of his birth and the circumstances of his parentage are unknown. He sang in the Covent Garden oratorios at some undertermined date and in the Handelian memorial concerts at Westminster Abbey and the Pantheon in May and June of 1784.

Atkins was first seen in theatrical bills at Drury Lane Theatre, singing in the chorus to *The Pirates,* on 16 May 1794. He repeated this service on 30 May. He lived at that time at No 8, Change Alley, Lombard Street. He was back in the Drury Lane company on 27 October and sang in the chorus from time to time during that season and the following one. If he was at the house in 1796–97 the fact is not recorded in the playbills, but he was again at Drury Lane at least from 8 November through 4 June of 1797–98 and from then on through at least 1806.

Atkins played the provinces in the summertime and sometimes in the winters too; he was on the Bath and Bristol stages fairly regularly from 1792 through 1799. He married the talented singer Eliza Warrell at Bristol on 9 August 1796. She joined him at Covent Garden in January 1799. At the time of their benefit of 22 May 1800, they lived conveniently at "No 31, Bow St, opposite the Box Door."

Atkins was unprepossessing in appearance and, according to the *Authentic Memoirs of the Green Room* (1801), "elder than his wife by a very potent disparity of years." She left him about 1805 and took up with and assumed the name of (or married) an actor named Hill.

Atkins was kept fairly busy singing in the choruses to such extravaganzas as *The Pirates* and *The Cherokees* in his early years at Covent Garden, standing in as a peasant in *Richard Coeur de Lion,* shaking a spear as an anonymous janizary in *Blue Beard.* Occasionally he filled inconsiderable roles like Oxford in *Richard III,* the first senator in *Othello,* Calvette in *The Castle of Andalusia,* or the Mate in *The Death of Captain Cook.*

The *Authentic Memoirs* described him in 1801: "His features are of that rough iron cast, which well accord with the personation of a bailiff, a tipstaff, or a turn-key. In such characters he is principally employed, and serves occasionally to swell a procession, or increase a mob." So he continued at Covent Garden for over 30 years, said his obituary in *The Gentleman's Magazine* of 1831, "and during the whole of that time never had a day's illness, and never neglected his duty by absence from rehearsal in the morning, or from the performance of his part in the evening."

He died at London on 6 February 1831.

*Harvard Theatre Collection*

ELIZA ATKINS, as Selima

by De Wilde

**Atkins, Mrs William, Eliza, née Warrell, later Mrs Hill** [*fl.* 1787–1808?], *singer, actress.*

Eliza Warrell was born into a well-known provincial theatrical family. Her parents, Mr and Mrs A. Warrell, were singing actors who had settled in the Bath-Bristol company after extensive experience at York. Eliza had three brothers, Henry, James and Thomas, all younger than she and all at some time on the stage. Evidently there was also a younger sister.

Eliza Warrell appeared in children's roles at Bath in 1788. For several years thereafter she studied singing with the eminent Venanzio Rauzzini. She obtained considerable success at Bath as a singer during the season of 1795–96. Although her parents and her brothers were acting in Philadelphia, New York, and elsewhere in America from 1793 to 1797, Eliza cannot have been the Miss Warrell who was on the bills with them, for she was married to William Atkins at Bristol on 9 August 1796. It was under her married name that she first appeared in London, at the Haymarket Theatre on 16 August 1797 in the title role in Brooke's *Rosina*. The *Monthly Mirror* gave her encouraging criticism after this occasion:

It is seldom that we have to record an appearance so promising as the present . . . Her voice has not capacity or strength to fill a very extensive theatre; but what there is of it is perfect. Well-bodied, equable, and firm, it commands the entire compass of the gamut, and is regulated by an ear of uncommon accuracy, which has received every assistance from taste and science, so as to give ease and agreeableness to her execution. Mrs Atkins, in common with most singers, is not much of an actress; but she speaks sensibly, and with sufficient distinctness.

This judgment was sustained in another review in the same journal on 5 January 1799, being altered only in favor of her acting, which the reviewer found much improved.

Mrs Atkins sang at the Haymarket from August to September 1797. By January 1798 she and her husband had obtained regular engagements with Covent Garden Theatre, where she was earning £6 per week, and she was also concerned in Ashley's oratorio program for the season. In 1800–1801 she was earning £7 per week, in 1801–2, £8. She was at Birmingham and Margate with William Atkins in the summer of 1802, but the 1806 edition of *Authentic Memoirs of the Green Room* stated that in the summers she "rusticates," but not with her husband. She was certainly the *"Miss* Atkins from Covent Garden" whom James Dibdin finds coming to Edinburgh from 2 to 16 August 1806, with a Mr Hill. Hill played young Meadows to her Rosetta in *Love in a Village*, to open their engagement, and Don Carlos to her Clara in *The Duenna* to close it. By September 1807 the *Monthly Mirror* was describing her as "Mrs Hill, formerly Mrs Atkins," but William Atkins did not die until 1831, and it is probable that the association with Hill was irregular.

Eliza Atkins was employed in the Covent Garden company in all the winter campaigns until at least 1806–7, singing Handelian songs in the spring oratorios, playing parts in ballad opera, warbling in "The Grand Triumphal Entry of Alexander into Babylon" in *Alexander the Great*, or mourning with others of the chorus in "The Dirge" at Juliet's tomb. In time she ascended to occasional leads and good secondary parts: Patty in *Maid of the Mill*, Polly in *The Beggar's Opera*, Sylvia in *Cymon*, Emily in *The Flitch of Bacon*, Nora in *The Poor Soldier*, Janetta in *False and True*, Clara in *The Duenna*, Huncamunca in *Tom Thumb*, Laura in *Lock and Key*, Maudlin in *Poor Vulcan*, and Margaretta in *No Song, No Supper*. She was applauded for doubling the parts of Sabrina and Pastoral Nymph in *The Brilliants*, singing both "Sweet Echo" and "Maria, or the Beggar Girl." She sang a well-received "Tantara" as a Huntress in *The Norwood Gypsies*, and on several occasions in *Abroad and at Home* she thrilled the auditory, with

the great tenor Incledon, in their duet "Together let us Range." Her husband, William, was a performer far her inferior.

There is in the British Museum a fine portrait of Eliza Atkins by Samuel DeWilde, in pencil and red chalk, tinted in water colours. She is portrayed as Selima in *Selima and Azor*. This likeness was engraved by Cooper for Cawthorn's *Minor British Theatre*. An oval portrait of her by S. Drummond was engraved by K. Mackenzie in 1801.

*Harvard Theatre Collection*
ELIZA ATKINS
by Drummond

**Atkinson, Mr** [*fl.* 1747–1751], *doorkeeper.*

Mr Atkinson was pit doorkeeper at Drury Lane Theatre during the seasons 1747–48 through 1751–52.

**Atkinson, Mr** [*fl.* 1750], *actor.*

A Mr Atkinson played Lovemore in *The Constant Couple* for four performances, 7, 8, 10, and 12 September 1750, at Phillips's

Great Theatrical Booth, Southwark Fair. He is conceivably the same person as the Drury Lane doorkeeper.

### Atkinson, Mr  [fl. 1781],  actor.

Mr Atkinson played Tally in *The Artifice* in an irregular company convened at the Haymarket Theatre for the benefit of the actor Walker on 16 October 1781. No other record of his performing is known.

### Atkinson, Master  [fl. 1783],  dancer.

A Master Atkinson danced with the two Misses Simonet and Miss Hall in "A Melange Ballet, in both Serious and Demi-Character, called Le Noce, Du Chateau," and also in a pantomime called *Harlequin, The Phantom of a Day*, on 18 October 1783, at Hughes's Royal Circus.

### Atkinson, Miss  [fl. 1771–1782],  actress.

Miss Atkinson first appeared in the London playbills on 15 April 1771 as a chambermaid in *The West Indian*. She was a member of a casual company performing out of season at the Haymarket Theatre at this time. She found no permanent situation in London during this season, however, and was probably the young Miss Atkinson who appeared at Norwich in 1772. At the Haymarket on 24 May 1773 a Miss Atkinson was advertised by Foote as being for the first time on the stage, when she played Lucy in *The Virgin Unmasked*, but since novices were considered to have power to draw audiences, we may believe that she was the Miss Atkinson of 1772. She was given many chances by Foote that summer and played Hyema in *Cupid's Revenge*, Dorcas in *The Mock Doctor*, Charlotte in *The Apprentice*, Maria in *The Register Office*, Cicely in *A Trip to Portsmouth*, and unspecified parts in several other plays. (The "Miss Atkins" who played in *The Modish Wife* on 18 September was doubtless Miss Atkinson.)

She was either acting in the provinces or not at all in the season of 1773–74, except for one appearance on 4 April 1774 for a benefit. In the summer seasons of 1775 and 1776 she was with the Birmingham company. On 6 May 1782 she was once again at the Haymarket playing an unspecified part; but she does not seem to have played anywhere thereafter.

### Atkinson, John. *See* ATKINS, JOHN.

### Atkyns [Atkins], Mrs Edward. *See* WALPOLE, CHARLOTTE.

### "Atlas"  [fl. 1787],  strong man.

At the Royal Circus in the summer of 1787 "ATLAS, the Strong Man" exhibited "his wonderful feats."

### Atterbury, Luffman  d. 1796, musician.

Luffman Atterbury was a carpenter and builder of Turn Again Lane, Fleet Market, London, who early became enchanted with music and dedicated his leisure hours to the earnest study of composition and harpsichord. Shortly after the death of his father gave him control of the family business, he sold it and took up residence at Teddington, where he devoted his energies to composing the three- and four-voice glees and catches for which he became notable. He was elected as a professional member to the Noblemen's and Gentlemen's Catch Club, formed in 1761, and was a member for many years, winning five of the Club's prizes before 1780. On 15 May 1765, he was admitted as a performing member of the Madrigal Society.

On 9 December 1775 Atterbury was sworn by William Fitzherbert, Gentleman Usher and Daily Waiter, "into the Place and Quality of Musician in Ordiny to His Majesty in the Room of Mr. Peter Bennell Deceased." Attached to the warrant in the Public Record Office is a letter of attorney of 6 June 1776 empowering Richard Duke, musical instrument maker of the parish of

St Andrew, Holborn, to demand all sums due him from the office of the Lord Chamberlain. (This assignment was inherited by Duke's executors Ann Lloyd and Thomas Libby at Duke's death in 1783.)

On 23 April 1773 Atterbury's oratorio *Goliath* came out at the Haymarket Theatre, advertised "for one night only" but repeated on 5 May. Despite the valiant vocal efforts of Mrs Barthélemon and Battishill and others and the superb violin playing of François Barthélemon, leader of the band, the oratorio was heard no more in the public theatres. It was, however, revived as a musical adjunct to the rather ludicrous ceremony in West Wycombe Church on 13 August 1775 when the heart of Paul Whitehead, politician and satirical poet, was inurned in the tomb of his patron Lord Le Despencer.

In June 1784 Atterbury sang in the chorus at the Handel Commemorations at Westminster Abbey and the Pantheon. In 1787 he was one of a group of 21 (which also included Samuel Arnold, Samuel Harrison, James Bartleman, Thomas Aylward and Thomas Linley) which met at the Newcastle Coffee House in the Strand and established the original Glee Club.

In September 1790 Atterbury married Miss Elizabeth Ancell of Downing Street, Westminster, and Doane's *Musical Directory* of 1794 (which lists him as organist, member of the King's Band and composer) gives him both this address and Teddington. Soon after, he gave up his Teddington residence and moved to Marsham Street, Westminster, where he lived in much reduced circumstances. He died at his home on 11 June 1796 while one of the series of benefit concerts to assist him was in progress. Yet when he made his will on 7 June, three days before his death, he was denominated "Gentleman"; he spoke of "pieces of music . . . Debts . . . ready Monies standing at Interest in my Name . . . either in the Public Bank Stock or ffunds," all of which he left to his wife Elizabeth

Atterbury. To his sister Elizabeth Luffman Eurly and her husband Samuel he left a guinea apiece, as likewise to Charles and Hannah Dorrington.

About 1790 Atterbury published a collection of 12 glees and catches. His most popular works in his own day, some of which are still sung, were: "The undaunted Britons," "At the peaceful midnight Hour," "Come, let us all a-Maying go," "With horns and hounds in chorus," "Take, oh take, those lips away," "Sweet enslaver," "Joan said to John," "Lay that sullen garland by," "Oh! thou sweet bird," and "Adieu, ye streams"; but the British Museum *Catalogue of Printed Music* lists another collection, *Apollonian Harmony*, published during his lifetime and a third published by Mrs Atterbury after his death, as well as a dozen separate songs. He also composed the music for Mark Lonsdale's *Mago and Dago* (1794).

**"Atterino, Signor"** [*fl. 1754*], *dancer.*
"Signor Atterino" was a pseudonym used by one of the dancers in Christopher Smart's ("Mrs Midnight's") company.

**Attilio.** *See* **ARIOSTI, ATTILIO.**

**Attwood, Mr** [*fl. 1784*], *violinist.*
A "Rev Mr Attwood" is on Charles Burney's list of players among the first violins of the band supporting the choruses of the Handel Memorial Concerts at Westminster Abbey and the Pantheon on 26, 27, and 29 May and 3 and 5 June 1784.

**Attwood, Miss** [*fl. 1794*], *harpsichordist.*
The Miss Attwood, harpsichordist, who was listed in Doane's *Musical Directory* of 1794 as living at No 20, Eaton Street, Pimlico, was very likely one of the four daughters of the elder Thomas Attwood, who were: Ann, then aged 30, Susannah, 27, Pheby, 21, and Lucy, 20. She was consequently sister, also, of Thomas the younger

and Francis, both musicians. Her address was at that time the address also of Francis and Thomas Jr and Thomas Sr.

### Attwood, Francis  b. 1775, violist, violinist, violoncellist.

Francis Attwood, youngest of the six children of Thomas Attwood the elder, was born about 1775 (he was said to be seven years of age in April 1782). By 1794 he was already a veteran of the Covent Garden oratorios, had played in one of the Handelian concerts at Westminster Abbey, and had assisted at the Oxford music meetings. In each of four years beginning in 1790, he was named to the list of musicians appointed by the Governors of the Royal Society of Musicians to play at the benefit concert for the clergy at St Paul's Cathedral. He was living at his father's address at No 20, Eaton Street, Pimlico, in 1794.

When the great cellist Joseph Reinagle left the concerts at Oxford's Music Room from 1796 to 1800 his place there was taken by Francis Attwood. He introduced many of his father's compositions to the program. His last benefit at Oxford was on 14 March 1800.

### Attwood, Thomas  b. 1737, trumpeter, violist.

Thomas Attwood the elder, No 20, Eaton Street, Pimlico, was proposed for membership in the Royal Society of Musicians on 7 April 1782 by the distinguished violoncellist William Waterhouse. In his address of nomination Waterhouse called Attwood "a married man aged forty-five years [who] performs on the Tenor and Horn at several private concerts. Is one of his Majesty's Band of Musicians and Page to his Royal Highness the Prince of Wales. A very sober, discreet man." He was said to have six children—Ann, then aged 18, Thomas, 16, Susannah, 15, Pheby, 9, Lucy, 8, and Francis, 7. At least three of these children—Thomas, Francis, and one of the girls—became musicians. Attwood was ad-

mitted to the Society in 1782. At that time his wife's name was stated as Ann.

Attwood's principal instrument was the trumpet, though he also played expertly the horn and the viola. He was listed among the trumpets playing at the first Handel Memorial Concerts at Westminster Abbey and the Pantheon in May and June 1784 and several years subsequently; and from 1785 through the 1790's he played often in the annual benefit concerts for the clergy at St Paul's Cathedral, his instrument usually being the trumpet.

Attwood was often in the band at the Concerts of Ancient Music and was among the most generously paid of the instrumentalists concerned. (A surviving account-sheet of the season of 1787–88 shows him to have been paid £9.) In 1791 he was in the band, led by J. B. Cramer, during the Pantheon's season of 55 nights of operas and ballets, 17 February through 19 July. He had played at the Oxford Music Room at the concerts of the Music Society on 24, 25, and 26 June 1789, and he returned in 1793.

Attwood was proposed to be a Governor of the Royal Society of Musicians at the general meeting of 3 June 1792. The "Attwood senior" on the Minute Books of the Society in January 1807 may refer to him. An Attwood was in the band at Drury Lane, earning £1 10s. per week, in the seasons of 1800–1801, 1803–4, and again in September 1807.

### Attwood, Thomas  1765–1838, singer, violoncellist, composer.

Thomas Attwood the younger was born in London on 23 November 1765 and baptized at St Martin-in-the-Fields on 5 December, the son of Thomas and Ann Attwood. His father, an excellent musician connected with the Royal Household, and later page to the Prince of Wales, obtained for him a place as chorister in the Chapel Royal when he was nine years of age. There he was fortunate in the tutelage successively of James Nares and Edmund Ayrton, both competent organists and both composers.

His father's master, the Prince of Wales, heard him play at Buckingham House in 1781 and sent him in 1783 to Naples with a generous allowance to study with Fillipo Cinque and Gaetano Latilla. After two years Attwood proceeded to Vienna where he was accepted for instruction by Mozart, who praised his abilities. In 1787 he returned to England with the Storaces.

The Prince of Wales welcomed him, confirmed his emolument, and placed him as tenor player in his Chamber Band. On 1 February 1789 his father proposed him for membership in the Royal Society of Musicians. The proposal states he had "studied and practised music for a livelihood more than seven years—was brought up in the Kings Chapel plays the Piano Forte and Tenor and composes—is at present in the service of H. H. the Prince of Wales as Musician and page." He was "a Single man." He was admitted on 7 June 1789. (Attwood was in 1813, 1814, and 1821 a member of the Society's Court of Assistants and in 1817 one of its governors.)

Soon after his return from Vienna Attwood became deputy organist to F. C. Reinhold at the church of St George the Martyr. In 1789–90 he was pianist at the oratorios, and when on 25 March 1790 he played "a new concerto" on the *pianoforte,* he was styled "Attwood, Jun., Musician to His Royal Highness the Prince of Wales." In 1791 after the marriage of the Duke of York with the Princess Royal of Prussia, he became her teacher and he was naturally chosen by his patron to instruct the Princess of Wales in 1795. Doane's *Musical Directory* of 1794 located him at his father's address, No 20, Eaton Street, Pimlico, and asserted that he had performed at Drury Lane Theatre. The younger Thomas is probably the Attwood who was paid £28 15*s.* on 29 October 1792 and £33 4*s.* 4 *d.* on 5 May 1794 for copying music parts "and attendance" at Drury Lane Theatre,

according to the manuscript account books.

In 1796, Attwood succeeded John Jones as organist of St Paul's Cathedral. On the death of Dupuis the same year he was appointed composer to the Chapel Royal. He composed new music for *The Fairy Festival,* which was performed at Drury Lane first on 13 May 1797. He was at Covent Garden in 1798–99 and in that and the subsequent season was paid £6 per week as composer to the theatre. On 5 March 1804 he was appointed to play the violoncello at the annual Dublin Commemoration Concert and on 2 April was proposed as an honorary member of the Irish Musical Society. In 1821 George IV added to the chain of royal favour by appointing him to the sinecure position of organist at the royal Pavilion at Brighton, and in 1836 he succeeded John Stafford Smith as organist of the Chapel Royal. Among his pupils were John Beale and Joseph Hart. He was a friend and early champion of Mendelssohn, whom he entertained at his villa at Norwood and who inscribed one of his works to him. He died 24 March 1838 and was buried under the organ in St Paul's Cathedral.

Attwood's brief will, dated at Eaton Street, London, in 1807 and proved in 1838 by oath of Mary Attwood, his widow and executrix, left his entire unspecified personal estate to her. No children were mentioned.

A writer for the *Monthly Mirror* in 1800 remarked of Thomas Attwood the younger, "In addition to a more than common portion of musical science (acquired under Mozart) he possesses the well cultivated understanding of a gentleman." In addition to his royal charges, he taught many of the journeyman musicians of London, the theatrical singer Miss Wheatley and the imminent organist, teacher, and composer Thomas Walmisley the elder. He was both godfather and teacher of Thomas Walmisley the younger, organist and composer.

Grove lists 33 light operatic and melodramatic works to which Attwood contributed music. Much of his early work in this field was concerned with artful pastiche arrangement, and his first four stage works heavily reflect his admiration for his teacher Mozart. To the end of his career his deft handling of the orchestral effects from wind instruments was a mark of his style. He apparently made little money from his early works. A critic observes tartly, in reviewing Thomas Dibdin's *True Friends* (Covent Garden, 19 February 1800) "It seems to be the peculiar and distressing fate of Mr. Attwood to compose music for pieces that have proved unsuccessful in the representation." But as his reputation grew, he was more successful in attaching himself to successful *libretti*.

In addition, Attwood composed coronation anthems for three successive reigns and saw many of the songs from his operettas published separately. A good many are listed in the British Museum's *Catalogue of Printed Music*. He wrote a number of glees and devoted much of his later life to church music. His godson, Thomas Attwood Walmisley, published a volume of this music after his death.

The Garrick Club owns a picture painted in 1820 by George Clint in which, according to the catalogue, Thomas Attwood the musician appears in a scene from *A New Way to Pay Old Debts*. This is probably a mistake, as there is no record of Thomas Attwood's having acted.

### Atwood, Mr  [*fl.* 1734–1735], *house servant?*

A Mr Atwood is listed as distributing tickets for a benefit performance for Robinson, sub-treasurer of Drury Lane Theatre, on 23 May 1735. He was probably a minor servant of the playhouse.

### Atwood, John  [*fl.* 1735], *musician?*

A concert for the benefit of John Atwood was performed on 11 December 1735 at Hickford's Great Room in Panton Street.

### Aubert, Mons  [*fl.* 1715–1725], *dancer.*

In the fall of 1715 at Lincoln's Inn Fields a Monsieur Aubert performed three times, on 7 and 14 October and 10 November, the last being a comical dance with Laetitia Cross. This seems to have been his only stay in England; between 1718 and 1725 he was performing at Lille.

### Aubert, Isabella  [*fl.* 1715–1720], *singer, author.*

The first notice of Isabella Aubert (or Obert) suggests a previous performing history which has yet to be discovered: on 15 March 1715 at Hickford's Great Room a benefit concert was given her, at which the violinist Castrucci played and, presumably, she sang. On 27 August 1715 at the King's Theatre in the Haymarket a Signora Aubert sang Mandane in *Hydaspes,* the Mancini opera which Mrs Aubert was later to parody, and it is probable that the singer and parodist were one and the same. Signora Aubert was billed as lately arrived, and this could account for Mrs Aubert's sudden appearance on the musical scene in March 1715 as well as the gap of two years before her name was mentioned again. In 1717 Mrs Aubert was a member of the Lincoln's Inn Fields company, singing in *Camilla* on 2 January, *Calypso and Telemachus* on 27 February, and the title role in *Thomyris* on 1 June. This singer was presumably the same as the Signora Aubert and Mrs Aubert of 1715.

She was active again in 1719, starting with a benefit concert on 20 January at the King's Theatre, at which she sang between the acts with a troupe of French comedians; she was billed as making her first appearance on that stage this season. During March she sang at the King's Theatre and at Hickford's, and on 27 May 1719 her *Harlequin Hydaspes,* a parody of the Mancini opera, opened at Lincoln's Inn Fields with Mrs Aubert as Harlequin and Christopher Bullock as the Doctor. The parody had originally been scheduled for 22 May but was postponed when Bullock, for some reason, was arrested.

In 1720 Mrs Aubert sang at Lincoln's Inn Fields "after the Italian manner" in February and was given a benefit concert at York Buildings on 1 June 1720. After this date, records of her cease and she may have returned to the Continent.

**Aubert, John** ₁*fl. 1695–1716*₁, *oboist.*
John Aubert (or Ober) was one of the musicians who played at the King's birthday ball on 4 November 1694. An oboist, he was assigned to Princess Ann of Denmark in October 1699 and played at two balls and a play at court (title unknown). He may have remained active for some time after this, but within 15 years he was on a pension: as a former member of the Prince of Denmark's Music he was paid for the period from 1 October 1714 to 24 June 1716.

**Auberval, de.** *See* DAUBERVAL.

**Aubin, Mrs** ₁*fl. 1724–1729*₁, *orator.*
Mrs Aubin was given a benefit at Lincoln's Inn Fields on 2 January 1724 at a performance of *The Spanish Friar*, but whether or not she was a participant is not known. In April 1729 at York Buildings, in Topham's Great Room called "now The Lady's Oratory" she was pitted, apparently in a debate, against the more famous Mr. ("Orator") Henly. On 22 and 29 April at the same place she participated in, or perhaps sponsored, a "concert" which was probably oratorical in nature. Her *The Merry Masqueraders* was performed on 9 December 1730 at the Haymarket Theatre, and on 11 December at a performance of it "Mrs Aubin, the Oratrix" spoke the Epilogue. This Mrs Aubin may be the authoress Penelope Aubin who flourished about 1722. In any case she was apparently the first woman to take advantage of the vogue for public oratory.

**Auger, Mr** ₁*fl. 1783*₁, *dancer.*
A figure-dancer named Auger was on the company list at the English Opera House at some time in 1783. He returned for the entire season of 1784–85.

**Auguste, Mlle M.** ₁*fl. 1741–1753*₁, *dancer.*
Mlle M. Auguste came rather explosively upon the London theatrical scene in 1741. Fleetwood announced that she "(who never appeared on the English stage before)" would dance at Drury Lane on 4 December, but she did not. Instead, on 7 December she danced with Lalauze at Covent Garden and denounced Fleetwood in the *London Daily Post and General Advertiser*: "Being informed that a letter from Mr Fletewood was read on the stage of Drury Lane Theatre on Friday last (greatly to my prejudice) compels me to attempt this justification of my conduct to him in particular and the town in general." She continued to complain of "several unkind and displeasing proceedings" for which she had demanded redress. Receiving none, she had offered her services to Rich at Covent Garden. Fleetwood had nevertheless insisted that she was contracted to Drury Lane and had put her name in the bills.

Mlle Auguste was dancing at Covent Garden in the 1741–42 and 1742–43 seasons. She danced a duo with "Signor Grimaldi, detto Gamba di Ferro" on 1 November 1742, his English debut. In April 1743 she was living "at her house in Monmouth Court, Hedge Lane." She returned to Drury Lane during 1743–44. She appeared nowhere in London for the next nine years.

In 1752–53 a *Madame* Auguste danced for Garrick. (That she is probably the same person is suggested by the fact that Mlle Anne Auretti is also called "Madame" by the bill-printer this year.) "Mlle Auguste" was again present at Drury Lane the next season. After this she was not seen again in London. On 26 March 1753 she was living "at Mr Harris's, Hosier, in Tavistock Row, Covent Garden."

**Aumer.** *See* ST AUMER.

**Aunuciati.** *See* ANUNCIATI.

**Auretti, Anne** [fl. 1742–1754], *dancer.*

Anne Auretti danced, with a girl who was presumably her younger sister, at Covent Garden Theatre on 23 October 1742—"Les Demoiselles Anne and Janneton Auretti, Two French Girls, being the first time of their appearing on the English stage." Evidently they had been accompanied to town by the dancer Cooke, since his appearance on this night was "the first time of his performance since his arrival from the Opera at Paris." Cooke and Anne Auretti were featured in "A Grand Ballet," supported by the entire corps of dancers.

Anne and Delamaine also did the "Dutch Skipper Dance" on 25 October and for a succession of several nights thereafter. Janneton made her debut in solo performance also on 25 October. Throughout the seasons 1741–42 and 1742–43 Anne and Janneton were named in the company lists and frequently in the bills and were thus easily distinguishable. As of 6 April 1743 Anne lived at "the Golden Head in Newport Street, near Long-Acre." From the spring of 1743 through the summer of 1748 the sisters do not seem to have danced in London at all.

In the seasons 1747–48 and 1748–49 both Anne and Janneton were at Drury Lane, advertised on their first appearance as "The Two Mademoiselles Auretti." Which of them appeared there as "Mlle Auretti" in 1749–50 and which as simply "Madam Auretti" in 1750–51 is moot, and if both were present they were never dancing on the same night. From about 1749 through 1759 one Mlle Auretti was living "at the second house on the left hand, the corner of Panton St, Leicester Fields." On

*Harvard Theatre Collection*

ANNE AURETTI
by Amiconi

29 November 1749 one sister "strain'd her Leg upon ye Stage," and the prompter Cross, who left us this note, complicated matters by calling her "Mrs," which may mean anything. A month later, 29 December, "Mrs Auretti danc'd first since she hurt her leg."

Max Fuchs identified the "Dlle Auretti" who danced at London in April 1754 (almost certainly Janneton) as the *danseuse* among the "secondes soubrettes" at Bordeaux in 1762–63, where there was also an Auretti, *danseur,* in 1773–75 and 1778 who retired in January 1779.

Their flatteries and importunities were certainly a bane to Garrick, who never had very good luck with French dancers. In a letter of 28 August 1752 to his brother George, he was vexed enough to say: "Miss Auretti, Mon$^{sr}$ Pitro. Mad$^{me}$ Janeton, ye Father, Mother & all their Generation may kiss my A——se; I am so sick of their no Meaning Messages & Compliments, that every time I see her Name in a Letter, my Stomach falls a heaving." The most reasonable interpretation of all these data seems to be that Anne and Janneton were sisters, perhaps with a younger brother who danced in France but never in London, and that they were accompanied to London by non-performing parents. Pitro also seems related.

Both the Aurettis were capable in the then-current school of Mlle Camargo, but they appeared very often also in character dances and in national dances of several countries.

A portrait of Anne Auretti, dancing, by C. Amiconi was engraved by T. Ryley.

**Auretti, Janneton** [fl. 1742–1763], dancer. See **AURETTI, ANNE.**

**Austen, Mr** [fl. 1744], actor.

A Mr Austen played Sir Charles in *The Careless Husband* in Charlotte Charke's irregular company, assembled for her benefit at May Fair on 27 June 1744. He was not heard of again.

**Austin, Mr** [fl. 1757–1767], scene painter, candle snuffer.

A Mr Austin was on the company pay list of Covent Garden Theatre at 12s. per week in 1757–58; he had the same salary per week during the season of 1759–60, with extra payments for snuffing candles. He advanced to 15s. in 1760–61. He is probably to be identified as the Austin who was painting scenes at Covent Garden under Dall and Lambert in 1759–60 and in 1766–67 under Dall. He still earned 2s. 6d. per day in 1767, after which his name disappeared from the lists. He may have been related to the Austin who painted scenes at the Haymarket in the summer of 1804. Austin was not a designer but a painter-executant who could be pressed into other theatrical service.

**Austin, Mr** [fl. 1794], singer.

A Mr Austin of Litchfield was listed by Doane's *Musical Directory* (1794) as an alto who had at some time sung in the Handelian performances at Westminster Abbey.

**Austin, Mr** [fl 1794], violinist.

A Mr Austin, violinist, was a professional musician residing in Denmark Street, St Giles's parish, in 1794.

**Austin, Miss** [fl. 1766–1767], actress.

A Miss Austin, a child, was paid £2 2s. on 10 May 1767 for performing eight nights in the afterpiece *The Fairy Favour* at Covent Garden during the season.

**Austin, Miss** [fl. 1794], pianist.

A Miss Austin, performer on the pianoforte, was living in Denmark Street, St Giles's parish in 1794.

**Austin, Joseph** 1735–1821, actor, provincial manager.

Joseph Austin early in his career seems to have been associated with Tate Wilkinson in various provincial theatres in the north and west of England.

He was introduced to London at Drury Lane Theatre on 22 February 1757 as a "Young Gentleman" making his first appearance on the stage. The prompter Cross identified him in his diary, calling his attempt at Bertram in *The Spanish Friar* "Indiff." But he repeated the role on 26 February and on the 28th played Aboan in *Oroonoko*. He was Beau in the afterpiece, *The Toyshop*, on 9 May but apparently learned no more parts that season. But that he was either already an experienced actor or a "quick study" is demonstrated by the fact that he was in the company playing Buckingham in *Henry VIII* on 27 September 1757, had an unidentified part in *The Rehearsal* on 29 September, did young Cape in *The Author* on 15 October, Antonio in *The Tempest* on

20 October and on 7, 9, 14, 21, and 23 November, and Burgundy in *King Lear* on 10, 12, and 17 November. But he was not seen again until 1 February 1758 when he played his debut part of Bertran. He was employed but sparingly for the rest of that season. On 13 October 1758 the prompter Cross notes in his diary: "Mr. Fleetwood in ye fight with Paris in ye last act *Romeo and Juliet*, having a sword by his side instead of a foil, run Mr Austin (Paris) into the belly, he lay some time but at last taken off—a surgeon was sent for—no harm, a small wound, & he is recover'd."

At Drury Lane in 1758–59 Austin played a variety of parts including Silvius in *As You Like It*, Worthy in *The Recruiting Officer*, Malcolm in *Macbeth*, Guildenstern, and Noodle in *Tom Thumb*. He was important enough to take his 16 May 1759 benefit with Wood the subtreasurer and was probably by this time assistant prompter. Certain surviving letters to him from David Garrick show that by October 1760 he supervised preparation of the Drury Lane playbills. In the season 1759–60 his parts included Garcia in *The Mourning Bride*, Strut in *The Double Gallant*, Malcolm in *Macbeth*, Douglas in *1 Henry IV*, Buckingham in *Henry VIII*, Canidius in *Antony and Cleopatra*, Burgundy in *King Lear*, Truman in *The London Merchant*, and Jeremy in *Love for Love*. In 1760–61 he expanded his Shakespearean roles to Tressel in *Richard III*, Dauphin in *King John*, and Laertes. He acted at Portsmouth a few times in the summer of 1760, but he was not there in 1761–62, 1762–63, or 1763–64.

In 1761 Austin went to Ireland to act briefly at Crow Street. He was seen with Barry at Cork on 28 October and was there again in August and October of 1762, on 3 October 1764, and at Drogheda on 26 August 1765.

He seems to have formed his managerial partnership with Michael Heatton while they were acting together at Crow Street.

In July 1766 they crossed together to Wales, playing first at Wrexham, Denbighshire, where they stayed into September, moving on later that fall to Denbigh and then to Oswesty. In the spring of 1767 they proceeded to Shrewsbury, Bridgenorth, and finally to Chester, where they set up their scenery in a tennis court. Their company was excellent, for, besides Heatton and Austin (who naturally allotted to themselves leading roles), John Edwin had joined them, Heatton's daughter had much talent, his wife some, Mahon was a dependable journeyman, Vandermere was beginning his solid career, and the others seemed adequate. On 22 April 1769 Austin returned to London for a single performance at Covent Garden, being advertised as "from the Theatre Royal, Dublin" and playing Ogleby in *The Clandestine Marriage*, for the benefit of Mahon who had now come to London.

In 1769 they moved their Chester performances to the Wool Hall, which in 1772 they fitted out in a permanent condition. In this year their company was joined by William Siddons.

Heatton seems to have dropped out of the partnership about 1775, but in 1780 Whitlock joined Austin to help supervise a circuit which by this time was one of the most extensive in England. James Winston, in his *Theatric Tourist* (1805), states: "An estimate may partly be formed of the laborious life of an itinerant player, when we state that Austin and Whitlock's circuit, consisting of Newcastle, Lancaster, Chester, Whitehaven, and Preston, occasioned the performers a necessity of travelling eleven hundred miles each year, in addition to the constant weariness and fatigue of studying and acting." Actually, in the 1780's Sheffield, Warrington, and Manchester were also in the circuit.

Austin died in London on 23 March 1821, at his house in Crowne Street, near Brunswick Square. His will, signed 22 March 1820 and proved 26 April 1821, assigned to his son Edward Frederick Richard Austin "all his right title and interest in the ground building premises known as Theatre Royal Situate in Chester together with his share in the patent" and also £800 in three per cent bank annuities. To his daughter Maria Frances, the wife of Martin Poulaire, Austin left the interest of £800 in bank annuities, and to his friend Robert Rawlins of Red Lion Square, Holborn, £5 for a mourning ring. All the rest of his estate, property, and effects, he left to his daughter Henrietta Ann, the wife of John Worrell of Cromer Street, St Pancras parish.

Mrs Austin acted with Joseph Austin at Drogheda, in Ireland, August 1765, and a Mrs Joseph Austin is listed by Clark at Crow Street, Dublin, in 1789, billed as "from Covent Garden." Yet not only is there no note of a Mrs Austin acting in London, but Burney notes that on 21 October 1771 Joseph Austin was married "to a Lady worth £14,000 near Whitehaven in Cumberland," one of the towns in the circuit. It may be that there were two Mrs Austins.

Austin was a skillful manager and a sound actor. He was particularly proud of the careers he had helped advance, and a manuscript ledger in the Folger Library and a collection of playbills annotated by Austin and now in the British Museum speak with satisfaction of Courtney Melmoth, of Murray of Covent Garden ("Raymur" at Chester), Miss Duncan as a child, Mr and Mrs Nunn, Berry, Mrs Belfield, Thomas Knight, John Edwin, Elizabeth Siddons (who married Whitlock), Joseph Munden, George Frederick Cooke, and others.

**Auvigne, d'.** *See* D'AUVIGNE.

**Avelloni, Signora.** *See* DURASTANTI, MARGHERITA.

**Avelloni, Casimiro** [fl. 1721], *musician.*

Casimiro Avelloni was a minor musician in London, though his wife, Signora Margherita Durastanti, was an accomplished and popular *prima donna.* Avelloni probably performed in London, perhaps in the King's Theatre band, though there is no specific evidence of his musical activity. His daughter was christened on 2 March 1721 with the King standing as godfather and the Princess and Lady Bruce as godmothers.

**Avery, Thomas** [fl. 1768], *master carpenter.*

Thomas Avery was described as "the Master or Managing carpenter" of Covent Garden Theatre in a legal deposition taken in 1768.

**Avison, Charles** 1709–1770, *organist, composer, violinist, harpsichordist, flutist.*

Charles Avison was baptized in St John's Church, Newcastle-on-Tyne, in February 1709. Both his parents were accomplished musicians. It has been said that, after studying with them at home, Charles was sent for further experience to Geminiani in Italy. Though this assertion has been questioned, he was certainly a partisan of Geminiani's music in later life.

Avison played the flute, violin, and harpsichord, and he advertised as a teacher of the German flute. He may have conducted concerts at Hickford's Great Room in London in 1734, for there survives a notice of an instrumental concert for his benefit in that locale on 20 March 1734.

On 12 July 1736 Avison was appointed organist at St John's Church in Newcastle, and in October he obtained appointment to the much larger church of St Nicholas. From 1736 until his death he conducted the first subscription concerts ever given in Newcastle.

In 1752 Avison published his *Essay on Musical Expression,* which stimulated a controversy in musical circles because of its heretical depreciation of the Handelian school in favor of the French and Italians. He was answered anonymously and successfully by Dr William Hayes, the Oxford musicologist, in 1754 in a pamphlet, *Remarks On Mr Avison's Essay on Musical Expression*. Avison, assisted by Dr Jortin, replied with some effect the following year. The exchange constitutes the first serious musical criticism in England.

Avison's talents were much in demand, and it is said that he refused the posts of organist at Charterhouse, succeeding Pepusch; at York Minster, succeeding Nares; and of two churches in Dublin. He also waived the opportunity to direct the concerts at Edinburgh. He was essentially provincial and much attached to his hometown of Newcastle, where he was the admired center of an extensive circle of music-lovers to whom his word was law. Meetings at his house were frequent.

Avison's best music is found in the five "sets," containing 50 concertos, which he published for a full band of stringed instruments. On 13 February 1765 the oratorio *Ruth*, which he composed in collaboration with his friend Geminiani, was performed at the Lock Hospital Chapel in London. The work may have been conceived during Geminiani's visit to Avison at Newcastle in 1760.

Avison was an excellent and persuasive writer and a capable classicist and linguist. In 1757 he and John Garth edited Marcello's *Psalms*, and he wrote an accompanying "Life of Marcello".

Charles Avison died at Newcastle on 10 May 1770 and was buried there in the church of St Andrew. His will, proved 20 February 1771, is of touching interest, showing his devotion to his family.

New Castle June 24, 1767 Having made a Deed of Gift of my Stock of One thousand Pounds in the Old South Sea Annuities— Namely to my Daughter Jane Eight hundred pounds, to my Son Edward One hundred pounds, to my Son Charles One hundred Pounds after my Decease, & herewith add the following Bequests. To my Daughter Jane the Double Harpsichord made by Slade and the Cabinet in her own Room. To my Son Edward the Double Harpsichord made by Kirman and the Scrutoire in the best Parlour to my Son Charles the Double Harpsichord made by Willbrook and the [Viol?] in the red Room All my other Musical Instruments and my Collection of Music with the Plates of my Concertos in [Sets?] I bequeath to my son Edward not Doubting but he will make a proper Use of them My Reading Books may be Sold if Occasions should require If not I Desire they may be Divided among my Children This is my Last Will and Testament Blessing the Infinite Goodness and Mercy of the Almighty who has Given me Hopes of Eternal Happiness through the Mediation of my Saviour Jesus Christ . . . P. S. All my Household Goods Linnen and Plate Excepting the Scrutoir above mentioned, I bequeath to my Daughter Jane

Should my Decease happen in New Castle I Desire that my remains may be laid near the South Porch in Saint Andrews Church yard near the Remains of my Dear Wife and that the least possible Expense may be laid out in my Interment . . . May every Blessing attend my Dear Children and that they may be a Comfort to theirs, as their Parents have been to them.

As is evident from the will both sons Charles and Edward were musicians. One of them was apparently either manager or in charge of musical affairs at the Durham theatre and entrepreneur at the Newcastle concerts instituted by Charles Avison, the elder. In 1770 this young Avison employed his father's pupil and friend William Shield as leader of the band at both places.

Avison is found among Robert Browning's *People of Importance in Their Day*, as the poet "parleys" with the musician thus:

*Not too conspicuous on the list*
*Of worthies who by help of pipe or wire*
*Expressed in sound rough rage or soft*
    *desire,*
*Thou whilom of Newcastle organist!*

**Avoglio, Christina Maria** [fl. 1740–1744], *singer.*

Signora Christina Maria Avoglio (sometimes "Avolia"), an Italian coloratura soprano, was in London by 1740. In the fall of 1741 Handel went to Dublin at the invitation of the Duke of Devonshire, then Lord Lieutenant, and brought with him several London performers, among them Signora Avoglio. According to Handel's letter to Charles Jennens of 29 December 1741 she "please[d] extraordinary" in the series of subscription concerts at the new music hall in Fishamble Street. She presumably sang in all the cantatas, oratorios, and operas performed, which included among others *L'allegro, Acis and Galatea, Esther, Alexander's Feast,* and *Saul.* Along with Mrs Cibber, Church, and Roseingrave, Signora Avoglio was a featured soloist in the first performance of the *Messiah,* which occurred at Fishamble Street on 13 April 1742 before 700 of Dublin's elite. At the time of her first Dublin benefit, on 5 April 1742, she was living in lodgings "at Mr Madden's in Strand-street." She took a second benefit on 23 June.

In London in 1743 Signora Avoglio sang in the first London performance of the *Messiah,* and she took the part of the Israelite woman in *Samson,* probably repeating the highly successful rendition in 1744. Also in 1744 she performed Iris in *Semele* and probably Merab in *Saul.* She was assigned a part in the planned revival in 1743 of *Athalia.* On 11 June 1744 she assisted at Ruckholt House, Essex, in *Alexander's Feast,* and so far as is known this was her last appearance before a British audience. Her career outside Britain is completely obscure.

**Avolia, Avolio.** *See* AVOGLIO.

**Avory, Mr** [fl. 1738], *house servant?*

A Mr Avory shared a benefit with other employees of Covent Garden Theatre on 8 December 1738.

**Axt, John Mitchell** [fl. 1748], *kettle-drummer.*

At a special performance for the benefit of the bass singer Gustavus Waltz at the Haymarket on 9 December 1748, a number of first-rank musicians played and sang a program which included these two numbers:

"A *Grand Concerto* with Trumpets, French Horns, and four Kettle Drums beat by John Mitchell Axt, who has had the honour to perform before several Sovereigns and English General Officers with great applause. Between the Acts: *Preamble on Kettle Drums*—Axe . . ."

**Aylett, Mr** [fl. 1726–1729], *gallery doorkeeper.*

Mr Aylett was a Lincoln's Inn Fields house servant who seems to have taken over his gallery doorkeeper station in 1726 from a relative, possibly his mother or aunt, a Mrs Aylett. His name appears in the theatre account books in October and November 1726 and from September 1727 through February 1729.

**Aylett, Mrs** [fl. 1716–1726], *gallery doorkeeper.*

Mrs Aylett (or Lylett, Elliot) was a Lincoln's Inn Fields house servant whose first recorded benefit, shared with two others, was on 18 July 1716. Though the records are not complete, she was apparently active through the 1724–25 season, usually sharing her benefits but on at least one occasion (11 June 1719) having a benefit by herself. From 1726 through 1729 the only mention of her in the theatre account books concerns free tickets for her, which suggests that she was by then retired. When she relinquished her position, a Mr Aylett, possibly a son or nephew, took it over.

**Ayleworth.** *See also* ALEWORTH.

**Ayleworth, Mr** [fl. 1721], *dancer.*
In his *Anatomical and Mechanical Lec-*

*tures upon Dancing* John Weaver listed a Mr Ayleworth as a dancing master active in England in 1721.

## Ayleworth, Jonathan [*fl. 1739*], musician.

Jonathan Ayleworth is listed as one of the original subscribers ("being musicians") to the Royal Society of Musicians of Great Britain, in the Declaration of Trust establishing the Society on 28 August 1739.

## Ayleworth, [Joseph?] [*fl. 1708–1710*], violinist.

A Mr Ayleworth (or Aleworth, Ailsworth), whose first name was possibly Joseph, was a theatre musician active in the early 18th century; he may have been related to Jeoffrey Aleworth, who was sometimes erroneously identified as Joseph, a court musician of the Restoration. In 1708 Mr Ayleworth asked £1 10s. nightly for playing at the opera, a fee comparable to that asked by such well-known musicians as Paisible, Babel, and Banister. Ayleworth apparently did not get the position he sought in 1708, but by 24 December 1709 he was hired as one of the first violins in the Queen's Theatre band.

## Ayliff. *See also* ILIFF.

## Ayliff, Mrs [*fl. 1690–1697*], singer, actress.

Mrs Ayliff (or Aglyffe, Alyfe, Aliff, Ayloff) may have made her first appearance on stage in Betterton's version of *The Prophetess* when it was brought out by the United Company in June 1690 at the Dorset Garden Theatre, though this would place her in the company two years before any other record of her. She was certainly in *The Fairy Queen* when it opened at that playhouse on 2 May 1692; the airs assigned her were "Sing whilst we trip it" and "Thus happy and free." Her performance in *Regulus* in June drew high praise

from Motteux in the *Gentleman's Journal*: "The first of the three Songs which I send you ('Ah me! Ah me! to many, many deaths') is set by *Mr. Purcell* the *Italian* way; had you heard it sung by Mrs *Ayliff*, you would have own'd that there is no pleasure like that which good notes, when so divinely sung can create!"

She was busy at the theatre again in the early months of 1693 and sang for the Queen's birthday at court on 30 April. When *The Prophetess* was revived at Dorset Garden in May 1693, she was certainly in the cast. It was during the 1692–93 season that Anne Bracegirdle began singing; previously the songs in plays were sung by professionals like Mrs Ayliff who were not actresses. It may have been this competition which in time led Mrs Ayliff to take up acting.

She sang in United Company productions throughout the 1693–94 season, and when the troupe split in late 1694, she managed to remain on good enough terms with the two new groups to perform with both during the next few years. Her first appearance as an actress seems to have been as Prue in *Love for Love* which opened the new Lincoln's Inn Fields playhouse on 30 April 1695; she was a last-minute replacement for Mrs Verbruggen, who demanded too high a salary, failed to get it, and deserted the troupe. Following up her advantage, Mrs Ayliff both acted and sang the next season: in September 1695 she sang in *Bonduca* at Drury Lane, and in December she acted Jacond in *Lover's Luck* at Lincoln's Inn Fields. Her last recorded appearance was in *The Loves of Mars and Venus* at Lincoln's Inn Fields on 14 November 1696 when she acted Terpsichore in the Prologue and played Euphrosyne in the masque proper. What happened to her after that is not clear; Mrs Manley's semifictitious autobiography, *Rivella* (1714), implies that Mrs "Alyfe" was a kept woman and was shown great respect by Mrs Barry and other performers of stature because she lived so finely. Perhaps, as the prompter Downes quaintly phrased such matters, she was "by force of love erept the stage."

Willard Thorp hazarded the guess that she may have been the "maiden Lady in Hanover-sq." who, according to the *Gentleman's Magazine*, died on 2 November 1737, but there seems to be no clear evidence to support this.

### Aylmer, Christopher [*fl. 1662*], *musician*.

Christopher Aylmer was appointed to the private music of Charles II on 18 January 1662, but his position was "extraordinary"—that is, he served without salary until a position became vacant. There is no record of a permanent position materializing for him.

### Aylmer, George [*fl. 1787–1801*], *singer, actor*.

A Mr Aylmer was among the tenor singers listed by Charles Burney as singing at Westminster Abbey and the Pantheon in the first Handel Memorial Concerts in June 1784. According to a surviving manuscript pay-list, G. Aylmer was paid £6 for some employment by the Academy of Ancient Music in their concerts in the season of 1787–88. The singer's first name is given by Doane's *Musical Directory* (1794), in which he is said to have assisted at the Oxford Music Meeting of 1793, to have taken a part in the oratorios at Drury Lane, and to have been clerk at Bow Chapel. Aylmer was paid as a chorus singer at Drury Lane every season from 1791 to at least 1801, and in the summers he sang at the Haymarket from 1788 until after 1801. At Drury Lane in 1791–92 he sometimes took small acting parts.

### Ayloff. *See* AYLIFF.

### Aylward, Theodore 1730–1801, *singer, organist, composer*.

Nothing is known of the early life or musical education of Theodore Aylward except that he was probably born at Chichester around 1730 and as a child sang in the chorus at Drury Lane Theatre.

Aylward became organist of Oxford Chapel, in London, about 1760, of St Lawrence Jewry in 1762, and of St Michael's, Cornhill, in 1768. He remained at St Michael's for 20 years. He was elected a member of the Royal Society of Musicians in 1763 and was one of its Governors in 1785. He was active in the Madrigal Society for many years and also in the Catch Club, which in 1769 awarded him its Gold Medal for a glee, "A Cruel Fate."

On 5 June 1771 Aylward was appointed Professor of Music at Gresham College, upon the recommendation of Edmund Burke, David Garrick, and other influential people. He was one of the assistant directors who organized the Handel Memorial Concerts, involving hundreds of singers and instrumentalists, which were given at Westminster Abbey and the Pantheon in June 1784 and revived in several later years.

On 10 May 1788 the Dean and Chapter of Windsor elected Aylward "probationer Organist and Master of the Boys; and also sub-chanter" of the Chapel of St George, Windsor, to succeed Edward Webb. He was evidently at that time furnished with a house, stable, and garden at Windsor. In November 1791 he took the accumulated degrees of Bachelor of Music and Doctor of Music at Oxford.

Aylward died on 27 February 1801 and was buried, as his will implored, in St George's Chapel at Windsor, "in a vault near Dr Child." A memorial tablet there bears the inscription of his Chichester friend, the poet William Hayley:

*Aylward adieu, my pleasing gentle Friend,*
*Regret and Honours on thy Grave attend.*
*Thy rapid Hand harmonious skill possest*

*And moral Harmony enrich'd thy
   Breast
For Heaven most freely to thy Life
   assign'd
Benevolence, the Music of the Mind!
Mild as thy Nature, all thy mortal Scene!
Thy Death was easy, and thy Life serene.*

Aylward collaborated with others in the music for Garrick's "Shakespeare Jubilee" Procession in 1769, and he furnished other theatrical pieces, as reflected in the publication of *Six Songs in Harlequin's Invasion, Cymbeline, A Midsummer Night's Dream,* and some of the songs he wrote for *Mago and Dago* in 1794. He also published *Six Lessons for the Organ, Elegies and Glees, Eight Canzonets for two Soprano Voices, Six Lessons for the Harpsichord, Organ, or Piano Forte, Ode on the Dawn of Peace,* the two songs *Oft Have I Seen at Early Morn* and *Sweet Tyrant Love,* and *Canzonets for two Soprano Voices,* but most of his very estimable music is still in manuscript. He was for a time a teacher also, and his most successful pupil was William Dance.

The most important bequest in Theodore Aylward's will directs his executors, John Collick and Thomas Bingley Senior of Birching Lane, London, insurance broker, to liquidate his properties, including a collection of musical instruments, and to use the proceeds (after subtraction of other bequests) toward "Educating and bringing up a ffemale child born on the Body of Susan Small and Christened as I have been informed in the Parish of Lambeth and now is living with her Mother until the said Child shall attain the Age of twenty one years." She was at that time to have £500 in cash. To his "kinsman John Aylward of Salisbury, Wilts, Parchmentmaker" he left £300. The "several children" of his late kinsman James Wheeler of Cooley Street, Southwark, each received £100. To his servants Richard Adams and Ann his wife he left "thirty pounds a year Long Annuities of the Bank of England," and to Richard, moreover, "all my wearing

Apparel both Woollan and Linen and also my second best Bedstead Bed Blankets and ffurniture thereto belonging and four pair of Sheets, half a dozen good chairs and two Armed Chairs one Grate and ffire Irons . . . one Carpet and all my Brewing Utensils," as well as £30 immediately to buy mourning.

Other bequests were as follows: "Old Musical ffund" £100; Theodore Freehorn, cabinet maker £100; Rev Mr Toghill of Chichester £20 "as a small acknowledgment of my ffriendship"; his "worthy and good ffriend Mr John Bright of Islington," £100; ten guineas apiece to his "ffriends and acquaintances John Crossdall[,] Thomas Blake and Mr Shields Musicians"; to Saxton, his "deputy" at Windsor £50; to Mr [William] Hayley of Eartham, in Sussex, and to John Yein of the Board of Works ten guineas each for mourning rings; to Mr George Richard of Berners Street £20 for a ring; " and to each of the Laymen or Singers in the Chapel at Windsor" £10.

**Aylworth.** *See* **ALEWORTH, AYLEWORTH.**

**Aylyffe.** *See* **AYLIFF.**

**Ayme,** [Mr?] [*fl.* 1726–1727], *house servant?*
One Ayme was cited on the free list for the 1726–27 season at Lincoln's Inn Fields; he appears to have been one of the house servants.

**Aynscomb, Mr** [*fl.* 1761–1762], *singer.*
An Aynscomb was among the singers on the company list at Drury Lane Theatre in the season 1761–62. Tenducci and Miss Brent sang a program of "Songs from Artaxerxes" for his benefit at the Haymarket on 20 May 1762 when he was so ill as to be "incapable of waiting upon his friends personally." He was not noticed after this date.

**Ayres, [James?]** [*fl.* 1729–1744], *actor, playwright?*

A Mr Ayres was on the Haymarket bills for the spring of 1730, acting very small parts in farce. His first appearance was as Charon, in *The Author's Farce*, on 30 April. He remained with the company in 1730–31, after acting in September at Southwark Fair in Lee and Harper's booth. He was again with Lee and Harper at Bartholomew Fair in August of 1731, but he did not appear again anywhere in the London area, so far as the bills show, until 26 December 1733 when, billed as "Eyres," he played the part of Mat in *The Beggar's Opera* at Goodman's Fields. The printer again thus spelled his name on 8 January 1734 when he was Dick in *Flora* and on 9 January when he was Montano in *Othello*. Meanwhile and thereafter, "Ayres," he regularly obtained roles like Pearmain in *The Recruiting Officer*, Sir Harry in *The Double Gallant*, and Micher in *The Stage Coach*. But he continued as well to act small roles like Cinna the poet in *Julius Caesar*.

Some of his other characters were: Gibbet in *The Stratagem*, Tragedio in *The Author's Farce*, Doodle in *Tom Thumb*, Sebastian in *The False Count*, Sulky Bathos in *The Battle of the Poets*, Davy in *The Generous Freemason*, Sir Charles in *The Stratagem*, Richard in *The Provok'd Husband*, Nicodemus Stitch in *The Jealous Taylor*, Ben in *Love for Love*, Alphonso in *The Spanish Fryar*, and Foodle in *The Tragedy of Tragedies*.

Hogan furnishes the first name James for this Haymarket actor. If this is correct, he may perhaps also be the James Ayres who wrote the words for *The Queen of Spain*, an operetta with music by J. F. Lampe produced at the Haymarket on 19 January 1744, and for Lampe's music to *The Kiss Accepted and Returned*, produced at the same theatre on 16 April 1744. This James Ayres is also credited by Nicoll with *Sancho at Court: or, The Mock-Governor*, designed, according to its title-page, for acting at Drury Lane, but never staged, and published at Dublin in 1742. (This title-page asserts also: "Written by a Gentleman, Late of Trinity College," but the assertion was evidently only bait for students, since the College's Admission Registers yield no James Ayres.)

**Ayres, Matthew** [*fl.* 1702], *actor.*

On 8 September 1702 the *Post Man* listed Matthew Ayres as one of the strollers required to pay town constables 2s. per day when performing. It is not clear whether or not he acted in London.

**Ayrton, Edmund** 1734–1808, *organist, composer, concert organizer, singer.*

Edmund Ayrton was born in 1734 the son of a "barber-chirurgeon" who became borough magistrate and finally Mayor of Ripon. Sainsbury says that the three immediate ancestors of Edmund's father had "held, successively, the consolidated livings of Nidd and Stainley, within the liberty of that town."

Edmund was educated at the free grammar-school, the intention being that he should follow his forebears into the church. He was a contemporary there of Beilby Porteous, later Bishop of London. But a proclivity toward music and perhaps also the example of his older brother William, who was soon to become organist of Ripon Cathedral, sent Edmund to study under Robert Nares, the great organ executant and teacher at York Cathedral. At this time began his long and close friendship with Nares.

In 1754, when he was only 20, Ayrton was elected organist, auditor, and *rector-chori* of the collegiate church of Southwell, Nottinghamshire. Sainsbury tells us that he resided in this town for "some years, and married a lady of good family by whom he had fifteen children." (Sainsbury adds that "only three daughters and one son are now [1827] living.") His wife was Ann Clay, daughter of Benjamin Clay, Gent of Southwell, by Elizabeth his wife. Ann was born at Southwell on 28 December 1739. She and Edmund Ayrton were married there on 20 September 1762.

Ayrton left Southwell in 1764 to accept an appointment as one of the Gentlemen of the Chapel Royal in London, where he was also lutenist. Three years later he was installed as a vicar-choral of St Paul's Cathedral. In 1780 he was promoted to be Master of the Children of His Majesty's Chapels when Nares resigned the office and also became a lay-clerk of Westminster Abbey. He was in 1785 one of the Governors of the Royal Society of Musicians. Ayrton on some occasions hired out his choir-boys of the Chapel Royal to sing background choruses at the public theatres. The accounts of Covent Garden show payments to him "for his Boys" for £18 18s. on 13 July 1787; the end-of-season accounts of 1789–90 carry the notation: "Dr Ayrton in ful for 8 nts £25.4," and on 7 June he received £6 6s. "for the boys in the Crusades" (i.e., the melodrama by Frederick Reynolds).

It was doubtless these associations which, along with his musical abilities, made him an excellent choice as one of the assistant organizing directors of the Handelian Memorial Concerts at Westminster Abbey and the Pantheon in June, 1784. He continued to act in this capacity for all the succeeding years in which the Concerts were held and seems also to have sung alto.

Ayrton was created Doctor of Music by the University of Cambridge in 1784 and admitted *ad eundem* by the University of Oxford in 1788. His wife died on 16 May 1800. In 1805 he relinquished the mastership of the Chapel Royal. He died in 1808 at his son's house in James Street, Buckingham Gate, and was buried beside his wife in the North Cloister of Westminster Abbey.

Five of Edmund and Ann Ayrton's 15 children are also buried near their parents in Westminster Abbey: Catharine, born 9 July, died 16 October, buried 19 October 1772; William, born 31 January, baptized 27 February, died 12 July, and buried 13 July 1776; Sarah, born 31 July, and baptized 2 September 1773, at St Margaret's Westminster, died 29 December 1777 and buried 2 January 1778; Peter-Thomas Ayrton born 1 October, baptized at St Margaret's 4 November, died 25 December, and buried 29 December 1779; his twin James-Nares Ayrton, born 1 October, baptized at St Margaret's 4 November 1779, died 17 October and buried 20 October 1780.

Edmund Ayrton's will, signed on 6 October 1802, gives only £20 to his "Eldest Son Edmund Ayrton" and £5 to his "third son Benjamin Ayrton" inasmuch as "they have already received from me more than the rest of my Children can reasonably expect." To his daughter Elizabeth Clay Paris of Cambridge he left £150 and to her husband Thomas Paris "my harpsichord made by Baker Harris and my portrait by [William] Pether as a small token of my affection." To his daughter Mrs Ann Ward of Bridgeworth, Shropshire, he left £50, she "having already received considerable of my property as a marriage portion and to her husband Jabez Ward Doctor of Medicine I bequeath a plain mourning Ring as a trifling proof of my esteem."

To his second son William he left £100, "my Old ffamily Organ with the Cloughs arms upon it," a portrait of himself by Hoppner, all his music in manuscript, and "all the pictures paintings Drawings and Copies of Drawings Painted and drawn by my late Brother in Law Nicholas Thomas Dall."

To his youngest son, Scrope Ayrton, he left £100. He bequeathed a mourning ring to each child and to each of his executors. He desired all his musical and mathematical instruments, household furniture, and books to be sold and placed in trust to "Robert Nares of the British Museum Clerk Master of Arts Thomas Paris of Cambridge my son in Law [and] my Son William Ayrton, to be put out at interest for benefit of My Daughter Catherine Ayrton." By a codicil of 15 May 1808 Edward Edmund Ayrton was additionally to receive £180, Ann £150, and William £120 and "My Silver Cup I received from my Brethren at Saint Pauls I [also] give to him my two Commemoration Medals I also give to him my Doctors Robes Hoods and Cap also my harpsichord made by Tabel." Scrope was to receive £100 additional. Ayrton revoked the appointment of Thomas Paris as an executor "as his health is so precarious" and appointed in his stead Thomas Littlewood of Poplar, Middlesex.

Edmund Ayrton had many relationships to the world of music and the theatre: his brother, nephew, and son, all named William, were all musicians. On 17 May 1803, the son William married Marianne, the daughter of the composer and manager Samuel Arnold and the sister of the playwright-manager Samuel James Arnold. This William was a distinguished music critic and founder of the *Harmonicon* and for a time managed the English Opera House, where he first introduced to England Mozart's *Cosi fan tutte* and *Die Zauberflöte.* As Edmund's will shows, his sister Ann married the academician Nicholas Thomas Dall, who was a scene painter at Covent Garden theatre where his wife supplied the company as a linen draper. His eldest son Edward Edmund may be the "Edward Ayrton organ. Tenor-Swansea, Wales" listed by Doane's *Musical Directory* in 1794.

Ayrton wrote church music, principally. He contributed two complete morning and evening services and a number of anthems. Much of his music remains unpublished. It is not very often played today.

### Ayrton, Edward Edmund  (fl. 1784–1794), singer, organist.

A "Mr Ayrton (Jr)" was listed by Burney as a tenor in the Handel Memorial Concerts at Westminster Abbey and the Pantheon in 1784. He is perhaps to be identified with the tenor singer and organist placed by Doane's *Directory* at Swansea in 1794. Very likely he was Edward Edmund Ayrton, the elder son of Edmund Ayrton, who was a principal organizer and director of the 1784 concerts.

### Ayrton, William  1777–1858, singer, music critic, manager.

A Mr W. Ayrton of Yorkshire was a countertenor in Burney's list of vocalists who sang at the Handel Memorial Concerts at Westminster Abbey and the Pantheon in June 1784. Since Edmund Ayrton was one of the principal organizers of this massive tribute, it seems probable that his son William was singing in it. William, who married Marianne, the daughter of the composer Dr Samuel Arnold, went on to a career as a writer on musical topics. In 1816 he was Director of Music at the King's Theatre. He was the first impresario to produce Mozart's *Don Giovanni, Cosi fan tutte,* and *Die Zauberflöte* in England. William Ayrton was born at London on 24 February 1777, the son of Edmund Ayrton (1734–1808).

Ayrton was for many years on intimate terms with Charles and Mary Lamb. There survives a pleasantly nonsensical letter to him in Lamb's "lapidary style," indicating that the friendship was very close in May of 1817; and an urgent invitation to visit Lamb at Enfield, dated 14 March 1830, mentions Ayrton's sister at Cambridge and sends "Our very kindest loves to Mrs A. and the younger A's." William Ayrton was honorary musical and literary critic for the *Morning Chronicle* from 1816 to 1826 and for the *Examiner* from 1837 to 1851. He was a fellow of the Royal and Antiquarian Societies and a member of the Athenaeum Club. He helped found the Philharmonic Society in 1813.

He is often confused with his cousin, William Francis Morrall Ayrton (1778–1850).

## Ayrton, William Francis Morrall
*1778–1850, singer, organist.*

William Francis Morrall Ayrton was the
son of William Ayrton (1734–1799),
organist, and the nephew of Dr Edmund
Ayrton (1734–1808), organist, composer,
and concert manager. He was born in 1778
in Ripon, the city of his family for many
generations, and he ended his life there.
But, like some of the other Ayrtons, he
was apparently drawn for part of his career to London.

He was doubtless the "Morrell Ayrton,
canto" of No 24, James Street, Westminster, listed in Doane's *Musical Directory*
(1794). He sang in the concerts of Ancient
Music and belonged to the Academy of
Ancient Music and was a member of the
Chapel Royal Choir, his uncle Edmund being at that time Master of the Children
of the Chapels Royal.

He was appointed organist of Ripon
Cathedral on 25 June 1799 to succeed his
father and remained in the post until 1802.
He died at his dwelling, Abbott's Grange,
Chester, on 8 November 1850.

A will signed on 1 June 1841 left his
considerable estate of Abbot's Grange, near
Chester, and all its contents to his widow
Ellen, with his three children residuary
legatees, except that his two sons' shares
were to be diminished by the amount they
would receive from their mother's father,
Francis Nicholson. A codicil of 7 August
1846 gave to his son William Francis Ayrton "the portrait of his Grandfather painted
by himself," to his son Alfred the portrait
of his mother painted by Mr Hough, and to
his daughter Elizabeth Margaretta the portrait of herself by Liversage and one of
himself by Junes. The will was proved by
Ellen the widow on 24 February 1851.

# = B =

**B., Sʳ F.** ₁fl. 1720₁, *singer.*

A Sʳ F. B. sang *When absent from the Nymph I love,* a song published in London about 1720.

**"Bab Allen."** *See* **KNEPP, MARY.**

**Babb, Mrs** ₁fl. 1706–1707₁, *actress.*

Mrs Babb's first appearance was on 24 October 1706 at the Dorset Garden Theatre where, as one of "the *deserted company* of Comedians of the Theatre Royal," she spoke the prologue to *The Recruiting Officer.* A year later, on 18 October 1707, she spoke the prologue at a performance of *The Committee.* On 1 November she played Rose again and spoke a new prologue, but when the play was repeated on 26 November the part of Rose was omitted; following this Mrs Babb's name disappeared from the bills. An Anna-Leinda Babb from St Clement Danes, possibly the actress, married a Henry Pratt at St Paul, Covent Garden, on 15 October 1710.

**Babbini, Matteo** *1754–1816, singer.*

Matteo Babbini was born at Bologna on 19 February 1754. His father, a hair dresser, intended him for the practice of medicine, but when Matteo's parents died he went to live with his mother's sister, the wife of the singer Arcangelo Cortoni, who instructed him in music. Babbini made a brilliant debut as a second tenor at Modena about 1773 in an opera by Paisiello. He was engaged immediately for the Italian opera of Frederick the Great at Berlin, and after a year went to the court of St Petersburg where he remained until 1781. After singing also at Vienna, Madrid, and

*Instituti di Storia e D'Arte, Milan*

MATTEO BABBINI
by Monotti

Lisbon he went to London in 1785.

Babbini made his first appearance in England at the King's Theatre in the role of Artabano in *Artaserse* on 16 April 1785. The opera was repeated five times that season. On 28 May he made his first appearance "in the Comic," singing Giannetto in *I viaggiatori felici,* a role he repeated six times. In the following season, he sang: Giorgino in *Il marchese di Tulipano,* Enea in *Didone abbandonata,* Il Conti di Bandiera in *La scuola de gelosi,* Sabino in *Giulio Sabino,* Conte Rifinito in *L'Inglese in Italia,* and Ubaldo in *Armida.* In the last role, he took a benefit on 25 May 1786 ("Tickets to be had of Babbini, No

17, Great Pulteney-street, Golden-Square")
and made his final London appearance on
11 July 1786.

After leaving London, he continued to
sing in the principal Italian cities (and
again at Berlin in 1792) for a number of
years. He also lost a large part of his money
in commercial ventures at Bologna, where
he died on 22 September 1816. An *Elogio
di Matteo Babbini* was published by his
friend Dr Pietro Brighenti at Bologna in
1822.

Three years after Babbini had left London, Burney wrote in *A General History of
Music* that he had a sweet, though not
powerful, voice and an elegant, pleasing
style of singing: "It is easy to imagine that
his voice *had* been better; and not difficult
to discover, though his taste was modern,
and many of his *rifforamenti* refined and
judicious, that his graces were sometimes
redundant and his manner affected." Babbini made no great impression in London.
An account of his continental career may
be found in the *Enciclopedia dello spettacolo.* He was pictured in a painting by
Antonio Fedi of a large group of musicians,
an engraving of which was printed between
1801 and 1807.

### Babel, Charles [fl. 1697–1716], in-strumentalist.

Charles Babel, father of the more famous
William, played the bassoon in "*la troupe
de Sa Majesté Britannique*" at the Hague
in 1697–98 at 21 *sols* per day. By 1707–8
he had come to England and taken a position at the Queen's Theatre in the Haymarket playing bassoon, bass, and violin at 15*s.*
daily. One concert outside the theatre is
recorded for Babel: at Nottingham during
the races in August 1707. Along with
Pepusch he was his son William's teacher.

By 1714 he was retired. As one of the
musicians of the "late Prince of Denmark's
Musick" he received an unspecified pension
from 1 October 1714 to 24 June 1716. His
son's will, written in December 1720 makes

no mention of Charles Babel, so by that
time he may have died. Hawkins stated,
without supplying evidence, that Babel
played at Drury Lane until he was 80; there
seem to be no documents connecting him
with that theatre.

### Babel, William c. 1690–1723, com-poser, instrumentalist.

William Babel was born about 1690,
probably in London, and received his early
musical training from his father Charles
and Dr Pepusch. By 1707–8, perhaps
through the influence of his father, he was
playing second violin in the band at the
Queen's Theatre in the Haymarket for 8*s.*
per day; at about this time he petitioned
for a £1 5*s.* salary, but no document of the
Queen's Theatre shows him earning more
than 10*s.*

By the time he was about 19 the younger
Babel had published three volumes of harpsichord transcriptions of favorite opera arias
and duets, each called a *Book of the Ladys
Entertainment.* The third book came out in
1709 and a fourth followed within five
years. His transcriptions, though scorned by
the purists, proved extremely popular. Burney said Babel was

. . . wire-drawing the favourite songs of the
opera of Rinaldo, and others of the same
period, into showy and brilliant lessons, which
by mere rapidity of finger in playing single
sounds, without the assistance of taste, expression, harmony, or modulation, enabled
the performer to astonish ignorance, and
acquire the reputation of a great player at a
small expense.

Burney was probably justly harsh, but he
might have recognized Babel's obvious talent even if it was, perhaps, misdirected. In
addition to these pieces, Babel turned out
a number of highly regarded compositions
and was particularly facile at composing
for the flute and oboe, instruments which,
however, he seems not to have made a profession of playing.

Most of his orchestral playing at the theatre was on the treble violin or on the Ripieni violin, but his concert work—as at the Homes Dancing School on 24 April 1711 or at Hickford's music room on 25 March 1713—seems to have been solely on the harpsichord, an instrument upon which he was reportedly very proficient.

At the accession of George I in 1714 Babel became a member of the King's private music; the *Calendar of Treasury Books* for 1715 records a payment of £40 to him for 237 days from 1 August 1714 to 25 March 1715 plus the next quarter. Perhaps it was this security that encouraged him to marry. On 18 February 1718 Babel, of St Giles in the Fields, wed Alice Green of St Paul, Covent Garden, at his parish church. He did not withdraw from the public music world, however: in 1717 he gave concerts at Stationer's Hall; on 26 April 1718 he had a benefit at the Lincoln's Inn Fields Theatre; and in 1719 he composed songs for plays and performed as an accompanist at the same playhouse. On 6 March 1723 he made his last recorded public appearance, playing the harpsichord at Stationer's Hall.

At some point in his career he was appointed organist of All Hallows, Bread Street, a position he held until his death at the age of about 33 on 23 September 1723 at Canonbury House, Islington. Though they cite no authority for it, most older musical dictionaries attribute his death to intemperance. Babel was buried on 26 September at All Hallows, and his will, which he had drawn up on 30 December 1720, described him as from the parish of St Andrew, Holborn. The will was proved on 30 October 1723 by his wife and executrix, Alice, to whom he left all his estate.

**Babini.** *See* **BABBINI.**

**Baccelli, Giovanna** *d. 1801, dancer.*
The Italian ballerina "Mademoiselle"

Giovanna (sometime Gianetta) Baccelli made her debut at the King's Theatre on 8 November 1774 in a grand ballet *Pirhame et Thisbe* and in *Le ballet de fleur.* That season she danced regularly after the operas in such divertissements as a *Grand chacone* and a *New Pastoral Ballet* and took a benefit on 11 May 1775. In the following season she danced in two new pantomime ballets, *Le triomphe d'Euthime sur le genie de libra* and *Pigmalion amoureuse de la statue*, and also appeared with Fierville in the ballet of *Diane et Endymion.*

Mlle Baccelli remained as a featured dancer at the Opera for the next seven years through May 1783, during which time she became the mistress of John Frederick Sackville, Duke of Dorset, and lived with him at Knole House in Kent. Horace Walpole, who mentioned in a letter to General Conway on 16 June 1779 that he had seen "the Bacelli and the dancers of the Opera dance" at a *fête* at the Pantheon recently, described an uncomfortable visit to Knole caused by "a trapes of a house keeper, who, I suppose, was the Bacelli's dresser, and who put me out of humour." Fanny Burney also gave an account of a visit to Knole with the Thrales in 1779: "The Duke of Dorset was not there himself; but we were prevented seeing the library and two or three other modernized rooms, because Mlle Bacelli was not to be disturbed."

Mlle Baccelli's relationship with the Duke seems to have prevented a full-time commitment to her profession, and in some years she did not come on until mid-season or later. On 29 March 1781, she danced the role of Creusa in *Medée et Jason*, one of the great ballets by Noverre which in this London production the elder Vestris cavalierly took credit for as his own work. With the cast also including Vestris as Jason, his son as the young Prince, Simonet as Creon, and Mme Simonet as Medea, the event was impressive. A lovely painting of a moment from this performance is in the Cia For-

*Courtesy of Lord Sackville, Knole House*

GIOVANNA BACCELLI
by Gainsborough

naroli Collection and was engraved by Boy-dell in 1781.

After passing the earlier part of 1782–83 at Paris, Mlle Baccelli appeared at the King's Theatre on 10 April 1783 in Le-picq's new ballet *The Amours of Alexander and Roxana*, with entirely new music by Barthélemon, and danced a *Pas de deux* with Mlle Rossi (who was dressed in boy's clothes). In announcing this event the *Morning Herald and Daily Advertiser* of 31 March 1783 commented that Mlle Baccelli "must feel bold indeed . . . to encounter such a rival as Madamoiselle Rossi, who besides her acknowledged merit, has this advantage, that having practised the whole season, she must be far more *en train* than the former, whose limbs must be stiffened with the chill of idleness, she having

spent the whole of her time since her return from Paris in a kind of *otium cum dignitate!*" She danced in another ballet, *Les caprices de Galatée*, with Mme Simonet on 1 May and again in the *Pas de deux* with Mlle Rossi on 8 May 1783.

For the next four years, Mlle Baccelli did not perform in London although she may have been dancing in Italy. She returned to the King's Theatre on 23 March 1786 to dance with Vestris in a grand pantomime ballet *Le premier navigateur* about which performance the *Public Advertiser* remarked on 25 March: "Vestris and Baccelli, tho' incomparable in some parts of the art, are far inferior as *actors* to Lepicq and Rossi." She also danced in *L'Amour jardiner* on 1 April and in a *Pas de trois* to the tune of "Bon André," taken from the

*Dance Collection, New York Public Library*

GIOVANNA BACCELLI

by John Jones, after Gainsborough

French comic opera *L'Epreuve villageoise*, and in a *Pas de quatre*, from the opera *Panurge*, on 27 April, all got up under the direction of Vestris. At the end of the opera *Armida* on 1 June, she performed in Gardel's comic ballet *Ninette à la cour*, a piece in which she was reputedly most charming, and in *Les Amants surpris*, which she had last danced there on 30 June 1781. Her final performance at the King's took place on 11 July 1786, again in *L'Amour jardiner* and *Ninette à la cour*.

Mlle Baccelli's later years are obscure. She danced at the Paris Opéra in 1788 with a blue bandeau around her forehead inscribed "Honi soit qui mal y pense?"—or at least so reported Horace Walpole to Hannah More on 4 July 1788, adding, "Now, who can doubt but she is as pure as the

Countess of Salisbury? Was not it ingenious? And was not the Ambassador so to allow it?" According to a memorandum by John Philip Kemble, she died in Sackville Street, Piccadilly, on 7 May 1801, generally respected for her benevolence. By the Duke of Dorset she had had a son, who became an ensign in the army and married a pastry cook's daughter. He was sent by his father to the West Indies, where he caught yellow fever and died.

Possibly the dancer listed as Giovanna Baccelli in the *Enciclopedia dello spettacolo* was the same person who danced in England, although no mention of that aspect of a career is made in the Italian entry; nor is any alliance with the Duke of Dorset reported there. That Giovanna Baccelli is reported to have made her debut in the ballet *Adriano in Siria* at the Teatro San Benedetto in Venice at carnival time 1783, under the patronage of a rich Venetian woman named Cecilia Zen Tron, and was also dancing in that city as late as 1789.

In addition to the above-mentioned painting of her in *Medée et Jason*, Mlle Baccelli was painted full length, in flowing gown, by Gainsborough. The original at Knole House was copied and engraved by John Jones. Also at Knole House is a pencil sketch by Gainsborough showing her posing on a dais in the ball room; the sketch also depicts a man playing on a harpsichord, various female figures holding music sheets, and the Chinese boy, Wang y Tong, who was at Knole at the time. Mlle Baccelli was also done by O. Humphrey and engraved by T. Trotter, for a plate published by William Holland in 1785. J. Roberts did a picture of her dancing in *Les Amants surpris*, which was engraved by Thornthwaite for a plate to *Bell's British Theatre* in 1781.

**Bacchelli, Miss.** *See* CORRI, MRS DOMENICO.

**Bach.** *See also* LA BACH.

### Bach, Johann Christian *1735–1782, composer, instrumentalist, concert entrepreneur.*

Johann Christian Bach was born in Leipzig 5 September 1735, the youngest son of the great Johann Sebastian Bach and his second wife, Anna Magdalena Wilcken Bach. His schooling was apparently very thin. His godfather was Johann August Ernesti, rector of St Thomas's School, but there is no record of Johann Christian's enrollment there. Unlike his brothers, he did not attend a university.

His father's death in 1750 left him in the care of his half-brother Friedemann, who took him to Berlin where another half-brother, Carl Philipp Emanuel Bach, was musician to Frederick of Prussia. Johann Christian was taught by Emanuel for some six years, until the outbreak of the Seven Years' War. He left Berlin for Milan in 1756.

Bach's conversion to Roman Catholicism and his consequent interest in ecclesiastical music, his appointment as organist at Milan Cathedral, and his turn toward opera in 1760 are important successive stages in his early development. In 1761 came productions of his operas *Artaserse* (at Turin) and *Catone in Utica* (at the San Carlo Theatre in Naples), with Pietro Metastasio furnishing the *libretti*. In 1762, also at Naples, Bach took Metastasio's *Alessandro nell' Indie* as the subject for his next operatic attempt.

In the summer of 1762 Bach came to England at the invitation of Signora Mattei, *impresaria* of the King's Theatre, to succeed Gioacchino Cocchi. Bach thought the London singers as a group very inferior, but before long he discovered, singing in his *pasticcio, Tutore e la pupilla*, the Neapolitan soprano Lucia de Amicis who had up to that point been confined to *opera bouffe*. Immediately recognizing her marvelous powers, Bach began to write serious parts for her. He produced his first opera in England, *Orione*, at the King's Theatre, on 19

*Civico Museo Bibliografico Musicale, Bologna*

JOHANN CHRISTIAN BACH
by Gainsborough

February 1763, with the Royal Family attending for the first two performances. It ran nearly three months, and Bach's music virtually preempted the rest of the season, for on 7 May his *Zaida* was introduced and stayed on the boards until 11 June.

Not everyone was pleased by the operatic muse of J. C. Bach. The *Theatrical Review* in 1763 published what purported to be a translation of a letter from Arcangelo Bimolle, "a Florentine fidler" in London, to "the Signora Chiara Aquilante (the famous Opera Broker) at Naples," complaining that the "ponderous harmony of Handel outweights, by far with [the English] the elegant taste of Italian malody [*sic*]. This, *Bach*, at first, did not suspect; but finding it, by experience, has prudently changed his style; and now his chorusses roar, his basses thunder, and his airs float in an ocean of symphony. In a word, he has *Handelized*; and acquired a reputation here, by the very thing which would have ruined him in

Italy." Bach, continued Bimolle, had "discovered the vitiated taste of the town" and had "prudently resolved . . . to comply with it."

Bach was soon appointed music-master to Queen Charlotte, no doubt in recognition of popular approval of his music, but also, perhaps, because of the influence of Karl Friedrich Abel, the *viola da gamba* virtuoso, then a member of the band at the King's Theatre. Johann Sebastian Bach had taught Abel and had been godfather to his sister, so there is good reason to suppose that the two young German strangers to London had been well acquainted before they began in 1763 to share the house at No 9, Dean Street, Soho.

On 29 February 1764, Bach and Abel gave the first of their famed subscription concerts at Spring Gardens, presenting Bach's serenata *Galatea*, with libretto by Metastasio. In 1764 also, they welcomed the young Mozarts to London. For seventeen years, at Spring Gardens, at Almack's Rooms, and at Carlisle House, the concert series continued, terminating on 9 May 1781.

Bach produced several other operas and *pasticci*, including other works of his own, in London: *Berenice* and *Adriano in Siria* (1765), *Carattaco* (1767), *Manalcas* (with a chorus from Handel) and the oratorio *Gioas rè di Giuda* (1770), and *La clemenza di Scipione* (1778), as well as operas of Gluck and Piccinni containing his own additions. He set some music for singers at Vauxhall Gardens in 1771, and he may even have performed there.

Bach left London in 1772 for Mannheim and there brought out his *Temistocle.* He was there again in 1774 when he produced *Lucio Silla*. Probably early in 1774 he married the aging singer Caecilia Grassi, who had been engaged at London in 1766 as *prima donna seria*. (Hester Lynch Thrale noted in her *Diary*: "Grassi the Old Singing Woman was married to Bach the Harpsichord Player, but says Burney she will bring no children." She brought none.)

In 1778 Bach went to Paris on invitation from the Opéra, and there met again Mozart, his friend the singer Giusto Ferdinand Tenducci, and his brother Johann Christoph Friedrich Bach. His opera *Amadis des Gaules*, produced in December 1799 at the Royal Academy of Music in Paris, found little critical favor.

Johann Christian Bach died in London on 1 January 1782 and was interred at old St Pancras burying ground. His will, made on 14 November 1781, left everything he had to "Cecilia Bach late Cecilia Grassi," a sadly ironic bequest, for his widow was left also with debts of over £4,000. Bach's old patron Queen Charlotte helped her with a gift, and, further assisted by a benefit, she made her way back to Italy.

Bach was a competent teacher and took pupils when he could find time during the crowded London years in which he gained the sobriquet "English Bach." Among his more celebrated students were Mrs Billington and her mother Mrs Weichsel, G. B. Zingoni, and Joseph Mazzinghi, who made such rapid strides under Bach's tutelage that he was appointed organist to the Portuguese Chapel at the age of ten. Bach also taught his nephew Wilhelm Friedrich Ernst Bach for several years in London, but there is no evidence that the boy played in England professionally.

Gainsborough painted two portraits of Johann Christian Bach. One is owned by Lord Hillingdon and one by the Liceo Musical at Bologna. There is another portrait, by Matthieu, in the Prussian State Library in Berlin. Bartolozzi and J. F. Schröter engraved medallions of him.

For a detailed and competent life of Bach and a catalogue of his works, see Charles Sanford Terry, *J. C. Bach* (Oxford, 1929).

**Bach, Johann Christoph** *b. 1764, clavier player, teacher.*

Johann Christoph, second son of Johann Christoph Bach (1642–1703) and his wife Maria Elisabeth Wedemann Bach, was born at Eisenach on 27 August 1674. Very little is known about him. He taught the clavier in Erfurt and in England, where he probably was living by 1720, for Baker in his biography of the first Duke of Chandos finds a payment to him for a harpsichord in that year. It is possible that he was the Bach who played a solo in a *concerto grosso* organized by Pepusch at Hickford's Great Room on 16 April 1729.

**Bachelor.** *See* BATCHELOR.

**Back.** *See* LA BACH.

**Backington, Miss** [fl. 1734], *actress*.
Miss Backington played Ramilie in *The Miser* at the small theatre in James Street on 31 May 1734.

**Bacon, Mr** [fl. 1784], *singer*.
Mr Bacon was listed as one of the tenor vocal performers in the Handel Memorial Concerts at Westminster Abbey and the Pantheon in May and June 1784.

**Badcock,** [Mr?] [fl. 1796–1799], *house servant*.
The Covent Garden accounts list one Badcock, servant, at a constant salary of 12s. daily for the 1796–97 through the 1798–99 seasons. Badcock's duties are not known.

**Baddeley Junior** [fl. 1781], *actor*.
*See* BADDELEY, MRS ROBERT.

**Baddeley, Richard** [fl. 1661–1662], *sub-treasurer*.
Richard Baddeley was a sub-treasurer of the Duke's Company on 24 September 1662, but how long he had been with the troupe and how long he continued in it are not known.

**Baddeley, Robert** 1733–1794, *actor*.
Robert Baddeley was born on 20 April 1733 and was orphaned at an early age. As a young man he is said to have been a cook for the actor-manager Samuel Foote from whom he acquired his interest in the stage. Supposedly he also spent three years on the Continent as valet to a travelling gentleman, thereby acquiring the smattering of foreign languages and a knowledge of foreign customs which later were to serve him so well as an actor.

Baddeley's first appearance on the London stage was in the role of Sir William Wealthy in Foote's new comedy, *The Minor*, at the Haymarket on 28 June 1760. He played that part throughout the summer and then offered it for his debut at Drury Lane several months later on 20 October 1760. He repeated the performance on 22 November. His other roles in his first season at Drury Lane included Frankly in *The Register Office*, Gomez in *The Spanish Fryar*, and a part in the new act to Foote's comedy *Taste*. He shared a benefit with Kear on 11 May 1761. Baddeley spent the next summer with Foote again at the Haymarket where he played Sir William Wealthy again, Sir Jasper Wilding in *The Citizen*, a role in *All in the Wrong*, and Pantaloon in *The Wishes; or, Harlequin's Mouth Open'd*. In the fall of 1761 he went to play at the Smock Alley Theatre in Dublin, where he was seen as Gomez. Where he passed the season 1762–63 is not known—perhaps touring Irish provincial towns—but by the fall of 1763 he was back at Drury Lane making a reputation for himself in low comedy roles. In this, his first full season at a patent house, he took on well over 20 roles including: the Old Captain in *Philaster*, Old Philpot in *The Citizen*, Paris in *The Jealous Wife*, Lockworth in *Love at First Sight*, Fabian in *Twelfth Night*, Biondello in *Catherine and Petruchio*, Flute and Bottom in *A Midsummer Night's Dream*, Sir Jacob Jollup, Surly, and Kastril in *The Alchemist*, Dr Caius in *The*

*Merry Wives*, Petulant in *The Way of the World*, the Frenchman in *The Recruiting Officer*, Fetch in *The Stage Coach*, Sir Philip in *A Bold Stroke for a Wife*, and Polonius in *Hamlet*.

Baddeley was to become an established member of the Drury Lane company throughout the remaining 31 years of his career. On occasion he acted in summer at the Haymarket (1772, 1776, 1780–82, 1789), at Bristol (1767), and at Richmond (1766). He made one appearance at Covent Garden, as Polonius, on 21 April 1772.

Despite the fact that Baddeley is often best remembered for the terms of his will, described below, he did not become wealthy; but he was apparently comfortable. In 1764–65, early in his engagement at Drury Lane, he was on the pay list for £3 per week. By 1774–75, he was being paid only £4 per week and by 1789–90, £9 per week. His annual benefits brought him an average of about £100 after house charges, although in some years, such as 1782–83, he seems to have had a deficit. His largest benefit recorded in the extant account books came on 12 April 1792, when he cleared £247 19s. 6d. In several seasons Baddeley accepted payments of £60 or £70 in lieu of a benefit. According to benefit notices, he was living in Tavistock Row, Covent Garden, in 1772; at No 2, Little Russell Street, between 1780 and April 1787; and from late 1787 until his death he lived at his house, No 10, New Store Street, Bedford Square.

Enjoying some reputation as a dandy, Baddeley, it was said, "loved as great variety in his amours as in his clothes." About 1763 he eloped with Sophia Snow, eighteen-year-old daughter of Valentine Snow, serjeant-trumpeter to George II and sometime musical performer at the theatres. Life with Sophia Baddeley was to be tumultuous and unhappy because of her extraordinary beauty, vanity, and recklessness. Baddeley arranged for her introduction on the

Drury Lane stage in 1764–65, and she soon became a favorite performer, especially in musical pieces. In 1770 Baddeley was involved in a bloodless duel with George Garrick, David Garrick's brother and assistant at Drury Lane, over the reputed escapades of Mrs Baddeley. After an earlier connection with Mr Mendez, a man-about-town and a merchant of considerable wealth, Mrs Baddeley had taken up with the physician Dr Hayes. David Garrick insisted that she stop living with Hayes, and she consented on the condition that Garrick pay her salary directly to her rather than through her husband. Baddeley agreed to the new arrangement provided that she should pay some of his debts. But George Garrick, hearing of the arrangement, and apparently incensed by what he regarded to be false charges against the actress, expressed his resentment to Baddeley who then challenged him. George engaged a Mr S——s, an attorney, for his second, and Baddeley asked Mendez, his early rival, to be his second. Meeting George Garrick in

*Harvard Theatre Collection*

ROBERT BADDELEY, as Sir Harry Grubbin

after De Wilde

Hyde Park early on the morning of 17 March 1770, Baddeley fired first and missed; at that point Mrs Baddeley arrived on the battlefield, threw herself upon her knees, and entreated Garrick to spare her husband. George fired into the air. The report of the duel in *Town and Country Magazine* (March 1770) was accompanied by a wood engraving.

A separation was soon agreed upon before James Wallace as referee and John St John and Arthur Murphy as legal counselors. On 28 March 1770 it was reported by *Town and Country Magazine* that Mrs Baddeley, who had not been heard of for some days, had "gone to Ireland with an officer in the army." She was back at the London theatres during the 1770's but certainly did not live with her husband. On 1 March 1778, a Robert, "son of Robert Baddeley," was buried at St Paul, Covent Garden. A "Mr Baddeley, Jun" played Harlequin in *The Genius of Nonsense* at the Haymarket on 24 July 1781. In an autographed letter in the Harvard Theatre Collection, undated but written in 1782, Mrs Baddeley mentioned her "children," particularly a boy who was then five years of age. Considering her various amorous adventures, these children were not necessarily by Robert Baddeley. In his latter years Baddeley lived with Catherine Sherry, near whom he asked to be buried at St Paul, Covent Garden, and then with Mrs Catherine Strickland, "generally called and known by the name of Baddeley."

On 30 May 1780 Baddeley suffered an "Apoplectic Fit" in Heming's Row which rendered him temporarily speechless, and it was necessary for the Haymarket prompter, Hitchcock, to read his announced part of Catchpenny in *The Suicide*. But the attack seems not to have seriously curtailed his career. By 6 June following he was back on the Haymarket stage and continued to be a consistent performer for the next 14 years. On 15 October 1794, two days before he added codicils to his will, he suf-

fered another "very serious fit." Several months later on Wednesday evening, 19 November 1794, while dressing at Drury Lane for the role of Moses in *The School for Scandal*, the character he had created in the original performance on 8 May 1777, Baddeley fell ill. He died early the next morning, 20 November 1794, at his house in New Store Street. According to a notation by John Kemble on the account book, he was 61 years old. His remains, as requested in his will, were interred on 27 November 1794 in the churchyard of St Paul, Covent Garden, near the tomb of Catherine Sherry. The funeral was attended by leading London actors, including a group called "The School of Garrick," a society formed after Garrick's death of which Baddeley was a member. Just a few days before his death, according to a manuscript in the Folger Library, he had been excluded from a group insurance policy because he could not produce a certificate of his birth.

Baddeley's will, which was drawn on 23 April 1792, and proved at London on 18 December 1794, is one of the most interesting of all theatrical dispositions. At the same time it is a rich biographical source. To the above-mentioned Mrs Catherine Strickland he left his freehold dwelling, with garden and effects at West Moulsey, Surrey, as well as his home in New Store Street, Bedford Square. Naming her his executrix, he also gave her to use for life his "Garrick's head" and all his theatrical prints, drawings, paintings, and books. After her death the two houses and £650 (kept in trust) were to revert to the Drury Lane Theatrical Fund—of which he had been a founding committee member in 1774—for the relief of indigent members of the profession, with the house in West Moulsey to be used as a retreat home for theatrical folk on the fund who "from Accident or Misfortune may have been prevented continuing their subscription long enough to entitle them to an Annuity." A sign reading "Baddeley's Asylum" was to

*Permission of the Lady Lever Collection*

ROBERT BADDELEY, as Moses

by Zoffany

be placed on the building in easy sight of passengers on the road. His theatrical effects, pictures, and books were to be kept at the Asylum. On 20 April of each year—which Baddeley stated to be his birthday—the oldest inhabitant of the asylum was to wear his medal and ribbon from the "School of Garrick Society." The inhabitants were also to receive pensions once the annual interest from the properties and money bequeathed reached £350. Each year on 20 April the directors of the Fund were obliged to reprint Baddeley's letter to the *General Advertiser* of 24 April 1790 —"as various printed books and pamphlets have . . . grossly misrepresented the disagreements between my late unhappy wife and myself" he wished by this means to let posterity know he had not merited the villainy imputed to him.

Baddeley also bequeathed the interest of £100 to provide the actors at Drury Lane with cakes and ale on Twelfth Night, a ceremonial custom observed to this day at that theatre. To the actor Richard Wroughton he left £10 and asked him to be an executor; to the actor John Bannister he left his mourning ring for David Garrick, at whose funeral in 1779 he had been an official deputy. Another bequest, suggesting an earlier serious illness perhaps connected with his fits (or strokes?), was one of £20 to the surgeon Thomas Brand of Soho Square, another executor, in expression of a "grateful heart" that could never repay the fact that to Brand he owed "many years" of his life. By a codicil of 17 October 1794, he gave mourning rings to his godson John Burgoyne Caulfield and to John's sisters, the children of General Burgoyne by Susan Caulfield.

As an actor, Baddeley never demonstrated such enormous talents as to excite the enthusiasm of the town. The roles of the great tragic heroes were not his line. He was skilled in portraying national characters such as Dr Druid in *The Fashionable Lover* and Fluellen in *Henry V*. His Swiss,

Germans, and Frenchmen "were admirably characteristic," although he achieved less success in playing Frenchmen of an elevated rank, according to a verse in *The Secret History of the Green Room* (1795):

> His skill in Frenchmen has procur'd his
> name
> No scanty portion of theatric fame.
> Yet, though we own that BADDELEY
> can trace
> Their mean servility and pet grimace,
> He poorly labours to depict by these
> The polish'd Frenchman's elegance and
> ease.
> His chief defect's a kind of snarling
> brawl,
> The testy tone of misanthropic gall;
> Which, though it well his general cast
> pourtrays,
> Invariably appears in all he plays.

His best characterization was Moses, the German Jew in *The School for Scandal*, which he "created" in 1775 and played over 200 times until his death, missing only one performance of that play at Drury Lane during his career. Among the secondary class of actors, he excelled as a low comedian. William Hawkins accounted him a good Varland in *The West Indian*, a decent Trinculo in *The Tempest*, and "not a bad Touchstone." His conception of Polonius was "just and natural" and never degraded itself into buffoonery. From his playing of peevish old men in comedy he received the nick-name of "Old Vinegar," after a character in O'Keeffe's *Son-in-Law*. Among his other roles were Canton in *The Clandestine Marriage*, which he played in its first performance on 20 February 1766, Roderigo in *Othello*, Medecin in *The Anatomist*, Old Groveby in *The Maid of the Oaks*, Cutbeard in *Epicoene*, Major Oakly in *The Jealous Wife*, Colonel Baton in *Love in the East*, and the Lord Mayor in *Richard III*. Garrick thought highly enough of him in this last role to send him to instruct the Mayor of Stratford in etiquette in preparation for his official duties at the famous Shakespeare Jubilee of 1769. Baddeley had his detractors, of course. Francis Gentleman, agreeing that he would "never miss A crouching Frenchman, or a flatt-ring Swiss . . ." found his talents for anything else "but small." The harsh John Williams (as "Anthony Pasquin") summed up his opinion in *The Children of Thespis* (1786):

> *With crab-apple phiz, and a brow that's disdainful,*
> *See Baddeley smile with fatigue that is painful;*
> *From his dissonant voice, and the form of each feature,*
> *You'd swear him the favorite child of Ill-nature . . .*
> *He snarls thro' his parts, be they easy or hard . . .*
> *As an actor he's slovenly . . .*
> *And changes his dress in so careless a hurry.*

Some years later, the same critic, in *A Pin Basket to the Children of Thespis* (1797), had mellowed and he then confessed that although Baddeley's manner remained coarse and seldom excited enthusiastic bursts of applause, "so it less frequently incurred censure." He applauded Baddeley for always studying so that he never came on less than perfect, even after a long interval had elapsed from his last playing a role.

Baddeley seems also to have written some plays. Hogan suggests that *The St Giles's Scrutiny*, the second piece played at Drury Lane on 11 April 1785 for his benefit, and *A Lesson for Lawyers*, the third piece played there on 5 May 1789, also for his benefit, were by him. He did create a number of specialty solo acts, such as the two short interludes *A Specimen of Jewish Education* (17 April 1780) and *A Specimen of Jewish Courtship* (23 April 1787) in which he presented the comic characters of Shadrack Moses, obviously capitalizing on his reputation in *The School for Scandal*. On 9 May 1767 he offered *A Humorous Descriptive Search after Scrubs* and in May 1773 a *Dissertation on Macaronies*. Similarly he appeared frequently in such specialty interludes as Garrick's *Bucks Have at Ye All*. He also devised an entertainment called *The Modern Magic Lanthorn*, which he first offered at Lebeck's Head on 5 September 1774, then at Panton Street, 10–15 April 1775, during Lent, and at Marylebone Gardens, on Thursday and Saturday nights from 30 May through 20 June of the same year.

An excellent painting of Baddeley as Moses in *The School for Scandal* was done by Zoffany and exhibited at the Royal Academy in 1781; it is now the property of the family of Mrs Keith Hutchison, whose ancestor received it from the Treasurer of Drury Lane. Baddeley is also shown in the anonymous engraving of the gallery scene from the same play with Yates as Sir Oliver, Smith as Charles, and Farren as Careless. A portrait of Baddeley by Thomas Hardy was exhibited at the Royal Academy in 1792 and was probably the painting now in the possession of the Garrick Club which shows him, head and shoulders, with powdered hair, dark coat, and wearing the badge of the Society of the School of Garrick around his neck. It was engraved by W. Ridley and published as a plate to Parsons' *Minor Theatre*, 1793.

Also in the Garrick Club is a large canvas by Zoffany of a scene from *The Clandestine Marriage* with Baddeley as Canton, Mrs Baddeley as Fanny, and Thomas King as Lord Ogleby. This picture was painted, it is said, by the express command of George III as a result of the monarch's delight at seeing a performance of the play at Drury Lane on 12 October 1769. It was engraved in mezzotint by Richard Earlom in 1772. Another picture of him as Canton, a vignette, was painted and engraved by S. Harding and published by him in 1794. A miniature of him as Canton, done after Cosway, is in the Garrick Club. A canvas of Baddeley as Sir Harry Grubbin in *The Tender Husband* was done by Samuel De Wilde and is also in the Garrick Club; it was engraved by P. Audinet for a plate in *Bell's British Theatre*, 1791, and copied anonymously for a plate to *British Drama*, printed by C. Cooke in 1807. A drawing in India ink by M. Brown of him as Peter in *2 Henry IV* is in the British Museum and was engraved by Thornthwaite for a plate to *Bell's British Theatre*, 1786. A colored drawing by Thomas Parkinson of him as Trinculo in *The Tempest*, also in the British Museum, was engraved by the artist for *Bell's Shapespeare*, 1776. Another drawing in India ink of him as Trinculo, artist unknown, is in the British Museum and was published as a plate to an edition of the play in 1778 by I. Wenman. The Harvard Theatre Collection has an anonymous engraving of Baddeley in *The Commissioner*. A painting by J. Roberts of him as Petulant in *The Way of the World* was engraved by Thornthwaite for a plate to *Bell's British Theatre*, 1777. Baddeley also is said to appear in George Carter's large canvas of "The Apotheosis of Garrick," c. 1782, in the Stratford Art Gallery of the Shakespeare Memorial Theatre, where Baddeley is shown as Dr Caius in *The Merry Wives of Windsor*.

### Baddeley, Mrs Robert, Sophia, née Snow *1745?–1786, actress, singer.*

A woman of exceptional beauty, Mrs Sophia Baddeley was one of the most popular and controversial stage personalities of her time. She was born in the parish of St Margaret, Westminster, in 1745, according to a biography written shortly after her death, but obituary notices at the time of her death suggest variously 1744, 1749, and 1750 as the year of her birth. The biography was published in six volumes in 1787, bearing the name of Mrs Elizabeth Steele, a person who claimed to have been

*Harvard Theatre Collection*

SOPHIA BADDELEY
by Zoffany

her companion and friend; but it has been attributed to the pen of Alexander Becknell, the author of a life of Alexander the Great. In the tradition of many period "memoirs" of stage figures, the work is romantic, imaginative, novelized, and highly unreliable; it seems to have been written, in the words of the *Dictionary of National Biography*, "for the purpose of extorting money from the men of rank implicated in the adventures it describes."

Sophia Baddeley was the daughter of Valentine Snow, serjeant-trumpeter to George II and theatrical musician, and his wife Mary Snow. Her grandfather was Moses Snow, the royal musician. She had at least one brother, Jonathan Snow (b. 1741), who as Master Snow appeared as a juvenile harpsichordist at the Haymarket in 1751. Almost certainly the Robert Snow (widower of Valentina Snow) who left a substantial estate to his four minor children by his will, which was proved on 14 December 1771, was also a brother.

Sophia was educated in music by her father. About 1763, at the age of about 18, she ran off with the actor Robert Baddeley, whom she soon married. He was influential in obtaining her first theatrical engagement, which Becknell claims was as Cordelia in *King Lear* at Drury Lane, when she went on in place of an ill actress, never having seen the play performed:

When Edgar came in, as Mad Tom, his figure and manner gave her such an unexpected shock, that through real terror she screamed and fell down motionless, and it was some time before she recovered. The audience, to an individual, sympathized with her, and she resumed her character, encouraged by the thunder of reiterated applause from every quarter of the house.

The fact of the matter was that Mrs Baddeley did not play Cordelia at Drury Lane until 29 April 1766. Her debut took place some 19 months earlier on 27 September 1764 when, listed in the bills as a young gentlewoman, she played Ophelia to Holland's Hamlet and Mrs Pritchard's Gertrude. Her second appearance was in the same role on 22 November 1764; on 27 April 1765, again as Ophelia, she was identified in the bills by name, for her third appearance on any stage. She played Polly in *The Beggar's Opera* a week later on 7 May. In her first season at Drury Lane she and her husband were on the pay list together at 10s. per day, or £3 per week. Mrs Baddeley's early appearances should not be confused with those of a young dancer named Miss Snow, perhaps her sister, who made her first appearance on any stage at Covent Garden on 10 May 1765 in a hornpipe.

In the summer of 1765 Mrs Baddeley joined the company at Manchester while her husband engaged at Liverpool, this being the earliest of the separations made necessary by the irregular demands of their respective careers. At Manchester she ap-

parently found great comfort in the attentions of the actor John Edwin. She returned to Drury Lane in 1765–66, when on 13 January she again played Ophelia, at which time the prompter William Hopkins wrote in his manuscript diary, "very bad, all but the singing." In the summer of 1766 she joined her husband at the new Richmond Theatre, under the management of Love, where among several other roles she played Juliet to young Cautherley's Romeo.

The next five years were to be very busy ones for her professionally. From 1766 to 1770 she was a regular member of the Drury Lane company and played a number of roles for the first time including Emily in *The Runaway*, Cecilia in *As You Like It*, Fidelia in *The Foundling*, Patty in *The Maid of the Mill*, and Urganda in *Cymon*. On 10 October 1767 she acted Imogen in *Cymbeline*, a performance in which the prompter Hopkins noted she did "pretty well,–but an indifferent figure in Breeches," a comment on her figure somewhat contrary to the opinion of Hugh Kelly, who in *Thespis* (1776) wrote that he found her form to be as sweet as her voice.

Mrs Baddeley appeared at Covent Garden, announced as from Drury Lane, on 13 April 1769 as Patty in *The Maid of the Mill* for the benefit of Mrs Vincent. She also played at the Haymarket, out-of-season, in 1768–69 and under Foote's management there in the summer of 1769. At the end of that summer, in early September, she sang in Arne's oratorio *Judith* at the great Shakespeare Jubilee at Stratford under the stewardship of Garrick. About this time she was also engaged as a singer on "high terms"– her biographer claims at 12 guineas per week–at the pleasure gardens of Ranelagh, Vauxhall, and Finch's Grotto, where some of her more popular renditions included the songs "My Jockey is the blithest Lad," "No more shall Buds or Branches spring," and Potter's "Sandy."

Although Mrs Baddeley's sweet voice,

SOPHIA BADDELEY, as Joan
by J. Roberts

vivacious personality, and exceptional beauty were making her the fashion, they were also contributing to her increasing personal problems. In 1768 she began an affair with the actor Charles Holland, and "under a pretence of being privately instructed by him" in acting, she used to call at his lodgings three or four times a week. When he died in 1769, his physician Dr Hayes assumed his place in her affections. Her husband—himself a man of "great variety in his amours"—seemed not much troubled over his wife's diversions, though he insisted that she continue to contribute to his expenses. Baddeley's cavalier attitude, however, provoked George Garrick to challenge him. A famous bloodless duel resulted, on 17 March 1770. Although George Garrick and Baddeley were reconciled by the pleading intervention of Sophia on the battlefield, the rift between husband

and wife apparently never closed. On 25 March 1770, it was reported that she had set off for Dublin, "induced by her husband's behaviour," accompanied by an army officer. (She was, however, advertised for singing Rhodope in *A Peep Behind the Curtain* at Drury Lane on 26 March.) During the summer Baddeley had his lawyer, a Mr Levey of Fetter Lane, draw up a case against his wife, which according to David Garrick's letter to his brother George on 30 August 1770 was full of falsehoods; and the manager hoped that the testimony of Mrs Baddeley and her father would "shew him in his proper Colours." With Arthur Murphy and John St John of the Middle Temple as counselors and before James Wallace as referee, a separation was soon agreed upon.

Mrs Baddeley spent the summer of 1770 in Ireland with her army officer, William Hanger, the eldest son of the Irish nobleman Lord Coleraine, who provided her with carriage, house, purse, and a prodigious amount of genteel company, according to her early biographer. It was an easy arrangement in several respects, for when Hanger's brother John seemed to be suffering from a passionate disorder she moved in with him to effect a cure.

She returned to Drury Lane for the 1770–71 season and continued to play on the same stage with her husband, although reportedly they never addressed each other "except when the utterance was dramatic." The story is told that during a command performance of *The Clandestine Marriage* Mrs Baddeley played with such pointed coyness the scene in which Baddeley (as Canton) urged King (as Lord Ogleby) to make love to her (as Fanny) that the delighted George III ordered her to be painted by Zoffany in the character, the result being one of the loveliest of eighteenth-century theatrical illustrations.

While singing at Marylebone Gardens in the summer of 1771, Mrs Baddeley had a dispute with Garrick over her salary which caused her to quit Drury Lane before the 1771–72 season began. The breach was brought on by a compliment paid to her by Samuel Foote in his play *The Maid of Bath*, which was played at the Haymarket in June 1771. In one scene the character Flint, upon hearing the character Miss Linnet sing, says, "Enchanting! ravishing sounds! not the Nine Muses themselves, nor Mrs Baddeley, is equal to you." Garrick wrote to Foote on 24 September 1771 to chide him about the line, which Mrs Baddeley had considered so great a compliment that she now demanded an increase of £3 per week along with other conditions in respect to her roles and the timing of her benefit. Claiming that she had a gentleman admirer who would lose his life for her — apparently now Lord Melbourne — and therefore did not value a thousand pounds, she refused to "come to her business." She did not appear as Polly for the opening night at Drury Lane on 21 September 1771, and Miss Wrighten had to go on in her place. The result was that Mrs Baddeley was not in the company of that theatre for that and the following season, but her whereabouts are unrecorded. Probably she passed the time with her admirer Lord Melbourne. Her biographer recounts several other connections about this same period — with the Duke of York, with Sir Cecil Bishop, who sent her a valuable service of plate, and with Stephen Sayer.

Mrs Baddeley returned, however, to Drury Lane on 26 March 1774 in the role of Lady Elizabeth in *The Earl of Warwick*, announced as her first appearance there in three years. In the following season, in which she was paid £7 per week, she played Olivia in *Twelfth Night* for the first time on 11 January 1775. She left that theatre again in 1775–76 (Garrick's last on the stage) but made her debut that summer as Violante in *The Wonder* on 27 August 1776 at Brighton, where she lodged "in apartments near Pool Valley, at the south extremity of East Street." She also was at Brighton in 1777. She reengaged at Drury Lane in 1776–77 at a salary of £8 and an allowance of £4 to £6 per week for clothes, and there she remained for the next four seasons, making her last appearance there on 1 December 1780 in the title role of Arne's *Artaxerxes*. For a benefit on 11 April 1778 she cleared £139 9s. She also played at Dublin and at Cork in 1778.

By 1781, Mrs Baddeley's fortune and health began to decline. She apparently had squandered her money, and a nervous disorder which she had developed earlier in life was taking its toll. Early in 1782 she was singing at De Loutherbourg's scene-and-light spectacular, the *Eidophusikon*, when from her lodging at No 37, Princes Street in Leicester Fields, she wrote to Mrs Sheridan that De Loutherbourg had reduced her salary from £6 to £3 per week, of which she had the expenses of her dresses, and she found herself with "little more than two shillings a week left for my subsistence." She asked Mrs Sheridan to pass along a letter of appeal to the Duchess of Devonshire: "I mean to address her Grace in Behalf of my Children — in order to Enable me to put my Boy who is now 5 years of Age to School." She feared that in his "Present Situation" he was "learning nothing that's good."

Sophia wrote again to Mrs Sheridan on 18 May 1782 to remind her of her plight and once more to solicit her intercession with the Duchess, in behalf of her "Unfortunate Child whom I so earnestly wish to Snatch from Destruction." This notice of her "Children," especially of the five-year-old son, provokes speculation about the father or fathers. A Robert, "son of Robert Baddeley," was buried at St Paul, Covent Garden, on 1 March 1778, some three years before Mrs Baddeley's letter to Mrs Sheridan. The register entry does not mention Mrs Baddeley as the mother. But on 24 July 1781, a "Mr Baddeley, Jun" played Harlequin in *Genius of Nonsense* at the Haymarket. Performers as young as five

*Harvard Theatre Collection*

ROBERT and SOPHIA BADDELEY with THOMAS KING
in *The Clandestine Marriage*

by Zoffany

were usually listed in the bills as "Master," not "Mr . . . Junior." Nevertheless, perhaps this was the son—possibly now under the influence of Robert Baddeley, who may have been exploiting him or leading him into a theatrical life—about whom Sophia was so distressed. Given the legends of Mrs Baddeley's own amorous wanderings, this boy need not have been sired by Robert, but if he had been, then the belief that the couple was estranged to the point of no communication after 1770 must be suspect. According to her biographer, "Elizabeth Steele" (whose chronology is uncertain), Mrs Baddeley, having no children of her own, had adopted the son of her cook.

Sophia had certainly lived for a while with the actor William Brereton. By report of her early biographer she also lived with an actor named Webster for two or three years and had her first child by him when she went to play with him in Ireland. The child died upon her return to London. Webster also died, leaving her pregnant. (But the biographer says nothing about a birth.) Sophia next took up with a fellow named "John," who had been Webster's favorite servant and with whom she lived for a while in a small house in Pimlico.

Whether or not the Duchess of Devonshire ever responded with charity is unknown, but soon Mrs Baddeley was "compelled to take refuge from her creditors" and leave London. First she went to Dublin where she played at the Smock Alley Theatre on 2 December 1782. While in Dublin she apparently became the mistress of Richard Daly, the manager there. Mrs Inchbald had tea at Mrs Hitchcock's on 20 January 1783, "and heard the truth of Mrs Badeley and Mr Daly." Next she seems to have gone to act for Tate Wilkinson at York, where according to Genest she enjoyed great popularity. By now her health was in fast decline. Besides being very lame at her last benefit at York she was stupid with laudanum and almost unable to act. Wilkinson wrote that by now the "quantity of laudanum she indulged herself with was incredible." But she struggled on to Edinburgh, making her first appearance in that city on 1 February 1783 as Clarissa in *The School for Fathers*. On 5 February she played Ophelia, then Mrs Lovemore in *The Way to Keep Him* on 26 March, Harriet in *The Jealous Wife* on 2 April, and Imogen in *Cymbeline* on 9 April. Her benefit came on 26 April, when she played Lady Teazle in *The School for Scandal* and Lady Bab Lardoon in *The Maid of the Oaks*, singing the air of "No Flower that Blows" in the latter piece. She was living then at Mrs Cumings, Scale Stairs, at Dickson's Close in the Exchange. Her final role that season seems to have been Jane Shore for the benefit of Miss Farren on 3 May.

She remained in the Edinburgh company in 1783–84 and 1784–85. Then, according to her *Memoirs*, "she fell into consumption" and could play no longer. In her last year she was supported, said the *Gentleman's Magazine*, by a small stipend from the Drury Lane Actors' Fund, although "Mrs Steele" wrote that the Edinburgh players "subscribed a weekly sum, to afford her all the comforts a sick bed required, and a proper person to attend her." After lingering a few months she died on 1 July 1786 at her apartment in Shakespeare Square, Edinburgh, and was buried in the Calton burial ground, attended by the actors from the theatre. At the time of her death she was, according to her *Memoirs*, aged 46; however, other obituary notices give her age at death as variously 37, 38, and 42. As a warning to other performers of the consequences of a life of vice, Anthony Pasquin wrote of her death in *The Children of Thespis* (1787):

Turn your fancy to Scotia, where rigorous
  snows,
Envelope her rocks, and stern Eolus
  blows;
There view lovely Baddeley stretch'd on
  her bier,
Whose pallid remains claim the kindred
  tear:
Emaciate and squalid her body is laid,
Her limbs lacking shelter, her muscles
  decay'd.
An eminent instance of feminine terror,
A public example to keep us from error.

It is to be expected that in an age when drama was pointing constantly to a sentimental moral that accounts of Mrs Baddeley would stress the "public example" she offered of the dangers of seduction. While in the bloom of her life, her reckless extravagances, her vanity, and her undeniable loveliness of face and figure all contributed to creating the kind of public personality so often equated with the profession of actress. The remarks of William Hawkins, *Miscellanies in Prose and Verse* (1775), are typical of the satire she invited. Hawkins judged her to be an agreeable actress and a useful singer: "but for virtue, modesty cries hush! . . . Our heroine in particular pleads the part of chastity in her characters, with so much grace, simplicity, and propriety, that were we not sensible to the contrary, we might, without doubt, imagine it to be her natural qualification." In a letter to the *Morning Post* in August 1774, Mrs Baddeley protested the earlier publication by that paper of confidential correspondence between "a beautiful actress" and "a noble Lord" as an invasion of her privacy, asking what family in the kingdom could be safe or happy when an editor of a paper would expose their most confidential concerns brought by a malevolent enemy or a treacherous servant. "I have this consolation," she concluded, "if I have my follies, they are *innocent,* and make up but part of the errors of an imperfect world." The editor defended himself by pointing out that the correspondence had been published as anonymous, and that when Mrs Baddeley and her brother had rushed into the shop after the printing of the first letter, he withdrew the second in the series from his forms and printed a public apology. "Mrs Baddeley wishes to have a veil thrown over what she calls her innocent follies," he concluded, "but surely this is not the way to accomplish so desirable an end!" He was "in possession of vouchers," he claimed which would make her conduct appear "far from Innocent with respect to the Community at Large."

If suspected by the larger community, she was adored by a certain male coterie of fashion. Once when she was refused admission to the Pantheon—because of the management's decision to exclude women of doubtful character—fifty gentlemen, supposedly headed by Captain George Hanger, with drawn swords, pushed by the constables and "escorted her in triumph to the rooms" and then demanded an apology from the management. Two bust portraits in oval frames, of Mrs Baddeley and Captain Hanger, alluding to the event, were published in *Town and Country Magazine* in June 1772.

As an actress her strength was in the roles of innocent young women in genteel comedy. She did not often appear in tragic parts, although she was highly regarded as Mrs Beverley in *The Gamester*, a role she took on with success from Mrs Barry when that actress became suddenly indisposed. During her best years, however, she displayed her engaging talents in singing roles like Polly in *The Beggar's Opera* and

in entertaining at the pleasure gardens. "As a singer, wherever pathetic expression was necessary, she stood unrivalled," and her rendering of "Sweet Willy O!" according to the *Scots Magazine*, contributed greatly to the huge financial success which Garrick enjoyed when he restaged his Jubilee Celebration at Drury Lane in 1769–70.

In addition to the painting by Zoffany of *The Clandestine Marriage*, mentioned above, that artist did a lovely portrait of her which was engraved by R. Laurie and published by R. Sayer in 1772; a copy was engraved by H. R. Cook and published by Payne in 1814. J. Roberts did her as Clarissa in *Lionel and Clarissa*, engraved by Thornthwaite for *Bell's British Theatre* in 1781, and as Joan la Pucelle in *1 Henry VI*, engraved anonymously for *Bell's Shakespeare*, 1776. A picture of her as Mrs Strictland in *The Suspicious Husband* was done by T. Parkinson, engraved by J. Taylor, and published by T. Lowndes as a plate to *New English Theatre*, 1776.

**Baderdon.** *See* BETTERTON.

**Badini.** *See also* BEDINI.

**Badini, Signora** [*fl.* 1792], *singer.*
In *The First London Notebook* (1792), Haydn mentioned a female singer named Badini among the musical people he encountered. She is not otherwise known, though she may have been related both to Carlo Francesco Badini the librettist and to Signora Bedini the dancer, both of whom were in London in this period.

**Badini, Carlo Francesco** [*fl.* 1770–1793], *librettist, poet, journalist, manager.*
The contemporary records concerning Carlo Francesco Badini present some baffling problems, but it seems probable that he was born in Italy, came to England at a fairly early age (perhaps with his father, who may have had the same name) and pursued a varied career that encompassed

both music and literature. His fame rests on his work as a librettist, and his earliest recorded text was to the comic opera *Nanetta e Lubino*, produced at the King's Theatre on 8 April 1769. His *Il disertore*, published in London in 1770, and given one performance at the King's Theatre in the Haymarket on 19 May 1770, was printed again in Lisbon in 1772. Whether or not he was in England during this period is unknown, but the Lisbon publication suggests that perhaps he went to the Continent after his work was performed in London.

Badini's *Le pazzie di Orlando* was given at the King's Theatre on 23 March 1771 but not printed until 1773 in Milan. On 14 January 1772 at the same house his libretto for *Carnevale di Venezia* was performed, and on 29 February 1776 *Le ali d'amore* had its London premiere. After this successful beginning it is surprising to find in the *London Advertiser* of 11 May 1779 a report that "Yesterday . . . at the Public Office in Bow-street, Mr. Badini was bound over to the peace, at the suit of [the dancer?] Mr Le Texier." No details of the case seem to have survived, nor is it clear whether or not the Badini cited was, in fact, the librettist. Just a few days after this, on 15 May, his libretto for *La governante* was given its first performance at the King's Theatre—a work based on Sheridan's *Duenna* and indicative of the librettist's fluency in English. *Il duca d'Atene* had its premier performance on 9 May 1780 and *Il trionfo della costanza* was presented on 19 December 1782—both at the King's Theatre.

In 1783 Badini published what the *Catalogue of Five Hundred Celebrated Authors* (1788) called "a very heterogeneous poem" entitled "The Flames of Newgate." The *Catalogue* also reported that "About the same period he was for a short time editor of the newspaper, called the Morning Post," and that he had recently contributed two operas to "the Italian Theatre in London" which played with moderate success.

(The operas referred to were probably works that came out shortly before the *Catalogue* was published in 1788.) In 1783 a report circulated that one Charles Francis Badini was dead. If Badini's father had the same name and anglicized it (as the librettist later did), perhaps the report was a case of mistaken identity, but the librettist was alive and well and about to embark on his most active period.

For the 1784–85 season Badini was hired as a staff librettist (or "poet," as they called him) at the King's Theatre at a salary of £100 per year. The following season he was raised to £150, and this may have been because he took on the additional duties of acting manager.

His first libretto under this new association with the King's was *L'Inglese in Italia*, done in collaboration with the composer Anfossi. When it was performed on 20 May 1786, the librettist was billed as Charles Frances Badini, but he did not need this bow to the English to win the critics' praise. The *General Advertiser* of 22 May said "The Author has . . . struck out ideas to excite the utmost powers of harmony. We do not think that he has been sufficiently seconded by Signor Anfossi. The music evidently labours under a tedious monotony." Badini was careful not to work with Anfossi again, but having won his own praise, he reverted to his Italian name. There followed a series of works, probably including the two that the *Catalogue* described as moderately successful. He altered Metastasio's *Demetrio* into *Alceste* for a 23 December 1786 production; on 1 May 1787 his *La vestale* was performed; at the Haymarket Theatre on 2 June 1789 *La generosità d'Alessandro* was given; and on 28 May 1790 *Andromaca* had its premiere. Badini apparently remained on the King's Theatre staff in 1790–91, but something must have happened during the following season to disrupt the association.

On 11 February 1792 Badini, signing himself Charles Francis again, wrote from his house at No 11, Broad Street, to Edward Jerningham:

*Most Honoured Sir*

Though I have not the honour of your personal acquaintance, yet, Sir the sublimity of your talents, and the renowned benevolence of your character encourage me to solicit your generosity in my unfortunate and surely deplorable circumstances. Having, from a cruel persecution, been deprived of my bread at the Opera-House, I am so reduced, as to be literally starving, and almost in the gulph of despondency like Chatterton. I take the opportunity of submitting a short poem to the sagacity of your judgment, and remain with the greatest respect

Most Honoured Sir
your very much devoted, and most
respectful humble servant
*Charles Francis Badini*

The letter must have done some good, for Badini was back on the King's Theatre staff in 1792–93. After this, however, records of him cease, and one wonders whether the report of his death in 1783 was perhaps a scribal error for 1793.

The dancer Signora Bedini, who was with the King's Theatre in 1787–88, and Mademoiselle Bedini, who danced there in 1793, may have been related to the librettist; if spelling errors were made in the records, perhaps they were actually husband, wife, and daughter. Haydn mentioned a female singer named Badini in his list of musical people in London in 1792, and she, too, may have been a relative of Carlo Francesco.

**Badouin.** *See* **BAUDOUIN.**

**Baer, Mr** [*fl.* 1774], *clarinetist.*
Mr Baer's playing of a clarinet concerto on 10 February 1774 in a concert at the King's Theatre was announced as his first performance in England. There is no record of subsequent appearances.

**Baetty, Mr** [*fl.* 1795–1797], *house servant?*
A person named Baetty was put on the Drury Lane pay list at 2s. per day on 25 April 1795. A Battye was taken off the list on 4 February 1797, and at that date was being paid 1s. 6d. per day.

**Bagg, Mr** [*fl.* 1767–1769], *doorkeeper.*
Mr Bagg was paid 2s. per day as a doorkeeper at Covent Garden in 1767–68 and 1768–69. (A Mr Bagg was discharged from the Norwich Theatre by order of the proprietors on 6 May 1784).

**Baggs, Zachary** [*fl.* 1685–1710], *treasurer.*
Though most of the references to Zachary Baggs (sometimes Baggly) date after 1700 and clearly identify him as treasurer of the Drury Lane company under Chistopher Rich, a letter from Aphra Behn to a creditor dated 1 August 1685 implies that Baggs was then connected with the United Company:

. . . I am indebted to Mr Bags the sum of six pownd for the payment of which Mr [Jacob] Tonson has obleged him self. Now I do here by impowre Mr Zachary Baggs, in case the said debt is not fully discharged before Michaelmas next, to stop what money he shall hereafter have in his hands of mine, upon the playing my first play till this aforesaid debt of six pownd be discharged.

Since Ralph Davenant was the United Company treasurer at this time, Baggs may have been a sub-treasurer.

From 1701 onward and perhaps earlier, Baggs was the Drury Lane treasurer. In the *London Gazette* of 9–13 October 1701, acting for the manager, he advertised the loss of the score of Purcell's *The Fairy Queen* and offered a 20 guinea reward; some parts were found, but the whole score was not discovered until the twentieth century. The first mention of a benefit for

Baggs was on 31 October 1702, and he was active with the company through the 1709–10 season.

How much authority he had is difficult to determine, but it seems to have been considerable. Steele, in treating with the company for his plays, seems to have settled the financial arrangements as much with Baggs as with the manager, Christopher Rich. On 8 July 1709 Baggs published an *Advertisement Concerning the Poor Actors*, a pamphlet which he and Rich seem to have concocted in an attempt to quell the rumor that Rich had been underpaying his players; the *Advertisement* detailed the incomes of Wilks, Betterton, Estcourt, Cibber, Mills, and Anne Oldfield, and it showed Baggs to be a careful accountant.

Baggs shared a benefit with Hall on 9 March 1710 and was still working at Drury Lane as late as 5 June of that year, but after that date his name disappeared from the records. If he had been working in the theatre since 1685 or earlier, by 1710 he may have reached retirement age. The parish registers of St Bride, Fleet Street, contain three entries which probably refer to Baggs—or perhaps his father: Dianah, daughter of Zacharah Baggs, Esq, and his wife Elizabeth, was baptized on 20 February 1672, with Lord Lagingbuvoe(?), Lady Margaret Sheldon, and Lady Dinah Harwood standing as godparents; Sheldon, son of Zacaria and Elizabeth Baggs, was baptized on 4 October 1676; and a Zacharia Baggs was buried on 14 February 1677.

**Bagnage, Mr** ₁*fl. 1716–1717*₁, *pitkeeper.*

Mr Bagnage was pitkeeper at the King's Theatre in the Haymarket at least during the 1716–17 season; the accounts for the opera *Cleartes* on 15 December 1716 show that he took in 72 people for a sum of £18.

**Bagnal, Mrs** ₁*fl. 1764–1765*₁, *candlewoman.*

Mrs Bagnal was paid 12*s.* a week as a candlewoman at Drury Lane in 1764–65, first appearing on the paylist on 9 February 1765.

**Bagnall, Mr** ₁*fl. 1734*₁, *harpsichordist.*

The Earl of Egmont's diary for 1734 twice mentions a Mr Bagnall who played harpsichord at concerts on 15 February and 22 March; he was apparently a member of the Vocal Music Club, but whether or not he was a professional is unclear. The concerts were private or semi-private, but the participants were a mixture of amateurs and public performers.

**Bagnolesi, Anna, stage name of Signora Giovanni Battista Pinacci** ₁*fl. 1731–1732*₁, *singer.*

Anna Bagnolesi (or Bagnoleti), a contralto, was billed as "lately arriv'd from Italy" when she sang in *Admeto* at the King's Theatre in the Haymarket on 7 December 1731; in the 1731 second edition of the opera she was listed as having sung Alceste, though the *Daily Courant* reported at the time that Signora Strada took that role. It is probable that at the 7 December performance Signora Bagnolesi sang Antignona, though later she may have appeared as Alceste. Her husband, Giovanni Battista Pinacci, a tenor, probably sang Ercole. During the rest of the 1731–32 season she sang Valentiniano III in *Ezio* (15 January 1732), Erenice in *Sosarme* (15 February), Veturia in *Coriolano* (25 March), either Flavio or Teodata in *Flavio* (18 April), Servilio in *Lucio Papirio* (23 May), and Filli in *Acis and Galatea* (10 June). Whether or not Signora Bagnolesi and her husband remained in England for the following season is unknown, though there is a possibility that they stayed to sing in *Alessandro* on 25 November 1732—he taking the role of Leonato and she Cleone.

**Bags.** *See* **BAGGS.**

Bagwayes. *See* RAGOIS.

### Baildon, Joseph *c. 1727–1774, composer, organist, singer.*

Joseph Baildon was one of at least three members of his family active in London musical affairs during the middle years of the eighteenth century. In contemporary notices and records it is often impossible to know which of them is intended. The Joseph of this notice was born around 1727.

Listed as Joseph Baildon, bachelor, of Christ Church, London, our subject married Charlotte Marriott of the same parish on 7 March 1752 at St Paul's Cathedral. Perhaps he was the Baildon who sang at Aungier Street Theatre, Dublin, in 1743. Singers of this name were occasionally performing at Covent Garden and Drury Lane in mid-century, and in the concert rooms. One Baildon sang in Handel's *Alexander's Feast* at Ruckholt House, Essex, in October 1743 and in the Three Choirs Festival at Worcester in September 1755. Singers listed as Baildon and Baildon, Junior, were in the paylists for performances of the *Messiah* at the Foundling Hospital in 1754, 1758, and 1759. (Possibly, however, these were the two Thomas Baildons, one of whom may have been the brother of Joseph and the other either his father or his nephew.)

A lay vicar of Westminster Abbey by 1762, Baildon that year was also appointed organist of the London churches of St Luke, Old Street, and All Saints, Fulham. In 1763 he was listed in Mortimer's *London Directory* as living in Rolls Buildings, Chancery Lane. He was reported as playing organ concertos at Ranelagh Gardens in 1767.

Baildon was buried in St Paul's churchyard "near the pump" on 2 May 1774, at which time he was identified in the burial register as from the parish of Fulham and as an organist of the Cathedral. Administration of his estate was granted to his daughter and only child, Charlotte, spinster, on 21 May 1774, when he was listed as a widower of the parish of St Giles in the Fields.

Ten catches and four glees by Baildon were published in Warren's collections, and others are in print, including a collection of songs in various editions of *The Laurel* and *Four Favourite Songs sung by Mr Beard at Ranelagh Gardens*. His other songs for the pleasure gardens included "How pleasing is beauty," sung by Lowe at Marylebone Gardens about 1750, and "On pleasure's smooth wings," sung by Gearle at Ranelagh about 1770. In 1763, he contributed songs to *Love in a Village*. In the same year, he received one of the first prizes given by the Catch Club, and in 1766 he won another for his glee "When gay Bacchus fills my breast." About 1770 he wrote a song for Jessica in *The Merchant of Venice*, "Haste Lorenzo, haste away."

### Baildon, Thomas *d. 1760, singer, composer.*

Two persons by the name of Thomas Baildon were active in London music during the mid-eighteenth century. Probably they were father and son. The one commonly regarded as the brother of Joseph Baildon (but who may have been his father) probably was the one buried on 31 October 1760 at St Paul's Cathedral churchyard, "near the pump," in the same location where Joseph was to be interred in 1774. The burial register described him as vicar choral of that church and as living in the parish of St Margaret, Westminster. According to obituary notices in the *Gentleman's Magazine* and the *London Magazine*, another Thomas Baildon, a vicar choral of St Paul's and Westminster Abbey, also belonging to the Chapel Royal, died on 1 October 1762.

Because of the ambiguity of contemporary notices, it is impossible to discriminate all of the various activities of the two Thomas Baildons from each other, or, often, from those of Joseph. One of the Thomases contributed seven songs to *Clio and Eu-terpe*, a collection published in 1758. Sing-ers listed as Baildon and Baildon, Junior, were paid £1 10s. and 10s. 6d. respectively for singing in the Foundling Hospital per-formances of the *Messiah* in 1754, 1758, and 1759.

**Baildon, Thomas** *d. 1762, singer, composer.* See **BAILDON, THOMAS** *d. 1760.*

**Bailey.** *See also* **BAILY** *and* **BAYLEY.**

**Bailey, Samuel** [*fl. 1694–1707*], *actor.*

Samuel Bailey was a player of mostly minor roles in the United and Betterton companies. His first recorded role, though he was acting earlier, was Courtall in *The She-Gallants* at Lincoln's Inn Fields in late December 1695. Between then and 1703 he appeared in such secondary parts as Selim in *The Mourning Bride*, the Earl of Lancaster in the Betterton version of *Henry IV*, Lucio in the Gildon version of *Measure for Measure*, and Lorenzo in the Granville version of *The Jew of Venice*. By 1707 he was apparently earning be-tween £40 and £50 yearly—the lowest scale among the men in the acting com-pany but a level comparable to that of Mills and Griffith, both actors who later gained some fame. After 1707 Bailey's name dis-appeared from the bills; perhaps the Sam-uel Bayley who died about April 1708 was the actor.

**Bailey, William, stage name of Wil-liam O'Reilly** *d. 1791, actor, man-ager.*

William Bailey began adult life as a merchant in London. By 1772 (or earlier) and in 1774 (and perhaps later) he was manager of a theatrical circuit based on Norwich and including also Colchester, Bury, Bungay, and Aylsham. He was pro-prietor of a theatrical booth at Stourbridge

Fair, near Cambridge, in September of 1772 and again in 1773 and 1774.

William was probably the "Baily" who acted several times at Richmond, Surrey, in August 1776, his first recorded per-formances anywhere near London. For a benefit on 26 January 1778 Bailey played Gomez in *The Spanish Friar* in a company of casuals at the Haymarket, usually dark at that season. Also, for benefits, he acted there on 9 February as Ratcliffe in *Jane Shore* and Sir Patrick O'Neale in *The Irish Widow* and on 23 March as Captain O'Cutter in *The Jealous Wife*. On the latter occasion Bailey's wife came forward for the first time we notice, playing the part of Toilette in the mainpiece. Bailey was Peri-winkle in *A Bold Stroke for a Wife* on 31 March, Ernesto in *The Orphan* (while his wife played Florella) on 9 April, and Sir John English in *The Country Lasses* on 29 April.

Bailey's considerable ability to shift from one to another of a multiplicity of parts is demonstrated by his brief and financially unfortunate experience as proprietor and actor-manager of the little summer theatre called China Hall, located between Rother-hithe and Deptford. It is not known when he began his association with China Hall, but he was managing and acting there when it opened for a season on 25 May 1778. Be-tween that date and the enforced interrup-tion of the season on 26 June, the surviving bills show him acting at least 17 different parts in addition to performing managerial duties: Jollup in *The Mayor of Garratt*, Beau Trippit in *The Lying Valet*, Gibby in *The Wonder*, Catesby in *Jane Shore*, Sir Jealous Traffic in *The Busy Body*, Hard-castle in *She Stoops to Conquer*, Biondello in *Catherine and Petruchio*, Brush in *The Clandestine Marriage*, James in *The Mock Doctor*, Peter in *Romeo and Juliet*, Duke in *Venice Preserved*, Nottingham in *The Earl of Essex*, Mortimer in *The Fashionable Lover*, Old Grub in *Cross Purposes*, Blunt in *Richard III*, Blunt in *The London Mer-*

*chant*, and Simon Pure in *Bold Stroke for a Wife*.

Bailey's wife played such parts as the chambermaid in *The Clandestine Marriage*, Charlotte in *The Mock Doctor*, Melinda in *The Ghost*, Harriet in *The Miser*, and the Widow Brady in *The Irish Widow* ("with an Epilogue song").

Shortly after the performance of 26 June 1778 the China Hall house caught fire. (Cape Everard, who was of the company at the time, believed it was set afire, either by competitors at nearby St Helena Gardens or by the Methodists.) The theatre was completely consumed, along with its wardrobe, scenery, machinery, and properties. Everard says that Bailey, determined to continue, employed a carpenter who, with the company assisting, fashioned a makeshift theatre: "he obtained the lend of nearly a hundred pounds worth of sail-cloth, bays [baize] and canvass, and, in about a month, we opened a theatrical tent, or booth." The company flourished for six weeks more before performances were closed down by officers of the peace.

Bailey took the insurance money which was paid him after the destruction of the first China Hall Theatre and with it erected a second, but almost immediately upon its completion it was blown down in the wind storm of 25 November 1778.

Mr and Mrs Bailey went to Edinburgh for the winter season of 1779–80 and were announced there as "from Dublin." Mrs Bailey was in Tate Wilkinson's summer company in Edinburgh in July 1780, and both she and her husband were announced as "from Edinburgh" when they went with Wilkinson to the York circuit in August. Both remained with the York company in 1781 and 1782. On 15 January 1782 Wilkinson's account book noted that Mrs Bailey forfeited a week's salary for refusing to dance in *Love in a Village*.

Bailey made his Smock Alley, Dublin, debut on 2 November 1782 under what was apparently his real name, O'Reilly. He played an unspecified part in *Cheapside* at the Haymarket on 17 September 1783, billed as "from the Theatre Royal, York." Except for a brief interval in 1786 when he was again in Edinburgh, he made his career in Ireland, not only in Dublin, but also in Cork, Limerick, Belfast, Kilkenny, and Waterford. Clark places him at Galway in 1793 and at Belfast in 1796, but is confusing him with another actor of the name, for the William Bailey we have been following died on 23 May 1791. He was buried at St James's Church, Dublin, on 27 May. His will, filed under the name of William Reilly, left his property to his wife, who is identified as Mary Sophia, née Arnold.

*The Mirror* (1790) commended Bailey's versatility:

> There's a twang on his tongue but you
>   never will find,
> That his talents are cribbed by a twang
>   of the mind;
> It varies with character, ever appearing
> The point to possess, and the actor en-
>   dearing

**Bailey, Mrs William, stage name of Mrs William O'Reilly, Mary Sophia, née Arnold** [*fl.* 1778–1782], *actress, singer.* See BAILEY, WILLIAM.

**Baillie.** *See* BAILEY.

**Baily.** *See also* BAILEY *and* BAYLEY.

**Baily, Mrs** [*fl.* 1742–1746], *actress.*
A Mrs Baily first appeared in a few unspecified roles in plays performed at the James Street Theatre under Julian's management in 1742. She may be the Mrs Baily who acted with the Smock Alley company in June 1743. She acted such parts as Lady Easy in *The Careless Husband*, Lucinda in *The Conscious Lovers*, and Almeda in *Don Sebastian*.

There was a "Mrs Bayley," possibly the same, at Aungier Street Theatre, Dublin, on 28 November 1743. A Mrs Bailey played Cherry there in *The Beaux' Stratagem* on 6 August 1746; and on 18 April 1748 a Mrs Baily was given a benefit at Smock Alley Theatre.

**Bain.** *See* **BAYNE.**

**Bainbridge.** *See* **BAMBRIDGE.**

**Baines.** *See* **BAYNES.**

**Baini, Cecilia** [*fl. 1763–1764*], *singer.*
Cecilia Baini made her first appearance at the King's Opera on 26 November 1763 in the role of Mitranes in *Cleonice*. She sang this role and Eurito in *Senocrita* several times that season and probably appeared in the several other operas which were performed but for which no casts were listed.

**Bainville.** *See* **D'BAINVILLE.**

**Baites.** *See* **BATES.**

**Baker, Mr** [*fl. 1683*], *actor.*
A Mr Baker played the old servant Mrs Frances in *Dame Dobson* at Dorset Garden on 31 May 1683; this could be a misprint for Mrs Baker, though actors frequently played such roles. The only male Baker otherwise known to be active at this time was Francis Baker, but he was in Dublin from about 1670 to 1685.

**Baker, Mr** [*fl. 1729–1730*], *singer.*
A Mr Baker sang a solo at Lincoln's Inn Fields Theatre on 14 May 1730 and probably at other times in the choruses, for he shared a benefit on 21 May.

**Baker, Mr** [*fl. 1729–1730*], *singer.*
A Mr Baker was on the roster as a singer at Drury Lane Theatre in the season of 1729–30.

**Baker, Mr** [*fl. 1732*], *dancer, actor.*
A Mr Baker played Mephistopheles in *The Metamorphosis of Harlequin* in performances at the "Great Theatrical Booth in the Cherry-Tree Garden near the Mote" during the Tottenham Court Fair in August 1732. He was very likely the same Baker who danced at the New Haymarket in the following season. He was accorded a special benefit, "By Desire of several Persons of Quality," at Drury Lane Theatre on 31 December 1733.

**Baker, Mr** [*fl. 1740*], *actor.*
A Mr Baker was listed as playing Triton in *Neptune's Palace* at Hallam's theatrical booth during Bartholomew Fair in August 1740.

**Baker, Mr** [*fl. 1742–1745*], *pit door-keeper.*
Mr Baker, pit doorkeeper at Drury Lane Theatre and "late Linen Draper in Wood Street," was given a benefit at Drury Lane on 17 May 1742 because of his recent failure in business. He remained in the office of doorkeeper through the season of 1744–45, but his name does not occur in the house lists after the benefit which he shared on 6 May 1745.

**Baker, Mr** [*fl. 1744–1745*], *singer.*
A Mr Baker appeared infrequently at Drury Lane Theatre, singing between acts in the season of 1744–45.

**Baker, Mr** [*fl. 1749–1750*], *singer.*
A Mr Baker sang at Marylebone Gardens about 1749 and 1750, in which years were published editions of the music to the air *When Beauty and Wit at First did Conspire,* as he rendered it.

**Baker, Mr** [*fl. 1752–1757*], *house servant.*
A Mr Baker took benefits among others identifiable as house servants and technical personnel at Drury Lane in the seasons of 1752–53, 1753–54, 1754–55, and 1756–57.

**Baker, Mr** ₍fl. 1760–1761₎, *box office keeper.*

A Mr Baker was on the house salary list at Covent Garden Theatre as box office keeper in the season 1760–61. He earned 15*s.* per week.

**Baker, Mr** ₍fl. 1760–1769?₎, *dancer, actor. See* **BAKER, SARAH.**

**Baker, Mr** ₍fl. 1770₎, *singer.*

In the summer of 1770 a Mr Baker sang at Finch's Grotto Gardens, St George's Field, Southwark.

**Baker, Mr** ₍fl. 1775₎, *actor.*

A Mr Baker played Belcour in *The West Indian* at the Richmond Theatre on 14 June 1775 in what was said to be his first performance on any stage. It is not known whether or not he re-appeared, though he may have been the Baker who was at Drury Lane in the season of 1776–77.

**Baker, Mr** ₍fl. 1776–1777₎, *actor.*

A Mr Baker was introduced at Drury Lane Theatre on 28 September 1776 as "A Young Gentleman (first appearance on any stage)" in the part of Jerry Sneak in *The Mayor of Garratt.* In his diary, the prompter William Hopkins identified Baker and commented that "he is a tall, thin, awkward Figure, looked like a Pinmaker is a very strong Copy of poor [Thomas] Weston, has some Requisites, may in Time be a tolerable Actor in low Comedy—pretty well received." John Philip Kemble added to this his own note: "Mr Baker, I have heard, had at this Time received an Inheritance of fifteen thousand Pounds, which he so quickly dissipated as to be reduced within five years after to the Condition of Coachman to a Bristol Diligence."

During this 1776–77 season Baker earned £2 per week, playing very infrequently in such roles as Maw-worm in *The Hypocrite* and the Gardener in *The Drum-mer.* He played Jerry Sneak again when the farce followed the historic first performance of *The School for Scandal* on 8 May 1777. His final appearance in London was in the same part on 6 June 1777. But he carried the part to the China Hall company at Rotherhithe in the summer and, so far as the record shows, ended his career playing it and Davy in *The Mock Doctor,* Diggory in *She Stoops to Conquer,* and Tester in *The Suspicious Husband.* After the destruction of the China Hall theatre and the dispersal of its company in November 1778 he was not heard from again.

**Baker, Mrs** *d.* 1760?, *singer, actress, dancer.*

The Mrs Baker who was first seen in London as a dancer at Drury Lane Theatre in 1749–50 may be the same performer who was advertised as acting at Covent Garden for the first time on 2 November 1753 as Corinna in *The Confederacy.*

Mrs Baker's success in such parts as Corinna, requiring youth and vivacity, was instant, and her versatility secured for her in her first season the frequent if not unrivalled possession of such roles as Jenny in *The Provok'd Husband,* Serina in *The Orphan,* Lucinda in *The Conscious Lovers,* Biddy in *Miss in Her Teens,* Lucy in *Oroonoko,* Ann Page in *The Merry Wives of Windsor,* Miss Prue in *Love for Love,* Cherry in *The Beaux' Stratagem,* Sylvia in *The Old Bachelor,* and Lettice in *The Schoolboy.* Among the other characters she annexed during the decade or so in which she played in London were: Isabella in *The Revenge,* Cleone in *The Distress'd Mother,* Charmion in *All for Love,* Parisatis in *The Rival Queens,* Oriana in *The Inconstant,* Betty in *The Refusal,* Valeria in *The Rover,* Flametta in *A Duke and No Duke,* Inis in *The Wonder,* Lucia in *Cheats of Scapin,* Cynthia in *The Double Dealer,* and Drusilla in *The Prophetess.*

Though the name "Mrs Baker" appears in the Covent Garden bills almost continuously from 1753–54 until the later 1770's, the Mrs Baker we have been following here appears to be the lady alluded to in a contemporary manuscript notation: "Mrs Baker, actress dyed this day [10 October 1760] at Coventry on her Journey from Liverpool to London." Furthermore, there are no female Bakers in the London bills in 1761–62.

This Mrs Baker is not to be confused with the actress known to have married the elder Thomas Baker late in 1764 and who acted only after September 1762, at first as Miss Miller, nor with Mrs David Erskine Baker, who was at Covent Garden for a few seasons. It is at least possible, however, that the Mrs Baker who died in 1760 was the *first* wife of Thomas Baker the elder.

**Baker, Mrs** *[fl. 1770]*, *puppeteer.*

In or about the year 1770 a Mrs Baker was proprietress of an obscure puppet show in and around London and Westminster.

**Baker, Mrs** *[fl. 1780]*, *actress.*

A Mrs Baker was the Lady Brainless in *The Modish Wife* in a special benefit performance at the Haymarket Theatre on 3 January 1780. Advertised as from "the Theatre Royal, York," a Mrs Baker, probably the same, assumed the parts of Mrs Increase in *The Detection* and Mrs Magnum in *The City Association* at the Haymarket on 13 November 1780. Most of the other performers that night were either novices, minor players, or from provincial houses.

It is doubtful that Mrs Baker was in London at any other time, unless she is to be identified with the singer Mrs Thomas Baker the younger, who had disappeared from the metropolitan scene about 1775. It is possible that she was the Mrs Baker who was at Edinburgh in 1777 and at Bristol in 1782–83. She may have been related to Joseph Baker, who managed at York from about 1750 to about 1769.

**Baker, Miss** *[fl. 1746–1747]*, *dancer.*

Miss Baker, a juvenile dancer, first appeared in a *Peasant Dance* with Master Morgan at Goodman's Fields Theatre on 27 October 1746 and repeated the dance many nights thereafter. She is probably related to the Mr T. Baker who played minor roles at the theatre that season.

**Baker,** *[Miss?]* *[fl. 1766–1767]*, *singer.*

A female singer named Baker was on the Covent Garden company lists at a salary of 11s. 8d. per day in the 1766–67 season.

**Baker, Miss** *[fl. 1773–1774]*, *actress.*

A Miss Baker was carried on the Covent Garden Theatre's company lists as an actress in the season 1773–74, though she was given no parts in the bills. She was probably related to Mr and Mrs T. Baker, who also performed at the theatre in this season.

**Baker, Ann** *1761–1817*, *actress.*

Ann Baker was the elder daughter of a Mr Baker whose first name is unknown and of his wife Sarah Wakelin Baker. Both parents are thought to have been on the London stage before moving permanently to the provinces, where Ann's mother Sarah Baker became the most redoubtable female British theatrical entrepreneur of the eighteenth century.

Ann may possibly have danced or acted with her parents and in-laws at Sadler's Wells, and it is perhaps she who appeared in an irregular performance at the Haymarket on 15 March 1779, in the walk-on part of a maid in *The Humours of Oxford*. She acted with her mother's excellent provincial company for a number of years, able, in the words of Miss Norma Hodgson, to "play Lady Macbeth or Little Pickle in *The Romp* with equal facility." She died on 8 October 1817, just four days before the death of her younger sister Sarah, who had married the famed comedian William Dowton.

### Baker, Bartholomew  (fl. 1615?–1679), actor.

Bartholomew Baker, probably born between 1610 and 1620, was a member of the King's Company under Thomas Killigrew during the 1662–63 season and was involved financially and legally with several actors in the troupe during the following 12 or so years, but no roles of his are known and his direct connection with the company may have ended after a season or two.

On 10 June 1663 Baker, Michael Mohun, Robert Shatterell, Walter Clun, William Wintershall, and William Cartwright —all King's Company players—leased to Margery Nephway, a widow, one of three houses they had recently built in the parish of St Martin-in-the-Fields, for 21 years at £24 annual rent. About this time Clun sold his two theatre shares at a tremendous profit and Pepys reported how rich and proud some of the actors had grown; Baker was probably one of them. On 31 July 1663 Baker petitioned against Shatterell for payment of a debt, and there seems to have been a good deal of buying, selling, and borrowing going on among the players about this time. In late 1667 and early 1668 Baker was again at law against Shatterell.

Over the years Baker acquired a considerable estate, and one of the pieces of property he owned was detailed on John Lacy's 1673 map of the parish of St Paul, Covent Garden. Baker owned a 30′ by 135′ strip of land touching the northeast corner of the Theatre Royal property—the Bridges Street playhouse on this land had probably burned down by the time the map was drawn and the new Drury Lane may have been under construction. Baker's property was on the corner of Russell Street and Drury Lane, the long side fronting the former.

By an indenture dated 18 April 1678, Baker, from St Clement Danes, made over the bulk of his estate, the actual transfer occurring on 19 December 1679, apparently after his death. The indenture listed four properties, all in the parish of St Martin-in-the-Fields, one of which was the plot shown on the Lacy map; this property Baker himself held, while the other three he transferred to his son, Bartholomew, Richard Leighton of the Inner Temple (apparently the husband of Baker's niece Mary Lea), and his brother, George Baker of Salop. The property on Russell Street and Drury Lane which the elder Baker kept must have been very valuable, for out of its income Baker felt he could will £120 a year for life to various relatives. In his will he named a brother John Baker of Worcester, whose daughter Elianor Chilton, a widow, was to receive £20 yearly; Sarah Bayly, one of the daughters of his brother George, was left £20; and John, William, Sarah, and Mary Leighton, grandchildren of Baker's sister Mary Lea, were left £20 each. The rest of his estate Baker split between his brother George, his son Bartholomew, and Richard Leighton but held it in trust until his death, which must have occurred between 18 April 1678 and 19 December 1679.

Bartholomew Baker the younger was born about 1637. Young Baker received a license on 11 June 1672 to marry Anne Lacey; he declared himself a gentleman, bachelor, age about 35, from Worcester, and she a spinster of about 25 from Ipsley, Warwickshire, where the couple were married.

### Baker, Benjamin  (fl. 1730–1736), kettle-drummer.

Benjamin Baker's name first appeared on the Drury Lane playbill of 13 May 1730: "Handel's Water Music, with a preamble on the Kettle Drums," the same musical specialty made famous by his kinsman Job Baker. The performance was for the benefit of Chetwood the prompter. On the next evening Baker repeated his preamble at the Lincoln's Inn Fields Theatre for the benefit of Houghton, prompter of that theatre.

Benjamin Baker played in "a grand Concerto composed by Dr Pepusch," a piece "to which the kettle drums are principal," at Lincoln's Inn Fields on 9 May 1732, but for the several other benefits for which he played at that theatre and at Covent Garden in 1733 and 1734, he returned to the "Water Music." This standard offering was also his contribution to the concert of prominent vocal and instrumental musicians at Mercers' Hall on 11 February 1736 and at his last recorded performance, at Covent Garden on 11 May 1736.

**Baker, Berkley** *[fl. 1775–1805]*, *actor, manager.*

Berkley Baker made his theatrical debut at Richmond on 14 June 1775 in a role not now known. He was acting at Capel Street Theatre, Dublin, from 27 December 1783 through 1784, in which year he was joined there by his wife.

When Baker performed for the first time in London—as Grub, in the farcical afterpiece *Cross Purposes*, at Drury Lane on 10 December 1789—he had most recently been at Margate but was advertised as "from Dublin." The reviewer for the *European Magazine* thought that, despite his obvious imitation of Parsons, and a certain "coarseness," he had "spirit and freedom" and might "by practice and discipline . . . become a useful performer." But John Philip Kemble, the Drury Lane manager, thought far otherwise: "This farce," he wrote, "was revived to introduce Mr Baker in Old Grub—he was recommended to me by Parsons & Wroughton, yet he was nothing!"

Baker was given no permanent employment in London, and the *Thespian Dictionary* located him, in the same year as his Drury Lane attempt, as manager of a company of itinerants at a barn near Windsor, "where he afterwards opened a public-house 'The Merry Wives of Windsor.' "

In 1790–91 the Bakers played at Salisbury and elsewhere in the English prov-

inces. Baker was at Richmond and the Haymarket for casual appearances in the summer of 1792 and then, evidently, he returned to Ireland. The announcement of his appearance of 2 June 1794 at the Haymarket as Governor Harcourt in *The Revenge* specified that he was "from Dublin."

Nothing more was recorded of either Baker or his wife until he bobbed up again at the Haymarket for two fugitive performances on 23 and 26 January 1797, first as Sir David Dunder in *Ways and Means* and then as the title character in *Barnaby Brittle*. He was probably the Baker who played Isaac in *The Duenna* in a special benefit for the Lying-In Hospital at Covent Garden on 21 June 1797.

The account in the *Thespian Dictionary* relates that by 1805 the family had gone to America, where the daughter (who had acted in Ireland and the English provinces, but not in London) was then "well married." It is probable that this account confuses details in the lives of the families of Berkley Baker and J. S. Baker, unless the two are the same.

**Baker, Charles** *[fl. 1758–1770]*, *gallery office keeper.*

Charles Baker identified himself in a letter to David Garrick dated 4 October 1770 as "12 years your one shilling gallery office-keeper" at Drury Lane Theatre.

**Baker, David Lionel Erskine** *1730–1767?*, *actor, playwright, theatre historian.*

David Lionel Erskine Baker was born in the parish of St Dunstan in the West, London, on 30 January 1730 and named after his godfather, the Earl of Buchan. He was the elder son of Henry Baker, F. R. S. (1698–1774), natural scientist and poet, and his wife Sophia, who was the youngest daughter of Daniel Defoe. David's younger brother Henry Baker (1734–1766) was a well-known poet and writer on legal subjects.

*Harvard Theatre Collection*

DAVID ERSKINE BAKER
by S. Harding

Through the good offices of the Duke of Montague, Master of the Ordnance, David was trained in the drawing-room of the Tower for service in the Corps of Royal Engineers. He early showed extraordinary talent for the mathematical studies to which he was there introduced, but he also developed on his own a taste for languages. According to a letter from his father to Dr. Doddridge, he had by age 12 translated from the French all 24 books of *Telemachus*. By the time he was 15 he had "translated from the Italian, and published, a treatise on physic of Dr Cocchi of Florence concerning the diet and doctrines of Pythagoras, and last year [1746] before he was seventeen, he likewise published a treatise of Sir Isaac Newton's 'Metaphysics' compared with those of Dr Leibnitz, from the French of M. Voltaire. He is a pretty good master of Latin and understands some Greek, is reckoned no bad arithmetician for his years, and knows a great deal of natural history."

It is not clear at what point David Baker forsook these studies for the theatre. John Nichols, in his account of Baker's father in his *Literary Anecdotes*, says only that "unfortunately marrying the daughter of Mr Clendon, a revered empiric, who had like himself a most violent and infatuated turn for dramatic performance, he repeatedly engaged with strolling companies, and provincial Theatres, in spite of every effort of his father to reclaim him."

The listing of David Erskine Baker as an actor at Dublin's Smock Alley Theatre in 1742 in the appendix to Professor Clark's *The Irish Stage in the County Towns* is an error. At this time the twelve-year-old child was at his books in London. But Clark is perhaps correct in placing him in Sheriffe's Belfast and Drogheda company in the spring of 1758, though no mention is made of Baker's roles. According to Isaac Reed, his successor editor of the *Biographica Dramatica*, he had been at one stage of his youth "adopted by an uncle, who was a silk throwster in Spital Fields, [and] he succeeded him in his business; but wanting the prudence and attention which are necessary to secure success in trade he soon failed." It is possible that the effort to interest him in commerce was one of the devices employed to keep him from the stage.

The question of possible London acting appearances by David Baker is complicated by the presence onstage somewhere in the metropolis of one Baker or another virtually at any given moment during 35 years in the middle of the century. There is at least a possibility that David acted minor roles at Covent Garden while his wife was there, from 1762 until perhaps 1765. There is no evidence that he acted with her in Edinburgh, though his two dramatic works were produced there in 1763. He is credited with a prologue written for a benefit of the Canongate Poor House on 17 April 1765, and he may have preceded his wife to Edinburgh. The editor of the Sarah Ward-West Digges correspondence in 1833 identified a singer and his wife at Liverpool in August 1758 as the David Erskine Bakers. A Baker, possibly D. E., was in Roger Kemble's company at Coventry, Worcester, Droitwich, Bromgrove, and Bath in 1767. He left the company "clandestinely," according to Kemble, on 1 June 1768, apparently for Richmond.

David Erskine Baker's principal contribution to the theatre of his day was the publication in 1764 of his highly useful *Companion to the Playhouse* in two duodecimo volumes. They included brief notes on plays, authors, and actors. The work was expanded and revised by Isaac Reed in 1782, as the *Biographia Dramatica*, and again, in 1812, by Stephen Jones. Baker's other works include his juvenile translation *The Metaphysics of Sir Isaac Newton* (1747); a "dramatic poem," *The Muse of Ossian*, performed at Edinburgh in 1763 and published there the same year; a comic opera, *The Maid the Mistress*, essentially a translation of *La serva padrona* of Gennaro Antonio Federico, which was produced at Edinburgh in 1763; and a life of Colley Cibber published with Cibber's *Works* in 1777.

Stephen Jones wrote that Baker died about 1770. John Nichols gave 16 February 1767 as the date of death. Maidment, editor of the Digges-Ward letters, says that Baker "died in a state of indigence" in Edinburgh "about the year 1780." Nichols's testimony is likely to be correct.

An engraving of Baker by H. R. Cook after a portrait by S. Harding is furnished in Harding's *Biographical Mirror* (1810).

### Baker, Mrs David Lionel Erskine, Elizabeth, née Clendon   *d. 1778, actress.*

Mrs David Lionel Erskine Baker was born Elizabeth Clendon, the daughter of a clergyman. The year of her marriage to the writer and actor Baker is unknown, but it was certainly before her London debut at Covent Garden Theatre on 6 October 1762.

She then played Roxana in *The Rival Queens* and was advertised as coming "from Bath" and as appearing for the first time on the Covent Garden stage.

The *Theatrical Review* said of this performance that "she evinced some sensibility and much judgment; but her person, which is short, and inclinable to the lusty, is unhappily adapted to the heroines of tragedy; though . . . [her] judicious accuracy of speaking is deemed a sufficient compensation."

Except for the previous season, 1761–62, there had been at least one Mrs Baker (otherwise unidentified) in the Covent Garden company every season since 1753–54, and the name continued to appear in the lists of that theatre through 1774–75. However, the bill announcing Mrs Elizabeth Baker's second appearance in the season 1762–63 (as Lady Easy in *The Careless Husband*) insisted that she was then appearing for only the second time at Covent Garden; and from 1765 until her death in Scotland in 1778, she was firmly identified with the Edinburgh stage. It seems certain, then, that from 1762–63 through 1764–65, there were at least two Mrs Bakers at Covent Garden.

Elizabeth Baker's other parts in her first London season, as shown in the surviving notices, were more in her subsequent line, roles such as the Queen in *The Spanish Fryar* and the Countess Rousillon in *All's Well that Ends Well*.

Precisely when Eliza Baker took up residence in Edinburgh is obscure, but the context of a notice in the Edinburgh *Courant* for a performance of 3 March 1756 persuades that she was an established local figure at that date: "We hear that Mrs Baker, although she never played Juliet before and is fully conscious of the impropriety of her figure for that character, has consented to do it on Monday for Mr Aiken's Benefit, and hopes that the audience will accept of her performing it in the best manner she is able."

That Mrs Baker acted in Edinburgh regularly in the winter seasons from 1767–68 is probable. In 1766 she and Sarah Ward engaged in a protracted newspaper dispute over precedency in that theatre's published advertisements. Dibdin lists her as certainly a member of the company in 1769–70 and following until her retirement at the end of the 1773–74 season. Her husband had died, probably in February 1767.

She had long been interested in elocution and either after she quit the stage or some time before that date she established herself as a fashionable tutor of the King's English to the Scots, and she quickly grew prosperous. Tate Wilkinson, who knew her well, believed that she left the theatre to pursue her new profession because of a quarrel with the manager, West Digges "(for her temper was soon ruffled, and she was too apt to rush into the different extremes of love and hate)."

Mrs Baker's interests in speech teaching extended to theatrical management, and she was treating for a share in the Edinburgh house with Bland the patentee when she died. Dibdin's account, that she died of excitement the night before the day on which articles of agreement between her and Bland were to be signed, is perhaps too imaginative.

Mrs Baker died late in January 1778, and the following lines were published in the Edinburgh *Courant* of 2 February:

*Ah! cruel death, thou unrelenting foe!*
*To taste and love, why giv'st thou such*
*a blow?*
*Could'st thou no other find (on whom to*
*try*
*Th' unerring aim of thy artillery),*
*But her, who, with a more than common*
*art,*
*To you and age rich knowledge could*
*impart?*
*Whose speech each grace of eloquence*
*possest,*
*While genuine wit was her convivial*
*guest,*

*Nor aught of female but the form was*
*seen,*
*For all her mental powers were*
*masculine.*
*As Shakspere wrote, so she instruction*
*gave;*
*Ruler of language, and not grammar's*
*slave.*
*But now, since gone to that uncertain*
*bourn,*
*From whence no travellers shall e're*
*return,*
*Those left behind, when they their loss*
*deplore,*
*May aptly say, what Hamlet said of yore,*
*Take her for all in all, and own 'twere*
*vain*
*To hope to look upon her like again.*

Dr Samuel Johnson spoke of her as a friend, in a letter of 24 October 1767 to William Drummond; and Tate Wilkinson had considerable praise for her abilities:

Mrs Baker was a woman of strong understanding, aided by a good and highly finished education, wonderful natural abilities, and an actress of great capacity; and she had performed three or four parts at Covent Garden, where they could not deny she possessed much merit. Her features were very good, but her figure was short, clumsy, and against her in many parts which otherwise she was well calculated for. If a line had been drawn of competitorship, the first of that or the present day [1790] would have shrunk in the debate as to comprehension and real understanding, and yielded to her courtesy. Use is of greater importance than the London or any other audience are aware of. Mrs Pritchard was a striking instance, who, with a large figure, was esteemed the best Rosalind, though Mrs Woffington, the beautiful, was her opponent. Prejudice for some time prevailed much against Mrs Baker, at York, when she acted during the races in August, 1768, and one winter, 1769; but at the latter part of the season she surmounted those prejudices. At Edinburgh, where she resided many years, she was in universal esteem as an actress.

**Baker, Frances** ₍fl. 1677₎, actress.

Frances Baker ("Mrs Baker Senior") may have been the mother of Katherine Baker, who was also an actress in the King's Company in the 1670's, or the two women may have been unrelated but were referred to as Senior and Junior simply because Frances was older. Often the printed casts made no differentiation, but there were two roles which were certainly taken by Frances: Amasia in *Wits Led by the Nose* in mid-June 1677 and Alfreda in *King Edgar and Alfreda* in October 1677—both at Drury Lane.

**Baker, Francis** ₍fl. 1670–1690₎, actor.

Francis Baker was active at the Smock Alley Theatre in Dublin from about 1670 to 1685 before coming to London. According to Chetwood he made a considerable name for himself in two roles of importance, Falstaff and Sir Epicure Mammon. In addition to being an actor he was a master paver and "used to pave with his part pinn'd upon his sleeve and hem [fit the paving stones together] and rehearse alternately." One time when he was rehearsing Falstaff this way he was working with two new assistants; bending over his work he said aloud, "Who have we here?—Sir Walter Blunt!—There's honour for you!" Whereupon the two assistants thought him mad, trussed him up, and carried him home.

His first recorded role in London was a double one: Grandpree and Allan in *The Bloody Brother* on 20 January 1685 at Drury Lane. Supposedly he played Falstaff in London, but no specific evidence of this has survived. He acted through late October 1690, when he was last listed as acting the Persian Magi in *The Distress'd Innocence*—another elderly role. A Francis Baker who had a son Francis buried at St Paul, Covent Garden, on 19 February 1687, may have been the actor, or related to him.

**Baker, George** 1773?–1847, organist, violinist, pianist, composer.

George Baker was born the son of John Baker, Esq, of Exeter in 1773. (*Grove's Dictionary* dates his birth 1768, but he gave his age as 24 when he matriculated at Oxford in 1797.) From his mother's sister he received instruction on the harpsichord and when he was seven he was able to perform with precision Handel's and Scarlatti's lessons for that instrument.

Baker next studied under the locally renowned composer Hugh Bond, lay vicar of Exeter Cathedral and organist of St Mary Arches. He was a little later the pupil of William Jackson, the celebrated organist at the Cathedral, and of the violinist Ward. By his sixteenth year he was leader of concerts in his neighborhood.

When he was about seventeen Baker came to London as protégé of the Earl of Uxbridge, a musical enthusiast, who, according to Sainsbury, received him into his family and subsidized his lessons on the violin under Cramer the elder and on the *pianoforte* under Dussek. Uxbridge also arranged public performances in the Hanover Square Rooms, where Baker performed his famous piece "The Storm" and was publicly praised by Dr Burney.

In 1794 Baker was appointed organist of St Mary's Church, Stafford, which had recently installed a new organ built by Geib. The *Alumni Oxoniensis* states that he was 24 years of age when he matriculated at St Edmund Hall on 1 July 1797. The Corporation Books of Stafford contain several cryptic entries which imply that he had an unhappy tenure at Stafford. On 5 March 1795 there is an entry ordering "that the organist be placed under restrictions as to the use of the organ, and that the mayor have a master key to prevent him having access thereto," and on 16 July 1795 it was "ordered that Mr George Baker be in future prohibited from playing the piece of music called 'The Storm.' " On 19 May 1800 the entry reads "Resignation of Baker."

Baker was appointed in 1810 as organist

at All Saints, Derby, and in 1824 he went as organist to Rugeley where he remained in tenure until his death on 19 February 1847, although from 1839 his duties were performed by a deputy, due probably to his increasing deafness.

There has been speculation as to his right to the title of Doctor of Music, which he seems sometimes to have used. No record of the granting of such a degree is known.

In 1799 Baker married the eldest daughter of the Rev E. Knight of Milwich. If he was the George Baker of No 4, Euston Crescent, "Music-Master" whose children were baptized at St Giles in the Fields in 1817 and 1818, his wife's first name was Maria.

Baker composed many songs for the theatrical singer Incledon, his fellow-pupil under Jackson. He also composed some glees, printed and dedicated to the Earl of Uxbridge, and a number of organ voluntaries, *pianoforte* sonatas, and anthems.

He was said to have been handsome, generous, and exceedingly eccentric.

*Harvard Theatre Collection*

J. S. BAKER, as Gustavus Vasa

by Lovett

### Baker, J. S. *fl. 1787–1800*, *actor, manager.*

J. S. Baker is said by Seilhamer to have acted minor roles at the Haymarket Theatre in London in 1787, though no evidence is given for the assertion. His wife is said to have performed as actress, singer, and dancer in pantomimes at Sadler's Wells from 1785 to 1792.

Baker appears to have served as Charles Stuart Powell's stage manager in the first season of the Federal Street Theatre in Boston, Massachusetts, and he played Gustavus in Henry Brooke's *Gustavus Vasa* at the opening of that house on 3 February 1794. Mrs Baker filled the role of Augusta in the mainpiece and of Mrs Camomile in the afterpiece, John O'Keeffe's *Modern Antiques*.

Baker and Powell quarrelled in public and in print before the end of the first season, and the Baker family, which included the daughter Eliza, then 16, withdrew from the theatre to present in opposition a series of "Dramatic Olios" at the Boston Concert Hall. At this time they were also managing the Shakespeare Hotel in State Street, Boston.

The family returned to the Federal Street boards under the management of Colonel J. S. Tyler in the season of 1795–96 and remained there during the successive managements of J. B. Williamson, J. J. L. Sollee, Giles Barrett, and Joseph Harper. J. S. Baker may have been the actor of the name who played at Halifax, Nova Scotia, on 15 September 1797.

In 1797 Eliza, the daughter, married Thomas Paine (d. 1811), the poet and second son of Robert Treat Paine, the signer of the Declaration of Independence. The marriage aroused bitter opposition in Paine's family and caused his estrangement for some years from his father. (At the death of his elder brother in 1801, Thomas assumed his name and was known as Robert Treat Paine throughout his stormy political career.)

On 16 April 1798 the elder Bakers played under their son-in-law's direction at the Boston Haymarket Theatre in David Everett's *Daranzel*. Absent from the roster of the Federal Street Theatre in the season of 1799–1800, they returned when Barrett resumed its direction in 1799–1800. After the close of this season the Bakers appeared no more in the bills.

S. Hill engraved a picture of J. S. Baker in his role of Gustavus in 1794.

**Baker, Mrs J. S.** [fl. 1785-1800], actress, singer, dancer. See **BAKER, J. S.**

**Baker, Job** [fl. 1709–1744], kettle-drummer.

"The ingenious Mr Job Baker" was for nearly 20 years an ubiquitous figure in the shifting musical and theatrical society of London.

Baker was a musician in the band of the Second Troop of Horse Grenadier Guards. He made his first known public theatrical appearance under that identification with "a Preamble beat on the Kettle Drums" before a benefit performance at Lincoln's Inn Fields on 10 May 1727. His services came to be considered by many actors the difference between a profitable and unprofitable benefit. Baker exploited the enormous popularity of Handel's "Water Music" by beating his "Preamble" to it at Lincoln's Inn Fields on every occasion which offered during the next two years.

At Goodman's Fields on 23 March 1731 he was introduced incorrectly as "Joab Baker, who never appear'd on the Stage before." He played both at that theatre and at Covent Garden in 1730–31 and 1731–32. At Goodman's Fields on 11 May 1732 he departed from his formula so far as to announce that, after his usual preamble, "Mr

Baker will perform 'Tollet's grounds' on a Side Drum, accompanied with a Violin, the like having never been attempted by any Person before."

Baker is traceable at the Haymarket Theatre in November 1734, at the New Wells near the London Spa in the summer of 1739, at the James Street Theatre in 1743, and at the Haymarket again in 1744. In August 1744, at a *fête* of fireworks and music at Mulberry Garden, Clerkenwell, Baker beat the same "trevally on the side drum" which he had beat before the Duke of Marlborough after the victory of Malplaquet in 1709. Sixteen hundred people heard him at this performance, and over 500 were turned away.

Job Baker's relationship to the kettle-drummer Benjamin Baker is not understood.

**Baker, John** d. 1679, trumpeter.

John Baker, trumpeter, may have been related to the two Robert Bakers who were attached to Charles I's musical establishment: Robert Senior played the recorder and Robert Junior the oboe, sackbut, and cornet. John Baker replaced Anthony Franck as trumpeter in the King's Musick on 19 December 1661 at a salary of £60 annually. Much of his time in the musical service seems to have been spent travelling: a trip to Tunbridge with the King in June and July 1663, one to Bath in August and September of the same year under Sergeant Trumpeter Gervase Price, attendance on the ambassadors to the United Netherlands Lord Hollis and Henry Coventry in 1667, and a similar assignment to Breda in the summer of 1674. The gaps in the record of Baker's career may be indications of periods spent out of England: 1664–1667, 1668–1674, and 1675–1679. On 27 June 1679 he was replaced as trumpeter in the King's Musick by William Shore. His will had been written on 17 June and was proved by his wife and executrix, Catherine, on 4 July; he probably died sometime between 17 and 27 June 1679.

Baker's will described him as from Lambeth Marsh, Surrey, gentleman, "sick and weake of Body," and a musician. He requested burial in his parish church and left a considerable estate. To his fellow trumpeters Gervase Price and William Bounty he left £5 each for mourning; to his brother-in-law Bray(?) Chune(?), his wife Mary, and their children Thomas and Barbary he left mourning rings; to his youngest daughter Martha he bequeathed £50, to be paid from an investment of £833 6s. 8d. he made through Sir Robert Viner between 30 April 1677 and 29 April 1678; to Martha, too, he left all the property which his wife had settled upon him: the Queen's Head Tavern in Smith Lane, St Martin's, Cornhill; property in Pike Yard, Fenchurch Street, St Katherine Coleman; property in Penford, Essex, called the Red Lyon Inn; and the Lyon Mead in Springfield, Essex. He specified that the £600 which he had lent his brother-in-law was money belonging to his daughter Dinah and should be repaid to her. To his daughters Martha and Dinah he left £12 in silver, and to Dinah went the rest of his estate, including arrears in his wages from the King. Though his wife Catherine was made his executrix, he left her nothing, possibly because she had a sufficient income of her own. By 1686 she may have been dead, for on 13 January of that year the "executors" of John Baker were paid £75 14s. 3½d. for livery due Baker in 1676.

Baker and his wife may have had connections with the public playhouses, though their names are so common that one cannot be certain: a John Baker was involved on 21 July 1674 with leasing the Dorset Garden playhouse to Nicholas Davenant and John Atkins, and a Katherine Baker acted with the King's Company during the Restoration period.

### Baker, Katherine  *d. 1729, actress.*

There may have been two actresses named Katherine Baker, one called "Mrs Baker Junior" who was active in 1677–78 and a second who performed from 1699 onward. The existing records are too imprecise to make a clear distinction, and Katherine Baker is here treated as a single person.

In the King's Company in 1677 there were two Mrs Bakers, Frances and Katherine, not always distinguishable in the cast lists. Katherine was the younger and possibly called Mrs Baker Junior simply to indicate the age difference, though she could have been the daughter of Frances. It was probably Katherine who played Margaret in *The Country Innocence* in March 1677 and Parisatis in *The Rival Queens* on 17 March, and it was certainly she who acted the young Heroina in *Wits Led by the Nose* in mid-June. She may have been one of the performers who had just come from the Nursery—the training ground for fledgling actors sponsored by the patent companies. In October 1677 she played Hillaria in *King Edgar and Alfreda*, and the following March she acted Jocalin in *The Man of Newmarket* and spoke the epilogue. The youthfulness of the roles assigned her during this brief period of activity suggests that she was probably in her early 20's, but not quite young enough to be styled "Miss." Unless there were two separate Katherine Bakers, this actress retired or acted away from London until 1699 when she resumed her career.

At the very end of the century Mrs Baker reappeared in casts at Christopher Rich's Drury Lane Theatre, playing small roles, usually servants, such as Aegina in *Achilles* in December 1699, Pert in *The Reform'd Wife* in March 1700, and Betty in *Courtship à la Mode* on 9 July 1700. For the next decade she seems to have played regularly, though not in significant roles, at Drury Lane until 1705, at Lincoln's Inn Fields briefly in 1705, at the new Queen's Theatre in the Haymarket from 1705 to 1707, back at Drury Lane for the 1708–9 season, and at the Queen's again in 1709–10. By this last season she was able to contract with Owen Swiney for a salary of £40 annually, to be paid in nine installments, and a vacation from 10 June to 10 September.

From 24 June through 9 September 1710 at Greenwich in William Pinketh-man's troupe Mrs Baker had her first op-portunity to play important roles: during this brief summer season she acted Belvi-dera in *Venice Preserv'd*, Miranda in *The Tempest*, Lady Macbeth, Jocasta in *Oedi-pus*, Mrs Fribble in *Epsom Wells*, the title role in *The Island Princess*, Lavinia in *Caius Marius*, and Amanda in *The Relapse*; most of her roles were leads or second leads and, usually, of mature women.

She played at the Queen's Theatre for two seasons, and when it was given over to operas in late 1711 she transferred, ap-parently, to Drury Lane and dropped into semi-oblivion for several seasons. Until the 1714–15 season she either acted very little, or played roles too small to have been mentioned on the bills, though she re-ceived yearly benefits, usually shared with one or two other performers. About 1715 she began playing more frequently, taking such elderly roles as the Aunt in *Greenwich Park* (1 July 1715), the Duchess of York in *Richard III* (6 December 1715), and Mrs Otter in *The Silent Woman* (25 May 1717), and beginning in 1715 she also be-gan to receive unshared benefits. After her brief fling at major roles in 1710, she seems to have regressed, but then she grad-ually started rebuilding a modest but use-ful career habitually playing elderly comic characters. In the 1720's she made a spe-cialty of playing such roles as Mrs Day in *The Committee*, Lady Townly in *The Man of Mode*, Lady Laycock in *The Amor-ous Widow*, the old Nurse in *The Relapse*, and Lady Wishfort in *The Way of the World*. One of the few more serious roles she tried during this last decade of her career was Emilia in *Othello*.

By the 1727–28 season she was playing less frequently, and after it she retired from the stage. In January 1729 she died;

the *Universal Spectator* of 11 January re-ported her funeral on the fifth: "Last Sun-day Night Mrs Baker, the Actress of Drury-Lane Theatre, was buried in a very hand-some Manner at St Clement's Danes, the Master of the House and most of the Actors attending the same."

The character of Bella in Mrs Manley's long semi-fictitious autobiography, *Rivella* (1714), was supposed to be based on a Kitty Baker who acted in the early eight-eenth century, and though the evidence is very untrustworthy, what Mrs Manley said of the actress may have some bearing on Katherine's early years. Kitty was a girl of 17 or 18 who sometimes frequented the playhouse but could not find employment, and she used to visit Mrs Manley in hopes that the authoress might speak to the man-agers for her. The girl was the daughter of a poor woman in the neighborhood, some-times helped serve at Mrs Manley's, but oc-casionally sat at table and entertained with readings from plays. She had "a round Face, not well made, large dull Eyes, but she was young, and well enough complexion'd, tho' she wanted Air, and had a Defect in her Speech, which were two Things they objected against as to her coming into the Play-House." Once, when Mrs Manley was away, Kitty met Christopher Monk, a booby, a conniver, and a married man, the son of Colonel Monk; he fell in love with her and she, wanting to get on the stage and be a kept woman, was attracted to him. Upon her return Mrs Manley tried to break up the couple, but Kitty finally became Monk's mistress. In time he left her and "she was put for some time to Pension by a feign'd Name at a poor Woman's House in an obscure Part of the Town, with daily Promises of being sent into *Flanders* to her Beloved." At length she was forgotten.

**Baker, Mary.** *See* KING, MRS THOMAS.

**Baker, Richard** [*fl.* 1778–1779], *singer, actor.*

The Lord Chamberlain's records contain a reference to a license granted Richard Baker for a special performance in August 1775 at the Haymarket Theatre. Nothing is known about the performance. A singing actor identified as Richard Baker by *The London Stage* was cast as Mat o' th' Mint in *The Beggar's Opera* at the Haymarket on 8 and 9 June 1778 and 27 August 1779. He may have been the elder Thomas Baker, however.

### Baker, Sarah, née Wakelin  *c. 1736–1816, actress, manager.*

Sarah Wakelin (or Wakelyn) was born probably in 1736 in London. Her father was perhaps the minor actor Wakelin whose presence in London was recorded only in a bill for his own benefit performance at the Haymarket on 16 May 1749 (though this person could have been Sarah's brother). Her mother, it is certain, was the Ann Wakelin, acrobatic dancer at Sadler's Wells, who conducted her own small company of performers from the Wells to provincial fairs.

Sarah grew up performing as a dancer in her mother's company, in London as well as on tour. She married Mr Baker, also a dancer in Mrs Wakelin's employ, before 1761 and had by him a son and two daughters before his death about 1769.

Almost immediately after her husband's death Mrs Baker emulated her mother and embarked on a managerial career, at first with her children only, and then perhaps succeeding her mother as the executive of provincial adventurers from Sadler's Wells. At any rate, from 19 November 1772, the date on which her first advertisement appeared in the *Kentish Gazette*, announcing a performance for Canterbury, until 1777 when Mrs Wakelin retired, the mother occasionally performed for the company of which her daughter was billed as manager.

Sarah's three children Ann, Henry, and Sarah (later Mrs William Dowton) and several of her cousins, the Irelands, were also in her troupe for many years. The elder Ireland served as leader of the band, Mrs Baker's son Henry acted young heroic parts, Ann was dependable in both tragic and comic leads, and Sally sang sweetly. Sister Mary Wakelin served in the fourfold capacity of dancer, actress, wardrobe mistress, and cook. More importantly it seems, Mrs Baker attracted to her service a number of competent and faithful outsiders to complete the durable *cadre* which carried the company to success over some determined country opposition. First was an accomplished clown named Lewy Owen, excellent enough for the metropolis but evidently preferring rural strolling, whose performances were vastly attractive to the farmers and villagers of Kent. Later there was Garner, Sarah's shrewd stage manager, who remained with the company for at least 15 years, and Bony Long his successor, who was manager for over 21 years.

Mrs Baker moved gradually from programs of singing, rope dancing, burlettas, and tumbling to a more balanced bill offering both old and new comedies and tragedies. As time went on she brought down from London for short engagements a long procession of the finest actors, and she also introduced or helped advance the careers of many notables, from her son-in-law William Dowton to Joseph Grimaldi the younger: Kean, Harley, G. F. Cooke, Incledon, Palmer, Mathews, Thomas Dibdin, Emery the elder, Fawcett, Mrs Jordan—all were connected with her enterprise at one time or another.

From 1772 through 1777 Mrs Baker's touring company was regularly at Dover, Rochester, Canterbury, and Faversham and sometimes made brief stands at Deal, Folkestone, Sandwich, Lewes, and Sittingbourne. From 1778, when she widened her repertoire to embrace straight drama as well as operas, she began to construct a circuit around Canterbury, Rochester, Faversham, Maidstone, and Tunbridge Wells, with occasional visits to Deal, Lewes, Sandwich, and Sittingbourne. After 1789 she gradually forsook the smaller towns in order to build permanent theatres in the larger ones. She finally relinquished direction of the company to her son-in-law William Dowton in June 1815. She died on 20 February 1816.

Mrs Baker was an eccentric figure about whom many colorful anecdotes are preserved and no doubt exaggerated in the *Memoirs* of Grimaldi and those of Thomas Dibdin and others, and in manuscript letters and memorabilia collected by James Winston. Gossip spoke of her love affairs with Gardner, Rugg, and others of her subordinates. She was supposed superstitious, illiterate, and arbitrary, but her shrewdness, theatrical sense, and courage made her usually more than a match for Hurst, Glassington, and other male managers with whom she tilted.

**Baker, Thomas** *c. 1686–1745, singer.*

Thomas Baker must have been born about 1686, inasmuch as he was 59 when he died in 1745. On 8 August 1715, when four additional positions were granted the Chapel Royal by George I, Baker was sworn a Gentleman of that group. On 15 August 1722 the *St James's Journal* reported that on the day before in the King Henry VIII Chapel at Westminster Abbey, members of the Chapel Royal rehearsed the music for the Duke of Marlborough's funeral; Baker, Samuel Weely, Bernard Gates, Mr Lee, and Mr King were the leading singers.

At some point in his career Baker was ordained, and from at least 10 May 1743 to 11 December 1744 he swore in members of the Chapel Royal, apparently as Subdean, replacing George Carleton. He died on 10 May 1745 and was buried in Westminster Abbey on 13 May, apparently intestate. On 24 May administration of his estate was granted Rev Thomas Baker, clerk, who declared himself the natural and lawful son of the deceased. On the administration the elder Baker was described as

late of St Margaret, Westminster, clerk, widower.

**Baker, Thomas** [*fl.* 1745–1785?], *actor, singer, dancer.*

A Mr Baker, very likely the Thomas of this entry, appeared on the Drury Lane bills and boards for the first time, as a chorus singer, in the "Historical Musical Drama" *Alfred the Great* in March and April of 1745. He went to Goodman's Fields in 1745–46 to fill small roles like a Demon in the Dryden-Davenant version of *The Tempest* or only slightly larger ones like Zama in Rowe's *Tamerlane*, Ned in *The Beggar's Opera*, Blunt in *Richard III*, the Second Murderer in *Macbeth*, and Rugby in *The Merry Wives of Windsor*. He was probably also the same Baker who danced on several occasions this last season of the Hallam company. The female juvenile dancer who appeared in the company during the season was doubtless a relative, perhaps a sister.

Both a Baker and a Miss Baker were dancing in Rich's pantomimes at Covent Garden by 1748–49; and Thomas Baker deposed in a legal document of 1768 that he "Now is and has been a Performer at Covent Garden Theatre for 19" years. A Mrs Baker and a Miss Baker, dancers, turned up at Drury Lane in 1749–50, but our subject was again at Covent Garden that season. Baker now in addition to his dancing assumed such roles as Jack Stanmore, in *Oroonoko*, Haly in *Tamerlane*, Aethiopian in *Perseus and Andromeda*, and one of the attendant spirits in *Comus*. Retaining some of these parts in 1750–51, Baker also sang in the chorus to the current version of *Macbeth*, and performed as Arthur in *Tom Thumb*, Mystery in *Apollo and Daphne*, Gloster in *1 Henry IV*, and Montjoy in *Henry V*.

During the next thirty years, until the end of the season of 1781–82, Thomas Baker was always at Covent Garden in the winter. He was probably the singing Baker who was cast as Roger in *The Gentle Shepherd* at the special benefit for Riddle at the Haymarket on 8 March 1779. (A Miss Baker played a juvenile part there the same month but did not reappear.) In the summers Baker often played at the Haymarket. He was at Stratford in 1771 and Brighton in 1783 and 1786. His last recorded London performance was at Covent Garden on 18 October 1784 in his most constantly-recurring character, Sileno in Kane O'Hara's popular burletta, *Midas.*

Thomas Baker was evidently an actor-singer of modestly capable talents to whom were entrusted at first only a few minor parts in tragedy, afterpiece farces, and pantomimes, but who grew slowly to more frequent and better-regarded employment. His singing, both in *entr'acte* and in chorus was often demanded. Over the years he won for himself such secondary and tertiary roles as: the Shade of Leander in *Harlequin Doctor Faustus*, Crylove and Gaylove in *The Honest Yorkshireman*, Mercury in *Harlequin Skeleton*, Earth in *The Rehearsal*, True Blue in *The Press Gang*, the Magician ("with an Incantation Song") in *The Humourous Lieutenant*, Mercury in *Lethe*, Hilliard in *The Jovial Crew*, Loveless in *Double Disappointment*, Gamut in *The Englishman in Paris*, Ascalax in *Harlequin Sorcerer*, Beaufort in *The Citizen*, Mat-o'-the-Mint in *The Beggar's Opera*, Mervin in *The Maid of the Mill*, Benvolio in *Romeo and Juliet*, Laertes in *Hamlet*, Lord Bardolph in *2 Henry IV*, Eustace in *Love in a Village*, Higgins in *Rose and Colin*, and Ati in *The Two Misers*. He sang frequently from 1750 through 1770, at least, at Marylebone Gardens and Finch's Grotto Gardens, Southwark. He was listed among the tenor vocal performers at the Handel Memorial Concerts at Westminster Abbey and the Pantheon in June 1784.

Thomas Baker was the author of the prologue to *Tunbridge Walks: or, The Yeoman of Kent* and the epilogues to *The Fine Lady's Airs*, *The Pilgrim*, and *The Platonick Lady*. He was a singing-master of some repute, among whose pupils were Miss Brown (later Mrs Cargill); Miss Morris (later Mrs George Colman); Miss Dayes (later Mrs Morgan); and Sarah Wewitzer (later Lady Tyrawley).

Baker married Miss Miller of Covent Garden Theatre in November or December of 1764. "Thomas Baker, Comedian, of Covent Garden Playhouse" was in 1767 left £5 in the will of the eccentric painter-dramatist James Worsdale. He witnessed the will made by George Mattocks the actor in 1768. The Thomas Baker who acted in London from about 1787 to about 1797 was evidently his son.

(The "History of the Stage," in the *Monthly Mirror* for August 1799, furnished a note to a 1759 performance of a Mrs Baker, in the part of Flora in *She Wou'd and She Wou'd Not*, remarking: "This lady was but a very indifferent actress and singer, though often entrusted with characters of consequence. Her husband, who belonged to the same theatre, commenced a teacher of music, and in that character succeeded better than on the stage. . . . He is still alive, and resides in Martlett Court, Bow-street [in 1799]." The author of this note seems either to be conflating inadvertently the careers of the actress Mrs Baker who died in 1760 and of Mrs Thomas Baker who was Miss Miller until 1764 or confirming our conjecture that the Mrs Baker who died in 1760 was the first wife of Thomas Baker, the subject of this entry. The Martlett Court resident may have been the younger Thomas Baker.)

**Baker, Thomas** *c. 1765–1801, actor, singer.*

A Thomas Baker, probably the son of Thomas Baker (fl. 1745–1785) was acting with Giordani at the Capel Street Theatre in Dublin in 1783. There he gained some applause impersonating old men, though he was said to be only 19 years old. He can be traced to Cork in 1784, from whence he came, apparently, to the English provincial circuits.

In 1787 Baker made two summer appearances at the Haymarket, on 18 May as Laertes and on 25 May as Borachio. On 7 November 1787 he was first seen at Hull and afterwards disappeared from the record until his name was included in the Margate bill of 11 August 1789 as Caleb in *He Would Be a Soldier*. He was probably Varanes in the *Theodosius* presented by an irregular winter company at the Haymarket on 23 February 1789, at which time he delivered also "A Monody on the Death of the Late Mr Henderson."

The younger Thomas Baker acted for the first time at Drury Lane as Grub in the afterpiece *Cross Purposes* on 10 December 1789. Evidently this was a trial performance and the only one at that theatre. He performed in four out-of-season benefits at the Haymarket between September 1791 and March 1792: as Roger in *The Gentle Shepherd*, Jaffeir in *Venice Preserved*, Othello, and Bassanio. He played Young Norval in *Douglas* there on 26 December 1792. He was at the Hammersmith Theatre on 24 March 1794, as Sir Benjamin Backbite in *The School for Scandal*, and on 2 June following was once more at the Haymarket, playing Governor Harcourt in *The Chapter of Accidents* and advertised again as "from Dublin," though his Dublin days may then have been far in the past. In 1795 he played one or two unrecorded parts in irregular companies at the Haymarket.

A Thomas Baker, presumably our subject, was granted a license for plays and entertainments at the Haymarket for 23 January 1797. He witnessed the will of Dr John Randall the musician, in 1792. He was residing in Martlett Court, Bow Street, in 1799.

The *Thespian Dictionary* (1805) stigmatized him for heavy drinking, and be-

lieved that, though he never appeared on the stage in a visible state of inebriation, his intemperate habits hastened his death, "which happened in a public house in Fleet Street, 1801."

(There were two Thomas Bakers married in 1792 at St George Hanover Square, one to Hannah Alexander on 5 July and the other to Ann Ford on 21 August.)

**Baker, Mrs Thomas, Elizabeth, née Miller** [*fl. 1761–1792*], *actress, singer, dancer.*

Miss Miller made her professional debut under the conventional anonymous designation "A Young Gentlewoman" at Covent Garden Theatre on 9 October 1761 as Arethusa in *The Contrivances*. The *Theatrical Review* noted that her roles that season were "trifling," but judged "from the elegance of her figure, the delicacy of her deportment, and the sweetness of her voice" that she would prove "a shining ornament to the theatre." Her salary this first year was 3s. 4d. per day.

Elizabeth appears to have caught the public attention swiftly in 1762–63 and during the following two seasons appeared repeatedly both as the pert young women of straight comedy and in singing roles in opera, musical farce, and pastorals. Eventually she added to her repertoire some 25 such roles as: Anne in *The Jovial Crew*, Isabella in *The Double Disappointment*, Ann Page in *The Merry Wives of Windsor*, Bridget in *Every Man in His Humour*, Phillida in *Damon and Phillida*, Harriet in *The Upholsterers*, Semira in *Artaxerxes*, Nerissa in *The Merchant of Venice*, Euphrosyne in *Comus*, Isabinda in *The Busy Body*, Belinda in *The Fair Quaker of Deal*, Ann Bullen in *Henry VIII*, Ceres in *The Rape of Proserpine*, Melinda in *The Recruiting Officer*, Margery in *Love in a Village*, Meriel in *The Jovial Crew*, Lucy in *The Beggar's Opera*, both Sally and Dorcas in *Thomas and Sally*, Harriet in *The Miser*, the Shade of Helen in *Harlequin Doctor Faustus*,

Nancy in *Tom Jones*, Margaretta in *Rule a Wife and Have a Wife*, and Theodosia in *The Maid of the Mill*. She was also pressed into service in choruses, vocal processions, and "Solemn Hymns" and dirges in tragedy; and she was for several years an attraction as soloist at London pleasure gardens.

Miss Miller married the well-known actor Thomas Baker, the elder, in 1764. Mrs Baker retired (or, possibly, went to a provincial company) at the end of the season 1774–75, though the Mr Baker who so long paralleled her career at Covent Garden, and who was probably the elder Thomas Baker her husband, remained at the theatre until the early 1780's. John Philip Kemble left a manuscript note identifying her as the wife of Thomas Baker, from whom, he said, she was separated as of 1792. Latterly, Kemble thought, she had performed "only at Sadler's Wells in Pantomimes."

Mrs Thomas Baker should not be confused with the Mrs Baker who apparently left Covent Garden before Miss Miller's debut and who died in 1760. She is also liable to be confused with Mrs David Erskine Baker, who played a few seasons at Covent Garden. There is a possibility that she may have been related to John Miller (d. 1770) and George Miller (fl. 1763), both musicians in the Covent Garden Theatre band.

### Baker, William *fl. 1784–1796*, singer.

A William Baker was among the bass singers on Burney's list of performers at the Handel Memorial Concerts at Westminster Abbey and the Pantheon in 1784. Conjecturally he was the William Baker (perhaps the father of the bride?) who, with John Taylor, witnessed the marriage of Daniel Thurston to Ann Baker at St Paul, Covent Garden, on 31 August 1796. (A Thurston is among the violinists at the 1784 concert, and there are several Taylors among the performers.) William was very

likely a teacher of voice who apprenticed young singers to him, for an entry of 23 October 1782 paid one Baker £50 "in consideration of his giving up Miss Elizabeth Satchell's Article."

### Bakewell, [Mary?] *fl. 1771–1787*, actress.

Mrs Bakewell made one recorded appearance in London, at the Haymarket, on 30 April 1787, as the laundress in *The Musical Lady*, having spent her earlier theatrical life in the provinces. On 2 March 1771 she played Ursula in *The Padlock* at Stratford and was also a member of a strolling company which played at Cooper's Hall, King Street, Bristol, from November 1772 to April 1773, then at Richmond, Surrey, for the summer and again at Bristol from October 1773 to February 1774. A Miss Bakewell, her daughter and then a child, was also a member of the Bristol group. A Mr Bakewell acted at Norwich in 1758.

Mrs Bakewell may have been the Mary Bakewell, wife of Robert Bakewell, whose daughter Hannah, born on 30 September 1804, was christened at St Paul, Covent Garden, on 28 October 1804. If so, by then she (and probably her husband) appears to have retired from acting. Perhaps there were connections between Mrs Bakewell and the theatrical families of Pritchard and Palmer, which intermarried. In a will of one Mary Palmer, widow, proved 16 March 1814, a small bequest was given to her sister, Mrs Hannah Bakewell.

### Bakley. *See* BULKLEY.

### Balatri, Filippo *1676–1756, singer.*

Filippo (or Dionisio) Balatri (or Salatri) was born in Alfea, near Pisa, in 1676, the son of a poor father from an old Florentine family with good connections and a mother who had been a lady in waiting to the Grand Duchess of Tuscany. From them Filippo inherited a delightfully whimsical nature that ultimately led him to write a

long, jaunty autobiographical poem (*Frutti
del mondo, esperimentati da Filippo Balatri nativo del'Alfea in Toscana*) and a
serio-comic will which have fortunately
preserved most of the details of his fasci-
nating life.

At some point in his early years Balatri
was castrated by the specialist, Accoramboni of Lucca; this may have been at the
urging of Balatri's earliest patron, Cosimo
III. About 1691, when the young singer
was 15, Cosimo sent him to Moscow with
Prince Galitzin to investigate the culture
there. Though much of the visit was uncomfortable and drew Balatri into numerous fights with the Russian guards who
taunted him, he learned much from his stay
and was able to make a trip to Tartary
where he charmed the Grand Cham with
his singing ("I scatter passages and trills by
the hundred").

From Russia Balatri went to Vienna
with the Russian ambassador and there
studied under Gaetano Orsini for two years
and perfected his singing ("My voice is
high, clear, and without fault"). He sang
before the Emperor and at masses and began to win considerable praise which, he
admitted, turned his head. After Vienna,
Balatri returned to Florence where he was
flatteringly received by the Grand Duke
and then went to Pisa whence his parents
had moved. His travels had spoiled him,
and he found bourgeois life ugly. For some
time after this he was used by the Grand
Duke of Florence for various tasks—interpreter for the Russian ambassador, teacher
of a pair of children given by Peter the
Great to the Grand Duke—and he was not
able to pursue his singing career. He therefore asked for and received permission to
go to England, where Italian opera was the
rage and where he hoped to make his fortune.

His trip took him through France, where
his singing was laughed at by the provin-
cials but appreciated by Louis XIV. Sometime before August 1714 he arrived in
England, was comfortably housed by the

*Bayerisches Nationalmuseum, Munich*
FILIPPO BALATRI

by Horemans

English envoy who had accompanied him
from Florence, and was scheduled to sing
before Queen Anne; but this honor was
cancelled by her death on 1 August 1714.

Filippo was joined in England by his
brother Ferrante, and they apparently spent
several happy months there. Socially, he
was much appreciated by the aristocracy,
for he was far more gentlemanly in his behavior than other Italian singers they had
encountered. Curiously, Balatri's verse autobiography makes no mention of his
having performed publicly in London, and
Heriot's splendid work *The Castrati in Opera*, which was the major source of information for this biography, does not speak
of it either. Balatri was engaged, however,
by the impresario Heidegger, possibly for
the whole 1714–15 season but certainly for
at least two productions: *Arminius* on 23
October 1714 and *Ernelinda* on 16 November. In the former Balatri sang Valen-

tino's old role of Segestes and in the latter the part of Rodoaldo which Margherita de l'Epine had previously sung. By March 1715 when *Arminius* was revived, Balatri was no longer in the cast, so it may be that he performed only from October to December, the last month in which the two operas were performed during their initial run. Colman's "Opera Register" contains a clue as to the reason for Balatri's rather brief public career in England: the manager called him, after his performance in *Ernelinda*, "a bad singer." This might also explain why Balatri did not care to include the event in his life story. His performances in England were his first appearances anywhere in public theatres.

The Grand Duke summoned Balatri to Düsseldorf, but the singer fell ill on the way when his boat was becalmed in the English Channel. He finally arrived in Munich on his way to Italy, but there Maximilian II offered him a post in the electoral chapel at 1000 florins a year, starting 1 October 1715. Balatri accepted the position, but within a short while his stomach troubles recurred and he went home to Tuscany for a short stay. He returned to Bavaria but remained only three months before illness again forced him to leave ("The beer which I love to idolatry / is undoubtedly the cause"). He travelled to Eichstätt hoping that worship of the bones of St Walburga there would help him, and then he visited Würzburg where he sang for the Prince-Bishop.

In 1724 he performed on stage again, this time in Munich, and was successful enough to be invited to Vienna by Emperor Charles VI to sing with the celebrated Faustina on 28 August 1724. He was, he said, terrified at the thought of appearing with so fine a performer:

> She sings in such a way that my art
> can scarcely appear in the presence of
>    hers.
> What can a crane do next to a canary?

> But patience, I must perforce obey.
> I do as well as I can,
> My voice does not displease, nor does my
>    acting.
> Then Faustina sings. You tell the rest,
> world, who told me to gnaw my knuckles.

After his profitable season in Vienna he travelled in northern Italy and eventually returned to Germany to serve under the new elector, the Bishop of Ratisbon.

Balatri had been a devout Catholic throughout his life and chose to end his days in a monastery. On 13 July 1739 he was consecrated parson at Ismaning, near Munich, and joined the monastery of Fürstenfeld as Brother Theodore. He had made his will on 27 November 1737 before his consecration, a sprightly document which opened with jaunty comments on himself: "You have found the buffoon in all my writings; but you know that the reason was because I could not do otherwise. So, if you find the same in this, you will be all the more certain it is mine. He who was born a fool will never be cured, says the proverb." Then, after parodying legaleze in untranslatable Italian, Balatri wrote, "I, by the grace of God, by my industry and thanks to the surgeon Accoramboni of Lucca, never took wife, who after loving me for a little would have started screaming at me." He then asked that his body not be submitted to the custom of being washed by women: ". . . I do not want them to amuse themselves by examining me, to see how sopranos are made."

His good humor seems never to have deserted him, and one may see it in the amused look on his face in the painting in the National Museum in Munich in which he is depicted at a musical party, seated at the harpischord. Balatri died on 10 September 1756 at his monastery in Fürstenfeld, having spent his last years directing the sacred music and occasionally singing. Abbé Gerhard reported that when Balatri was 76 "one could still hear the ruins of a voice which once had been the admiration of all."

**Balbi, Rosina**  [fl. 1748–1760], *dancer.*

An Italian dancer at the Court of Bayreuth between 1748 and 1754, Sga Balbi arrived in London with the dancer Frantzel on 1 November 1754, both having been engaged for Covent Garden. Although not listed in the bill, they made their first appearance on 18 November, the same night on which a new company of Italian singers performed the burletta *L'Acadia in Brenta.* The following night Sga Balbi appeared with Frantzel in a new pantomime entertainment, *L'Hôte du village,* which the *Public Advertiser* reported as their second appearance on the English stage. Throughout this season, Sga Balbi performed with Frantzel, with Lepi, and with Villeneuve in such pieces as a *Pas de quatre,* a *Peasant Dance,* and a *Comic Minuet.* Her last billed appearance was on 22 April 1754 in a *Louvre and Minuet* with Villeneuve. After this season she returned to Bayreuth, where she was known to be dancing in 1760.

**Baldassari, Benedetto**  [fl. 1712–1725], *singer.*

When Benedetto Baldassari sang Darius in *L'Idaspe fedele* at the Queen's Theatre in the Haymarket on 27 March 1712, replacing Margherita de l'Epine, he was billed as a servant to the Elector Palatine and "newly arriv'd." The same opera was given on 26 April for his benefit, after which he must have returned to the Continent, for his next recorded London appearance, when he was again billed as lately arrived, was at a concert at Drury Lane on 11 March 1719 for his benefit. He gave a second concert at the King's Theatre (previously the Queen's) on 21 March. The next season he sang Remo in *Numitore,* Fraarte in *Radamisto,* and Cefalo in *Narciso.* He also appeared in a summer

BENEDETTO BALDASSARI
by Belluzi

concert in 1720 at Pinkethman's theatre in Richmond. During the 1720–21 season he apparently sang little except at a benefit concert for himself on 9 January 1721 at York Buildings.

The 1721–22 season, on the other hand, was a busy one for him: Timante in *Floridante,* Costante in *Crispo,* Ernesto in *Griselda,* and opera house potpourri concerts. From October to December 1725 he was in Dublin for a series of 16 successful concerts, after which he seems to have left Great Britain. Though the date of his death is not known, Musgrave's dictionary records a Benedetti, presumably the singer, dying in England.

Steele chided Baldassari for his touchiness, in the 8–12 March 1720 issue of *The Theatre*; apparently the singer had complained at having to sing a captain of the guard in some opera when his usual role was that of a sovereign. Vertue did an engraving of the tenor (or possibly he was an *alto castrato*) from a painting by Belluzzi, a copy of which is at the British Museum.

**Baldi, Signor** [*fl.* 1726–1728], *singer.*

Signor Baldi, an Italian countertenor whose only superior while he was in England was the famous Senesino, seems first to have appeared on the London stage as Annabale in *Elisa* at the King's Theatre in the Haymarket on 15 January 1726. This season he also sang Scipione in *Scipio* and Tassle in *Alessandro*. The next season Baldi sang Thrasymede in *Admeto*, and a part unknown in *Astianatte*. In his last London season, 1727–28, he sang Sivenio in *Teuzzone*, Oronte in *Riccardo I*, Medarses in *Sirce*, and Alessandro in *Tolomeo*, in addition to revivals of earlier roles. His last performance in England was probably as Thrasymede in *Admeto* on 1 June 1728. The following season the King's Theatre was closed and the cluster of great Italian stars—Faustina, Cuzzoni, Senesino, and their fellow singers—had left.

**Baldisarri** *See* **BALDASSARI**.

**Balducci, Signor** [*fl.* 1739], *mechanist.*

Signor Balducci was a maker of mechanical statues which he exhibited at New Wells and at Bullock's booth at Bartholomew Fair in the summer of 1739. The newspaper announcements promised "Three Mechanical Statues of the famous Signor Balducci, which have surprised all the *virtuosi* of the several kingdoms they have hitherto been shewn in, and have not been equalled by any piece of moving machinery: exposed to Public View at 1*s.* each person."

**Baldwin, Mr** [*fl.* 1774–1775], *actor.*

A Mr Baldwin was a member of a company which gave 10 performances of eight mainpieces and seven afterpieces at the Haymarket during off-season in 1774–75. The only roles he was listed for were a servant in *Love in a Village* and a cook in *The Devil to Pay*, both on 2 February 1775. He may have been connected to the Baldwins noted in the entry of J. Baldwin, music porter.

**Baldwin, J.** [*fl.* 1783–1794], *music porter, musician?*

One J. Baldwin was music porter at the King's Opera House in 1783 and in 1784–85. He may have been the John Baldwin who received £31 10*s.* from Covent Garden on 17 October 1787, perhaps for copying music. He was doubtless the same Mr Baldwin who received £4 4*s.* on 7 October 1794 for four weeks' attendance as music porter at the Opera. Listed in Doane's *Musical Directory* (1794) by that occupation, he was living then at No 9, Upper Rathbone Place. Doane identified him also as belonging to the Academy of Ancient Music (and in their concerts) and a participant in the grand performances at Westminster Abbey and in other professional concerts, but in what capacity is not clear. Perhaps he was a performing musician as well as porter.

Many persons by the name of Baldwin were entered in the eighteenth-century registers of the "Actors' Church," St Paul, Covent Garden, and our subject may have been related to the Samuel Baldwin, son of Joseph Baldwin, who was buried there on 11 May 1754. (A Samuel Baldwin of the Custom House received £10 in the will of the actor Charles Holland in 1769, and someone of the same name was witness in a law suit brought against George Colman of Covent Garden Theatre in 1770. Another Samuel Baldwin, son of Samuel and Elizabeth Baldwin, of St Andrew, Holborn, was born on 28 May 1787 and was chris-

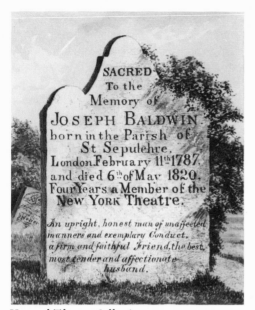

Tombstone of JOSEPH BALDWIN

tened at St Sepulchre, Holborn, on 24 June 1787. Also there may have been connections with the American actor, Joseph Baldwin, whose tombstone inscription in Trinity Churchyard, New York, states he was born in the parish of St Sepulchre, London, on 11 February 1787 and died on 6 May 1820. T. Allston Brown notes the latter as the "first burlesque singer that visited America.")

**Baldwin, Mary** ₁fl. 1703–1706₁, *singer.*

About 10 June 1703 Mary Baldwin, a singer with Betterton's company at Lincoln's Inn Fields, petitioned the Lord Chamberlain, complaining that she had made an agreement with Betterton and Mrs Barry to perform for 15s. weekly but that they had stopped her salary, promised her a benefit instead, and then had admitted so many people free that she had made no profit. She apparently was successful in getting redress, for she was taken back into the

company the next year and sang there in the summer.

After the Queen's Theatre in the Haymarket opened in 1705 she joined the troupe there, her last recorded appearance being Venus in *The Temple of Love* on 7 March 1706. Several printed songs name her as the singer, one in *Wit and Mirth* spelling her name "Ballden." Very little else is known of her stage career, and of her personal life about all that has been discovered is that her mother was probably the Elizabeth Baldwin who, late in the seventeenth century, petitioned in behalf of her daughter, but even the details of the case are not known.

**Balelli, Antonio** ₁fl. 1786–1789₁, *singer.*

Antonio Balelli, an Italian singer, was engaged at the King's Opera for three seasons 1786–89. (His first name is found on a libretto of *Pizzarro*, published at Florence in 1784.) He made his first appearance singing Olinto in *Alceste* on 23 December 1786. That season he also sang Achilla in *Giulio Cesare in Egitto* (a *pasticcio* of Handel's works selected by Arnold), Licinio in *La vestale*, and leading roles in *Virginia* and *Didone abbandonata*. Next season, between 8 December 1787 and 28 June 1788, he sang Gafforio in *Il re Teodoro in Venezia*, Arminio in Sarti's *Giulio Sabino*, and Licida in *L'Olimpiade*. In his final season, 1788–89, he received £225 for singing Ulisse in Cherubini's *Ifigenia in Aulide*, Corradino in *Il disertore*, Licida again in *L'Olimpiade*, and a principal character in *La buona figliuola*. His last role in London was Gandarte in *La generosità d'Alessandro*, which opened on 2 June 1789 at the King's. When that theatre burned down on 17 June, the opera moved to Covent Garden where Balelli sang Gandarte three more times, on 27 and 30 June and 7 July 1789. Grove calls him a bass, but several contemporary newspaper notices, including an official list of singers for the King's Opera printed in *The World*, 16 December 1788, described him as a second soprano. The roles he sang suggest he was capable in both serious and comic opera.

**Baletti, Signor** [*fl.* *1755–1756*], *dancer.*

Signor Baletti was one of the many dancers brought to London in 1755 by Noverre. He made his first appearance at Drury Lane on 3 November 1755 in a new dance with Monsieur Lauchery; the prompter Richard Cross wrote in his manuscript diary for that night that they were "pretty well receiv'd." The tenor of the reception was soon to change, however, when Baletti and the other foreign dancers tried to perform Noverre's *Les Fêtes Chinoises*. The ballet opened on 8 November to hissing and anti-French catcalls, and each night the tumult grew until it erupted into a riot on 15 November and again on 18 November, after which Garrick was "oblig'd to give up the Dancers." Signor Baletti may have been related to the famous Baletti family of dancers at the Comédie-Italienne in Paris.

**Balicourt, Simon** [*fl.* *1735–1748*], *flutist.*

A player of the German flute and a composer for that instrument, Simon Balicourt (sometimes Balincourt, Bellicourt, or Pelicour) was active in the concert life of London from 1735 to at least 1748. He first played in England at the Swan Tavern, "lately arrived from abroad," on 26 November 1735. His next notice was at a concert given by the Young family of musicians and singers at Mercers' Hall on 11 February 1736. A week later, on 18 February, Balicourt performed for his own benefit at the Castle Tavern in Paternoster Row, and then on 27 April of the same year he played at Goodman's Fields Theatre. Other appearances at the London theatres included solo performances at Covent Garden on 22 April 1747 and at the Haymarket on

10 March 1743, 14 February 1745, and 9 December 1748. He was listed as one of the original subscribers in the "Declaration of Trust" which established the Royal Society of Musicians on 28 August 1739.

**"Balino."** *See* FABRI, ANNIBALE PIO.

**Ball, Mr** [*fl.* *1799–1804*], *house servant.*

A Mr Ball was entered as doorkeeper at a salary of £1 12*s.* per week in the Drury Lane account book for 1799–1800. The following season he was a stage doorkeeper. In the summer of 1804, a Mr Ball was a scene man at the Haymarket.

**Ball, Mrs** [*fl.* *1789*], *singer.*

A Mrs Ball performed the role of Wowski in *Inkle and Yarico* on 16 September 1789 at the King's Head Inn at Southwark.

**Ball, Miss** [*fl.* *1781*], *actress.*

A Miss Ball played Belinda in the afterpiece *The Ghost* at the Haymarket on 16 October 1781.

**Ballard, Signor** [*fl.* *1752–1753*], *animal trainer.*

Signor Ballard and his trained menagerie came from Italy to perform a *Pantomime Entertainment* which opened 11 December 1752, as part of "Mrs Midnight's" (Christopher Smart's) enterprise at the Haymarket Theatre in 1752–53. In *The Adventurer* for 9 January 1753, a reporter applauded, with some irony, the amazing docility of the dancing bears and the "exalted genius" of the monkeys and dogs.

The price of monkeys has been considerably raised since the appearance of Signior Ballard's cavaliers; and I hear, that this inimitable preceptor gives lectures to the monkeys of persons of quality at their own houses. . . . Lady Bright's lapdog, that used to repose on downy cushions, or the softer bosom of its mistress, is now worried every hour with begging on its diminutive hind-legs.

On 1 March, Ballard announced that his "Animal Comedians" were engaged to perform at the Hague and Vienna "after some days more" and that his big monkey, Mango, would talk the prologue that evening. Although the last performance was announced for 6 March, the animal pantomime was given again, for the sixtieth and final time, on 10 March 1753.

**Ballard, Jonathan** ₍fl. 1755–1762₎, treasurer.

On 19 May 1756, Jonathan Ballard shared a benefit with other house servants at Covent Garden and in the next season was identified as the treasurer, a position he held through 1761–62. His first name is known from the will of the actor Isaac Ridout, which he witnessed on 6 February 1761. In 1760–61, Ballard was on the pay list for a salary of £1 per week, so his benefit on 4 May 1761 was extraordinary: he distributed 1299 tickets, a near record for any recipient of a benefit, and thereby gained a profit that evening of £187 14s. 6d., the equivalent of more than three years' salary. His last benefit in that position was on 3 May 1762. In the following season, he received a benefit on 6 May 1763, as "late treasurer," perhaps having left his position because of illness.

**Ballarini, Mr** ₍fl. 1778₎, puppet-show-man.

In January 1778, a company of Italian and French shadow players, directed by Messrs Ballarini, Antonio, and Gabriel, opened at the Great Room in Panton Street. Their repertory, described as the *New Ombres Chinoises*, played until May.

**Ballatri.** *See* BALATRI.

**Ballden.** *See* BALDWIN.

**"Balletino, Signor"** ₍fl. 1753–1754₎, dancer?

Signor and Sga Balletino were pseudonyms for unidentified performers who were among Christopher Smart's imported "company of Lilliputians" at the Haymarket in 1753–54.

**"Balletino, Signora"** ₍fl. 1753–1754₎, dancer? *See* "BALLETINO, SIGNOR."

**Ballon.** *See* BALON.

**Balmat, Mr** ₍fl. 1785–1787₎, acrobat.

Mr Balmat (or Bellemotte) performed at Astley's Amphitheatre on 7 April and 27 September 1785 as part of a team of tumblers; in the summer of 1787 he was at the Royal Circus, serving as a principal dancer and performing on the trampoline.

**Balmforth, ₍John?₎** ₍fl. 1784₎, singer.

A Mr Balmforth was listed as one of the bass vocal performers in the Handel Memorial Concerts at Westminster Abbey and the Pantheon in May and June 1784. Perhaps he was connected with the John Balmforth, bachelor, of St Paul, Covent Garden, who married Anne Warriner, of the same parish, on 18 August 1771. (A Mr Warriner was a box keeper at Covent Garden in the 1730's.)

**Balon, Jean** ₍fl. 1698–1699₎, dancer.

Jean Balon was the son of a French dancer who taught the Dauphin's three children and, presumably, his own son. In 1698–99 Thomas Betterton, hoping to boost lagging attendance at Lincoln's Inn Fields, negotiated with Jean Balon, then one of the dancers at the Paris Opéra, to come to England. Balon was released by the Opéra for five weeks, and on 8 April 1699 Narcissus Luttrell noted that Betterton would pay Balon an extravagant 400 guineas for that brief stay, on top of which Lord Cholmley promised the dancer a 100-guinea gift; Betterton, by comparison, probably earned about £75 over this same five-week period. The *Post Man* for 4–6 April 1699 announced that Balon, lately arrived from France, would perform "an entertainment of Dancing" at the theatre on the tenth. The event proved so popular that in less than a week the rival company at Drury Lane advertised that they had engaged the famous *castrato* Clementine; the race was on to engage foreign performers, and for the next few years contemporary writers paid more attention to the popularity of the imported artists than to the quality of their work. The Epilogue to *Feign'd Friendship*, done about May 1699, commented:

> *Of late your Stomachs are so squeamish grown,*
> *You are not pleas'd with Dainties of our own,*
> *And 'tis meer folly now to think to win ye*
> *Without Balon or Seignior Clementine.*

*Harvard Theatre Collection*

JEAN BALON

*A Comparison Between the Two Stages* (1702) commented that "the Town ran Mad" to see Balon, "and the prizes were rais'd to an extravagant degree to bear the extravagant rate they allow'd him."

Gildon, in his *Life of Betterton*, had the old actor state that

All that could be said of *Ballon*, (or any other Dancer of more Reputation) is, that his Motion was easy and graceful, the Figures he threw his Body into, fine, and that he rose high with Freedom and Strength; or, in short, that he was an active Man. But is that, or would indeed the *Roman Pantomimes*, be a sufficient Ballance for the Loss of the *Drama* to any Man of common Sense?

Balon represented the rigid traditions of the Paris Opéra, and these were not always to the taste of the English. John Weaver classed Balon as the best French dancer seen on the English stage, yet he thought Balon

pretended to nothing more than a graceful motion, with strong and nimble risings, and the casting of his body into several (perhaps) agreeable postures. But for expressing any thing in Nature but modulated Motion, it was never in his head. The imitation of the Manners & Passions of Mankind he never knew anything of, nor ever therefore pretended to shew us.

Balon's fame was still remembered in England when Marie Sallé and her brother first appeared in 1716 and billed themselves as scholars of his.

**Balph, Mme** [*fl.* 1784], *equestrienne.*

An equestrienne advertised as "Madame Balph, the Spanish Lady" performed trick riding at Hughes's Royal Circus in St George's Fields on 17 September 1784.

**Balsart** or **Balser.** *See* BALTZAR.

**Balshaw, Jarvis** [*fl.* 1794], *singer.*

Jarvis Balshaw, tenor, was listed in Doane's *Musical Directory* (1794) as belonging to the Choral Fund and the Handelian Society, as a participant in the oratorios at Covent Garden, and in the grand performances at Westminster Abbey. He lived at that time at No 8, Green's Alley, Coleman Street.

**Balshaw, Peter** *[fl. 1794], singer.*

Peter Balshaw, tenor, was listed in Doane's *Musical Directory* (1794) as a participant in the oratorios at Covent Garden and in the grand performances at Westminster Abbey. He lived at that time at Mr Dower's Academy, Highgate.

**Baltazar.** *See* **BALTZAR.**

**Balthazar.** *See also* **BALTZAR.**

**Balthazar, Mr** *[fl. 1760–1763], dancer.*

Mr Balthazar's name first appeared in the bills as a dancer at the Haymarket on 2 June 1760. In 1760–61, he was on the Covent Garden pay list for 5*s.* per day, as a member of the dancing company. The only mention of him in the bills that season, however, was as one of the many dancers in a comic ballet, *The Hungarian Gambols*, on 9 March 1761. The following season, 1761–62, he was employed at Drury Lane. There he danced in *The Drunken Swiss* with Grimaldi and Miss Baker on 24 April 1762 and in *The May Day Frolic* on 1 May with Nancy Dawson. The last mention of him in the bills was on 24 May 1762, when he again danced with Nancy Dawson at Drury Lane, but in 1763 he was found on a company list for Sadler's Wells.

**Baltzar, Thomas** *c. 1630–1663, violinist.*

A violinist with an astonishing technique which greatly influenced the playing of the instrument in England, Thomas Baltzar was born in Lübeck about 1630, spent some time in the royal chapel in Sweden (hence his sometimes being called a Swede), and came to England in 1655. He stayed for a time with Sir Anthony Cope of Hanwell, Oxfordshire. Evelyn heard him and recorded his impressions in his diary on 4 March 1656:

This night I was invited by Mr Roger L'Estrange to hear the incomparable Lubicer on the violin. His variety on a few notes and plain ground, with that wonderful dexterity, was admirable. Tho a young man [of 26], yet so perfect and skilful, that there was nothing, however cross and perplexed, brought to him by our artists, which he did not play off at sight with ravishing sweetness and improvements, to the astonishment of our best masters. In sum, he played, on the single instrument a full concert, so as the rest flung down their instruments, acknowledging the victory. As to my own particular, I stand to this hour amazed that God should give so great perfection to so young a person. There were at that time as excellent in their profession as any were thought to be in Europe, Paul Wheeler, Mr [Davis] Mell, and others, till this prodigy appeared. I can no longer question the effects we read of in David's harp to charm evil spirits, or what is said some particular notes produced in the passions of Alexander, and that King of Denmark.

Anthony Wood also heard Baltzar, on 24 July 1658, and was equally dazzled by his virtuosity:

Thos. Baltzar, a Lubecker borne, and the most famous Artist for the Violin that the World had yet produced, was now in Oxon. and this day A. W. was with him and Mr. Ed. Low, lately Organist of Ch. Church, at the Meeting-house of Will. Ellis. A. W. did then and there, to his very great astonishment, heare him play on the Violin. He then saw him run up his Fingers to the end of the Finger-board of the Violin, and run them back insensibly, and all with alacrity and in very good time, which he nor any in England saw the like before. A. W. entertain'd him and Mr. Low with what the House could then afford, and afterwards he invited them to the Tavern; but they being engag'd to goe to other Company, he could no more heare him play or see him play at that time. Afterwards he came to one of the weekly Meetings at Mr. Ellis's house, and he played to the wonder of all the auditory: and exercising his Fingers and Instrument several wayes to the utmost of his power. Wilson thereupon, the public Professor (the greatest Judg of Musick that ever was) did, after his humoursome way, stoop downe to Baltzar's Feet, to see whether he had a Huff on, that is to say, to see whether he was a Devil or not, because he acted beyond the parts of a man. About that time it was, that Dr. Joh. Wilkins, Warden of Wadham College, the greatest curioso of his time, invited him and some of the musicians to his lodgings in that College purposely to have a Concert, and to see and heare him play. The instruments and books were carried thither, but none could be perswaded to play against him in consort on the violin. At length, the company perceiving A. W. standing behind in a corner neare the dore, they haled him in among them, and play, forsooth, he must against him. Whereupon he being not able to avoid it, he took up a violin and behaved himself as poor Troylus did against Achilles. He was abashed at it, yet honour he got by playing with and against such a grand master as Baltzar was.

Roger North was also impressed but noted the Lubecker's flaws: "Baltazar had a hand as swift as any, and used the double notes very much; but alltogether his playing, compared with our latter violins, was like his country rough and harsh. But he often used a lira manner of tuning, and hath some neat lute-fashioned lessons of that kind, and also some of his rough peices behind him."

Before the Restoration Baltzar played in Sir William Davenant's *The Siege of Rhodes* at Rutland House in 1656, shortly after his arrival, and it may be that this relationship with Davenant helped him to his appointment in 1661 as the leader of the violins in the King's private music. He served from at least 5 September 1661 on-

ward at a salary of £110 annually, on top of which he was paid for his instruments and strings.

Anthony Wood provided a clue to Baltzar's death in 1663: "being much admired by all lovers of musick his company was therefore desired; and company, especially musical company, delighting in drinking, made him drink more than ordinary, which brought him to his grave." Baltzar was buried in his thirty-third year in Westminster Abbey in July 1663. He left a few compositions, chiefly for the violin, some of which Dr Burney thought to be of great merit.

**Balzago.** *See* **BUZARGLO.**

**Bambridge, Mr** [*fl.* 1731–1743], actor.

A Bambridge (sometimes Bainbridge) and his wife were given trial employment in Giffard's small company at Goodman's Fields Theatre in the 1731–32 season. Bambridge's first appearance was as an anonymous sailor in *The Fair Quaker of Deal* on 8 November 1731. On 18 November he was Catesby in *Jane Shore*, and those were his parts, once or twice repeated, in the bills which survive for that season.

Mrs Bambridge had preceded her husband on the Goodman's Fields boards, her debut there on 11 October 1731 as Angelica in *The Constant Couple* being advertised "Mrs Bambridge, who never appear'd on this stage before," a probable indication of previous experience elsewhere. She was Trusty, in *Provok'd Husband* on 13 October, the servant Betty in *Woman's a Riddle* on 15 October, and Lucetta in *The Rover* on 17 December, and this ended her first flight in London, so far as the bills show.

The Bambridges reappeared in August 1736 as members of the Bartholomew Fair booth company of Hallam and Chapman. After that, they were absent from London entirely until August 1736, when they showed up in *The True and Ancient History of Fair Rosamond*, that favorite of fair booths, he as Cardinal Columbus and she as fair Rosamond, with Hallam and Chapman at Bartholomew Fair. Bambridge was at Hallam's booth in August 1741, playing the Cardinal, and unless another of his name was present at the fair, he (as "Bambridge") also performed Barberino in *The Devil of a Duke* "At Hippisley and Chapman's Great Theatrical Booth in George-Inn Yard."

On 25 September 1741 Mrs Bambridge appeared once more at Goodman's Fields, playing Lady Wronghead in *The Provok'd Husband*, having been forgotten sufficiently as to allow the managers to present her as playing for the "first time on this stage." On 9 November she was Lady Davers in the first performance of *Pamela*, James Dance's adaptation of Richardson's novel, which ran for 13 successive nights. From December to March she was Margaretta in *Rule a Wife and Have a Wife*, Belinda in *The Old Bachelor*, Widow Lackit in *Oroonoko*, Mrs Fainall in *The Way of the World*, Lady Graveairs in *The Careless Husband*, and Goneril (on 25 March, with the young novice Garrick acting Lear). She thus showed during the season the ability to move from youthful maidens to superannuated women, which was her most notable ability during her entire career.

When Giffard, under pressure from the Licensing Act, had to abandon the Ayliffe Street theatre and move his company for a new start to the old house at Lincoln's Inn Fields, Mrs Bambridge went along. But that enterprise was doomed, and after some fifty performances following its late opening on 24 November, the company disbanded in mid-April 1743. Mrs Bambridge had worked unusually hard. Among the new parts she played were: Mrs Day in *The Committee*, the Nurse in *The Relapse,* Lady Manlove in *The School Boy*, Duchess of York in *Richard III*, Lady Bountiful in *The*

*Stratagem*, Lady Loverule in *The Devil to Pay*, Town Lady in *Bickerstaff's Unburied Dead,* Widow in *All's Well that Ends Well*, Mrs Coaxer in *The Beggar's Opera*, Nurse in *Love for Love*, Mrs Wisely in *The Miser*, and Mrs Foresight in *Love for Love*.

On 23 August 1743 Mrs Bambridge was in Turbutt and Dove's Booth in Hosier Lane, Smithfield, for Bartholomew Fair, performing the Queen in *The Glorious Queen of Hungary*. On 8 September she was in the Great Tiled Booth on the Bowling Green for the time of Southwark Fair, playing Lady Westford in *The Blind Beggar of Bethnal Green*. In this latter performance her husband reappeared as Westford, but he was absent from the bills again when his wife joined William Hallam's company at Goodman's Fields for the 1744–45 season.

At Goodman's Fields Mrs Bambridge played about the same variety of roles that she had with Giffard, her new characters being: Queen Mother in *The Massacre at Paris*, Aurelia in *The Twin Rivals*, Mrs Prim in *A Bold Stroke for a Wife*, Scentwell in *The Busy Body*, Lady Trueman in *The Drummer*, Diana Trapes in *The Beggar's Opera*, the Queen in *The Spanish Fryar*, Hostess in *1 Henry IV*, Marcia in *Cato*, Altea in *Rule a Wife and Have a Wife,* Queen Elizabeth in *Richard III,* Villetta in *She Would and She Would Not,* Belinda in *The Fair Quaker of Deal*, Mrs Goodfellow in *Tunbridge Walks*, Mrs Peachum in *The Beggar's Opera*, and Necessary in *A Woman Is a Riddle*.

Mrs Bambridge remained at Goodman's Fields in the season 1745–46 and was given a benefit on the last night of the season, jointly with the elder Hallam. She returned to the same parts in the season of 1746–47. Evidently she lacked regular employment after 1746–47, although she played twice more in London, at the New Wells on 4 April and at the Haymarket on 2 May 1748. Her last recorded appearances were as a member of the Richmond and Twickenham summer companies in 1751.

**Bambridge, Mrs** [*fl. 1731–1738*], *actress.* See **BAMBRIDGE, MR.**

**Bambridge, Mrs** [*fl. 1749*], *house servant?*

A Mrs Bambridge was on the Covent Garden pay lists, earning 5*s.* per day in some capacity now unknown, from 29 September 1749 until 28 April 1750.

**Bambridge, Mrs** [*fl. 1757–1767*], *dancer.*

A Mrs Bambridge was in the corps of dancers at Covent Garden Theatre from the beginning of 1757–58 until 1766–67. She earned only 1*s.* 8*d.* per night throughout the whole period.

**Bamfield, Mr** [*fl. 1671*], *actor, dancer.*

Mr Bamfield (or Bampfield) played Ossolinsky in *Juliana* in June 1671 for the Duke's Company at the Lincoln's Inn Fields Theatre and sometime this same year danced in Cartwright's *Lady-Errant*. In 1673 a Mrs Bampfield owned a triangular piece of property on the corner of Long Acre and St Martin's Lane, beside the Cross Keys and not far from the Theatre Royal property, measuring about 150′ by 150′ by

*By Permission of the Huntington Library*

EDWARD BAMFIELD

80'; she may have been related to the performer.

**Bamfield, Edward**  *1732–1768, giant.*
Edward Bamfield, a giant, performed the role of the dragon in *The Dragon of Wantley* at Covent Garden during the 1760's. He appeared in the role on 30 March and 29 November 1762 and four times in May 1767. In 1767–68 he was on the Covent Garden pay list at 3s. 4d. per day, again for playing the dragon, which he last performed on 11 February 1768. He died on 6 November 1768 at the age of 36. A print of Bamfield is at the Huntington Library. Bamfield is pictured in a group entitled "Mirth and Friendship," drawn and engraved by Charles Mancourt; copies of this are at the British Museum and the Huntington Library.

**Bamshaw.** *See* BARNSHAW.

**"Banbaregines, Signor"**  *[fl. 1752–1754], dancer.*
"Banbaregines" was a pseudonym used by an unidentified actor in Christopher Smart's ("Mrs Midnight's") company which played at the "Oratory" at the Haymarket Theatre, 56 performances from December 1752 through March 1753.

On the evening of 4 July 1754 at the Haymarket a program of dancing followed the play. The featured dancers were "Banbaregines and Rerriminonies (just arrived from Piemons)."

The program was repeated on nine nights through 26 July. The bills of the London playhouses do not record any further appearances of Banbaregines.

**Banberry, Mr**  *[fl. 1746], actor, singer, dancer.*
Banberry was listed in no casts previous to his appearance as Hamlet for his benefit at Goodman's Fields Theatre on 31 January 1746, on which night he also played the title role in *Captain O'Blunder,* sang an Irish song, and did both a "wooden shoe

dance" and a hornpipe. He repeated these varied delights for the patrons of the Lee and Yeates booth at Bartholomew Fair in August 1746. He cannot be followed further and must be considered a novice whose attempt to attract attention in the metropolis failed.

**Bancroft.** *See* BENCRAFT.

**Bandiera, Anna**  *[fl. 1756], singer.*
Anna Bandiera was a singer in Giuseppe Giordani's opera troupe at Covent Garden Theatre from 12 January and apparently on through the spring season of 1756.

**Bane, la.** *See* L'ABBÉ.

**Banester.** *See* BANISTER, BANNISTER.

**Banford, Mr**  *[fl. 1728], boxkeeper.*
The Lincoln's Inn Fields Theatre accounts show a Mr Banford as a boxkeeper on 29 April 1728 when *The Stratagem* was performed; he was also named on the free list during 1727–28 and 1728–29.

**Banister.** *See also* BANNISTER.

**Banister, Mr**  *[fl. c.1676], dancer.*
It is not certain whether or not Mr Banister ever performed in London, but he replaced the elder John Weaver as dancing master at Oxford about 1676.

**Banister, James**  *[fl. 1676–1686], violinist.*
James Banister was probably related to the other musical Banisters of the Restoration period, but no precise connection can be established. He was appointed to Charles II's band of violins on 8 May 1676, replacing Henry Comer, who resigned, and it is likely that he was the James Bannister of St Giles in the Fields who married Mary Burch of Burchin Lane, London, on 28 April 1678 at his parish church. Serving under Louis Grabu, Banister received a salary in 1679 of £46 12s. 3d. annually.

Perhaps he was the James Banister of the "coleyard" whose son James was buried at St Giles on 29 April 1684. Banister was still performing on 26 January 1685 when an order directed him to practice at the court theatre for a ball.

The bulk of the records pertaining to James Banister, however, have more to do with his debts than his musical life. William Cooke petitioned against him on 29 August 1681 for unpaid rent; John Smyth did the same for a debt on 28 November of the same year; and James Mercy of Newmarket, where Banister had apparently gone as part of the King's entourage, petitioned against him for a debt of £41 10s. for food and lodging at Maypole Alley. On 19 March 1686 Banister sensibly made his wife Mary his attorney "to demand and receive all sums of money due to him as salary."

### Banister, Jeoffrey _1641–1684, violinist._

The violinist Jeoffrey Banister was almost certainly the Jeffrey Banister, son of Jeffrey (and Beatrice), who was baptized at St Giles in the Fields on 24 October 1641. This matches well enough with the marriage of a Jeffrey Banister of St Giles, bachelor, about 23, son of Jeffrey Banister, gentleman, to Katherine Fletcher of the same parish, spinster, age 21, at her own disposal, which was alleged on 28 May 1663. The marriage would have occurred in the spring following violinist Jeoffrey Banister's appointment to the King's Musick (on 27 October 1662), a likely time to set up housekeeping. Katherine Fletcher Banister died not long after the couple were married, for on 19 August 1664 Banister married a second time, the register now describing him as a widower, age 24, from St Martin-in-the-Fields. His new wife was Elizabeth Howell of St Andrew, Holborn, spinster, age 20, whose parents were dead. It is possible that John Howell the singer was related to her.

Jeoffrey Banister's appointment in 1662 was as a musician in ordinary but without fee, there being at the time no salaried position vacant; when Edward Strong died the following year, Banister was appointed, on 24 December 1663, to replace him at £46 12s. 8d. annually, retroactive to 29 September. In addition to playing in Charles II's band of violins, Banister also served occasionally in the Theatre Royal band; an order dated 20 December 1664 commanded him and others to perform at the Bridges Street playhouse whenever manager Thomas Killigrew should require them. The wording of the order suggests that Banister performed there only when an augmented orchestra was needed. He was also regularly chosen to travel with the King to Oxford, Hampton Court, Tunbridge, Dover, and Windsor.

A good many of the entries in the Lord Chamberlain's accounts that have to do with Banister concern finances. On 21 March 1668 he was assigned £26 12s. 6d. by violinist William Youckney; on 28 June 1672 singer Thomas Finall assigned him £10 at the usual 6 percent interest (on this document Banister was described as being from the parish of St Clement Danes); on 1 June 1674 he assigned £267 16s. 6d. to attorney or broker William Parkes (here Banister was cited as from St Dunstan in the West); on 29 April 1676 he assigned all the wages due him to Parkes in return for £150 in ready money; and on 4 July 1676 he assigned the £46 12s. 8d. annual salary due him to musician Thomas Bates in return for £150 in cash.

Like the other musical Banisters, to whom he was probably related, Jeoffrey was a poor manager of his financial affairs, though during this period, when Charles II was retrenching, many musicians in his employ were caught by the pinch and their salaries were frequently in arrears. In 1668 Charles had his band of 24 violins split into two groups, each to wait upon him on alternate months; this made them available for other duties, such as playing at the Chapel Royal, and Banister, in 1671, was one of the musicians assigned to play at the Chapel every third month.

In 1674 a "Banister Junior," who was probably Jeoffrey, not John Banister the younger, was named in the account books; this was meant to distinguish him from John Banister the elder, though why his first name was not used instead is unclear. He was cited again in 1675 as "Junior" in a livery warrant.

By 1676 Jeoffrey Banister and James Hart had set up a boarding school for young ladies in Chelsea in Sir Arthur George's old house (later to be used by Josias Priest for the premiere of *Dido and Aeneas*). There, in 1676, Banister and Hart produced Duffett's masque, *Beauties Triumph*.

Banister's service with the King's Musick continued at least until 17 May 1682, when the last record of his musical activity was entered in the *Calendar of Treasury Books*. At this time he would have been only 42, but perhaps he was in ill health. He died about September or October 1684. His will, dated 29 August and proved 13 October 1684, described him as of the Liberty of the Rolls in the parish of St Dunstan in the West, gentleman. George and Alice Howell were two of the witnesses—probably relatives of Banister's wife. The violinist left everything to his wife Elizabeth and asked her brother Henry Howell to assist her.

### Banister, John   1630?–1679, *instrumentalist, composer, impresario.*

John Banister was probably born in London in 1630—though some sources give 1624—the son of one of the waits of the parish of St Giles in the Fields, from whom he presumably received his early musical training. In 1656 he played (the violin, probably) in a small band that Sir William Davenant assembled for his production of *The Siege of Rhodes* at Rutland House. Since among others in the group of instrumentalists were Christopher Gibbons, Thomas Baltzar, and Dr Charles Coleman —all musicians of considerable stature— Banister by this time must have been fairly skilled. Though he gained fame with his musical concerts starting in 1672, as early as 1660 he may have held some public performances, for on 21 January 1660 Pepys wrote that he had gone to "the Mitre; where I drank a pint of wine, the house being fitted for Banister to come thither from Paget's"—though this could have been for a private musical gathering.

Banister seems to have been appointed to the King's Musick during the summer or fall of 1660, the first clearly dated reference to him in the Lord Chamberlain's accounts being a livery payment of £16 2s. 6d. on St Andrew (30 November) 1660; but his name was crossed off the list of musicians and "vacatur" noted beside it, which suggests that he was in the King's service but away from London at the time. On the following 12 April 1661 he was named on a livery warrant that indicated his participation in the coronation of Charles II on 12 April.

He had come to the attention of the King by this time, for he was sent by Charles on a mission to France; his passport, dated 2 December 1661, called him the King's servant "on Special Service." The purpose of his trip is not known, though it may have been connected with the King's plans for the royal musical establishment. By April Banister was back, and on 18 April 1662 he was appointed to take charge of eleven other violinists and attend Charles to Portsmouth to receive the Queen. On 3 May he was officially granted a position as one of the violinists in ordinary in the King's private music, in place of Davis Mell, deceased, at £110 annually.

Probably by this time Banister had married; it is likely that his son John was born about 1662.

In July 1663 he was given a new assignment; upon the death of the famous Baltzar he was made leader of the King's band of 24 violins and organizer of an even more elite group of 12, with almost dictatorial powers:

Where wee have beene pleased to appoint our welbeloved servant John Banister to make choice of twelve of our fower and twenty violins, to be a select Band to wait on us, wheresoever there shall be occasion for musique, And that he doe give his attendance on us constantly to receive our commands, and to see that our service be performed by the said twelve persons; And in consideracon of their extraordinary service done and to be done unto us, and the smallenesse of their wages already settled, Wee are willing to augment the same. Our will and pleasure therefore is, That you prepare a Warrant fitt for our royall signature for the payment of six hundred poundes per annum to passe by our Letters of Privy Seale unto the said John Banister, to be by him received at the receipt of our Exchequer for himselfe and twelve of our said violins. And upon receipt thereof to be equally divided to such persons, as he hath already made choice of, or shall from time to time for our said service, And the first payment of the said six hundred poundes per annum to commence from the five and twentieth of March, which was in the year of our Lord one thousand, six hundred sixty and two. And the arreares that have accrewed and growne due since the said five and twentieth of March 1662 to the fower and twentieth day of June last past to be paid off, And from thenceforth to be paid quarterly by equall porcons, out of the Receipt of our Exchequer during our pleasure. And our further will and pleasure is, That if any of our said Band of Violins nominated, or to be nominated, by the said John Banister, Master of our said Band, shall either neglect practices or performance before us in Consort upon his summons, or mix in any musique whatsoever otherwise than for our particular service in our said Band, without the knowledge and allowance of the said John Banister, That upon his complaint to the Lord Chamberlaine of our household, such person or persons so offending shall be discharged from this our

private musicke and such others of our other twelve violins taken into their roomes for the performance of this our said particular service, as our said Lord Chamberlaine shall thinke fitt and allow of upon the recommendacon of the said John Banister.

Having been granted the power to control his band's participation in musical activities outside the court, Banister immediately curtailed his own extra-courtly work. He had, in early 1663, begun a secondary career as a composer for the theatres. For Stapylton's *The Slighted Maid*, done at Lincoln's Inn Fields on 23 February 1663, Banister had written music for three masque sequences, and to the Dublin premiere of Katherine Phillips's *Pompey* in February he had contributed four songs. Not until 1668 did he write more theatre music—or at least have it performed in public.

The King was not against Banister's composing, however, as long as it was for him; when the violinist was listed to attend Charles at Windsor on 10 July 1663, Banister was labelled "composer." For the next few years his position at court was a splendid one, and he probably looked forward to taking Nicholas Lanier's place as Master of the King's Musick when Lanier, now in his seventies, retired. He moved in good social circles and the King smiled upon him; why under these circumstances he should have risked his career—which he certainly seems to have done in the mid-1660's—is very strange.

Like the other musical Banisters, John was careless with money, and his manipulation of the finances of his band of violins finally brought about his dismissal. A petition by members of the band dated 29 March 1667 revealed what had gone on over the years:

Wee the band of violins now under the direction of Mons.^r Grabu, Master of his Majesties musique, doe humbly represent to your Lordshipp [Lord Arlington]—That it was his Majesties will and pleasure to give unto his Band of Violins late under the direction of John Banister 600*l.* per annum for doeing extraordinary service. This John Banister undertakes it for himselfe and demanded of the Company 20*l.* a peice, or all the arreares that was due to them from the Queenes comeing in untill Michaelmas 1663, which, if we refused, hee swore wee should be turned out of the Band, for said hee, I am to carry upp the names to morrow morning to the Councell Chamber, and they that will not doe this, their names shall be left out, and others put in: But instead of putting in ours or others into a Privy Seale to receive the said 600*l.*, hee onely put in his owne name unknowne to us, soe wee consented to give him all that was due to us before that time, for 20*l.* a peice could not be raysed by us and in doeing this hee did promise that we should have 10*l.* a peice every quarter of him, whether he did receive it or not, and wee should begin from Michaelmas 1663, but unknowne to us hee had gott it granted a yeare and an halfe before, and since this Agreement he hath received 950*l.* for this Augmentation, of which said 950*l.* some have received of him 20*l.*, some 10*l.*, and one but 7*l.* 10*s.* and others more. And in 1663 wee played to the Queenes dancing which was her Birth Day, and wee presumed to speake to the Lord Chesterfield to speake for our accustomed fee, and the Lord Chesterfield spake to the Queene for us, but the Queens Treasurer being by, told the Queene, we had received great summes of money already, about 230*l.* which Mr. Banister keepes from us, as his owne right by giving him our arreares, and setting our hands to it, but it was that hee should performe his bargaine with us. The Queene hearing hee had such a summe of money was very angry, but wee never did speake before, and if we had not spoke then, wee never had knowne of the money, for Mr. Banister would not suffer us to looke after any money that is due to us, hee sayes, how dare wee doe it. That the said Banister received 50*l.* from the Queenes Majestie at the Bath, and paid to those that attended only 5*l.* each, keeping 20*l.* for himselfe. Also a person of honour giving us 10*l.* in gould for attendance, the said Banister kept fower peeces for himselfe. And 20*l.* he received from the Duke of Buckingham for

us, of which wee never had one penny, besides severall other things of that nature. And this last birthday of the Queenes he gets the fee of 10*l.* into his hands, and gives money to some, and to others not a penny, neither did hee waite on the Queene himself. Likewise Mr. Banister hath kept sometimes five or six of us out of wayting, according as hee is pleased or displeased, and three of us he hath turned out of his Band, his Majesties pleasure not being knowne therein, nor the Lord Chamberlaines, by this meanes, hee thinkes to put all our arreares in his owne purse, whereby the King's service is abused, and his poore servants utterly ruyned. Wee therefore most humbly desire that your Lordshipp would be pleased to order the Caveat to be taken off, that soe the Seale may passe. And if any objecčon be made by the said Banister, wee are ready and willing humbly to submitt to what your Lordshipp shall please to order therein.

The *caveat* referred to concerned the new master of the band, Frenchman Louis Grabu, who had not yet been appointed head of the select band of 12; the petitioners clearly thought their position would improve under Grabu, and, certainly, it could hardly have gotten worse.

On 12 November 1666—probably after the band had aired at least some of the grievances that they finally put in writing above—a warrant was issued replacing Banister with Grabu as head of the band of 24 violins; Banister was furious, as Pepys reported on 20 February 1667: "the King's viallin Bannister, is mad that the King hath a Frenchman come to be chief of some part of the King's musique, at which the Duke of York made great mirth." Anthony Wood reported that Banister had been dismissed because the King had called for the Italian violins and, within the hearing of the royal ear, Banister had retorted that "he had better have the English."

On 4 August 1667, after the band had lodged its official complaint, Manchester wrote:

The grant of the Privy Seale which Bannester had for a particular Band of Violins [the elite dozen], was by his Majesties especiall command given to Mons. Grabu, Master of the Musick; and a stop was made, upon Bannesters petition, that hee might receave the arreares due in the Exchequer. But the whole Band of Violins complayning severall times that Banister had wronged them in their share and dividend; I did thinke it fitt upon hearing all parties and by the consent of all, to order that the Master of the Musick should receave it, and that I would see it justly distributed hereafter: wherewith I acquainted his Majestie, and his Majestie was well pleased therewith and comanded that the Master of Musick should receave it, and should have his Privy Seale pass as it is drawne.

Banister's dismissal was probably brought about by a combination of his manipulation of the funds, his impolitic statement before the King, and his jealousy of Grabu. The odd thing is that after losing his post, Banister continued as a member of the band under Grabu, playing with the very musicians who had complained against him, so perhaps in the hearings it was discovered that the situation was not so serious as the surface facts might imply. The gambling that Banister was doing with the band funds was a common practice of the times, for the King was frequently in arrears with his payments to employees, forcing many of them to use unpaid salaries as collateral for loans. Banister may have been doing just that.

As soon as he lost his position as head of the violins, Banister was apparently free —or at least felt free—to engage in outside musical activities again. With his colleague Pelham Humphrey he wrote the music for the first Restoration version of *The Tempest*, produced at Lincoln's Inn Fields on 7 November 1667. Whatever money he received for this work, plus his salary of £45 10s. 10d. annually as a member of the band at court, plus his £16 2s. 6d. annual livery, plus arrears in his salary, must have given him a very reasonable income, though probably nothing like what he commanded earlier.

He seems also to have spent more time relaxing with friends now, and his theatrical contacts brought him into new circles. Pepys on 26 March 1668 wrote of entertaining Banister and others, including performers Henry Harris and Mrs Knepp, at the Blue Balls near the Lincoln's Inn Fields playhouse, where they all sang and danced until midnight. On 29 March he invited Harris and Banister to his home for dinner and found them

most extraordinary company both, the latter for musique of all sorts, the former for everything: here we sang, and Banister played on the theorbo, and afterwards Banister played on his flageolet, and I had a very good discourse with him about musique, so confirming some of my new notions about musique that it puts me upon a resolution to go on and make a scheme and theory of musique not yet ever made in the world.

A month later, on 26 April, Pepys entertained the pair again, though he started feeling guilty about the expense and felt that "the pleasure of these people was not worth so often charge and cost to me." On 7 May Pepys saw Banister again, this time at Mrs Knepp's house where the composer brought a song he had set for Sedley's new play, *The Mulberry Garden*, done on 18 May at the Bridges Street playhouse. Banister had written the song ("Ah! Cloris, that I now could sit") for Mrs Knepp, and Pepys recorded that "this he did, before us, teach her, and it being but a slight, silly, short aire, she learnt it presently." When Pepys saw the play performed he was even more displeased with Banister's music: "there never was worse musick played— that is, worse things composed, which made me and Captain Rolt, who happened to sit near me, mad."

If some Banister music struck Pepys as poor, other works by him sent the diarist into ecstasy. At the party at Mrs Knepp's house on 7 May Pepys got Banister "to prick me down the notes of the Echo in 'The Tempest,' which pleases me mightily."

Pepys had been enchanted with the echo song ever since he first heard it at the theatre on 7 November 1667: "a curious piece of musique in an echo of half sentences, the echo repeating the former half, while the man goes on to the latter, which is mighty pretty." After Banister supplied Pepys with the music, Harris wrote down the words for him.

From 1668 to 1672 Banister wrote music for a number of plays: *The Man's the Master* (26 March 1668 at Lincoln's Inn Fields), *The Royal Shepherdess* (25 March 1669 at the same theatre), *The Conquest of Granada* (December 1670 at the rival Bridges Street Theatre), *Juliana* (June 1671 at the same), *The Adventures of Five Hours* (1670–71 at the same), and *The Gentleman Dancing Master* (6 February 1672 at Dorset Garden).

Banister, if the following records pertain to him and not to another man of the same name, received a marriage license on 11 January 1671. He described himself as of the parish of St Margaret, Westminster, a widower, age 46 (which would place his birth in 1624 rather than 1630); his bride was Mary Wood of the same parish, a widow, age 50. To this second marriage Banister brought at least one son, John, age about nine.

About this same time Charles II was trying to cope with his financial problems by retrenching. Banister was probably affected by this pinch, but he was at this point in his life ready to support himself outside the court if necessary. Not only was he now well established as a composer for the theatre, but he was ready to embark on a third career, that of *impresario*.

Banister had been one of the important members of the Corporation of the Art and Science of Musick for some time. He had been elected to membership on 24 November 1663, replacing Symon Hopper, who had resigned. The Corporation tried to protect musicians by means of the old guild system, but by 1672 their effectiveness had

deteriorated and their medieval outlook was outmoded. It was in 1672 that Banister reinstituted the public concerts upon which his real fame now rests, and it was probably the weakening power of the old establishment which made his concerts possible. In the *London Gazette* of 26–30 December 1672 he printed his first announcement: "These are to give Notice that at Mr John Banisters House, now called the Musick School, over against the George Tavern in White Fryers this present Monday, will be Musick performed by Excellent Masters, beginning precisely at four of the Clock in the afternoon, and every afternoon for the future, precisely at the same hour." Roger North later reported on Banister's project and noted that it was the beginning of a great blossoming of musical interest among Londoners:

But how and by what stepps Musick shot up in to such request, as to croud out from the stage even comedy itself, and to sit downe in her place and become of such mighty value and price as wee now know it to be, is worth inquiring after. The first attempt was low: a project of old Banister, who was a good violin, and a theatrical composer. He opened an obscure room in [*recte*, across the street from] a publik house in White fryars; filled it with tables and seats, and made a side box with curtaines for the musick. *is.* a peice, call for what you please, pay the reckoning, and Welcome gentlemen. Here came most of the shack performers [i.e. vagabonds] in towne, and much company to hear; and divers musicall curiositys were presented, as, for instance, Banister himself, upon a flageolett in consort, which was never heard before nor since, unless imitated by the high manner upon the violin. But this lasted not long . . .

In a slightly different description that North wrote of Banister's room he located it "neer the Temple back gate" and noted that the raised box for the musicians had curtains because of the modesty of the musicians— whatever that implies. North was incorrect in remembering that the concerts did not continue for long; Banister presented them regularly until his death in 1679, though the later ones were not as ambitious as those given during his first season.

Banister's original scheme was to perform daily, and this he did in 1673, but on 20 November 1673 he altered his system somewhat and promised new music on the first day of every month; he probably found that daily performances were far too ambitious. Banister was not only presenting the first regular public musical concerts in England, but he was probably the earliest advocate of music by new composers (himself included, to be sure). The fact that he called his place a "Musick-School" suggests that in addition to the concerts he may well have been doing some teaching. He needed what money he could get, for his salary at court was in arrears and in February 1674 he still had not received his livery payment for 1665. On 20 May 1674, describing himself as from the parish of St Dunstan in the West (Jeoffry Banister's parish, incidentally), he assigned to attorney William Parkes £116 7s. 1d. in court wages unpaid for the past two and a half years; this was probably collateral for a loan. Though he remained in the royal service until his death, as numerous warrants show, he earned little cash—though, to be fair, he seems to have contributed little in return.

In the *London Gazette* of 21–25 January 1675 Banister announced a change of address: "Mr John Bannister that lived in White-Fryers, is removed to Shandois-street [i.e. Chandos Street], Covent Garden, and there intends to Entertain, as formerly, on Tuesday next, and likewise every Evening for the future, Sundays only excepted." He managed to return to his daily schedule and still rehearse and perform in the court masque *Calisto*, which had its premiere on 15 February 1675.

In April 1675 Banister was again manipulating his finances; describing himself now as from the parish of St Martin-in-the Fields, he assigned to Mr John Hill his yearly livery of £16 2s. 6d. in consideration of £40 in cash. Hill agreed to suffer the loss if Banister's livery fee was not paid on schedule, but if it was discontinued or made void, Banister was to take the loss. This was again typical of the gambling that went on among court employees at this time; Hill was, in a sense, betting that Banister would get paid and Banister was betting he wouldn't—and was willing to sacrifice his livery fee for life in return for ready money.

In 1676 Banister wrote the music for Duffett's *Beauties Triumph*, done at Jeoffrey Banister and James Hart's school in Chelsea. For the production of *Circe* at Dorset Garden on 12 May 1677 he set all the music, and, according to the prompter Downes, "being well Perform'd, it answer'd the Expectation of the Company." Three of his *Circe* songs have survived in print: "Young Phaon strove," "Give me my lute," and "Cease, valiant hero."

By December 1676 Banister had moved his public concerts again:

On Thursday next the 14th instant, at the Academy in Little Lincolns-Inn Fields, will begin the first part of the Parley of Instruments composed by Mr John Banister, and perform'd by eminent Masters, at six a clock, and to continue nightly, as shall by Bill or otherwise be notifi'd. The Tickets are to be delivered out from one of the clock till five every day, and not after.

In 1678 he moved once more, this time to "the Musick School in Essex Buildings, over against St Clement's Church in the Strand" where he began presenting his concerts on 22 November. He was still there on 9 January 1679 and perhaps for several months thereafter, but on 23 May 1679 he was granted permission to travel abroad for six months or more. Whether he made the trip or not we do not know. On 3 October 1679 Banister died, and on the following day he was buried in the cloisters of Westminster Abbey. He apparently died intestate, and on 20 October 1679 his estate was administered; he left a wife, Mary, and a son, John, who took his place in the band of violins at court and had a considerable musical career of his own.

### Banister, John   *1662?–1736, violinist.*

John Banister was the son of John Banister the concert impresario and, like him, a violinist. His birth date has sometimes been given as c.1652–1655, but at his death in January 1736 the *Grub Street Journal* spoke of him as aged 74, which would place his birth about 1662, presumably in London. If the records concerning a 1671 marriage of John Banister the elder are correct, young John was the child of the first Mrs Banister.

The "Banister Junior" referred to in the Lord Chamberlain's accounts between 1674 and 1679 was probably Jeoffrey Banister, not John the younger; the first clear indication of the younger John Banister's musical activity was his appointment on 6 November 1679 to the place in the King's band of violins made vacant by the death of his father on 3 October. His wages, as indicated in a warrant dated 24 April 1680, were 1s. 8d. daily plus livery. He supposedly would have been about 17 when he took his father's place, and it is likely that he had trained under him.

John the younger continued as part of the private music of James II, periodically traveling with James to Windsor and elsewhere. A warrant dated 8 December 1690 shows that he was selected to attend William III on a trip to Holland, but his name was canceled in favor of Henry "Eagles" (that is, Eccles); Banister stayed behind to attend the Queen. For his royal service during the 1690's he was paid £40 annually, plus livery.

Not until 1698 did he engage in musical activity outside the court. On 10 and 17 January of this year he and Robert King had benefit concerts; on 23 March Banister played at a concert at Frank Roberts's

rooms; in July 1700 he sold subscriptions to a set of Corelli sonatas; and during the early years of the new century he began making theatrical appearances.

By this time Banister had married and was trying, with a pathetic lack of success, to raise a family: of twelve children listed in the St Giles in the Fields parish registers as offspring of John and Elizabeth Banister, only four survived the violinist, and most died in infancy. His son John, who became a flutist, was born on 27 December 1686; a daughter Elizabeth was born on 29 January 1688 but died within ten years; a son Windham was baptized on 16 May 1689 and buried on 18 March 1690; a son James was born on 18 May 1690 and died sometime before 1730; a daughter Ann was born on 29 August 1691 and buried on 1 August 1692; a daughter Mary was born on 21 August 1692 and buried the following 3 September; a second Mary was born on 12 November 1693 and lived to

*Harvard Theatre Collection*

JOHN BANISTER, Jr
by T. Murray

execute her father's will; a son William was baptized on 20 March 1695 and buried on 6 May 1700; a daughter Henrietta was born on 9 April 1696; a daughter Elizabeth was baptized on 29 August 1698 and buried on 17 June 1699; a son Thomas was baptized on 24 September 1701 and buried on 10 January 1704; and a daughter Charlotte was born on 19 March 1703.

On 7 July 1702 Banister and his son John, then 15, appeared together at Drury Lane playing new music set to flutes. The pair played there again on 11 August; Banister alone performed there on 23 October 1702 and 19 April 1703; and father and son appeared there again on 18 June. Banister had become a member of the Drury Lane band, and at some point—probably after 1710—he was made its leader. During the first decade of the eighteenth century, however, he frequently performed as a soloist elsewhere, usually on the violin and often at York Buildings.

Many court musicians, on 1 December 1707, were granted royal permission to play at the new Queen's Theatre in the Haymarket and thus augment their incomes. Banister offered to play for manager Heidegger for £1 10s. per performance—the top rate requested except for an exorbitant £3 asked for by Dieupart. Banister was one of the musicians hired, though at 5s. less than he had requested. Since he and others were at the time members of the Drury Lane band, manager Christopher Rich of that playhouse tried to fire them for negotiating with Heidegger, but they were apparently reinstated and held positions in both theatres concurrently. At first Banister was among the second rank of musicians at the Queen's Theatre, but by about 1709 he was earning the top salary of £40 annually. He must have been engaging in too many outside activities, for a royal restraining order was issued on 24 December 1709 cautioning him not to leave the Queen's musical establishment without permission, and apparently about this time, at least temporarily, he severed his connection with the court.

The *Tatler* No 222 in 1710 noted another source of income for musicians of the time: young lovers often hired waits to help with their courtship. The *Tatler* reported that "my friend Mr Banister has told me, he was proffered five hundred pounds by a young fellow to play but for one winter under the window of a lady that was a great fortune, but more cruel than ordinary."

Banister joined Thomas Britton's music club in 1712, and at some point he assumed the leadership of the Drury Lane band, a post he held until about 1720. The last contemporary notice of him before his death, however, was on 9 May 1715 when he played at a performance at the Lincoln's Inn Fields Theatre.

He made his will on 5 September 1730, six years before his death, naming his eldest daughter, Mary, his executrix. He asked that his estate be equally divided, among his daughters Mary, Henrietta, and Charlotte. To his son John, whose musical career had not come to much, he left £10 for mourning plus £200 which young John had borrowed from him. His will made no mention of his wife Elizabeth, so perhaps by 1730 she had died. Since 1718 John Banister had lived at No 32, Brownlow (Betterton) Street, Bloomsbury, and there he died on 9 January 1736, still cited in the papers as "one of His Majesty's Band of Musick which place he has held for many years." The wording suggests that he had been active up to his death and that he had rejoined the group of musicians at court. Mary Banister, with inappropriate haste, proved her father's will on the day of his death.

John Banister was not the composer his father had been, though he wrote a few small works. In 1698 he published *The Compleat Tutor to the Violin*, though no copy now exists. T. Murray painted Banister, and engravings of his work were made by I. Smith, R. Williams, and C. Grignion.

## Banister, John  b. 1686, flutist.

John Banister, the third of that name, was the grandson of the impresario and son of the violinist. He was born on 27 December 1686, and his parents, John and Elizabeth, baptized him at St Giles in the Fields four days later. His first appearance, billed as "Banister Junior," was with his father on 7 July 1702 at Drury Lane when they played "New Musick set to Flutes"; the pair performed again on 11 July and on 18 June 1703. On 28 April 1704 the younger Banister played at a concert for his own benefit held at York Buildings. Perhaps he abandoned his musical career after this, for the next mention of him was in his father's will, dated 5 September 1730. John was left £10 for mourning and £200 which he had earlier borrowed from his father.

## Banister, Thomas  [fl. 1673], musician.

Thomas Banister was one of the musicians playing at the Nursery—the training playhouse for actors operated by the patent houses in the 1670's; for reasons not specified, he was apprehended on 15 April 1673 but discharged on 19 April.

## Banks, Mr  [fl. 1723], actor.

Mr Banks, possibly an amateur, acted Kite in *The Recruiting Officer* on 15 April 1723 at the Haymarket Theatre with a pickup company that played irregularly during the 1722–23 season.

## Banks, Mr  [fl. 1746–1749?], actor.

A Mr Banks played one of the witches in *Macbeth* at Goodman's Fields Theatre on 5 January 1747. He was at the New Wells, Goodman's Fields, at some time in June 1748 as the Miller in *Harlequin Collector*. He did not appear again in the bills of that house, but he may have been the Banks who is listed by *The London Stage* as acting in fair booths in the summer of 1749. He may also have been the Banks who was at Sad-

ler's Wells in some capacity in 1753, 1755, and 1768.

## Banks, Mr  d. 1752, door keeper, office-keeper.

A Mr Banks was evidently constantly in the seasonal employment of Covent Garden Theatre from the season of 1737–38 (when he shared a benefit with several other servants of that house on 16 May 1738), until at least the spring of 1750. The benefit bill of 11 May 1742 identifies Banks and companions sharing the benefit as "Pit and Gallery Door-Keepers." He was too ill to solicit tickets for his benefit on 17 April 1752, at which time he was called office-keeper, and by 30 April he was dead.

The "Widow Banks" shared a benefit with house personnel on 7 May 1752 and again on 21 May 1753.

## Banks, Mr  [fl. 1780], carver?, actor. See BANKS, WILLIAM.

## Banks, Mr  [fl. 1789], actor.

A Mr Banks performed once at the King's Head Inn in the Borough High Street, Southwark, on 16 September 1789, as Sir Christopher Curry in *Inkle and Yarico*. Mrs Banks played Narcissa. The company was apparently assembled for this single performance. They may have been Mr and Mrs Thomas Banks.

## Banks, Mr  [fl. 1800–1827], dancer, actor.

Charles Dibdin the younger mentioned in his *Memoirs* a Banks who was harlequin at Sadler's Wells in 1800 and who at the time of writing, 1827, was keeping "the Harlequin Chop, or Eating House" in London. Dibdin, however, may have been confusing Thomas "Harlequin" Banks, who died in 1810, with another Banks.

## Banks, Mrs  [fl. 1789], actress. See BANKS, MR  [fl. 1789].

### Banks, Henry *1744–1829, theatrical tailor, wardrobe keeper.*

Henry Banks was resident theatrical tailor at Drury Lane Theatre at or near the turn of the nineteenth century. It is impossible to determine whether some of the payments in the account books of the end of the eighteenth century were to him or to the scene painter and harlequin Thomas Banks, who may have been a kinsman. Henry seems, however, to have been employed in some capacity in the theatre from 1789–90 onward.

Banks's weekly salary in 1803–4 was £1 6s., and from 1805–6 through 1811–12 he signed his full name to receipts for £2 per week; he apparently replaced Colquhon as wardrobe keeper in 1806, at least temporarily. As master tailor at £2 10s. a week he paid salaries to several subordinates after the 1811–12 season, and from then until at least 1818–19 he earned a constant salary of £3 per five-day week. It is not known when he retired.

Banks the tailor was probably the Henry Banks of Henrietta Street, Covent Garden, whose will, witnessed by Griffith and Edward Foulkes and Abraham Jones on 12 November 1827, was proved 9 November 1829. He left his "two freehold houses being No 15 Bridges Str Covent Garden and No 8 Princes St Drury Lane and also my three shares in Drury Lane Theatre, together with the money allowed by the Amicable Society Serjeants Inn for my 2 shares" to four of his daughters—Caroline, Susanna, Elizabeth, and Lydia Banks; £25 to his eldest daughter Mrs Ann Price; £10 to his son George; and "the gold watch chain & seals that I usually wear" to his son John, who with Henry's sister Mrs Ann Hathaway of Knightsbridge, was appointed to execute the bequests.

"George Son of Henry Banks by Su-[s]anna his Wife Born November 26 1792" was christened at St Paul, Covent Garden, on 30 December 1792.

Henry Banks "Aged 85" was buried in St Paul, Covent Garden, churchyard on 5 November 1829.

### Banks, Mrs John. *See* KNIVETON, MRS THOMAS.

### Banks, Thomas *1756–1810, scene painter, dancer, actor.*

Thomas Banks was the son of William Banks of Fleet Street, the carver, gilder, and Covent Garden dancer. His father's association with the stage apparently drew Thomas early to a career of dancing and acting.

*The Secret History of the Green Rooms* (1790) says that Banks made his debut (but does not specify when) at Covent Garden "in some trifling part, and was under the tuition of Mr Younger, who afterwards took him to Liverpool." Along with other performers, a Thomas Banks signed a letter to George Colman, of the Covent Garden management, on 5 November 1768. However odd it may seem to find a twelve-year-old boy signing among adults, he apparently did so, though why his father, who was at the theatre with him that season, did not also sign, is not known.

The *Green Rooms* account asserts that Tom prospered in the provinces. In the theatres of the North he was called "Little Banks, in contradistinction to the gentleman, who lived with Mrs Barresford, who was called Big Banks." This was John Banks, the Liverpool and Manchester manager, who was perhaps a relative. Thomas Banks "had discovered a good taste and execution in scene painting; and in most of the companies to which he has belonged, he has superintended that department." He was "universally acknowledged a good harlequin . . . yet never appeared in London until some friends told him of the extravagant praise W[illiam] Lewis had given his performances in Liverpool," and "suggested he visit London."

This account appears generally correct. Banks is traceable in surviving Liverpool theatrical account books in 1776 through 1778 and again in the summer of 1786. His salary was in the 15s. range weekly and he administered substantial sums for materials, probably for scenery. In the summers of 1776 and 1777 at least he was also described as "property man" and "property maker" and was paid £1 per week. He shared a benefit with Sydney on 11 August which cleared £82. In the winter season of 1782–83 he was at Edinburgh, along with another Banks, probably John.

When Banks came back to London in the fall of 1788, John Philip Kemble is said to have met him in the street and immediately to have engaged him at a "genteel" salary. His name first appeared in a London patent house bill predicting his portrayal of Younger Brother in *Comus* at Drury Lane on 8 November 1788, but he may not have played the part, actually, since his performance as Harlequin in the afterpiece of *Harlequin Junior* on 10 November is called his first London appearance, and according to *The London Stage* he hailed from Manchester. He repeated the part on 13 November and was Stukely in *The West Indian* on 15 November. Thereafter during his first season at Drury Lane he seems to have performed but seldom (Harlequin in *Robinson Crusoe*, Balthazer in *Romeo and Juliet*, and the Knight in *The Law of Lombardy*) and he very likely was devoting much time to assisting in the scene room. His salary was 10s. per week. In 1789–90 it was raised to £3 per week at which salary he remained through 1795–96. It is possible that the Banks who played, along with his wife, in suburban London theatres in 1789 was Thomas.

In the summer season of 1795 at the Birmingham theatre the bills several times carry credits for scenery he painted; he was on the roster there in 1791 and 1792 and every summer from 1795 until 1800, when he again was specifically credited with scenes. In August–September 1794 he was employed at Covent Garden as an assistant

painter at 10s. 6d. per week. In 1796–97 his salary as an actor at Drury Lane dropped to £1, but he probably received substantial extra sums for painting. In 1798 Banks helped the younger Thomas Greenwood paint the scenery for Richardson's traveling theatre. He assisted Capon, the younger Greenwood, Blackwood, and Demaria in 1799 with the spectacular scenery for *Pizarro* and *Feudal Times*.

By 1799, according to the *Authentic Memoirs*, "His situation [at Drury Lane was] precarious; for there being but little dependence on him, he [was] only employed occasionally, sometimes at one place, sometimes at another." But this does not appear to be entirely correct. For though in the summer season of 1801 Banks assisted S. Whitmore and Wilkinson at the Haymarket in executing Whitmore's designs for the "New Grand Ballet Romance" of *The Corsair*, he continued to be carried on the Drury Lane winter roster as an assistant painter, and after 1798 he was again at a constant weekly salary of £3 until the end of the season 1808–9. He was also the Banks who was assisting Greenwood in creating scenery for John Cartwright Cross at his Royal Circus from 1799 through 1808. He was also probably the Banks who was actor and dancer on the pay-list of 1799–1800 at Drury Lane, but in the latter part of his career he seems seldom to have exercised this more arduous capacity. He claimed a pension from the Drury Lane Fund in 1809.

A fair selection of his roles might include: John in *Man of Ten Thousand*, Spirit in *Comus*, Pedrillo in *Don Juan*, Pedro in *Loves Makes a Man*, Servant in *The Fugitive*, Quildrive in *The Citizen*, Kitteau in *Englishman in Paris*, John in *The Humourist*, one of the Lazzaroni in *The Pirates*, and Frank in *The First Floor*.

He may have been the Banks dancing at Sadler's Wells and living in Shoemaker Row, Blackfriars, in May 1803. Thomas Banks died on 26 December 1810, aged

54, according to the burial register of St Paul, Covent Garden. In his will, dated from Clare Court, Drury Lane, on 21 January 1805 and witnessed by one N. Shirts, he designated property unspecified but valued above £450 to his wife Jane, whom he also made his executrix. On 28 December 1810, two days after Banks died and two days before he was buried, Jane, probably already gravely ill, made her own will. She died at 48, sometime between 28 December 1810 and her burial in St Paul, Covent Garden, churchyard on 18 January. On 19 January both wills were proved. Jane's friend Sarah Shirts of No 5, Bridges Street, widow of the witness to Thomas's will, was made executrix. Jane's will is specific:

Whereas I am entitled to a debt belonging to my aforesaid husband Thomas Banks late scene painter of Drury Lane Theatre twenty-four pounds with interest from a trust Deed signed by the said Thomas Banks likewise twenty pounds nineteen shillings for scene painting I give and bequeath unto Ann King sister to my late husband Thomas Banks and her heirs now living in Water Lane North End Deal in Kent the above debt if it can be obtained.

Of "Three hundred pounds in the five pᵣ cents in the Bank of England" Jane left to her four sisters (Martha Milner, Elizabeth Taylor, Ann Asworth and Orlio Prince, all of Manchester) an equal division of £100; to Caroline Farquharson "my adopted niece now at school," £100, as well as her "Gold Watch and all my Silver Spoons" and other household goods. Smaller amounts were to be given to Hanley Hatter of Holborn; Sarah Tourneur, "Wife of Joseph Nicholas Tourneur now living with Lord Heathfield"; Elizabeth Ruse, daughter of a chop house keeper in Great Mays Buildings; and Sarah Shirts and her sons Nathaniel and George. Jane's will was witnessed by John Brandon, of White Horse Yard, very probably the theatrical concessionaire.

A Thomas and Elizabeth Banks witnessed the marriage of the Reverend Mr Edward Foster, of the parish of St George, Hanover Square, widower, to Lavinia Banks, spinster, of St Marylebone parish, on 3 August 1799.

**Banks, W.** *[fl. 1796–1812?]*, *actor, singer, dancer.*

A W. Banks appeared first in some small unspecified part in the new afterpiece *Harlequin Captive*, at Drury Lane on 18 January 1796, when another Banks, identified by *The London Stage* as Thomas Banks, was harlequin. The pantomime was repeated four times through 17 March. On 9 November 1796, W. Banks played again in the pantomime, this time assuming the part of Harlequin. On 26 December he was one of the principal savages in *Robinson Crusoe*, repeated on 5, 6, and 9 January. He was listed as a singer from 16 January to 16 May 1798 and was paid £1 per week for a few trifling roles. In 1798–99 he was listed as a dancer. He was entirely absent from Drury Lane but turned up at Covent Garden from 17 February through 1 May 1800, playing a domestic in *Raynard and Agnes* and dancing a few times. He may have been the Banks who played comic parts during the summer and until 6 October 1800 at Shrewsbury, and was doubtless the one acting small roles at the Royal Circus up until at least 1812.

A William Banks, bachelor, married Jane Wilson, spinster, on 20 March 1799 at St Paul, Covent Garden.

**Banks, William** *d. 1776, dancer, actor, designer.*

William Banks was a Fleet Street carver and gilder whose failure in business apparently precipitated him onto the stage. He is reported from several sources to have danced at Sadler's Wells early in his career, and a Banks is shown to have been present there by a surviving bill of 1753.

A Banks, probably William, danced in pantomime and occasionally acted small parts at Covent Garden Theatre from 4 October 1766 when a Banks, dancer, was added to the pay list at 5s. per day until at least 13 October 1775, when the bills last noticed him. He did chorus and pantomime dancing and assumed very small parts, hardly ever ascending above such roles as Doctor in *The Royal Chace* and Pantaloon in *The Metamorphosis of Harlequin.* In view of his apprenticeship he was probably the "Banks" who was paid £4 8s. 6d. for "masks, &c." on 23 May 1772, £1 1s. for two masks on 15 February 1773, and on 16 December 1773, £1 1s. for a head of a figure. The Banks who furnished three masks to the theatre on 29 May 1780 is not identified, but it is perhaps worth suggesting that William may have taught a son (the W. Banks, fl. 1796–1812?) his trade.

William Banks died on 25 September 1776 at his lodgings in Crown Court, Fleet Street. He is sometimes confused with his son Thomas and sometimes with John Banks the Manchester manager, both much more important figures.

**Banner, Mr** {d. 1800?}, *doorkeeper.*
One Banner, doorkeeper, is listed in the Drury Lane account book under date of 16 November 1799. A payment of £5 5s. to "Mrs Banner on acct to Bury her husband" is noted on 25 January 1800.

**Banner, Mr** {fl. 1801}, *doorkeeper.*
An individual named Banner is listed as doorkeeper at Drury Lane Theatre in 1801.

**Banner, Mr** {fl. 1801}, *sweeper.*
An individual named Banner is listed as a sweeper at Drury Lane Theatre in 1801.

**Bannester.** *See* BANISTER and BANNISTER.

**Bannet.** *See* BENNET.

**Bannister.** *See also* BANISTER.

**Bannister, Mr** {fl. 1790–1797}, *puppet showman.*
A puppet showman named Bannister appeared sporadically at Bartholomew Fair in the summers from 1790 through 1797.

**Bannister, Mrs** {fl. 1793–1794?}, *actress.*
The anonymous author of *A Peep Into Paris* (1794) to a superficial discussion of Mrs John Bannister's roles provides a footnote: "I have particularly mentioned Mrs J. Bannister, to distinguish her from another actress of the Haymarket Theatre, who *assumes* the same name." No other Mrs Bannister is to be found in the playbills of the Haymarket, however.

**Bannister, Master J.** {fl. 1773}, *actor.*
*See* BANNISTER, JAMES.

**Bannister, Charles** 1741–1804, *actor, singer.*
Charles Bannister, son of John and Rebecca Powell Bannister, was baptized at some time between May and October 1741 in the parish church of Newland, Gloucestershire. *The Thespian Dictionary,* which incorrectly states the year of his birth as 1738, says that when Charles was seven his father received an appointment to the victualing office of the Navy at Deptford. The local theatre was an irresistible attraction to the boy, who soon was on familiar terms with all the actors. Before he was 18 he had played Richard III and Romeo in amateur performances, and it was not long before his passion for theatre carried him off to London brashly to apply to David Garrick for a place at Drury Lane.

Rebuffed by Garrick, he was taken on in the company which played the Norwich-Ipswich circuit and found immediate favor with country audiences. More importantly, he attracted the attention of Samuel Foote, the London manager and mimic, who was just then, in 1762, evading the licensing act at the Haymarket with a series of dramatic

*Harvard Theatre Collection*

CHARLES BANNISTER, as Polly Peachum
by J. Sayer

ness and the *castrato* Tenducci. The composer declared that the imitations were well enough but that the voices projected by Bannister were better than the originals.

Notwithstanding several such legends, it does not appear that the theatrical managers of London rushed to sign the young man to articles. He seems to have sung a few times in 1762 at taverns and pleasure gardens and then to have returned to performances in the provinces. The London sojourn had been darkened at the end by the death of Charles, his first son, who was buried at St Paul, Covent Garden, on 5 September 1762. His second son, John, had been born in 1760 and presumably also accompanied his parents in this first foray into London.

Charles Bannister was at Crow Street, Dublin, in 1764 and back at Norwich in 1766–67, where the call finally came to join the Drury Lane company for the following season. He had probably re-activated Garrick's interest when he played several roles at Richmond, Surrey, in the summer of 1766.

He did not come this time unheralded. Pinn, in his popular *Roscius* (1767), reviewed his performances of the previous Norwich season and gave him points as a countryman, as Gloster in *Jane Shore*, and as the Tyrannic Dane in the masque of *Alfred*. He was a "gallant ruffian," and

> *In fam'd Macheath, unseen, these many*
> *years,*
> *Now first restor'd, Lo! Bannister appears*

Somewhere along the line he had made an enemy, however, for the anonymous author of *Momus* (1767) stormed bitterly at his imitations

> *An arrant stroller, from the lord knows*
> *where,*
> *A true itinerant, now here, now there,*
> *Who oft from barn to barn, from town*
> *to town,*

entertainments denominated "Oratorial Lectures." Foote's first production in this vein was an engaging trifle called *The Orators* on 28 April (repeated nine times by 29 May) in which Foote, onstage, was supported by various "pupils" planted in the boxes. In the performances Bannister purported to be one Will Tirehack, an Oxford student, and was highly successful in imitating well-known players during his colloquy with Foote. John Adolphus, in a memoir of John Bannister, says that Charles had an untutored but good natural voice "uniting in extraordinary perfection, the extremes of a deep bass and high-toned falsetto" when he spoke or sang and was from the beginning expert in "taking off" other performers, especially foreign singers. Garrick is reported to have brought the composer Giardini around to listen to Bannister's imitations of the bass singer Champ-

*Ten nights has labour'd for a single*
    *crown;*
*See* B-nn———r *assume* (*unaw'd by*
    *shame*)
*A mimic's vile and despicable name* . . .
*A very monkey with a human name;* . . .
B-nn———r *a* Wilkinson *would be,*
*But can't so truly imitate as he.*

On 22 September 1767 the Drury Lane prompter William Hopkins noted in his diary: "Mr Bannister made his first Appearance on this Stage in Merlin [in Garrick's *Cymon*] with a new Song introduced. – He was received with Applause, – is a tall Figure, – good Voice and sings well." Hopkins's approbation may have been strongly tested by Bannister's appearance in an afterpiece a month later. On 23 October the talented mimic played the part of "Hopkins the Prompter" in the first production of *A Peep Behind the Curtain; or, The New Rehearsal*, written by Garrick.

The next time Bannister was named in the bills he was playing the kind of odd old man who was to be one of his mainstay sub-lines from then on, Old Wilding in *The Lyar*. Yet, perhaps partly because of a plethora of seasoned talent that year (especially Dodd as an eccentric and Vernon as a singer) but doubtless also because of the management's heavy preference for the tragic and the sentimental, Bannister was underemployed. He was used for chorussinging and walk-ons, but aside from several repetitions of the roles cited above, he played no named parts, and he may not even have remained in the theatre after 3 February, for on 13 and 15 February Aickin took Merlin in *Cymon*, and Bannister was omitted from the bill of *A Peep Behind the Curtain* on 5 March 1768.

But Bannister turned up the next summer in Foote's Haymarket company, playing first Matthew Mug in *The Mayor of Garratt* and then Squire Sullen in *The Stratagem*. In other performances that summer season he was: Cacafogo in *Rule a Wife and Have a Wife*, Worthy in *The*

*Statesman Foil'd*, Squintum in *The Minor*, Major Rakish in *The School Boy*, Tirehack again in *The Orators*, and, for his first attempt in London in a leading part in a ballad opera, Macheath in *The Beggar's Opera*. After his lean Drury Lane repertory, Bannister was in Foote's debt for displaying his varied abilities to a London audience. But the relationship was symbiotic, for Bannister drew excellent houses to the Haymarket.

Charles Bannister became a well-applauded standard at Drury Lane from the season of 1768–69 through that of 1782–83. In 1783–84 he defected for one season to Covent Garden – to his profit, for his salary was doubled, from £6 to £12 per week, and remained at that figure when he returned to Drury Lane from 1784–85 through 1786–87. In the season of 1787–88 he was named in none of the bills of either patent house. He returned to Covent Garden on 15 September 1788, where he

*Harvard Theatre Collection*

CHARLES BANNISTER, as Steady
by Pye

remained, still at £12 per week, through the season of 1790–91. He was absent from the record again until 27 December 1791, when he showed up at Drury Lane and played until 14 June 1792 at £210 for the season. He does not seem to have had any London engagements in the fall of 1792, but he returned to the Drury Lane company at the reduced salary of £6 per week to sing in the chorus to *Macbeth* on Boxing Day. During this whole period he lived at No 7, Suffolk Street, Charing Cross.

His career was now in decline, but he played with Colman's hastily-recruited company at the Haymarket after the Drury Lane troupe was dismissed to await the re-building of the theatre in the fall of 1793. He rejoined the company when the magnificent new playhouse opened with a "Grand Selection of Sacred Music from the Works of Handel" on 7 March 1794. Bannister was not named in the bill as a "Principal Singer" but was probably among those supporting Incledon, Florio, Bartleman, Madame Mara, and the other first-rank voices, for the bill assured the presence of "a Complete Set of Chorus Singers."

He remained for the rest of his career in the Drury Lane roll, always at £6 a week, through the season of 1797–98. His withdrawal from theatrical activity was evidently well planned, for in August 1797 *The Monthly Mirror* anticipated it by a year: "Mr. Bannister, senr. retires from the stage with a liberal provision from the managers."

Throughout his service in London he had performed profitably almost every summer at the Haymarket, first under Foote and then under Colman. And just as it was that theatre which first introduced him to London, so was it the last to bid him good-bye, at the end of the summer season of 1799.

He had already claimed his pension from the Drury Lane retirement fund, to which he had first subscribed his 10s. 6d. in 1775.

Except for his early youth and a few summer excursions, Bannister had been a London actor. Clarke is probably correct in identifying him as the Bannister who was at Cork on 31 July and 20 September 1769; and at Waterford on 18 July, Limerick on 31 July and 15 August, and Cork on 17 August and 9 September 1786. He also "went through most of his best characters" successfully in July 1779 at Birmingham.

Charles Bannister's strong point was his voice, which he used (and once or twice abused to a dangerous hoarseness) both as a tool of the mimic's trade and with near-operatic skill in dramatic singing. An anonymous contemporary correspondent to a London newspaper wrote

It is a curious fact that Mr Bannister, who never sang out of time or out of tune, did not know one note of music. He had his songs, &c. paroted to him by a worthy friend of mine, Mr Griffith Jones, who was at that time pianist to Covent Garden theatre.

Anthony Pasquin, in his poem *The Children of Thespis* (second edition, 1786), painted a most attractive word-picture of the elder Bannister, "laughing Charles . . . As he journies thro' life, Love and Wine lead the Way," and

*In thunder harmonious, his cadences roll,*
*And the full tide of Melody pours on the*
*soul*

The German traveller Brandes remembered, in 1795, "eine herkulische figur mit eine sehr schönen Bass Stimme, der erste Ganger zu Drury-Lane . . . Er hat ein sehr richtige komische Aktion."

But Bannister had other attributes besides herculean figure, pleasant bass voice, and personality. In private he could draw tears with sentimental song but usually preferred to set the table on a roar with his drollery. On the stage of the patent theatres, at Marylebone Gardens and Ranelagh, from the rawest mimicry of fellow singers and actors through stirring rendi-

*Harvard Theatre Collection*

CHARLES BANNISTER
by R. Dighton

tions of patriotic ballads and "anacreontic songs" to some of the best depictions of certain standard comedy characters to be seen in his part of the century, he rollicked along, his audiences adoring. In 1788 *The Modern Stage Exemplified* celebrated his versatility:

> *Of various pow'rs is BANNISTER possess'd*
> *At once with pathos, and with humour bless'd.*

He was best, thought the author, the folly to "disclose" of "quacks, bloods, taylors, or apprentice-beaux."

Perhaps the fairest appreciation of Bannister at his apogee came from Francis Godolphin Waldron, the actor who wrote *Candid and Impartial Strictures*, in 1795:

The many, many winters that have rolled over the head of this veteran of the stage, have not so much impaired his powers as one would reasonably expect. In his time he was much the finest English bass the theatre could boast of, and we have always thought him the best actor we ever saw that established himself as a singer. Indeed some of his comic performances were fraught with humour of the most rich and luxuriant kind, although we never could discover in any of them much display of genius, as their style and manner appeared to us to be in part taken from something before seen.

A contemporary quoted in Mathews's *Gallery* (1833) thought that

No actor was ever more celebrated for his jeux-d'esprits, or more admired as a singer. His voice was a strong, clear bass, with one of the most extensive falsettos ever heard; they were finely contrasted in a Pantomime performed at the Haymarket, in which he was dressed one half like a Huntsman and the other half like a Beau, in which he sung a duet: one part in the rough tone of a sportsman, and the other with the most feminine shrillness.

Sylas Neville had heard Bannister sing, at the beginning of his London career, in *The Maid of the Mill* and entered in his diary in March 1769 the opinion that "Bannister is the best Giles I have seen since Beard left the stage." Many people still felt that way after he had sung the part for a quarter of a century. Because of his ability as a mimic, Bannister was exceptionally good in dialect characters of all kinds: Cadwallader in *The Author*, O'Flannagan in *The Cozeners*, O'Flam in *The Bankrupt*, Macfable in *Widow or No Widow*, Owen in *Coeur de Lion*, and Don Diego in *The Padlock*; but he was most applauded when he mimicked Italian singers. The *Public Advertiser* of 17 August 1779 thought that he was "exceedingly happy in speaking the broken English" when he played Signor Arionelli in *The Son in Law*, a part he had originated three days previously at the Haymarket. He "had made up his figure admirably for the representation of a castrato, add to which his mimickry of Tenducci in the favourite air of 'Water parted from the Sea' was excellent." So excellent was it, in fact, that, according to the *Morning Chronicle*, on the second night "A parcel of Italians from the Theatre over the way [the Opera] had placed themselves in different parts of the Theatre, in order to hiss off Arionelli," but Bannister's performance elicited such approval from the rest of the audience that "the impudent eunuchs were obliged to abandon their project."

By 1786 Bannister's fame had spread so far that he himself was being imitated by George Saville Carey at Edinburgh in a "Lecture on Mimicry," and by 1789 Moses Kean had inserted an imitation of Bannister into his "Evening Lounge" at Margate.

But the greatest testimonial to Bannister's comic effectiveness came in a way that he could hardly have wished. Mrs Fitzherbert, the widow of a Northamptonshire clergyman, had been with some friends to Drury Lane on the evening of 17 April 1782 to see the transvestite *Beggar's Opera*, in which Charles Bannister played Polly. This lady was overcome by laughter to the extent that she had to leave before the end of the second act. She continued in hysterics until the morning of 19 April, when she died.

A selection of Bannister's characters might include: Tugg in *The Waterman*, Bonoro in *A Christmas Tale*, Hatchway in *The Fair Quaker*, Scander in *Selima and Azor*, Captain Seagull in *Old City Manners*, Russet in *The Deserter*, Don Ferolo Whiskerandos in *The Critic*, Steady in *The Quaker*, Hawthorn in *Love in a Village*, Rashly in *The Lord of the Manor*, Lucio in *The Carnival of Venice*, Major Sturgeon in *The Mayor of Garratt*, Punch in *Harlequin Skeleton*, Bounce in *Follies of a Day*, Gammer Gurton in *The Genius of Nonsense*, and Pan in *Midas*. His Shakespearean characters were a famous Caliban in *The Tempest*, Hecate in *Macbeth*, Antonio in

*The Merchant of Venice*, Apemantus in *Timon of Athens*, Casca in *Julius Caesar*, Host in *The Merry Wives of Windsor*, Henry IV in *1 Henry IV*, Henry VI in Colley Cibber's revision of *Richard III*, Tybalt in *Romeo and Juliet*, Claudius in *Hamlet*, Jaques in *As You Like It*, and Snug in George Colman's revision of *A Midsummer Night's Dream* called *A Fairy Tale*.

Bannister was rather bibulous and he was also more than a trifle careless about money, but he managed to stay out of the hands of the bailiffs and quietly raise and train his two children. They followed him to the stage—John, who overshadowed his father's fame in Charles's final years, and Jane, later married to the London actor and provincial manager James Swendall. Charles Bannister was extremely popular with his fellows—a popularity perhaps best illustrated by his standing as second to *both* combatants in the bloodless duel of 1792 between Francis Aickin and John Philip Kemble.

Many anecdotes center on his backstage pranks and tavern japes. At Drury Lane on 8 November 1777 *The Beggar's Opera* was in progress when, said the *Public Advertiser*, "Jenny Diver forgot her song . . . and continued inflexibly silent till a Wag behind the Scenes assumed her Voice, and sung the Song for her." The wag was, of course, Charles Bannister.

Charles was one of the original Committee elected to establish the Drury Lane actors' fund. He was often sent out to pacify audiences disgruntled by changes in the bills. He was a charter member of the Glee Club which was formed in 1798 to which Shield, Johnstone, Incledon, Dignum, Charles Ashley, and W. T. Parke also belonged. They met at the Garrick's Head Coffee House in Bow Street, Covent Garden, once a fortnight, for singing and supper. He also belonged to the Anacreontic Society, an exclusive group of noblemen and professional singers founded in 1766, which met in the Crown and Anchor Tavern in the Strand. Their constitutional song was "Anacreon in Heaven," the tune of which is now that of "The Star Spangled Banner." He was a leader in the organization of Drury Lane friends and contemporaries, a sort of survivors' club of people who had acted with the century's greatest player, called "The School of Garrick." Some 20 of the songs Bannister made popular on the stage, and with which he regaled such gatherings, are in the British Museum's collection of printed music.

Charles Bannister died, aged 63, at his house in Suffolk Street, on 19 October 1804, three days after an overflow house at Drury Lane had proffered him a last benefit. The *Gentleman's Magazine* reported that "His remains were interred, on the 25th, in the family-vault under the communion-table in St Martin's church . . . the coffin was placed on those of the deceased's mother and brother." Six mourning coaches carried 20 of the most prominent comic actors and singers to his obsequies. " 'Live while we can' was his motto throughout his mortal career."

On 25 November 1808 an administration of the goods of the happily improvident Bannister, amounting in value to a paltry £200, was granted to his son John, "Sarah Bannister the relict dying without having taken upon her the letters of Ad-[ministrati]on of goods of the deceased."

Charles Bannister was painted full length by John Zoffany. This formal portrait was engraved by an anonymous engraver. He was depicted as Steady in *The Quaker* by Thomas Pye, and Ridley engraved the picture for the *European Magazine* in 1804. His daughter Jane did an informal study of him in tinted pencil. All of the originals of these portraits are in the Garrick Club. In a volume in the Folger Shakespeare Library entitled "Portraits of Eminent Actors Taken from Life by W. Loftis 1787–1815" are hand-colored drawings of Bannister as Inkle in *Inkle and Yarico*, Jonas in *The Island of St Marguerite*, and Shift

in *The Minor*. W. C. Lindsay painted a formal portrait which was engraved by W. Dickinson for publication in 1801. A profile sketch was published 1 November 1804 for E. Scott by E. Walker. Ridley engraved a portrait from a drawing by Spicer for publication in 1791 in Parsons's *Minor Theatre*. W. Richardson published R. Dighton's portrait of him in 1787. He was drawn by J. Sayer and engraved by J. R. Smith as Polly Peachum in *The Beggar's Opera* in 1781, and from this engraving an etching with acquatint was subsequently made. J. Roberts painted and Pollard engraved him in the character of Steady in *The Quaker* in 1777, and anonymous artists prepared an engraving of him in the same character for publication in the *European Magazine* in 1801. About 1785 an anonymous engraver depicted him as Thomas in *Thomas and Sally*.

### Bannister, James [fl. 1771–1783], actor.

Both a "Bannister" and a "J. Bannister" were in the Drury Lane company of 1772–73 and 1773–74. There was also a third Bannister, a "Master J. Bannister," who played the young Lord William in *The Countess of Salisbury* for Cautherly's benefit on 23 April 1773, the same performance at which "Bannister" was Sir Ardolph. The actor called only "Bannister" was, from his roles and a number of other indications explained in his entry, the singer-actor Charles Bannister. J. Bannister cannot have been Charles Bannister's son John, since John is from several sources known to have begun his London career in 1778. (He himself, when invited to sign the book of the Haymarket Theatre on 19 August 1829, wrote "John Bannister, who made his first appearance on the stage of this theatre 1778. Huzza!")

James Winston, an old staff member of Drury Lane, took particular care in his "Manager's Notebook" to distinguish the "Master J." from John Bannister but was

wroth with an anonymous historian who asserted that Master J. was the same J. Bannister who "previously acted Alexis in 'All
for Love,' and Callipas in the 'Grecian
Daughter' . . . How this very little boy
could previously have acted two characters
which required full-grown men as their
representatives" Winston was at a loss to
say; and he assures us that the boy was "the
son of a very subordinate performer in Garrick's company, at a salary of thirty shillings a week."

Apparently this "subordinate performer"
was the "Bannister, from Dublin" who first
came to Drury Lane on 12 March 1771 as
Beau Clincher in *The Constant Couple*. He
had been seen at Smock Alley in 1769, as
"from Drury Lane." He was in minor parts
of fops and rakes at Drury Lane until the
spring of 1774. Nevertheless some sort of
relationship to Charles Bannister is suggested by the fact that Charles was absent
from Drury Lane the year before James
came and departed temporarily the year
James left permanently. It is sometimes
difficult to discriminate them in the bills
for they often played similar roles.

James Bannister occasionally appeared
in the Drury Lane bills as "Banister," a
spelling which was used for him later at
Norwich, where he played with some applause for several years. The identification
of this actor as Charles Bannister in *The
Committee Books of the Theatre Royal
Norwich 1768–1825*, edited by Dorothy
H. Eshleman, 1970, is incorrect.

In a letter to the editor of the *Morning
Chronicle*, published 29 November 1777,
and relative to the Norwich Company,
James Bannister's full name appears. There
is a notation in the Norwich Committee
books, dated 24 August 1771: "If Mr Bannister offers, Mr Griffith may engage him &
Mrs Bannister at £2.2 a week." On 11 May
1775 it is "Ordered that Mr & Mrs Bannister be not allowed any Increase of Sallary
for the present." On 8 February it was ordered that the Treasurer should bring "to

his Acct the Sums advanced to the several
Performers." James Bannister was indebted
in the amount of £12 12s., and was to be
mulcted 18s. a week. On 25 April 1777 the
couple were to be articled with the condition that they pay £24 for their benefits instead of £21 as formerly. On 23 January
1778 it was "Ordered that Mr & Mrs
Banister be advanced to £2 12s 6d per
week." On 3 January 1781 it was "Ordered
that Mrs Bannister's salary be advanced
to five and twenty shillings P week." According to manuscripts in the British Museum there were at Colchester in August
1782 a Mr and Mrs Bannister "when both
C. & J. Bannister were at H[ay]M[arket]."
Mrs Bannister played Lady Freelove in *The
Jealous Wife* there on 12 August. On 31
January 1783 permission was given by the
Norwich Committee to "Banister (on his
own Request) to be absent from Business a
Month or two—and that his Salary be continued"—a probable indication of illness,
for on 15 August 1783,

In consideration of the declined State of
Health of Mr Banister which no longer per-
mits his being a Performer, and in Consideration of his numerous Family, this Committee
do recommend that the Salary of Mr Banister
be advanced to £1.11.6 to commence at the
next Norwich season.

James Bannister was probably given
lighter duties than acting to carry out in the
operation of the Norwich theatre. Nothing
more was said about him, and he may have
died not very long afterward. On 24
February 1784 the Committee Book entry
is surprisingly harsh after the previous indulgent treatment: "Mrs Bannister having
applied for an Increase of Salary is rejected." How poor Mrs Bannister had offended we may never know, but on 23(?)
April 1784 it was ordered that she was "to
be discharged at the End of the present
Season at Norwich." A Mrs Bannister appeared on a manuscript list of the Norwich

company in 1787, but after this year she disappeared permanently.

James Bannister had a daughter named Harriet who acted and to whom John Howe, Baron Chedworth of Chedworth, who died 29 October 1804, left £2,500, largely it seems in admiration of her father's services with the Norwich players, to whom Chedworth was devoted.

It is tempting to believe that the Master J[ames?] Bannister of the one Drury Lane performance of 23 April 1773 was the son of the James Bannister, also then at Drury Lane and subsequently at Norwich. He could also have been either the James Bannister who on 3 April 1809 was married to Rebecca Emery at St George, Hanover Square, or the one to whom in 1837 Joe Grimaldi left £25—or both. So far as is known the James Bannister who published two translations from the Greek classics in 1780 and 1791 was none of these persons.

**Bannister, Jane.** *See* SWENDALL, MRS JAMES.

**Bannister, John** *1760–1836, actor.*

John Bannister the comedian left a diary which was drawn on by his friend John Adolphus to piece out Adolphus's recollections. Adolphus produced in 1839 the two-volume *Memoirs of John Bannister*, a work of great circumstantiality and authority. The *Memoirs* form a groundwork for the present notice of Bannister but are supplemented and corrected from numerous other sources.

Bannister was born at or near Deptford on 12 May 1760, the son of the Charles Bannister who was later to become a much-loved London singer and comic actor. Charles Bannister was then employed with his father, John, in the government victualing office at Deptford, but shortly after young John's birth he began acting, first as an amateur at Deptford, and then professionally with the Norwich company. The

*Harvard Theatre Collection*

JOHN BANNISTER, as Uncle Toby with MRS CRAWFORD

by Leslie

infant John and an elder brother, Charles, accompanied their parents to London in May of 1762, and there the father Charles had a brief success in the summer company led by Samuel Foote at the Haymarket Theatre. His son Charles died in late August and the saddened family returned to country touring in the fall of 1762, crossing to Ireland and back to Norwich. They did not return to London until 1767.

Perhaps the hardships of his profession determined Charles Bannister to turn his son John another way. At any rate, the boy possessed a talent for drawing "and his father encouraged this propensity by giving him a shilling, as pocket money, for each production of his pencil." In 1777 John entered the Royal Academy, to study with De Loutherbourg, but the painter is said to have demanded £200 for four years' instruction, far beyond the resources of Charles Bannister, who then was only a £6-per-week singer. John remained at the Academy, but with another teacher, until his mimicry and foolery so upset "poor old George Michael Moser, the keeper," that the boy left his fellows (among them Rowlandson, the caricaturist) and presently gravitated to his father's calling after all.

Bannister dined out for years on his description of his interview with David Garrick, who received him kindly while shaving and listened to the youth's recitation of Hamlet before his father's ghost. Garrick was sufficiently impressed by the lad to coach him to play for Charles Bannister's benefit on 27 August 1778. John's tryout part was Dick in Arthur Murphy's farce *The Apprentice*, a role which the recently dead Henry Woodward had made famous. The young actor immediately stamped his own personality on the character, employing his inherited talent in "A Variety of Imitations," and taking off the foibles of well-known actors so successfully that the veteran Bensley, one of those satirized, called on him and begged for mercy.

The gratified Garrick instructed John line-for-line and gesture-by-gesture for his debut in tragedy, as Zaphna in *Mahomet*, opposite "Perdita" Robinson as Palmira, on 11 November 1778. But the incipient patronage of the great actor and Bannister's career as a tragedian ended together, with the death of Garrick in January 1779.

At the commencement of the winter season of 1779–80 John Bannister was regularly engaged at Drury Lane, where his father, for years a greatly popular and respected figure, could smooth his way and offer instruction. In the summer, he followed his father to the Haymarket. They frequently played on the same bill, as in the strange transvestite *Beggar's Opera Metamorphosed* in the summer of 1781, when Charles played Polly, and John was bedizened as Jenny Diver. They sometimes offered a "sketch," as at Digges's benefit the

same year, in which they vied in their powers of mimicry.

The two Bannisters were staples of the Drury Lane fare until the retirement of Charles in 1799. Little by little John took over parts identified with his father and began to surpass him in fame. By 1789–90 John was commanding £10 per week, while his father remained at £6. In 1795–96 John was at £16, his father still at £6. But the growing disparity does not seem to have affected their relationship adversely.

Except for the season of 1793–94 when he was from 19 September to 8 April at the Haymarket, while the disbanded Drury Lane company awaited the rebuilding of their house, John Bannister played with the company in every season from 1779–80 through February 1809, when Drury Lane burned. In the fall of 1807 he was appointed stage manager but, says Adolphus,

his powers were limited, his authority unsupported, and the treasury in distress; consequently his exertion could not be expected either to enforce regularity in the company, or procure for the public attractive entertainment, and he soon resigned his situation to Mr Wroughton.

Nevertheless, his popularity did not wane, and that April he drew the immense sum of £740 11s. to his benefit.

The Drury Lane players faced real hardship after the destruction by fire of the playhouse on 25 February 1809. Bannister's own loss, however, was lessened by the outright gift of £500 pounds sent him on 27 February by an admirer of his acting, his wife's uncle, the wealthy Philip Rundell of Ludgate Hill. He had also been preparing for a long while a lecture-entertainment which he called "Bannister's Budget," and he now took it on an extensive tour of provincial towns where it gleaned him such profit that, according to George Colman's own testimony, he generously canceled Colman's bond of £700. He was in Ireland

JOHN BANNISTER when an old man
by Clint

for some time after 5 January 1810, for a
letter of that date speaks of his having
landed safe "after a tedious and dangerous
passage of thirty hours."

Bannister brought his Budget before the
judgment of London audiences during Lent
in 1810 at the Freemasons' Tavern, where
formerly Sheridan and Henderson had delivered memorable readings. From there he
moved the act to the Haymarket Theatre,
where he finished triumphantly on 14
April. His audiences were large, the critics
were kind, and profits were great. After a
long engagement from 11 June through
23 July, Bannister took to the road again.

He returned to Drury Lane to "warm
and general applause," after a three-year
absence, on 15 October 1812, playing Bob
Acres in *The Rivals*. But after mid-Novem-
ber his old enemy the gout laid him off for
10 weeks.

Bannister's final season on the boards
was that of 1814–15, when he was somewhat overshadowed by the phenomenal Edmund Kean, whom he, with characteristic
generosity, admired and assisted. He was
reconciled to retirement by the departure
from the stage of his old friend Harriot
Mellon, for whose final benefit he played
Touchstone; by the retirement also of his
close comrade Richard Wroughton; and by
the death of his benefactor Samuel Whit-
bread, who, when the new Drury Lane was
being built, had written to him permitting
him to subscribe to the new building.
When John Bannister took his farewell
benefit on 1 June 1815, playing the favorite and sentimental part of Walter in *The
Children in the Wood*, he was given an
ovation by the audience and by fellow performers crowding the stage and spoke an
affecting farewell to his 37 years as a
trouper.

His long service at Drury Lane was,
however, only a part of Bannister's professional story. Like his father, he played summer after summer at the Haymarket and
contracted a warm friendship with the Colmans. After Edwin's death in 1790 a whole
new field of characters opened to him, particularly at the summer theatre. Over a
space of 17 consecutive years at the Haymarket he acted more than 150 different
characters. But, better than almost any
other first-rank London actor of his period,
he was known also to the provinces. In
1797 his friend Colman refused to raise his
pay from the £12 per week which he had
been receiving, so that summer he began to
go to the Manchester theatre in the London
off-season to act for James Swendall, who
had married his sister Jane. He went on to
Birmingham, where he played to overflow
houses, producing £148 for his benefit, said
to be a larger sum than Mrs Siddons had
obtained there. From Birmingham he proceeded to Newcastle and then on to Edinburgh. He wrote his friend Harry Angelo
on 8 August 1797 that he had "already
sent near £900 to London."

In subsequent summers Bannister was: in 1798 at Manchester, York, Liverpool, and Margate; in 1799 at Weymouth (where his perhaps artful refusal to accept payment for a command performance reached the ears of the King and founded his fortunes with the monarch, who at once invited him to sail in the royal yacht); in 1800 at Windsor (at the King's insistence), Dublin, Birmingham, Liverpool, and Plymouth; in 1801 at York; in 1802 with the Weymouth manager to the Isle of Guernsey (but suddenly recalled to Weymouth by the arrival of the royal family); in 1803 to crowded houses at Glasgow (where he handsomely returned his night's pay to the aging Mathews on that actor's benefit night), and then to Edinburgh, Berwick, Harrowgate, Leeds, and Brighton; in 1804, all summer at the Haymarket; in 1805, to Manchester, Liverpool, Birmingham, Belfast, and Richmond; in 1806, mostly at the Haymarket, but also at Manchester; in 1807, at Worthing; in 1809, at Arundel, Manchester, and Dublin; in 1810, at Southampton, with Mrs Siddons and Pope, and at Bath; in 1812 at Bath. In the summer of 1814 he availed himself of the first good opportunity Englishmen had had for more than twenty years to travel in France and left on a tour with Nield the solicitor, Heath the engraver, and the singer Michael Kelly, who gave in his memoirs an interesting account of the trip.

Throughout his whole career Bannister waged a cheerful and energetic fight against seizures of gout which occasionally disabled him for weeks at a time. In the autumn of 1806 the bursting of a fowling piece cost him several joints from three of the fingers of his left hand. His acting was delayed until 2 December 1806.

In the appendix to his *Memoirs*, John Adolphus listed some 425 characters which were played by Bannister in the course of his career. Even when the fact is considered that many of them are relatively short roles in comic afterpieces, the total is a tre-

*Harvard Theatre Collection*

JOHN BANNISTER, as Ben
by De Wilde

mendous testimonial to his abilities. A selection of his characters might contain: Bob Acres in *The Rivals*, Almaviva and Basil in *The Spanish Barber*, Autolycus in *The Winter's Tale*, Beau Clincher in *The Constant Couple*, Belcour in *The West Indian*, Ben Bowsprit in *A Trip to the Nore*, Bobadil in *Every Man in his Humour*, Bowkit in *The Son in Law*, Brazen in *The Recruiting Officer*, Bombardinian in *Chrononhotonthologos*, Caleb Quotem in *The Review*, Lord Chalkstone in *Lethe*, Colonel Oldboy in *Lionel and Clarissa*, Dicky Gossip in *My Grandmother*, Dabble in *The Humourist*, Doctor Pangloss in *Heir at Law*, Goldfinch in *The Road to Ruin*, Inkle in *Inkle and Yarico*, Jerry Blackacre in *The Plain Dealer*, Job Thornberry in *John Bull*, Lovewell in *The Clandestine Marriage*, Mercutio in *Romeo and Juliet*, Mother Cole in *The Minor*, Razor in *The Upholsterer*,

Scrub in *The Stratagem*, Sheva in *The Jew*, Sir Fretful Plagiary in *The Critic*, Sir John Brute in *The Way to Keep Him*, Touchstone in *As You Like It*, and Tony Lumpkin in *She Stoops to Conquer*.

John Bannister had married the Haymarket singer Elizabeth Harper at Hendon on 26 January 1783. She was evidently a girl of determined character who suppressed his convivial habits and made of him an ideal husband. Their daughter Elizabeth was baptized at St Paul, Covent Garden, on 23 January 1784, and a second daughter, "Rosenna" (Rosina) on 6 April 1785. No baptismal records can be found for two other daughters, Ann and Frances, nor for either of the couple's sons, John and Charles.

Elizabeth married Stephen Morgan, Esq, a merchant who traded to Russia; she accompanied him to Moscow in June of 1806, and a son was born to them there on 25 April 1809. There were subsequently four other children born to the Morgans.

Rosina married a man of ample fortune, William Gelston, Esq, a captain in the service of the East India Company. They had no children.

Ann married John Eieke, Esq, and had two sons and two daughters. Both she and her husband were dead by 1839, she in childbirth at Madeira, when brought to bed of the sons, twins.

Fanny, Bannister's fourth daughter, married Major Rotton, son of Colonel Rotton, and nephew of Richard Wroughton, Bannister's old friend the actor who, for obvious reasons of professional prudence, had changed his name.

John, the Bannisters' elder son, became an officer in the Navy and eventually retired to Exeter with a wife and children. He may have been that John Bannister who married Frances Milward at St George, Hanover Square, on 28 July 1799. Charles became a prosperous solicitor and he and his wife produced nine children. His character was supposed to be almost saintly. On 18 February "Charles George Bannister of Grays Inn Esq" appeared to attest the handwriting of Richard Wroughton.

According to Adolphus, who had known five generations of Bannisters from Charles the elder to one of John's great-granddaughters, John's family was "reared on strict religious principles, aided by his wife who after performing for so many years all the duties of a wife, a mother, and a friend, was still as unaffected, as simple in manners, as gentle in disposition, as when she was Miss Harper."

The comedian George Bartley, one of several who half-seriously addressed Bannister as "father," said that in 30 years' acquaintance he never saw John without a smile on his face. Bannister possessed a guileless joyousness which drew to him people of all kinds. His list of acquaintances, from king to charwoman, may have been the longest in London. He was a favorite of the Earl of Barrymore and a participant in his Wargrave Theatricals during his frequent visits (but Adolphus was sure he "never permitted himself to be initiated in the gross scenes of prodigality and debauchery which assimilated it to the court of Comus"). From the Queen and the princesses who so delighted to see him act and to talk with him, to Harry Angelo the dandy and swordsman who made a unique stage appearance for his benefit in 1800, everyone wanted to be in his company and to assist him. The Duke and Duchess of Bedford, the Marquis and Marchioness of Lansdowne, Lord and Lady Holland, Sir Richard Ford, the Earl of Egremont, Sir Joshua Reynolds, Sir Thomas Lawrence, William Linley the musician, Samuel Rogers the poet, the banker Thomas Coutts, Richard Brinsley Sheridan, Sir William Beechey, Henry William Bunbury the artist and amateur thespian, Lord Essex, General Phipps, John Hunt the publisher and Leigh Hunt the essayist, the novelist Jane Porter, William Hazlitt—the list of the friends whom he charmed and commanded would be virtually a social and professional bluebook for his times.

Bannister seems, in short, to have been that rarity, a practicing Christian who lived in the world untouched, and so amiably disposed that he invested everyone else with his own amiability and unconsciously endowed them with his unselfish character. The most competitive of professions turned only its good side toward Bannister:

I have often thought that I was very fortunate in making one of this pleasant, professional, amicable coterie. I think there was as little mixture of envy, jealousy, or malevolence prevailing among us, as ever could exist around so many competitors for the same prize—the applause of the public.

He was extremely clubbable, and like his father he belonged to that association called the School of Garrick, formed originally by those who had been contemporaries of Roscius (as he barely was) but replenished "as death thinned the ranks" by younger ones, and including Kelly, King, Dodd, Moody, Parsons, Mathews, Suett, and Dowton. He belonged also to the "Keep the Line" Club of practical jokers.

His original London address had been an apartment in Bedford Street, Covent Garden. By 1794 he was at No 2, Frith Street, Soho. In 1815, he moved to his house in Gower Street, No 65. One by one his old friends dropped away, Nield in 1828, Sir Thomas Lawrence in 1830, Lord Mulgrave and John Quick in 1831, Joseph Munden in 1832, Heath in 1834, and Charles Mathews in 1835. Bannister suffered a severe attack of gout on a visit to the Earl of Egremont at Petworth in February 1836 and returned home weak and ill. He recovered sufficiently to go to Brighton in June, but through the summer and fall his strength ebbed away, and he was so far declined that he was never allowed to know of the death of his oldest friend, George Colman, on 26 October.

At two o'clock in the morning of 7 No-vember 1836 John Bannister died at his house at No 65, Gower Street, Bedford Square. His last words were "My hope is in Christ." He was buried on 14 November in St Martin-in-the-Fields in the family vault close by his father. The eminent divine Sir Henry Dukinfield read the service in a simple ceremony limited to the family. The principal performers of both patent houses assembled outside, beneath the portico.

From 14 August through 12 September 1818 Bannister had taken a tour of some of the principal galleries of the Low Countries, at Rotterdam, Bruges, and Ostend, keeping a journal in which he recorded his appreciation of the paintings, especially of Rubens, Rembrandt, Wouverman, and Berghem. He got much quiet pleasure from his knowledge and talent in painting, which was often of use to his theatrical employers, who consulted him about costumes and scenery. "Rowlandson and Morland were from his youth, his constant friends," Adolphus remembered, "and in the study of Gainsborough he passed those hours which he reckoned among the most agreeable of his recreations. When the great artist was in town, their meetings were almost daily." Gainsborough called him "Tom Fool," a nickname which stuck, among his intimates. The production of *The Tour of Dr Syntax* was due to hints and suggestions by him. He was also present at the party at which Alderman Boydell's project of illustrating Shakespeare was germinated.

Considering his devotion to painters and painting, it is not surprising that Bannister was drawn, painted, and engraved by a great many artists, both competent and not so competent. Condé, only an adequate draftsman, has left us a formal portrait in his drawing and engraving for the *Thespian Magazine* of 1793, showing a rather solemn and priggish-looking young man, whose lineaments may be like Bannister's but who lacks his spirit.

Samuel DeWilde painted him as Don

Whiskerandos in *The Critic*, and an engraving of the picture by R. Smith was published by John Cawthorn in 1807. In the Somerset Maugham Collection there is a painting by DeWilde of Bannister as Sylvester in *Sylvester Daggerwood*, with Richard Suett as Fustian. DeWilde also painted him "As Ben the Sailor," engraved by Condé, for Bell's *British Theatre*, and also engraved by W. Bromley. DeWilde also painted him twice as Scout in *The Village Lawyer*, with Parsons in the scene as Sheepface—once in 1792 (picture now in the Garrick Club), and again in 1795 (version in the City of Leicester Museum and Art Gallery; this was engraved by J. R. Smith in mezzotint in 1796). Other DeWilde portraits of Bannister are: as Dick in *The Apprentice*, engraved by E. Scriven and published by John Cawthorn in 1805; as Ben in *Love for Love*, published in an engraving by Bromley in 1791 for Bell's *Library*, as Echo in *The World*, engraved by Scriven; in water color on paper as Storm in *Ella Rosenberg*; and a formal portrait in black and red chalk, which is in the Victoria and Albert Museum.

J. Condé drew and engraved him as Bottom for the *Thespian Magazine* in 1793, and the original pencil sketch is in the Garrick Club. A portrait of him by George Dance is in the National Portrait Gallery. John Zoffany painted him as Scout, with William Parsons as Snarl, in *The Village Lawyer*. John Russell did a portrait in pastel of him as Lenitive in *The Prize* in 1802, which is in the Garrick Club. C. Pye drew him in the character of Polly Peachum in *The Beggar's Opera*, and W. Ridley engraved it. There are three versions of him as Colonel Feignwell in *A Bold Stroke for a Wife*, two by J. Russell, engraved by J. Heath, and one by Russell, engraved by J. Thomson. George Clint drew and engraved him as Ben in *Love for Love*. A drawing by Wageman, engraved by T. Wright, of Bannister as Gradus in *Who's the Dupe* was published by Simpkin and Marshall in

1821. A sketch by G. P. Harding from a drawing by Russell was engraved by W. Greatbatch and published by R. Bentley in 1839. J. Sayer also painted him, and J. R. Smith engraved the portrait. He appears as Uncle Toby, with Mrs Crawford as the Widow Wadman in *The Devil in the Wine-Cellar*, drawn by C. R. Leslie and engraved by L. Stocks. There are two versions of him as Captain Bobadill in *Every Man in His Humour*, one by an anonymous artist, published by J. Roach late in the 1780's; and one by H. Moses and J. Chapman, prepared as a plate for *The British Drama* in 1817. Barlow engraved him as Jonas in *The Island of St Marguerite's*. J. Roach published in 1790 a plate depicting Bannister with Signora Storace, as Leopold and Lilla in Cobb's *Siege of Belgrade*; and another impression was published in 1791. There are anonymous prints of him as Lovell in *High Life Below Stairs*; as Major MacPherson in *False Alarms* (1807); and as Mrs Cole in *The Minor*.

A portrait by Bannister's friend Sir William Beechey was engraved by Ridley in 1797 for the *Monthly Mirror*. There is an anonymous engraving of the comedian as Zaphna. In 1811 Asperne published a bust portrait of him by Drummond, engraved by Ridley. A pencil sketch of him, done by J. Varley in 1816 for publication in the *Graphic Telescope* of that year, is in the Garrick Club. There is an undated likeness of Bannister by Smith, engraved by Ridley, and there is another drawn and engraved by Roberts.

The popularity of his songs and recitations inspired from Cruikshank and others engravings to accompany published ballads. See 11202–4 and 10359 in the British Museum's collection of Personal and Social Satires.

**Bannister, Mrs John, Elizabeth, née Harper** *1757–1849, actress.*

The only contemporary biographical notice of Mrs Bannister, of any size, that in the *Thespian Magazine* (1793), is more encomiastic than informative. It does tell us that she was born to a Mrs Harpur (*sic*) "now a mantua-maker at Bath," who, having displeased her family by marriage, was "obliged to educate her daughter to her business." She was also said by several accounts to have been the niece of a wealthy man of Norwich, described by Winston as the "wealthy Mr Rundle of Ludgate-hill," and identified by John Adolphus in his *Memoir* of John Bannister, as "Philip Rundell of Ludgate Hill," and elsewhere as "the eminent goldsmith" who in 1809 was to send £500 to John, in admiration of his acting, when Drury Lane Theatre burned and the company was thrown out of work. (Philip has been confused with Francis Rundell, the sometime Drury Lane actor and patentee of the theatre at Calcutta, India. Francis was his brother, and Miss Harper's mother was their sister, as the will of Francis Rundell, proved at London on 24 September 1792, indicates. In this document, Francis Rundell, Esq, at his death with the East India Company, left "to my sister Harper two hundred pounds which I hope will assist in removing her from her difficulties.") Elizabeth Harper's father was apparently in no way connected with Joseph Harper and the others in that acting family. She had a sister who never acted and who died on 5 September 1781.

The account in the *Thespian Magazine* of 1793 added that a "Mr Paul, a gentleman of musical taste," was so charmed with her powers that he obtained for Miss Harper an engagement at the Haymarket in 1778. Elizabeth Harper made her theatrical debut at the Haymarket, as Rosetta in *Love in a Village* on 22 May 1778. The *Gazeteer* of 23 May 1778 reported that

Miss Harper, the young Lady who made her first appearance last night at this theatre . . . is possessed of power very capable of being improved; her voice is not powerful, but

*Harvard Theatre Collection*

ELIZABETH BANNISTER
by J. Condé

distinct & harmonious, her dialogue remarkably correct. Indeed, Miss Harper sung with more taste & spoke with more sensibility than we can remember at a first appearance; her whole deportment was easy and unembarrassed, without the least tincture of affectation.

On 11 September 1778 the *Morning Chronicle* said of another performance that

Miss Harper in Lucinda gave us a specimen of her talents as a performer of the sprightly cast of females in comedy, a specimen which did her great credit. Her dress became her so well, & her deportment was so graceful, both throughout the part and in the minuet which she danced with Mr. Harris, that she put us more in the mind of a woman of fashion in the ballroom on a birth night than any stage lady in our memory. From the blunder of some person whose business it was to have the guittar ready, she was much disconcerted when she was to sing the song, and was obliged, after sitting some time, to leave the stage while the instrument was put in tune behind the scenes.

But she had already been heard in public in London a year previously, singing at Marylebone Gardens, with her future father-in-law Charles Bannister on the same program doing "Musical Imitations." On 8 June she sang Polly in *The Beggar's Opera* for the first time. The *Gazette* of 9 June 1778 was representative of all the journals:

Miss Harper's Polly was what Gay really intended, her deportment was genteel, a modesty mixed with a proper degree of female sensibility; she sang with taste, and through the whole character kept nature closely in view.

On 8 July 1778 she was given the attractive little role of Patty in *The Maid of the Mill* and on 17 August was well received as Eliza in *The Flitch of Bacon*. She repeated each part.

According to the *Morning Chronicle*, she was at once "engaged by the proprietors of the Pantheon, for two years, at the salary of *One Thousand Pounds*." But in the summers of 1779 and 1780 she was also at the Haymarket. Tickets for her benefits of 25 August and 29 August were to be obtained at Guy's, No 19, Catherine Street, Strand. Elizabeth Harper was an instant success as a singing actress in her first season at Covent Garden, 1781–82, when she was paid the very high salary, for a debutante, of £12 per week. In March she collected £80 in lieu of a benefit. She was rehired in 1782–83, when she appeared, again at £12 per week, billed as Miss Harper, from 25 September to 25 January and thereafter as Mrs Bannister, having then married John Bannister the comedian, at Hendon on 26 January 1783. They were living at No 6, Great Russell Street, Covent Garden, at the time of her benefit on 5 April. She continued as Mrs Bannister in the winter seasons 1783–84 through 1785–86 at Covent Garden. She was seen no more at the patent houses. In the summer of 1786, she was

again at the Haymarket, the favorite theatre of both her husband and her father-in-law, and she returned there in the summers of the next six years. On 1 April 1786 her address was No 29, Bow Street, Covent Garden, and on 26 July 1791 it was Frith Street, Soho.

At the Haymarket on 5 September 1792 Elizabeth spoke a farewell address written by George Colman (which overstated her service by two years: "Full sixteen summers now have roll'd away / Since on these boards I made my first essay"), played Emma in *Peeping Tom* and her favorite character, Laura in *The Agreeable Surprise*. According to Anthony Pasquin in *The Children of Thespis* (1788) "She quitted the STAGE, to fulfill her desire, / And trim Friendship's lamp round her family fire."

*Harvard Theatre Collection*

ELIZABETH BANNISTER, as Rosetta

artist unknown

Adolphus agreed that the prime motive for her retirement while at the peak of her powers was to give her "increasing family . . . the constant care and personal attention which a virtuous and affectionate parent alone can bestow," but he admitted another motive—the coming of Elizabeth Billington to Covent Garden in 1786 and the consequent impossibility of Mrs Bannister's being any longer considered, in comparison, of first rank.

Though in 1780 she played Ophelia for her husband's benefit, her roles were almost invariably in comedy and comic opera. A representative selection might include: Clara in *The Duenna*, Olivia in *Twelfth Night* ("with a song"), Mandane in *Artaxerxes*, Laura in *The Agreeable Surprise*, Daphne in *Midas*, Rosina in *Rosina*, Rosina in *The Spanish Barber*, Cecilia in *The Son-in-Law*, Amelia in *Summer Amusement*, Caroline in *The Dead Alive,* Seraphina in *The Birthday*, Perdita in *The Sheep Shearing* ("with *songs*"), Amelia in *The English Merchant*, Maria in *Gretna Green*, Charlotte in *Two to One*, The Lady in *Comus* (singing the song of "sweet Echo"), Editha in *The Noble Peasant*, Clarissa in *Lionel and Clarissa*, and Emma in *Peeping Tom*.

Elizabeth Bannister died at her house in Gower Street on 15 January 1849, aged 92, and was buried beside her husband in the Bannister family's vault in St Martin-in-the-Fields.

The brief account of her career in the *Thespian Magazine* of August 1793 spoke of "a prize of one or two thousand pounds which she had the good fortune to gain in the lottery," which, added to her great earnings singing at the Pantheon and elsewhere, "realized a genteel and independent fortune." On 1 February 1849 administration of her estate, worth £4000, was granted to her son John.

Her portrait was drawn and engraved by J. Condé, for the *Thespian Magazine* of August 1793. Robert Dighton painted her portrait when she was Miss Harper and R. Laurie engraved it for publication by W. Richardson in 1780. Roberts drew her as Patty in *The Maid of the Mill*, and the likeness was engraved by Thornthwaite for Bell's *British Theatre* in 1781. There is an anonymous engraving of her as Rosetta in *Love in a Village*, which was published by J. Bew in 1778. She was paired with George Mattocks, she as Patty and he as Lord Aimworth, for Lowndes's *New English Theatre* in 1782. An undated engraving by J. McGoffin, probably of the early nineteenth century, depicts her as Mrs Page and Anne Crawford as Mrs Ford in *The Merry Wives of Windsor*.

**"Banquo."** *See* PALMER, JOHN.

**Banson.** *See also* BENSON.

**Banson, Richard** [*fl.* 1777–1794], *scene painter.*

Richard Banson received payments regularly for scene painting at Covent Garden from 1777 through 1794. The first payment of £12 19s. 6d. was made on 10 October 1777, with another of £15 9s. following on 24 November 1777. On 23 June 1781 he was paid £51 19s. for full salary that season. Bills paid to him on 10 April 1783 and 23 June 1784 amounted each to £42 15s. In 1787–88 he was paid £32 12s. 6d., and from 19 July to 13 September 1794 he was paid 7s. 6d. per day, apparently for summer work preparatory to the 1794–95 season. The "Benson" who was paid various small sums at Covent Garden in the seasons of 1789–90 and 1790–91 and who was paid, with the painter Bromley, £22 at Drury Lane on 2 November 1780 is doubtless Richard Banson.

**Banti, Signora** [*fl.* 1756–1758], *dancer.*

Signora Banti was a minor member of the *corps de ballet* at the King's Theatre in

the Haymarket from at least her first recorded *duo* appearance with Lucas on 30
March 1756 through 1757–58. It is to be
supposed that she was the mother of Master
Banti, a scholar of the elder Poitier, who
danced at Covent Garden on 11 April 1758
and who was probably Zaccaria Banti. If
so, then it would seem that she was also the
mother of the dancer Felicità Banti.

### Banti, Felicità [*fl.* 1777–1788?], dancer.

Felicità Banti was a member of the *corps
de ballet* and sometime featured dancer at
the King's Opera in the season 1777–78.
Though she is called "Mlle" in the bills,
she is doubtless of an Italian family of
dancers, and the "Mons" Banti who was her
partner on occasion was Zaccaria Banti
and very likely her brother. Felicità may be
the daughter of the dancer Signora Banti
(fl. 1756–58). Felicità is obscurely satirized
in the text accompanying an anonymous
print of 1770 for some connection with the
Earl of Rochford. She was at Milan in
1788.

### Banti, Zaccaria [*fl.* 1758?–1802], dancer.

Zaccaria Banti is almost certain to have
been the Master Banti who, as a scholar of
the elder Poitier, danced with his fellow
scholar Miss Wilford at her debut at Covent
Garden Theatre on 11 April 1758. He was
probably also the son of the dancer Madame Banti (fl. 1756–58) and the brother of
Felicità Banti.

Banti danced at the King's Theatre from
November 1777 until July 1779. His first
and second appearances at Covent Garden
Theatre on 19 and 21 December 1781 were
in a ballet of his own composition, *The
Double Surprise*, which was repeated several times until May 1782. He was paid
£150 for the season. As an artist and a
personality he was overshadowed by his
wife, the opera singer Brigitta Giorgi. The
couple had at least two children.

### Banti, Signora Zaccaria, Brigitta, née Giorgi *c. 1756–1806, singer.*

The Italian soprano singer Brigitta
Giorgi was born about 1756 at Monticelli
d'Ongina, near Piacenza. She was reputedly
the daughter of a Venetian gondolier,
though this fact has been doubted.

The circumstances of her early musical
education and career are not well established, but she was said to have been when
a child a street singer in her native place.
At about the age of nineteen she sang her
way to Paris where she was heard singing
in a cafe by De Vismes, director of the
Opéra. On 1 November 1776 she made her
debut at the Opéra with a song inserted between the second and third acts of a performance of Gluck's *Iphegenie en Aulide*.

Giorgi went next to London where the
managers of the Pantheon employed her to
fill a vacuum left in their concerts by the

*Harvard Theatre Collection*

BRIGITTA GIORGI BANTI
by Hopkins

departure from London of the celebrated Agujari. But Giorgi was at this point in her career by no means a trained singer and despite the raptures of the public her managers knew it. Thus her articles stipulated that £100 a year should be deducted from her salary to pay for singing lessons. Her first master under this arrangement was Sacchini, who, according to Sainsbury, found her "idle and obstinate" and soon gave over tutelage to Piozzi, who was in turn succeeded very soon by Abel.

At some time between 1777 and 1780 Giorgi married the ballet dancer Zaccaria Banti. (They had at least two children: a daughter, who married a Dr Barbieri, and a son, Giuseppe Banti, S. J., who published a short life of his mother in 1869.)

In 1780 Signora Banti left England without her husband and made a highly successful tour of German courts and Italian towns. Lord Mount-Edgecumbe, who heard her sing at Reggio in 1785, was enthusiastic in her praise. At the San Carlo Theatre in Naples in 1790 she was acclaimed for her performance in an opera by Francesco Bianchi called *La vendetta di Nino*. In 1795 Madame Banti established a residence at No 3, Haymarket, and was reported engaged as "principal woman" at the King's Opera for the sum of 2,000 guineas a season. She made her first appearance on the English operatic stage at the King's Theatre on 26 April 1794 as Semiramide in Bianchi's work of that title. Her appearance was the greatest musical event of that season.

To celebrate the sea victory of Lord Howe over the French, Banti, in a performance before the King and Queen on 3 June 1794, introduced in one of her cantatas the national air of "God Save the King," singing it, according to the *Morning Chronicle*, "with as perfect articulation as if she were a native of England, and never were the few notes of the anthem so exquisitely uttered."

From 21 May until 1 June 1795, Banti was one of the star performers at a series called the "Opera Concerts" at the King's Theatre. In 1794–95 and 1795–96 she remained with the Opera as principal singer and in the latter season earned £1400 and two benefits. Her benefit ticket for 1795 was designed at her request by the celebrated Francesco Bartolozzi. On 16 January 1796 she was cruelly hissed when she had to discontinue singing for some minutes after one of the sentinels stationed on the stage fainted at her feet.

Banti continued to sing leading roles until near the end of the season 1801–2, although she had been much affected by the death of her brother in 1797, a serious illness in December of 1798 had left her in chronic poor health, and in a letter to Damiani in 1799 she had declared her intention of retiring "at the end of the next season of operas." The Earl of Mount-Edgcumbe wrote new music to Metastasio's *Zenobia of Armenia* for her benefit in 1800. At this time she lived at No 24, St Alban's Street.

On the night of her benefit, 28 March 1802, Banti prevailed upon Mrs Billington to appear with her, Banti taking the male tenor role of Polifonti in Nasolini's *Merope*, while Mrs Billington acted the part of the heroine. Mme Banti died in Bologna on 18 February 1806. Her operatic roles had included Ines in *Ines de Castro*, Galatea in *Aci e Galatea*, Arsene in *La bella Arsene*, Tisbe in *Piramo e Tisbe*, Ifigenia in *Ifigenia in Tauride*, Selene in *Medonte*, Giletta in *I due Svizzeri*, Serpina in *La serva padrona*, Taide in *Alessandro e Timoteo*, and the title-roles in *Alceste*, *Antigona*, *Evelina*, *Merope*, *Didone*, *Elfrida*, and *Alzira*.

Signora Banti's range and agility, and her consequent ability in the *bravura* style, were praised by all contemporary critics, as were her acting and her delivery of *recitativo*. And though she was always incorrigibly inattentive to instruction, her natural gifts carried her to both critical acclaim and popular adoration. Many songs and arias "as sung by" Banti were published and sold widely.

A portrait of Signora Banti was drawn

and engraved by Pietro de Angelis and published at Leghorn in 1785. J. Hopkins drew and J. Singleton engraved her in costume in 1785. There is an undated and anonymous Italian engraving bearing the legend "Ecco la Banti: ecco l'imagin vera" in the Milan Gallery. Other engravings were published at Venice in 1785 and in 1804. Banti also appears among a large group of Italian singers in an engraving of c. 1801 by Antonio Fedi.

**Banyard, Mr** [fl. 1785], actor.
Mr Banyard is recorded in one performance only in London: as Bishop Juxon in *King Charles I*, at the Haymarket Theatre on 31 January 1785.

**Baptist.** See also **DRAGHI, GIOVANNI BATTISTA**, and **VERBRUGGEN, JOHN**.

**Baptist, Mr** [fl. 1691], oboist.
A Mr Baptist was listed as one of the oboists paid to accompany William III to Holland from 1 January to 13 April 1691. This might have been Giovanni Battista Draghi, though Draghi was not a member of the King's Musick, nor was he known as an oboist; he was, however, sometimes referred to as Baptist. The same Mr Baptist may have been the one who shared a benefit concert at York Buildings on 24 March 1701 with Mrs Hodgson.

**Baptist, Mr** [fl. 1784–1785], dancer.
A Mr Baptist danced several times in pantomimes and ballets at the Haymarket Theatre during the early spring of 1785. These were irregular, out-of-season performances.

**Baptista.** See **DRAGHI, GIOVANNI BATTISTA**, and **LOEILLET, JEAN BAPTISTE**.

**Baptiste.** See also **LOEILLET, JEAN BAPTISTE**.

**Baptiste, Mr** [fl. 1724], flutist.
At Hickford's music room on 20 April 1724 one Baptiste, "lately arriv'd from Paris," played flute at a concert given for his benefit.

**Baptiste, Mr** [fl. 1782], clown, equestrian, tumbler.
From 21 March through 12 October 1782 Mr Baptiste entertained audiences at Astley's Amphitheatre with a variety of equestrian clown acts. On 23 April and 8 June he was billed as having ridden "the camel, or Dromedary from Grand Cairo and the Elk from Bombay." For his 12 October performance he vaulted from the off side of a horse, tumbled backwards and forwards, and did somersaults "with the greatest ease."

**Baratti, Francesco** [fl. 1754–1755], singer.
Francesco Baratti (or Baretti) was a member of a small group of opera singers from Italy who, at Covent Garden Theatre on 18 November 1754, joined several compatriots already performing in England to present the first of what they hoped would be a successful season of burlettas. On opening night the company presented Galuppi's *L'Arcadia in Brenta* and repeated it on 22 November. From 9 November until 3 January 1755 they sang Ciampi's *La famiglia di Bertoldi alla corte del re albino*.
The company attracted little interest, and the sponsor, whose name is not known, deserted them shortly after he had persuaded them to the enterprise. Being left with debts, they appealed in letters to the newspapers for public support of a series of three benefit performances. The benefits were held on 22 and 29 January and 7 February, being performances of Pergolesi's *La serva padrona*.

**Barbandt, Charles** [fl. 1754–1761], organist, harpsichordist, woodwind player, composer, teacher.
Charles Barbandt (sometimes Barbant or Barbault) appeared in minor theatres in London from 1753 onward as a flutist and

oboe player, and in the season of 1754–55 he was carried on the list of Covent Garden Theatre as organist. But the first London notice taken of his compositions seems to have been on that occasion of 11 February 1755 when, "At the instance of several of the Nobility and Gentry," he caused to be performed at the Haymarket Theatre his musical setting of Alexander Pope's "Universal Prayer" "in the manner of an Oratorio." On this night he himself played a "Concerto on the Hautboy, and a voluntary on the Organ."

His second subscription oratorio, based on a text from the first book of *Paradise Regained*, was at the Haymarket on 25 March 1756 when he again played the oboe. (He was living at this time at the house of a Mr White in Marshall Street, Carnaby Market.) His *Universal Prayer* was repeated at the Haymarket on 15 February 1760, when he played the harpsichord as well as the oboe. Barbandt's third endeavour in this vein was the presentation of his oratorio *On the Divine Veracity*, the words by Mrs Elizabeth Rowe, at the Haymarket on 9 March 1758. His final oratorio was *David and Jonathan*, again at the Haymarket, on 28 January 1761.

Barbandt composed a good number of instrumental pieces. In 1766 he published a collection of music for sacred services and, in 1759–60, *Mr B's Yearly Subscription of New Music*.

Barbandt also taught music, and among his pupils was the celebrated composer of glees Samuel Webbe.

**Barbaregines, Signor.** *See* "BANBAREGINES."

**"Barbara S."** *See* BARRY, MRS SPRANGER, ANN, NÉE STREET.

**"Barbarina, Barbarini, La."** *See* CAMPANINI, BARBARINA.

**Barbault.** *See* BARBANDT, CHARLES.

**Barber,** [Mr?] [*fl.* 1708], *house servant.*

A list of the Queen's Theatre staff dated 8 March 1708 has "Barber" down for 7*s.* 6*d.* per day, the second highest rate among the entire group of house servants. His duties were not specified. Every other entry on this Harvard document is clearly a person's name, though perhaps in this case the duty rather than the name was noted.

**Barber, Mr** [*fl.* 1725–1728], *house servant?*

The accounts for the Lincoln's Inn Fields Theatre for the period 1725–27 show three payments to "Barber:" 5*s.* on 27 May 1725, 6*s.* on 16 September 1726, and 6*s.* 6*d.* on 14 June 1727. Barber may have been one of the house servants—possibly the entries refer to the company barber, Sorine —or a merchant. During the 1727–28 season a "M^r Barber from the Opera" was on the Lincoln's Inn Fields free list; this may have been the same person.

**Barber, Mr** [*fl.* 1780], *actor.*

A Mr Barber appeared as Lovemore in the afterpiece *No Wit Like a Woman's* in an irregular out-of-season performance at the Haymarket Theatre on 5 April 1780.

**Barber, Mr** [*fl.* 1784?–1794], *violist.*

A Mr Barber of Chichester is listed in Doane's *Musical Directory* for 1794 as having been concerned in at least some of the several annual Handelian commemorative performances in Westminster Abbey. He is called "alto," which probably, according to the terminology of the day, meant viola player.

**Barber, William.** *See* SPENCER, WILLIAM.

**"Barberini, La."** *See* CAMPANINI, BARBARINA.

## Barbier, Jane  *d. 1757, singer.*

Jane Barbier's birthdate is unknown, but since she was a leading member of the Queen's Theatre company by 1712, yet still under the protection of her parents in 1717, she was probably born in the 1690's. Perhaps she was Jane Barber, daughter of Priestwith and Jane, who was baptized on 28 May 1693 at St Giles in the Fields. Her first appearance was at the Queen's on 14 November 1711 as Almanzor in *Almahide*, a role previously sung by the male contralto Valentino Urbani. An anonymous young gentleman who was quite taken with her wrote a poem in *Miscellaneous Poems and Translations by Several Hands* (1712) entitled "On Mrs Barbiere's First Appearance on the Stage at the Rehearsal of *Almahide*."

> *No Pleasure now from Nicolini's Tongue,*
> *In vain he strives to move us with his Song;*
> *On a Fair* Syren *we have fix'd our Choice,*
> *And wait with longing Ears for* Barbiere's *Voice.*
> *When lo! the Nymph by bashful Awe betray'd!*
> *Her faultring Tong denies her Looks its Aid;*
> *But so much Innocence adorns her Fears,*
> *And with such Grace her Modesty she wears;*
> *By her Disorder all her Charms encrease,*
> *And had she better Sung; she'ad pleas'd us less.*

She had not conquered her stage fright at her first performance, for Addison wrote in the *Spectator* on 24 November 1711 that he was pleased "at the Opera of *Almahide*, in the Encouragement given to a young Singer, whose more than ordinary Concern on her First Appearance, recommended her no less than her agreeable Voice, and just Performance." Her fright prompted Addison to discuss "Bashfullness" and what he called "Elegant Distress" in performers and public speakers.

Miss Barbier must have overcome her distress, however, for she went on to sing another of Valentino's old roles, Eustachio in *Rinaldo*, on 23 January 1712, and she concluded the season by being the first to sing the role of Telemachus in *Calypso and Telemachus* on 17 May. Her specialty—male roles—was already established but she enjoyed switching occasionally to female characters during her career, as she did when the next season opened.

When the new Rossi and Handel opera, *Pastor Fido*, was performed on 22 November 1712, Jane Barbier sang Dorinda; at court on 6 February 1713 she performed in Handel's *Ode for the Birthday of Queen Anne*; and for her benefit on 9 May she chose *Rinaldo*, this time taking the title role which *castrato* Nicolini had sung in earlier seasons, but her proceeds were a disappointing £15. She continued at the Opera during the 1713–14 season, but half way through she moved to Drury Lane where she was Venus in the premier performance of *Venus and Adonis* on 12 March 1715. Adonis was sung by Margherita de l'Epine, and this pair continued singing in the popular afterpiece for several years. At Drury Lane the following season she was Daphne in the premiere of *Apollo and Daphne* on 12 January 1716 and Aeneas in *The Death of Dido* on 17 April.

After the 1716–17 season Jane went to the new Lincoln's Inn Fields Theatre under John Rich where she sang Turnus in *Camilla* on 2 January 1717, her old role of Telemachus on 27 February, and Orontes in a revival of *Thomyris* on 1 June. But, as the Earl of Cork is said to have remarked, "She never could rest long in a place; her affectations increased with her years. I remember her in the parts of Turnus and Orontes, when the operas of Camilla and Thomyris were represented at Lincoln's-Inn Fields. She loved change so well, that she liked to change her sex."

She did not change her sex for her next performance, however, for it was a non-operatic escapade. Sometime in 1717, the story goes, she fled the protection of her parents and eloped with a lover. Hawkins placed her flight before her engagement at Lincoln's Inn Fields, and there is a gap in her record between April 1716 and January 1717, but if she fled in 1717 it may have been between June of that year and 22 March 1718 when, again, her whereabouts are unaccounted for. In any case, John Hughes burst forth with an amusing and informative poem on her elopement and her character:

> O yes!—hear, all ye beaux and wits,
> Musicians, poets, 'squires, and cits,
> All, who in town or country dwell,
> Say, can you tale or tidings tell
> Of Tortorella's hasty flight?
> Why in new groves she takes delight,
> And if in concert, or alone,
> The cooing murmurer makes her moan?
>     Now learn the marks by which you
>         may
> Trace out and stop the lovely stray!
>     Some wit, more folly, and no care,
> Thoughtless her conduct, free her air;
> Gay, scornful, sober, indiscreet,
> In whom all contradictions meet;
> Civil, affronting, peevish, easy,
> Form'd both to charm you and displease
>         you;
> Much want of judgment, none of pride,
> Modish her dress, her hoop full wide;
> Brown skin, her eyes of sable hue,
> Angel, when pleas'd, when vex'd a
>         shrew.
>     Genteel her motion, when she walks,
> Sweetly she sings, and loudly talks;
> Knows all the world, and its affairs,
> Who goes to court, to plays, to prayers,
> Who keeps, who marries, fails, or thrives,
> Leads honest, or dishonest lives;
> What money match'd each youth or
>         maid,
> And who was at each masquerade;
> Of all fine things in this fine town,
> She's only to herself unknown.
>     By this description, if you meet her,

> With lowly bows and homage greet her;
> And if you bring the vagrant beauty
> Back to her mother and her duty,
> Ask for reward a lover's bliss,
> And (if she'll let you) take a kiss;
> Or more, if more you wish and may, ⎫
> Try if at church the words she'll say, ⎬
> Than make her, if you can—"obey." ⎭

After her elopement, from which she returned rather quickly—and unmarried—she sang again at Lincoln's Inn Fields; it may have been this second engagement of which Hawkins spoke. Now, instead of operas, she chose to sing *entr'acte* selections—often operatic arias—or participate in musical afterpieces. Among her many new roles were the Sultaness in *The Sultan*, Proserpine in *Harlequin a Sorcerer*, Ceres in *The Rape of Proserpine*, Venus in *Apollo and Daphne*, Syrinx in *Pan and Syrinx*, and Perseus in *Perseus and Andromeda*. For her solo assignments she frequently sang in Italian and English to display her bilingualism. Her 1718–19 season under John Rich was an extremely busy one, but in the following season she made only one appearance: on 7 April 1720 she sang at a performance of *Oroonoko* for her benefit and was billed as "being the first and only Time she will Perform this Season in Publick." The reason was probably that she did not have to work: she made a large profit on a South Sea speculation at about this time—reportedly £5000—and in her quixotic way she took most of the season off. Then she announced her retirement.

Perhaps because the South Sea Bubble burst, Jane returned to the stage on 23 February 1722, this time back at Drury Lane, to sing a concert for her benefit. She sang another concert in February and one in March before disappearing from the playbills for another year. On 11 January 1723 she performed at a concert at Buckingham House but then was not heard again until April 1724, at Lincoln's Inn Fields; she had a benefit on 13 April and completed the season singing specialties. She went back to Rich's company for the 1724–25 season at an annual salary of £200, specializing in Italian songs but occasionally singing in English. Occasionally she reverted to straight operatic singing, as in the 1726–27 season when she sang Turnus in *Camilla* again after 10 years.

Her unpredictable nature made her much trouble as, for example, when without authority she advertised in February 1728 that *The Beggar's Opera* would be done for her benefit. Rich quickly placed a notice in the *Daily Journal* of 28 February saying, "Whereas Mrs Barbier has advertised that the Beggar's Opera is to be performed for her Benefit, on the 16th of March next; This is to inform the Publick, That such Advertisement was published without Consent of Mr Rich, and that the same will not be allow'd of." According to the 5 March issue of the paper, the singer waived her rights to the tickets that were out for the sixteenth and stated that she would, instead, sing at the performance of *Hamlet* on 18 March for her benefit. The manager had prevailed, but the receipts for her benefit, £87 19s. in money and £73 11s. in tickets, indicated that she was still a popular attraction.

At the end of the 1729–30 season at Lincoln's Inn Fields Mrs Barbier announced her retirement again; on 16 March 1730 she was billed as having her last benefit in England, a phraseology which suggests that after this she may have toured on the Continent. This time her retirement was again of two years' duration; she was back to sing a concert at Lincoln's Inn Fields on 22 March 1732, and on 20 November of the same year she sang Xarino in *Teraminta*. On 7 March 1733, after Rich's company had left Lincoln's Inn Fields for their new Covent Garden Theatre, the Arnes did a production of *Rosamond* at the old playhouse with Mrs Barbier singing the King. *Rosamond* was performed seven times, but the next production, *Ulysses*, was given only once, on 16 April 1733, with Mrs Barbier

again offering one of her male impersonations in the title role. The 1733–34 season found her at Drury Lane after the reunion with the seceders; she sang Britannia in *Love and Glory* on 21 March 1734 and Cupid in *Cupid and Psyche* on 15 April.

Though it was probably a slip of the pen, she was recorded as dead on 5 February 1737 in Musgrave's *Obituary*, and she was carefully identified as "Cantatrix, an opera singer." She was still, however, very much alive and well, for in the 1740–41 season she returned to the stage, this time at Covent Garden. She appeared there for the first time on 16 December 1740 singing her old role of Syrinx in *Pan and Syrinx*, but time had taken its toll, and she performed so unsatisfactorily that she was hissed. This may have been the end of her career, for her name was not listed in the bills for later seasons.

Sometime between 12 November and 9 December 1757 Jane Barbier died, following a long illness at her house on St James's Street in St James's parish. She had drawn up her will on 16 May 1756, adding codicils on 12 September 1756 and 12 November 1757, styling herself "spinster" and spelling her name both "Jane" and "Jeane." The will was proved on 9 December 1757 by her executors Thomas Gardner and Pomeroy Needler. In addition to leaving these two gentlemen £21 each for their services, she gave Mrs Kissandra Stevens various items of dinnerware in thanks for Mrs Stevens's affectionate behavior to her during her illness. She directed that her British Bank annuities and French tontines be sold and the proceeds used to give 50s. to each prisoner in White Chapel toward his discharge, and she left £5 to the poor of her parish. Her will mentioned no relatives, though the Lincoln's Inn Fields free list for 1726–29 cites her brother, mother, and son — the son was perhaps by the lover she ran off with in 1717; the accounts unfortunately mention no names.

Fear of burial alive was not uncommon

in the eighteenth century, but it was typical of Jane Barbier to express her concern. In her will she stated, "My desire is that I shall be kept for (six days) . . . in the Bed I shall dye in before I am buried as many have come to life who have been thought dead." She asked for burial at St Margaret, Westminster, if she died in London, and then staged her funeral procession: she wanted to be interred "in a very decent and genteel manner at eleven a clock at night the Clergyman to have white gloves and scarf the pall-bearers the same and the clerk to have white gloves and hatband the ffeathers of the Hearse and horses to be white likewise and the whole Expenses of my ffuneral not to exceed the sum of fforty ffive pounds."

**Barbo.** *See* **Barbott.**

**Barbott, Mr** ₁*fl. 1794*₁, *violinist, dancing master?*

Doane's *Musical Directory* (1794) lists both a Mr Barbo of "Hanover-Street, Hanover-Sq," a performer on the violin and dancing master, and a Mr Barbott of "No 19, Hanover Street," a performer on the violin and subscriber to the New Musical Fund. They are probably the same person.

A John Barbot was married to Maria Gwynn at St George, Hanover Square, on 11 April 1784, but there was no indication of his profession in the register.

**Barcavelle,** ₁Mrs?₁ ₁*fl. 1786*₁, *dancer? house servant?*

Among the theatrical notations of James Winston in the Folger Library are two relative to a female performer at Drury Lane named Barcavelle, whose name is preserved nowhere else, apparently. The first, dated 14 January 1786 is to the effect that adding her to the company list increased it 3*s*. 4*d*. *per diem*. The second notation calls her "Mrs" Barcavelle and records a payment to her of £4 "to compleat Sal.ʸ from 8th Decr."

She was very likely a dancer, though she may have been a minor house servant.

**Barclay, Mr** ₁*fl. 1741–1744*₁, *actor.*

Mr Barclay appeared for the first time in the bills in the trifling part of the porter in the afterpiece *The Harlot's Progress* at Drury Lane on 31 October 1741. On 4 December and many times afterward that season he was one of the Haymakers in *Harlequin Shipwrecked* but was not named as playing any part after 18 March. He had a partial benefit on 24 May (as "Berkeley"). There is no information on the other roles he took that season, if any, but they are certain to have been inconsequential. He was probably the "Berkly" who played Ratcliff in *Richard III* at Richmond on 8 September 1744. He shared a benefit on 16 May 1744, with Ray, Green, and Mrs George, and received another one (as "Berkeley") on 8 May 1745, with five other minor actors. He played King of the Antipodes in *Chrononhotonthologos* on 30 April 1745. He may have died soon after, as he is not listed with the company in the following season, and as a Mrs Barclay, not a member of the company, was accorded partial benefits on 19 May 1746 and 11 May 1747. She was also loaned £4 by the theatre on 15 December 1749. (The Mrs Barclay who came on at Edinburgh as Cordelia on 3 January 1756 is almost certainly not to be identified as the widow of the London Barclay.)

**Barclay, Caroline, later Mrs Whalley** ₁*fl. 1792–1794*₁, *actress.*

Caroline Barclay was said by contemporary accounts to have been the daughter of a clergyman who was also a peddler of patent medicines. She trained for the musical stage under the tutelage of Thomas Linley and made her debut, advertised as his pupil, on 24 February 1792 at the King's Theatre, singing a selection from one of Handel's oratorios. On 24 January a "Miss Berkeley" had been paid £20 "per Mr Kemble," ac-

*Harvard Theatre Collection*

MISS BARCLAY, as Olivia
by De Wilde

cording to the manuscript account books. On 9 February: "Miss Berkeley for 5 years 2 at £5 2 at £6 and 1 at £7 Ben[efit] pay-[in]g Charges." On 14 February: "Miss Barkley put on List & paid for two Prior weeks 10.0.0," and "Miss Barkley added to list 0.16.8 per diem."

On 23 May 1792, however, she was again advertised as appearing for the first time "on any stage" when she sang the role of Anna in the revival at Drury Lane of the opera *Dido, Queen of Carthage*. The opera was repeated several times to approving audiences before the season's end.

George Colman, warned of the approaching departure of Mrs Bannister from the Haymarket, engaged Caroline Barclay for the summer season of 1792. Her first role at the Haymarket was as Charlotte in the farce *Two to One* on 23 July. The critic

of the *European Magazine* was kind but cautious: "This was her first comic appearance and being in a character which required no extraordinary exertions she was not unsuccessful. . . . Her person, face, voice and musical powers united to a proper degree of industry cannot fail of producing a great effect, if properly exerted."

But, according to the perhaps suspect account of the *Secret History of the Green Room,* the young actress began to be both arrogant and lazy, refusing to appear for ten-o'clock rehearsals and flatly refusing to sing in choruses, though her predecessor had done so.

After taking a vocal part in *The Surrender of Calais* on 10 September 1792 and playing Laura in the afterpiece *The Agreeable Surprise* on 11 September she disappeared from the bills. But two notations of 2 November in the account book tell of a reduction of 8s. 6d. per week in her pay.

She probably returned to occasional concert singing, for sometime just prior to the publication of Doane's *Musical Directory* in 1794 a Miss Barclay, singer, was living at No 6, Manchester Buildings, Cannon Row. Apparently shortly thereafter she married a Mr Whalley and retired permanently from the stage.

Miss Barclay was said to speak with more elegance than energy and to possess a weak but sweet singing voice. Testimony to her great beauty is unvarying, and DeWilde painted her as Olivia in *She Stoops*. The painting was engraved by Leney for John Bell's *British Library*.

**Barcock, Mr** [fl. 1730–1733], *actor*.
Mr Barcock was first seen at the Oates-Fielding booth in Bartholomew Fair on 20 August 1730 playing the King of Tunis in *The Generous Free Mason*, which was repeated 13 times through 7 September. He was recorded next at the Miller-Mills-Oates booth at Southwark Fair on 8 September 1731, playing the King in *The Banish'd General*.

Barcock was first named in the bills of a regular theatre on 8 March 1732, when he played Loveworth in *Tunbridge Walks,* at the Haymarket. The occasion was a benefit and the company was an irregular one which only fitfully illuminated that house from March onward. Barcock played Worth in *The Recruiting Officer* on 27 April and Trueman in *The London Merchant* on 1 June. On 4 August he played the Good Genius in *Metamorphoses of Harlequin* at the "Great Theatrical Booth in the Cherry Tree Garden near the Mote" at Tottenham Court Fair, and on 23 August Wolsey in the droll, *The History of King Henry VIIIth and Anna Bullen* at the Miller-Mills-Oates booth at Bartholomew Fair. He was not seen in London thereafter.

## Bardin, Peter  *d. 1773, actor.*

Peter Bardin "bent his Thoughts towards the Stage very early in Youth," according to Chetwood, "and, having seen the Performance of the best Actors in England, upon the London stages (where, at various Times, he has made one in most of the Theatres in that City), if he has not improv'd it must be owing to himself." Even as early as 1749, when these remarks were written, Chetwood thought him not "amiss" in parts of any persuasion—tragedy, comedy, or farce. Surviving bills confirm the estimate.

Bardin's first recorded London appearance was under Henry Giffard's management at Goodman's Fields Theatre on 22 January 1730 as Humphrey in *The Conscious Lovers.* He remained in the winter company there until November 1735. During the 1734–35 season he lived in lodgings "opposite the Hoop Tavern in Mansfield Street, Goodman's Fields." He was also playing seasonally at Richmond (1732 and 1735, summers) and at various fair booths (Pinkethman and William Giffard in 1730; Miller-Mills-Oates in 1731–32–33; Fielding and Oates in 1734). On 16 December 1735 and 3 January 1736 his name occurred opposite the parts of Young Fash-

ion in *The Relapse* and Subtleman in *The Twin Rivals* at Drury Lane. From April 1736 he was with the summer company at Lincoln's Inn Fields and in the fall with Giffard's regular company there. But the Giffard company was dispersed at the end of the season of 1736–37 by the effects of the Licensing Act, and, though Sir John Taylor said that Bardin was at Goodman's Fields when Garrick made his debut there in 1741, the comedian was almost certainly not even in London.

Bardin was rumored to be managing strollers for a season or so before he turned up on 11 October 1740 at the Aungier Street Theatre in Dublin, acting Archer to Mrs Elmy's Mrs Sullen in *The Stratagem,* an appearance billed as the first for each "in this Kingdom." Bardin was billed falsely as "from Drury Lane." On 11 December both he and Mrs Elmy were appearing for the first time at Smock Alley.

Bardin was again at Aungier Street in 1744 where he had a benefit on 1 March, but his regular employment was at Smock Alley Theatre, at least through 1746–47, for in February of 1747 he was one of 51 actors petitioning the Lord Lieutenant to allow the theatre to reopen. He was also of that company in 1749–50 and 1750–51. There is a gap in the records until 16 January 1762 when *Faulkner's Dublin Journal* mentions him as Treasurer of Smock Alley Theatre.

Bardin was next heard from again in London when he acted with Barry at the Haymarket on several nights in August and September 1766. But if he had thought to return permanently to London he was disappointed, for he joined none of the capital's patent theatres. Taylor said that Bardin played Gloucester to Barry's Lear in the summer of 1766 under an assumed name. Hogan points to "Johnston," the Gloucester of 25 and 29 August at the Haymarket, but Bardin's assumption of the pseudonym may actually have been in the next summer when, on 2 July as Zacharias in *The Taylors* and on 15 July as Gloucester, one "Thompson" was seen at the Haymarket. "Thompson" appeared also on 22 and 27 July in Bardin's old part of Moody in *The Provok'd Husband*; on 31 July as Aristander in *Alexander*; on 3 August (and several times thereafter) as Lockit in *The Beggar's Opera*; and finally on 16 August as the chaplain in *The Orphan*. If this was indeed Bardin, he was not seen again in London by any name, so far as the records show. He presumably retired to Ireland, where he was granted a benefit at the Capel Street Playhouse on 11 May 1772.

Bardin acted some serious secondary parts in tragedy, though this was not his favorite line. He was about equally at home in comic eccentrics and fops and beaux and gallants, and occasionally he even assumed old men. His great usefulness to the theatres he served by singing, acting, and managing may be indicated by a partial list of his parts, arranged roughly chronologically:

Foresight in *Love for Love*, Basset in *The Provok'd Husband*, Caius in *Merry Wives of Windsor*, Voice in *The Fashionable Lady*, Antonio in *The Rover*, Lawyer in *Love's Last Shift*, Trusty in *The Man's Bewitched*, Osric in *Hamlet*, Hob in *Flora*, Duke in *Othello*, Stanmore in *Oroonoko*, Manuel in *Love Makes a Man*, Sir Charles in *The Beaux' Stratagem*, Doctor in *Devil of a Wife*, Kent in *King Lear*, Macheath in *Beggar's Opera*, Rossano in *The Fair Penitent*, Axalla in *Tamerlane*, Marcus in *Cato*, Obadiah in *The Committee*, Renault in *Venice Preserved*, Petit in *The Inconstant*, Sir Timothy Gripe in *The Jealous Clown*, Keeper in *The Pilgrim*, Rako in *The Wedding*, Farewell in *Sir Courtly Nice*, Psyllus in *The Cynic*, Fantome in *The Drummer*, Crafty in *The Careless Husband*, Day in *The Committee*, Pyfleet in *The Cobler's Opera*, Polydor in *The Orphan*, Monsieur in *Love Makes a Man*, Topmast in *The Sailor's Wedding*, Archer in *The Stratagem*, Trueman in *The London Merchant*, Mopsus in *Damon and Phillida*, Vernon in *1 Henry IV*, Varole in *The Lovers' Opera*, Castro in *Rule a Wife and Have a Wife*, Garcia in *The Mourning Bride*, Sussex in *The Lady Jane Gray*, Judge in *Father Girard the Sorcerer*, Charles in *The Footman*, Richmond in *Richard III*, Strut in *The Double Gallant*, Decius in *Julius Caesar*, Captain Woud'be in *The Harlot's Progress*, Malcolm in *Macbeth*, Attall in *The Mad Captain*, Lysander in *Scanderbeg*, Young Worthy in *Love's Last Shift*, Juan in *Rule a Wife and Have a Wife*, Laertes in *Hamlet*, Raleigh in *The Unhappy Favourite*, Lodovico in *Othello*, Brazen in *The Recruiting Officer*, Albany in *King Lear*, Garcia in *The Mourning Bride*, Frederick in *The Wonder*, Perdiccus in *The Rival Queens*, Lorenzo in *The Mistake*, Bertran in *The Spanish Fryar*, Diego in *Don Quixote*, Orbellan in *The Indian Emperor*, Duart in *Love Makes a Man*, Waterman in *Britannia*, Pylades in *Distres't Mother*, Mad Captain in *Mad Captain*, Young Fashion in *The Relapse*, Frederick in *The Wonder*, Aboan in *Oroonoko*, Standard in *The Constant Couple*, Foppington in *The Careless Husband*, Lord Modely in *A Tutor for the Beaus*, Duke of Richmond in *Charles I*, Marquis in *Sir Harry Wildair*, Sir Philip in *A Bold Stroke for a Wife*, Mlle D'Epingle in *The Funeral,* Sir Novelty Fashion in *Love's Last Shift*, Elder Stanmore in *Oroonoko*, Sir Avarice Pedant in *The Temple Beau*, Lothario in *The Fair Penitent*, Gibbet in *The Stratagem*, Grig in *Phebe*, Num in *Man's Bewitched*, King in *Wat Tyler and Jack Straw*, Bellmour in *Jane Shore*, Father in *Devil of a Wife*, Clincher Junior in *The Constant Couple*, Harry Pystreet in *The Cobbler's Opera*, Octavio in *She Could and She Could Not*, Sapscull in *The Honest Yorkshireman*.

Peter Bardin seems to have been a contentious man who was reproved by Chetwood for failure to keep his disputes out of the theatre. Several times his performances were disrupted by verbal exchanges between him on the stage and opponents in the gallery. But his boldness stood him in excellent stead on at least one occasion. *The General Advertiser* for 8 January 1745 reported: "Last Monday night Mr Bardin the Comedian was attacked by four fellows in Peter's Row near the Church; but on his pulling out a Pistol two of the Villain's ran away and he seiz'd the other two who are since committed to Newgate."

Bardin died in Dublin on 24 October 1773, at which time he was described as "Master of the Hotel College-Green."

**Bardoleau, Mr** [*fl.* 1794–1801?], *singer.*

Mr Bardoleau, a countertenor, was employed in the chorus at Drury Lane Theatre parts of each season from about 1794 until at least 1800–1801. On 17 March 1800 he was apparently earning £1 15*s.* per week.

**Bardoni.** *See* FAUSTINA.

**Baretti.** *See* BARATTI.

**Barfield, Mr** [*fl.* 1784], *actor.*

A Mr Barfield played some small, unspecified part in the afterpiece called *The Reprisal; or, The Tars of Old England* in an out-of-season performance at the Haymarket Theatre on 23 February 1784.

**Barford, Mr** [*fl.* 1794], *musician, music seller, actor?*

Mr Barford played the violoncello in several of the Handelian celebrations in Westminster Abbey. In 1794 he kept a music shop in Cambridge. He may have been the Barford who on 28 May 1792 was advertised as playing the part of Lord Gayville in *The Heiress* under Briggs's management at Barnstable, Devonshire.

**Barghetti.** *See* BRAGHETTI.

**Barker, Mr** [*fl.* 1752], *actor.*

A Mr Barker appeared once at the Theatre, Richmond, Surrey, as Tattoo in *Lethe* on 25 August 1753. Apparently he did not act in the patent theatres.

**Barker, Henry Aston** [*fl.* 1787?–1823?], *panorama exhibitor.*

Henry Aston Barker helped his father Robert Barker paint and exhibit the views called the "Panorama" in London from about 1789, at first in the Haymarket and then in Leicester Square. He had been trained in painting, first by his very capable father and then in the schools of the Royal Academy, where J. M. W. Turner was his school-fellow. At his father's death in 1806 Henry assumed the chief direction of the exhibit, sharing principally in the profits. In 1809 he opened a second panorama at No 9, the Strand, while maintaining the one in Leicester Square. His pupil and apprentice John Burford became his partner at both locations in 1816, but Barker's name disappeared after 1818, when he either sold out to Burford and retired, or died. The enterprise was carried forward first by Burford (until 1826), then by his son (until 1844), and finally by the younger Burford (d. 1861) and Selous (until 1860). From Lord Howe's victory at sea on "The Glorious First of June," through Waterloo, to Sebastopol, every British triumph was celebrated. In addition, as Tom Taylor testified, "every scene of interesting incident and discovery, every locality of special natural beauty, every great public ceremonial, has been illustrated in this ingenious pictorial invention."

Henry Aston Barker and his heir were probably concerned also in a similar project in Liverpool until about 1824. He painted or designed most of his panoramas himself until late in his career, travelling abroad for his ideas. Though early enamoured of Jane Porter the romantic novelist, H. E. Barker married one of the six daughters of Admiral William ("Breadfruit") Bligh, of *Bounty* fame.

**Barker, Robert** *c. 1739–1806, panorama exhibitor.*

Robert Barker was an Edinburgh artist who, apparently acting under the inspiration of De Loutherbourg's successful "Eidophusikon," painted his first "Panorama," a view of Edinburgh, in the guard-room of Holyrood Palace about 1788 and exhibited it first that year in the Scottish capital and then in Glasgow. He presented it to London spectators in the spring of 1789, in a room at No 28, Haymarket.

No one has been able to say exactly in which respects the Panorama was an advance over the changing and dissolving views called collectively the Eidophusikon with which De Loutherbourg had charmed London some half-dozen years earlier. But apparently there was a difference, judging from the reactions of Sir Joshua Reynolds, who had been the enthusiastic admirer of the Eidophusikon, who had dismissed as impractical the plans of Barker, but who, when he saw the finished machine, said: "I find I was in error in supposing your invention could never succeed, for the present exhibition proves it to be capable of producing effects and representing nature in a manner far superior to the limited scale of pictures in general."

There survives also the testimony of Benjamin West, who permitted Barker to advertise his opinion that the invention was the greatest advance in the art of painting in history. Barker himself and his son and assistant Henry both laid emphasis on the fact that it was an "invention" of great novelty. Barker was cautious enough to patent it before he completed it, and in his specification of patent (No 1612 of the year 1787) he called it only *La Nature à coup d'oeil*. It was only in 1789, according to the *Oxford English Dictionary*, that Barker coined the inevitable neologism $\pi \alpha \nu$ (all) + $\partial' \rho \bar{\alpha} \mu \alpha$ (view). In attempting to define the Panorama, however, the *Dictionary* calls it: "A picture of a landscape or other scene, either arranged on the inside of a cylindrical surface round the spectator as a center (a *cyclorama*), or unrolled or unfolded and made to pass before him, so as to show the various parts in succession," without deciding which mode was Barker's. That the former arrangement was the one Barker

*Harvard Theatre Collection*

ROBERT BARKER
by Allingham

exhibited in London is probably established by the *Encyclopaedia Britannica* in 1801, which explains "Panorama" as "a word employed of late to denote a painting . . . which represents an entire view of any county, city, or other [*sic*] natural objects, as they appear to a person standing in any situation, and turning quite round." Also, the dimensions of Barker's second place of exhibition, which can be found in *The Pleasure Haunts of London*, suggest a spectator surrounded by the exhibit.

An exhibition room in Leicester Square, larger than the one in the Haymarket, was occupied from 1793, and the paintings were extremely popular with all classes of people, including the Royal family and members of the Royal Academy. The new hall was divided into three circular rooms, the largest of which was 90 feet in diameter and 40 in height. It was opened with a "View of the Grand Fleet moored off Spithead in the year 1791" which was visited by King George and Queen Charlotte, the

Queen declaring the waves to be so realistic that they made her seasick.

After Robert Barker's death his son Henry Aston Barker continued to exhibit and paint and was in turn succeeded in the proprietorship by his pupil John Burford, who left the property to his son Robert Burford. Robert Burford was the last proprietor of the enterprise, which finally closed in 1860. There is evidence that at the time of his death Robert Barker was also managing a similar exhibition in Liverpool.

Robert Barker died at his house in West Square, Southwark, on 8 April 1806, aged 67. His will, proved 21 May 1806, reveals his financial success. He left the management of his London exhibition, valued at over £2000, to his son Henry Aston Barker, advising that he pay himself a salary of £300 clear after taxes, and Robert's widow Catherine a salary of £200. After expenses of running the exhibition were paid, the profits were to be divided on a share basis among Catherine, Henry Aston Barker, another son, Francis Lightfoot Barker, and a daughter, Tessy. Two other sons, Joseph and Thomas Edward Barker, were specifically excluded and cut off with bequests of £100 and £20 respectively. A codicil obscurely mentions Robert Barker's Liverpool properties.

J. Flight engraved a portrait of Barker after a painting by C. Allingham.

**Barkhurst, Mr** [fl. 1691–1692], musician.

At the St Cecilia Day celebration on 23 November 1691, Mr Barkhurst was chosen one of the six stewards of the St Cecilia Society for the ensuing year; he was identified in the Gentleman's Journal as one of the two stewards chosen from among the Gentlemen of the Chapel Royal or the "chief masters in town," and since his name does not appear in Chapel Royal accounts, he was probably one of the latter.

**Barkley, Miss.** See BERKLEY, MISS.

**Barkwell, Mr** [fl. 1686], musician.

On 30 September 1686 Mr Barkwell, one of the "masters in music" in London at the time, joined Henry Purcell and others to judge the quality of a new organ at St Katherine Cree.

**Barlow, Mr** [fl. 1745–1746], actor, singer.

Mr Barlow was a member of the small company with which the Hallams valiantly tried to establish a third theatre in London in Lemon Street, Goodman's Fields, in the season of 1745–46. On the opening night, 28 October, and for four more nights, he filled the small role of Columbière in the anti-Catholic play Massacre at Paris with which the Hallams hoped to capitalize on the anti-Jacobite feelings in this year of the Rebellion. He seems to have acted only twice more: on 16 November as a shepherd, in The Humours of Purgatory, and on 3 January 1746 in the good part of Chamont, in The Orphan. But he was often employed as a singer between the acts. He did not return to Goodman's Fields in the season of 1746–47.

**Barlow, Edward** [fl. 1785–1800], treasurer.

Edward Barlow was treasurer of Covent Garden Theatre and a power in its financial and artistic management from at least 1785–86 until 1793. A notation of 16 September 1793 in a theatrical account book in the Folger Library states that "This is the year that Mr [Richard] Hughes became Treasurer after the dismissal of Mr Barlow"; and a proof-copy of A Statement of the Differences Subsisting Between the Proprietors and Performers of the Theatre Royal, Covent Garden, London, 1800, with annotations by Samuel James Arnold, describes him as "formerly Treasurer of Covent Garden Theatre." At the time of the dispute over salaries in 1799, Richard Hughes was Treasurer. But Barlow was still a functionary of some sort and drew a salary until at least 1798.

Barlow had a reputation for querulousness, and *The Secret History of the Green Room* (1792) describes a dispute between him and the actor Ralph Wewitzer:

The quarrel happened at Richmond, where Mr. Wewitzer was performing, and in the vicinity of which (Kew Lane) Mr. Barlow had country lodgings. What the subject of the disagreement was we cannot precisely say, but the consequence of it is well known to have been Mr. Wewitzer's discharge. His antagonist's countenance depicts his temper; he is not remarkable for either flexibility or politeness; he exercises his power with an iron hand; nor do we find that he wishes to number *forgiveness* among his *many* virtues.

Notwithstanding his personal deficiencies, Barlow seems to have discharged his complex duties as treasurer honestly and efficiently. They included, in addition to receipt and disbursement of funds to professionals and tradespeople and a share of the decisions regarding the financial articles which actors signed, probably also a partial responsibility for artistic affairs where they involved budgetary considerations. We know that Barlow acted not only as paymaster and often as banker on behalf of the theatre to impecunious actors, but that he also handled such matters as occasional reception of subscriptions for the publication of plays, preparing statements for the press, and the painful duty of informing the public (as in September 1792) of the necessity of advancing prices for tickets.

**Barman, Mr** [*fl. 1735–1736*], *actor? house servant?*

One Barman was allowed by the Treasurer of Covent Garden Theatre 105 days' salary at 2s. 6d. per day and was charged with the moiety of a benefit levy of £30 at the end of the season 1735–36, according to a contemporary manuscript notation.

**Barmazon.** *See* **BOIMAISON.**

**Barnard.** *See also* **BERNARD.**

**Barnard, Mr** [*fl. 1744–1748*], *actor.*

A Mr Barnard acted Mercutio in *Romeo and Juliet* with Theophilus Cibber's illegal company at the Haymarket on 29 September and 2 October 1744. He was probably the Barnard who was briefly in the Covent Garden company, playing minor and unnamed parts in the season of 1747–48.

**Barnard, Mr** [*fl. 1750–1754*], *house servant.*

A Mr Barnard, minor member of the house staff at Covent Garden Theatre, was granted partial benefits in the seasons 1750–51, 1751–52, 1752–53, and 1753–54.

**Barnard, Mrs** [*fl. 1744*], *actress.*

A Mrs Barnard played the part of Edging in *The Careless Husband* at the James Street Theatre on 10 December 1744. She was not seen again in London.

**Barnard, Mrs** [*fl. 1779–1785*], *actress.*

A Mrs Barnard played Patch in *The Busy Body* on 18 October 1779 and Doll Tricksy in *The Tobacconist* on 21 March 1782; and occasionally at various other times she played in unspecified parts in the fugitive winter companies at the Haymarket from 1783 through 1785.

On 15 December 1783 she was the Duchess of York in *Richard III* on the occasion on which Miss Barnard, presumably her daughter, was introduced as the Duke of York, a traditional part for the debut of young children.

The Barnards evidently never succeeded in finding employment in the regular winter companies of the London playhouses.

**Barnard, Miss** [*fl. 1783*], *actress.* *See* **BARNARD, MRS** [*fl. 1779–1785*].

**Barnard, John** *d. 1773?*, *musician.*

John Barnard was listed in the "Declaration of Trust," establishing the Royal Society of Musicians of Great Britain on 28

August 1739 as one of the original sub-scribers, "being musicians." In Mortimer's *London Directory* of 1763 he is called "One of his Majesty's and the Queen's Band," and was said to reside at that time in "Stafford-road without Buckingham Gate."

"John Barnard, Esq, Page of the Back Stairs to the Prince of Wales" was left a mourning ring of the value of two guineas by the will of the eminent violinist Michael Christian Festing in 1750; and there is a memorandum in the Lord Chamberlain's records establishing that:

Administration of the Effects of the late John Barnard, Esq$^r$, Page of the Bedchamber and Musician to the King, was granted the 17. July 1773. to Frederick Augusta Barnard, Esq$^r$, son & residuary Legatee of the Deceased (the sole Executor William Reynolds Esq$^r$ in the Will named, having first Renounced) with the Will annexed, of all the Goods, Chattels, and Credits of the said Deceased.

The will itself is not extant.

**Barnardi.** *See* **BERNARDI.**

**Barnes.** *See also* **BARNS.**

**Barnes, Mr** [*fl.* 1721], *actor.*
A Mr Barnes played Captain Scout in *The Chimera* on 19 January 1721 at the Lincoln's Inn Fields playhouse, but no other roles are recorded for him.

**Barnes, Mr** [*fl.* 1743?–1759], *door-keeper.*
The house functionary Barnes who shared a benefit at Covent Garden Theatre in 1743 is possibly the same man who shared there again in 1758 and 1759 with many others, when he was called "lobby door-keeper." After these years he was not listed.

**Barnes, Mr** [*fl.* 1757–1760], *constable.*
A pay list of Covent Garden Theatre for 11 October 1760 carries the notation "Mr Walker entered as Constable the 6th inst. incl. in the place of Mr Barnes who resigned." He had been paid 2*s.* per day from the beginning of the 1757–58 season.

**Barnes, Mr** [*fl.* 1777–1782], *actor.*
A Mr Barnes played minor and unspecified parts in several scattered performances of casual companies out of season at the Haymarket Theatre during the winters and springs of 1777–78 and 1781–82. Nothing is known of him thereafter.

**Barnes, Mr** [*fl.* 1795–1798], *dancer.*
A Mr Barnes danced at Covent Garden Theatre, only on 12 May 1795 and on 19 March 1798.

**Barnes, Mrs** [*fl.* 1782–1808?], *actress.*
Mrs Barnes appeared billed only as "a Lady" in the character of Alicia in *Jane Shore* at Covent Garden on 21 January 1782, for the "first time on any stage." If this declaration was true and if the Miss Barnes who was already performing at Drury Lane in the previous season was her daughter—as seems likely—then Mrs Barnes was already a mature woman.

She repeated Alicia on 23 and 28 January. So far as the bills show she played no other role until 17 April, when she took the male role of Rutland in *The Earl of Essex* for Maddox's benefit performance. She repeated Alicia and presented also Mrs Oakly in *The Jealous Wife* for her benefit on 3 May. At that time she was living at No 21, Crown Street, Westminster. She played Mrs Belville for the first time on 11 May, and this apparently completed her contribution to the season, and to Covent Garden.

Her conjectural daughter Miss Barnes was still at the Drury Lane house the next season, and Mrs Barnes played there also on 18 December 1782 in her debut part of Alicia, when the fact of her first appearance on that stage was remarked in the advertising. If the performance was a test upon which her permanent engagement there depended she failed it.

Mrs Barnes may then have been discouraged for awhile from further theatrical attempts. But it is more likely that she joined strollers in the country to use the rubric "from Covent Garden," which at any rate the managers employed when on 22 November 1784 she turned up at Smock Alley Theatre in Dublin. She was at Cork early in 1785 but came back to London in time for one performance, as Old Nun in *'Tis Well It's No Worse*, at the Haymarket on 25 April 1785. In 1787 she was at Bristol, billed as "from Dublin."

(A Mrs Barnes, actress of Manchester,

*Harvard Theatre Collection*

MRS BARNES, as Anne Boleyn
by E. F. Burney

was reported to have died in Chester on 28 December 1808, but there is no indication that this was the London and Dublin actress.)

Mrs Barnes was painted as Anne Boleyn in *Henry VIII* by E. F. Burney, and the portrait was engraved by Thornthwaite as a plate to accompany John Bell's *British Theatre*, published 1786.

**Barnes, Miss** [*fl* 1781–1792], *actress, singer, dancer.*

Miss Barnes made her "first attempt on any stage" singing between the acts at Drury Lane on 10 May 1781. She was probably a young girl at the time. She returned the next season on 19 October as Matilda in *King Arthur*. During the two seasons following she established the line of minor parts, often involving singing and dancing, in pantomime, farce, and comic opera, which she was to fill over the next 10 years: Miss Trippit in *The Lying Valet*, the Chambermaid in *A Trip to Scotland*, Miss Biddy in *Love in a Village*, the Milliner in *The Suspicious Husband*, Corinna in *The Confederacy*, the Jew's Daughter in *Dissipation*, Flammetta in *Duke and No Duke*, Country Girl in *The Elopement*, Myrtilla in *The Provok'd Husband*, and unspecified parts in the much-repeated harlequinade *Lun's Ghost*, in *The Ladies' Frolic*, and other entertainments.

Miss Barnes was lowly and faithful, the very type of the utility actress-singer-dancer of the eighteenth century, now submerged in the chorus, now stepping from small roles in farce to sing a specialty song or reinforce the *corps de ballet*. Only one story survives to humanize her, and it probably does not do her diligence justice. James Winston, who had perhaps known her, recounts it in his *Theatric Tourist* of 1805:

Miss Barnes performing Wilhelmina, in the Waterman, not having learned the second act, found it necessary (to prevent the odium of incorrectness from attaching to her study), to excite the commisseration of the audience, by fainting on the stage. The stratagem would infallibly have answered, had she not exposed the trick, by telling the carpenter, who ran to her assistance, *to be careful of her gown,* before he had borne her out of sight and hearing.

Miss Barnes was paid £1 per week in 1789–90, and £2 in 1790–91. She was gone from the list at Drury Lane by the 1791–92 season and appeared only briefly in an irregular Haymarket company the following fall. A manuscript notation in J. P. Kemble's handwriting before 1791–92 season informs us: "Miss Barnes is married." She always shared benefits with several others. She subscribed to the actors' retirement fund 10*s.* 6*d.* from 1781 to 1792. Her home addresses were given on benefit bills as at "Cateman's 52 Drury Lane" in 1786 and No 23, Clare Street, Clare Market, in 1789–90 and 1790–91. She was almost certainly the daughter of the actress Mrs Barnes (fl. 1782–1808?) who was at both London patent theatres in 1782.

### Barnes, Charles  *d. 1711, singer.*

Charles Barnes was sworn a Gentleman of the Chapel Royal extraordinary—without pay until a vacancy occurred—on 10 September 1694. He replaced John Howell as Epistler on 10 December 1695 and, on the death of John Frost, was sworn a full Gentleman of the Chapel on 1 June 1696. He was a countertenor who was, according to Rimbault, much in demand at musical performances. Barnes died on 2 January 1711.

### Barnes, Edward  *d. c. 1703, rope dancer, booth operator.*

Edward Barnes inserted the following advertisement in the 5–8 September 1696 *Post Man*:

At Mr Barns's Booth in Southwark Fair, near St. Georges Church, will be seen the only

English, Dutch, Spanish, High German and Indian Companies of Rope-Dancers, who are all five joined together, and will perform such variety of Dancing, Walking, Vaulting and Tumbling; the like was never seen in England before. 1st, you will see the famous Indian Woman and her Company. 2. You will see the High German Company. 3. You will see the Spanish Company dance excellently well on the low Rope. 4. You will see the two famous Dutch Children, who are the wonder and admiration of all the Rope Dancers in the World of their Sex and Age. 5. You will see the two famous Englishmen, Mr Edward Barns of Rederiff, and Mr Appleby, who are the only two Master Ropedancers and Tumblers in the old world; also you may see Mr Edward Barnes dance with a Child standing on his shoulders, and with 2 children at his Feet, in Jack-boots and Spurs, and cuts Capers a yard and a half high, and dances a Jig on the Rope with that variety of steps, that few, or no Dancing Masters can do the like on the ground: He likewise walks on a slack Rope no bigger than a penny Cord, and swings himself 6 or 7 yards distance. Afterwards you will see the famous Indian Woman Vault the High Rope with great dexterity. Likewise you will see the famous Mr Appleby, who is the only Tumbler in all Europe, fling himself over 16 mens heads, through 12 Hoops, over 14 Halbards, over a Man on Horseback, and a Boy standing upright on his Shoulders. You will likewise be entertained with good Musick. The merry Conceits of Harlequin and his Son Punch. You will see the English and Dutch Flag on the top of the Booth. Vivat Rex. We shall play at this place 12 days.

At Bartholomew Fair in August 1697 Barnes was located between the Crown Tavern and the Hospital Gate, against the Cross-Daggers, in West Smithfield Rounds. This year he was reduced to only four companies in one: English, High German, French, and Moroccan.

In August and September 1698 Barnes operated his booth jointly with his fellow performer Appleby. They were at the same place in Smithfield for Bartholomew Fair, their chief feature being "the German

Maiden outdoing all Men and Women, that ever Danc'd before her, both for high leaping and fine Dancing, and whatever has been done by any person on the Ground, as side, upright, cross or back capers, is performed by her on the Dancing Rope, and rises to that prodigious height, as will startle all that see her." With the same bill, Barnes and Appleby entertained the crowds at Southwark Fair, in the Coachyard near St George's Church.

The pair had their booth again at Bartholomew Fair in August 1699, and Ned Ward in *The London Spy* recorded his impressions of the entertainment. Having paid sixpence each for tickets, he and his friend went within the booth, "where a parcel of country scrapers were sawing a tune" while the audience assembled. Heading the bill was

a little animal, that looked as if it had not been six weeks out of a go-cart, and that began to creep along the rope, like a snail along a cabbage stalk, with a pole in its hand not much bigger than a large tobacco-stopper. This was succeeded by a couple of plump lasses, who, to shew their affection to the breeches, wore 'em under their petticoats, which, for decency's sake they first danced in. But to show the spectators how forward a woman once warmed is to lay aside her modesty, they doffed their petticoats after a gentle breathing, and fell to capering as if Old Nick had been in 'em. These were followed by a negro woman and an Irish woman . . . This was succeeded by a pragmatical brother of the same quality [probably Barnes himself], who mounted the ladder next, in order to ascend the rope, who had such a Tyburn look that I was fearful of his falling, lest his hempen pedestal should have catched him by the neck. He commanded the rope to be altered according to his mind, with an affected lordliness, and looking steadfastly in his face, I remembered I had seen him in our town, where he had the impudence to profess himself an infallible physician. . . . The person that danced against him was the German maid, as they style her in their bill, who does wonder-

ful pretty things upon the rope, and has fine proportion to her limbs and much modesty in her countenance. She as much out-danced the rest as a greyhound will outrun a hedgehog, having something of a method in her steps, and air in her carriage, moving with an observancy of time and play with her feet, as if assisted with the wings of Mercury.

Then Doctor Cozen-Bumpkin mounts the slack-rope, and after he had lain down and swung himself a quarter of an hour in his hempen hammock, he comes down, believing he had done wonderful things . . . Then up steps the negress to the top of the booth, and began to play at swing-swang with a rope, as if the devil were in her, hanging sometimes by a hand, sometimes by a leg, and sometimes by her toes, so that I found, let her do what she would, Providence or Destiny would by no means suffer the rope to part with her.

This scene being ended, they proceeded to the conclusion of their entertainment, the tumbling [probably by Appleby], and indeed, it was very admirable to think that use should so strengthen the springs of motion, and give that flexibility and pliableness to the joints, nerves, sinews, and muscles, as to make a man capable of exerting himself after so miraculous a manner.

In August of 1700 Edward Barnes operated his booth with a new partner, Mr Finley (or Findley). Plays and interludes had been forbidden by the authorities this year, but other entertainments were allowed. Barnes and Finley had a booth at May Fair in 1701 as well as at Bartholomew Fair in August, and they appeared at both fairs again in 1702. At May Fair, according to their 1702 advertisement, they were situated at the lower end of Brookfield Market. The pair were at May Fair in 1703 but apparently not at Bartholomew Fair the following August, and it is probable that Barnes died in the summer of 1703, for at May Fair in 1704 Finley worked with Mrs Barnes, and the following August she ran a booth alone, styling herself Widow Barnes.

**Barnes, Mrs Edward**  *(fl. 1704–1711),*
*fair booth operator.*

Mrs Edward Barnes may have helped her
husband operate his fair booths starting in
1696 when the first notice of his activity
occurs, but her name did not appear in the
advertisements until May Fair in 1704, after
her husband's death. In 1704 she ran a
booth with her husband's old partner, Mr
Finley (or Findley), at May Fair, and
later in the summer at Bartholomew Fair
she worked alone, styling herself Widow
Barnes. At May Fair in 1705 and 1706 she
was in partnership with Finley and Evans.
Though no other fair activity is recorded
for her, she continued leading a company
of rope dancers, for they performed at
Punch's Theatre on 19 January 1711.

**Barnes, Elizabeth.** *See* ELRINGTON,
MRS RICHARD.

**Barnes, Richard**  *(fl. 1675–1691),* *ac-*
*tor, singer.*

The Barnes who was active at the Smock
Alley Theatre in Dublin from about 1675
to 1680 is probably to be identified as the
Richard Barnes who appeared in minor
roles with the United Company in London
between 1689 and 1691. His first recorded
performance in England was as Boozer in
*The Widow Ranter* at Drury Lane on 20
November 1689. In London he seems to
have been used more as a singer than as an
actor.

**Barnet, Mr.** *See also* BERNARD, JOHN.

**Barnet, Mr**  *(fl. 1778–1845?),* *actor.*
The name "Barnet[t]" is ubiquitous in
the London and provincial theatres of the
late eighteenth and early nineteenth cen-
turies. Thus it is seldom certain which minor
or major actor may be referred to in the
casual and fragmentary accounts of the
time.

For instance, the Mr Barnett who played
at Edinburgh during the race season of Au-

gust 1777 was likely the one who was at
Richmond's summer theatre on 27 June
1778. Conjecturally also he was the Barnet
who played an unspecified part in *The Tay-*
*lors* in a casual company at the Haymarket
on 25 November 1782.

Was this the same Barnet who made his
Edinburgh debut on 26 January 1795 as
Lorenzo in *The Merchant of Venice*? James
Dibdin says that the latter was from Covent
Garden and was a tenor singer (though
there is no other record of a Barnet then at
Covent Garden). Perhaps, then, he was the
husband of the Mrs Barnet, also a singer,
who achieved only a single humble per-
formance in London as one of innumerable
Indians in the chorus of *The Cherokee*, at
Drury Lane on 30 October 1795.

How often Barnet played at Edinburgh
is not known, but he seems to have been on
the roster through 1796–97. A Barnet is recorded in a single performance at the Haymarket Theatre in the trifling walk-on of a
mutineer on 4 December 1797.

**Barnet, Mrs.** *See* BERNARD, MRS
JOHN.

**Barnet, Mrs**  *(fl. 1795),* *singer.*
A Mrs Barnet was listed among many
other singers in the chorus accompanying
the presentation of *The Cherokee* at Drury
Lane Theatre on 30 October 1795. She
did not appear again.

It is possible that she was Miss Catherine
Barnett, who was otherwise absent from
the theatre that season.

**Barnet, Master**  *(fl. 1750),* *actor. See*
BARNET, JARVIS.

**Barnet, Jarvis**  *(fl. 1748–1750),* *actor.*
Jarvis Barnet first appeared on the London stage on 2 December 1748 at Drury
Lane Theatre. He substituted for Berry in
the role of Old Capulet and it is therefore
certain that he was already a professional
actor when he came to the metropolis. He

apparently satisfied the star, Barry, and the management, for he retained the part for the last 12 performances of this run.

But Barnet did not succeed in carving a place for himself in the talent-packed Drury Lane of Garrick's early management, and though he was enrolled with the company for a season and a half he was seldom named in the bills in parts of importance, being relegated to such serious and comic roles as Lovewit in *The Alchemist*, Lennox and Duncan in *Macbeth*, Blunt in *Richard III*, Tradelove in *A Bold Stroke for a Wife*, and various walking gentlemen.

According to MacMillan Mrs Barnet came on at Drury Lane as Wheedle in *The Miser* on 25 January 1749, but the *London Stage* gives the part to Mrs Bennet and does not place a Mrs Barnet in the company. A Master Barnet, presumably a son, played Areo, one of the Infernals in *A Duke and No Duke* on 26 December 1750. He did not reappear.

**Barnett, Mr.** *See also* **BERNARD, JOHN.**

**Barnett, Mrs** ₁*fl. 1729*₁, *actress.*
A Mrs Barnett was among the minor actors in Reynold's troupe at Bartholomew Fair on 25 August 1729, playing in *The Beggar's Wedding*.

**Barnett, Catherine** ₁*fl. 1786–1800*₁, *actress, singer.*
Catherine Barnett was probably the Miss Barnett who was singing at Vauxhall Gardens in 1786. She was one of the unnamed "Vocal Characters" in the lyrical presentation of *Douglas* which was performed at Drury Lane on 20 December 1790. She was in choruses and very small vocal parts at that theatre until near the end of the season of 1793–94, when her salary was £2 per week. Her first appearance in an important character was on 1 June 1793 as Rosetta in *Love in a Village*.

Miss Barnett was at Edinburgh some part of the season of 1794–95 and at York

in the winter-spring seasons (beginning in January) of 1796 and 1797.

She married Richard Phillips, bachelor, of the parish of Marylebone at St Paul, Covent Garden, church on 10 October 1800. They were the parents of the singer Henry Phillips.

**Barnett, John** ₁*fl. 1794*₁, *bass viol player.*
Doane's *Musical Directory* of 1794 lists John Barnett of No 3, Cockspur-Street, as a participant in concerts by the Long Acre Society, and the Surrey Chapel Society, and at Westminster Abbey. He must have been related to musician Thomas Barnett of the same address.

**Barnett, Thomas** ₁*fl. 1794*₁, *oboist, tenor horn player.*
Doane's *Musical Directory* of 1794 lists Thomas Barnett of No 3, Cockspur-Street, as a participant in concerts by the Choral Fund, the Long Acre Society, the Surrey Chapel Society, and at Westminster Abbey. He must have been related to John Barnett of the same address, and he may have been the Thomas Barnett of St Pancras, a bachelor who married Susannah Lillington of St George, Hanover Square, on 20 February 1800.

**Barns.** *See also* **BARNES.**

**Barns, Mr** ₁*fl. 1794–1795*₁, *house servant.*
A Mr Barns was paid 15*s.* per week as "Cap[tain] of ye Supernum[erarie]s" at Covent Garden in the season of 1794–95.

**Barns, Mrs** ₁*fl. 1725*₁, *actress?*
*The Spanish Friar* and *Silvia's Revenge* were performed at the Haymarket Theatre on 27 December 1725 for the benefit of a Mrs Barns; no role was listed for her, and her function in the company, if any, is not known.

**Barnshaw, John** [*fl. 1768–1783*], *actor, singer.*

Barnshaw acted first at Covent Garden on 27 April 1768, in the role of Giles in *The Maid of the Mill*, and repeated that part on 19 September. In both appearances he was billed only as "a Gentleman." (His name appeared on 18 October.) Francis Gentleman found him unsuitable for the farmer Giles, "having more of the Clare Market knock-me-down knowing-one than rustic simplicity." He is mentioned in the bills at Covent Garden only occasionally during the next three years, in rustic and eccentric pairs like Hawthorn in *Love in a Village*, a sailor in *Thomas and Sally*, Hecate in *Macbeth*, Jobson in *The Devil to Pay*, and Damaetas in *Midas*. His salary was £2 per week.

During the summer of 1768 he was at Bristol, singing in choruses and playing secondary parts like Sileno in *Midas*. Occasionally in the summers of 1769 through 1771 he sang in ballad operas and interludes and was featured in solo ballads at Finch's Grotto Gardens.

Barnshaw left Covent Garden after 1770–71 and cannot be traced further until 1774–75, when he reappeared at York. In the summer seasons of 1775 and 1776 he was in the Birmingham company, and during the winter seasons of 1776–77 and 1777–78 he was at Liverpool, earning from 12s. to 18s. per week. In this latter season he received £48 18s. 9d. as his half of a benefit after £15 in charges were paid, indicating a degree of local popularity. Still advertised as "from Covent Garden," Barnshaw made his Irish debut at Fishamble Street, Dublin, on 11 April 1777.

John Barnshaw came next to public notice acting with a small company which staged 10 nights of plays at China Hall, Rotherhithe, between 18 June and 23 July 1777, under the management of the father of S. T. Russell. According to the bills, however, Barnshaw played only one speak-ing role, that of Sir John Loverule in *The Devil to Pay*, on 2 July.

The following summer he engaged for Joseph Fox's first season as lessee at Brighton and seems to have been an itinerant in Ireland in the fall of that year. In 1780 and 1781 he was named in the bills at Cork. In 1782–83 he engaged at Capel Street in Dublin, according to John Bernard. He faded finally from sight after singing again at Liverpool in the summer of 1783.

**Barnwell, Mr** [*fl. 1794–1795*], *dresser.*

A Mr Barnwell was paid 8s. per week as a men's dresser at Covent Garden Theatre in the season 1794–95.

**Baron, Mr** [*fl. 1800*], *singer.*

Mr Baron was one of the members of the singing chorus that participated in the initial run of Cumberland's *Joanna*; the work opened on 16 January 1800 and ran intermittantly until 7 February.

**"Baroness, The,"** stage name of Joanna Maria Lindelheim [*fl. 1703–1717*], *singer.*

The singer who ultimately adopted the stage name of The Baroness made her first appearance in London as Signora Joanna Maria Lindelheim at Drury Lane on 23 January 1703 singing several songs in Italian and French; the next week, on 1 February, she was billed simply as Signora Joanna Maria, and her last name was not used again. Her name suggests a German birth, but the "Signora" possibly indicates an Italian training; it is likely that she was the singer described by Evelyn on 28 February 1703:

A famous young woman, an Italian, was hired by our Commedians to sing on the stage, during so many plays, for which they gave her 500 pounds: which part (which was her voice alone at the end of 3 Scenes) she performed with such modesty, & grace above all by her skill, as there was never any (of many Eunichs & others) did with their Voice, ever anything comparable to her, she was to go hence to the Court of the K: of Prussia, & I believe carryed with her out of this vaine nation above 1000 pounds, every body coveting to heare her at their privat houses, especially the noble men.

She was back in England by 1705, and, with musician Nicola (or Nicolini) Haym as her agent, she entered into articles of agreement with managers Swiney and Congreve of the opera company, soon to open the new Queen's Theatre in the Haymarket. On 14 January 1705, in connection with his alterations to the opera *Camilla*, Haym persuaded manager Christopher Rich of Drury Lane that when the Queen's Theatre opened in April, Haym could accompany his scholar Joanna Maria there. Haym appears to have served the young singer not only as agent but as accompanist and tutor as well.

When the Queen's Theatre opened on 9 April 1705 with *The Loves of Ergasto*, done by "a new set of Singers, arriv'd from Italy," no names were listed, but from Haym's contract with Rich it seems likely that Joanna Maria was in the cast. The opera lasted five performances—only three, according to Cibber—after which the theatre was given over to the production of straight plays. This created an awkward situation for the managers, for in anticipation of more operatic performances, they had made contractual agreements with their singers which they now could not keep. According to a letter dated 1 March 1706 that reviewed the situation of the previous year, Swiney and Congreve had agreed to pay Haym's scholar, The Baroness (Joanna Maria's new stage name), 100 guineas for 10 performances before November 1705. By November she had sung only five times, demanded her full 100 guineas, and asked permission to sing elsewhere. She had been paid less than half of her fee, and Congreve, according to Haym, offered to settle for £50 and give The Baroness her liberty. Before any agreement was reached, Congreve withdrew his offer and Sir John Vanbrugh stepped into the picture with a possible solution. He suggested that The Baroness might be paid the same salary as Mrs Bracegirdle—£100 annually—for singing twice a week, or half the profits of a benefit in the fall of 1706. This, quite naturally, did not satisfy the singer or her agent; she proposed singing the other five times if the managers would pay her £100 (instead of the original 100 guineas), and if this was paid, she offered to sing five more times free and 10 times before the end of May (1706 apparently) at eight guineas a performance. The Lord Chamberlain was appealed to, and though he felt that the theatre should certainly pay The Baroness according to the original contract and have her sing the other five times she had agreed to, he hoped the theatre folk could straighten out the matter themselves. From Vanbrugh's letters it appears that he and the singer never reached an agreement; henceforth she was paid for each performance rather than on a yearly contract.

While all this wrangling was going on, between April 1705 and March 1706, The Baroness participated in performances at the Queen's Theatre, but the extent of

*Courtesy of Theatre Notebook and the Major Christopher Turnor Collection*

"THE BARONESS"

detail from a larger picture by M. Ricci

her activity is unclear. On 17 November 1705 "la Signiora Maria, as of late taught by Signior Nicolini Haym" sang in Italian and English, and she probably made other similar appearances during the winter. On 30 March 1706 Haym's alteration of *Camilla* opened at Drury Lane with the Baroness reverting to her older billing of Mrs Joanna Maria and singing Lavinia. The opera was quite successful and ran into August. After this the singer may have returned to the Continent, for she was not a member of the Drury Lane troupe during the 1706–7 season, nor was she affiliated with the Queen's Theatre.

She was active again in the spring of 1707 when she sang a concert on 2 April at Hickford's music rooms, and she was busy at the theatres in 1707–8. *Camilla* was revived at Drury Lane on 15 November 1707, and possibly The Baroness played in it; she was certainly present for the 6 December performance, singing Lavinia. This revival was a linguistically peculiar one: Mrs Tofts sang in English, Valentino Urbani sang in Italian, and The Baroness and Mrs de l'Epine sang mostly in Italian and partly, apparently, in English. Haym's tutoring of his scholar had not yet yielded very satisfactory results; Chetwood later described The Baroness as "a Dutchwoman, that committed Murder on our good old English, with as little Understanding as a Parrot."

In mid-January the Drury Lane singers switched to the Queen's Theatre, a house better suited to opera than plays, and for this engagement Haym worked out a new contract for his protégé. According to a letter of his dated 12 January 1708, the day before the company opened, The Baroness was to receive £300 for singing 30 times and Haym would take his agent's fee from her salary; if she should sing more than 30 times, she was to be paid at the same rate per performance. The letter stated that she would sing in *Camilla*, *Pyrrhus and Demetrius*, and the role of Eurilla in *Love's Triumph*, which she had just learned.

Whether or not the singer actually received the stipulated fee is problematical; a Queen's Theatre document at Harvard from this period indicates that she may have settled for £200. The Baroness sang as planned in *Camilla* and *Love's Triumph*, and on 10 April she replaced Mrs de l'Epine in the title role in *Thomyris*.

It was not until the following 14 December 1708 that she sang Deidamia in *Pyrrhus and Demetrius*. By this time she was established as a major member of the Queen's Theatre company, though her salary scale was about half that of her colleagues Mrs Tofts and Mrs de l'Epine; where she was listed for £200, they were listed for £500 and £400, and where she was listed for £3 per day, they were listed for £7 10s. She seems, however, not to have accepted a flat yearly contract but preferred to be paid by the performance, so the annual figure of £200 should be taken as a total cost to the managers rather than a contracted salary.

In 1709–10 Drury Lane and the Queen's Theatre returned to their competitive arrangement, both offering plays and the Queen's also presenting operas. Though the operas which The Baroness had done before were still being performed, the bills do not name her and *The London Stage* does not list her as a member of the troupe for either this season or the next. She was in the company, however, for an order dated 24 December 1709 mentioned her and warned Queen's Theatre personnel not to work elsewhere without permission. She must have been with the company for the 1710–11 season as well, for *Pyrrhus and Demetrius* was done for her benefit on 12 May 1711. During these two seasons, though, she seems to have lost her standing in the company; she was rarely mentioned in the bills, and in December 1710 a tally of the annual charges to the company showed her costing them £200—the lowest sum on the list.

After the 1710–11 season she either gave up her operatic career or went out of England to pursue it. The next London notice of her is two years later, on 24 April 1713, when she sang at a concert at Hickford's organized by her old mentor Haym. A month later, on 27 May, she sang another concert there for her benefit. In March or April of every year thereafter, through 1717, The Baroness sang at Hickford's for her benefit, though no other activity for her has come to light. After 12 April 1717, her last benefit, nothing more is heard of her.

Marco Ricci painted several pictures of singers of the period around 1720 in rehearsal. One, owned by Major Christopher Turnor, shows the Baroness standing with a fan partly hiding her face—apparently a habit she carried even into performance. Variants of this painting, also done by Ricci, are in the collections of Mr George Howard and Sir Watkin Williams-Wynn, Bart. Still another rehearsal scene by Ricci, formerly in the collection of Mr A. W. Holliday, shows the Baroness less hidden, though her features are not very clear.

**Barowby, Miss** *[fl. 1766]*, *actress, dancer.*

Miss Barowby first attempted the stage dancing in a minuet with Mons Curtet at Covent Garden Theatre on 22 May 1765. Her first acting role was the confidant Lucilla, a secondary character in *The Fair Penitent*, on 7 November 1766 at Covent Garden. Evidently she succeeded only indifferently well, for she was next seen dancing with numerous others in the pantomime *Harlequin Doctor Faustus* on 18 November; and after that she was named in no bills or company lists in London. Her salary was £1 5s. per week.

No connection with the theatrical physician Dr William Barrowby (fl. 1740–45) has been traced, but one is probable.

**Barques.** *See* DESBARQUES.

**Barr.** *See also* BARRE.

**Barr, Mr** *[fl. 1749–1750]*, *stage door-keeper.*

One Barr was entered on the Covent Garden pay list at the beginning of the 1749–50 season, at the rate of £1 per week, as a stage doorkeeper.

**Barr, Mr** *[fl. 1788–1795]*, *actor.*

A Mr Barr who was described by the *Ipswich Journal* when he acted in that town on 30 July 1789 as "late a printer of the Morning Herald" had first come on the stage at Drury Lane on 1 December 1788. His character was Tancred in *Tancred and Sigismunda*, and he was announced simply as "A Gentleman" but later was identified by J. P. Kemble by an annotation on the bill.

The playbills record no further appearances of a Barr in London during the eighteenth century or in the first quarter of the nineteenth. But the Drury Lane account book of 1791 records on 7 February: "Mr Barr from Commencement of this season 34/13/4" without specifying his occupation in the theatre; and on 12 February: "Mr Barr added to List –/6/8 per diem." Finally, on 25 April 1795, he was added to the company list at 6s. per day.

Barr may possibly be Joseph Barre.

**Barr, Benjamin** *[fl. 1794]*, *bass viol player?*

Doane's *Musical Directory* of 1794 lists Benjamin Barr of Orange Street, Leicester Square, as playing the bass viol (or singing bass?) in concerts by the Choral Fund and at the Handelian concerts at Westminster Abbey.

**Barr, John.** *See* FARR, JOHN.

**Barrand, William** *[fl. 1793]*, *bass viol player?*

Doane's *Musical Directory* of 1794 lists William Barrand of No 10, Aldersgate Buildings, Goswell Street, as a bass (viol player or bass singer?) in concerts at Westminster Abbey, and at the Oxford Music Meeting in 1793. Mary Barrand, possibly a sister of William, married a John Jones at St George, Hanover Square, on 20 May 1783.

**Barras, Joseph** [fl. 1756], proprietor.

Joseph Barras, proprietor of the Bowling Green House pleasure garden in 1756, announced that year that he had made extensive alterations to the house and fitted it up in a "genteel manner."

**Barrati.** See **BARATTI.**

**Barratt.** See also **BARRETT.**

**Barratt, Mr** [fl. 1784?–1794], bass viol player.

Doane's *Musical Directory* of 1794 lists a Mr Barratt who played bass viol in some of the Handelian Commemorative performances at Westminster Abbey (the first of which was in 1784) and who lived at Salisbury in 1794.

**Barre.** See also **BARR.**

**Barré, Mons** [fl. 1796–1798], choreographer, dance director.

Mons Barré was present at the King's Theatre during some part of the 1795–96 season and also during 1797–98 and 1798–99. Apparently he did not dance there, but he furnished several successful ballets and rehearsed and directed at least one of them.

On 13 December 1796 he revived and brought forward Noverre's ballet *L'Amour et Psiché*, the music by Mazzinghi. For Mlle Parisot's benefit on 25 May 1797 he composed a new ballet, *Le Triomphe de Cupidon; ou les nymphes vaincues par l'amour.* On 26 December 1798 he presented, to music by Bossi, his *Le Marchand de Smyrne.* On 29 January 1799 he presented his *Les Deux Jumelles; ou la méprise,* the music also by Bossi.

**Barré, Mlle** [fl. 1795–1796], dancer.

Mlle Barré was a member of the *corps de ballet* for the opera at the King's Theatre from 16 February 1796 until the end of that season. On 25 May 1796 she danced in a special performance at Drury Lane, with other dancers from the opera house.

**Barre, Joseph.** See **BARRE, MRS** [JOSEPH? CATHERINE?].

**Barre, Mrs** [Joseph?, Catherine?], née Groce [fl. 1768–1797?], actress, singer.

Miss Groce was said to be appearing the "first time on any stage" when on 30 April 1768 she sang the lead, Polly, in *The Beggar's Opera* at Covent Garden for the singer Mrs Mahon's benefit. She was billed simply as "A Young Gentlewoman." She repeated the part under her own name on 25 May. The Miss Grace who played an unnamed character in the afterpiece *The Statesman Foil'd* at Foote's summer company at the Haymarket on 8 July 1768 was doubtless Miss Groce.

She made her first appearance at the Crow Street Theatre in Dublin on 26 November 1768 in Lady Townly in *The Provok'd Husband,* again anonymously. By 19 December she was playing Rosetta in *Love in a Village,* advertised as her fifth appearance on any stage. In 1770 she had gone over to Smock Alley.

Both Hitchcock and the *Hibernian Magazine* of 1771 were agreed that Miss Groce became Mrs Barre, but neither gives a date for her marriage. It was before she came on again in Dublin in 1771, and it may have caused a short retirement after her Dublin debut. She signed a document, along with 17 other actors, promising "to perform and attend our business regularly" under Macklin's management at Crow Street, and she apparently played there through 1774. She also made appearances at Limerick in October 1771 and July and August 1772. She was at Cork briefly in October 1772.

On 1 May 1775 Mrs Barre came to Drury Lane for the first time, playing Euphrosyne in *The Mourning Bride*. On this occasion the bills spelled her name "Barree." But she did not catch on at Drury Lane, and probably she retired to some country company before going to the Edinburgh Theatre Royal, which she joined in April 1776. If the Mrs Barre who came to the Haymarket on 18 September 1797 to play Miss Biddy in *Miss in Her Teens* is our Mrs Barre, she was a durable ingenue indeed.

The Mrs Barre of 1797 was almost surely the actress Catherine Barre (who may also have been known as Mrs Barrett) who signed articles of employment with James Winston at the Richmond, Surrey, Theatre in 1799, and whose address was then Stafford Street, Bond Street. In the same company was Joseph Barre of the same address, doubtless her husband, and about whom we have no other information, unless he was the Mr Barr who was at Drury Lane in 1788.

**Barrem, Mr** ₁*fl. 1795*₁, *house servant?*

Mr Barrem was listed as an employee of Drury Lane on 25 April 1795 at 8*s.*, but his precise function in the theatre was not mentioned.

**Barrenstadt.** *See* BERENSTADT.

**Barrer, Elizabeth.** *See* BARRY, ELIZABETH.

**Barresford, Mrs Ebenezer.** *See* BULKLEY, MRS GEORGE.

**Barret, Mr** ₁*fl. 1730–1732*₁, *actor.*

A Mr Barret was first seen professionally on 20 October 1730 at Goodman's Fields Theatre, as Freeman in *A Bold Stroke for a Wife*. He was Fenton in *The Merry Wives of Windsor* on 30 October, the Prince in *Tamerlane* on 5 November, and

Livius in *Cato* on 12 November. Despite this evident utility he was not seen in London the next season, and he played only a couple of minor parts in a casual company at the Haymarket in November 1732 before quitting the London field.

Barret exploited his scanty metropolitan experience by advertising as "lately arriv'd from London" when playing for the first time at Smock Alley, Dublin, on 24 April 1732 and following.

**Barret, R.** ₁*fl. 1784–1785*₁, *actor.*

An R. Barret is placed by Hogan among the actors in the irregular winter performances at the Haymarket in 1784–85 and identified as the "R. Barret, comedian" who was one of the subscribers to John Cunningham's *Poems* of 1766. He was present as Wingate in *The Apprentice* on 17 September 1784 and thereafter disappeared.

**Barrett, Mr** ₁*fl. 1722*₁, *actor.*

With a relatively inexperienced troupe, a Mr Barrett played Ratcliff in *Jane Shore* at the Haymarket Theatre on 28 June 1722; he may also have performed in *The Orphan* and *The Revenge* which the company produced that summer.

**Barrett, Mr** ₁*fl. 1736–1737*₁, *musician?*

A Mr Barrett, probably a musician, was benefited by a concert given by a group of eminent instrumentalists, including Michael Christian Festing playing the violin and Weideman on the German flute, at the Devil Tavern in 1737.

**Barrett, Mr** ₁*fl. 1776–1805?*₁, *boxkeeper, constable.*

A Mr Barrett (who may have been the wax chandler with whom Drury Lane Theatre dealt in November 1775) was listed in the account book of the theatre for 1776–77 as a boxkeeper. He was living in "Angel-Court, Strand" when in 1779 he shared a benefit and addressed his patrons: "Mr

BARRETT begs the Favour that none of his Friends will go without Tickets; as there are others concerned with him; and hopes they will come early, that they may find no difficulty in getting good Places." Joint benefits are also recorded for 1779, 1780, 1781, 1783, and 1785.

On 10 February 1787 there was an account book notation: "Mr Blandy off.—Mr Barret in his Place of Constable," when the boxkeeper assumed the new duties. He was the Barrett who was drawing a weekly salary of £1 5s. through at least 1804–5.

### Barrett, Mr  *d. 1777? actor.*

According to James Winston's manuscript notes on subscribers to the Drury Lane Actors' Fund, a Mr Barrett subscribed 10s. 6d. in 1776. He left the theatre shortly afterward and apparently he died in 1777. He cannot, however, be identified by an appeal to the playbills for those years, and there is not any trace of his burial or his will.

### Barrett, Mr  [*fl.* 1784–1794], *double-bass player.*

Doane's *Musical Directory* of 1794 lists a Mr Barrett of No 22, Clement's Lane, Cannon Street, who was a double-bass player. He belonged to the New Musical Fund, the Amicable Society, and the band at Sadler's Wells Theatre. He was among the double-basses who assisted at the Handel Memorial Concerts of 26, 27, and 29 May and 3 and 5 June 1784 at Westminster Abbey and the Pantheon.

### Barrett, Mr  [*fl.* 1797–1800], *violinist.*

A Mr Barrett was among the first violins at the Handel Memorial Concerts of May and June 1784 at Westminster Abbey and the Pantheon. He played violin in the pit band for an out-of-season oratorio performance under Dr Arnold at the Haymarket Theatre on 15 January 1798. In the season of 1799–1800 he was in the band at the Covent Garden Theatre with the Ashleys.

### Barrett, Mrs  [*fl.* 1776], *actress.*

A Mrs Barrett played Toilet the maid in *The Jealous Wife* on 2 May 1776 in an out-of-season benefit performance at the Haymarket Theatre for "Mrs Newton and a Lady who has not appeared upon the stage these seven years," the lady being unidentified. Mrs Barrett was not heard from again in London.

### Barrett, Mrs  [*fl.* 1790–1816], *actress, dancer, singer.*

A Mrs Barrett was on and off the Drury Lane roster at various times from the fall of 1790 until the spring of 1797. She began dancing in the company for £1 5s. per week and went on to such nameless parts as one of several vintagers in James Cobb's *The Pirates* (its first night coinciding with her first appearance, 21 November 1792). She danced for the first time in an afterpiece on 27 December with many others.

Mrs Barrett is recorded as appearing only on 16 and 30 May in 1793–94, again in *The Pirates,* but she doubtless danced and "walked on" at other times during the season. She was first carried on the roster as a singer in the 1794–95 season but was named in the bills only on 20 and 22 December, when she appeared among a great many red Indians singing "The War-Whoop Chorus" in the drama of *The Cherokee.* She was a singer again in 1795–96 when she again swelled a chorus of many in *Harlequin Captive* on 18 January before falling back into even greater obscurity.

Mrs Barrett's 1796–97 season fell into this same pattern of anonymous chorus singing and pantomime and ballet, with an occasional half-identified part, such as the occasion when, in a ballet of 1 October called *The Triumph of Love,* she was one of eight "nymphs."

Mrs Barrett continued to earn her constant weekly salary of £1 5s. as a dancer at

Drury Lane until the season of 1815–16, after which we are unable to follow her.

**Barrett, Mrs** [fl. 1797]. *See* **BARRE, Mrs** [JOSEPH?].

**Barrett, Miss** [fl. 1776], *actress or singer.*

A Miss Barrett sang or spoke an "Epithalamium," with Millar on the occasion of a special benefit performance for Mrs Fisher at the Haymarket Theatre on 22 April 1776.

**Barrett, Miss** [fl. 1784], *actress.*

A Miss Barrett was at the Haymarket Theatre as Jenny in *The Romance of an Hour* on 16 November 1784. She was not noticed again.

**Barrett, Giles Linnett** *1744–1809, actor, manager.*

A Mr Barrett appears on the Richmond bills for 1775. The *Town and Country Magazine* identifies Giles L. Barrett "from Norwich and Richmond" as the actor appearing at the Drury Lane Theatre early in 1777. He was, then, the Mr Barrett who was given Sir Harry Beagle in *The Jealous Wife* at Drury Lane on 28 February, advertized as first acting on that stage. On 3 March he was Horatio in *Hamlet* for the first time and repeated the part twice more during the season. Whether he was given only occasional engagements or taken formally into the company but obscured in minor parts not named in the bills is uncertain, but his roles were rare that season, judging from extant evidence. Yet his parts which were named continued good: Don Carlos in *The Revenge*, Manly in *The Provok'd Husband*. If they were not more frequent it was probably because he was competing in his line of gallants and rakes with the young Palmer and the aging but potent "Gentleman" Smith, as well as with Waldron and Lamash.

After a summer at Richmond, where he

*Harvard Theatre Collection*

GILES LINNETT BARRETT, as Charles
by Dunthorne, Jr

was a successful Belcour in *The West Indian*, Barrett helped open the 1777–78 Drury Lane season on 20 September playing Harry Stukely in the afterpiece *All the World's a Stage*, and several nights later he repeated his debut character, Beagle. On 27 September he was Bogg in *Harlequin's Invasion*, on 10 November Scaramouch in *The Elopement*, on 24 November Hastings in *2 Henry IV*. After a repeat performance of Scaramouch on 27 December he was seen no more at Drury Lane or in any London patent theatre, though he turned up again at Richmond in the summer of 1778.

For the rest of his extended English career Barrett was identified with peripatetic provincial playing, often as an actor-manager. He was probably the Barret who came with Joseph Glassington to Stourbridge Fair in Cambridge in the summer

*Harvard Theatre Collection*

GILES LINNETT BARRETT, as Sir Gilbert Pumpkin

by De Wilde

of 1780. On 11 August 1780 the Committee at Norwich "unanimously agreed . . . that Mr Giles Linnett Barrett be appointed to succeed Mr Griffith" in the management. By the following February he was manager at Norwich at £1 5s. per week and for the next several seasons ousted Glassington and other competition from Stourbridge Fair with his Norwich company. He curried favor there every summer until 1786 with the Mayor and Corporation, the Vice Chancellor of Cambridge University, the students, the local gentry, and townspeople. He built a semi-permanent theatrical booth of considerable opulence, rehearsed his good company thoroughly, and gave parts of his proceeds to local charities.

The Norwich Committee Book entry of 13 August 1781 shows that "Mr Barret is

desired to go to London from Colchester to supply the Places of the Performers who are leaving the Company." Evidently Barrett combined personal profit with company business for he was at Richmond, playing Charles Surface as "from the Theatre Royal, Norwich," in September 1781. He continued at Norwich as manager at least until 1788 and acted at Ipswich, Bury, and other, smaller, towns on the Norwich circuit. In 1784 he signed a lease from the proprietors and paid them a rental of £180 per year.

On 21 November 1788 Barrett made his Irish debut at Dublin as "from Norwich." But this year he also fell desperately ill and had to treat from his bed with the proprietors in the matter of assigning his leasehold of the several theatres on the circuit to John Brunton. In the summers of 1789 and 1790 he was playing at the Royal Circus for Hughes the equestrian manager but was also several times at Brighton. In 1791 he can be traced to Derby, Nottingham, and Margate. By 1793 he was managing the company at Plymouth.

Barrett took two spouses. His first wife was said to have been a daughter of a Norwich alderman who took up acting after she met Barrett. He left her about 1791 for an actress named Mrs Rivers, née Ranoe, who was known by a more picturesque stage name, Mrs Belfield. (She should not be confused with the Mrs Belfield [really Mrs Marian Burnell] [1783–1819] who acted at York and Edinburgh and who stabbed herself to death.) Allston Brown says that she made her debut "in London, as Portia, to Macklin's Shylock," but there is no record of this performance. She is also said to have been Macklin's pupil. It is not known when or whether she married Barrett. At any rate, the Committee of Proprietors of the Norwich Theatre compassionately "in consideration of all the necessities of [the first] Mrs Barrett" and "also of her Father having been a very respectable and worthly magistrate of this City" granted her an annuity of £50 at her husband's desertion, and it was continued when William Wilkins leased the theatre in 1799.

The Barretts were engaged in England by Charles Stuart Powell for the first season of Boston's Haymarket Theatre, 1796–97. They arrived in the United States early in the fall with their infant son George Horton Barrett. Barrett taught fencing while awaiting the opening of the Boston theatre.

He made his American debut on 28 December 1796 in the Boston Haymarket as Ranger in *The Suspicious Husband*, a favorite part. Mrs Barrett played first in America at the Haymarket on 30 December as Mrs Beverley in *The Gamester*.

Barrett was in his middle fifties when he went to America, but he had apparently boxed himself into a line of young gallants in comedy and was unsuited to the heavier tragic characters which Powell, having no good tragic actors in the company, required. A dispute with Powell developed in the press. At the close of the season Mr and Mrs Barrett joined Joseph Harper in Newport, Rhode Island.

When the Boston Theatre Company opened on 6 December 1797 the Barretts were on the rolls. Barrett and Harper assumed the management on 22 January 1798, and after the theatre burned on 2 February 1798 he went back to the expedient of teaching fencing.

Once again Barrett tried Boston management in the season which opened in December 1799, but though he was hardworking and ingenious, rising expenses in an inflationary year forced him to close in April 1800. Boston remained a kind of home base for the Barretts, but after their last failure in management they became more or less itinerant, acting for Sollee in his challenge to Hodgkinson and Dunlap at the John Street Theatre in New York from August 1797, with Dunlap in the 1798–99 season, and in various New York theatres to 1806. In 1802 Barrett and Hodgkinson offered some entertainments at the Southwark Theatre in Philadelphia. William B. Wood hired Mrs Barrett at the Chestnut Street Theatre in the season of 1802–3. She had delivered the monody on the death of Washington on 10 January 1800 at Boston's Federal Street Theatre. She was still acting roles of old women in some New York theatres as late as 1814. But Barrett died in poverty and obscurity in Boston on 18 November 1809. The second Mrs Barrett died in 1832, also in Boston.

The Barretts' son, George Horton Barrett, was born in Exeter, England, on 9 June 1794. He made his debut in Boston in 1796 as the Child in *Pizarro*, according to T. Allston Brown, but the appearance may have been at the Park Street Theatre in New York on 10 December 1798. By 1806, a little after the height of the "Infant Roscius" craze in England, he was being billed as the "Young American Roscius." Unlike the original "Young Roscius," Henry West Betty, he succeeded as an adult, and he was sometimes called the best light comedian the American stage possessed. He was applauded for his genteel address and a manly beauty and aristocratic bearing which he inherited from both parents. On 24 June 1825 he was married to Mrs Anne James Henry the dancer. He died on 5 September 1860.

Samuel De Wilde painted G. L. Barrett as Sir Gilbert Pumpkin in *All the World's a Stage*; J. Dunthorne, Jr painted him as Charles Surface in *The School for Scandal* and as Lingo in O'Keeffe's *Agreeable Surprise*. Both pictures were engraved by E. Scott.

**Barrett, Mrs Giles Linnett, née Ranoe, formerly Mrs Rivers, stage name Mrs Belfield** d. *1832*, actress. See **BARRETT, GILES LINNETT.**

**Barrett, John** c. *1674–c. 1720, organist, composer.*

Grove gives John Barrett's dates as c. 1674–c. 1735, but the death date is clearly in error, for Barrett was spoken of as deceased as early as 28 January 1720. He was probably the John Barrett, former boy singer and student of John Blow, who was granted livery on 8 December 1691. By about 1707, when he was appointed music master at Christ's Hospital, he had composed a great number of songs which had already appeared in published collections, and several of these were composed for the theatre. When D'Urfey's *Wit and Mirth* was printed in 1719 Barrett was heavily represented, and he seems clearly to have been one of the most popular song writers of his day. He composed songs and/or instrumental music for *The Pilgrim* (1700), *The Generous Conqueror* (1701), *Tunbridge Walks* (1703), *The Albion Queens* (1704), *Love's Last Shift* (1707 revival), *The Fine Lady's Airs* (1708), *The City Ramble* (1711), *The Lancashire Witches* (1712 revival), *The Wife of Bath* (1713), and *The Country Lasses* (1715).

On 28 January 1720, according to the Christ's Hospital Court Minutes, Peter Horwood was elected music master, replacing John Barrett, deceased, and on 25 October 1720, when *The Lancashire Witches* was performed at Drury Lane, the music was billed as by "the late Mr Barret."

### Barrett, John  *d. 1795, actor.*

The first recorded London appearance of John Barrett was at the Haymarket on 6 June 1780, as a watchman in *The Apprentice*. Thereafter that season he played Scrub in *The Stratagem*, Lint in *The Mayor of Garratt*, Roderigo in *Othello*, Jackides in *The Tailors*, Simon in *The Wedding Night*, Lucianus in a revision of *Hamlet*, Trapland in *Love for Love*, Transfer in *The Minor*, and unspecified parts in several other productions. If all of these parts were studied during the summer season between 6 June and 15 September, Barrett must have been remarkably retentive. But he had stage experience in the provinces, for Tate Wilkinson was referring to him as of

1782 as Barrett "of the Hay in the summer and Manchester in the winter."

A hint as to the character of his provincial training is in the admonitory critique with which the *Morning Chronicle* of 10 June 1780 noticed his Scrub:

He seems to have something of the bad habit which infects most actors who have their stage education in the old-fashioned *Thespian* schools, and have learnt their profession in *moving* seminaries, viz. a desire to court the favour of the galleries, at the expense of character. This vicious habit he must learn to despise and avoid, if he would pass for a good Comedian in the eyes of the Haymarket audience.

A Barrett was placed at Dublin "during Mossop's and Ryder's Management" by the *Thespian Dictionary* of 1805, and this seems to have been John:

[He was] excellent in some small parts, as Orator Mum, Vinegar, &c. [His] features had a peculiar cast of saturnine acidity, well suited to his confined line. He obtained the name of Jew from his lending out small sums, from half-a-crown to half-a-guinea (no more at a time) to his distressed brother sufferers . . . on stage properties, shirts, clothes, &c. At this time no pawnbroker had opened in Dublin, and the traffic was carried on by usurers. How Barret, to whom the managers were *minus,* as well as the rest, could *compass the cash,* his salary and his wife's jointly not amounting to £3 per week, still remains a secret, and is probably buried with him. He was a man of dry humour . . . His wife was but a coarse substitute for Mrs Heaphy in the old women.

Despite the *Dictionary's* specific assertion that he was not the Haymarket Barrett who died in 1795, John seems to have been that individual. W. C. Oulton, for example, speaks of John Barrett as the comic actor of "Crazy, Orator Mum, &c" at the Haymarket, and says he died "previous to its opening" for the 1795 season: "This gentleman from a peculiarity of voice and manner, was an original in many eccentric characters, and though unnoticed by the Managers, was deemed of much service to this theatre in the O'Keefian line."

"Little Barrett" is celebrated by the author of *The Thespian Mirror . . . of the Theatres Royal, Manchester, Liverpool, and Chester* (1793):

> *His face is a compound of laughter and*
> *    grin;*
> *His voice and appearance accords with*
> *    his spirit,*
> *And equally serves to establish his merit:*
> *With spirits on fire and body tip-toe*
> *He looks like a Bantam preparing to*
> *    crow*

John may have been the Barret, actor, who was reported by the *Morning Chronicle* to have married a Mrs Hinde (possibly widow of a member of the theatrical family) at the New Church in the Strand on 31 August 1774. The "wife of John Barrett of the Hay-market Theatre" died at Bushy on 26 August 1790. She does not appear to have acted in London, but only in Ireland.

John Barrett continued a well-known public figure, but playing the same round of low-comic parts, at the Haymarket through the summer season of 1794. The death of "the quaint little actor" occurred while he was touring with the Manchester company on 9 May 1795.

### Barrett, Mr [John?] [fl. 1799], actor.

A Mr Barrett performed an unspecified part in the afterpiece *The Jew and the Doctor* at Covent Garden Theatre on 12 June 1799 for the benefit of Becky Wells Sumbel. The *Hibernian Magazine* for June 1806 reported that a John Barrett "of Covent Garden" Theatre had lately married a Miss Devereux.

### Barrey. *See* BARRY.

### Barrimore. *See* BARRYMORE.

### Barrington, Mr [fl. 1783], actor, singer.

The Barrington who was making his "first appearance on that stage" at Drury Lane on 25 January 1783 as Don Diego in the afterpiece of *The Padlock* was also making his last appearance in London, so far as the bills tell. He can hardly have been a son, but may have been a relative, of John Barrington (d. 1773) and his wife Ann Hallam Barrington. Mrs John Barrington's ward and niece, Mrs George Mattocks and her husband, were playing at Covent Garden that season.

Barrington was also on a Sadler's Wells bill of 14 May 1783 as a singer. He was at Capel Street, Dublin, from 18 December 1783, and he may still have been playing in 1800 when a Barrington appeared in the summer company at Margate.

Conceivably he could have been the William Barrington whose child Charles James by Mary his wife was baptized at St Paul, Covent Garden, on 10 April 1785.

### Barrington, Mrs [fl. 1732–1733], actress?

A Mrs Barrington, presumably a minor actress, was given a partial benefit, along with the actor Aston and the actress Miss Oates at Covent Garden Theatre on 10 May 1733. Apparently she was not connected with the Barringtons of a later date.

### Barrington, John 1715–1773, actor.

John Barrington was born into a good family of County Cork, Ireland, in 1715 and was bred to the law, according to Chetwood's account, which esteemed him "an excellent comic Actor, of Infinite Humour, a much-desir'd pleasing Companion and (what is not always to be met with) a Person of Sincerity."

Barrington's engagement at the Rainsford Street Theatre, Dublin, in 1735 seems the start of his long career. In its early stages, when he played much in the Irish countryside, his rambles are impossible to follow. He was doing comedy turns and imitations, including a "squeeking Punch and Monkey" at Smock Alley on 17 May 1737. His name appeared in what Clark calls the earliest known reference to the Waterford theatre when the *Dublin News-Letter* of 25 June 1737 announced that Lewis Duval with his Smock Alley company was "in a short time to set out for Waterford to open there with *The Committee*, Teague [the original stage Irishman] to be perform'd by Mr Barrington." Some London players were to accompany the Dubliners as guest actors, among them Adam Hallam, later to become Barrington's brother-in-law. He received a benefit at Aungier Street Theatre on 13 February 1739.

Tate Wilkinson, a connoisseur of "national" parts, later said that Barrington's Teague was the best stage Irishman he ever saw. The young actor sensibly used this, his best "line," in his attempt to storm London in 1739. He was accompanied from Ireland by his friend Luke Sparks. He played Teague in *The Committee* at Covent Garden as "from the Theatre in Dublin" on 5 April, *another* Teague (though substantially and broguishly the same) in *The Twin Rivals* on 12 April, Jobson in *The Devil to Pay* for his benefit, jointly with Sparks, on 30 April, and the second Teague again on 18 May.

Barrington was back at Aungier Street in 1741 and still or again there from 1743 through 1744–45. On 19 September 1745 "Barrington from the theatre in Dublin" played Foigard in *The Stratagem* at Drury Lane; and on 2 January his Teague was received with wild applause, "he being allowed by the whole audience to be the most complete Teague that ever appeared on the stage," the more so because of his introduction of several Irish songs.

Barrington remained at Drury Lane into the season of 1747–48, playing at Jacob's Wells Theater in Bristol every summer from early June until September and enjoying a variety of Irish and eccentric parts. (He was also probably the "Barronton" who played Hastings in *Jane Shore* at the Haymarket on 2 May 1748.) He spent the 1748–49 season at the Smock Alley Theatre in Dublin. Chetwood also saw him there in a booth managed by Madame Violante.

In the summer of 1749 Barrington married the recently-widowed Mrs Sacheverel Hale, née Ann Hallam, and they appeared together at Covent Garden in the season of 1749–50. Ann, the sister of George, William, Adam, Lewis, and the naval officer who was later Admiral Thomas Hallam, had first come upon the stage in 1733 while Thomas her father and her mother and other members of the family were strolling through Canterbury and other southern towns. She played the Duke of York in *Richard III* and spoke an epilogue of thanks to the audience. Her early acting history is largely unknown, but she married the journeyman actor Sacheverel Hale just before the opening of the Covent Garden season of 1739–40 and began playing pert servants like Cherry in *The Stratagem* and more sophisticated young women like Philadelphia in *The Amorous Widow*. She also essayed breeches parts like that of Young Fashion in *The Relapse* and was esteemed both for her voice and her excellent figure. Hale died in the summer of 1746, and she was left with one daughter, Mary Anne.

The Barringtons liked to tour the provinces in the summers of their 24 years together. They were at Bath in August 1750. They were at Bath and Bristol and Maidstone in Kent in June of 1754. At Maidstone they were managed by John Wignell and played in a booth in the Star Yard in a company which included Tate Wilkinson, Jefferson, and the Hulls, as well as little "Miss Hallam," who was probably Isabella, later Mrs George Mattocks. Mrs Barrington's Andromache on this occasion was much admired by young Tate Wilkinson, who played Orestes, and she dazzled him with "Peg Woffington's tragedy Jewels." The Barringtons lived in style and amazed "the eyes and ears of the little streets with a very handsome one horse chair," according to Miss Rosenfeld, in which every noon they "took a genteel airing." Where they got this affluence is not recorded. Gilliland says that "In some weeks the shares were not six shillings each."

But in the winters the Barringtons played at Covent Garden continuously from 1749–50 through 1762–63, during which latter season Mrs Barrington dropped temporarily out of sight. She was back in 1763–64, but he was gone in 1764–65. (He was in the Bristol summer company in 1746, 1747, 1748, 1751, 1754, 1756, 1759, 1761, 1762, 1763 and 1764.) Both he and she returned to Covent Garden in 1765–66 and remained until 1770–71, when he again vanished. He came back to join her in 1771–72, but after this year both left the London stage for good.

Thus, Barrington had been acting perhaps continuously for some 37 years. Mrs Barrington was probably on for more than 40, for she was still playing at Liverpool, as Mrs Peachum in *The Beggar's Opera*, in 1773. We do not know when she died.

Mrs Barrington's parts naturally ranged widely, acting as she did from early childhood to old age. They included Nerissa in *The Merchant of Venice*, Celia in *As You Like It*, Belinda in *The Provok'd Wife*, Hillaria in *Love's Last Shift*, Araminta in *The City Wives' Confederacy*, Mrs Strictland in *The Suspicious Husband*, Lady Macduff in *Macbeth*, Lady Capulet in *Romeo and Juliet*, Lady Grace in *The Provok'd Husband*, and Dorcas Zeal in *The Fair Quaker*.

John Barrington was, first of all, the pre-eminent stage Irishman of his day, playing not only his inimitable Teague and Foigard, but Macahone in *The Stage Coach*, Outside in *Humours of the Army*, O'Blun-der in *The Double Disappointment*, Mackmorrice in *Henry V*, O'Brallaghan in *Love a la Mode*, the Irishman in *The Apprentice*, O'Cutter in *The Jealous Wife*, O'Connor in *A Summer's Tale*, and MacShuffle in *The Oxonian in Town*. But he also played parts like Thunder in *The Rehearsal*, Swagger in *The Funeral*, Jeremy in *Love for Love*, did a specialty called "Cries of Dublin," and sang Irish ballads.

The Barringtons, competent and hardworking actors as they were, were probably more important for the training and nurture they gave to their beloved niece, Isabella Hallam, who lived with them, toured with them, and was educated by them after the departure of her family for America.

John Barrington died on 15 January 1773 and was buried on 25 January in the burying ground of St George the Martyr near the Foundling Hospital.

**Barrington, Mrs John, Ann, née Hallam** *[fl. 1733–1773].* See **BARRINGTON, JOHN.**

**Barrisford.** *See* **BERRISFORD.**

**Barrois, Mons** *[fl. 1754–1755],* dancer.

A Barrois was on the Drury Lane company list for 1754–55 as a dancer. He did not show up in a London company again.

**Barron,** [Mrs?] *[fl. 1760–1761],* charwoman.

The Covent Garden accounts list one Barron as charwoman in 1760–61 at 1s. daily.

**Barron, John** *[fl. 1784–1794],* singer, pianist, violinist?

John Barron may have been the "Mr Barron" whom Burney lists among the first violins at the Handel Memorial Concerts of 1784 at Westminster Abbey and the Pantheon. If so, he was probably the father or older brother of the violoncellist distinguished as "Barron Jr" and identified in Doane's *Directory* of 1794 as W. A. Barron.

John Barron is listed by Doane as a "Tenor," which may mean in the terminology of the time either singer or instrumentalist, and as a player on the *pianoforte* who had performed in some undescribed fashion in the Abbey concerts and who belonged to the Chapel Royal Choir. He had played at the Oxford Music Meeting of 1793. In 1794 he was resident at No 11, Clifford Row, Chelsea.

(A John Barron was acting at Belfast in February and April of 1776. There were also Barrons identified only as "Barron Senior" and "Junior" in the Liverpool Theatre's company in the seasons of 1777 and 1778, carried as "extras," but there is small chance that any of these were the musicians.)

### Barron, William Augustus  *fl.*
*1760?–1794,  violoncellist.*

William Augustus Barron played in public for the first time when he was 13. Young Barron and a group of other juvenile instrumentalists and singers, including Miss Schmeling (later Madame Mara), Miss Burney, and James Cervetto, played and sang in concert at the Haymarket on 23 April 1760. Neither their instruments nor their selections were given.

Our subject certainly is the "Mr Barron, Jr" whom Charles Burney lists among the violoncellos at the first Handel Memorial Concerts at Westminster Abbey and the Pantheon in May and June of 1784. He belonged to the New Musical Fund. In 1794 he lived at No 16, Rathbone Place.

### Barronton. *See* BARRINGTON.

### Barrot. *See* BARRETT.

### Barrow, Thomas  *1722?–1789, singer, harpsichord teacher.*

Thomas Barrow the singer was born probably in 1722, a son of Berea Barrow

of Monmouth, County Monmouth, and was early educated under Bernard Gates as one of the Children of the Chapel Royal. He was apparently the Thomas Barrow who matriculated at Wadham College, Oxford, on 10 July 1739, paying fees as a plebeian. He proceeded B. A. on 9 May 1743.

Barrow was one of the most accomplished altos or countertenors of his day. His singing career seems to have begun when he was 10 years old, as one of the choir of the Chapel Royal. He was an "Israelite Officer" in a private performance of the oratorio *Esther* at the Anchor Tavern in the Strand on 23 February 1732. He sang in the presentation of *Alexander's Feast* at Ruckholt House on 11 June 1744.

He was made a Gentleman of the Chapel Royal, one of the Westminster Abbey choir, and lay vicar of the Abbey. Handel heard and admired his "high, loud" voice, befriended him, and involved him in the oratorios. He led Handel's choral altos in the performances of the *Messiah* at the Foundling Hospital in 1754, 1758, and 1759. The Treasurer's Minutes show that he was paid for the first performance 10s. 6d. and for each of the others £1 10s.

In 1763 he was described in a London directory as "one of the Gentlemen of the Chapel Royal and Teacher of the Harpsichord." He was then living in Northumberland Court, Charing Cross. On 1 August 1769 a son, George, age 13 months, died, and was buried on the fourth in Westminster Abbey.

The *Oxford Journal* of 13 March 1779 announced for the Oxford Music Room "Chorusses by several good voices in Oxford assisted by Messrs Barrow, Randal, and Real from London." In May and June of 1784 Barrow was among the countertenors for the Memorial Concerts for his friend Handel which were given in Westminster Abbey and the Pantheon. On 19 February 1779 he appeared to attest the handwriting in the will of his friend the notable composer Dr William Boyce. In

1783 "Thomas Barrow of Little Cloyster Westminster Abbey . . . Gentleman" came forward to perform the same service for the organist and tenor singer Edward Edmund Ayrton. By 1785 Barrow was Secretary of the Royal Society of Musicians.

Barrow died on 13 August 1789 and was taken from his house in the Little Cloisters and buried on the seventeenth, with musical services, in the North Cloister of Westminster Abbey. On 6 September the Royal Society allowed his widow Mrs Mary Barrow £2 16s. 6d. per month and £8 additional for funeral expenses.

Thomas Barrow's will names the actor Thomas Hull of Bow Street, Covent Garden, and Barrow's son-in-law William Watkins, optician of St James's Street, trustees of £212 6s. 7d. bank stock for the benefit of his widow. They were also to assume direction of £150 in annuities which he had been administering for his late brother in behalf of the brother's widow (then remarried) Mary Nash of Warfield, Berkshire. The residuary legatee of this sum was to be Thomas Barrow's sister Elizabeth Barrow of Clapham Common. Small sums were given immediately to his children— John, Thomas, Lydia, and Lucy Barrow and Mrs Catherine Watkins—and to his sister Elizabeth. The will was signed 22 January 1788, witnessed by A. Palmer and Francis Dollman, and proved 19 August 1789.

Thomas Barrow's widow Mary died on 10 June 1810, aged 78, and was buried beside her husband in the North Cloister.

## Barry. *See also* BERRY.

## Barry, Mr [fl. 1699], actor?

A Mr Barry, not to be confused with Thomas Berry, was a member of Christopher Rich's troupe at Drury Lane and Dorset Garden in 1699. On 11 November 1699 a fight occurred involving Henry Arthur and "one Barry of the playhouses." Perhaps he was a performer, though he may have been a house servant.

## Barry, Mr [fl. 1799], actor.

A person billed as "Barry Jun." acted unnamed principal characters in *Lover's Vows* and *The Jew and the Doctor* at Covent Garden on 12 June 1799. He also spoke the epilogue to the first piece.

## Barry, Elizabeth c. 1658–1713, actress.

Elizabeth Barry, the first great English actress, was born in 1658—or possibly a year or two earlier—the daughter of barrister Robert Barry. Barry raised a regiment for Charles I at his own expense and came to be called Colonel Barry, but the cost of it ruined him financially, and, according to Curll (*The History of the English Stage*, 1741, authorship questionable), he was forced to let his children make their own way in the world. Who Elizabeth's siblings were is not known.

Anthony Aston said that Elizabeth became woman to his godmother Lady Shelton of Norfolk, but this may have been wishful thinking on Aston's part, for she would have had to enter this service at a very tender age indeed, since she was certainly in London and under the protection of Sir William Davenant before he died in 1668. Through the Davenants she received a good education and an acquaintanceship with people of rank and breeding.

The stories of her early attempts at acting vary, and certainly Curll's claim that Davenant tried to train her, found she had a poor ear, and rejected her thrice as a member of the Duke's Company cannot be true, for this also would have had to happen before she was 10; she may, on the other hand, have undergone discipline in acting with Sir William's son Charles in the early 1670's. Curll also told of the Earl of Rochester's training her for the stage, on a wager that he could make an actress of her in six months, and this may have been partly true. In this anecdote Rochester and his friends supposedly saw her in a performance, found her wanting, and struck

ELIZABETH BARRY
after Kneller

have been cast in it, Rochester's training notwithstanding.

It is more probable that her first role was Draxilla in Otway's *Alcibiades* at the Dorset Garden Theatre in late September 1675 — a small part, suited to her age and inexperience. Cibber later said that her first appearance was unsuccessful and that she was dismissed at the end of the season; if so, perhaps the whole episode of Rochester's wager and instruction took place between September 1675 and 3 July 1676, when she made her next recorded appearance, as Leonora in *Abdelazer*. She was then cast as Elvira in *The Wrangling Lovers* on 25 July and Theodocia in *Tom Essence* in late August. Her 1676–77 season was remarkably busy for a new member of the company: Constantia in *Madam Fickle* (4 November 1676), Phaenice in *Titus and Berenice* (December), Lucia in Otway's *The Cheats of Scapin* (December), Hellena in *The Rover* (24 March 1677), Emilla in *The Fond Husband* (31 May), Clorina in *The French Conjurer* (June), and Philisides in *The Constant Nymph* (July).

No sooner had Rochester made his protégé fit for the stage than he begged her to relinquish it; a poem he wrote about 1677 probably refers to Elizabeth:

the wager; Rochester then "made her Rehearse near 30 times on the Stage, and about 12 in the Dress she was to Act in." He recognized that she had no ear for music and could not learn effective line readings through imitation, so he "made her enter into the Nature of each Sentiment; perfectly changing herself, as it were, into the Person, not merely by the proper Stress or Sounding of the Voice, but feeling really, and being in the Humour, the Person she represented, was supposed to be in." The role for which Rochester trained her, Curll said, was the Hungarian Queen Isabella in *Mustapha* which, he claimed, was done before Charles II about 1673 or 1674; there are, however, no records of the play having been performed at this time, and though Elizabeth Barry probably played the role later in her career, it is highly unlikely that at about 17 she would

> *Leave this gawdy guilded Stage*
> *From custome more than use frequented;*
> *Where fooles of either sex and age*
> *Crowd to see themselves presented.*
> *To loves Theatre the Bed*
> *Youth and beauty fly together*
> *And Act soe well it may be said*
> *The Lawrell there was due to either:*
> *Twixt strifes of Love and war the difference Lies in this*
> *When neither overcomes Loves triumph greater is.*

The strife between the two was apparently exasperating for Rochester, and he complained bitterly of being driven mad and being forsaken for others. But he finally lured her to love's theatre, and between July 1677 and the following April no roles are recorded for her.

Elizabeth's daughter by Rochester was born shortly before 17 December 1677 and named after her. On that date, prodded by Nell Gwynn, Saville wrote to Rochester, urging the rake to look to Mrs Barry's financial plight. Not long after this, Rochester wrote to his mistress:

Your safe Delivery has deliver'd me too from Fears for your sake, which were, I'll promise you as burthensome to me, as your Great-belly cou'd be to you. Every thing has fallen out to my Wish, for you are out of Danger, and the Child is of the Soft Sex I love. Shortly my Hopes are to see you, and in a little while to look on you with all your Beauty about you. Pray tell no Body, but yourself open the Box I sent you; I did not know, but that in Lying-inn you might have use of those Trifles; sick and in Bed as I am, I cou'd come at no more of 'em; but if you find 'em, or whatever is in my power to use, to your service, let me know it.

Sometime after this Rochester took charge of the infant for reasons only hinted at in another letter he wrote Mrs Barry:

I am far from *delighting* in the *Grief* I have given you by taking away the *Child*, and you, who made it so absolutely *necessary* for me to do so, must take that *Excuse* from me, for all the *ill Nature* of it. On the other side, pray be assur'd I love *Betty* so well that you need not *apprehend* any *Neglect* from those I employ; and I hope very shortly to *restore* her to you a *finer Girl* than ever.

The girl was apparently returned to Mrs Barry at some later date, but when is not certain. When the Earl died in 1680 he left a £40 annuity to Elizabeth Clerke, an infant child, and this was doubtless the actress's daughter. The girl died at about the age of 12 or 13.

Elizabeth Barry's first stage appearance after this experience was probably on 5

April 1678 when she spoke the epilogue and played Mrs Goodvile in Otway's *Friendship in Fashion*. She completed the season delivering the epilogue and playing Clara in *The Counterfeits* on 28 May and acting Sophia in *Squire Oldsapp* in June. In 1678–79 only two roles are known for her, Polyxena in *The Destruction of Troy* and Cornelia in *The Feign'd Curtizans*, but the records are woefully incomplete.

It was in the 1679–80 season that Mrs Barry's acting talent blossomed and she was given her first great role. During the season she is recorded as delivering one prologue and four epilogues—a sure sign of her growing popularity and skill—and she acted Mrs Gripe in *The Woman Captain*, Olivia in *The Virtuous Wife*, Lavinia in Otway's *Caius Marius*, Camilla in *The Loving Enemies*, Lady Dunce in Otway's *The Soldier's Fortune*, and Corina in *The Revenge*. But putting all of these in the shade was Monimia in Otway's *The Orphan*, which she "created" in late February 1680, setting a standard that virtually every great tragic actress of the following century tried to match. The prompter Downes cited it as one of the three roles that "gain'd her the Name of Famous Mrs Barry, both at Court and City; for when ever She Acted any of these three Parts [Monimia, Belvidera in *Venice Preserved*, and Isabella in *The Fatal Marriage*], she forc'd Tears from the Eyes of her Auditory, especially those who have any Sense of Pity for the Distress't."

She had acted in all of the plays Thomas Otway had written up to 1680, and the playwright had tailored roles to her special talent. He also, perhaps, starting as early as his first association with her in April 1678, developed the hopeless passion for his favorite actress that he later proclaimed in a series of heart-rending letters. When *The Orphan* came out, Mrs Barry's liaison with Rochester was probably ended, and in any case he died on 26 July 1680. Whether or not she gave Otway any en-

ELIZABETH BARRY and ANNE BRACE-
GIRDLE

a detail from a large painting by Kneller of
William III

couragement at this time is not known, but
she may have, and some of his letters may
have been written this early; most of them,
however, probably date from 1682 when
he created another great role for her.

By the 1680–81 season Elizabeth Barry
was the leading lady in the Duke's Company, usually playing opposite Betterton,
then in his prime. During this season she
acted, among other parts, the title role in
*The Princess of Cleve*, Athenais in *Theodosius*, Leonora in *The Spanish Friar*, and
Cordelia in the Tate version of *King Lear*.
She played in both comedy and tragedy, but
her temper was best suited to serious roles,

as was Betterton's, and the pair must have
been ideal for Otway's purposes when he
wrote *Venice Preserved* for them. The premiere was probably on 9 February 1682,
with Mrs Barry as Belvidera and Betterton
as Jaffeir.

If Mrs Barry excelled in exciting pity in
spectators when she acted tragic roles, in
her private life she drove men wild when
she acted the jilt—especially when the man
in question was Otway. She was free with
herself, and Otway knew it; there had been
Rochester, there was Sir George Etherege,
and there was possibly Sir Henry St John,
Bt., father of the Tory statesman, apparently among others. They received some
satisfaction from her, but Otway, who had
made her the gift of his talent, was only
tormented by her indifference. His letters
to her, written about this time, were not
published until 1697 (anonymously) and
not attributed to Otway until 1713. They
have now been accepted as his, and they reveal as much about Mrs Barry as they do
about the poet.

The first letter strikes the main theme:
"I love you, I dote on you; Desire makes
me mad, when I am near you; and Despair,
when I am from you. . . . I lov'd you
early; and no sooner had I beheld that soft
bewitching Face of yours, but I felt in my
Heart the very Foundation of all my Peace
give way: But when you became another's,
I must confess that I did then rebel." Yet
he could not forget her: "Your Commands
have been always sacred to me; your
Smiles have always transported me, and
your Frowns aw'd me." The second letter
mentioned "the Child your Bowels are
most fond of," Betty, who was perhaps by
now back with her mother.

The third makes an unexplained comment: "Since you are going to quit the
World, I think my self obliged as a Member of that World to divert you from so ill
natur'd an Inclination; therefore by reason
your Visits will take up so much of this
Day, I have debarr'd my self the oppor-

tunity of waiting on you this Afternoon, that I may take a time you are more Mistress of." If Elizabeth Barry had considered retiring from the stage, this would seem to be the only reference we have; perhaps she had, or perhaps she had simply tantalized Otway with a false suggestion that she might retire.

In the fourth letter is a clearer indication of Mrs Barry's response to Otway's passion, and of a magnetic quality she must have had onstage and off:

Everything you do is a new Charm to me; and though I have languish'd for seven long tedious Years of Desire, jealousy and despairing; yet, every Minute I see you, I still discover something new and more bewitching. Consider how I love you, what would not renounce, or enterprize for you? I must have you mine, or I am miserable; and nothing but knowing which shall be the happy hour can make the rest of my Life that are to come tolerable. Give me a word or two of comfort, or resolve never to look with common goodness on me more, for I cannot bear a kind Look, and after it a cruel Denial. This Minute my Heart akes for you, and if I cannot have a Right in yours, I wish it would ake till I could complain to you no longer.

And the fifth is even more explicit:

You cannot but be sensible that I am blind, or you would not so openly discover what a ridiculous Tool you make of me. I should be glad to discover whose satisfaction I was sacrific'd to this Morning; for I am sure your own ill nature could not be guilty of inventing such an Injury to me, meerly to try how much I could bear . . . [Y]our whole Bus'ness is to pick ill-natur'd Conjectures out of my harmless freedom of Conversation, to vex and gall me with . . . I cannot bear the thought of being made a Property either of another Man's good Fortune, or the Vanity of a Woman that designs nothing but to plague me.

Part of Otway's torment was probably of his own making, yet the letters, plus other evidence, point to Mrs Barry's sometimes being capricious, cruel, taunting, mercenary, faithless—but always captivating.

Of the other men in her life at this time and later less is known. To Etherege she was apparently warmer than she was to the impecunious Otway, though Etherege called her a jilt; she is said to have had a child by him and he is supposed to have settled £5000 or £6000 on Mrs Barry, but there is no evidence of any other child than Betty, and it is unlikely that Etherege had so great a fortune as to be that extravagant with his money. The Earl of Dorset was reputed to have had an affair with Mrs Barry at some point, according to *The School of Venus* (1715), but that may have been a fiction. She was free with her affections, certainly (except to Otway), and later satirists were to be merciless in their attacks on her private life.

In 1682 the King's and Duke's companies united, and in the new troupe Elizabeth Barry was still the acknowledged leader among the actresses. Otway wrote one more role for her, Porcia in *The Atheist*, which she played in July 1683 at Dorset Garden. During the life of the United Company (1682–95) she acted mostly at Drury Lane, playing, among other roles, Olivia in *The Plain Dealer*, Lucina in Rochester's *Valentinian*, the Queen of England in *Richard III*, Mrs Loveit in *The Man of Mode*, Laetitia in *The Old Bachelor*, and Lady Touchwood in *The Double Dealer*. For a few other roles from this period we fortunately have some commentary.

She acted Isabella in *Mustapha*, perhaps on 6 October 1686 (though no cast was listed), the role Curll assigned her in the mid-1670's for her debut. She would have been suited for it now, and Curll said that Mrs Barry so pleased the Duchess of York "that from Mrs Barry she learned to improve in the English Language, made her a Present of her Wedding-Suit, and favoured her in so particular a Manner, not only whilst Dutchess, but when Queen, it is said, she gave Her her Coronation Robes to act Queen Elizabeth, in the Earl of Essex [Banks's *The Unhappy Favorite*]."

Another Curll story must refer to this same period. One of Elizabeth Barry's important roles, which she started playing as early as, or earlier than, March 1690, was Roxana in *The Rival Queens*. At one performance, possibly during the 1689–90 season (though the incident could also belong to the period 1694–96), she had an almost mortal combat with Mrs Bowtell, who was playing Statira. They

unfortunately had some Dispute about a veil which Mrs. *Boutel* by the Partiality of the Property-Man obtained; this offending the haughty *Roxana*, they had warm Disputes behind the Scenes, which spirited the Rivals with such a natural Resentment to each other, they were so violent in performing their Parts, and acted with such Vivacity, that *Statira* on hearing the King was nigh, *begs the Gods to help her for that Moment*; on which *Roxana* hastening the designed Blow, struck with such Force, that tho' the Point of the Dagger was blunted, it made way through Mrs. *Boutel's* Stayes, and entered about a Quarter of an Inch in the Flesh.

(Curll then went on to say that some Londoners thought the dispute stemmed from Mrs Barry being jealous of Mrs Bowtell and Rochester, but this would place the incident about 1677, when the play was the property of the King's Company and Mrs Barry could not have acted in it.) Mrs Barry's Cassandra in *Cleomenes* in mid-April 1692 drew the praise of the author, Dryden, though one would wish he had been more specific: "Mrs Barry, always Excellent, has, in this tragedy excell'd Herself, and gain'd a Reputation beyond any Woman I have ever seen on the Theatre." It would be useful, too, to have more information on her playing of her third most memorable role, Isabella in *The Fatal Marriage*, which she created in February

1694; a surviving unidentified letter of 22 March said, "I never saw Mrs Barry act with so much passion as she does in it; I could not forbear being moved even to tears to see her act."

In addition to her commanding position as an actress, Mrs Barry became increasingly involved during the late 1680's with the finances of the United Company, sometimes (as on 8 May 1686) being named in warrants from the Lord Chamberlain's office to receive payments for plays performed by the troupe before royalty. This led, in later years, to her serving with Betterton as a co-manager. What she may have been paid at this time is not known, though Cibber said she was the first performer to receive a benefit in addition to her regular salary; this happened, Cibber said, during the reign of James II, but not until later in the century did it become a common practice.

The passion with which Elizabeth Barry acted, her enviable financial security, her haughtiness, and her promiscuity were bound to be lampooned, and one of the earliest and most scurrilous attacks was in the anonymous *Satyr on the Players* of about 1684:

> *There's one Heav'n bless us! by her*
> *cursed Pride*
> *Thinks from ye world her Brutish Lust to*
> *hide*
> *But will that pass in her, whose only*
> *Sence*
> *Does lye in Whoring, Cheats, & Impu-*
> *dence?*
> *One that is Pox all o're, Barry her Name,*
> *That mercenary Prostituted Dame, . . .*

In late April 1688 Mrs Barry became ill when playing Barzana in the premiere of Crowne's *Darius*. The author commented on it in his dedication when the play was printed:

A misfortune fell upon this play, that might very well dizzy the judgments of my audience.

Just before the play began, Mrs Barry was struck with a very violent fever, that took all the spirit from her, by consequence from the play; the scenes she acted fell dead from her; and in the fourth act her distemper grew so much upon her, she cou'd go no farther, but all her part in the act was wholly cut out, and neither spoke nor read.

On 5 May Lord Granville wrote to Sir William Leveson: "she was forced to be carried off, and instead of dying in jest was in danger of doing it in earnest." The illness was probably as serious as he intimated, for she did practically no further acting until the fall of 1689. There may have been a connection between this incident and the death of her daughter, but too many details are missing to be certain. In 1689 an unknown author wrote a poem "To the most Virtuous and most devoted Overkind, Notorious Mad^m Barry:"

> *Retyre thou Miser from thy Shop the*
> *Stage*
> *Retyrement will befit thy Sins and Age:*
> *The Vitious Treasure thy base ways have*
> *gain'd,*
> *Which for thy Daughters sake was still*
> *obtain'd,*
> *Give to some Pious Use, or thou'lt be*
> *damn'd.*

This was a cruel attack, apparently written shortly after Mrs Barry's daughter died in 1689; if young Betty had a prolonged illness before her death, Mrs Barry's collapse in April 1688 and her absence from the stage during the months following may well have been caused by this private calamity.

In late 1694 the situation of many of the older players in the United Company under manager Christopher Rich became so intolerable that, with Betterton as their leader, they petitioned for a separate license (granted on 25 March 1695) and withdrew to form their own troupe at Lincoln's Inn Fields. In the documents connected with the rebellion, Mrs Barry appears to have been second in command to Betterton, and with Mrs Bracegirdle as a third party, they managed the new company for several years. The documents also reveal that her financial situation about this time was very sound indeed: in April 1693 she had been able to loan Alexander Davenant £400 in return for a share in the United Company, and her salary by 1694 was 50s. weekly plus an annual benefit which, if it did not bring in £70, would be made up to that figure by the management.

The satirists could not let her financial status go unheeded; Tom Brown in his *Amusements* (c. 1695) pictured Betterton and Mrs Barry:

Now for that majestical man and woman there; stand off, there is no coming within a hundred yeards of their high mightiness. They have revolted, like the Dutch, from their once lords and masters, and are now set up for sovereigns themselves. See what a deference is paid 'em by the rest of the cringing fraternity, from fifty down to ten shillings a-week; you must needs have a more than ordinary opinion of their abilities. Should you lie with her all night she would not know you next morning, unless you had another five pounds at her service . . . nor will her celebrated modesty suffer her to speak to an humble servant, without a piece or two to rub her eyes with and to conceal her blushes; while she sluggishly goes through a vacation she might take more pains in, did she not grudge a pennyworth for a penny.

There would seem, indeed, little reason for Mrs Barry to have acted during her summer vacations, especially so "sluggishly," unless she was as mercenary as the satires of the time indicate.

Mercenary Mrs Barry may have been, but careless about her acting she was not, according to most other sources, and Brown may have been exaggerating. After the new company opened at Lincoln's Inn Fields on 30 April 1695 with *Love for Love* (with Mrs Barry as Mrs Frail), she continued acting a remarkably heavy schedule and was frequently praised for the care with which she prepared all roles, good or bad. Gildon reported Betterton as saying,

Whereas it has always been mine and Mrs. *Barry*'s Practice to consult e'en the most indifferent Poet in any Part we have thought fit to accept of; and I may say it of her, she has often so exerted her self in an indifferent Part, that her Acting has given Success to such Plays, as to read would turn a Man's Stomach; and tho I could never pretend to do so much Service that way as she has done, yet I have never been wanting in my Endeavours.

Mrs Manley was perhaps one of those "indifferent" playwrights who gained from Mrs Barry's willingness to do her best even in imperfect roles. In *The Royal Mischief* (1696) Mrs Manley said, "Mrs. Barry, who by all that saw her [as Homais, in April] is concluded to have exceeded that perfection which before she was justly thought to have arrived at; my Obligations to her were the greater, since against her own approbation, she excell'd and made the part of an ill Woman, not only entertaining, but admirable." And when Dilke's *The City Lady* was done in December 1696 with Mrs Barry as Lady Grumble, the author wrote, "I think my self oblig'd to applaud the Justice I receiv'd from the Incomparable Mrs Barry." Even in roles written for others Mrs Barry excelled; Aston wrote that she "outshin'd Mrs. *Bracegirdle* in the character of ZARA in the *Mourning Bride* [acted on 20 February 1697], altho' Mr. *Congreve* design'd Almeria for that Favour."

Mrs Barry may have contemplated marriage about this time, though the only reference to it seems to be another satire, "On Three Late Marriages" (c. 1696) in the manuscript "Choyce Collection" at Ohio State University:

*At thyrty eight a very hopefull whore,*
*The onely one o' th' trade that's not profuse.*
*(A policy was taught her by the Jews),*
*Tho' still the highest bidder shee will choose.*

The satire referred to her as "slattern Betty Barry" but probably contained more gossip than truth.

The theatrical records for the last few years of the seventeenth century contain many gaps, but at least a few of Mrs Barry's more important roles are known. She was the original Lady Brute in *The Provoked Wife* in mid-April 1697; in November 1697 she had the title role in *Boadicea*; she was Armida in *Rinaldo and Armida* in November 1698; in December 1699 she played the Queen in *Iphigenia*; and on 5 March 1700 she acted Mrs Marwood in the premiere of *The Way of the World*. No commentary seems to have survived in connection with these roles, though a rather pleasant letter from Mrs Barry to Lady Lisburne dated 5 January 1699 spoke of her part in Dennis's work: "As for the little affairs of our house I never knew a worse Winter only we have had pretty good success in the opera Rinaldo and Armida where the poet made me command the Sea the earth and Air." There is a slightly amused air about her comment that suggests that the capricious and bedevilling Elizabeth Barry of earlier years had mellowed at about 41 into a trouper. She was playing mostly more mature characters now, having given up her youthful parts, very sensibly, to the younger Anne Bracegirdle, and her concentration appears to have been on tragic roles and, in comedy, the parts with darker hues.

About 1700 Robert Gould published his satire, *The Playhouse*, an attack on a number of players that seems to have been written about 1685 and revised before publication. Gould had been a friend of Otway and was furious after the playwright's unnecessary death at the treatment Otway had received at the hands of Mrs Barry:

The shame, the guilt, the horror and dis-
    grace,
Light on the Punk, the Murderer and the
    Place.
. . . . . . . . . . . . . . .
How well do those deserve the general
    hiss,
That will converse with such a thing as
    this?
A ten times cast off Drab, in Venus Wars
Who counts her Sins, may as well count
    the Stars.
So insolent! it is by all allow'd
There never was so base a thing, so
    proud:
Yet Covetous, she'll prostitute with any,
Rather than waive the getting of a penny;
For the whole Harvest of her youthful
    Crimes
She hoards, to keep her self in future
    times,
That by her gains now she may then be
    fed,
Which in effect's to damn herself for
    bread.
Yet in her Morals this is thought the
    best;
Imagine then the lewdness of the rest.

(The last five lines appear in a slightly different form in Summers's *The Restoration Theatre*.)

This portion of the satire, which seems to date about 1685, may have circulated at that time, or Gould may have been responsible for the *Satyr on the Players* (c. 1684), for in 1696 when he brought his play *The Rival Sisters* to Betterton and Mrs Barry, they were cool to it, and Mrs Barry is supposed to have said, "I am not so good a *Christian* as to forgive." Other parts of the satire belong to 1700, including one section that calls Mrs Barry "Zara" and introduces the comedian Joe Haines:

And hence has Zara all her Thousands
    got:

Zara! that Proud, Opprobious, Shameless
    Jilt,
Who like a Devil justifies her Guilt,
And feels no least Remorse for all the
    Blood sh'has spilt.
But prithee Joe, 'since so she boasts her
    Blood,
And few have yet her Lineage under-
    stood,
Tell me, in short, the Harlot's true De-
    scent,
'Twill be a Favour that you shan't repent.

    Truly said Joe, as now the Matter goes,
What I shall speak must be beneath the
    Rose.
Her mother was a common Strumpet
    known,
Her Father half the Rabble of the Town.
Begot by Casual and Promiscuous Lust,
She still retains the same Promiscuous
    Gust,
For Birth into a Suburb Cellar hurl'd,
The Strumpet came up Stairs into the
    World.
At Twelve she'd freely in Coition join,
And far surpass'd the Honours of her
    Line.
As her Conception was a Complication,
So its Produce, alike, did serve the
    Nation;
Till by a Black, Successive Course of Ills,
She reach'd the Noble Post which now
    she fills;
Where, Messalina like, she treads the
    Stage,
And all Enjoys, but nothing can
    Asswage!

After all that venom, it is a relief to turn to a less caustic but still critical commentary, *A Comparison Between the Two Stages* (1702). One of the characters, Critick, notes that for *The Orphan* Otway had "some of the best Tragedians in the World to Act it, and who knows not the Advantage a Play receives from their Mouths? Who knows not the effect of *Betterton*'s fine Action? Who is not charm'd with Mrs. *Barry*? What Beauty do they not give every thing they represent?"

In another place in *A Comparison* Sullen calls her "Cleopatra," a role in *All for Love* which she must have played by this time, though no performance date is known. "By that Nickname," replies Critick, "so unfortunate to poor Anthony, as the other has been to many an honest Country Gentleman, I shou'd guess whom you mean. . . . In her time she has been the very Spirit of Action every way; Nature made her for the delight of Mankind; and till Nature began to decay in her, all the Town shar'd her Bounty." Ramble then enters the discussion: "I do think that Person the finest Woman in the World upon the Stage, and the ugliest Woman off on't." Sullen agrees: "Age and Intemperance are the fatal Enemies of Beauty; she's guilty of both, she has been a Riotter in her time, but the edge of her Appetite is long ago taken off, she still charms (as you say) upon the Stage, and even off I don't think so rudely of her as you do: 'Tis true, Time has turn'd up some of her Furrows, but not to such a degree."

Sullen was right, and Mrs Barry in 1702 still had some of her best performing years ahead of her. Before her temporary retirement in 1708 she played a number of significant parts in addition to her old ones: Calista in *The Fair Penitent*, Lady Easy in *The Careless Husband*, Mrs Ford in *The Merry Wives of Windsor*, Calpurnia in *Julius Caesar*, Evadne in *The Maid's Tragedy*, Queen Katherine in *Henry VIII*, and, on 27 December 1707, the role one would have expected her to have done much sooner, Lady Macbeth. Though she must have been adequate in this role, Cibber pointed out that Mrs Barry "could not in that Part, with all her superior Strength and Melody of Voice, throw out those quick and careless Strokes of Terror from the Disorder of a guilty Mind" that Mrs Betterton had earlier done, and Lady Macbeth seems not to have been one of her better roles.

She was still in full command of her powers, however. After she played Sakia in Dennis's *Liberty Asserted* on 24 February 1704, the author paid her a handsome compliment:

This Play indeed receiv'd all the Grace and Ornament of Action in most of the principal Parts, and in all the Womens. But that of *Sakia* by Mrs. *Barry* was acted so admirably and inimitably, as that no Stage in *Europe* can boast of any thing that comes near to her Performance; or if the Foreign Stages can shew any thing like it, they are at least prodigiously improv'd since I was upon the Continent. That incomparable Actress changing like Nature which she represents, from Passion to Passion, from Extream to Extream, with piercing Force, and with easie Grace, changes the Hearts of all who see her with irresistible Pleasure.

For this excellence Mrs Barry was probably being paid £150 annually, or, if profits were insufficient, a minimum of £120. Only Betterton, by virtue of the extra pay he received for training the younger actors, had a higher salary.

From 1705 to the spring of 1708 the Betterton troupe was playing at the Queen's Theatre in the Haymarket, after which they moved to Drury Lane. Mrs Barry played Sophonisba on 17 June 1708 and then retired from the stage temporarily. On 7 April 1709 she came back for a sentimental benefit for Betterton, playing Mrs Frail in *Love for Love* and speaking an epilogue written by Rowe.

It was with Mrs Barry's retirement in mind that Steele wrote an amusing piece on 26 April 1709 in *The Tatler*, describing how he would like to have his funeral arranged:

[S]ince all mourners are mere actors on these occasions, I shall desire those who are professedly such to attend mine. I humbly, therefore, beseech Mrs Barry to act once more, and be my widow. When she swoons away at the church-porch, I appoint the merry Sir John Falstaff [probably Betterton], and the gay Sir

Harry Wildair [probably Robert Wilks], to support her. . . . To make up the rest of the appearance, I desire all the ladies from the balconies to weep with Mrs. Barry, as they hope to be wives and widows themselves.

Mrs Barry returned to the stage full time in 1709–10 at the Queen's Theatre, playing Queen Elizabeth in *The Unhappy Favorite*, Isabella in *The Fatal Marriage*, the Queen in *The Spanish Friar*, Angelica in *The Rover*, Margaretta in *Rule a Wife and Have a Wife*, Alcmena in *Amphitryon*, Lady Easy in *The Careless Husband*, Lady Cockwood in *She Would If She Could*, Lady Macbeth, Almeria in *The Indian Emperor*, the Queen in *Edward III*, and, at Betterton's last appearance on 13 April 1710, Evadne in *The Maid's Tragedy*. Her last appearance was on 13 June when she played Lady Easy.

Though Mrs Barry went into retirement, she was still kept on the company books at £100 annually and was promised a benefit before the end of April with £40 house charges. Her roles were passed on to Mrs Rogers and Mrs Bradshaw, but a promising young tragedienne, Mary Porter, who had been discovered at Bartholomew Fair by Mrs Barry and Mrs Bracegirdle, was soon to succeed to most of Mrs Barry's great roles.

Still a spinster, Elizabeth Barry retired to the quiet of Acton, apparently well off financially, but, according to Curll, beginning to feel an "inward decay." She had not been forced, as had Betterton, to act past her prime to earn a living, and her last season had probably seen her still in command of most of her powers. In 1713, according to Davies, she was bitten by her favorite lap dog, who was discovered to have rabies. On 4 November, "sick in body," she drew up her will. To a Mr Gabriel Ballam she gave her estate at Newbury, consisting of mills; to a Mrs Cary, £20; to Mrs Hawker, wife of the painter Thomas, £20; to a Mrs Phubs, £20; to

Anne Bracegirdle, £20 (probably for mourning) plus £200 "to save M$^{rs}$ Bracegirdle harmless from any debt of the Play-House"; and to her executors John Custis and Abigal Stackhouse she left the rest of her estate. Her bequest to Anne Bracegirdle, who probably did not need it, is most revealing; the two actresses were of quite opposite temperaments, and one might have expected them to be cool toward one another, but they were, it appears, warm friends. On 7 November 1713, when she was about 55, Elizabeth Barry died; she was buried in the churchyard at Acton where, according to Curll, her daughter Betty had been buried in 1689. The memorial there describes Mrs Barry as from the parish of St Mary le Savoy. Her will was proved on the day of her death. (As late as 1 March 1747—or possibly 1747/48—administration of the residue of this estate was granted to Mary Sayer, formerly Overton, wife of James Sayer; Mrs Sayer was the administratrix of the estate of Abigail Overton, formerly Stackhouse, wife of Philip Overton).

In Gildon's *Life of Mr. Thomas Betterton* (1710), Betterton was quoted as saying that Mrs Barry's acting was "always just, and produc'd naturally by the Sentiments of the Part, which she acts, and she every where observes those Rules prescrib'd to the Poets by *Horace*, and which equally reach the Actors." Whereupon Gildon provided Lord Roscommon's translation of the pertinent passage:

*We weep and laugh as we see others do,*
*He only makes me sad, who shews the*
*          way,*
*And first is sad himself; Then* Telephus
*I feel the Weight of your Calamities,*
*And fancy all your Miseries my own;*
*But if you* ACT *them ill I sleep or laugh.*
*Your Look must needs alter as your*
*          Subject does,*
*From kind to fierce, from wanton to*
*          serene.*
*For Nature forms and softens us within,*

*And writes our Fortune's Changes in our
Face.*
*Pleasure enchants, impetuous Rage
transports,*
*And Grief dejects, and wrings the
tortur'd Soul;*
*And these are all interpreted by Speech.*
*But he, whose Words and Fortunes
disagree,*
*Absurd, unpity'd grows a public Jest.*

Gildon then had Betterton continue:

She indeed always enters into her Part, and
is the Person she represents. Thus I have
heard her say, that she never said, *Ah! poor
Castalio!* in the *Orphan*, without weeping.
And I have frequently observ'd her change her
Countenance several Times as the Discourse
of others on the Stage have affected her in
the Part she acted. This is being thoroughly
concern'd, this is to know her Part, this is to
express the Passions in the Countenance and
Gesture.

Her acting was frequently, like Betterton's,
called just or judicious, suggesting a high
degree of control over her work, despite
the high pitch of the emotions she portrayed.

Though in the early days she had had
difficulty with her ear—and consequently
her voice—she must have remedied this as
she gained experience, for she was frequently praised for her power and melody.
Cibber tried to describe it:

I take it for granted that the Objection to Mrs.
Barry at that time must have been a defective
Ear, or some unskilful Dissonance in her manner of pronouncing. . . . [But in time she
gained] a Presence of elevated Dignity, her
Mein and Motion superb and gracefully ma-
jestick; her Voice full, clear, and strong, so
that no Violence of Passion could be too much
for her: And when Distress or Tenderness
possess'd her, she subsided into the most affecting Melody and Softness. In the Art of exciting Pity she had a Power beyond all the
Actresses I have yet seen, or what your Imagination can conceive. Of the former of these

two great Excellencies she gave the most delightful Proofs in almost all the Heroic Plays
of *Dryden* and *Lee*; and of the latter, in the
softer Passions of *Otway's Monimia* and
*Belvidera*. In Scenes of Anger, Defiance, or
Resentment, while she was impetuous and terrible, she pour'd out the Sentiment with an
enchanting Harmony.

Despite the control that Mrs Barry obviously exercized over her voice and body,
she, like Betterton, strove for what would
then have seemed a natural quality. Curll
quoted Mrs Bradshaw as saying that Mrs
Barry taught her a useful rule: "to make
herself Mistress of her Part, and leave the
*Figure* and *Action* to *Nature*." Curll himself was especially taken with Mrs Barry's
Roxana in *The Rival Queens*; in her jealousy speech she "seemed to feel a Fever
within, which by Debate and Reason she
would quench. This was not done in a
ranting Air, but as if she were strugling
with her Passions, and trying to get the
Mastery of them." Cibber, too, liked her
best in compassionate roles, or in "the no-
bler Love of *Cleopatra*, or the tempestuous
Jealousy of *Roxana*" to which she brought
such a feeling of reality.

Anthony Aston, typically, commented
very specifically on her acting. In tragedy
he found her solemn and august, in comedy
alert, easy and genteel, pleasant in face
and action, and full of variety in her gestures. Her face, he said, "somewhat preceded her Action, as the latter did her
Words, her Face ever expressing the Passions." He thought she had no "tone" in
her speaking, like most actors of her day,
but apparently that was better than many
of the mid-eighteenth-century performers
who had too much; precisely what he
meant by tone is not certain, but it seems
to have been what Victor called "the good
old manner of singing and quavering out
. . . tragic notes." The chances are that
for a barnstorming comedian like Aston,
Mrs Barry was *too* natural.

What is most remarkable about Mrs

Barry is that she was able to conquer not only a vocal deficiency, but a physical one as well. She dazzled audiences with a beauty she did not have. Aston was, again, very candid about her looks: "She was not handsome, her mouth opening most on the right side, which she strove to draw t'other way, and at times composing her face, as if sitting to have her picture drawn—she was middle-sized and had darkish hair, light eyes, dark eyebrows, and was indifferent plump. . . . She could neither sing nor dance, no, not in a Country-Dance." When *The Rape* was produced on 19 January 1692, Shadwell helped the playwright Brady get it on the stage; he wanted Mrs Barry for a role and wrote to the Earl of Dorset that "I would have had it acted in Roman habits and then w$^{th}$ a Mantle to have covered her hips Mrs Barry would have acted y$^e$ part." But she managed to radiate a kind of beauty, captivating men quite completely, and Curll noted that she had "a peculiar Smile . . . which made her look the most genteely malicious Person that can be imagined."

Otway was probably right in the little poem he wrote for "Under Mrs. B——'s Picture" by Kneller:

> *I am the Famous She, Whose moving*
> *Arts*
> *Give Life to Poetry, to Poets Fame:*
> *I Charm Spectators Eyes, and Chain their*
> *Hearts,*
> *'Till their Applause and Love are but*
> *the same.*

Kneller used Mrs Barry as an emblematic figure in his painting of William III at Hampton Court; she is pictured kneeling, as Britannia, and beside her stands Anne Bracegirdle as Flora. Another Kneller at Strawberry Hill served as the basis for the Knight engraving published in Harding's *The Biographical Mirror*, and a third, done by Kneller in preparation for the Hampton Court painting, is now in the possession of Mr Cyril Hughes Hartmann.

The Garrick Club has a painting after Kneller, similar to the one at Strawberry Hill. A portrait by Dahl has been reported at the City of York Art Gallery; it may represent Mrs Barry as Magdalen. The Duke of Buccleuch's collection includes a group picture, based on the Hampton Court Kneller, but showing Mrs Barry as Abundance rather than Britannia. The Huntington Library reports an anonymous engraving of Mrs Barry different from the Harding-Knight, and the frontispiece to Rowe's 1709 *Shakespeare* shows Mrs Barry as Gertrude, with Betterton as Hamlet, but their features are hardly distinguishable.

The Hartmann and Hampton Court Knellers capture best Mrs Barry's magnetic intensity—the quality that made her the first great English actress and helped her set a standard which few of her successors could achieve.

**Barry, Mrs I.** *See* **BARRY, THOMAS.**

**Barry, Spranger** *1717?–1777, actor, manager.*

According to early sources, Spranger Barry was born in Skinner Row, Dublin, on 20 November 1719, a date which would suit the information in the *Westminster Abbey Registers* to the effect that when he died in January 1777 he was 57 years of age. In *Notes and Queries*, 2 October 1948, however, J. W. Montague-Smith cited his baptismal entry at St Werburgh's, Dublin, on 13 November 1717. (Another Spranger Barry, presumably his elder brother who died young, was buried at St Nicholas Without, Dublin, on 20 June 1716.)

Spranger's parents were William Barry, a wealthy silversmith of Skinner Row, and his wife Catherine. William Barry was evidently a son of Edmund Barry, whose marriage to Catherine Sprainger, daughter of Thomas Sprainger, was mentioned by Archdall in his edition of Lodge's *Peerage of Ireland*. Edmund, Spranger's grandfather, born 17 April 1639, was the second son of the Reverend William Barry, rector of Killucan, who in turn was the younger brother of Sir James Barry of Santry Court, created Lord Santry in 1662 and later made Lord Chief Justice. The Barrys can be traced through Lord Santry back to Sir Robert Barry of the Rock, County Cork, who lived during the early part of the fifteenth century and was a brother of an early antecedent of the Earls of Barrymore.

Apprenticed to his father, who brought him up in his silversmith business, Spranger Barry was intended for retail trade. With a "tolerable fortune" from his father and a £1500 dowry from his first wife, Anne, he set up in a "mechanical business," but about the third or fourth year of his marriage, according to *Theatrical Biography*, mismanagement brought on bankruptcy. (He may also have been a publican. The Office of the Registry of Deeds, Dublin, records a sale of the Black Lion by Spranger Barry to one Thomas Sutton on 18 January 1740.)

His impulse to perform apparently inflamed by frequent visits to the theatre, and possessed of a handsome figure and a fine voice, Barry turned next to acting. He made his first appearance "on any stage" as Othello at the Aungier Street Theatre, Dublin, on 15 February 1744; according to Chetwood, the prompter who took credit for instructing him in the "first rudiments," Barry "seem'd a finish'd Actor dropt from the Clouds." He next played Pierre in *Venice Preserv'd* and Varanes in *Theodosius*. On 2 March 1744 he took a benefit at Smock Alley Theatre as Othello and another at Aungier Street on 26 April (when his address was given as Skinner Row).

Barry's immediate emergence as a first-class actor gave impetus to the flagging fortunes of the Aungier Street and Smock Alley theatres, both under the same management. Hitchcock could not conceive of a figure "more perfect" and described a voice "the harmony and melody of whose silver tones were resistless." According to the *Theatrical Review* (1757), nature had been so favorable in her gifts that "she did it with a view to fit him out for the exhibition of Othello," the graces of his manly beauty blended with a majesty and a softness, "as equally to make him look the warrior, command the respect due to a general, and make the greatest excess of love appear natural." When Barry later played the role in London, Francis Gentleman wrote that if any performer had been born to play one part in particular, it was Barry for the Moor. Garrick, who realized that in this instance at least all the advantage was with Barry, gave up playing Othello himself.

Barry continued for the next two seasons at Smock Alley, where he worked with Samuel Foote, Thomas Sheridan, and two other young actors, David Garrick and

*Harvard Theatre Collection*

SPRANGER BARRY, when a young man

artist unknown

George Anne Bellamy. He had an especially busy season in 1745–46, playing Bajazet in *Tamerlane*, Castalio in *The Orphan* (with Sheridan as Polydore, Garrick as Chamont, and Miss Bellamy as Monimia), Antony in *All for Love*, Torrismond in *The Spanish Fryar*, Edgar in *King Lear*, Orestes in *The Distrest Mother*, Varanes in *Theodosius*, Altamont in *The Fair Penitent*, Hotspur in *1 Henry IV*, the title role in *Oroonoko*, and Pierre in *Venice Preserv'd*, happily establishing for himself the name of the "Irish Roscius."

In May 1746 he missed several performances when he had the misfortune to be overturned in a coach. At about this time he had a dispute with Sheridan, his manager, and wrote to Garrick at London on 6 June 1746 that he had not received a penny of his salary since Garrick had left Dublin at the end of that season. James Lacy, the manager of Drury Lane, had offered Barry a bonus of £100, "by way of a present," to engage for one or more seasons, but Barry told Garrick—who had written to friends that Barry was the best lover that he had ever seen on the stage— that he preferred to link his future with him. Barry was prepared to stay at Dublin if Garrick planned to return the next winter or to go to England to assist in any scheme Garrick would promote. As it turned out, Garrick engaged at Covent Garden for 1746–47. Barry accepted Lacy's offer and made his debut at Drury Lane on 4 October 1746 in the role of Othello. In a letter to Horace Walpole on 20 October 1746, Thomas Gray described the impression Barry made upon him:

he is upwards of six Foot in Height, well & proportionally made, treads well & knows what to do with his Limbs; in short a noble graceful Figure; I can say nothing of his Face, but that it was all Black, with a wide Mouth & good Eyes. his Voice is of a clear & pleasing tone. . . . when high strained it is apt to crack a little & be hoarse; but in its common Pitch, & when it sinks into any softer Passion,

*Harvard Theatre Collection*

SPRANGER BARRY, as Alexander

artist unknown

particularly expressive & touching. in the first Scenes, especially where he recounts to the Senate the Progress of his Love, & the Means he used to win Desdamona, he was quite mistaken, & I took a Pique against him: instead of a Cool Narration he flew into a Rant of Voice & Actions, as tho' he were relating the Circumstances of a Battle that was fought yesterday. I expected nothing more from him, but was deceived: in the Scenes of Rage & Jealousy he was seldom inferior to Quin: in the Parts of Tenderness & Sorrow far above him. these latter seem to be his peculiarly: his Action is not very various, but rarely improper, or without Dignity: & some of his Attitudes are really fine. he is not perfect to be sure; but I think he may make a better Player than any now on the Stage in a little while.

Other critics confirmed Gray's impression. *A Guide for the Stage* (1751) observed that the youthful Othello did not please the judgment as well as he struck the eye and that grace was not sufficient compensation for unemphatic speech, but it forecast Barry's ripening into "a proper manhood." The early applause Barry received, it was stated, "was in consequence of what he promis'd, not what he perform'd."

His first season at Drury Lane was extraordinarily ambitious. After opening with Othello (which he played 14 times more that season, once by command of the Prince and Princess of Wales on 17 October), he acted Macbeth on 7 November 1746 (and six times more). "Barry ought not to have attempted that which was so opposite to his natural manner," wrote Davies of the less-than-successful performance. For Francis Gentleman, Barry "made but a lukewarm affair of Macbeth, his amorous harmony of features and voice could but faintly, if at all, describe passions incident to a tyrant, in such circumstances."

There was no question whatever, however, about his suitability for his next role, that of Castalio in *The Orphan* on 15 November, with Lacy as Chamont, Delane Polydore, and Mrs Giffard Monimia. In five consecutive nights of the play's run (and again on 10 December, 27 January, and 2 March), Barry established himself without reservation as the Town's foremost sighing lover. Gray, very impressed, in a letter to Chute on 23 November 1746 confirmed his insistence that Barry might become the best player on the stage—presumably even better than Garrick—and wrote, "I am glad Castalio has justified himself & me to You. he seem'd . . . more made for Tenderness than Horrour." Barry then acted Varanes in *Theodosius* on 15 December (and four times more), Lord Townley in *The Provok'd Husband* on 3 January (and 15 times more), and Hotspur on 15 January (and three times more)—Davies thought Hotspur to be

outside his range: "there is a military pride and camp-humour, if I may indulge the expression, to which Barry was a stranger" —Antony in *All for Love* on 26 February (and four times more), Pierre in *Venice Preserv'd* on 16 and 17 February, Bevil Junior in *The Conscious Lovers* on 12 March (and four times more), Hamlet on 24 March and 11 April, and Antony in *Julius Caesar* on 28 March and 2 April.

In 1747–48, Barry continued at Drury Lane (that theatre having newly come under Garrick's management) while living in the corner house on the west side of Bow Street, formerly Will's Coffee House. His line of capital roles included Bajazet in *Tamerlane*, Dumont in *Jane Shore*, Horatio in *The Fair Penitent*, and Orestes in *The Distrest Mother*. He played Castalio again on 15 November 1747, with Delane as Polydore, Garrick as Chamont, and Mrs Cibber as Monimia, no doubt the finest cast that ever performed the play—"they were formed by nature for the illustration of each other's talents," wrote Davies; "there was no passion of the tender kind so truely pathetic and forcible in any player as Barry, except in Mrs Cibber," who could be "styled indeed the daughter of Mr Garrick . . . but could be only the mistress or wife of Barry." For Tate Wilkinson, "Barry, without doubt, possessed the art of pleasing persuasion beyond any man I ever saw. . . . He was bewitching to hear, and dangerous to believe." Wilkinson was about 11 years old when he saw the production and recalled "Mr Barry, in Castalio, in a neat bag wig, then of the newest fashion, in his bloom and prime of life; and was certainly one of the handsomest men ever seen on or off the stage." When he saw *The Orphan* later, on 12 December 1755 at Covent Garden, Wilkinson felt Barry acted Castalio so excellently that he was the only one he wished to remember in the role. Barry had made it an overwhelming part which Wilkes said had suffered for many years "under the hands of ignorance and incapacity." In *The Actor* (1750), John Hill ascribed his success in Castalio to the fact that he was "the very first" to get the most out of the long speeches in which there was not really very much dramatic meat. Until Barry's time, Castalio had always seemed to be "not the first, but the second, sometimes the third character in the play."

Garrick and Barry, an enormous dual attraction for any repertory theatre, alternated during 1747–48 and the next season in roles such as Hamlet and Macbeth and appeared together as well in the same pieces, such as *The Orphan*, or *The Foundling* on 13 February 1748, in which Garrick played Young Belmont, and Barry Sir Charles Raymond, with Macklin as Faddle, Mrs Woffington as Rosetta, and Mrs Cibber as Fidelia. On 6 February 1749 Barry played Mahomet to Garrick's Demetrius and Mrs Pritchard's Irene in the first performance of Samuel Johnson's Tragedy *Mahomet and Irene*. Despite the best efforts of the company, the play was hissed in the fifth act, but Garrick kept it on for eight more performances in deference to his old friend Johnson. Aaron Hill, disappointed by Barry's performance of Mahomet, felt that he indulged in "an unpointed restlessness of leaping levity, that neither carried weight to suit his dignity, nor struck out purpose to express his passions"—really somewhat contrary to Barry's usual form and style.

The rivalry between the two great actors was inevitable. Barry, feeling somewhat repressed under Garrick's management, became restless; Garrick reputedly was roused to some jealousy after Barry's success as Romeo on 29 November 1748. Too often to suit Garrick, Barry was too "indisposed" to play, and the manager felt the young actor was overly involved in social pursuits. On 20 November 1749, Barry took space in the *Public Advertiser* to deny what had "been industriously given out . . . to prejudice" him, that he had "fre-

quently of late refused to act" when his health would have permitted, indignantly affirming he scorned "to make use of tricks or Evasions of this kind." At the close of the 1749–50 season he quitted Drury Lane; the prompter Cross wrote in his diary on 8 September 1750: "Mr Barry flew from his articles & engaged with Mr Rich." He was joined by the inimitable Mrs Cibber, who had not played at London in 1748–49. They provided Covent Garden with the opportunity to make a serious challenge against Drury Lane for supremacy in serious drama.

Barry made his first appearance on the Covent Garden stage on 28 September 1750 as Romeo, with Mrs Cibber as Juliet and Macklin as Mercutio, on the same night that Garrick, Miss Bellamy, and Woodward appeared in the same roles at the rival house, thus beginning the famous *Romeo and Juliet* war between the two theatres. After 12 consecutive performances at each house, the play was withdrawn from Covent Garden when Mrs Cibber tired, and a thirteenth triumphant performance was played at Drury Lane. An epigram in the *Daily Advertiser* summed up the irritation of the public over the battle:

*'Well, what's today' says angry Ned,*
*    As up from bed he rouses;*
*'Romeo again!' and shakes his head—*
*    'Ah, pox on both your houses!'*

A controversy raged for days in the coffee houses over the better Romeo. The balance of critical opinion tipped toward Barry. "The amorous harmony of Mr Barry's features, his melting eyes, and unequalled plaintiveness of voice, and his fine graceful figure gave him a great superiority," wrote Kirkman in *The Life of Macklin*. It was Wilkinson's opinion that Barry "was as much superior to Garrick in *Romeo*, as York Minster is to a Methodist Chapel." With his natural physical and vocal advantages, along with a great gift for trag-

SPRANGER BARRY, as Macbeth

by Gwinn

edy, Barry was more ideally suited to the role, but Garrick's genius, extended to its fullest by the challenge, allowed him nearly to equal Barry's performance. Gentleman in the *Dramatic Censor* reported that Garrick drew the most applause while Barry drew the most tears. The report that best summarizes the respective performances was that given by a practical female: "Had I been Juliet to Garrick's Romeo,—so ardent and impassioned was he, I should have expected he would have *come up* to me in the balcony; but had I been Juliet to Barry's Romeo,—so tender, so eloquent, and so seductive was he, I should certainly have *gone down* to him!" Mrs Garrick, who naturally preferred the performance at Drury Lane, saw Barry at Covent Garden and wrote "that Mr Barry is too jung (in his ha'd) for Romeo, & Mrs Cibber is too old for a girl of 18. . . . I wish thie

woold finish both, for it is too much for My Little Dear Spouse to Play Every Day."

Now in the zenith of his career, Barry remained at Covent Garden through 1753–54. Among the many roles he played during this period were Lothario in *The Fair Penitent* (19 January 1751), Oroonoko (22 April 1751), Phocyas in *The Siege of Damascus* (5 December 1751), Hastings in *Jane Shore* (10 November 1752), Osmyn in *Zara* (12 December 1752), and the title role in the new tragedy, *The Earl of Essex* (12 February 1753). He acted Pierre in *Venice Preserv'd* for the first time at Covent Garden on 16 December 1751 (he had played it at Smock Alley and at Drury Lane). Pierre was not one of his best roles. Arthur Murphy believed the character did not suit him—"his voice was too soft and tender for that young hero." Although Gentleman in the *Dramatic Censor* (1770) found Barry "very agreeable" in the role, the "melifluous flow of expression, and harmonious consonance of features" contradicted the public's expectation of a bold militarian, and in the critical view, Barry was pronounced an "indefensible Pierre."

On 21 December 1752, he made his first attempt at Jaffeir in the same play, a role he had not been able to play at Drury Lane after Delane gave it up because Garrick, himself, preempted it. Again the public had an opportunity to compare the two great actors in the same role, and in the words of Edward Cape Everard, they were "powerful rivals" in Jaffeir for nearly eight years. Barry enjoyed an advantage from his handsome figure and "smoothness of tone," Garrick from his energy and dignity. Each actor stressed that which he did best, and neither could excel the other in his rival's strength. Garrick could not easily make the transitions "from anger to sorrow," nor could Barry from "elegant distress" to rage and violence. Gentleman, usually partial to Garrick, admitted that the two had "such an equality of merit," that "to draw a fair parallel requires the nicest equilibre of criticism."

By 1753, Barry's first wife, Anne, presumably was dead, the last notice of her occurring at the christening of their son, also named Spranger, at St Paul, Covent Garden, on 10 August 1748. (Another son, Thomas Barry, had been born to them in Ireland in 1743.) Barry formed a liaison with young Maria Isabella Nossiter, who made her first appearance on any stage at Covent Garden on 10 October 1753 as Juliet to his Romeo. "The delicacy of her figure and her graceful distress obtained for her the warmest applause"; she succeeded for several years under Barry's instruction, living with him in Bow Street. When Barry later built the Crow Street Theatre in Dublin, he gave her one-eighth of his share in the profits. Miss Nossiter died of consumption in 1759, and in her will, naming Barry as executor and proved on 11 August 1759, she returned her interest in Crow Street and left him almost all of her own estate. No figures were provided in her will, but the *Theatrical Biography* (1772) claimed the legacy to be worth upwards of £3000.

When John Rich would not accede to the exorbitant salary demands made for Miss Nossiter in 1754–55, Barry took her off to act at Smock Alley, whose manager Benjamin Victor offered him £800 for the season and also reluctantly agreed to £500 for Miss Nossiter. In his pamphlet, *A Humble Appeal to the Public* (1758), Thomas Sheridan claimed credit for pushing Barry out of Covent Garden, by an agreement he had with Rich to act on shares there.

Barry returned to Covent Garden, however, in 1755–56, where he remained through 1757–58. In a revival of *The Rival Queens* on 15 January 1756—not acted in 12 years—Barry, by his portrayal of Alexander, appeared "Himself the leading God," according to Wilkinson. "He looked, moved and acted the Hero and the Lover in a manner so superiour and elevated," wrote Davies, "that he charmed every audience and gave new life to a play, which had not been seen since the death of Delane." In the scene with Clytus, "In his rage he was terrible, and in his penitence and remorse affecting." In his final agony, "his delirious laugh was wild and frantic, and his dying groan distressing."

In the same season, on 26 February 1756, Barry played Lear for the first time, once again inviting a comparison with Garrick, whose fame in the role was so immense that it persists until this day. Barry acquitted himself nobly, but he was "a faint apology" by comparison. Dignified, impressive, but unequal to the mad scenes in which Garrick excelled, Barry was characterized as "Every Inch a King," while Garrick was "Every Inch King Lear." Barry's Lear was too dependent upon study, rather than inspiration, and sprang, according to Gentleman, from "a hundred different critical opinions jumbled." He was, nevertheless, "truly striking" in parts. A somewhat detailed account of Barry's interpretation of Lear in Tate's version was provided by Mrs Frances Brooke, writing under the pseudonym of Mary Singleton, in her periodical *The Old Maid* on 13 March 1756:

I think it a great mark of judgment in *Mr Barry* that he has thrown so strong and affecting a cast of tenderness into the character: he never loses sight of the Father, but in all his rage, even in the midst of his severest curses, you see that his heart, heavily injured as he is, and provoked to the last excess of fury, still owns the offenders for his children: without this circumstance, his concessions when he meets them at *Gloster's* Castle, and his offering to return with *Goneril*, with only fifty of his Knights, would appear a degree of meanness; but we see in his whole manner that paternal fondness in combating his resentments; and that he endeavours, in spite of all appearances, to think them innocent . . . . His figure is so happily disguised that you lose

*Mr Barry*, and have no other idea on his first appearance than that of a very graceful, venerable, kingly, old man: but it is not in person alone he supports the character; his whole action is of a piece; and the effects in his voice, which are uncommonly beautiful, seem the effect of real, not personated, sorrow.

I am inclined to imagine, from his masterly performance of *Lear*, that this actor is capable of playing a much greater variety of characters than he has yet attempted; and that he is yet far from knowing half of his dramatic powers.

A month after playing Lear, he acted the title role in *Busiris, King of Egypt* (not acted in 30 years) on 22 March 1756, and he played Osmyn in *The Mourning Bride* for the first time on 30 March. In the following season he created the famous title role of *Douglas* on 14 March 1757. He was now one of the Town's most popular players, both on and off the stage, enjoying a reputation for amiability and cordiality. The *Theatrical Review* reported in 1757 that "Barry keeps a plentiful board, and gives many orders; his friends gratefully rise from the table to attend him at the theatre, and there clap hands for joy."

While in Ireland in 1756 Barry had begun negotiations for building a new theatre in Dublin. On 14 May 1757 he took a lease on the old Music Hall in Crow Street, and soon after, he acquired four contiguous lots of land. On 20 August of that year he mortgaged the properties to William Chaigneau, Richard Benson, and Hosea Coates for £1000 at 5% interest. He then had the Music Hall torn down and started the building of a theatre which was to be much larger than any then in Dublin and was predicted to be "as ample and magnificent as that of Drury-lane." Thomas Sheridan tried in every way "to divert Mr Barry from so strange a course," and verbal and written arguments flourished pro and con about the advisability of erecting another theatre in Dublin.

The many pamphlets, according to Davies, "(except of that which was written by Mr Sheridan), published on both sides were drawn up in the stile of resentment and malevolence." The contending parties strove to outdo each other with vituperation and "unjustifiable language." Despite rumors that he had quitted the London stage Barry played at Covent Garden in 1757–58, but by the fall he migrated to Dublin to work full-time at his new project. Macklin was to be his partner, but before the indenture of partnership was drawn up, he withdrew and went back to England, apparently dissatisfied with Barry's conduct and worried over the ill-health of Mrs Macklin. Barry then persuaded Woodward, who had a very comfortable situation with Garrick, to become his partner. Woodward was confused about his plans and delayed for some time, but Barry worked upon his two great passions, love of money and lust for power, thus prevailing upon him to sign the articles of partnership on 29 July 1758. Barry's brother William was established as treasurer of the new theatre.

The Crow Street Theatre was opened on 23 October 1758 with Cibber's *She Wou'd if She Cou'd*; in the opening prologue Barry promised Shakespeare as his chief dramatist, and for comedy he summoned Jonson, Congreve, and Vanbrugh. Barry himself did not act until 3 November when he played Hamlet. The rivalry for Dublin's audience proved a catastrophe for both Crow Street and Smock Alley. On 18 June 1759 Barry took another mortgage for £3000, stating in the document that he had spent £8000 in the fitting up of the theatre. He seemed not to worry about his perilous financial situation. "It was not so material being in debt, for that never disturbed his rest," informed Wilkinson. On the other hand, Woodward, who reportedly lost some £11,000 on the venture, was "quite contrary, for his dinner, good or bad, would not digest unless he was certain it was paid for." The partners quarreled finally in 1762 and Woodward returned to London. He eventually compromised a law suit with Barry and agreed to take £600 in settlement and an insurance policy on Barry (which after Barry's death he found had been neglected). Barry also started a venture at Cork which he left in the hands of his son Thomas, who eventually ran it into the ground. On 21 July 1766 Barry took yet another mortgage on Crow Street, yet despite his efforts to survive he was obliged in 1767 to give up the premises to Mossop, who as manager of the Smock Alley house had been a strong rival and now was in control of both theatres.

During the 1760's Barry also had to sell off other property he owned at Dublin. On 10 May 1760 he sold a farm to Richard Cranfield, on 26 April 1762 a dwelling and 22 acres of land to William Austen, and on 14 July 1762 another five acres to Austen.

Barry had returned to London in the summer of 1766 to share the King's Theatre with Samuel Foote's company. According to Garrick's letter to Colman on 31 July 1766, Foote was to give Barry half the profits, "but the expenses will be great and all his friends think he [Foote] had made a mistake to engage them." With a company of actors largely from Dublin, Barry gave 21 performances in August and early September, on nights alternately with Foote's; many of the actors, in fact, appeared in both companies. With Barry was Mrs Ann Dancer, who had acted in his Dublin theatre. Her husband, William Dancer, an Irish actor, had died on 26 December 1759, and she, it is said, despite her obvious readiness for success in the London theatre, had decided to remain at Dublin in order to be with Barry (see her as BARRY, Mrs Spranger). She made her first appearance at London on 8 August 1766 as Desdemona to Barry's Othello. On seeing them in the play, "Dramaticus" wrote in *Jester's Magazine* (September 1766):

> *What Hart so hard, what Temper so severe,*
> (*This Question let the most Obdurate answer*)
> *As not to drop a tender, gen'rous Tear,*
> *BARRY, Othello; Desdemona, DANCER?*

Again at Dublin in 1766–67 in an attempt to settle his theatrical affairs there, Barry returned to London with Mrs Dancer and his son to engage with Foote's company at the Haymarket, where they drew crowded audiences in July and August. Sylas Neville saw several of the performances: on 15 July he wrote in his diary, "Barry played Lear very well. His broken voice is appropriate . . . though I am apt to imagine that certain nice inflections of voice in expressing the language of passion are mistaken for a failure of the voice itself"; and on 5 August, "Barry is a good Macheath, but most persons who have seen him when young observe he has not the activity & fire that he had then. He sings tolerably as does Mrs Dancer; but both are greatest in the acting part. Mrs D: is the best Polly I ever saw."

Barry and Mrs Dancer both engaged with Garrick in 1767–68 for a total of £1300 per year, a figure which Lacy told Davies was advanced during the season to £1500. Garrick, who was then acting little, gave Barry the choice parts. After a ten-year absence Barry reappeared on the Drury Lane stage on 21 October 1767, as Othello. Sometime between 5 December 1767 and 26 February 1768, he married Ann Dancer (in a letter on the former date he referred to her as Mrs Dancer and in one on the latter date as Mrs Barry). On 27 February 1768 the Barrys created the roles of Rhadamistus and Zenobia in the first performance of Murphy's *Zenobia*. Their performances were acclaimed and the play was offered every acting night through 10 March when Mrs Barry's "illness" made it necessary to abort the run.

Barry also then fell ill and subsequently the death of his son Thomas in that spring prevented additional performances.

Except for occasional trips to Dublin to attend business affairs or to perform, Barry remained at the Drury Lane Theatre through 1773–74, living in 1768 at Mr Gilbert's, near Exeter Exchange in the Strand, by September 1770 at Streatham, and in 1774 in Norfolk Street. In November 1768, Barry was sued in the Court of Common Pleas at Westminster by William Bates, the musician, "for a large sum of money due to him from the Defendent," for the performance of Miss Slack, Bates's apprentice, at the theatre in Cork. After a short hearing, the verdict was given in favor of Bates.

The relationship with Garrick was uneasy, made more difficult by the endless trouble the Barrys gave the vexed manager over playing dates and by their airs and affectations. Garrick, for example, could not assure Thomas Francklin on 25 February 1769 that the Barrys could appear in the fall in a new play that author had submitted because they had not yet engaged with him for the next season and he thought they would not (they did finally) —"it is not in the power of a Manager to force such Performers against their Will."

The prompter William Hopkins provided a running account of the "illnesses" of the Barrys and their subterfuges to avoid playing in *The Jubilee* and other pieces in the fall of 1769. On 21 September Hopkins wrote to them asking when they would be ready to play; they replied that as they had been ill the earliest they could appear would be "the latter end of next week." Accordingly, *King Lear* was set for 7 October, a commitment they kept. A rehearsal was called for *The Fair Penitent* on 10 October for a performance the following night, but Barry wrote that "he was so ill that it would be impossible for him to play for sometime & that he would give up his salary till he was able." *Man and Wife* was therefore substituted for the eleventh. On Thursday, 12 October, the Barrys agreed to walk in the procession of *The Jubilee* on Saturday, 14 October (she did, but he did not). A rehearsal of *As You Like It* called by desire of Mrs Barry for ten o'clock that Thursday morning was eventually cancelled—"The Performers staid for her till past Eleven, but she not coming they went away." Hopkins waited on Mrs Barry on 16 October to know "if it would be agreeable to her to play Lady Townley with Mr Reddish. She said she had no cloaths for it."

A performance of *The Mourning Bride* scheduled for 23 October was cancelled by her illness and replaced by *1 Henry IV*. On 26 October *Tancred and Sigismunda* was deferred because Mrs Barry was ill. Hopkins called at their house, but Barry was not at home: "In the afternoon I sent him a note desiring they would send notice when they were able to perform. He sent me an angry note in answer on Fryday." On 28 October Hopkins received another message "that Mrs Barry was better & she would be able to Rehearse on Monday & that Mr Barry would be able to play Lord Townley on Thursday next [2 November]"; Barry did perform it.

Several months later Barry could not play in *The Siege of Damascus* on 1 February and *Amphitryon* was substituted. That day Hopkins inquired "if he should be able to play in *The Conscious Lovers* on Saturday [3 February]. His answer was that he could not," so Reddish played Young Bevil for the first time. On 3 February Hopkins inquired if Barry could play in *The Siege of Damascus* on Tuesday, 6 February, and the actor replied he could not determine until the next day; on 4 February Hopkins asked if *Zenobia* might be advertised for Saturday, 10 February. "His answer was he would let me know when he was able to play." It turned out that Barry did play Phocyas in *The Siege of Damascus* on 10 February but did not appear as Rhadamistus in *Zenobia* until 26 March.

Similar problems continued into 1770–71, and finally on 3 May 1771 Garrick wrote a hard letter complaining that Barry had acted only 19 times that season for which he had received a great sum of money despite the full forfeits taken by the management for the loss of business when Barry did not act. Garrick laid down the regulations upon which any new agreement must be based if the Barrys were to continue to be engaged at his theatre:

*First.* A reasonable Number of times shall be ascertain'd for your performing, your Sallary be divided into the same Number of parts, & so many parts forfeited as You fall short of your performance, (when call'd upon by us) as Shall be Stipulated in the Agreement.

*Secondly.* You must receive certain Characters which we will mutually settle upon closing our Agreement; and take your Share of the New ones.

*Thirdly.* You must make no Objection to perform without Mrs Barry, the ill consequences of which Objection, have been Severely felt.

*Fourthly.* Mrs Barry must likewise agree to play without you if the Business requires it.

*Fifthly.* Upon these terms, we make no Objection to your Salary and we have no New Conditions to propose to Mrs Barry.

On the following day, Barry answered, accepting the terms. By now, however, Barry's age and growing infirmities were becoming obvious to many. In 1772, in *A Letter to David Garrick*, David Williams criticized Garrick for miscasting Barry—"Why is Mr Barry made to appear in characters, for which his age must now disqualify him; and why not in others, where it could be no objection?"—and implied that the manager, being vain, avaricious, and unable to brook rivals, was trying to destroy Barry's reputation. Francis Gentle-

man in *The Theatres* (1771) claimed that Barry was "brought out" again after Garrick's refusal to reengage him only by the intervention and persuasion of Thomas Sheridan, a friend to both. In a verse Gentleman wrote:

> *Barry was banish'd when his powers could shine,*
> *Now ta'en [by Garrick] to sneer at in his sad decline;*
> *Or, what is worse, upon the verge of life,*
> *View'd as a mere appendage to his wife.*

Despite the agreement, and no doubt because of real illnesses now, Barry continued to play at Drury Lane spasmodically. In 1771–72 he did not make his first appearance until 12 November, as Horatio in *The Fair Penitent*. That season he enjoyed success and high praise as the elderly Evander in Murphy's *The Grecian Daughter*, a role he created on 26 February 1772, drawing copious tears from the audience by "a masterpiece of impersonation." With his wife as Euphrasia—"Mrs Barry rose beyond herself," wrote the *Theatrical Review*, 26 February—they received "uncommon Applause." Bills were put out for the 23 March announcing him in the title role in *King Arthur* ("Being his First Appearance here in that Character"), for his benefit, with Mrs Barry as Emmeline, but the play was put aside and *The Wonder* substituted. Not until 23 April was a new benefit scheduled for him, on which night his wife played Sir Harry Wildair in *The Constant Couple*, and he, "continuing ill," did not play. Except for additional performances in *The Grecian Daughter* on 30 April and, 14 and 28 May, Barry did no other roles for the rest of the season.

At the conclusion of the London season of 1771–72, the Barrys went to Dublin where they took the Smock Alley Theatre for 12 nights at the season's end and planned to remain the ensuing season, according to a letter by the actor William Dawson to Macklin on 21 May 1772.

Barry had previously assigned the Crow Street Theatre on 26 February 1772 to Tottenham Heaphy. At the time, Thomas Sheridan was trying to persuade Commons to give him a monopoly of the Dublin stage, and in his petition charged that since the building of the Crow Street Theatre Barry had laid out above £20,000 in its wasteful decoration and beautifying. In a pamphlet, *An Appeal to the Public Against Mr Sheridan* (1772), Barry protested he had been able to pay his several creditors by avoiding the benefit of bankruptcy and by returning to Dublin to play and "appropriating his earnings for that purpose."

The Barrys were back in Drury Lane in 1772–73 at a total salary of £50 per week. Illness continued to plague him. Although announced for Bajazet in *Tamerlane* on 4 November, the role had to be taken on by Palmer at the last moment, Barry "being taken suddenly ill." Barry was playing again on 19 November in *The Grecian Daughter*. On 8 December he created the role of Melville in O'Brien's comedy *The Duel*—"It was very much hiss'd from the 2d Act & with the greatest difficulty we got thro' the Play," wrote Hopkins, "amidst hisses & c." The audience would not suffer the play to be given out again.

In May 1773 Barry went again to perform for a few nights at Dublin in an attempt to meet more debts and to sell or let his theatre. Dawson, who owed him £800 and who had been a nominal manager under Heaphy's lease, also had to give up, so except for the few weeks when Barry returned to play in the summer of 1774 and 1775, the theatre was closed down. (For details see La Tourette Stockwell, *Dublin Theatres and Theatre Customs*, 1938, and Esther Sheldon, *Mr Sheridan of Smock Alley*, 1956.)

At the end of 1773–74, Barry left Drury Lane for Covent Garden where he remained until his death in 1777. His last years were marked by a complicated distemper and the pains of gout. He now played principally mature roles, with success, but his infirmities intruded more and more on his artistry. His roles included Lusignan in *Zara* (3 December 1774), Jaques in *As You Like It* (20 December 1774), Sciolto in *The Fair Penitent* (11 February 1775), Selim in *Edward and Eleonora* (27 March 1775), Old Norval in *Douglas* (15 January 1776), and Orellan in *The Fatal Discovery* (18 March 1776), all for the first time. After praising him lavishly in his *Miscellanies in Prose and Verse* (1775), William Hawkins reluctantly described Barry's imperfections in his action, brought on no doubt by the agonies of gout:

[his action] is sometimes rather flat and unmeaning to the true sense of his words, and likewise a stoop in his shoulders, and a bend in his knees, as if he was ashamed of his superior stature . . . and desirous to level it to the common standards; but I forget that he is bordering on the vale of years, consequently such blemishes as those must be pardoned and forgiven.

The Barrys were at Edinburgh for the race season in the autumn of 1776 for a triumphant engagement of ten performances, opening in their parts of Evander and Euphrasia in *The Grecian Daughter*. They were still remembered for their Drury Lane performances of these parts in 1772.

At Covent Garden on 28 November 1776 Spranger Barry made his last appearance on the stage, in the fitting role of Evander. He was scheduled for Lusignan on 3 December, but he being taken "suddenly extremely ill," the bill was changed to *Ethelinda*. A letter from Walpole to Mason several months earlier on 8 October 1776 had informed that Barry had lost all his teeth and sputtered his lines.

He died on 10 January 1777—"with a philosophic resignation"—and was buried in the North Cloister of Westminster Abbey on the evening of 20 January, in a private, yet decent manner:

The pall was supported by Mess. Wallace, Home, Maleveron, Linden, Atkinson, and Portis, who attended the hearse in mourning coaches. To these followed a few of the deceased's old friends and fellow labourer's in the field, in others; amongst whom was Mr Macklin, the father of the present stage, who all seemed much affected at the loss of a man who, in his professional line, leaves so gloomy a prospect of 'ever looking upon his like again.'

Mrs Barry had asked Garrick to write an epitaph for her husband's tomb—"I can't refuse her, & yet I don't like ye office," wrote Garrick—but apparently he did not write it as none appears on the tomb at Westminster Abbey. In his will dated 24 January 1770, and proved on 1 February 1777, Barry left his estate to his widow, whom he named as his sole executrix, including: "my House held by Lease for ffifty years at Streatham in Surrey with all the ffurniture belonging to the same and also the Theatre Royal in Crow Street Dublin with the Dwelling House adjoining to it and the ground near thereto . . . Together with the Wardrobe Scenes ffurniture and other things belonging to the said Theatre," the same being subject to two annuities of £60 and £40 payable to James Carter, during the lives of Ann Carter and Julia Carter, under an indenture dated 23 April 1768. Ann Barry still retained the properties in Crow Street at the time of her marriage to Thomas Crawford in 1778, and on 17 February 1789 she assigned them to Edward Featherston. When she died, under the name of Mrs Crawford, on 29 November 1801, she was buried beside Spranger Barry in the North Cloister.

Barry's death touched a melancholic-romantic spring in the poetasters of the day. A flood of newspaper verse and eulogies followed, including an elegy in *Pursuit After Happiness* (1777). Mrs Barry seemed genuinely crushed. She was persuaded, however, to speak a somewhat tasteless prologue at her first appearance after his death (at Covent Garden on 3 March 1777 when she played Lady Randolph in *Douglas*), in which she expressed doubt for her ability to weep for Douglas while oppressed with such real grief "Of the lov'd Pilot of my life bereft" and solicited their protection. As late as 1786, the well-remembered dignity of Spranger Barry was being exploited when in April of that year at Leeds George S. Carey imitated his Othello and Richard III in a "Lecture on Mimicry."

All testimony supports the impression that Barry was a most congenial man, with little formal education, but possessing an irresistible power of conversation and being an expert raconteur of Irish stories. He was the easiest man in the world, according to Davies, to live with as a friend and companion. Off stage he styled himself a Marc Antony, living high, never within the confines of his income, opening his doors for expensive and splendid dinners and entertainments. A glimpse of his private life was provided by Frederick Reynolds, who when a boy about 12 saw the Barrys act in *Othello* and afterwards was invited to sup at the house in Norfolk Street, the Strand:

Supper was on the table, and according to Barry's invariable custom after acting, a boiled fowl. Mrs. Barry cut off both the wings, placing the one on her husband's, the other on my plate. Trifles have caused discussions between more kings and queens than those in theatrical life, unfortunately mine was the liver wing. By signs and winks Barry endeavoured to attract his wife's attention, but she was too much engaged by her hospitality to me to heed him. Barry's visage began to approach the hue it had just worn in Othello, and Desdemona at length discovered this second jealously of her hero. But the tide of luck in her affairs was that evening on the ebb, or, in plain language, owing to the ardour of my appetite, the moment of rectification had just vanished with the wing of the fowl. Rendered irritable by pain [of the gout], he made some sharp remark on her neglect, she replied on his gluttony, and they quarrelled.

According to Boaden, Barry's gout and his wife's temper gave rise to frequent scenes. But if they quarrelled often, there is no hint that Barry was anything but devoted to her during their marriage, and she to him. Their marriage produced no children of record. Thomas Barry, his first son by his first wife, died in Dublin in 1768; what happened to the second Spranger, born in 1748, is not known. A person billed as "Barry Jun." acted unspecified roles in *Lover's Vows* and *The Jew and the Doctor* at Covent Garden on 12 June 1799 and may have been related to Spranger Barry or to his brother William Barry. It is extremely unlikely, however, that he was Spranger the younger, not only because Spranger's age at the time would make against the conclusion, but because any son of the greater Barry would have been so heralded in bills for any patent-theatre debut. The Julia Carter mentioned in Barry's will was no doubt his sister; the original indenture by which he bound himself to the two annuities on 23 April 1768 gives the names as James Carter and Julia Barry.

Despite his early training in business, Barry by nature seemed not cut out for theatrical management. Joseph Knight in the *Dictionary of National Biography* suggested he was "destitute of tact, knowledge, and judgment," which may have been the case, but an essential laziness and lack of devotion to the daily exigencies and demands of theatrical affairs, as evidenced by his constant problems with other managers, may have been the more likely reason. There was no doubt, however, that Barry was one of the finest actors of his age, equal to Garrick in many respects and inferior to him in few. Renowned in tragedy, he also excelled in a few comic characters such as Sir Charles Raymond in *The Foundling* and Townley in *The Provok'd Husband*. Generally, however, he enjoyed less success

in comedy, the language and situations usually being "too familiar to sit easy on him," requiring, in the words of the *Theatrical Examiner* (1768), "something more to actuate him."

He was less comfortable on stage in a modern dress than in a Roman shape or a regimental uniform. The habits and characters of by-gone heroes sat more easily upon him, and when he played Othello he looked so like the Moor it was no easy matter for the audience to remember he was not a real Negro; the story was told of a simple country girl in the gallery who cried out, "Lord! Lord! where did they hire that Néeger to act for 'm!" However much Davies admired Garrick, he stated that "Of all the tragic actors who have trod the English stage for these last fifty years, Mr. Barry was unquestionably the most pleasing." He gave dignity to the hero and passion to the lover as few others, and "in his person he was tall without awkwardness; in his countenance, handsome without effeminacy; in his uttering of passion, the language of nature alone was communicated to the Audience." For Macklin both Barry and Garrick were "extraordinary actors." He regarded the former as better "in all scenes of love and domestic tenderness" and superb also in "the blended passages of rage and heartfelt affection." John Hill, who apparently preferred actors of medium size, commented that Garrick was perhaps the shortest man to have acted a hero and Barry among the tallest—"Mr Barry looks a unnatural lover for a very short woman." His height was no real liability, however, because by his skill in dancing and fencing he "was so much in the free and easy management of his limbs, as never to look encumbered, or present an ungraceful attitude."

The following portraits and prints of Spranger Barry are known: 1. A portrait by Reynolds painted about 1758, engraved by E. Harding in 1776 and published as a plate to Harding's *Biographical Mirrour*,

1796. The original portrait is not listed by E. K. Waterhouse in *Reynolds* (1941), and its whereabouts is not known. 2. A portrait of Barry as a young man. 3. A small canvas by an unknown artist of head and shoulders, profile to right, with a gray mask in his left hand, in the Garrick Club. 4. A portrait by Nathaniel Dance, in the Huntington Library. 5. As Alexander in *The Rival Queens,* an anonymous engraving. 6. As Bajazet in *Tamerlane,* an engraving by Thornthwaite, after J. Roberts, with Mrs Barry as Selima, published as a plate to *Bell's British Theatre,* 1776. 7. As Jaffeir in *Venice Preserv'd,* an engraving by J. Collyer, after J. Roberts, with Mrs Barry as Belvidera, published as a plate to *Bell's British Theatre,* 1776. 8. As King Lear, an anonymous engraving, with Mrs Barry as Cordelia, published as a plate to the *Universal Museum,* September 1767. 9. As Timon in *Timon of Athens,* an engraving by W. Walker, after J. Roberts, published as a plate to *Bell's Shakespeare,* 1776. 10. As Timon, an engraving by Taylor, after D. Dodd, published by Harrison, 1780. 11. Speaking the prologue to *The Earl of Essex,* an engraving by T. Cook, after D. Dodd, published by Fielding and Walker, 1779. 12. As Hotspur, an anonymous engraving, colored in the Harvard Theatre Collection version, published by Smith and Sayer (1747?). 13. As Macbeth, an engraving by M. Jackson, after J. Gwinn, 1777. 14. As Othello, an anonymous engraving, published by Wenman, 1777. 15. As Romeo, an engraving by W. Elliott, after R. Pyle, with Miss Nossiter as Juliet, printed for John Ryall (1753). 16. As Varanes in *Theodosius,* an engraving by Terry, published by Harrison, 1779. 17. As Hamlet, a painting by James Roberts, about 1775, with Mrs Barry as Gertrude, in the Garrick Club. 18. As Hamlet, a painting by Francis Hayman, about 1751, with Mrs Elmy as Gertrude, in the Garrick Club. This picture has sometimes been reproduced erroneously as being Betterton and Elizabeth Barry. 19. Rehearsing Romeo, a painting by Joseph Highmore, sometimes attributed to Hogarth; others in the group are Miss and Mrs Pritchard, Fielding, Quin, and Lavinia Fenton; owned by Sir Charles Tennant, London. 20. An anonymous print of "A View of the House in which the late Mr Barry resided, in Castle Street, Oxford Road," published 30 April 1806.

**Barry, Mrs Spranger, Ann, née Street, formerly Mrs William Dancer, later Mrs Thomas Crawford** *1734–1801, actress.*

Mrs Spranger Barry was born in 1734 at Bath, the daughter of an "eminent apothecary" of that city named Street. She was sent to boarding school there, where she continued after her father's death while her mother and eldest brother kept up the

*Harvard Theatre Collection*

ANN BARRY

by Kettle, in the engraving by Paul (De Wilde)

*Harvard Theatre Collection*

ANN BARRY, as Constance
by J. Roberts

business. At the age of 17, she became engaged, according to some accounts, to a gentleman of extensive fortune, the brother of a peer, but he left her and went off to London. To help her forget him, her family sent her to stay with relatives at York, where she became an actress. James Winston said that she made her first appearance at Portsmouth in the role of Monimia in *The Orphan*, but he provided no date. Miss Street did act Cordelia at York on 28 February 1752, and she played at Bath in 1753 and 1754.

In a private ceremony at Bath in 1754 Ann married William Dancer, an actor in the York company who had played Lear to her Cordelia and whom the *Town and Country Magazine* described in January 1777 as "one of the most disagreeable men, as to person, that ever existed." Apparently the marriage took place against her relatives' wishes, and the couple were obliged to place an advertisement in the *Bath Journal* absolving people accused of encouraging them:

Whereas it has been wickedly and maliciously reported, that Mr Richard Stephens and wife were privy and accessory to our late private wedding: In justice therefore, we think it our indispensable duty to certify their innocence, they being in no way concern'd or acquainted with it.

The story that her relatives used their influence to have the couple "dislodged" from York and that thereafter wherever they tried to play in the provinces they found an order from a magistrate forbidding it has little basis in fact.

The Dancers were, indeed, engaged at York in 1755 and 1756 and at Newcastle in 1756 and 1757. Despite the opinion of Charles Macklin, who saw her at York, that she "would never make an actress" because of her shrill and dissonant tones, Mrs Dancer became a local favorite, earning the name of the "York Heroine." Her roles at York and Newcastle included: Jessica in *The Merchant of Venice*, Juliet, Calista in *The Fair Penitent*, Elizabeth in *The Earl of Essex*, Cleopatra in *All for Love*, Zara in *The Mourning Bride*, Thyra in *Athelston*, Ophelia, Lady Macbeth, Lady Sadlife in *The Double Gallant*, Clarissa in *The Confederacy*, Hippolito in *The Tempest*, Mrs Riot in *Lethe*, Rosalind in *As You Like It,* and the Queen in *Richard III.*

Mrs Dancer's mother left her a small weekly pension on the condition that she give up acting. She was allowed, however, to retain the allowance even though she failed to meet the condition because the person who would have benefited from it otherwise declined to claim the forfeit. In 1758–59 she and her husband were engaged by Spranger Barry at his new Crow Street Theatre, Dublin—"at a venture," according to Hitchcock—her debut being 8 November 1758 as Cordelia to Barry's Lear. In her first season at Dublin she was received with little enthusiasm, but under the instruction of Barry, with whom she appears to have been immediately smitten, she so improved that within a year or so she became, in fact, the "queen of the theatre" there. "Like a second Stella," it was said, "she sucked in the poison of love by the vehicle of tuition."

Stories were circulated of her domestic discord with her huband, who it seems was jealous of her professional success and agitated by her many admirers. Such reports, whether true or not, made Dancer the subject of puns and epigrams. Dancer died on 27 December 1759 (and therefore should not be confused with the Mr Dancer who acted at Norwich in the 1770's and at York in the 1780's and who may have been his son), leaving the way clear for Mrs Dancer to take up openly with Barry. Her constancy to him kept her at Dublin for nine years although she had the requisites to succeed on the London stage. In 1759 appeared an anonymously written account of her early life entitled *Rosalind, or An Apology for the History of a Theatrical Lady*. Her characters during this period included Millamant, Andromache in *The Distrest Mother*, Juliet, Desdemona, Belvidera in *Venice Preserv'd*, and Jane Shore. Although her line was tragedy, she played with success Angelica in *Love for Love* and Polly Peachum in *The Beggar's Opera*. She also acted in Barry's summer company at Cork from 1760 through 1765.

Under Barry's tuition in Ireland, Mrs Dancer became recognized for "some of the finest notes of the tender and pathetic," in the words of Macklin's biographer, Cooke, and she was regarded as "a young actress who looks tenderness and distress better than anybody; and acts them passing well." In the summer of 1766 she joined Barry for 21 performances in the King's Theatre at London, making her first appearance in that city on 8 August as Desdemona, and following with Belvidera, Juliet, Cordelia, Lady Townly in *The Pro-*

*vok'd Husband*, Monimia, Indiana in *The Conscious Lovers*, Rosalind, Calista, and Athenais in *Theodosius*. Verses in the press "On seeing Mrs Dancer, in the Character of Belvidera," acclaimed her as a new Mrs Cibber:

*What envious mind this witness'd truth denies,*
*Ask all those throbbing breasts, those streaming eyes,*
*Did ever madness move the passions so?*
*Did ever phrenzy wear such comely woe?*

Not all the critics were as enthusiastic. She was described as a pleasing person, but with little animation, having "an agreeable face, though it has not much expression," and a musical voice. Not yet was she really fitted for the strong roles of Belvidera and Juliet, according to the *London Magazine* (July 1767), and "her passion very frequently rises into turbulence." She did not yet enjoy "that full applause," wrote Davies, "which afterwards a better acquaintance with her merit drew from the audience." Desdemona was her most successful role at this time of her life, for there was "an invariable simplicity in this part to which she is happily suited; and the only feelings which she has occasion to assume are the feelings of innocent distress."

After another winter season at Dublin, Mrs Dancer returned to London in May of 1767 with Barry, who had finally been obliged to give up his struggle to make a financial success of the Crow Street venture. Taking lodgings in Bow Street, Covent Garden, they accepted an engagement with Foote at the Haymarket for the summer. She was accounted by Sylas Neville, in his diary, a tolerable singer in the role of Polly Peachum in *The Beggar's Opera*, which he saw on 5 August, yet "the best Polly I ever saw, having that sensibility which your mere singing Pollys generally want." Her success remained, however, indifferent, as suggested by a verse in *Momus* (1767):

> See Dancer *now each high-rate part possess,*
> *And try to picture virtue and distress,*
> *But judgment seems to leave her in the dark,*
> *Whene'er she aims to hit the doubtful mark.*

In the fall of 1767 she and Barry joined Garrick at Drury Lane, at a combined salary of £1300, which according to the prompter Hopkins was soon raised to £1500. Her first appearance at Drury Lane was as Sigismunda in *Tancred and Sigismunda* on 14 October; Hopkins wrote in his diary that she "was well received and great applause,—She is a good figure, and has a great deal of merit,—and is an acquisition to the theatre." On 21 November she played Monimia for the first time at Drury Lane and apparently by then had matured considerably as an actress. Compared favorably to Mrs Cibber—"though not so strikingly conspicuous in particular places," she was "more equal through the whole"—she became the main attraction in keeping *The Orphan* alive during the remainder of her career. The *Theatrical Review* later reported in 1772 that her

Excellence in Monimia beggars all Description; she seems to have united the Perfections of all her Predecessors . . . and except in a few instances where we think she rather overfigures the Character, she has acquired what few Actresses ever did; viz. an equal degree of Conception, in the Passages of delicate Sensibility, with those of Rage and Distress.

Sometime between 5 December 1767 and 26 February 1768, Mrs Dancer married Spranger Barry; in a letter to Garrick on the former date, Barry still referred to her as Mrs Dancer, but in another letter to Garrick on the latter date he called her Mrs Barry. On 22 September 1768, when she played Lady Macbeth, she was first listed in the bills as "Mrs Barry, late Mrs Dancer." She remained at Drury Lane for seven years, during which time her reputation reached its highest point, but she gave Garrick considerable difficulty in settling on plays and performance dates because of her temperament and her many illnesses, both real and feigned (see BARRY, Spranger). In addition to the roles already cited, during this period she also acted Alicia in *Jane Shore*, Mrs Beverley in *The Gamester*, Octavia in *All for Love*, and the title roles in *Merope* and *Isabella*. As Imogene in *Cymbeline* on 1 December 1770, she was "not so well as expected," reported the prompter Hopkins, but she achieved great triumphs in the title role of *Zenobia* on 27 February 1768 and as Euphrasia in *The Grecian Daughter* on 26 February 1772, roles she created for the first performances of these two plays by Murphy. Her performance of Rosalind in *As You Like It*—with a "song of the Cuckow"— was the finest portrayal of the character John Taylor ever saw. Her admirable performances at Drury Lane were credited with saving several new plays of little merit. Because of her acting of the title role in Mrs Celisia's *Almida* (11 January 1771), the play, though a poor one, had a considerable run—"she rises like perfection out of chaos," reported the *Gentleman's Magazine* for February 1771, "and therefore those who have not yet seen it represented should by no means be deterred by these strictures on the composition." Similarly, Home's *Alonzo* met with great applause on 27 February 1773 owing to her inimitable performance of Orisminda, of which Hopkins wrote in his diary: "Indeed Mrs Barry Seem'd inspir'd She never appear'd to moor Advantage." On the second night (1 March), however, she was not in good form—"Mrs Barry Fail'd greatly tonight from what she did the first Night"—and there was not much applause. She rallied, though, and kept the play on for nine nights.

*Harvard Theatre Collection*

ANN BARRY, as Sir Harry Wildair
by D. Dodd

During these years she returned periodically with Barry to play at Dublin and at Cork in summer. In London in 1772 they lived in a house in Norfolk Street, Strand. In that year Francis Gentleman, in *The Theatres*, praised her "sterling merit" and affirmed he could see her every night and even gaze "with transport on her eyes" — this in response to the author of *Thespis*, who complained that Mrs Barry was nearsighted and who was rude enough to call her a "wall-ey'd Idiot." In the same year also appeared a fifty-three-page pamphlet, *Granny's Prediction*, written by one Elizabeth Franchetti, a supposed relative, who attacked her on aesthetic grounds, commenting on each of her characters, and also condemned her on moral grounds, suggesting polygamy, a charge which at this date seems to have had no basis in fact.

Because of constant disagreements with Garrick, the Barrys moved over to Covent Garden in 1774–75, where she made her first appearance on that stage on 31 October 1774, as Euphrasia. On 8 November 1774 she acted Beatrice in *Much Ado About Nothing*, a role Garrick had refused to allow her to play because it belonged at Drury Lane to Jane Pope. She followed with Lady Townly, Cordelia, Zara, Desdemona, and her other familiar roles. On March 20 she played Clarinda in *The Suspicious Husband* for the first time. In June 1775 Garrick tried to persuade her to accept a three-year contract, but when they could not agree on salary she remained at Covent Garden, where on 20 March 1775 she acted Horatia in *The Roman Father* to Thomas Sheridan's Horatius and on 16 March 1776 the Lady in *Comus*, both for the first time. Her first attempt at Millimant at Covent Garden was made on 2 November 1776. With Barry she acted at Edinburgh in June 1776.

Spranger Barry died on 10 January 1777, leaving to her by his will, dated 24 January 1770 and proved 1 February 1777, his leasehold house at Streatham and his holdings in the Crow Street Theatre, Dublin, with its contents, and a house adjoining, subject to two annuities of £60 and £40 payable to James Carter (see BARRY, Spranger). Mrs Barry seemed genuinely and deeply grieved, and on her first appearance after his death, as Lady Randolph in *Douglas* at Covent Garden on 3 March 1777, she expressed her doubts, in a prologue, of her ability to weep for Douglas while suffering such real sorrow "Of the lov'd Pilot of my life bereft."

On 17 March 1777 Mrs Barry made her first appearance in the character of Viola in *Twelfth Night*, for her benefit, tickets available from her at No 10, the Terrace, New Palace Yard, Westminster. On 1 May 1777 she received "the Sum of Three Hundred & Seventy pounds in full for my Salary this Season." That summer she made her usual excursion to Dublin where she reaped an enormous financial harvest. According to a London newspaper, "It is an undoubted Fact (though singular and extraordinary) that for sixteen nights only she has cleared upwards of £1100. Such Success, such Applause, and such Profits, were never known, heard, credited, or achieved by an other Performer." Returning to Covent Garden, she acted Mrs Sullen in *The Stratagem* for the first time on 28 March 1778, and for her benefit a week earlier on 23 March (when she gave her address as at No 26, Henrietta Street, Covent Garden) she took a profit of just over £200. According to the Covent Garden account books her salary in 1777–78 was £31 13*s*. per week.

Sometime in the middle of July 1778, Mrs Barry married Thomas Crawford (1750–1794), a young Irish barrister, who later turned actor. On 13 July 1778, in view of her intended marriage, she secured "to herself by law the Crow-street Theatre properties left to her by her late husband Spranger Barry," according to a manuscript in the Dublin Office of the Registry of Deeds. At the end of the summer season of 1778 she acted a few nights at Bristol, now as Mrs Crawford, taking nearly £300. Hannah More saw her there and wrote to Garrick on 22 September 1778:

Her new husband is handsome, volatile, and noisy, a dozen years younger than herself, and by his own account not worth a penny, but in debt. He is most desperately in love with his new wife, and in mourning for his old one. . . . Poor man! I believe he thinks her an angel; — pity those fine delusions cannot last.

Crawford—named Thomas but familiarly called Billy—proved to be an eccentric individual and an unprofitable husband, "who spent her money, and broke

her heart." He made his debut as an actor in the role of Pierre in *Venice Preserv'd*, for Mrs Crawford's benefit at Covent Garden on 22 March 1779 (at which time their address was No 3, Adam Street, the Adelphi). So awed was he that he "could do little more than rehearse his part." When they went to play at Crow Street in May 1779, she rejected the more suitable role of the Countess in Jephson's *Count of Narbonne* in favor of the virgin Adelaide in order that she might play the love scenes with her youthful husband who was in the part of Theodore. Crawford failed to make a mark as an actor, though according to Boaden he "made a fine figure." On 17 July 1779 the Dublin press announced that "Mr Crawford and his wife intend to take command of Crow-street theatre the ensuing winter." Thomas Ryder, as it turned out, took the management of the theatre but the Crawfords were employed at £25 a night for forty nights.

Mrs Crawford returned to London in the summer of 1780 to engage at the Haymarket, making her first appearance on that stage in some 13 years on 2 June as Lady Randolph in *Douglas*, one of her most effective roles, "which if not her theatrical chef d'oeuvre," remarked the *Morning Chronicle* the next morning, "is certainly one of her most capital exhibitions." She acted Phaedra in *Phaedra and Hippolitus*, for the first time in six years on 26 June, and Desdemona for her benefit on 24 July, when tickets could be had at her house in Salisbury Street, the Strand. In the fall she engaged at Drury Lane at £14 per night, making her first appearance there in six years on 5 October 1780 as Euphrasia. She played a round of her regular characters that season and was still important enough to receive the first of the benefit nights. In the following season, however, she failed to meet her commitment to act at Drury Lane. On 11 October 1781, *The Lord of the Manor* was substituted for *Zara*; "Mrs Crawford refusing to fulfill her Engagement at this Theatre, *Zara* cannot be performed."

She was, instead, at Dublin where her husband had assumed the management of Crow Street. Announced to perform there "one night every week," she had secured the theatre to herself and had rented it to him. If a mediocre actor, Crawford was an even worse manager, and in the face of stiff competition from the theatres in Smock Alley and Fishamble Street, Crawford's actors played to thin houses. The disillusioned Mrs Crawford, it was said, finally refused to appear unless she was paid in advance, a demand which compelled her husband to collect the receipts from the doorkeepers and turn them over to her before she would make her entrance. The situation had become so dismal by December 1782 that Crawford gave up the management, and the theatre was rented out at £150 for three months to William Dawson, Robert Owenson, and others, all members of Crawford's company. Mrs Crawford continued to act, being paid £17 1s. 3d. for every night she acted. But Crow Street fared no better and was closed in 1783 (until Daly took it in 1787). After this debacle Mrs Crawford apparently separated from her husband, making him an allowance of £100 a year until he died in June 1794 (see CRAWFORD, Thomas).

Having returned to London in the fall of 1783, Mrs Crawford played for two seasons at Covent Garden (at £21 per night), but her power was waning, and a new tragedy queen, Mrs Siddons, had taken over the fancy of the Town. When Mrs Crawford appeared as Lady Randolph on 13 November 1783, her older style suffered by comparison. There was no question in Boaden's mind about the superiority of Mrs Siddons in the roles, for her "passions were displayed in the tones of harmony," whereas Mrs Crawford "seemed to me the first of a school, in latter periods much admired, which deemed discordance the natural ally of anguish, and tortured the ear to

overpower the heart." The *Public Advertiser*, 24 December 1783, compared the portrayers of Lady Randolph at the rival theatres: "The Siddons, young and more rich in natural Gifts, certainly offers much to the Mind, and yet much more to the Eye. The Crawford, by some means or another, offers more to the Heart."

Not everyone, however, gave the palm to Mrs Siddons. One reviewer who saw Mrs Crawford on 15 March 1785 gave her "a pre-eminence over the Lady Randolph of Mrs Siddons," according to a clipping in the Enthoven Collection:

In every part and through every scene—the affectionate—the ardent—the exulting—and the wretched Mother—were so truly portrayed, and in tones so exquisitely expressive —that the house was more "the real house of mourning"—than we ever witnessed in a theatre.

When Mrs Crawford acted Euphrasia on 1 December 1783, she and Henderson, reported the *Public Advertiser*, 3 December, "In the shewy scenes of the Third and Fourth Acts . . . got a Plaudit for several Speeches together, after every Speech," but the role also became a great one in the hands of Mrs Siddons. When Mrs Crawford played Euphrasia again on 29 November 1784, the comparison by *The Gazeteer*, 30 November, seemed somewhat of a stand-off:

Nothing could be more affecting than [Mrs Crawford's] expression of the sorrows in the character; nor anything more languid and undecorous than her level recitation. . . . Discharge the fire, and she sinks into a tasteless disregard of the business, which injures, if it does not destroy the illusion. It is in this that Mrs Siddons triumphs over her. . . . But she cannot, so powerfully as Mrs. Crawford, assail at intervals the heart.

Windham confessed to a little prejudice in favor of Mrs Siddons when he went to see Mrs Crawford play Belvidera on 19 January 1784; on the following day, remembering her from better times, he entered in his *Diary*: "The chief faults that I should find would be, that her articulation was cramped and timid, her tones sometimes colloquial and vulgar, her action confined, and her countenance inexpressive." On 12 April 1785, as Calista in *The Fair Penitent*, Mrs Crawford gave her last performance in London until she was to return for a final farewell engagement in 1797–98.

No longer the great attraction in London and now somewhat old for many of the roles she had helped to make famous, Mrs Crawford played out most of her remaining career with sporadic performances in the provinces. She acted in the winter season at Edinburgh in 1786, and in May of that year she played a few nights for Wilkinson at Leeds and York. For her performance at York of Euphrasia on 20 May, Wilkinson was required to bring his admission prices up to London rates because of the considerable salary that he had to pay her. Of his experiences with her, Wilkinson wrote:

Though I wished her well, and admired her talents yet her temper was so variable (like a bad season, more rain than sunshine), that I never regretted her departure, though I did . . . respect her, not only as an actress, and think she has private worth; but if she never knows her own mind, nor when she is sick or well, such procedure gives a great shock to the nervous proprietor, and makes an audience very fretful. . . . She loves money, and would, I am assured, have obtained a great deal more but for her plaguing herself as well as other people, and fretting and fuming at every trifle.

Her merit in scenes of passion once so high but now greatly diminished—"because your fire is gone," wrote Leigh in *The New Rosciad* (1786)—Mrs Crawford retired from acting. In *The Children of Thespis*, John Williams, under the pseudonym of Anthony Pasquin, pointed the moral:

*In the caves of Neglect see poor CRAW-*
  *FORD retir'd,*
*To end a frail being abridg'd and be-*
  *mir'd. . . .*
*'Twas vicious desires gave birth to her*
  *pains,*
*They govern'd the Woman, and liv'd in*
  *her veins. . . .*
*[She] play'd 'till the tremors encreas'd in*
  *gradation,*
*And the frame was an orphan of tender*
  *vibration. . . .*
*In a moment when Vehemence fir'd her*
  *age,*
*An unprincipl'd ideot tickled her rage;*
*Like Eve, warm and panting, she met the*
  *temptation.*
*And laughing resign'd all her hopes of*
  *salvation.*

On 17 February 1789, Mrs Crawford assigned her Crow Street Theatre properties to Edward Featherstone. In that year she resided in Bath for the greater part of the winter and, it was reported, tried to procure "temporary access to the Theatre" to play for a few nights there but did not succeed because of a rule that performers had to sign on for the whole season—something she was not desirous of doing. In a codicil dated 28 April 1789 to the will of the actress Mary Elmy (proved 19 April 1792), she was left £50; here she was not named Mrs Crawford but Spranger Barry's widow, "though now call'd Mrs Brown at Colney near St Albans." According to a manuscript in the Folger Library, in September 1795 Mrs Crawford, the "once celebrated Ornam$^t$ of the Stage," was residing "in a private Manner at a small Village in Carmarthenshire." Another Folger manuscript, dated 1796, reports that she was engaged for a few nights at Dublin that year but did not play. She did, however, return to Covent Garden for a series of seven farewell performances in the fall of 1797, at £31 10*s*. per night and proved to be a melancholy spectacle. Playing Lady Randolph in *Douglas* on 23 October, her once celebrated part, she exhibited the ravages of time. For John Taylor, who remembered her from better days, she

held forth a lesson to people to watch over their manners as well as their conduct; for she, who was once so elegant in her deportment, became rough and coarse, and her person was so much impaired that . . . she had the appearance of an old man rather than of one of the softer sex.

Though she was old, the *True Briton* (24 October) was pleased to report that her abilities were not entirely lost—"The blaze is gone, but there is a richness in the setting lustre." She was received with reiterated applause throughout, though "Many parts of her performance . . . evinced the most evident decline of powers, and her tremulous accents, the debility of which was rendered the more striking from the want of several teeth, proclaimed that her days of *play* and *action* were nearly brought to a close." She repeated Lady Randolph on 26 October. When she offered Merope on 29 November 1797, the *True Briton* (30 November) gently closed the critical notices of her professional career with the observation that "Since Mrs Crawford's meridian another species of acting has arisen that adds the graces of demeanor to the ebullions of passion." She acted Alicia in *Jane Shore* on 27 December, Euphrasia on 5 January, Alicia again on 19 March, and on 16 April 1798 she made the final appearance of her career as Lady Randolph.

Mrs Crawford spent the last several years of her life at Bath, her native city, and in her apartments in Queen Street, Westminster, where she died on 29 November 1801, at the age of 68. She was buried on 7 December near the remains of Spranger Barry in the North Cloister of Westminster Abbey. Her will, made on 9 January 1801 and proved on 10 February 1802, denies the accounts of contemporary journals that she died devoid of relatives and reduced to poverty. She named as executor her nephew, the Rev Thomas

Street, the only surviving son of her brother the late William Street of Bath, of Lyncombe and Widcombe in Somerset, of which parishes she also described herself, bequeathing to him all "her messuages tenements, annuities, securities & personal estate," to be sold with convenient speed after her death. Out of the proceeds £300 was to be paid to her sister Edith Brome, widow, of Ipswich, and her daughters Edith and Elizabeth Brome. Of "All arrears of a certain Annuity of One hundred pounds that I am entitled unto and secured to me for my life by Mortgage upon the Crow Street Theatre in Dublin," she gave one half to her nephew Charles Brome and the other half to her nephew and executor the Rev Thomas Street.

No children of Ann Crawford by any of her three husbands are on record; however, the Mr Dancer who acted at Norwich between 1773 and 1775 and at York in 1783 and 1784 may have been her son by William Dancer. A serious illness in 1784 prevented this later Mr Dancer from acting at York and placed his wife (also a performer) and daughter in an "unhappy situation." There is no evident connection between Mrs Crawford and the dancer Miss Ann Street, who performed in London between 1760 and 1794, although both were members of Barry's company at the King's Theatre in the summer of 1766. In 1800 Charles Lamb met Mrs Crawford and made her the subject of his narrative "Barbara S." in *The Essays of Elia.* In 1803 was published *Funeral Stanzas to the Memory of Mrs Ann Crawford.*

As a younger actress, when she was, successively, Mrs Dancer and Mrs Barry, her personal attractions were often celebrated in print. Lichtenberg, who visited London in 1775, described her when she was still Mrs Barry as a "perfect beauty."

Being even by the light of day and without paint, they tell me, remarkable handsome. . . . Her beauty has something saint-like about it, and the prevailing impression made by her demeanour and the sound of her excessively charming voice is one of gentle innocence and an obliging amiability.

In manner she was charming, graceful, genteel, with a "certain modest *gaité de coeur.*" In person, according to Macklin, she was "above the middle size, of fair complexion, well made. . . . Her hair was of light auburn and fell gracefully on her shoulders. . . . Her features were regular . . . and though her eyes were not naturally strong, or distinctly brilliant, they gave a pleasing interest to her looks." In talent, she was clearly one of the leading actresses on the English stage during the eighteenth century. Indeed, Hawkins believed in 1775 that "her majestic deportment, elevated speech, expressive manner, and alacrity, all pronounce her to be the most accomplished actress on the English, perhaps on the European stage." In scenes of grief and rage, according to Hawkins, she was admirable, and her *forte* was the pathetic, in such roles as Belvidera, Monimia, Desdemona, and Lady Randolph. "Mrs Barry knows perfectly well the ready avenues to the human heart," wrote Davies of her impressive performance of Zenobia, "and can rouse every latent spring of human feeling; she, if any actress can, will force lamentations from the obdurate, and sensibility from the brutal." For Macklin, in the role of Desdemona she had no competitor, especially when playing opposite Spranger Barry. Lichtenberg thought her to be one of the most versatile of performers, "the only one who could bear comparison with Garrick," in this respect. Like Garrick also, she was extraordinarily impressive in portraying madness. "Every spectator unaquainted with the fable of the play trembled for her reason" when she began to betray traits of lunacy as Isabella and uttered: "Madness has brought me to the gates of Hell, / And there has left me." The author of *A Review of Mrs Craw-*

Harvard Theatre Collection

ANN and SPRANGER BARRY
in *Venice Preserv'd*

by J. Roberts

*ford and Mrs Siddons in the Character of Belvidera* (1782) declared that "perhaps there never was a finer piece of acting seen, nor could Bedlam exhibit anything so superior" as Mrs Crawford's last moments in Belvidera, "when her hands are folded on her breasts, and she expires laughing." She played the mad scene in a "loose undress," which pleased some but others thought "improper," especially when Mrs Siddons arrived to go mad in full dress. Her appeal to Jaffeir was given "in the most pathetic manner . . . her piercing tones, and tender breaks, searched the hearts of the most obdurate," and the scene "where Belvidera relates the indignities she met with from Renault . . . no woman on the English stage possesses that exquisite manner of inflaming a lover's soul to vindicate her wrongs in so elevated a degree as Mrs Crawford." She subdued a long succession of audiences by her storms of passion as Lady Randolph, moments of which "checked your breathing; perhaps pulsation," according to Boaden, and "made rows of spectators start from their seats." When she made her "terrific exit" as Constance at the close of the third act of *King*

*John*, when she lamented the loss of her son, concluding with the lines:

> *O Lord! my boy, my Arthur, my fair son!*
> *My life, my joy, my food, my all the world!*
> *My widow-comfort, and my sorrow's cure!*

she frequently "paralysed a crowded theatre—actually deprived the audience of the power of applauding." Yet in such roles as Desdemona and Cordelia she was "gentle, yielding and of as little satirical as heroic." For Lichtenberg, she possessed "the radiant countenance of the transfigured," when as Cordelia, "raising her large eyes, gleaming with tears, to heaven and silently wringing her hands, she hastens towards her forlorn old father and embraces him." Lichtenberg's tribute to her graceful and supple gestures—he would "pack all the German actresses . . . into a ship and take them to London, so that they might learn from Mrs Barry how to use their arms"—is supported by the many engravings of her in character.

Not all viewers were as taken by her as the German visitor was. John Hill denounced her habit of concentrating on the striking passages and slurring over the others, a habit she had acquired, it seems, from Barry. Some regarded her as the "mistress of the minutiae of acting," in an older fashion, and often her style was "vehement." According to Boaden—who wrote the *Memoirs of Mrs Siddons*—she "threw her arms out from side to side—struck the bosom with violence in bursts of passion, and took all *fair* advantage of her personal attractions." Mrs Siddons, herself, acknowledged the test she was being put to in taking on many of Mrs Crawford's characters, writing once to Dr Whalley: "I should suppose she has a very good fortune, and I should be vastly obliged if she would go and live very comfortably upon it. . . . Let her retire as soon as she pleases." The best summary perhaps of the comparisons of these two tragic queens was provided by John Bernard in *Retrospections of the Stage*:

The fact is, nothing could be more distinct than their respective spheres of preeminence. Mrs. Siddons, at the height of her powers and success, was the *matron* of the stage;—Mrs. Crawford, the *lover*. Mrs. Siddons claimed the dominion of the dignified, the vehement, the maternal, and the intellectual;—Mrs. Crawford, of the tender, the confiding, and the impassioned. . . . The fact that the former lady succeeded in the latter's characters during her lifetime, is of no great weight whatever. Young people can at all times assume elderly characters; but the most general of all outcries is that against elderly people putting our gravity to the old test, by representing young ones. Mrs. Crawford (for the stage) was an old woman when Mrs. Siddons appeared. She was not entitled, therefore, to play her *best* parts, and had to maintain her popularity by others in which her talent was but secondary.

Bernard's last comment, however, is not fully supported by the bills unless he was referring mainly to such young roles as Cordelia and Desdemona, for in the years of competition with Mrs Siddons (1783–85), Mrs Crawford did indeed act those roles which were commonly regarded as her best parts, such as Lady Randolph, Euphrasia, Belvidera, Zenobia, and Zara.

Mrs Barry acted approximately 82 different roles during her 46 years on the stage, which in addition to those already mentioned above included: Ethelswinda in *Alfred*, Helena in *All's Well that End's Well*, Zaphira in *Barbarossa*, Miranda in *The Busy Body*, Catherine in *Catherine and Petruchio*, Sir Harry Wildair in *The Constant Couple*, Countess in *The Countess of Salisbury*, Hermione in *The Distrest Mother*, Mara in *The Duel*, Eleanora in *Edward and Eleanora*, Mrs Harley in *False Delicacy*, Augusta Aubry in *The Fashionable Lover*, Perdita in *Florizel and Perdita*, Harriet in *The Guardian*, Lady Percy in *1 Henry IV*, the title role in *Iphigenia*,

Widow Brady in *The Irish Widow*, Tragic Muse in *The Jubilee*, Mrs Conquest in *Lady's Last Stake*, Patty in *The Maid of the Mill*, the title role in *Mariamne*, Donna Perriera in *Marplot*, Portia in *The Merchant of Venice*, Mrs Ford in *The Merry Wives of Windsor*, Almeria and Zara in *The Mourning Bride*, Imoinda in *Oroonoko*, Mandane in *The Orphan of China*, Elwina in *Percy*, Lady Brute in *The Provok'd Wife*, Sylvia in *The Recruiting Officer*, Statira in *The Rival Queens*, Deianira in *The Royal Suppliants*, the title role in *Sethona*, Eudocia in *The Siege of Damascus*, Arpasia in *Tamerlane*, Biddy Tipkin in *The Tender Husband*, Viola in *Twelfth Night*, Evanthe in *Timon*, Mrs Dogherty in *The True-Born Irishman*, Violante in *The Wonder*, Miss Montague in *A Word to the Wise*, the title role in *Zara*.

The following portraits and prints of Mrs Barry are known (and unless other locations are noted copies are in the Harvard Theatre Collection): 1. A portrait (the best of her) by T. Kettle and engraved by S. Paul (pseudonym for Samuel De Wilde). A reverse engraving was done by James Watson in 1769 and sometimes has been mistaken for a portrait of Lady Molineux. The Watson engraving, however, looks nothing like the portrait of Lady Molineux painted by Joshua Reynolds and engraved by Watson in 1770 and is undoubtedly Mrs Barry. The Paul engraving was published later by Bowles. 2. A portrait by Reynolds, engraved and published by S. W. Reynolds in 1821. A copy was published by Bowles. In the British Museum. 3. A portrait, full-length vignette, by an unknown engraver. 4. A portrait, bust, by an unknown engraver; a colored impression is in the Harvard Theatre Collection. 5. Speaking the prologue to *Douglas*, by an unknown engraver, published by Fielding and Walker, 1780. 6. as Almeria in *The Mourning Bride*, by James Roberts and engraved by the artist, 1781, copy in the Enthoven Collection.

7. As Almida in *Almida*, painted by T. Bonner and engraved by him. 8. As Athenais in *Theodosius*, an engraving by Thornthwaite, after James Roberts, published as a plate to *Bell's British Theatre*, 1776. This print appears also on a delftware tile in the Walker Art Gallery, Liverpool. 9. As Belvidera in *Venice Preserv'd*, with Spranger Barry as Jaffeir, an engraving by Collyer, after James Roberts, published as a plate to *Bell's British Theatre*, 1776. 10. As Calista, in *The Fair Penitent*, with Samuel Reddish as Lothario, by an unknown engraver, in the British Museum. 11. As Cleopatra in *All for Love*, by an unknown engraver, published by W. Turner, 1783, in the British Museum. 12. As Constance in *King John*, by an unknown engraver, after James Roberts, published as a plate to *Bell's Shakespeare*, 1775. 13. As Cordelia, with Barry as Lear, by an unknown engraver, published as a plate to the *Universal Museum*, 1767. 14. As Gertrude, with Barry as Hamlet, an oil painting probably by James Roberts, about 1775, in the Garrick Club. 15. As Mrs Ford in *The Merry Wives of Windsor*, with Elizabeth Bannister as Mrs Page, engraved by J. McGoffin. 16. As Horatia in *The Roman Father*, engraved by Terry, published by J. Harrison, 1780. 17. As Lady Randolph in *Douglas*, engraved by Cook, after Miller, published as a plate to Lowndes' *New English Theatre*, 1784. 18. As Lady Randolph, small vignette, by an unknown engraver, published by Harrison, 1780. 19. As Mariamne, in *Mariamne*, engraved by Thornthwaite, after James Roberts, published as a plate to *Bell's British Theatre*, 1777. Another version was engraved by W. Leney and published in *Bell's British Theatre*, 1794. 20. As Phaedra, in *Phaedra and Hippolitus*, engraved by Thornthwaite, after James Roberts, published as a plate to *Bell's British Theatre*, 1777. 21. As Rosalind, in *As You Like It*, vignette by an unknown engraver, printed by Smith and Sayer, 1772. Another version

was printed in *Gentleman's and London Magazine*, Dublin, 1777. 22. As Selima, in *Tamerlane*, with Barry as Bajazet, engraved by Thornthwaite, after James Roberts, published as a plate to *Bell's British Theatre*, 1776. For a discussion of this print see the end of the entry on Mrs William Barry. 23. As Sir Harry Wildair, in *The Constant Couple*, engraved by Goldar, after D. Dodd, published as a plate to *New English Theatre*, 1777. This print also appears on a delftware tile in the Walker Art Gallery, Liverpool. 24. As Sir Harry Wildair, by an unknown engraver, published by Wenman, 1777. 25. As Sir Harry Wildair, engraved by Terry, published by Harrison, 1779. 26. As Sophonisba, in *Sophonisba*, engraved by Thornthwaite, after James Roberts, published as a plate to *Bell's British Theatre*, 1778. Mrs Barry seems never to have acted this role. 27. As Widow Brady in *The Irish Widow*, with William Parsons as Whittle, by an unknown engraver. 28. As Violante, in *The Wonder*, with Garrick as Don Felix, by an unknown engraver, from an original picture belonging to the Duchess of Northumberland, printed for Smith and Sayer, 1769. 29. As the Widow Wadman, in *Tristram Shandy*, with John Bannister as Uncle Toby, engraved by L. Stocks, after C. R. Leslie. Mrs Barry never played this role. 30. As Zenobia, in *Zenobia*, by an unknown engraver, in the British Museum. 31. "The Tragic and Comic Muse Crowning her Favorite Daughters," by an unknown engraver: Mrs Yates as Calista, Mrs Barry as Belvidera, Miss Barsanti as Estifania, Mrs Abington as Clarinda, standing in a row; print in the British Museum.

**Barry, Mary** *[fl. 1698]*, *actress?*

A Mary Barry, along with the famous Elizabeth, was listed in the Lord Chamberlain's accounts as a member of Betterton's company at Lincoln's Inn Fields on 14 November 1698, though her function in the troupe was not mentioned.

**Barry, Thomas** *c. 1743–1768*, *actor.*

Thomas Barry was born about 1743 in Ireland, the son of the actor Spranger Barry and his first wife Anne (not to be confused with his second wife, the famous actress, also named Ann). O'Keeffe in his *Recollections* described Thomas Barry as a "fine, accomplished, well-educated young man," whose father brought him on the stage, according to O'Keeffe, as Romeo— "I saw him the first night; he had great success"; but actually Thomas Barry's debut took place at Cork on 2 October 1761 when he played Douglas, billed as "A Young Gentleman." On 17 November of the same year he appeared at Crow Street, again as Douglas, but now identified by name and as making his second appearance on any stage.

Young Barry continued to act for his father at Cork in the summers between 1762 and 1765. By 1766 he was married and had a family. In the summer of 1766, having gone with Mrs Dancer to play at London, Spranger Barry left him in charge of the Cork company, much to the dissatisfaction of the Cork public. On 28 July 1766 the *Cork Chronicle* announced that "the Quartermaster-general [Barry], his Lady, and family, arrived in town; as did also a few inferior's of the Marshall's Troops." Soon after the theatre opened on 8 August Barry was accused of failure as a manager, of "intolerable insolence," of turning the gallery into a "scene of obscenity," and of allowing players on stage "absolutely intoxicated."

Barry's acting also was bitterly attacked. The Cork critics despaired he would ever "shake that Socratical Gravity so unsuitable" to the role of Hastings in *Jane Shore* and wished that as the gay Lothario in *The Fair Penitent* he "would be more gay and smile a little." When Barry went to the *Chronicle*'s office to discover the identity of his critics, threatening to cane them, the publisher Busteed refused to give out the information. Barry then instituted a series "of contentions in court and out." He sued Busteed for £1000 and arranged to have two of his actors, Philip Glenvil and Robert Mahon appointed special deputy sheriffs to serve the warrant. They arrested Busteed on 5 September 1766, dragging him "like a common felon through the streets." Soon released on bail, Busteed gained the support of a group of local citizens—the "Friends of Liberty"—who raised money for the defendant's legal expenses. On 2 October the City Recorder, proclaiming the inviolable principle of the liberty of the press, discharged Barry's bill of libel. Anticipating a small audience at his benefit play of *Cato* on 15 October, Barry had his assistant Heaphy announce that "Mr Barry was suddenly and dangerously attacked with illness" and could not play, to which the *Chronicle* responded mockingly on 18 October:

*The mighty Cato sick—Oh! fatal Stroke!*
*Of empty Seats, and Boxes unbespoke.*

Busteed, however, was not through with him. On 10 November 1766, Barry was committed to the city jail "for having falsely and maliciously caused Busteed to be seized and imprisoned on an illegal action." Apparently satisfied with this indignity upon the proud Barry, the publisher dropped the complaint.

In the following summer, 1767, Barry joined his father and Mrs Dancer at London to play for Foote at the Haymarket. He made his first appearance at that theatre on 26 June 1767 as Pierre in *Venice Preserv'd*, to his father's Jaffeir and Mrs Dancer's Belvidera. On 6 July he played Dumont in *Jane Shore*—when Sylas Neville wrote in his diary: "but he will never be equal to his father"—and on 8 July he acted the title role in *Theodosius*. When he played Edgar to his father's Lear on 15 July, Neville wrote, "Young Barry was tolerable in some parts . . . but very inanimate in y⁰ last scenes." In that engagement

he also played Raymond in *The Countess of Salisbury* a number of times and Chamont in *The Orphan*. Evidently he did not make a good impression. The author of the poem *Momus* (1767), addressing the elder Barry, wrote, "thy son, when in each part he tries, / To copy thee, too oft from nature flies." The *London Magazine* of September 1767 gave a mild assessment:

Mr Tho Barry is in his person tall and extremely thin; has a face without meaning; and a voice without force; from the accounts we had received of this young gentleman in several Irish letters, we expected but little of him; and indeed he did not give us much; nevertheless, he surpassed our hopes, and convinced us, that where an actor is perfect in his part, and decent in his deportment, a good-natured audience will always overlook a number of natural imperfections.

Leaving his father in London, Thomas Barry returned to Dublin where he soon became ill and within a year died at his lodgings in Glassnevin Road in April 1768. About 12 May, Spranger Barry advised Garrick he could not play (in *Zenobia?*) because he had just heard of the unexpected death of his son, who, he said, had been dangerously ill for some time but seemed to be recovering.

Thomas Barry's wife went on the stage after his death. O'Keeffe acted with her at Drogheda for her benefit and reported "The young widow had a full and productive house." In a performance of *Phaedra and Hippolitus* at Drury Lane on 21 April 1774, in which Spranger Barry and his wife played Theseus and Phaedra, the role of Ismena was announced in the bills for "A Young Gentlewoman" whom the prompter William Hopkins identified by a manuscript notation on the bill as "Mrs I. Barry." We believe the "I" to be a scribal error or a misreading of "T" and that this person was Thomas Barry's widow. *Phaedra and Hippolitus* was repeated on 27 April. There is no other record of her appearance in London. A Thomas Barry, who was an actor and provincial manager at Brighton from about 1820 to 1825 and made his debut at Drury Lane on 15 May 1825, may have been descended from our subject.

**Barry, Mrs Thomas** *[fl. 1766–1774],* *actress. See* BARRY, THOMAS.

**Barry, William** *d. 1780, actor, treasurer.*

William Barry was the son of William Barry, a wealthy silversmith of Skinner Row, Dublin, by his wife Catherine, and was descended from the noble houses of Santry and Barrymore. He was also the younger brother of the famous actor Spranger Barry, in whose entry the family background is traced.

During the period of his brother's management of the Crow Street Theatre, and a provincial Irish circuit in the 1760's, William Barry served as his treasurer. He also acted on occasion, making his debut at Crow Street on 1 March 1765. In 1762 he married the young actress Jane Osborne. No doubt he accompanied her to London where she made her debut at Drury Lane in September 1767, and he was probably employed by that theatre from that time. His name, however, first appeared as a box office keeper there in 1771–72, when on 28 May 1772 he had benefit tickets in the amount of £38 2s. On 24 September 1772 the treasury advanced him 15s. for operating expenses and on 19 May 1773 he shared a benefit with J. Bannister. In the following season he was replaced as box office keeper by Archeveque.

After leaving Drury Lane, Barry went to work as treasurer at the Liverpool theatre, where he had been for a while in the summer of 1771 (on 12 June 1771 he witnessed the will of the actor William Gibson made at Liverpool). Barry was at Liverpool for the summer and winter seasons from at least 1776 through 1778, re-

ceiving £1 1s. per week in winter and £2 per week in summer. The last payment to him, of £2, was made on 19 October 1778. According to the *Town and Country Magazine* for February 1780, William Barry, the brother of Spranger Barry, had died "lately" at Liverpool. Barry's wife, Jane, had died in London on 13 October 1771, evidently without issue.

**Barry, Mrs William, Jane, née Osborne** *1739–1771, actress.*

Mrs William Barry was born Jane Osborne at London in 1739, the daughter of a Mr W. Osborne, who had been a butler to the Society of the Inner Temple but turned wastrel. Osborne's wife finally left him, taking her daughter Jane to live with relatives in Ireland. The story was told that one night a casual visitor to their house heard young Jane reading aloud from *Venice Preserv'd*, and so impressed was he that he brought his friend Spranger Barry, then joint manager at Crow Street, to hear her read the roles of Belvidera, Alicia (*Jane Shore*), and Almeria (*The Mourning Bride*). "Without further trial," it was said, Barry engaged her "for four years certain, at a very considerable salary," though her mother feared for her virginity. The *Theatrical Biography* (1772), which relates the above account of her early life, also states that Miss Osborne made her first appearance in Almeria; but actually she made her debut, billed as "A Young Lady," in the role of Juliet at the Crow Street Theatre on 27 January 1759. A month later, on 21 February, she played Juliet again, "2nd app. on any stage," this time with her name in the bills.

Miss Osborne soon gained the esteem and protection of "Lord Chancellor Bowes, and other personages of the first rank and distinction in Ireland," who, according again to the *Theatrical Biography*, gave her letters of recommendation to the first people of the towns she visited in summer tours of Ireland. She played at Cork in

August and October of 1760 and there again in October 1761.

In 1762 Jane Osborne married the actor William Barry, brother of Spranger Barry and at that time his treasurer at the Crow Street Theatre. She continued to act at Crow Street under her new name. She was evidently the Mrs Barry who acted at Crow Street in 1763 and at Cork in 1762, 1763, and 1765.

After acting at Bristol in the summer of 1766, Mrs William Barry made her first appearance at Drury Lane on 30 September 1766 as Juliet to Cautherly's Romeo. The reviewer in the *Public Advertiser* found her voice, figure, and face to be well suited to express the proper passions of the role but remarked that "She seemed to be so much in love with Romeo as to forget she represented a young and inexperienced virgin unused to men." That season at Drury Lane she also played Alicia in *Jane Shore* (24 October 1766), Eudocia in *The Siege of Damascus* (8 November), Lady Grace in *The Provok'd Husband* (9 February 1767), Statira in *The Rival Queens* (24 April), and the title role in Reed's *Dido* for its third performance on 14 May 1767 (Mrs Yates having created the latter role on 28 March 1767).

In 1767–68 Spranger Barry and Mrs Ann Dancer joined the Drury Lane company. Mrs Dancer made her first appearance there as Sigismunda on 14 October 1767, and then on 21 October she played Cordelia, Barry played Lear (his first appearance at this theatre in ten years), and Jane Barry played Goneril. It is presumed that other bills that season which list the name of "Mrs Barry" pertain to Jane Barry, since Mrs Dancer did not become Spranger Barry's wife until after the season closed. These roles include Zelmira in the first performance of Murphy's *Zenobia* on 27 February 1768, Mrs Strictland in *The Suspicious Husband* (26 May 1768) and Flavia in *The Absent Man*, a role she created in the first performance of that piece

JANE BARRY and SAMUEL CAUTHERLEY
in *Romeo and Juliet*

artist unknown

on 21 March 1768 and repeated for her benefit on 13 April, when she also spoke the prologue.

In the following season, 1768–69, her new sister-in-law began to act under the name of "Mrs Barry" and Jane Barry's name was billed as "Mrs W. Barry." Under that billing she continued at Drury Lane for three more years. When she appeared as Almeria in *The Mourning Bride* on 26 September 1768, the prompter William Hopkins noted in his diary, "Mrs W. Barry very bad in Almeria—imagine she was in Liquor." Some of her other roles were Harriet in *The School for Rakes* (5 May 1770), Fanny in *The Clandestine Marriage* (17 May 1770), and Monimia in *The Orphan* (30 May 1770). During summers from 1767 to 1770 she regularly was "the heroine of the Bristol Theatre" where she played many leading characters with great success.

Jane Barry died of unknown causes on 13 October 1771 at the age of 31. According to the *Memoirs of the Bristol Stage* she had been "a very pleasing and respectable . . . actress in tragedy and genteel comedy." At Drury Lane she was greatly overshadowed by her more talented sister-in-law Ann Barry. Her husband, William Barry, a house servant at Drury Lane for several of the years in which she acted there, later took up his career at Liverpool, where he died in 1780.

A small engraving crudely cut by an unknown engraver was published for William Tringham at an unknown date, depicting "Mrs Barry and Mr Cautherley" as Juliet and Romeo. As noted above, Jane Barry acted Juliet with Cautherly as early as September 1766. Both she and Ann Barry, however, acted the role with Cautherly in 1768–69. Since the drawing bears no resemblance to other likenesses of Ann Barry, we assume that it depicts Jane Barry. An engraving by Thornthwaite, after James Roberts, published as a plate to *Bell's British Theatre* (1776), depicts "Mr and Mrs Barry as Bajazet and Selima in *Tamerlane*." Ann Barry seems never to have acted Selima, but when the play was performed at Drury Lane in the 1770's, Jane Barry usually played the role, with Barry as Bajazet and Ann Barry as Arpasia. From the definite features of the woman's profile in this print, however, it appears that the artist, who did several other renderings of her in characters, intended to show Ann Barry as Selima, perhaps because of her greater popularity.

### Barrymore, Miss  *[fl. 1785]*,  *actress.*

A Miss Barrymore played the role of Molly Brazen in *The Beggar's Opera* on 15 March 1785 at the Haymarket. Perhaps she was the daughter of the actor William Barrymore.

### Barrymore, William  *1759–1830, actor, singer.*

William Barrymore, whose real name was Blewit, was born in 1759, the son of a hair dresser at Taunton. Various editions of

*Authentic Memoirs of the Green Room* differ as to whether he was apprenticed to a sugar baker in Bristol or to the counting house of Mr Ladbroke in London. In either case, he soon developed both expensive habits and ambitions for the theatre. He joined a company of strollers in the west of England—there is a record of his playing Don Ferdinand in *The Duenna* at

*Harvard Theatre Collection*

WILLIAM BARRYMORE

by T. Hardy

Plymouth on 19 July 1780—but could scarcely subsist on his meagre wages. His application to Linley for employment at Drury Lane was refused, but soon after he was seen at Brighton by Colman, who engaged him for the Haymarket. Colman, however, soon reneged on the offer and gave Barrymore some money instead of an appearance. Fortunately for Barrymore, the managers of Drury Lane now needed a substitute for Du Bellamy, who was leaving the London stage, and they employed him temporarily with the intention of soon finding someone of higher merit.

Barrymore made his first appearance at Drury Lane as Young Meadows in *Love in a Village* on 3 October 1782 without causing much stir. But despite the ostensibly temporary nature of his position he was ultimately to work at Drury Lane for most of his career, at least through the season 1808–9. For several years he was used infrequently and remained insignificant. On 4 November 1783 he played the Squire in *Thomas and Sally* and on 14 April 1784 the title role in *Cymon*. But when Farren went over to Covent Garden in September of 1784, many of that actor's considerable roles were assigned to him. A spirited performance of Carlos in *Isabella* on 12 October 1784 brought favor. Soon after, according to early biographers, another circumstance made a great impression on the public. One night Bannister, who regularly played Oakley in *The Jealous Wife*, became suddenly indisposed and the role was thrust upon Barrymore. After the proper apology was made to the audience, he began the performance with the part in hand, but soon after the beginning of the second act he put it into his pocket "and went through the whole of it, with a degree of ease and effect, that astonished every beholder, and in the highest degree charmed the audience." The death of Brereton in 1784 opened other opportunities for Barrymore's advancement. The author of the *Secret History of the Green Room* (1792) suggested that Barrymore was a studied opportunist who accelerated his career by "an obsequious demeanour and insinuating flattery."

For many summer seasons Barrymore was a leading actor at the Haymarket. He also acted at Liverpool in 1786, where on 9 August he took £46 15s. at his benefit, at Richmond in 1791 and 1792, and at Manchester in 1804. In December and January of 1791–92 he acted at the private

theatricals given by Richard, Earl of Barrymore (with whom the actor has often been confused) at Richmond. The next summer he was implicated by John Williams ("Anthony Pasquin") in a dispute that author had with Captain Wathen. Both Wathen and Williams published long and conflicting accounts of the matter in the *Thespian Magazine* along with affidavits and testimonials. It seems that after some words in the boxes of the Haymarket Theatre, Wathen, Harry Angelo, and Barrymore had assaulted Williams in the street. According to Williams, who was a sick man and possessed only one arm, Barrymore kicked him upon the ribs until he was at "the very threshold of death." Williams had to beg for his life.

Probably Barrymore well remembered what Williams had written about him in *The Children of Thespis* (1786):

> *With arms close enfolded, and gigantic stride,*
> *Denoting ill manners, defiance and pride,*
> *Who's that strutting round like a Tragedy king . . .*

Though typically cutting, Williams's verse confirms other reports that early in his career Barrymore was an awkward actor. He had a tall genteel appearance, which, when he grew more bulky in later years, gave him greater authority in many roles. Barrymore's detractors criticized his action and deportment as "constrained" yet at the same time accused him of moving "with terrible strides" and sawing the air with his hands. The hostile author of *Authentic Memoirs of the Green Room* (1792) found nothing in his portrayals which showed any intellectual discrimination or electric spark of genius. *The Druriad* (1798), another uncomplimentary epistle, called him an automaton, who acted with stiff knees, lengthened stride, arms expanded wide, unmeaning emphasis, and a theatric roar.

A more balanced assessment came from

Waldron in *Candid and Impartial Strictures on the Performers*, who observed in 1795 that many of Barrymore's faults were disappearing with experience. "He has in many instances of late, particularly this summer [at the Haymarket] . . . displayed abilities that plainly shewed him to possess a strong comprehensive mind, together with a soundness of judgment not inferior to any performer on the stage." His voice, while not heard to advantage in tender and pathetic moments, was clear and strong and, according to Waldron, "for certain tragic parts" was the best on the stage. His face, while not in any way extraordinarily expressive of the passions, was "by no means deficient of expression." Above all, Barrymore seems to have been industrious and steady, and, until his declining years at any rate, he served the theatre as a good second-rate actor.

Among his most effective roles was Osmond in the melodrama *The Castle Spectre*. As Laertes in *Hamlet* he spoke well but "there was at times a mandarin shake of the head which added nothing to the dignity of his appearance" (clipping dated 12 January 1787). His other roles included Scandal in *Love for Love*, Villamour in *Tit for Tat*, Plume in *The Recruiting Officer*, Octavian in *The Mountaineers*, Bassanio in *The Merchant of Venice*, Doricourt in *The Belle's Stratagem*, Orsino in *Twelfth Night*, Schedoni in *The Italian Monk*, Altamont in *The Fair Penitent*, Dumont in *Jane Shore*, Eustace in *The Surrender of Calais*, Sir Edward Mortimer in *The Iron Chest* and Macduff in *Macbeth*. When he played Pierre in a revival of *Venice Preserv'd* at Drury Lane on 15 January 1802, the *Monthly Mirror* (February 1802) found him to be "above mediocrity" with his appearance denoting the "fine, gay, bold-fac'd villain." In the words of the *Theatrical Repertory*, his Pierre was "truly respectable," but innocuous.

In 1789–90 Barrymore was on the Drury Lane salary list for £6 per week.

His wages increased gradually to £7 15s. in 1792–93, £8 in 1795–96, £9 in 1798–99, and in 1799–1800 finally levelled at £10 per week, where the figure remained through 1805–6. From about 1782 to 1792 he usually received an annual benefit alone, but from then on shared with another actor, usually Wathen, Sedgwick, or Miss Mellon. His benefit receipts averaged about £125 per season throughout his career, but with somewhat higher sums coming in the earlier years, the declining sums suggesting his declining popularity and importance at the theatre. He lived at No 8, Martlett Court, in 1786; at No 11, Queen Street, Bloomsbury, in 1787; at No 22, Church Street, in 1788; and at No 1, Southampton Street, in 1789. From 1790 through 1795 his address was No 11, Bedford Street, Bedford Row; and then from 1796 at least through 1800 it was No 20, Judd Place West, Sommers Town.

Despite his earlier triumph of memory, in later years he was not regarded as a good study. In 1798 he was accused by the

*Harvard Theatre Collection*

WILLIAM BARRYMORE, as Hubert
by Burney

*Monthly Mirror* of putting into his lines more of himself than of the author, and on 27 January 1800 he was almost hooted off the stage for being more imperfect in his role of Prince John in *Adelaide* than he had been on the first night, 25 January. A clipping in the Enthoven Collection recounts his going blank while delivering the prologue to *The Welch Heiress* in April 1795: "Barrymore *forgot* himself so far as to step forward and assure the audience that he never could speak a prologue in his life." After another couplet or two, and pleading that he had known the whole, word for word, three days ago, he read from the prompter's copy—"but his readings were by no means calculated to put the House in good-humour."

In 1796 Barrymore suffered some illness which confined him for many months and prevented his acting until after the summer. In a later year (on 19 January 1803) he was again seized with a serious illness, while playing Polydore in *The Orphan*. Some 18 months later, in June 1804, he suffered some accident on the Liverpool stage, and while the blood was streaming on his face the audience cried out, "Take away the Body, and bring forward the Farce" (*Thraliana*, II, 1052). Perhaps these events contributed to his decline on the stage. On 14 November 1807 he was announced in the Drury Lane bills for Claudio in *Much Ado About Nothing*, but having come late to the morning rehearsal, he was fined and in a huff refused to go on that night unless the fine was remitted. He was summarily discharged and Henry Siddons played Claudio. Genest, in describing the incident, remarked that Barrymore's absence was "no loss to this theatre." His last performance of record was at Brighton in the summer of 1809 when he played Charles Beverley opposite the Mrs Beverley of Mrs Siddons in *The Gamester*.

Barrymore died at Edinburgh in July 1830—on 7 July at age 71 according to the *Gentleman's Magazine*, but on 14 July at age 72 according to a notation in Smith's "Original Letters" at the Garrick Club. Little is known of his personal life. According to Gilliland he married a woman from Bloomsbury. A Miss Barrymore who acted at the Haymarket in the off-season of 1784–85 may have been his daughter. His son, William Henry Barrymore, was engaged in pantomimes and spectacles at the London theatres between 1814 and 1830 and went to America where he died in 1845. Many dramatic entertainments written by the son are listed by Nicoll.

A small water color portrait of Barrymore was done by Samuel De Wilde in 1813 and is now in the Garrick Club. A portrait of him by Thomas Hardy was engraved by Benjamin Smith and published in a number of impressions by J. Thompson in 1801 and later. A line drawing of him as Hubert in *King John*, done by Burney and engraved by Parker, was published by G. Kearsley in 1804. In a Folger Library art volume of "Portraits of Eminent Actors Taken from Life by W. Loftis 1787–1815" there are three meticulously detailed small water colors of Barrymore: as the Commandant in *The Island of St Marguerite* (13 November 1789), as the Dauphin in *Henry V* (1 October 1789), and as Young Raleigh in *Sir Walter Raleigh* (14 December 1789). In the Hall *Catalogue of Dramatic Portraits in the Harvard Theatre Collection* some illustrations of William Barrymore are listed under the name of his son: items one and five are of William Barrymore; the others are of William Henry Barrymore.

**Barsanti, Francesco** *b. c. 1690, instrumentalist, composer.*

Born at Lucca about 1690, Francesco Barsanti was trained for the law at the University of Padua but preferred to follow a career in music. He came to London in 1714 with Geminiani to play oboe and flute at the King's Theatre in the Haymarket, and though the flute seems to have been his favorite instrument, for which he composed several works, he was also proficient in strings and he wrote a few pieces for violin. From about 1740 (or, according to Meyer, 1719) he was at Edinburgh, where he became choir master at the Edinburgh Musical Society concerts and collected folk songs. In 1750 he returned to London to play viola at the King's Theatre and at Vauxhall. He apparently composed some theatre music, for the Covent Garden accounts show a payment to him on 20 April 1750 of £1 11s. 6d. Barsanti was also a theorist, one of his students of this discipline being Robert Rawlings. Grove gives his death date as some time before 1776; some sources suggest about 1772; and Meyer says he died about 1760.

Francesco Barsanti appears to have been the father and teacher of Jane ("Jenny") Barsanti, the singer and actress of the 1770's. Laetitia Hawkins wrote that Jenny "was the daughter of 'a little old Lucchese,' a humble musician, and of a Scotch woman, who, in later days, when her daughter Jenny acted in Dublin, was known by the Irish as 'the big woman.'" The father spoke broken English and was "interesting only as the father of the actress of that name." He trained her as a singer, but when her voice failed, she turned to acting; on the day of her debut at Covent Garden, perhaps because of anxiety, old Barsanti was seized with a paralytic stroke, and Jenny supported him in his old age. Laetitia Hawkins's dramatic report on the Barsantis has been questioned on several grounds, chiefly that Francesco Barsanti was hardly a humble musician of little interest, and he may well have been dead years before Jenny Barsanti started performing. She made her first public performance at Oxford on 22 June 1769, and her debut at Covent Garden was on 21 September 1772. There is no record of Francesco Barsanti, in London or elsewhere, after April 1750.

**Barsanti, Jane** later Mrs John Richard Kirwan Lyster; later Mrs Richard Daly; sometime stage name Mrs Lisley *d. 1795, actress, singer.*

Jane Barsanti was probably born to the violinist and composer Francesco Barsanti and his wife, a Scotswoman whose maiden name is not known. Neither is the place or date of Jane's birth recorded.

Jane was trained, first by her father and then by his patron Dr Burney, as a singer. She became Burney's favorite pupil and made her first public appearance at Oxford on 22 June 1769 as principal singer in the anthem performed as Burney's exercise for his degree of Doctor of Music. The eminent Dr Hayes conducted and the young girl was accompanied by such instrumentalists as Lates, Park, Pasquali, Malchair, and Charles Burney. Burney's anthem "gave much satisfaction" according to the testimony of his daughter Fanny's diary, but

Poor Barsanti was terrified to death, and her mother, who was among the audience, was so much affected that she fainted away; but by immediate assistance soon revived. However, notwithstanding her fears and apprehensions, Barsanti came off with flying colours, and met with great applause.

*The Oxford Journal* praised her, and she remained for two more performances in the Music Room.

Fanny Burney's journal details how she and Miss Allen, while Jane was visiting at Chesington in 1771, got up a performance of scenes from Cibber's *The Careless Husband* to prepare Jane for her London theatrical debut. It was performed before an audience of gentry who were week-ending at the country house. Burney, who had virtually adopted his protégée, approached Colman at Covent Garden on her behalf since "Drury Lane has actresses already in Barsanti's style." Colman deferred a decision until the fall of 1772, but he was so far convinced by an audition that he then wrote a dramatic "Occasional Prelude" for

*Harvard Theatre Collection*

JANE BARSANTI, as Helena
by J. Roberts

debut her father, perhaps even more anxious than Jane and her distrait mother, suffered a paralytic stroke. He seems to have expired shortly after Jane's first performances. The Barsantis lived at this time in Queen Street, Golden Square, and Jane and her mother continued in this residence for some years after Francesco's death.

Jane played Mrs Oakly in *The Jealous Wife* for the first time on 28 January 1773. During this season she seems to have been principally preoccupied with chorus singing and with the "New Occasional Prelude," which by the time of her appearance in the title role of the afterpiece *The Musical Lady* on 10 May, was being advertised as playing for the seventeenth time. For these services she earned £3 10s. weekly.

Those were also her endeavors and her emoluments in the 1773–74 to 1775–76 seasons except that in 1773–74 she added to her repertory Charlotte Rusport in *The West Indian*; she was the original Lydia Languish in *The Rivals* on 17 and 18 January 1775 and following; she made a good Lady Brumpton in *The Funeral* and a fine Maria in *The Citizen* and, on 26 May 1774, spoke a "Last New Occasional Epilogue, on the Departure of the Manager," establishing prologue- and epilogue-speaking as a specialty. So far as singing roles and occasional songs were concerned, she was up against the formidable competition of Miss Catley, Mrs Baker, and Miss Macklin. On two occasions she was borrowed by Drury Lane. She was also called to Bristol to play on separate occasions in 1774 and 1775. But there was a notation on her benefit bill of 5 May 1775:

The long continuance of Miss Barsanti's illness, together with a very recent affliction which has befallen the family [have] rendered it impossible for her to appear on the stage.

And Miss Hawkins testified that some years after her debut she fell into "a sad

her first appearance as an actress on 21 September, contrived so that she might during her part cleverly mimic some leading Italian and English singers. Though cautiously introduced only as "A Young Lady," she succeeded well, the prelude was repeated for 11 nights, and she was given her first big role, Estifania in *Rule a Wife and Have a Wife* and under her own name —"Miss Barsanti, who performed in the PRELUDE"—on 23 October.

Miss Barsanti was lucky enough, as a contemporary reviewer remembered, early to attract the friendship of the two most influential music historians of her day, Sir John Hawkins and Dr Burney, both of whom had diary-keeping daughters. Letitia-Matilda Hawkins in her *Anecdotes* remembered that on the very day of Jane's

continuity of ill health" and that "ill advised sea-bathing subjected her to excruciating pains in the head."

Jane went to Crow Street, Dublin, for the winter season of 1776–77, and the *Morning Chronicle* of 12 June 1777 thought that "Miss Barsanti is very much improved by her winter campaign in Ireland." A correspondent to the same paper lamented "an unlucky misunderstanding at Covent Garden Theatre which deprived us of this young actress" even for a season. "[T]wo years ago we gave her credit for the sprightly, genuine effusions of true comedy; we now behold her with equal delight in the sublime and the pathetic."

In addition to the new expertise which her Irish experience was thought to have brought, she came back to England provided with a fiancé of impressively aristocratic background. Young John Richard Kirwan Lyster, scion of an ancient Irish family and close friend of the Duke of Leinster, had secretly courted her and, despite the discovery of his ardor, and the consequent adamant opposition from his family, he came to London and married her on 9 June 1777 at St Martin-in-the-Fields.

Jane acted at Cork in 1779 as Mrs Lyster but her husband's family refused to allow her to employ the name on the stage, and so, after continuing to be billed as Miss Barsanti for a month or so she took the stage name of "Lisley" for the first time on 28 August 1777 when she played Constantia in *The Chances*.

J. R. K. Lyster died on 13 January 1779 at Dublin, and in a letter to Garrick reporting this melancholy fact, T. Wilkes lamented that "on the death of his father he was [i.e., would have been] entitled to an estate of upwards of £1500 a year." Naturally none of this came to Jane, although Miss Hawkins thought that the grandfather settled a small sum on a daughter of the marriage. Jane went on acting in Ireland and soon came under the influence of a man who was the very an-

tithesis of her gentle, meticulous, and courteous nature, the profligate Dublin duellist and actor-manager Richard Daly. She had married him by 14 September 1779 (she "remarried in her own natural rank," thought snobbish Miss Hawkins) and settled to the linked tasks of supporting his theatre and ignoring his depredations on decency. She loyally ran his household for him while he pursued other actresses and fought several of his innumerable duels; and her acting sustained the theatre through lean years in 1779–80 and 1784. She was still acting in Dublin in 1786–87 and 1787–88; and she acted at Cork, as Mrs Daly, off and on nearly every year from 1780 through 1793.

Jane Barsanti seems to have been a totally admirable person, approved by the rigidly correct Sir John and Lady Hawkins, and according to Letitia "religious, discreet, and made all she wore." She was also reported by Miss Hawkins to have been a model of filial piety, respectful of her father despite his difficult temperament, and living quietly with her mother, a fat, eccentric Scots woman who worried volubly and equally over her daughter's ill health and the death of a favorite lapdog (which she had had stuffed). Letitia thought Jane extremely correct and moral, fastidious in conduct, and of such great tact that when in Ireland she not only altered the patriotic English song-lines to Irish sentiments but even wore stage clothes of a conspicuously Irish manufacture. Yet, paragon as she seems to have been, she got on well with her less scrupulous colleagues in a theatre which, particularly in Ireland, was not distinguished always for its delicacy.

Jane Barsanti had and retained a fine figure "though her face," said Miss Hawkins, "had little but intelligent good-humour to recommend it." She is said to have modelled her social behavior on Mrs Abington's—or on that part of Mrs Abington's behavior which suited her strict moral canons. When she was acting early in her Irish career ladies were wearing very full petticoats in Dublin's fashionable salons, but "Jenny" made hers scantier and succeeded in dictating "Barsanti petticoats"; and other such triumphs are reported.

Jane Barsanti Daly died in 1795.

James Roberts drew her as Helena in *A Midsummer Night's Dream* and this representation was engraved by C. Grignion for Bell's *British Theatre* in 1776.

Two songs by Samuel Arnold, the words by John O'Keeffe, were published in Dublin in 1780 and 1781 as "Sung by Mrs Daly in The Son in Law." Copies are in the British Museum.

**"Bart."** *See* **BARTLEMAN, JAMES.**

**Barteeske, John** [*fl. 1660*], *drummer.*

John Barteeske was appointed a kettle-drummer in the King's Musick on 20 June 1660, but the records contain no further mention of him.

**Bartelman.** *See also* **BARTLEMAN.**

**Bartelman, Mrs** [*fl. 1767*], *singer.*

A Mrs Bartelman was concerned, with Mrs Arne and Champneys, in a performance of *Alexander's Feast* at Ranelagh on 1 June 1767. What relationship, if any, she bore to the famous bass-baritone singer James Bartleman is not known.

**Barthélemon, Master** [*fl. 1783–1784*], *singer. See* **BARTHÉLEMON, FRANÇOIS HIPPOLYTE.**

**Barthélemon, Cecilia Maria, later Mrs Henslowe** *b. 1770? singer, harpsichordist, harpist.*

Cecilia Barthélemon was born the daughter of François and Mary Barthélemon about 1770. She was named after her great-aunt Cecilia Young Arne, the celebrated singer and wife of Thomas A. Arne.

As a young child she traveled with her parents to the continent in 1776–77, and, according to her later letters, sat on the lap of Marie Antoinette while her parents performed. At the age of nine or ten, she made her debut at the Haymarket on 3 March 1779, singing an Italian duet by Vinci (*"Tu vuoi ch'io vivi o cara"*) with her mother. In a letter to the press on 13 April 1782, Mrs Barthélemon stated that Cecilia was then not quite 13 years of age. She appeared again on 27 April 1784 at the Haymarket, when after the oratorio she again sang a duet with her mother and played a concerto on the *pianoforte*, accompanied on the *viola d'amore* by her father, whose benefit the evening was.

In 1791, her aunt Isabella Young Scott left to Cecilia all her household goods, linens, plate, china, carriage horses, and the residue of her estate from the interest and principal of an unspecified sum in annuities. In 1792 Haydn listed her in his "London Notebook" as one of the musical people in London, and in 1794 Doane listed her as a soprano, a singer at Vauxhall Gardens, and a harpist, then living in Kennington Lane, Vauxhall, with her parents. At Brighton in August 1795, Cecilia, with her father, accompanied her mother in several airs of Handel in a benefit concert for the School of Industry and the Sunday School of the New Chapel.

Cecilia married W. H. Henslowe, the son of Sir John Henslowe, Commissioner of the Navy. Although she intended to write the memoirs of her illustrious forebears—the Arnes, the Barthélemons, and the Youngs—she never did. Her correspondence contains many letters asking other people to write the memoirs or at least to see that larger memorial stones were put on the graves of her ancestors. Her plan for an Arne Jubilee, similar to the Garrick Shakespeare Jubilee or the Handel Commemoration, never materialized. She did write a brief memoir of her father which was published as preface to an edition of the oratorio *Jefte in Masfa,* for which he wrote the music, in 1827.

## Barthélemon, François Hippolyte
*1741–1808, violinist, band leader, composer.*

François Hippolyte Barthélemon was born at Bordeaux on 27 July 1741. Grove states that he was the son of a wig-maker; the *Dictionary of National Biography* states he was the son of a French officer and an Irish lady; and a Sainsbury manuscript in Glasgow University Library states the father was a performer on the violoncello. When quite young, Barthélemon became an officer in the Irish Brigade, according to most accounts, but Van der Straeten suggests he was a French officer at Paris. He seems to have spent some years at Paris, in any event, studying the violin and composing some music. In 1764, Barthélemon also played the violin in the orchestra of the Comédie-Italienne.

Under the inducement of the Earl of Kelly, an amateur composer who was a patron of English music, Barthélemon came to London in 1764. There he was introduced by the Earl to influential social circles and soon became music master to the Dukes of Cumberland and Brunswick; he also received the patronage of the Prince of Wales.

Barthélemon's first public appearance of record in London was on 5 June 1764 when he played a violin solo at a concert in the Great Room, Spring Garden, St James's Park, on the same program in which the young Mozart and his sister made their first London appearances. He also played a violin concerto when the Mozarts gave their famous concert at Hickford's Room on 13 May 1765.

About this time Barthélemon was appointed leader of the band at the King's Theatre. He played, as well, for the Lenten oratorios at Covent Garden in 1766. At the latter theatre his serious opera *Pelopida* was first produced on 22 May 1766. Later in

that year Barthélemon married Miss Mary (Polly) Young, the daughter of the organist Charles Young and a niece of Mrs Thomas Arne. As Mrs Barthélemon she sang in many of the oratorios and concerts with which her husband became associated.

The story is told that David Garrick had been so impressed with Barthélemon's *Pelopida* that he approached him to inquire if the composer could set English words to music. When Barthélemon affirmed he could, Garrick sat down to write out the words of a song he wished to introduce into his play *The Country Girl,* during which time the musician looked over his shoulder and wrote down the notes as quickly. They finished together, and when Garrick handed Barthélemon the words, saying "There, sir, is my song," he was immediately replied to with "And there, sir, is my music to it." Delighted, Garrick invited him home that night for dinner with Dr Johnson. The song, which was introduced successfully in *The Country Girl* at Drury Lane on 25 October 1766, proved so successful it was, according to Sainsbury, encored every night it was sung, "and Garrick, in the fullness of his heart, promised to make Barthélemon's fortune."

Garrick commissioned him to compose music for a little burletta, *Orpheus,* which was introduced into the second act of *A Peep Behind the Curtain* at its first performance on 23 October 1767, but from a letter written by Garrick that very day it is apparent that Barthélemon's fortune was not coming from the manager. It seems that Garrick had neglected to pay Barthélemon for the music but promised he soon would. Reportedly he paid only 40 guineas instead of the 50 promised, because the "dancing cows" had cost him so much, but that story originates with Sainsbury, whose claim that Garrick netted over £2000 from the farce, "performed a hundred and eight nights in one year," is grossly exaggerated. In that season of 1767–68, *A Peep Behind the Curtain* was performed 23 times.

On 19 February 1768 Barthélemon played a violin solo for Dr Arnold's oratorio *The Cure of Saul* at the Haymarket. At the same theatre several weeks later, on 3 March, Barthélemon produced *Oithona*, "A Dramatic Poem from the celebrated *Ossian*," during which he played a concerto on the *viola d'amore* and a solo on the violin, and his wife played a "Lesson on the Harpsichord." On the bills for the evening "Barthélemon, the promoter," announced "that only two acts will be produced on this night, after one Act of a Concert. On the second night of performance of which timely notice will be given he will have the honour to present the piece complete." The second performance never occurred.

In the summer of 1768 Barthélemon composed songs which were sung by his wife at Marylebone Gardens and the Haymarket. He also composed for a new burletta afterpiece, *The Judgment of Paris*, which was performed at the latter theatre for the first time on 24 August 1768, with Mrs Barthélemon in the principal role of Oenone. After playing a concerto at the Haymarket on 7 October 1768, he then spent most of the 1768–69 season at Paris, where he had visited several times in the 1760's to play at the Concert Spirituel. On 22 December 1768 he produced his opera *Le Fleuvre Isamandre* at the Comédie-Italienne.

Barthélemon contributed music with Thomas A. Arne, Aylward, and Dibdin for a birthday performance of Garrick's *Shakespeare's Garland* at Stratford-upon-Avon on 23 April 1769. That September he played "a most enchanting solo on the violin" at the conclusion of the first act of Arne's oratorio *Judith*, which was performed in Trinity Church at Stratford as part of Garrick's Shakespeare Jubilee.

After playing in the Drury Lane oratorios in March 1770, Barthélemon succeeded Pinto as leader of the band at Marylebone Gardens, then under the proprietorship of Samuel Arnold. He remained at the Gar-

dens, where his wife also sang, at least until 1773, composing four burlettas which were performed there: *The Magic Girdle* (4 July 1770), *The Noble Pedlar* (21 August 1770), *The Wedding Day* (15 July 1773), and *La Zingara, or the Gipsy* (25 August 1773). During this period Barthélemon went to Dublin in the winter of 1771–72 to direct a subscription series of 12 burlettas which were given on a small stage in the Rotunda in the New Gardens. O'Keeffe recollected seeing the performances there: "he made a most admirable concerto rondo, on a common, but very pretty tune; his playing it was of the first order—most delightful. He was a very little man, but handsome, and a neat figure." Mrs Barthélemon, who sang the principal roles, was described by O'Keeffe as a "bewitching sprite" with a charming face and small figure.

Barthélemon and his wife sang in the oratorios at Covent Garden in the spring of 1773 and at the Haymarket on occasion in 1772–73 and 1773–74. He also played the violin at Drury Lane in 1774–75 and 1775–76. He wrote incidental music for *The Heroine of the Cave* at that theatre on 19 March 1774 and composed music for Miles Peter Andrews's *The Election*, which was performed on 19 October 1774. The latter piece, for which Barthélemon was paid £30, met with "great Applause," according to the prompter Hopkins's manuscript diary. The *Biographia Dramatica* commented, however, "What nauseous potions will not music wash down the throat of the public." The interlude was reviewed in the *Westminster Magazine* (October 1774): "We shall dismiss this musical trifle by observing, that if the writer [Andrews] was serious, he has been ridiculous. . . . It was preceded by a lively overture of Mr Barthélemon's, who composed the rest of the music; in which, however, we observed no peculiar novelty."

Garrick paid him £24 3*s*. for music to General Burgoyne's very successful entertainment, *The Maid of the Oaks*, which had its premier performance at Drury Lane on 5 November 1774. Barthélemon probably contributed some music to Henry Carey's setting of *Tit for Tat* at Sadler's Wells on 14 August 1775. He also provided one song to Charlotte Lennox's comedy *Old City Manners* at Drury Lane on 9 November 1775. A few weeks later, on 23 November, Barthélemon played violin in a performance of the *Messiah* at the Chapel of the Foundling Hospital.

In 1776 the Barthélemons embarked on a professional tour through Germany, France, and Italy. At the request of the Grand Duke of Tuscany, François set to music the Abbate Semplici's oratorio *Jefte in Masfa* for performance in the Teatro del Cocomero at Florence in the fall of 1776. It was performed in London later at the Hanover Square Rooms on 3 May 1782. The Queen of Naples was so pleased with him, it was reported, that she gave him a letter to deliver in person to her sister Marie Antoinette at Versailles.

Returning to London at the end of 1777, Barthélemon invented an instrument with five strings which he called an "Ipolito," an allusion to his middle name. Garrick paid him £36 15*s*. for music to Andrews's *Belphegor* on 16 March 1778 (with the songs being published the next day). At the Haymarket on 30 May 1778, for a benefit in behalf of the Westminster Lying-In Hospital, his wife sang his new cantata, "suitable to the occasion." He also played at the Haymarket oratorios during the winters of 1777–78, 1778–79, and 1783–84, with at times the orchestra under his direction. His "Victory, An Ode Inscribed to Admiral Keppel," was sung for the first time, at the Haymarket on 17 March 1779. On the same evening he provided the overture, a new cantata entitled "A Sea Storm" (sung by his wife), a canon, and a variation of "Lovely Nancy" ("as done in Italy"), and he also played on the violin. About 1780 he wrote the air "Awake, my soul," as a result of his acquaintance with the Reverend

Jacob Ducké, chaplain to the Female Orphan Asylum.

In the summer of 1779 Barthélemon became leader of the band at Vauxhall Gardens, appointed for life. In 1782–83 he was concertmaster at the King's Theatre, but lost the post the following season under difficult circumstances. In a letter from his house in Vauxhall to the trustees of the Opera on 18 November 1784, he and his wife claimed to be creditors of Mr Taylor, the previous manager, a fact which they said entitled them by provision of a deed of trust to priority in hiring. Barthélemon stated, however, that his wife had not been engaged in the season of 1784 or for the coming season, 1785. He, himself, two seasons previously, had been applied to by the singers and dancers of the Opera to lead the band for 12 nights for the Barthélemons' own benefits, at the King's and the Pantheon. "Messrs Giardini and Cramer having refused to lead, the Nobility wou'd have been depriv'd of their favourite Entertainment" had Barthélemon also refused. So he "sacrific'd" his position at Vauxhall "for that purpose," having been promised the first chair for four years by the trustees of the Opera. But in the last season, 1783–84, the trustees were obliged after a legal tangle to take Gallini's engagements, which included Cramer as the leader. Barthélemon was given a compensation of £100 instead of the £150 he had been promised as the concertmaster. Barthélemon now complained that although he expected to be reinstated this year, Cramer again had been engaged, and he demanded that the trustees restore him to the first chair "or else engage him to *Compose an Opera*, in which capacity he was engaged by M\*r\* Taylor before he gave the Deed of Trust to his creditors." He seems to have received no satisfaction. That season Cramer sat in the first chair and there is no record of an opera by Barthélemon for the King's Theatre.

Disappointed at the Opera, the Barthélemons went to Dublin for the winter season, but according to Mrs Billington's letters to her mother, they were not successful. On 14 February 1784 the actress wrote, "Mr and Mrs Barthelemon are here. He don't please; has only *squeaked* for two nights." On 22 June 1784 she reported, "Barthelemons are as much detested here as they are everywhere else: I have not heard the girl as yet. There was a fire in their lodgings, but they did not loose much."

Returning to London, Barthélemon was now less involved in professional activities as he took greater interest in theology and the newly established Swedenborg Society. He did play in a performance of *Acis and Galatea* at the Pantheon on 25 April 1786, in which his wife sang Galatea. For the 1787–88 season at the Academy of Ancient Music he was paid £37 16s. as the principal first violinist. On 18 August 1789 the press indicated that Barthélemon was to replace Richards as leader of the Drury Lane band and, in a reference to his small stature, stated that the carpenters were at work on raising a place for him in the music section. There is no record, however, that Barthélemon filled the position at Drury Lane in the ensuing season.

In 1794 the Barthélemons lived at No 8, Kennington Place, Vauxhall. They passed the summer of 1795 at Brighton, at No 66, West Street, next door to the Custom House. There in August Barthélemon accompanied his wife in several songs of Handel and in an anthem of her own composition, at a concert for the benefit of the School of Industry and the Sunday School of the New Chapel. Among his last professional activities was his leadership of the band for the performances of the *Messiah* at the Haymarket on 15 January 1798 and a year later on 24 January 1799.

Barthélemon's wife Mary died on 20 September 1799, and administration of her estate was granted to him on 4 October 1799. By Mary, Barthélemon had had a daughter, Cecilia Maria, born about 1770,

who was a pianist and singer in the Haymarket oratorios in the late 1770's and early 1780's. Cecilia later became Mrs Henslowe and wrote a brief memoir of her father which was prefaced to a selection from his oratorio *Jefte in Masfa*, published in 1827.

While we do not concur with Grove who states "there is little doubt" that the young singer James Bartleman was a son of François Barthélemon, we suggest a possibility. The first notice of James Bartleman was on 24 April 1784 when he sang at Covent Garden as Master Bartleman. A year earlier, however, on 6 May 1783, a "Master Barthélemon" sang with Brett, Reynolds, Perry, and Billington at Covent Garden, and several weeks later at the same theatre "Master Barthélemon" sang "Kate of Aberdeen" at the end of the mainpiece. Moreover, on 6 March 1786 a "J. Bartholomon" acted Roger in *The Mayor of Garratt* at the Haymarket. Yet when Isabella Young Scott died in 1791 and left bequests to her sister Mary Barthélemon, to her brother-in-law François, and to Miss Cecilia Barthélemon, she made no mention in her will of any male child of the Barthélemons. Our suggestion of progeny must be tempered further by the fact that in François's will of 1808, no mention is made of a son James (who may have been omitted for reasons of discretion), but a son George is mentioned. According to the will and letters of James Bartleman, that singer did have a brother George, but he also had three sisters, Jemima, Mary, and Selina Ann.

Sometime after the death of his wife Mary in 1799, François Barthélemon married a second time. He died on 20 July 1808 at his house in Hatfield Street in the parish of Christ Church, Surrey. In his will, drawn up on 7 June 1808 and proved on 5 August of the same year, he left all his possessions, musical instruments, and furniture to his "lawful wife" Sarah Barthélemon, whom he instructed to care for his two young children, evidently by her—his

"Dear Boy" George Barthélemon, godson to the Prince of Wales, and Angelica Augusta Barthélemon, who was the goddaughter of the famous singer Angelina Catalani. Neither Cecilia Maria nor any other children were mentioned in the will.

In addition to the theatrical music mentioned above, Barthélemon composed numerous instrumental works for violin, *pianoforte,* and orchestra. He also wrote dances, marches, and many songs for the pleasure gardens. A long list of his published pieces is found in the British Museum's catalogue of printed music. A Sainsbury manuscript at the Glasgow University Library mentions an oratorio entitled "The Nativity" and two services by Barthélemon which were still in manuscript after his death.

Among his pupils were General Christopher Ashley and George Bridgetower. As a violinist, Barthélemon excelled as an interpreter of Corelli, and reportedly his death elicited from Salomon, "We have lost our Corelli! There is nobody left now to play those sublime solos." Barthélemon was greatly admired by Burney, who wrote of the virtuoso's "powerful hand and truly vocal adagio."

**Barthélemon, Mrs François Hippolyte.** *See* **YOUNG, MARY** [**POLLY**].

**Bartholdi.** *See* **BERTOLLI.**

**Bartholomeo** or **Bartholomew.** *See* **ALBRICI, BARTOLOMEO.**

**Bartholomici.** *See* **BARTOLOMICI.**

**Bartholomon, J.** [*fl.* 1786], *actor.*
A J. Bartholomon played Roger in *The Mayor of Garratt* at the Haymarket, out-of-season, on 6 March 1786. He was perhaps James Bartleman, or possibly Barthélemon.

**Barthrope, Mr** [*fl.* 1775–1786], *house servant.*

A Mr Barthrope worked at Drury Lane at least from 5 October 1775, when he was listed as the first gallery cheque taker, to 29 May 1786, the last mention of him in the theatre accounts. Presumably he was the same person who was listed as a dresser at 9*s.* per week for the 1776–77 season, a position which he may have held for the bulk of his active career.

**Bartleman, James** *1769–1821, singer.*
James Bartleman, the English bass-baritone singer, was born on 19 September 1769, probably in Westminster. It has been repeatedly suggested that he was the son of the renowned musician François Barthélemon.

James was educated under Cooke in the choir school of Westminster Abbey after having been discovered and presented there by a wealthy office-holder named Royer. He sang soprano with the choir and was for a time "principal treeble singer" in the Chapel Royal.

Apparently his first notice in a public theatre was for 24 April 1784 when "Master Bartleman" sang two glees based on Shakespearean texts with Bannister, Brett, Davies, and Mrs Kennedy, at Covent Garden Theatre.

Young Bartleman had the good fortune to be taken up early by the musical historian Hawkins and became an intimate of the household. Laetitia Hawkins has left a striking memorandum of his character:

Though delicate in person and constitution, and often ill, Bartleman was lively and spirited to a remarkable degree. It used to puzzle me to find out when or how he learned; and, indeed, I have heard Dr Cooke say, "Those boys of mine learn of one another more than from *me.*" Of his early superiority he was as little vain as if it had consisted in spinning a top, or trundling a hoop; he never went further in setting himself above another, than by humourously caricaturing something ludicrously bad. In short, he was one of the most agreeable lads that ever had "the run" of a house.

*Harvard Theatre Collection*

JAMES BARTLEMAN
by Worthington

that group while his voice deepened, until 1791 when he became first solo bass (actually *baritano*) singer at the Vocal Concerts at the Hanover Square Rooms. His range extended from E below the bass staff to G above it. He sang in the oratorios at Covent Garden from 1792 through 1797 and in 1798–99, and at the Haymarket in 1797–98, and by 1793 had already established himself as without peer in the bass-baritone parts of all the works by Handel, Boyce, and Pergolesi which were sung in London. Callcott and Crotch wrote songs especially for him.

In the winter season of 1793–94 he sang for the first time under the baton of Dr Hayes at the great concerts of the Oxford Musical Society, and he revisited Oxford several times in the nineteenth century. He was also a regular singer at the Ladies' Catch and Glee Club. In 1794 Doane's *Musical Directory* credited him with membership in St Peter's Choir. He was living at the time at No 11, Clifford Row, Chelsea. He was at the fifth Chester Musical Festival in 1806. Despite bouts with wretched health, he kept singing in theatres and at concerts intermittently until 1813, and as late as 1814 was applying to the Lord Chamberlain, as joint conductor with C. and I. Knyvett and Greatorex, for a license to present the Hanover Square Concerts.

Bartleman was responsible for the revival of many of the great bass songs by Henry Purcell, and every critic esteemed him as one of the most sensitive and sincere interpreters of Handel's softer airs. His gentle, modest personality, rare in *virtuosi*, was doubtless involved. As Miss Hawkins said "Success never altered him, applause never elevated him."

James Bartleman died at Middlesex Hospital on 15 April 1821, aged 53, and was buried on 21 April (as from No 45, Berners Street) in the West Cloister of Westminster Abbey. His epitaph was by Dean Ireland, and on his memorial was chisled also the opening line of Pergolesi's "Lord

An instance of Bartleman's nice feeling I call to mind. My father had made him a present, annexing to the gift the condition that he should copy out some music for him . . . but just afterwards, having reached a point in his musical studies that left him less leisure, he found he had not time to do what he had promised [and] returned it, together with his present . . . saying, that "as he could not perform the task, it was not just to accept the reward". . . . I remember my own astonishment at this promptitude . . . but it appeared to me as if a boy had on a sudden, without the intervention of—what shall I say?—*ladhood?* started into manhood.

In 1788 Bartleman joined the Concerts of Ancient Music as a "tenoir voice" for an emolument of £5 and was a member of

have mercy upon me," one of his greatest vocal offerings.

He had never married and he apparently made no will. His sister Jane Bartleman administered his estate of under £5000 on 18 May 1821. According to subsequent letters of administration he had also a brother George and three other sisters: Jemima, wife of Thomas Godwin; Mary Gayntin, widow; and Selina-Ann Bartleman.

Bartleman left an extensive collection of song books of his and earlier periods which was sold by Mr White of Story's Gate, Great George Street, on 20 February 1822.

He was painted by Hargreaves, and an engraving of this pose, by I. Thomson, was published "by the Misses Bartleman" in 1830. There also survives a silhouette engraved by W. H. Worthington.

### Bartlett, Mr (fl. 1735–1741), musician?

A Mr Bartlett shared a benefit with a Mr Davis at the Haymarket on 21 March 1735 when the French company was playing there. Davis was a musician, so perhaps Bartlett was one too. It was possibly this same Bartlett who shared a benefit with three others at Drury Lane on 14 May 1741; again, the bill made no mention of his function.

### Bartolini, Vincenzio (fl. 1782–1792), singer.

Vincenzio Bartolini, a male soprano, made his first appearance in England at the King's Theatre in the Haymarket on 2 November 1782 singing Il Conte Polidoro, the second soprano, in the comic opera, Il convito. He sang in London for four seasons, his first one being the most demanding: in 1782–83, after his first appearance, he sang Evandro in Medonte (14 November), Il Barone di Ripa Verde in Il trionfo della costanza (19 December), Duarte in Cimene (7 January 1783), a principal role in Bertoni's Ifigenia (18 February), Azor in Zemire e Azor opposite Signora Alle-

granti (27 February), Licida in the pasticcio L'Olimpiade (6 March), Giacinto in I vecchi burlati (27 March), Filaco in Creusa in Delfo (29 May), a major role in La buona figliuola (3 June), and Felicino in L'avaro (14 June).

His 1783–84 season was almost as exhausting and included major parts in, among other operas, Silla, I rivali delusi, La schiava, Demofoonte, Issipile, and Le gemelle (sometimes called Le due gemelle). Twice he was specially noted as assuming one of the serious characters in comic operas. In May and June 1784, while still fulfilling his obligations at the King's Theatre, Bartolini sang in the Handel Memorial concerts at Westminster Abbey and the Pantheon.

The singer's season salary in 1784–85 was £300, but his burden was considerably reduced. He sang in only four operas, one of them a revival in which he took a role he had previously played—Il Conte in I rivali delusi. He had a principal part in Demetrio, sang Amenosi in Netteti, and finished the season performing a major role in Artaserse. His 1785–86 season was similarly light: Osmida in Didone abbandonata, Il Tenente in La scuola de' gelosi, a principal role in Perseo, Appius Claudius in Virginia, and Idreno in Armida. He also sang in the 1786 Handel Commemoration in May and June. After this season, Bartolini's name disappeared from the London bills, but he returned to the Continent to continue his career and was still singing to good notices at Cassel in 1792.

### Bartolomici, Luigi, d. 1800, dancer.

Luigi Bartolomici made his first public appearance dancing the role of Jack in a new comic ballet, The Happy Stratagem, at Drury Lane on 1 July 1799. The following season he was engaged at the King's Theatre, but before the season was out the Morning Herald (1 April 1800) reported that he had been murdered on 18 March.

A detailed account of Bartolomici's death

was given by the *London Chronicle* in its reports of the trial at the Bow Street Public Office of John Wilson respecting "the murder of Louis Bartholomici, the Opera dancer." According to the testimony of Bartolomici's widow, Wilson, an officer, had gone to arrest Bartolomici at his lodgings on Poland Street in connection with a suit brought against him for debt by a Mr Aldborough (or Harborough), a tailor. When the dancer and Wilson went downstairs and met John Lyne and William Crane in the hall, Bartolomici ran back upstairs, crying out he would be murdered, and locked himself in a front room on the second floor. The three men pursued him, forced the door, and beat him with a poker and sticks. Another witness, James D'Egville, balletmaster at the Opera, testified that at St Bartholomew's hospital, where the victim was taken because the keeper at Newgate would not take him in, Bartolomici had told him before he died that Wilson had pushed the poker down his throat. Mr Long, one of the surgeons at the hospital, testified that Bartolomici had died of wounds which he received under the tongue. On 3 June 1800 the defendant Wilson was found not guilty of manslaughter on the grounds that resistance was illegal in a warrant case and the violence of Bartolomici necessitated that the officer strike back in his own defense. During the trial Mrs Bartolomici was described as "a very genteel woman, of a most respectable family in Ireland, and had been married about five years to the deceased."

**Bartolotti, Girolamo** [*fl.* 1731], *trumpeter.*

A benefit concert for the trumpeter Girolamo Bartolotti was held at Hickford's music room on 19 March 1731.

**Barton, Mr** [*fl.* 1721], *dancer.*

John Weaver, in his 1721 lectures on dancing, listed a Mr Barton as one of the dancing masters active at that time.

**Barton, Mr** [*fl.* 1736], *actor.*

A Mr Barton played Sir Charles Easy in a performance of *The Careless Husband* at the Haymarket Theatre on 16 February 1736; the play was produced by Mrs Thomas Reading for her benefit.

**Barton, Mr** [*fl.* 1791–1792], *house servant? actor?*

A Mr Barton was on the payroll at Covent Garden Theatre throughout the season of 1791–92, earning 10s. per five-night week. His capacity is not known.

**Barton, Frances.** *See* ABINGTON, MRS JAMES.

**Barton, William** *d.* 1778? *musician, pleasure garden proprietor.*

William Barton, according to Haslewood, was proprietor of the place of public resort known as Ruckholt House at Leyton, Essex.

[It was] said to have been once the mansion of Queen Elizabeth; and is now mentioned as forming, for a short period, an auxiliary place of amusement for the summer to the established Theatres, and situate within the environs of London. It was opened about the year 1742 . . . with public breakfasts, weekly concerts, and occasional oratorios.

A William Barton "musician St James's St" was admitted to livery as a freeman of the Worshipful Company of Musicians on 17 July 1764, according to the Company's manuscript register at Guildhall. Conceivably the two William Bartons are the same. They may have been father and son.

A series of entries in the burial register of St Paul, Covent Garden, the "actors' church," may be relevant:

| | |
|---|---|
| 21 June 1764 | John son of William Barton |
| 19 April 1770 | Elizabeth wife of William Barton |
| 5 July 1770 | John son of Wil- |

| | liam Barton |
|---|---|
| 9 June 1773 | Thomas son of William Barton |
| 1 June 1775 | Sarah daughter of William Barton |
| 27 May 1776 | William son of William Barton |
| 26 February 1778 | William Barton |
| 2 April 1783 | Joseph son of William Barton |

**Barwell, Thomas** [*fl. 1677–1700*], *trumpeter.*

Thomas Barwell was appointed a trumpeter in the King's Musick on 5 June 1677, replacing James Castle, and probably served continuously until the end of the century despite the infrequent mention of him in the records. He also served as trumpeter in Captain Legg's troop until 8 March 1682, when he was replaced by Augustin Buckler. On 20 February 1686 the Lord Chamberlain's accounts begin a series of amusing entries concerning Barwell: "Received Thomas Barwell's trumpett, all broke to peeces, which was Culthrop's, weight 16 oz." This note was signed by the royal instrument repairman, William Bull, who also received, on the same day, a trumpet from Simon Pierson; it, too, was "broke to peeces, weight 27 oz." There is no indication in the accounts that Barwell and Pierson were enemies. Barwell must not have liked his repaired trumpet when he got it back, for though it was noted as "new made" on 12 May, he was delivered a silver trumpet, presumably a brand new one, on 2 August 1686, which must have been the envy of his colleagues.

In 1691 Barwell accompanied William III on his trip to Holland, and another indication of his high standing was his salary, which in 1697 was £91 5s. On 16 December 1697 he received another new silver trumpet, but he used it for only two years; on 5 January 1700 he stepped down from his position and was replaced by John Ernst.

**Bary.** *See* **BARRY.**

**Barzago.** *See* **BUZARGLO.**

**Barzond** or **Barzzond.** *See* **BAYZAND.**

**Basan.** *See* **BASSAN.**

**Basevi, Giacobbe.** *See* **CERVETTO, GIACOBBE.**

**Basil, Mr** [*fl. 1778*], *fair booth operator.*

Mr Basil operated a booth at Bartholomew Fair in 1778, but his offering is not known.

**Baskotin.** *See* **BOSKOTIN.**

**Basrier, Mr** [*fl. 1675*], *violinist.*

On 15 February 1675, when the masque *Calisto* was produced at Charles II's court, Mr Basrier performed as one of the regular band of 24 violins. This seems to be the only notice of him and perhaps it is a case of mistaken identity; most members of the King's band of violins were cited frequently in the records.

**Bass, Mr** [*fl. 1778–1784*], *actor.*

The Mr Bass who was a minor member of the acting company at Bristol in 1778 was probably the actor who played Roger in *The Mayor of Garratt* at the Haymarket Theatre in London on 8 March 1784.

**Bassan, Mr** [*fl. 1766–1784*], *house servant.*

The Covent Garden accounts connect Mr Bassan with the footmen's room at the theatre, but what his function was there is unclear. The earliest mention of him in the bills was on 15 May 1766, and the accounts name him almost every season through 1783–84, the last notice being on 3 June 1784. His salary seems to have remained at £1 5s. per week throughout his years of service, though one vague entry in 1766 lists him at 1s. daily—possibly for extra services.

Bassan was possibly related to the dancer Miss Bassan who was active at Covent Garden from 1773 to 1780. He may have been the Josiah Bassan whose wife Mary was buried at St Paul, Covent Garden, on 22 December 1744.

### Bassan, Miss [*fl.* 1773–1780], *dancer.*

Miss Bassan was a dancer at Covent Garden whose first appearance there was on 21 May 1773 when she danced a hornpipe. She seems not to have risen to any assignments of importance, and one of the few other specific references to her is on 9 May 1777 when she danced a double hornpipe with Rudd. Her salary that season was £1 5s. She may have been related to the Mr Bassan who worked for Covent Garden from 1766 to 1784; and the St Paul, Covent Garden, burial of a Mary Bassan, wife of Josiah, on 22 December 1744 could be a reference to her mother.

### Bassano, Henry *d. 1665, flutist, oboist.*

Henry Bassano was one of the last of a line of Italian-English musicians which stretched back at least to 1538 and was, in the sixteenth century, variously called Basson or de Basson or Bassano. He was related, but in what way is unclear, to Andrea, Anthony, Edward, and Jerome (or Jeronimo) Bassano, all of whom were active with him in the 1620's; only Henry, it seems, survived to perform in the reign of Charles II.

Bassano was part of the wind instrument group that played at the funeral of James I in 1625, and presumably he had served under that monarch. On 8 August 1626 he was admitted as a musician to Charles I in place of Andrea Bassano, resigned; the fee of 1s. 8d. per day and a livery allowance of £16 2s. 6d. for life, which had been granted Andrea, was turned over to Henry (lifetime grants were apparently rescinded

if one resigned from the royal service before retirement). Andrea Bassano may have been Henry's father, or at least it would appear that he was of an earlier generation. In 1628 Henry Bassano was listed among the oboe and sackbut players, and he was regularly cited among the wind instrumentalists up to 1642. Frequently during the 1630's he was in financial difficulties, occasionally assigning his livery payments to others or being petitioned against for debts.

What happened to Bassano during the Commonwealth period is not known; he may well have gone to the Continent, for he apparently kept up his court contacts and was returned to his old position in the King's Musick in 1660 under Charles II, at whose coronation he played. He seems to have performed regularly until shortly before his death in August 1665, and he was plagued with financial difficulties to the end. He was buried on 29 August 1665 at his church, St Margaret, Westminster. Apparently he died intestate; on 23 May 1666 administration of his estate was granted to Thomas Finell, Bassano's creditor (and fellow musician at court), in lieu of Susanna Swanley, alias Bassano, relict of the deceased, who renounced her claim.

On 5 September 1665, a week after Bassano's funeral, Isaac Staggins and William Young were appointed to replace him; on the following day Richard Hudson was designated to receive Bassano's livery fee. Young was a flutist and Staggins an oboist, so it appears that Bassano's position was split after his death or that he had occupied, as several musicians did, multiple appointments. Hudson was a violinist, but the wording of the warrant does not imply that Bassano had been proficient on that instrument. This granting of livery fees had, at that time, little bearing on reality, for the King was woefully behind in his payments; as late as 1667 Bassano's executors were still trying to collect livery payments due him for 1660, 1661, and 1662. It is little wonder that he died in debt.

**Bassanti.** *See* BARSANTI.

**Basset, Mr** [*fl.* 1799], *actor.*
A Mr Basset played a principal role in *Lover's Vows* at Covent Garden on 12 June 1799.

**Bassett, Mr** [*fl.* 1794], *bass viol player.*
Doane's *Musical Directory* of 1794 lists Mr Bassett, of Orpington, Kent, as a bass viol player in the Handelian concerts at Westminster Abbey.

**Bassett, John** *d. 1787, instrumentalist.*
John Bassett was already playing in the Drury Lane band on 2 February 1777 when he was recommended for admission to the Royal Society of Musicians; his entry in their books states that he had by then studied music upwards of seven years for his livelihood, was single, and worked at Drury Lane. The theatre accounts for 1778–79 list him as one of the first violinists, apparently doubling on clarinet, at a salary of £2 10s. per week. On 13 September 1780 Bassett married Barbara Maria Roworth of St James, Westminster, at St Martin-in-the-Fields, his church.

Bassett played in the Handel Memorial Concerts at Westminster Abbey and the Pantheon on 26, 27, 29 May and 3, 5 June 1784 as a first violinist, and he performed at St Paul's Concerts on 10 and 12 May 1785; he was presumably still on the Drury Lane staff at this time and continued playing there through the 1786–87 season. In July 1787, however, he was in great difficulty, as the records of the Royal Society of Musicians show. He petitioned for aid: "He being through Violent Illness, unable to retain an engagement for the summer season, on which he much depended, and at great expense without any Income is compelled to trouble the Society for their Assistance." He must have died shortly after this petition, for on 5 August 1787 his widow, Maria Bassett, was recommended for charity. The Bassetts had no children.

**Bassevi, Giacobbe.** *See* CERVETTO, GIACOBBE.

**Bassingwhite,** [John?] [*fl.* 1777], *actor.*
A Mr Bassingwhite, possibly John, played Sir William in *The Gentle Shepherd* at the Haymarket Theatre on 11 January 1779. When the work was repeated on 8 March an unidentified "Gentleman" took the role. It seems likely that the following information from the St Paul, Covent Garden parish registers refers to this actor: John, son of John Bassingwhite by Ann Gumley his wife, was baptized on 6 April 1771; and John Bassingwhite witnessed the marriage of Lewis Read to Mary Jane Devy on 9 June 1783.

**Basson.** *See* BASSANO and BASSAN.

**"Bastardella, La,"** or **"Bastardini."** *See* AGUIARI, LUCREZIA.

**Bastee.** *See* BAXTER, RICHARD *d. 1747, dancer.*

**Baster, Mrs John, Eleanor, née Green** [*fl.* 1799–1809?], *actress, singer.*
According to a perhaps heightened account in *The Authentic Memoirs of the Green Room* (1804), Mrs Baster's maiden name was Green, and she was the daughter "of a gentleman in a public situation of no mean emolument under government." She was also said to have received a fashionable education at a convent in France. But it is certain that, at the time of her debut, she was married to a Strand tailor named John Baster.

Although she was already well known in 1795 as a vocal performer in several private theatres in London's environs, Mrs Baster's brief professional career seems to have begun when James Winston (managing as "Neville" at Richmond) gave her a summer tryout in 1799. There she played

Edmund in the afterpiece *The Purse*, a "breeches" part.

At Covent Garden on 13 June 1800 as "A Lady, First Appearance," she played another role in breeches, Don Carlos in *The Duenna*. The audience was small, though the performance benefited the Bayswater General Lying-in Hospital; but it was generous with applause. Criticism was irritated by her corpulency but mollified by the sweetness of her voice which "amply compensated for this defect."

In the summer of 1800 Mrs Baster made a country tour, visiting several towns including Yarmouth and Norwich "where her vocal powers procured her great and general applause," if we credit the *Authentic Memoirs*, which continue:

At the opening of the winter theatres for the present season [1800–1801], she was engaged at Covent-Garden on the recommendation of Dr Kennedy, who had frequently witnessed her private performances, and spoke of her in terms of warm encomium to the manager.

Mrs Baster seems to have resisted stubbornly the pointed references to the inadequacy of her figure for the assumption of male roles. Her next essay was as Patrick in O'Keeffe's musical entertainment of *The Poor Soldier*, usually a dependable snare for applause. But again criticism was divided into encomiums on her voice and condemnations of her figure. She did little else that season except repeat *The Duenna*, sing a song "in the character of a Moss-Rose Woman," and assist in the choruses. One critic thought that in voice and *embonpoint* figure she resembled Mrs Lawrence Kennedy and lamented that at an earlier period of her life her richness of tone, her style, and her clearness of articulation would have made her a capital acquisition.

Mrs Baster's decline can perhaps be understood as much from her salary as from her roles. In 1800–1801 she received £3 for a six-day week; in 1801–2 her salary was £2; for a five-day week in 1802–3 she earned £1 13*s*. 4*d*. At the end of that season she left Covent Garden.

She was at Edinburgh during the winter seasons (beginning in January) of 1804 and 1805. She was at Glasgow under the management of Thomas Beaumont in the season of 1808–9.

Mrs Baster was reported to supplement her income "by instructing persons of her own sex in the rudiments of music, vocal and instrumental," though whether this was in London or in Scotland was not specified.

Her husband John Baster was a choleric man who, though he did not himself act, managed all of his wife's contractual and artistic affairs. Letters of 1799 from him to James Winston survive in which he objects to her assignment of characters and to her wages and threatens to sue if he is not allowed to inspect the financial accounts of the Richmond Theatre.

A list of bankrupts dated 12 October 1808, from one of London's newspapers, includes: "John Baster of the Strand, Tailor, to surrender Oct. 18, 26, and Nov. 22, at eleven, at Guildhall."

**Baster, Mrs** *fl. 1735–1736*, *dresser.*

A Mrs Baston served at Covent Garden as a dresser during the 1735–36 season and was paid £12 18*s*. for 172 days of work. She may have been the Miss Baston who made very little headway as a dancer the previous three seasons, or a relative, possibly the dancer's mother.

**Baston, Miss** *fl. 1732–1735*, *dancer, harpsichordist.*

Miss (sometimes, incorrectly, Mrs) Baston danced with John Rich's company at Lincoln's Inn Fields Theatre, her first notice being on 9 November 1732, when she replaced Mrs La Foy as the fourth Sylvan in the afterpiece, *The Rape of*

*Proserpine*. On 8 December 1732, the day after the troupe moved to their new theatre in Covent Garden, she was in a group comic dance; and so she continued, usually dancing in group numbers, to the end of the season. She had another talent, however, and she displayed it on 18 May 1733 when she not only danced but played a lesson on the harpsichord. The following fall, on 22 September 1733, she participated in a Scottish dance; on 13 October she played one of the Nymphs in *Apollo and Daphne*; on 26 February 1734 she was a Bacchante in *The Necromancer*; and she appeared in other similar groups in pantomimes during the season, never rising to a role of any importance.

She was re-engaged for the 1734–35 season and occasionally danced more distinguished parts: on 2 October 1734, for instance, she danced a Harlequin Woman to Le Sac's Harlequin Man in *The Necromancer*. But most of the season she was one of the corps of dancers playing unnamed characters. After this season, her name disappeared from the bills, though she may have been (or have been related to) the Mrs Baston who was a Covent Garden dresser in 1735–36.

**Baston, John** *[fl. 1709–1739]*, *flutist, composer.*

On 25 August 1709 at Stationer's Hall the two sons of a Mr Baston played a *concerto grosso*, apparently for violin and flute; they were advertised as having played it before with great applause, so this was not their first public appearance. Whether or not their father was also a musician is unknown, but the implication in the bill is that he was, though no record of his activity has survived. The brothers, John and Thomas Baston (or Bastor, Bastion) shared benefits on 20 December 1711 at Coachmaker's Hall and on 8 December 1712 at Stationer's Hall, presumably playing on both occasions; John was a flutist, though he composed for the violin as well,

and Thomas, sometimes called Baston Junior, was proficient on both instruments. On 25 January 1714 at Stationer's Hall Thomas shared a benefit with Mr Young, and on 25 April 1716 he and his brother joined again to play at Lincoln's Inn Fields Theatre.

The brothers Baston performed regularly at that playhouse for several years, usually as a team, and often featuring John's compositions. Their appearances at the theatre were occasional, however; they seem not to have been salaried members of the company at this time and were free to give concerts elsewhere. On 4 March 1720 John performed at Hickford's music room but, during this season made no theatrical appearances. On the other hand, Thomas played several times at the Lincoln's Inn Fields Theatre in May 1720, one of his selections being "A Concerto on the Sixth Flute" probably written by his brother. After this month, records of Thomas Baston cease, but his brother John continued active for at least two more decades.

On 23 December 1720 John Baston gave a concert at Lincoln's Inn Fields, and on 14 March 1722 he appeared at Drury Lane, playing a concerto on the "Little Flute" – the instrument he continued playing with great success during most of the 1720's. In July 1722 he played at a concert at E. Marriott's Great Room in Richmond; during the spring and summer of 1723 he carried a heavy schedule of performances at Drury Lane; and on 2 September 1723 he appeared at Pinkethman's playhouse in Richmond. Through the 1726–27 season he played at Drury Lane as a soloist, and he may have been a member of the theatre band as well; but after this season there is no notice of him until 13 March 1728, when he gave a concert at York Buildings. He was back at Drury Lane in the spring of 1730 for several performances; he had a benefit at the Academy in Chancery Lane on 5 April 1732; and he appeared at Drury Lane again on 9 May 1733. John Baston was still alive, and apparently playing, in 1739, for he was one of the original subscribers ("being Musicians") to the Royal Society of Musicians when it was established on 28 August 1739.

Six *concerti* for violin and flute by John Baston were published in 1730.

**Baston, Thomas** *[fl. 1709–1720], flutist, violinist.* See **BASTON, JOHN.**

**Bataglio, Matteo** *[fl. 1662?–1670], musician.*

Matteo Bataglio was probably one of the members of the Italian Musick of Charles II when it was established in 1662. On 27 June 1668 an order was written to present him with a gift from the King, and on 8 July 1670 a similar warrant awarded him a £40 gold chain.

**Batchelor, Miss** *[fl. 1750–1754], dancer.*

Miss Batchelor (or Bachelor, Batcheldor) joined the Covent Garden company in 1750–51 but seems not to have been significant enough to be mentioned in any of the bills for that season. In 1751–52 she was cited as playing one of four Scaramouch Women in *The Necromancer* on 11 November 1751 and one of the followers of Daphne in *Apollo and Daphne* on 4 December. The next season she transferred to Drury Lane, but her career there was no more successful. She was rarely mentioned in the bills, and only at the end of her last season, on 2 May 1754, was she mentioned as performing a specialty dance. It was a minuet, danced with Gerard, and the bill mentioned that tickets delivered by her would be accepted that night. On 1 May 1785 a Miss Batchelor was an honorary subscriber at one guinea to the Royal Society of Musicians, but there is no way of determining whether or not this was the dancer. Dancers were occasionally admitted to the Society.

**Bate.** *See also* **BATES.**

**Bate, Mr** *[fl. 1779], actor.*

A Mr Bate played at the Haymarket 15 March 1779, taking the roles of the Vice Chancellor in *The Humours of Oxford* and Mr McLofty in *A Mirror for the Ladies*. He may very well have been the same as one of the actors named Bates who was active at about this time.

**Bateman, Mr** *[fl. 1782], actor.*

A Mr Bateman played only once in London, as Dr Drench in *Don Quixote in England*, in a casual company assembled for Mrs Lefevre's benefit out-of-season at the Haymarket on 4 March 1782. He may have been only a venturesome amateur.

**Bateman, Mrs** *[fl. 1730], actress?*

Mrs Bateman was one of the women peasants in *Harlequin's Contrivance* on 14 September 1730 when it was presented at the Great Theatrical Booth in Bird Cage Alley at Southwark Fair; whether she was an actress or a dancer is not clear. The troupe was billed as from the Haymarket, and Mrs Bateman may have been one of the minor performers there.

**Bateman, John** *[fl. 1667], actor?*

John Bateman was named in a livery warrant dated 22 July 1667 as a member of the King's Company; he is not otherwise recorded, and his name on the list could be an error for actor Thomas Bateman.

**Bateman, Mrs** *[Mary? née Humphry?] 1765?–1829, actress, fencer, singer.*

The name of Mrs Bateman, a young woman of dim antecedents and some provincial stage experience, first sprang into prominence in London early in 1793. From 18 January at her house in Carlisle Street, Soho, she and the notorious transvestite fencer Madame D'Eon (*dit* "Chevalier") gave a series of subscription breakfasts for the curious nobility and gentry, which concluded around one in the afternoon with a display of sword-play by Madame D'Eon. Very likely Mrs Bateman, who had been D'Eon's pupil since 1792, also fenced.

Mrs Bateman was Bridget in *The Chapter of Accidents* at the Haymarket on 14 February 1793, under the untrustworthy statement "first time on any stage," but as the reviewer of her second performance of Bridget (in April) said: "This lady is not as generally supposed a novice in the profession, she having frequently trod the boards of a provincial theatre." Novice or not, her first performance was coolly received by periodical critics. The *European Magazine* was amazed at her "confidence." Kemble, in a manuscript note, succinctly decided: "Wretched!"

On 1 May she played the Widow Brady (with an Epilogue Song) in *The Irish Widow*; and on 30 May Lady Restless in *All in the Wrong* and Maria in *The Citizen*, all purporting to be first appearances in the several characters. On her benefit night the Chevalier D'Eon fenced with her and a masked "gentleman volunteer" from the audience. Kemble, whose profit from such displays scarcely assuaged his artistic anguish, noted simply: "Mrs Bateman acted—oh, Lord! D'Eon fenc'd—oh, Lord!" D'Eon had excited roars of laughter by fencing in a short petticoat and her "shift sleeves."

At least the publicity of *déjeuner* with fencing had kept these two odd women in the public eye, and in fact something called the Club D'Armes or Fencing Society seems to have supported their performances *en masse*. There was also some gossip about Mrs Bateman and the fashionable satiric writer and playwright Frederick Pilon.

The smaller theatres were glad to capitalize on all the notoriety, and Mrs Bateman secured three nights at Richmond in July 1793. The newspapers reported on 7 July that "Mrs Bateman is to play six nights at Brighton on very liberal terms." On 23 August Madame D'Eon and "her pretty friend," as Mrs Bateman was often called, were playing a benefit at Richmond. The *Thespian Magazine* reported that Mrs Bateman "murdered" both Lady Teazle in *School for Scandal* and Maria in *The Citizen* on this occasion. Mrs or Madame or Chevalier D'Eon "fenced with a nobleman." Both gave their addresses to be the house on Carlisle Street. By 26 October the two had been at Margate "Where they appeared, a few nights . . . more to the profit of the Manager than of themselves. A subscription begun by the Duchess of Cumberland, was presented, in the most respectful manner, to La [*sic*] Chevaliere."

In July of 1794 duelling and *déjeuner* again were advertized on Carlisle Street where "cold iron is always a standing dish to regale the loungers." On 16 September it was reported "Madame D'Eon and Mrs Bateman set out for Cork, where they were engaged to perform six nights in the Theatre Royal; from thence they proceed to Dublin, where they have a similar engagement."

The Cork experience was not fruitful. Mrs Bateman performed several standard comic parts and her friend fenced. But Mrs Bateman involved herself imprudently in an altercation with the explosive Irish audience which spilled over into the public prints. The pair recrossed St George's channel in late February 1795, and Madame D'Eon was was detained by illness at Liverpool.

James Winston records one performance by Mrs Bateman at the Tottenham Court Road private theatre in 1796, and after that there was apparently nothing to report.

A Mary Bateman of Bow Street, Covent Garden, was buried at St Paul, Covent Garden, on 12 July 1829, aged 64. Her dates, (1765–1829) would fit very plausibly the Mrs Bateman whom we have been discussing. The will of this Mrs Mary Bateman, signed 22 September 1826 and proved 9 July 1829, leaves small bequests to her "Niece Elizabeth the wife of my nephew Samuel Humphry, son of my late brother William Humphry"; to another niece, "Mary the wife of John Lownes and one of the children of my sister Elizabeth Brooks"; to other children of Mrs Brooks —William, Charles, Daniel, Elizabeth, Jane, and Ann (Mrs John Edwards); to the children of her sister Ann by her late husband Russell Hicmott, Charlotte, Susan, Eleanor, and Ann (Mrs Alexander Box); "and also the natural child of my sister Ann that is to say Mary the wife of James Macfee"; and to nephews John Humphrey and Samuel Humphry, the sons "of my late brother William Humphrey."

**Bateman, Thomas** ₁*fl. 1660–1669*₁, *actor.*

Thomas Bateman (or Batman, Batiman, Bateston) was a minor player in the King's Company whose first recorded appearance was as Wholesome in *The Alchemist* in December 1660 at the Vere Street Theatre. He may have been acting earlier at the Red Bull, and it is probable that he stayed with the King's troupe in the early 1660's even though his name is not mentioned again until 1665. On 18 March of that year he was among a group of actors ordered to appear before the Lord Chamberlain to answer an unspecified charge. A livery warrant of 22 July 1667, covering the period 1666–1668, includes a John Bateman, and this could be an error for Thomas, since he is clearly listed on a similar warrant dated 8 February 1668. He was probably the "Batman" who played Sganarelle's housekeeper in *Damoiselles à la Mode* on 14 September 1668 at the Bridges Street Theatre. The last certain reference to Bateman was on 17 April 1669 when he again played Wholesome at Bridges Street.

In the registers of St Margaret, West-minster, is a marriage license entry dated 10 December 1668 for a Thomas Bateman and Elizabeth Floyd which could pertain to the actor; there was, incidentally, an actor named Floyd in the early Restoration period.

**Baterton.** *See* BETTERTON.

**Bates.** *See also* BATE.

**Bates, Mr** ₁*fl. 1749*₁, *actor.*
A Mr Bates acted Plume in *The Recruiting Officer* at a booth at Southwark on 9 January 1749.

**Bates, Mrs** ₁*fl. 1678*₁, *actress.*
Mrs Bates was apparently one of the young actresses being trained at the "Nursery" operated by the Duke's and King's companies in the 1670's, and at Drury Lane in late February 1678 she played the small part of Emilia, a young girl, in *The Rambling Justice.*

**Bates, Miss.** *See* DIBDIN, MRS CHARLES ISAAC MUNGO.

**Bates, Miss, later Mrs Barfoot** ₁*fl. 1793–1820?*₁, *dancer, singer.*
A Miss Bates was on the lists at Sadler's Wells both in 1793 and 1806 as a dancer. About 1796 was published the song by Moorehead *How Can You Refuse Me,* as sung at the Wells in *Birds of a Feather,* by Miss Bates.

She carried on for some years a notorious affair with a Mr Barfoot, one of the joint proprietors of the Wells, and she bore him a child in 1806. They were later married after the death of his wife. In 1819 Barfoot was confined for debt, along with his partner at Sadler's Wells, Charles Dibdin, in the rules of the King's Bench Prison, No 3, London Road Terrace, St George's Fields. His poor wife then became an inmate of Clerkenwell workhouse. Already "worn out with drink and dissipation, she had become a spectacle," according to Dibdin.

She may have been related to another Miss Bates at Sadler's well, who later married Charles Isaac Mungo Dibdin.

**Bates, J.** [*fl. 1722*], *actor?*

J. Bates, who is otherwise unrecorded, was listed as a member of the Lincoln's Inn Fields troupe in an agreement drawn up on 12 April 1722 between Steele, Wilks, Cibber, and Booth of Drury Lane, and the Rich brothers of Lincoln's Inn Fields, in which they all pledged not to steal performers from one another. Bates's function in the Rich company was not specified.

**Bates, J.** [*fl. 1794*], *singer.*

A countertenor or *alto* singer named J. Bates was concerned in some of the Handelian memorial performances after 1784 at Westminster Abbey. In 1794 he was living in Halifax, Yorkshire. Bates was in London only temporarily. It is likely that he carried on or founded a line of musicians at Halifax.

The *Dictionary of Musicians* of 1827 speaks of a contemporaneous "Bates, junior, professor of music at Halifax" who was then "an eminent performer on the violin; his brother is also eminent on the double bass."

**Bates, Jacob** [*fl. 1760?–1770?*], *equestrian.*

Willson Disher declares that Jacob Bates the trick rider and showman performed at Sadler's Wells, Islington, before he departed to make "the Continent ring with his praises." But Caulfield's *Remarkable Persons* states that:

It does not appear he ever publicly exhibited in England, but on the Continent he met with so much applause and encouragement as induced him to reside there for several years. He seems to have been particularly patronized in Germany. . . . In excellence and ability as a horseman, Bates appears to have been in no way inferior to the riders of the present time

*Harvard Theatre Collection*

JACOB BATES
after Nusbiegel

[1820]; or in the exploit of firing pistols in full speed, under the belly of his horse, managing two, three, or four coursers at full speed, jumping, and dancing from the back of one to the other, was nothing behind them in dexterity, and it must have been a more difficult undertaking to perform these feats on a level plain, than aided, as at present, by an enclosed and prepared circular ride.

There is a notice in Bromley's *Catalogue* of English portraits, in the early nineteenth century, of a print which we have not seen, of Bates engraved by J. E. Ridinger. G. P. Nusbiegel also engraved his portrait at Nuremberg in 1766. The portrait as engraved by R. Grave was published by Caulfield in 1819. A French print, showing 14 different attitudes and achievements on horseback, was published in the *Journal Œconomique*, 1767. There is an anonymous engraving of him, after Nusbiegel, in riding clothes, undated, in the Harvard Theatre Collection.

### Bates, James *d. 1784, actor.*

The name "Bates" appears in number-less programs of London, and of English, Irish, Welsh, and Scottish provincial theatres, especially after the mid-eighteenth century and particularly at Covent Garden. No effort to distinguish them thoroughly or pursue them exhaustively can be more than marginally successful.

James Bates was probably the Master Bates who came on the stage at Covent Garden as the Child in *Medea* on 16 March 1768, his first recorded appearance in London. He had doubtless been brought to the theatre by Robert Bates, conjecturally his father, who was playing at that house at the time. Robert Bates had provincial connections, and he may have sent the boy out to Bristol to learn acting, for a Master J. Bates played pages and other juvenile roles at the Bristol theatre in the 1768 through 1774 seasons and again in 1777.

Where James was in the interim between Bristol and his return to Covent Garden on 21 September 1781 is not surely known. There was a Bates acting at 15s. per six-day week in Liverpool from 12 October through 20 December 1776, and at £1 1s. per six-day week from 4 October through 29 November 1777 and 1 June through 19 October 1778. This may, however, have been William Bates.

A selection of James Bates's parts at Covent Garden from 21 September 1781 (when he was earning £1 5s.) until 9 January 1784 (when he had risen only to £1 10s.) illustrates his usually narrow range and relative unimportance: Woodley in *Three Weeks After Marriage*; Paris in *Romeo and Juliet*; Officer, in *The Count of Narbonne*; Brother in *Comus*; Sailor in *The Positive Man*; Bellmour in *The Upholsterers*. His most frequently played part was one of his most trivial, Humane Scalper in the popular pantomime *Harlequin Teague*, much repeated in the final years of his service.

James Bates had married the actress Patty Ann Scrase at St James, Piccadilly, on 23 September 1783. The marriage was tragically short, for he fell ill in February or March following, died on 31 March, and was buried at St Paul, Covent Garden, on 9 April 1784.

### Bates, Mrs James, Patty Ann, née Scrase *d. 1787, actress.*

Patty Ann Scrase (or Scrace, sometimes Scarce and Scrates) was the daughter of the provincial and London actor Henry Scrase (1717–1807) and the sister of Henrietta, Mrs Walter Smith (1752–1822), the Hull, Bath, and Dublin actress who was the mother of Mrs Knight. She was the sister, also, of the Edward Scrase who died in May of 1787.

Patty Ann first came to the public's attention as "A Young Lady," playing Jane Shore on 18 February 1778 at the Crow Street Theatre, Dublin. Reed said that she was the original speaker of Robert Houlton's famous "Belles Have at Ye All" while she was at that theatre. She signed with other Crow Street actors a letter to the *Hibernian Journal* on 24 May 1779. She came to Liverpool as "from Dublin" on 12 June 1780 and to the Bath and Bristol company on 29 September 1781, again as "from Dublin."

At Bristol Miss Scrase played Almeria in *The Mourning Bride*, Adelaide in *The Count of Narbonne*, Elinor in *King John*, and other such important supporting roles with fair regularity the rest of the season. By the date of her benefit, 28 May 1782, she had so far succeeded as to attract the patronage for the night of the Duchess of Devonshire and the more important cooperation of Mrs Sarah Siddons, who consented to play Eleonora in *Edward and Eleonora* while Patty Ann played Daraxa. She netted £135 11s.

On 19 September 1783 she went from Bath to Covent Garden, along with Charles Bonnor, who spoke a prologue introducing himself, Miss Scrase, and Mrs Chalmers from York, all newcomers to the metropolis. She played on this occasion Sylvia in *The Recruiting Officer*. On 23 September she married the Covent Garden actor James Bates at St James, Piccadilly. He died on 31 March following.

Mrs Bates continued to play at Covent Garden during most of each season until her death. She also played, in 1784 and parts of other summer seasons, at the Haymarket. Her characters were the young heroines of comedy, with an occasional divagation into farce or sentimental tragedy: Elvira in *Loves Makes a Man*; Mrs Lovemore in *The Way to Keep Him*; Araminta in *The Confederacy*; Lady Rodolphia Lumbercourt in *The Man of the World*; Olivia in *The Plain Dealer*; Jane Shore in *Jane Shore*; Countess of Almaviva in *The Follies of a Day*; Mrs Casey in *Fontainebleau;* Lady Easy in *The Careless Husband*; Victoria in *A Bold Stroke for a Husband*; and Agnes in *Fatal Curiosity*. Her last appearance in London was at Covent Garden on 16 April 1787, when she played Mrs Tempest in *The School for Wives*. Probably it was her last appearance anywhere.

Mrs Bates was, as one contemporary critic said, "a good and useful actress," and Winston declared that "Mrs Knight [the actress] told me that Mrs Bates *not* the singer was her aunt and that just as she was getting to be a favorite she died." Her death occurred after a lingering and undiagnosed illness at her father's house in Bath on 25 or 28 September 1787.

There were two actresses named Bates at Drury Lane in the years following 1800, and one, in the season of 1816–17, earned the inconsiderable salary of £1 5s., according to the account books. A Miss M. Bates was on the company list of 1818–19 which belongs to the Garrick Club. Among the memorabilia of Mrs James Bates in the Folger Library is a provocative letter to Winston dated 1820 from one Caroline

Bates of 7 Hayes Court, Soho, who writes that she has been an actress for "so many years" at Drury Lane and asks Winston for employment. She may have been a daughter of Patty Ann Bates.

**Bates, Joah** *1740–1799, conductor, organist.*

Joah Bates was born at Halifax, Yorkshire, in 1740 and baptized on 8 March 1741. He was the son of Henry Bates, innkeeper and parish clerk of Halifax, a substantial man who procured the best possible educations for his sons. Joah's elder brother, Henry, a graduate of Dr Parnell's Manchester School, proceeded B. A. at Peterhouse in 1759, M.A. in 1762, and D.D. in 1782. He was rector of Freckenham, Suffolk, from 1773 until his death on 31 January 1816, in his eightieth year.

Joah followed his brother to Manchester School after studying at Halifax under Dr Ogden and taking music lessons from Hartley the organist at Rochdale. While at Manchester he studied organ under Robert Wainwright, organist of the Collegiate Church. On 26 August 1756 he obtained a scholarship to Eton, and although while there he was denied access to a keyboard instrument for nearly four years, he seems to have kept up his facility by practicing upon static keys marked off on a table. His musical isolation ended when one of his masters, Mr G. Graham, accidentally discovered his dedication and encouraged him.

On 31 July 1758 Bates was nominated for a scholarship to King's College, Cambridge, but was not admitted there till 1760. He obtained one of Lord Craven's scholarships and a tutorship at King's and was B. A. in 1764 and M. A. in 1767.

Bates's interest in organizing oratorios and concerts developed early. While he was still a student at Cambridge, he assembled at Halifax a group of musicians (among whom Sir William Herschel the astronomer was said to have been a first violin) for the first performance of the

*Messiah* – or for that matter any oratorio – north of the Trent.

Tutorship by Bates of the second son of the Earl of Sandwich led to Bates's becoming the Earl's private secretary and thence to an appointment in the Post Office worth £100 a year. From that point on he seems never to have wanted for a sinecure, being commissioner of the Sixpenny Office from 1772 to 1776, of Greenwich Hospital from 1775 until his death, and of the Victualling Office from March 1776 onward.

In 1776 also he began to put into effect the long-planned scheme of "The Concerts of Antient Musick," also known as the "King's Concerts," which were to continue until 1848. The committee of organization consisted of his patron the Earl of Sandwich, the Earl of Exeter, the Viscount Dudley and Ward, the Bishop of Durham, Sir Watkin W. Wynn, Bart., Sir R. Jebb, Bart., and Messrs Morrice and Pelham. Though several of the Committee were influential and helpful, it was Bates's energy which pushed the project. Bates was appointed "conductor" (i.e., principal manager) and the band was led by Hay. Miss Harrop (who became Mrs Bates in 1780), the Misses Abrams, and the Messrs Champness, Clarke, and Dyne, were conspicuous among the singers. Bates continued conductor, except for two years, until Greatorex succeeded him in 1793.

In 1783, with Viscount Fitzwilliam and Sir W. W. Wynn, Bates began to organize the Handel Memorial Concerts which were held in Westminster Abbey, near the burial place of the composer, and at the Pantheon. The first performance was heard in the Abbey on the morning of 26 May 1784, the second on the evening of 27 May at the Pantheon, and the third on 29 May, again at the Abbey. Charles Burney published a complete account of these events, including an enumeration of singers and instrumentalists. The first program at the Abbey, with Bates conducting at an organ especially erected by Green, utilized a wide selection of Handel's music and involved 525 performers, categorized by Burney as: 59 sopranos, 48 altos, 83 tenors, and 84 basses among the voices; 48 first and 47 second violins, 26 violas, 21 cellos, 15 double basses, 6 flutes, 26 oboes, 26 bassoons, 1 double bassoon, 12 trumpets, 12 horns, 6 trombones, and 4 drums. A total of 200 performers were at the Pantheon, again under Bates's sway.

The Commemoration of 1784 was enormously successful, with total receipts of over £12,736, which, after expenses were paid, was divided between the Royal Society of Musicians and the Westminster Hospital. The celebration was repeated in 1785, 1786, 1787, and 1791, in which latter year the total number of performers numbered 1068.

Bates was Vice President of the Royal Society of Musicians and a member of the Madrigal Society and the Sandwich Catch Club. Haydn, who visited "Mr Baze" on 15 December 1794 at his house at No 14, John's Street, King's Road, commended his organ playing. He was also a fine teacher, and among his pupils were the singers Samuel Ellis and Miss Ann Sharp(e), later Mrs William Palmer. Apparently he composed too, but by the time of his death none of his music had been published.

Miss Harrop brought Bates a considerable dowry, earned singing in concert, which he lost along with his own savings when the Albion Mills at Blackfriars Bridge burned in 1791. He died fairly prosperous, nevertheless, in London on 8 June 1799, as a will made on 21 May 1799 and sent to probate on 1 July that year shows. Some of its details are of interest:

I give and bequeath to my dear Wife Sarah Bates my double Key'd Harpsichord now standing in the Dining Parlour To my dear son Edward Bates I give my other Harpsi-

383                                                    BATES

chord which stands in a room upstairs together with my Old Amati ffiddle with its
proper Bow To my dear son Charles Bates I
give my other ffiddle which is in the same
case with the Amati ffiddle with its proper
Bow I give to my said Wife my Gold Watch
trusting that at her death she will leave the
same to my son Edward and I . . . bequeath
my Silver Watch unto my son Charles

Bates's share in the real estate of the
defunct Albion Mills went to his wife,
and the proceeds of an insurance policy
worth £1500 to Edward "for the purpose
of putting him upon an equal footing with
his Brother Charles to whom the late Earl
of Exeter left an annuity of one hundred
pounds for his life commencing at his age
of ffourteen years."
A portrait of Joah Bates with his wife
was painted by F. Cotes, R. A.

### Bates, Mrs Joah, Sarah, née Harrop
*d. 1811, singer, actress.*
Sarah Harrop was born to humble circumstances somewhere in Lancashire. Her
parents were reportedly poor but industrious, and ambitious for their daughter. She
was sent early and fortunately to a grammar school where music was well taught.
She was for a while a factory girl but found
also some employment as an occasional
singer. She was heard by Dr Howard of
Leicester, who predicted that she "would
one day throw all the English, nay, even
Italian female singers, far behind her; for
he had never before heard such a natural
delicacy of taste, and such surprising musical excellence out of any Englishwoman,
and but very few foreigners."
He spread the fame of "the Lancashire
St Cecilia" wherever he went, while she
continued to sing humbly in choruses and
for some time in the choir at Chester Cathedral. At length Joah Bates was depu-
tized by his companions of the Catch Club
to investigate the rumors of her great abilities. He was sufficiently impressed to bring
her at once to London.

*Harvard Theatre Collection*

SARAH BATES
by Pether

Sarah secured London concert engagements immediately, though she continued
her study, of Italian music under Sacchini
and of the Handelian style with Bates, her
future husband. The success of her dramatic soprano voice was great and instan-
taneous, although Susan Burney, in comparing her with the delicate Miss Linley,
thought some of her mannerisms "really
vulgar," and disliked her "howl and bad
manner of taking her notes."
When she sang a leading part in *Judas
Maccabeus* at Covent Garden on 14 February 1777, she was advertised as singing
for the first time in public. From that date
through 19 March following she sang in
*Messiah, Samson, Omnipotence, Jeptha,
Artaxerxes, The Prodigal Son*, and *Acis
and Galatea* (after which she sang a "Song
. . . with a violin obligato, the music entirely new, composed by Sacchini, accompanied by Lamotte").
Miss Harrop gained her London reputation—and a considerable fortune—by her

singing in Bach and Abel's concerts on Hanover Square and at the Pantheon, in the oratorios, and in occasional operas. Her *forte* was religious music, but several of her renditions of secular songs, notably of Purcell's "Mad Bess" and "Rosy Bowers," were famous.

Susan Burney's early criticism notwithstanding, Sarah Harrop developed a full, rich, steady voice of impressive range which finally could encompass contralto as well as soprano selections. Her expression, especially in interpreting the pathetic airs of Handel, was said to be matchless.

On 16 December 1794, Joseph Farington entered in his journal:

Wm Dance [the eminent violinist and leader of theatre bands] introduced Haydn, the composer of Music last night to Mr and Mrs Bates at their house in John Rd . . . Mrs Bates sang some of Haydn's songs, in so admirable a manner as drew from him the warmest eulogiums—He had never heard them sung so well.—Mrs Bates is about 40 Years of age,—Dance thinks her a sensible woman.

And Haydn himself says, in notes he made of his London visit: "On 15th Dec. 1794, I visited Mr Baze, who conducts the Ancient-Concert from the organ and plays quite well; his wife has a very pleasant, flexible voice, her pitch is very true and her pronunciation clear; she has Bachierotti's [Pachierotti's] way of singing, but her shake is a little too rapid."

The financial success of Mrs Bates was legendary, especially in the poorer districts of her native Lancashire. The writer of a contemporary biographical sketch thought that it "has had the same effect in Lancashire and Leicestershire as a twenty thousand pound prize falling to the lot of a poor labourer would have on people of the village where he resided."

Her wealth was dissipated, however, by an unfortunate investment. She had married her teacher, Joah Bates the organist

and conductor, in 1780 and is said to have brought him a dowry of between £6000 and £7000. But Bates sank all their joint capital in the scheme of the Albion Mills, on the Surrey side of Blackfriar's Bridge, and it burned to the ground uninsured in 1791. Farington remarked in his diary: "On the loss of £10,000 [*sic*] which she had saved . . . Lord Thurlow [the Chancellor] obtained for her a pension from the King of £500 a year. Lord Thurlow is very fond of musick, and Mr and Mrs Bates are frequently with him."

Sarah Harrop Bates died at Foley Place, London, on 11 December 1811.

Besides the picture with her husband painted by F. Cotes, R. A., there is another likeness of her alone which was engraved by W. Pether in 1793. She is depicted holding a volume of Handel's songs.

### Bates, John   [*fl. 1685*], *singer.*

As one of the children of the choir of Westminster, John Bates sang at the coronation of James II on 23 April 1685. He may have been related to the Restoration court violist Thomas Bates.

### Bates, Robert   *d. 1786, actor.*

A "Bobby Bates" was managing and acting at Shepton Mallet, Somersetshire, around 1755, for he introduced Francis Blisset to the strolling fraternity about that date, if James Winston's recollection in *The Theatric Tourist* (1805) was correct. One of Winston's manuscript jottings in the Folger Library establishes: "Bobby Bates at C[ovent] G[arden] during Colman's Man[agemen]^t." So he was the Robert Bates (or "Bates, Senior") who played at Covent Garden frequently in the seasons from May 1768 through 1785–86 (except 1775–76, and all but a brief period in the winter of 1776–77). He never rose to any eminence, and after his first season he always earned just £1 per week.

Robert Bates was the very type of the

actor of afterpieces and was, except for acting a few Shakespearean parts, almost always to be found in the lower half of the bill. A representative selection of his Covent Garden roles in a rough chronology would be: Charon in *Lethe*, Boatswain in *The Tempest*, Abhorson in *Measure for Measure*, Slender in *The Merry Wives of Windsor*, Pedro in *Isabella*, Member of the Mob in *Illumination*, Captain of the Guards in *Chrononhotonthologos*, Sternhold in *The Device*, Marrowbone in *The Humours of an Election*, Turpentine in *Seventeen Hundred and Eighty One*, Friar John in *Romeo and Juliet*, Hulk in *The Positive Man*, and Watchman in *The Wife's Relief*.

It is probable, since he is frequently denominated "Senior" in the pay lists, that Bobby Bates is the father of William Bates and James Bates, and possibly of a fourth Bates, who were at Covent Garden during most of the time he was there. He was joined, in 1768–69, by a "Master Bates" who was possibly the James Bates of later seasons. He also may have had some connection with the Bates who managed Hagget's Theatre in Scarborough and the Old Long Room there from before 1768 and, with Cawdell his nephew, from 1778 to about 1788.

Robert Bates was buried at St Paul's, Covent Garden, on 7 June 1786, and the register declared him to be "from St Martin-in-the-Fields."

**Bates, Thomas** *d. 1679, violist, teacher.*

Thomas Bates (or Baites) probably received a commission during the civil war, though nothing is known of his early life beyond the fact that during the Restoration he was sometimes called Captain. In 1651 he was listed as a teacher "For Voyce or Viole," and it was doubtless as a violist that he played in the small band that Sir William Davenant used at Rutland House in 1656 for the premiere of *The Siege of*

*Rhodes*. By 1 January 1661 he was a musician in ordinary for the viola in Charles II's private music, replacing both Alphonso Ferrabosco Junior and Henry Ferrabosco; for these two positions he received £90 annually plus the usual £16 2s. 6d. yearly livery fee – though the King was often years behind in actual payments.

The Lord Chamberlain's accounts contain regular and frequent references to Bates from this time to his death. On 22 October 1662, for instance, he was paid £12 for a bass viol and £5 for strings; on 23 May 1664, for reasons unstated, Richard Benyon petitioned against him – perhaps for an unpaid debt; on 7 February 1665 he was given £12 for another bass viol and £20 yearly for attendance at the Chapel Royal since Easter 1662; on 27 February 1674 he was to receive £43 7s. 6d. in livery arrears for 1671–1673; on 8 February 1675 a similar warrant said he should be given £64 10s. for arrears for 1665–67 and 1670; and on 15 February 1675 he played bass viol in the production of the masque *Calisto* at court. The unstable economy of the times led many royal musicians into borrowing and lending. On 7 July 1675 Bates, describing himself as from the parish of St Margaret, Westminster, assigned the 1675 livery due him to creditor Robert Gale, a London haberdasher, and appointed Gale his attorney. On 4 July 1676 the situation was reversed, and Bates gave £150 to Jeoffrey Banister in return for Banister's assigning to him the £46 12s. 8d. annual wages due him – but how much beyond £150 was due him was not mentioned. On 29 September 1677 Bates was again a debtor and assigned his unpaid yearly livery fees from 1661 to 1671 to John Broadhurst, a creditor.

He made an arrangement with fellow court violist William Gregory on 17 and 27 May 1678 whereby Gregory was to replace Bates in the King's private music as soon as Bates died and, consequently, receive the £90 annual salary Bates had regularly received (salaries were usually paid promptly enough, but livery fees were constantly in arrears). What Bates was supposed to get from Gregory in return is not known. He must, however, have been either in poor health or near retirement by this time.

On 15 April 1679 Bates made his will, leaving everything to his wife, Abigail, and in August of that year he died. He was buried in the cloisters of Westminster Abbey on 18 August 1679, and his will was proved on 21 August. In addition to his widow, Bates left three stepsons, James, Jeremiah, and Charles Hudgbutt, though James appears to have died at almost the same time as Bates, for his will was proved on 23 September 1679.

Thomas Bates wrote a few pieces of light music—airs and dances—which were published in Playford's *Musick's Recreation* in 1669.

### Bates, William  *d. 1813? actor, dancer, singer, machinist, manager.*

William Bates may have been the son of Robert Bates ("Bobby," or "Bates, Senior") and the brother of James Bates, both of whom played at Covent Garden during some of the years of his activity. Many of his roles were in their low comic line; but he is more often distinguishable from them than they are from each other because of his athletic abilities as a harlequin and because he concerned himself during part of his career with scenery and machinery.

John Bernard said that William Bates was in Bristol "before Powell and Holland," and the Bristol lists do indeed show a Mr and Mrs Bates in the company in every season from 1768 through 1773 and occasionally in 1774 and 1777.

The Bates whom *The London Stage* identifies as William appeared at Covent Garden for the first time on 16 October 1779 as Ralph in *The Maid of the Mill*. From 18 September 1780, when he was shown on the pay list at Covent Garden

as earning £3 per week, he acted frequently in comic parts and as a harlequin through 1782–83. He was at York in August of 1782. In the season of 1783–84 he joined Powell and Holland at Bristol. He next played and devised machinery at Norwich, from which place he was announced as coming when he returned to York in August of 1785. He was also on the York circuit at some times during the winter seasons of 1785 and 1786. On the occasion of his benefit at York on 9 March 1786 it was announced that the pantomime "got up at Bate's expense is his property reserved for his benefit."

Bates came back to London, but to Drury Lane, on 13 January 1787, where he was added to the list at £3 per week. According to James Winston he was discharged there on 10 November and reinstated on 12 December. The list shows that he was raised 10*s*. per week on 22 December, so apparently he ended the argument triumphantly. In that season he was also briefly with John Palmer's company in the ill-starred experiment of the Royalty Theatre. Nevertheless, his pantomimes *Harlequin Mungo; or, A Peep into the Tower* and *Gil Blas; or, The Fool of Fortune*, both with music by Reeve, were produced there with success. Both were published in 1788.

Bates's residence in 1781 had been No 12, Little Russell Street, Covent Garden, and it was the same again in 1787. But on the date of his last benefit at the Royalty, 25 August 1788, he was living at No 51, Pennington Street, Ratcliff Highway.

In the 1788–89 season Bates, "Harlequin and Mechanist at Drury Lane Theatre as well as [devisor] of the New Pantomimes at the Royalty" was at Bristol and at Bath's Orchard Street Theatre with Diamond and Keasberry. The next few seasons he apparently spent at Manchester, where Thomas Wignell found him and took him and Mrs Bates, along with 55 other recruits, to America on the ship *George Barclay*.

On 20 December 1793 Bates made his American bow in Annapolis, Maryland. A raging yellow fever epidemic had prevented Wignell from opening in Philadelphia. Bates was Pedrillo in *The Castle of Andalusia* before his first audience in the United States. After 24 January 1794 the company left Annapolis to open the new Chestnut Street Theatre in Philadelphia on 17 February. The first appearance there of Bates and his wife was on 24 February 1794, he as Sharp and she as Mrs Gadabout in *The Lying Valet*. They remained at Philadelphia (except for one hiatus) from then until July 1797. In 1796 Bates was engaged by J. B. Williamson for a short season at the Federal Street Theatre in Boston. Dunlap lured Bates to his management for a salary of $30 per week for himself and $8 for his daughter. He was also engaged to prepare pantomimes, for an extra 10 guineas. There was present from time to time during this season a "Master Bates." Mrs Bates was not mentioned.

In 1803 William Bates was at the Winter Street Theatre in Boston. He was in Providence, Rhode Island, in the summers of 1803 and 1804 and again in 1808. At Providence he took over Falstaff from Joseph Harper, the manager. Blake, the historian of the Providence stage, testified:

When he came under Mr. Harper's management he used to visit Providence every year, and then go with the company to Charleston and the other places in their regular circuit, but in the later years of his stay in Providence, he had become weakened by the approaches of age, and illness prevented him from fulfilling winter engagements. He had therefore to depend for subsistence solely on the profits of the summer campaign [in Providence] and in Newport, which were often very small. He, however, managed to eke out his means by giving one or two exhibitions of a humourous character in the winter season when there was a dearth of amusements. His distresses were also alleviated by the kind assistance of a benevolent gentleman, who yet lingers among us.

Blake remembered that Bates's benefits were always well attended and that audiences regarded him with affection, except on the unlucky occasion in 1809 when his interpretation of *The Beaux' Stratagem*, which he was then directing, proved too licentious for the puritan stomach. Bates then sustained for a number of weeks an attack in the Providence *American* by one who signed himself "Moralitas," but the actor capitulated with a public apology.

In 1810–11 Mr and Mrs Bates were acting with Hayman at the Thespian Hotel Theatre in Albany, and they transferred to John Bernard's management when he assumed direction of that company in late season. They were probably still with him when he opened at the Green Street Theatre in Albany in January of 1813. A benefit was arranged there on 17 April 1813 "for the widow and children of Mr Bates, who died recently." Mrs Bates seems to have continued acting. She was with William Twaits's company at the Circus on Broadway in 1813–14.

A fair selection of the characters which William Bates played (besides the harlequins for which he was best known) might be: Lopez in *The Duenna*, Sir Walter Blunt in *1 Henry IV*, Supple in *The Double Gallant*, Proteus in *The Humours of an Election*, Silver Tongue in *The Belle's Stratagem*, Lovelace in *Three Weeks After Marriage*, Jack Meggot in *The Suspicious Husband*, Spruce in *The School for Wives*, Kitteau in *The Englishman in Paris*, Diego in *The Regent*; Slender and Bardolph in *The Merry Wives of Windsor*, Furious in *The Wishes*, Lapelle in *The Seduction*, Justice Woodcock in *Love in a Village*, Captain O'Cutter in *The Jealous Wife*, and Sheepface in *The Village Lawyer*.

Thus, light and low comedy characters predominated, though early in his career he tried on a few beaux, and toward the end he did some elderly eccentrics in the Sir Peter Teazle line. He also seems to have yearned for Tragedy, but with no success. In harlequinade he was famous for his spectacular leaps, like the one advertised for his benefit at Covent Garden on 28 November 1782, later described by a newspaper writer: "The leap which Harlequin makes in the new pantomime is astonishing. Mr W. Bates, on the second exhibition, went clearly from one balcony to the other, and entered the window without touching." At the Royalty Theatre on 25 August 1788 he played for his benefit in "Harlequin's Vindication of Pantomime. At the Conclusion of which, [it was promised] he will (for that Night only) Leap through a grand transparent Sun, illuminated with fire-works."

According to Blake, "Bates was a true son of Momus, a fellow of infinite jest, equally amusing on the stage and in private life. . . . Like many other comedians he had in early life laboured under the mistaken idea that he was peculiarly adapted to tragedy."

Dunlap, on the other hand, described Bates as "a broad, short, strong-built man, with some comedy in his face, but it was all low, conceited, and cunning." He also frowned upon him as an inveterate practical joker.

Mrs Bates, who acted in the English provinces and all over eastern America but never, as far as is known, in London, portrayed spinsters and gossips, shepherdesses early and eccentric landladies later. Nothing is known of her personality.

**Batessen,** [Mr?] [*fl. 1783–1784*], *performer?*

One Batessen was noted in the Covent Garden accounts on 27 September 1783 at a salary of 16s. 8d. for five nights; the name appeared again at the end of the season, on 7 June 1784, at £1 10s. for nine nights. The salary suggests Batessen may have been a performer.

**Bateston.** *See* **BATEMAN.**

**"Bath Roscius, The."** *See* **HENDER-SON, JOHN.**

**Batichel.** *See* **BATTISHILL.**

**Batiere, Mrs** [*fl. 1784*], *actress.*

Mrs Batiere made her first, and apparently her last, appearance on any stage on 20 August 1784 as Lady Russel in the Rev Thomas Stratford's fiasco at Drury Lane, *Lord Russel.* Mrs Batiere also wrote and spoke the epilogue, but there is some question as to whether she was heard. The *Public Advertiser* of 21 August reported that the "performers . . . rendered the Doctor's Tragedy one of the most laughable farces at which we were ever present. [It] has much *Calimanco* in it, and where we could hear a sentence compleat (which was seldom indeed) it abounded with *Fustian.*"

**Batiman** or **Batman.** *See* **BATEMAN.**

**Batom, van.** *See* **VAN BATOM.**

**Baton.** *See* **BALON.**

**Batson, Mr** [*fl. 1774*], *actor.*

Mr and Mrs Batson were among the actors who performed "by authority" during the winter of 1773–74 at the Haymarket Theatre. The only record of their work is for 24 January 1774 when *The Busy Body* was performed; Batson played Sir Francis and his wife played Miranda. Later in the season *Catherine and Petruchio* and *The Beggar's Opera* were performed, but the casts were incomplete and it is not known whether or not the Batsons participated.

**Batson, Mrs** [*fl. 1774*], *actress. See* **BATSON, MR.**

**Batt, Mr** [*fl. 1734*], *actor.*

A Mr Batt, possibly an amateur, played Omar in a production of *Tamerlane* at York Buildings on 8 July 1734.

**Battel.** *See* **BATTLE.**

**Batterton.** *See* **BETTERTON.**

## Battishill, Jonathan  *1738–1801, instrumentalist, singer, composer.*

Jonathan Battishill (or Battishall, Batichel) was born in London in May 1738, the son of a solicitor named Jonathan Battishill (probably the person of that name who was buried in the churchyard of St Peter's Cornhill, on 25 May 1746) and grandson of the Rev Jonathan Battishill, rector of Sheepwash, Devonshire. Young Jonathan early showed a strong ability in music and in 1747 was placed in the choir of St Paul's Cathedral and articled to its leader William Savage. Reinhold, the singer, who was his contemporary in the choir, told R. J. S. Stevens, the composer, that "Battishill had by nature, what other Boys were obliged to fag hard and labour for."

By the end of his apprenticeship Battishill was not only an excellent countertenor singer but one of the finest *extempore* performers on the organ in England. About 1755 he became Deputy Organist to the great Dr William Boyce at the Chapel Royal. He was anxious to cultivate the good opinion of Boyce, but by a characteristic act of intemperance he ruined his chances, though Boyce was at first much impressed by his talents. The curious story of how the young man, coming to Boyce's house to receive praise and correction for his composition and invited to have some "Mountain wine" and "buiscuits" intoxicated himself by drinking the whole quart, was left by the composer Stevens in his manuscript memoirs (not published until 1932, by their owner J. B. Trend). Battishill said later:

By this one silly act I forfeited the esteem of the only man in the musical profession, whose friendship I had laboured for years to gain, and with whom I had assiduously endeavoured to be intimate. I never recovered the disappointment that I experienced in consequence of this foolish action to the end of my life.

Unhappily the "foolish action" was no isolated act of eccentric behavior but her-

By permission of the Trustees of the British Museum

JONATHAN BATTISHILL
by L. Sullivan

alded the uncontrolled alcoholism which many times was to mar Battishill's career. Stevens's memoir is replete with illustrations of the "violent and riotous behaviour," and even brutality, with which the unfortunate man offended his colleagues and friends when in liquor.

After leaving Boyce's protection, Jonathan drifted back to singing. He was doubtless the "Batichel" who, with Sga Passerini, Sga Mattei, Pazzaglia, and Miss Thomas, was a principal singer in *Alexander's Feast* at the Great Room in Dean Street, Soho, on 16 March 1756.

Battishill began composing for the theatre by contributing a song to the Rev James Townley's celebrated farce *High Life Below Stairs*, which was produced at Drury Lane in 1759. In 1760 he wrote a song for Edward Moore's *The Gamester*. He furnished a few of the songs for Garrick's operatic version of *A Midsummer Night's*

*Dream* in 1763. On 23 December 1763 he and John Potter collaborated on the pantomime *The Rites of Hecate*, Battishill writing the airs and choruses and Potter the overture and comic tunes. Another collaboration, that with Michael Arne in 1764 for the opera *Almena*, was not successful, due to Richard Rolt's inferior *libretto*. The piece had only six performances at Drury Lane. Battishill ended his contributions to music at Drury Lane with a song for a revival of Edward Moore's *The Foundling* on 3 October 1765.

About 1760 he had gone to Covent Garden Theatre as harpsichord player and leader of the band. There he met the well-known singer Elizabeth Davies. On 19 December 1765 he married her at St George, Bloomsbury. Stevens said that "Battishall's marriage did not tend to make him a happier or a better man. The cause I do not know, but they did not agree; and during my apprenticeship, Webster the actor lived in open adultery with Mrs Battishill next door to Mr Savage. 'If ever I meet that Rascal,' said poor Bat to some of his friends, 'I'll stick a knife in his heart.' " Evidently the dire encounter never occurred, for in the summer of 1777 Mrs Battishill ran off with Webster to Ireland, where she died in October of the same year.

Before reaching his majority Battishill was already turning the occasional shilling by writing songs for the singers at the public gardens, and he continued to produce them for Vauxhall, Sadler's Wells, and Ranelagh until late in life. He had moved into lodgings in Orange Street, Bloomsbury, in 1763 and there had set up as a teacher of harpsichord. At this endeavor he was successful, and Dr Kitchiner related anecdotes of his unorthodox teaching methods: "Are you a good-tempered fellow?" he would say to a new pupil. "Will you forgive me if I take you off? I know no other way of showing you the absurd tricks you play than by imitating them." He said he felt that "unteaching his pupils what they did

wrong" had priority over "teaching them how to do right."

Battishill continued as organist at Covent Garden, though perhaps not continuously, through 1777–78, but he evidently did not lead the band after 1763 except on special occasions. In addition, he had an income as organist to the united parishes of St Clement, Eastcheap, and St Martin Orgar, to which office he was elected in 1764. He then naturally turned his talents toward composing music for performance in churches. In 1767 he was given the additional post of organist of Christ Church, Newgate.

Despite his occasional social offensiveness because of his bibulous habits, Battishill's varied talents kept him in work and in company. In addition to his regular work in church and theatre he was in demand for concerts: he was in a program of sacred music at the Chapel on 18 May 1762, playing a concerto on the organ; he sang the countertenor part in an arrangement of the *Messiah* at Haberdasher's Hall on 10 December 1767; he sang in several specially-licensed dramatic performances at the Haymarket in the winter of 1772–73 and was organist there in the summer of 1778 and at some performances in the winter of 1778–79. Burney listed him among the countertenors at the Handel Memorial Concerts at Westminster Abbey and the Pantheon in May and June of 1784; and when Walter Claggett opened his Apollo Gardens on Westminster Bridge Road in 1788 with a concert of 70 vocal and instrumental performers before 1300 people, it was Jonathan Battishill who was chosen organist. From 1758 he had been a member of the Madrigal Society, and from 1761 of the Royal Society of Musicians.

Despite Battishill's successes, some prizes eluded him. Stevens reported that at the death of John Jones (1728–1796), organist of St Paul's Cathedral, Battishill, from his early connections with the Cathedral, had some reasonable expectations of being elected to the post but failed to gain it because of his reputation for inebriety, which had come to the ears of the Archbishop of Canterbury and the Bishops of London and Lincoln.

His drunkenness notwithstanding, Battishill was a man of cultivation and intellect. He collected a library of some 6,500 volumes, mostly the classics. He was possessed of a remarkable memory for music, so that "even the longest compositions of Handel, Corelli, or Arne, were alway sufficiently present to his recollection during the time he was playing them, to render the assistance of the text unnecessary," according to the *Dictionary of Music* (1827). In fact, "He was one day dining with Dr. Arnold, when he played, from memory, several passages of the doctor's oratorio of the *Prodigal Son*, which he had not heard for thirty years, and which the doctor himself had entirely forgotten."

Battishill died at Islington on 10 December 1801, after a long illness, and on 15 December was buried in accord with his death-bed request in the vault of St Paul's Cathedral near the remains of his estranged idol Dr Boyce. The service was composed by his old friend and pupil Dr Busby, and Battishill's own anthem "Call to Remembrance" was sung, accompanied by Attwood.

In his will of 8 December 1801, made when he was so weak that he could only subscribe his mark, he simply appointed his "good friend" John Page, Vicar Choral of St Paul's, his executor of unspecified "effects." There is no clue there or in the probation of 19 March 1805 as to how extensive his property was.

Battishill was a member of the Noblemen's and Gentlemen's Catch Club, which met at the Thatched House Tavern in St James's Street, and he won the Club's gold medal in 1770 for his Anacreontic glee "Come bind my brows." The British Museum's *Catalogue of Printed Music* lists 27 titles under Battishill's name. He is repre-

sented both in the *Apollonian Harmony* and in Page's *Harmonia Sacra*. In 1804 Page edited *Six Anthems and Ten Chants* by Battishill, with an engraved portrait of the composer. Battishill's most popular song was "Kate of Aberdeen," composed for Ranelagh Gardens.

L. Sullivan painted a miniature of Battishill in 1765 and this likeness was later engraved by S. Harding.

**Battishill, Mrs Jonathan.** *See* DAVIES, ELIZABETH, d. 1777.

**Battle, Ralph** *1649–1713, organist.*
Born on 11 April 1649, Ralph Battle was educated at Peterhouse, Cambridge, and in 1662 succeeded Humphry Talbot as the rector of All Saints at Hertford. On the death of Joseph Glanvill in 1680 he was appointed Prebendary of Worcester, and by 11 April 1689 when William and Mary were crowned, he was "Sub Dean" of the Chapel Royal and participated in the festivities. For the next 23 years, in addition to other activities, he swore in most of the new members of the Chapel. In 1704, with John Blow and Peter Hume (the latter from the Exchequer), he viewed three organs built by Bernard Smith at Windsor, Whitehall, and St James's, found them satisfactory, and by a warrant dated 3 July 1704, certified payment to the builder of £3180. Battle was a musical enthusiast and said to be proficient on the organ, but how much performing he may have done in public is not known. He was on intimate terms with many musicians of the time, and when John Blow's will was proved on 14 October 1708, Dr Battle was named trustee and asked to assist Blow's daughters in the will's administration. Battle died on 20 March 1713 and was buried in the cemetery of All Saints at Hertford. He left a wife, Elizabeth, to whom a £50 pension was bequeathed, and a son, Nathaniel, who was buried at St Margaret, Westminster, on 21

July 1715. The relationship between Ralph and William Battle has not been established, but they were in the Chapel Royal together.

### Battle, William  [*fl.* 1691–1711], singer.

William Battle was sworn a Gentleman of the Chapel Royal extraordinary – that is, without fee until a permanent position became available – on 10 December 1691; the officiating Sub Dean was probably Dr Ralph Battle, who may have been related. On 2 January 1711 William Battle, described as a "Chanter of Westminster," was sworn a full member of the Chapel in place of Charles Barnes. It thus appears that he served 20 years without a salary, so he must have had another source of income. On 5 July 1692, a half year after Battle joined the Chapel Royal, a marriage license was issued to a William Battell of St Benet, Gracechurch, bachelor, age 28, and Mary Thompson of St Edmund-the-King, spinster, age 25, daughter of Thomas Thompson of St. Andrew parish in Cambridge. This may have been William the singer.

### Battye. *See* BAETTY.

### Baudin. *See* DE BAUDIN.

### Baudouin, Mons  [*fl.* 1734–1745], dancer.

Monsieur Baudouin (or Badouin) was a member of the Moylin troupe that opened at the Haymarket Theatre on 26 October 1734, though the first mention of Baudouin in the bills was not until 25 April 1735 when he and de Lisle danced *Two Pierrots*. The company played about 116 performances during the season, including two at Goodman's Fields. Occasionally billing themselves as the French "Lilliputian" company, the group performed until 4 June 1735; Baudouin participated in the grand ballet at their last appearance at Goodman's

Fields on that date, after which the company apparently returned to the Continent.

Baudouin seems to have returned alone to England in the fall of 1735, but the only notices of him in the bills for the 1735–36 season are on 17 December 1735, when "Baudvin" danced a *Pierrot* at the Haymarket, and 20 February 1736 at the same playhouse, when he played Pierrot in a new comic dance called *The Pastoral*. During the next two seasons he was a member of John Rich's company at Covent Garden, taking such pantomime roles as an Infernal in *Perseus and Andromeda*, a Fury in *The Necromancer*, and tripling as Zephyr, Pluto, and a country lad in *The Royal Chace*; in addition, of course, he participated in *entr'acte* dances. In August and September of 1737 he was associated with Hallam at his booths at Bartholomew and Southwark Fairs, playing a role in *All Alive and Merry*.

During the 1738–39 and 1739–40 seasons Baudouin was a member of the Drury Lane company. There his pantomime roles included the Mandarin Gormogon in *Harlequin Grand Volgi*, Triton in *Harlequin Shipwreck'd*, and a follower of Mars in *Mars and Venus*. He left Drury Lane temporarily after the 1739–40 season. Baudouin danced at Sadler's Wells on 13 September 1740; on 4 December he was in Dublin performing at Aungier Street; and by the beginning of the 1741–42 season he had returned to London and renewed his affiliation with Drury Lane. Except for a brief summer stint at Sadler's Wells with Hendrick Kerman's group in June and July of 1742, Baudouin remained at Drury Lane for the rest of his London career, serving as one of the minor members of the dancing contingent. Rarely was his name specified in the bills during the early 1740's, and when it was it was usually one of several cited as participants in, for example, a *Tyrolean Dance* or a *Grand Turkish Dance*. Even his appearances in pantomimes were now usually not significant enough to warrant mention, yet the Sadler's Wells bill of 19 June 1742 placed Baudouin first among the dancers; perhaps he joined Kerman's summer company to get away momentarily from the anonymity of his Drury Lane position.

There seem to have survived no specific descriptions of his dancing, though a general comment made in 1742–43 by an anonymous Drury Lane actor was that when no afterpiece was performed at the theatre there were "long and tedious dances" by, among others, Monsieur Baudouin; the actor found the dancers "great performers but in bad taste and without grace."

Only at the end of his London career did Baudouin receive benefits. On 5 May 1744 and 8 May 1745 he shared benefits with several other performers. After the 1744–45 season, his name disappeared from the records.

**Baumgarten, Karl Friedrich** *1740–1824, organist, violinist, composer, teacher.*

Karl Friedrich Baumgarten was born in Lübeck, Germany, about 1740. He began his musical studies at the organ with J. P. Kunzen in Lübeck. He went to England, as a child, in 1757.

Circumstances of Baumgarten's early professional life are virtually unknown, except that he at some date before 1760 became organist of the Lutheran Chapel in the Savoy, London. By 1763 he was violinist and leader of the orchestra of the Haymarket Theatre, and in 1764 he was at Smock Alley Theatre, Dublin. He was invited by the Duke of Cumberland to lead his private band, a select group of musicians which included Shield, Parke, Waterhouse, and Cramer.

A Baumgarten, probably Karl Friedrich, was on the music lists at Covent Garden Theatre for 1767–68 at 10s. 6d. per day. In 1777–78 he was a violinist in the band for the oratorios at Covent Garden. He led the band at the annual St Paul's

Cathedral concert for the benefit of the Royal Society of Musicians on 1 May 1785, *vice* David Richards, who was ill.

From the season of 1780–81 through that of 1793–94 he was the first violinist and leader of the regular band at Covent Garden. Though in 1788 Baumgarten was complimented for leading the band "with great spirit," Haydn thought when he met him in 1792 that lack of spirit was his great deficiency—he led "a sleepy orchestra."

Baumgarten possessed technical proficiency and was a man of keen intellect and much charm, but seemingly lacked ambition. His theatrical compositions were few but respectable. He furnished the overture and other music for Richard Josceline Goodenough's pastoral *William and Nanny; or, The Cottagers* (Covent Garden 12 November 1779. The overture was reused for Leonard McNally's *Robin Hood* on 17 April 1784 and following). He composed the overture for the anonymous *Harlequin, Junior; or, The Magic Cestus* (Covent Garden, 7 January 1784), and all the music for *Blue Beard; or, The Flight of Harlequin* by Carlo Antonio Delpini (21 December 1791 – "Books of the Songs [W. Woodfall, 1791] to be had at the Theatre"). He also wrote some of the music for three *pasticcii* which came out at Covent Garden in 1794: William Pearce's operatic farce *Netly Abbey, Hercules and Omphale*, and *Mago and Dago*.

In addition to the music for the theatre, compositions by Baumgarten extant in the British Museum collection (all published in London) include: *Three Capriccios for the Piano Forte or Harpsichord* [1790?]; *A Grand Concerto for the Hautboy, Flute, or Clarinet Obligato* [1790?]; *A Celebrated Fugue or Voluntary for the Harpsichord or Organ* (No III) (No V) [1783–84?]; *Three Fugues for Organ, Harpsichord or Piano-Forte,* 1798; *Six Quartettos, three for a Violin, Oboe or German Flute, Tenor & Violoncello, and three for two Violins, Oboe, or German Flute, and Violoncello* [separate parts] [1785?]; and *Six Solos for a Violin with a Thorough Bass for the Harpsichord* [1785?].

Baumgarten was an excellent teacher who numbered among his many pupils William Dance and Thomas Welsh. In 1794 he lived at No 23, Russell Place, Rathbone Place. The Minute Books of the Royal Society of Musicians listed him as one of the Governors and one of the Court of Assistants of the Society in February, March, and April of 1785. On 3 January 1808 the Society ordered that, in consequence of his "age and infirmities," he be allowed £3 18s. 4d. per month and 10 guineas immediately for medical assistance.

Baumgarten died before 1 February 1824, when application was made to the Royal Society for his funeral expenses.

K. F. Baumgarten should not be confused with Samuel Baumgarten the bassoonist, who may have been related.

### Baumgarten, Samuel   [fl. 1752–1792], *bassoonist*.

Samuel Baumgarten first appeared to public notice on 11 January 1752 as a bassoonist on the program of a subscription concert led by Giardini at the Great Room in Dean Street, Soho. He was next seen in a list of Handel's musicians at the famous performances of the *Messiah* at the Foundling Hospital in May 1754, with an emolument of 10s. He played there again in May 1758, when his pay was raised to 10s. 6d.

In 1760–61 Baumgarten was on the list of the pit band at the King's Opera, Haymarket, and he was there again in 1761–62, though his service seems to have been only occasional. He returned again in 1765–66. He was doubtless the "Mr Bloomgarten" who played a concerto on the bassoon at the Haymarket on 13 November 1764.

Baumgarten was recruited to Covent Garden's band at a salary of 10s. 6d. per week in 1767–68 but was again a regular in the pit at the Opera in 1769–70, 1770–71, 1771–72, 1774–75, and 1775–76. Al-

though records are incomplete, he was probably at the King's Theatre until at least 1783 when his name last appeared on the list. But he was heard at the Pantheon as late as 1790–91, in concert. He had also been one of the woodwinds in the huge band which played for the Handel Memorial celebrations at Westminster Abbey and the Pantheon in May and June of 1784.

Samuel Baumgarten signed the Book of Admission of the Royal Society of Musicians on 2 September 1792 and paid the subscriptions to the Musicians' Fund of Lewis Henry Leander and Vincent Thomas Leander, presumably his pupils. His only recorded address is that in Mortimer's *London Directory* of 1763: "Cursitor's Alley."

### Baumgartner, Mr   [fl. 1742], *actor?*

*The Virgin Unmasked* was given "By Persons for their own Diversion" for the benefit of Evans and Baumgartner, at the little James Street Theatre on 25 January 1742. No cast was given by the bill, the James Street Theatre had no regular company, and it is not known whether or not Evans and Baumgartner were connected with the theatre.

### Baux, Julien   b. c. 1789, *violinist*.

Billed as not yet six years old, Master Julien Baux played a concerto on the violin by Viotti at the Haymarket Theatre on 22 May 1794. In 1795 he performed at Sadler's Wells in his sixth year, and he appeared at Hamburg in 1799, again playing *concerti* by Viotti.

### Baxter, Mrs   [fl. 1706–1711], *actress*.

Mrs Baxter played Maria in *The Siege of Barcelona* on 27 August 1706 at Pinkethman's booth at Bartholomew Fair. She was presumably the same actress who appeared during the 1710–11 season at Pinkethman's playhouse at Greenwich where she played Lord Foppington in *The Relapse* on 20 September 1710, Melesinda in *Au-*

*reng Zebe* on 28, and Arpasia in *Tamer-lane* on 30 September. When Pinkethman reopened the following spring, *Pastor Fido* was performed with an all-female cast for Mrs Baxter's benefit on 21 May 1711. The Greenwich playbills for the summer seldom mentioned performers, so it is not known whether Mrs Baxter continued with the troupe or not, although she probably did.

### Baxter, Mrs  [*fl.* 1741], *actress.*

A Mrs Baxter played Mrs Sullen in a production of *The Stratagem* given at the converted tennis court in James Street on 6 October 1741; the company's personnel varied considerably during the season, and Mrs Baxter's name was not mentioned again in the bills.

### Baxter, Eleanor  [*fl.* 1799–1801], *performer.*

An Eleanor Baxter signed articles of agreement with James Winston, the manager of the Richmond Theatre, for the summer season of 1799. At the time she was living "opposite Villars St Strand."

The pay ledger at Covent Garden Theatre "settled Eleanor Baxter" for the season 1800–1801 with the sum of £100. Elsewhere in the register she is called "Mrs Baxter." Her function is not recorded but there is no doubt that she was a performer.

### Baxter, John  [*fl.* 1663–1670], *scene-keeper.*

In the Lord Chamberlain's accounts, a list of King's Company members dated 17 April 1663 names John Baxter as one of the troupe's scenekeepers; *The London Stage* also lists him with the company in 1666–67 and 1669–70.

### Baxter, Richard  1618–c. 1666, *actor.*

Richard Baxter the elder, the father of the Restoration actor, was born in 1593 and married Joane Ellit at St James, Clerkenwell, on 2 October 1614. Their daughter Constance was baptized on 25 December 1616 but must have died in infancy, for a second Constance was christened on 21 October 1617. Richard the younger was baptized on 2 September 1618; Robert was christened on 23 August 1620 and Mychaell on 27 January 1622; Susan was buried on 2 December 1622; John was christened on 30 June 1624 and buried on 10 September 1625; Jane was buried on 26 January 1625; a second son John was baptized on 23 December 1629; and Elizabeth was baptized on 20 April 1631 – after which the Baxters are not recorded as having any more offspring.

Richard the elder acted with Queen Anne's company from about 1605 to 1623, when he joined the King's players. About 1630 Richard the younger appeared on stage for the first time on record, playing Stremon's boy to his father's Stremon and singing a song in *The Mad Lover*. The following year both Baxters were in *Believe as You List*, Richard the younger apparently taking a servant's role. In 1648 one of the Baxters performed illegally, and in January 1664 he testified in court about the incident; it is likely, though not certain, that this was the younger Baxter.

It was surely Richard the younger who joined a troupe styled His Majesty's Comedians, at the Cockpit in Drury Lane on 6 October 1660 for a month of performances before the two patent companies went into business officially. On 5 November Baxter played with the King's Company at the old Red Bull playhouse, and starting on the eighth the troupe performed at the Vere Street Theatre. When plans were laid for a new house in Bridges Street, Baxter agreed, on 20 December 1661, to act there; he was not, however, one of the eight actors who held building shares. Baxter worked with the King's Company until 1666–67, about which time he probably died. During these Restoration years his name was attached to only one play, *The Royall King*, acted about 1661–62; he was listed in a manuscript cast, but no role was assigned him. On 20 April 1671, curiously, a Robert Baxter, possibly related to Richard, was living "over agt ye Kings Theatre in Drury Lane in Drumm Alley."

### Baxter, Richard  d. 1747, dancer.

Richard Baxter, though of English birth, spent most of his career in France, where he was sometimes called "Bastee." His usual dancing partner was Monsieur Sorin, and it is likely that their first appearance in England was at Drury Lane on 22 August 1702 when there was presented a Night Scene by a Harlequin and a Scaramouch, after the Italian manner, by "Serene and another Person lately arrived in England." In A Comparison Between the Two Stages (1702) is a discussion of Sieur Allard and his two "sons"—probably Sorin and Baxter:

CRI[TIC]. Ay, the Sieur with a pox to him —and the two Monsieurs his Sons—Rogues that show at Paris for a groat a piece, and here they were an entertainment for the Court and his late Majesty.

RAMB[LE]. Oh—Harlequin and Scaramouch.

CRI. Ay; What a rout here was with a Night-piece of Harlequin and Scaramouch? with the Guittar and the Bladder! What jumping over Tables and Joint-Stools! What ridiculous Postures and Grimaces! and what an exquisite Trick 'twas to straddle before the Audience, making a thousand damn'd French Faces, and seeming in labour with a monstrous Birth, at last my counterfeit Male Lady is delivered of her two Puppies Harlequin and Scaramouch.

SULL[EN]. And yet the Town was so fond of this, that the Rascals brought the greatest Houses that ever were known . . .

A year later, on 7 October 1703, Baxter and Sorin were back at Drury Lane with their Night Scene and stayed at least until 29 October. They returned again to perform on the same stage on 18 August 1704, and on 8 October 1705 they did an Italian Scene at Lincoln's Inn Fields, their last recorded appearance in London for ten years.

In 1707 Baxter danced pantomimes with Nivelon at the St Germain fair, Baxter usually playing Harlequin. This pair worked together until 1711 when Nivelon's managerial ineptness forced him to disband his troupe. Sorin was apparently a member of this company, and when it broke up he and Baxter joined the Baron players. Baron died shortly after this, and his widow reorganized the company; to avoid her late husband's creditors, she used Baxter and Sorin's names as the troupe's leaders: Le Nouvel Opera Comique de Baxter et de Sorin. From 1712 to 1716 Baxter shared in the management and was successful as a performer, especially at the St Laurent fair. He played divertissements that were combinations of singing and dancing at the ends of acts or plays.

In late 1715 Sir Richard Steele, in an attempt to compete with the new Lincoln's Inn Fields Theatre and the productions of John Rich, wrote to the Earl of Stair, then minister plenipotentiary to Paris, asking him to negotiate with Baxter and Sorin for a London engagement. Steele's letter has not survived, but the reply has, dated 27 November 1715, Paris:

I received yr commands some time ago concerning Mr Baxter and his companion, they took some days to consider wt answer they should make, it is yt they are engaged to a woman here for ye fair of St Germain wch begins ye 2nd of February. Baxter has 5000 livres from her, so ye time being so short they are unwilling to make ye journey into England; when the fair is over you may command ym but I suppose yt wont answer to yr view wch was to have em for ye winter.

Madame Baron's troupe had to disband in 1716 due to the pressure of the Comédiens Français against foreign troupes, so Steele was able to lure Baxter and Sorin back to England after all. They appeared at Drury Lane on 4 April 1716, doing The Whimsical Death of Harlequin, with Baxter playing Harlequin and Sorin Scaramouch. They also did *La Guinguette* and their *Night Scene* plus *La Caprice*, and on 20 April and 10 May they received benefits. For one of Baxter's numbers the managers had a special door made "in ye flatt scene for Mr Baxter to leap through." On 14 May they left London.

Baxter and Sorin toured around France until 1721, in which year they went to Paris and formed a company to perform at the St Laurent fair. This was the *Opéra Comique*, of which Baxter was the manager. The project failed, however, not because of any incompetence in the troupe, but because a rage for gambling had ruined many of the theatre patrons, and business was poor. Baxter, in disgust, retired to a monastery where, according to some sources, he remained until his death in 1747. On 21 March 1732, however, a Mr Baxter, newly arrived from France, danced Harlequin in *Perseus and Andromeda* at Drury Lane, and this was doubtless Richard.

Baxter is said to have been a handsome, well-built man, a gifted dancer, actor, and mimic. He was especially skilled in satire and parody and often did droll imitations of the royal players in France and their pompous, declamatory style. He battled with considerable success the prejudice of the *Comédiens Français* against foreigners and became one of the very few Englishmen to make a successful career in France.

**Bay, Mr** (fl. 1724), *gallery keeper*.
The Lincoln's Inn Fields Theatre accounts for 25 November 1724 show a shortage of 4s., due to a mistake made by gallery keeper Mr Bay.

**"Bayes."** *See* CIBBER, COLLEY, and GARRICK, DAVID.

**Bayle** or **Baylery.** *See* BAILEY and BAYLEY.

**Bayley.** *See also* BAILEY and BAILY.

**Bayley, Mr** (fl. 1749), *house servant*.
On 29 September 1749, one Bayley was paid 3s. 4d. for two days' attendance at Covent Garden Theatre. His function is not known.

**Bayley, Mr** (fl. 1783–1785), *box and lobby keeper*.
A Mr Bayley is listed in the records of the Lord Chamberlain's office as a "Box & Lobby-keeper" at the King's Theatre in the Haymarket during the 1783–84 and 1784–85 seasons.

**Bayley, Mrs** (fl. 1780–1781), *singer*.
A Mrs Bayley sang several nights at the Haymarket in out-of-season performances in 1780–81.

**Bayley, George** (fl. 1662), *actor, manager*.
On 14 April 1662 a license was issued to George Bayley to present a play called *Noah's Flood* "with other Scenes"; he had a company of nine, including himself, and provincial authorities were advised to allow him to perform in the town hall, a guildhall, or a school house on any day except regular holidays. He apparently performed in London, though he was primarily a stroller.

**Bayly.** *See* BAILEY and BAYLEY.

**Baynham.** *See* BYNAM.

**Bayne, Mr** (fl. 1777–1790), *house servant*.
A Mr Bayne, evidently a minor house servant, shared a benefit with others at Drury Lane Theatre in every season from 1777–78 through 1781–82 and 1787–88 through 1789–90. In the latter season he was paid only 6s. per week. No connection can be seen with the Bayne (or Bain) who had acted at the Edinburgh Theatre in 1770–71, though one is possible.

**Baynes, Mr** ₁*fl. 1797–1800*₁, *actor, singer.*

Mr Baynes first bowed to the public at Norwich in 1797. He was given an opportunity in London on 13 June 1800 when performers from most of the city's theatres and circuses joined with a few novices in a performance for the benefit of the Bayswater Lying-in Hospital. He played on this occasion Don Jerome in *The Duenna*. Thomas Dutton, in his *Dramatic Censor*, thought that he "displayed much ability . . . he sings in a bold, manly style, and possesses talents, if he chose to follow the stage as an occupation."

He may have been the "Baines" who, shortly after the turn of the century, had taken over the public house in Russell Court from the father of the actress Miss Sims. The *Authentic Memoirs of the Green Room* describes the publican as "having been himself a performer of no mean abilities, as well as Manager of a Country theatre [who] possesses more than ordinary qualifications for an institution of this description."

There is no evidence of a relationship between Baynes and the Mrs Baines who was in the Orchard Street Theatre at Bath, playing minor roles, around 1787.

**Bayrand.** *See* BAYZAND.

**"Bays."** *See* CIBBER, COLLEY, *and* GARRICK, DAVID.

**Bazago.** *See* BUZARLGO.

**Bayzand, William** *d. 1802, dancer, actor.*

William Bayzand was member of the *corps de ballet* and was sometimes featured as a figure dancer, harlequin, and minor actor at Covent Garden Theatre. He appeared first there on 13 June 1791, returning briefly in the following season (from 22 December 1791 through 18 February 1792) at £1 5*s.* per week. He was at the house constantly in the winter seasons from 1792–93 through 1795–96, earning £1 10*s.* per week.

Bayzand was absent from London's patent theatres in 1796–97 and 1797–98, and when he returned in 1798–99 it was to Drury Lane, where he was paid £1 per week. He continued at the same theatre and earned the same salary through 1801–2. He danced ("for that night only") at Richmond on 1 September 1797.

William Bayzand married the singer Elizabeth Taylor at St Martin-in-the-Fields on 14 June 1792. He died on 12 June 1802, according to a notation in the Drury Lane account books.

Bayzand's patronymic baffled the treasurers, bill printers and theatrical scribes, who spelled it, according to their several whims, as: Besand, Bizan, Barzond, Bysand, Braysant, Bayrand, Bezond, Berond, Bisan, and probably in other ways.

**Bayzand, Mrs William, Elizabeth, née Taylor** ₁*fl. 1792–1796*₁, *singer.*

Elizabeth Taylor evidently never sang in London under her maiden name. She was married at St Martin-in-the-Fields on 14 June 1792 to the dancer William Bayzand. She was first noticed as one of the Aerial Spirits in the pantomime *Blue Beard; or, the Flight of Harlequin* at Covent Garden Theatre on 8 October 1792. Such was her humble line until she disappeared from the theatre after 31 May 1799—always one of a band of "Creolian women," or in a "Chorus of Country Girls," or among the "vocal parts" in "Solemn Dirges" and the like.

**Baze, Mr.** *See* BATES, JOAH.

**Bazon,** ₁**Mr?**₁ ₁*fl. 1784–1785*₁, *house servant?*

One Bazon is listed in the Lord Chamberlain's accounts as receiving a salary of £80 for the 1784–85 season at the King's

Theatre in the Haymarket, but his function in the company is not known.

### Beademore, Mr  [fl. 1786?–1794], singer.

A Mr Beademore, of Ashley, was a singer in some of the Handel Memorial Concerts at Westminster Abbey, according to Doane's *Musical Directory* of 1794. He was an alto or countertenor. There is a possibility that he was the theatrical singer John Beardmore, who has not been thought to have appeared in the London theatres until the nineteenth century.

### Beale, Mr  [fl. 1796–1815?], instrumentalist.

The Mr Beale who played some instrument in the band for the spring oratorios at Covent Garden in 1797 and 1799 was probably the Beale who was paid 15s. per week as a member of the band at the theatre in Richmond, Surrey, in the summer of 1799. But it is impossible with data presently known to identify him certainly, even though in the early nineteenth century records of the Royal Society of Musicians are several Beales, one of whom may be identical with this subject and all of whom are probably related to him.

William Beale, son of Robert and Elizabeth Beale of Cross Street, Kensington, who had been born on 1 January 1784 in Landrake, Cornwall, was proposed for membership by Thomas Attwood, Jr in August and elected on 1 December 1811. He had been educated as a chorister in Westminster Abbey. He engaged as a singer in concerts and also performed on the violin, tenor, and violoncello, and had "many scholars on the pianoforte and singing," as of 1811.

In May 1812 a Mr Beale was appointed by the Governors to the band playing at the Society's annual benefit concert at St Paul's Cathedral. "*W*. Beale" was given this duty appointment in May 1813. Appointed again a season later, he was granted permission to send a deputy. Probably the same Beale was elected as a New Governor of the Society on 4 December 1814. On 3 December 1815 he was elected to serve as Old Governor. He lived at No 8, Stacey Street in 1819.

On 4 June 1815 a John Beale was recommended as "a proper person" to be a member by William Dance and was elected "with 13 ayes" on 3 September. His teacher was J. B. Cramer, as a surviving letter to the biographer Sainsbury testifies, so he was probably the Beale who was Cramer's partner in a music publishing business in Regent Street in 1815. Domenico Dragonetti left this Beale all "the MSS quartets composed by me on the condition that he will carefully print them."

John Beale died shortly before 5 May 1823, and an allowance was granted to his widow, who was surely the Mrs Ann Beale who was the recipient of many benefactions for medicine until the last notation concerning her, on 1 March 1840, when it was stated that she would be given "£3 if she undergoes an operation for tapping, her complaint being dropsy."

When Robert Beale was proposed by William Beale on 5 October 1817; an affidavit affirmed:

He has been a Chorister in Westminster Abbey under Mr Guise and Mr R. Cooke and has studied Music ever since for a livelihood, and is a married man, has no children; aged twenty-five years. Performs on the flute and piano forte, is engaged at the Royalty Theatre, is Deputy Organist of Bow Church, Cheapside, and has many scholars.

An extract from the baptismal register of Christ Church, Surrey, submitted on 15 November 1815 shows Robert to have been the son of "Robert Beale, Callicoglazer and Elizabeth, born April 23$^{rd}$ 1792." He was a Governor of the Society in 1822 and 1823 and on the rolls until at least 1830.

Still another Beale, whose first name is not known, was elected to the Society on 4 January 1818.

### Beale, Simon  *d. c. 1695, trumpeter.*

Simon Beale was appointed a trumpeter in ordinary in the King's Musick on 11 June 1660. Pepys made his acquaintance on 16 December, and when he was with Beale eight years later he learned that the trumpeter had been one of Oliver Cromwell's guards and was, after the Restoration, one of King Charles's guards as well. Pepys found Beale "a very civil man."

On 27 August 1662 Beale was given a new silver trumpet, "his own being taken from him for his Majesty's service in Ireland." Between 12 November 1663 and 1668 Beale was not cited in the royal accounts, and perhaps he was on duty out of the country; when he was mentioned again he still held the same position. On 4 January 1670 he and William Bounty were to receive new trumpets after turning in their old ones, and on 24 January 1676 (the next mention of him) Beale was issued a new instrument, "as one of the silver trumpets in his custody was lately lost and stolen from off the Horse Guard and cannot be heard of." After this he seems to have had no further trouble with straying trumpets. The last record of him in the Lord Chamberlain's accounts is a petition of 6 February 1680 by Beale against a Joseph Walker, but the details of the case are not mentioned.

On 25 September 1691 Beale made his will, styling himself a gentleman from St James, Westminster. He left his property in Princes Street in that parish to his wife Frances and bequeathed mourning rings to his brother Edward, sister Mary Aston, nephew Charles Aston, and friend and fellow trumpeter Thomas Christmas. The rest of his estate, including a £150 debt owed him by Barnabee Love, he left to his wife. The exact date of his death is not known, but his will was proved on 11 February 1695, and he had probably died shortly before.

### Beall, Thomas  [fl. 1794–1803?], singer.

A Thomas Beall who is listed both as "Bass," and "Tenor," by Doane's *Musical Directory* in 1794, was at that time resident at Croydon, Surrey. He subscribed to the New Musical Fund, which should mean that his professional activities were prosecuted in London. He may have been the Thomas Beall, bachelor, who married Mary Wilson, spinster, on Christmas Day 1803 at St George, Hanover Square.

### Beard, John  *1716?–1791, singer, actor, manager, patentee.*

John Beard was born, probably in London, around the year 1716. His antecedents are unknown. He was early placed among the Children of the Chapel Royal under the tutelage of their celebrated master Bernard Gates, where he received a thorough education in Latin, mathematics, rhetoric, and history, as well as music.

On 23 February 1732 Gates presented to George Frederick Handel as a birthday present a private performance of the oratorio *Esther* at the Crown and Anchor Tavern in the Strand. The boy Beard sang, in his choir boy's "treeble," the part of the Priest of the Israelites.

By 1734 his voice had changed to the strong, clear tenor which was to make him the most celebrated English singer of mid-century. In October he was given an honorable dismission from the King's service and a present of clothing worth £10 by the Lord Chamberlain. Handel immediately engaged him for the role of Silvius in his new *Pastor Fido*, based on the pastoral romance by Guarini. It opened at Covent Garden on 9 November 1734 before the King and members of the Royal Family. According to Lady Compton, who was present in the shining assembly, "Mr Hendell is so full of [Beard's] praises that he says he will

Harvard Theatre Collection
JOHN BEARD
artist unknown

surprise the Town with his performances before the Winter is over." The prophecy was fulfilled as Beard won critical acclaim in a succession of roles that season: Lurcanio in the new *Ariodante* from 8 January 1735, Habdonah in *Esther* on 5 March, a role in *Deborah* on 28 March, Mathan in *Athalia* from 1 April, and Orontes in *Alcina* on 16 April.

Beard returned to Covent Garden on 23 January 1736 as Endymion in *The Royal Chase*, sang first tenor in *The Feast of Alexander* from 19 February, was Perseus in *Perseus and Andromeda* from 6 March, and Amintas in *Atalanta* on 12 May. He was also heard in concert at Hickford's Room on 8 and 20 April and 10 May. On 26 November at Covent Garden he sang Perseus again. He was Alessandro in *Porus* on 8 December, Varo in *Arminius* on 12 January 1737, repeated Endymion on 14

February, was Vitalino in *Justin* from 16 February, Placese in *Il trionfo del tempo e della verite* on 23 March, and Fabio in *Berenice* from 18 May.

In the performances of these three years before the failure of Handel's opera company and his departure for Aix-la-Chapelle, the great composer had thrust John Beard forward into roles of the type for many years previously reserved for the *castrati*. By doing so, he not only caused a major revolution in the musical taste of the London audiences but also might almost be said to have invented a kind of English singer thitherto unknown but long to be favored by the British public. He certainly founded the fortunes of Beard, for the popular and critical success of the handsome youth was great. His manly, natural voice was accepted by most of the *cognoscenti* as a relief from the *castrati*, despite some dissent from Walpole and others stubbornly devoted to the Italian style.

The meaning of his success was not lost on the alert managers of the patent theatres, and Beard was presently welcomed to Drury Lane where he helped open the season on 30 August 1737. He sang the part of Sir John Loverule in the afterpiece *The Devil to Pay*, Charles Coffey's ballad opera adaptation of Jevon's *The Devil of a Wife*. In his third night in the part he had the inspirational good fortune to introduce Galliard's hunting song "With Early Horn," in which he used the bugle notes of his upper register with thrilling effect. The ovation which followed secured his success with his new public, and it became one of his signature songs.

Beard was probably the "Board" singing the Roving Shepherd in *The Country Wedding* at Pinkethman's booth "over against the Hospital Gate" in the time of Bartholomew Fair in August of 1738. He returned to Drury Lane for the 1738–39 season. Handel engaged Lincoln's Inn Fields Theatre from Rich during the winter of 1739–40 and Beard sang in several operas for him. In the same busy season he sang in some 20 performances of musical entertainments at Hickford's Room, as well as in the regular company at Drury Lane.

He remained at Drury Lane (except for the 1740–41 season) until 1743 and then went to John Rich at Covent Garden, singing there almost constantly in the winter seasons until 1748. He then returned to Garrick's management until 1759 and remained at Drury Lane until his retirement in 1767.

During his years on the stages of the London patent houses, Beard was frequently heard in other places of entertainment. For example, he was Arete in the "semi-pasticcio" of Handel's music called *Jupiter in Argos* at the King's Theatre on 1 May 1739; he was at Hickford's Room on 13 December 1739 in *Acis and Galatea*; and on 22 February 1740 he was again there, singing "David's Lament over Saul and Jonathan." He sang in *Love and Friendship* at the Crown and Anchor Tavern on 21 March 1744. He was in the summer company at Richmond, Surrey, in 1746 and was frequently the most popular attraction at Ranelagh Gardens. He sang regularly in oratorios at the Oxford Music Room and at the Three Choirs Festival at Worcester. After his retirement from active concernment with the Covent Garden house, he was still carried on the list of musicians there as "Vocal Performer Extraordinary" at a yearly salary of £100, until at least 1782.

Handel composed for Beard, or encouraged him to sing, the great tenor parts in his religious and secular oratorios and masques *Israel in Egypt, Athalia, Messiah, Samson, Esther, Saul, Judas Maccabaeus, Jephtha, Acis and Galatea, L'Allegro and Il Penseroso, Alexander Balus, Deborah, Semele, Hercules, Balshazzar, Joshua,* and probably also *Theodora, Susanna,* and *Solomon.* Felice Giardini gave him the chief part in his *Ruth,* and T. A. Arne in *Judith.*

In the theatres the notable tenor roles in ballad opera, operetta, pastoral, panto-

mime, and melodic farce gravitated to him. He occasionally played in non-melodic comedy as well. His parts were not numerous, but he made them so popular that their frequent rotation in the bills seems to have caused no grumbling. In addition to some already named, among his well-worn roles were these: Joe in *The Miller of Mansfield,* Valentine in *The Intriguing Chambermaid,* Attendant Spirit in *Comus,* Edgar in *The Lover's Opera,* Conjuror in *Harlequin Restor'd,* Spaniard in *Columbine Courtesan,* Bully in *The Provok'd Wife,* Squire Freehold in *Robin Goodfellow,* Friendly in *The Committee,* King Henry in *Rosamond,* Mercury in *Lethe,* and Sir Timothy Flash in *Sir John Cockle.*

As popular as his melodic-dramatic roles were, however, and as impressive as he was to critics in sustaining his turns in the great Handelian oratorios, Beard's place in the hearts of his music-loving countrymen, whether they attended him at the patent houses or heard him at private ridottos or in the public gardens, was confirmed chiefly by his performance of English songs. Even his "straight" dramatic performances were laced with occasional song; and his "specialty acts," whether *solus* or with Vernon or Lowe or others in comic or pathetic dialogue, were the delight of the audiences. Just as Handel and Giardini created grand parts for him in oratorio, so Dr Thomas Augustine Arne and Dr William Boyce, John Stanley, Charles Burney, William De-Fesch, and Richard Davies vied in furnishing him with rousing beef-and-porter songs in the English tradition. He was enjoyed in sea chanteys, hunting songs, patriotic ballads, shouts of soldierly defiance, and college songs, as well as melting pastorals and love-lyrics touched with the fashionable "sensibility."

His "Mad Tom," in a setting by Henry Purcell, the "Come My Lads with Souls Befitting," celebrating the taking of Porto Bello, his version of Arne's "Sylvia wilt thou waste thy prime" and "School of Anacreon," the comic song of "The Cock and a Bull," his and Lowe's knock-down *duo* rendition of "Bumper Squire Jones," his own ballad "Stella and Flavia," or Oswald's "Robin's Complaint" and "Susan's Complaint"—all were applauded to the echo. Extracts from his oratorio parts and especially from Arne's music to Milton's *Comus* and the musical setting by Handel of Dryden's ode "Alexander's Feast" were enormously in demand. Beard sang Italian and French as well as English songs, and though he made no special point of dialect, he was well-received in songs "in character": "The Famous Sea Fight at la Hague" or "When Glory Invites what Briton so Mean" by "Beard in the character of a Sailor"; or, in tartans, the Scots ballad "And We are Gayly Yet"; or, as a West Countryman, "The Lass of the Mill," accompanied on the Welsh Harp by the blind harper Parry.

During and after "the '45," he reaped much profit from "Rule Britannia" and

*Harvard Theatre Collection*

JOHN BEARD, as Hawthorn

artist unknown

songs of loyalty to the Hanoverians and laudation of Cumberland and the English forces: "The English Hero's Welcome Home," "The Defeat of the Rebels," and many more. Dozens of the songs "as sung by" Beard were printed and published at the theatres and the popular music shops.

Beard's hearty outlook on life, his pleasantly genteel manners, and his gentlemanly and handsome appearance contributed as much as his extraordinary vocal powers to his generally rapid social and professional progress. Soon after his first vocal successes his engaging personality secured for him a bride from the upper reaches of London society. On 8 January 1739 he married the Lady Henrietta Herbert, the daughter of the Earl of Waldegrave and the widow of Lord Edward Herbert. The town was pleasantly aghast at what some thought the shocking *mésalliance*, and gossip as cruel as it was inaccurate flew between the lady's acquaintances. The Earl of Egmont entered in his diary five days after the wedding:

This week the Lady Henrietta Powis, a young widow 22 years old, married Birde the singing man. Her brother [James], an Ensign in the Guards, told her that her lover had the pox, and that she would be disappointed of the only thing she married him for, which was her lust; for that he would continue to lie every night with the player that brought them together, and give her no solace. But there is no prudence below the girdle. Birde continues to sing upon the stage. This lady had 600 l. a year jointure, 200 l. of which is encumbered by former debts, and 200 l. she has lately sold to pay his debts. To-day it is said her goods have been sold.

Lord Waldegrave turned his back forever on his daughter, ignoring a succession of affecting letters pleading for forgiveness. The Powis family defaulted on the jointure, and litigation ensued, as Mr Robert Halsband has shown; but though a child of Lady Henrietta's first union was eventually provided for, Beard's wife received little.

In the spring of 1740 the Beards were

living in a house in New North Street, just off Red Lyon Square, Holborn. They left England for some reason unknown and were living at Lille during the summer of 1740, and Beard was absent from the stage during the following season. When they returned in 1741–42 they were "in lodgings in Red Lyon Street, near Lamb's Conduit," according to his benefit bill. The next season, however, they returned to the house in New North Street, where they remained until about 1751. By May of 1752 they had moved to the poor neighborhood of Great Russell Street, Covent Garden.

There were other indications besides their *déclassé* address that the Beards were now perhaps in economic straits, for despite what must have been an increasingly good salary from the theatres Beard sought supplementary income. In December of 1752 he attempted without success to secure the sinecure office of Serjeant Trumpet to the King. (To make matters worse Beard had been robbed in his sedan chair on the early morning of 12 January 1750 and had probably suffered a physical attack, since he was reported ill and away from the theatre for over a week.)

On 31 May 1753 Lady Harriet died, perhaps sunk under financial worry and the obloquy of her family. She was buried in St Pancras churchyard. Except for the lack of money, the marriage had been an unusually happy one. And it had certainly broken new ground socially, for it was the first instance in which a male player of any degree whatever had contracted a regular union in England with a member of a noble family.

By the time of his benefit in March 1754, Beard had taken lodgings nostalgically "at Mrs Coleman's in East Street" in his old neighborhood of Red Lyon Square. His benefit bill of 29 March 1755 places his residence "next door to Old Slaughter's Coffee house," in St Martin's Lane, where he seems to have lived at least through 1763.

In 1757 he petitioned the Duke of Newcastle for "the Employment in his Majesty's Customs of a King's Waiter now Vacant by

the Death of Mr Newton," inasmuch as he was now getting old and has been "principally employ'd in the performance of the Birth-day and New-years Odes for twenty-four Years, for which he has never receiv'd any Allowance or Gratuity Whatsoever." Apparently the petition failed.

In 1759 Beard's fortunes took a decided turn for the better. He married Charlotte, one of the four daughters of John Rich, the patentee and manager of Covent Garden Theatre, and transferred his own services to that house at the beginning of the season of 1759–60. At the death of his father-in-law on 26 November 1761 Beard, who was already a shareholder through his wife's interest, assumed the active management (the will of Rich having specifically named him and Rich's widow Priscilla as empowered to act in all matters "jointly not severally"). Though at some time later he shared direction to some extent with the actor James Bencraft, who had married Henrietta Rich, Beard was always the decisive power. He had a successful career as manager, marred only by several paper exchanges with suppliant playwrights, a quarrel with the giddy actress Mrs Hamilton, and a serious riot in February 1763. Rioters led by one Thaddeus Fitzpatrick, who were intoxicated by a success over Garrick and Drury Lane, sought to force Beard also to grant admission at half price at the close of the third act of performance. Loss of property and of revenue finally forced Covent Garden, like Drury Lane, to submit when the malcontents ignored Beard's well-reasoned pleas in the newspapers.

The onset of deafness in 1766 made Beard prepare for a premature retirement despite the pleas of admirers, like the author of *The Rational Rosciad* (1767), who urged

*Continue Beard the knowing few to please*
*Who all applaud your elegance and ease.*

He appeared on the stage for the last time in his and the audience's favorite part of

Hawthorn in *Love in a Village* on 23 May 1767. He and his wife took their one-fifth share of the proceeds from the sale of the patent in the same year and retired to Hampton, where they bought a villa near that of David Garrick.

The latter few years of Beard's life were spent for the most part quietly at Hampton with his wife, as much at ease as his failing health would permit. In a letter to the musician Dr Samuel Arnold dated from Rose Gile on 1 December 1785, Beard spoke of "a most painful return of my Stranguary Complaint" which for a few days previously had been "so frequent, so violent."

Beard died on 4 February 1791, in his seventy-fifth year, and was buried in the church at Hampton. His second wife survived until 1818.

In a will made on 14 June 1786 and probated on 18 March 1791 Richard Hewetson (a lacemaker) and John Bellamy were named trustees of his estate, which totalled some £3000 in bank annuities plus the value of the property at Hampton. Provision was made for his widow Charlotte, for his sister "Catherine Beard (an Innocent) during her life," and for a "Mrs Mary Morice of Long Acre." After his wife's death legacies in varying amounts were to go to his "dear Nephew" William Beard "of Kenton in Devonshire" and his children, to his niece Harriet Crawford ("wife of William Crawford late of High Holborn cabinet maker"), to his niece Thomasin Jordan ("wife of John Jordan of Penryn in the County of Cornwall"), to his niece Elizabeth Withycomb, to his "dear ffriend Mr Thomas Hull [the actor] of Saint Margaret's Westminster and his Wife Anna Maria," and "to the ffund for the support of such persons who thro Age or Infirmity are Obliged to retire from the Stage Instituted by the performers of the Theatre Royal Covent Garden . . . the sum of One hundred Pounds."

John Beard was one of those theatrical persons whose private manners and personalities are to a degree identical with their projections in public. Whether acting, singing, managing, receiving guests at Hampton, or moving in the London society which never rejected him even after the indiscretion of his first marriage, his demeanor was always gentlemanly, frank, and amiable. He was early (1743) elected to the Sublime Society of Beefsteaks and later to the Royal Society of Musicians. Smollett, in *Sir Launcelot Greaves*, speaks of "the generous Johnny B[ear]d, respected and beloved by all the world" moving as a minister "of mirth, good cheer, and jollity" among the members of the Beefsteaks. The surviving testimony of Beard's contemporaries is uniform as to the sweet accord with which he lived with his wives and friends and to the probity and fairness of his professional dealings. He was a charitable man, and his benefactions were many. He alone among the performers at the annual performances of the *Messiah* for the benefit of the Foundling Hospital accepted no fee; and he was the star of numbers of benefits for actors and other citizens under misfortune.

Critics were unanimous on the greatness of his singing, and even those who attempted strictures on his rather formal action usually ended by paying him a compliment. Francis Gentleman, for instance, in *The Dramatic Censor* (1770) thought that "Mr. Beard's appearance and manner of singing were all that could be wished, but his speaking was intolerable, and he appeared too much of the gentleman." Of Hawthorn, in *Love in a Village*, "we may say he died with [the departure of] that truely great intelligent English Singer."

Giles [in *The Maid of the Mill*] is an extreme well-drawn, rural character, and Mr Beard did that honest, unaffected simplicity which distinguish him, particular justice; his humour was natural, forcible and intelligible. The farmer has never been quite himself since that very excellent singing actor left the stage.

Beard was the sort of actor to whom amiable legends attach and it would not be fair in any account of his life to separate him from the most famous. We may use it as it occurs in the manuscript commonplace book of Anne Matthews in the Folger Library (c. 1808):

When Beard the singer was rehearsing the character of Hawthorn . . . a small spaniel one morning walked upon the stage and attached herself to his side which she continued to do, and as it was not known from whence it came, Mr Beard adopted it and always appeared with it on the stage during each performance of the character while it lived, from the first night of the Opera being performed.

The dog's name was Phillis, or so it appears from a doggerel epitaph written at her death by William Kenrick.

An engraving was made by J. McArdell of a portrait of Beard by T. Hudson. An anonymous engraving of him "From [a] picture in his possession at Hampton," was published 17 December 1787. A portrait by J. M. Williams, engraved later by J. Faber, hangs in the Royal Opera House, Covent Garden. An anonymous portrait of him as Hawthorn, with a spaniel at his feet, was "printed for R Sayer, 1769." Finlayson engraved the group painting by Zoffany of Beard as Hawthorn, Shuter as Justice Woodcock, and Dunstall as Hodge.

**Bearda, T.**  (fl. 1794), violinist.
Doane's *Musical Directory* of 1794 listed T. Bearda of Buckingham House as a violinist in the King's band.

**Beardwell, John**  (fl. 1671), musician.
John Beardwell (or Beardnell), cited as Junior, was one of several musicians apprehended by an order issued on 31 March 1671 and repeated on 4 August 1671, though this may have been a second apprehension. The musicians had been performing or teaching without a license from the Marshall and Corporation of Musick.

**Bearnes, Hugh**  (fl. 1794), bass viol player.
Doane's *Musical Directory* of 1794 listed Hugh Bearnes of No 6, Old Street as a participant in concerts given by the Cecilian Society.

**Beates.** See BATES, JACOB.

**Beattie, Mrs.** See HALL, ELIZABETH.

**Beau.** See BEAW.

**Beaufield, Mrs**  (fl. 1784), actress.
Mrs Beaufield acted Miss Willoughby in *A Word to the Wise* at the Haymarket Theatre on 21 January 1784; and in the premier performance of the afterpiece, *The Talisman*, she played an unspecified principal role. On 8 March she was Laura in *The Man's Bewitch'd*. The *Gazetteer* for 8 March listed "Miss" Beaufield for the role of Laura, but this would seem to be a misprint.

**Beauford, Mr**  (fl. 1741), actor.
A Mr Beauford acted Cassander in *A Wife Well Manag'd* at Middleton's booth in Tottenham Court on 4 August 1741. He may have been the same as the Mr Beaufort who performed at Norwich in 1745.

**Beaufort, [Miss?]**  (fl. 1794–1795), singer.
Though there may have been both a Miss and a Mrs Beaufort in the Drury Lane singing chorus in 1794–95, it is likely that the scanty references are to only one woman. In the accounts for 25 April 1795 she was listed as receiving a weekly salary of £1 5s.

**Beaulieu, Mrs**  (fl. 1783–1785), figure dancer.
A Mrs Beaulieu was a figure dancer at the King's Theatre in the Haymarket 1783–85, and on 27 September 1785 a Miss Beaulieu was billed as a figure dancer

at Astley's Amphitheatre. There is a possibility that these represent a single person, though they could be mother and daughter.

**Beaulieu, Miss** ₁*fl. 1785*₁, *figure dancer. See* **BEAULIEU, MRS.**

**Beaumont, de.** *See* **D'EON DE BEAUMONT.**

**Beaumont, Mr** ₁*fl. 1731–1747*₁, *dancer, actor.*

The role of Parmenio in *The Cynick* was acted on 22 February 1731 at Goodman's Fields by a Mr Beaumont, and it was probably this same Beaumont who reappeared in the 1744–45 season in Hallam's company at the New Wells, Goodman's Fields. He was listed as both an actor and a dancer, though when he shared a benefit with Ravenscroft on 26 April 1745 he danced a hornpipe, and his activity in the troupe may have been confined to dancing. He and the dancer Ravenscroft shared benefits again on 11 March 1746 and 25 February 1747 at the same playhouse, and, again, at each of his benefits Beaumont danced a hornpipe. He was otherwise rarely cited in the bills and appears to have been only a minor member of the corps of dancers.

**Beaumont, Mr** ₁*fl. 1794*₁, *stage doorkeeper.*

A Mr Beaumont and a Mr Munday shared £1 16*s*. on 14 April 1794 for keeping the stage door for 12 nights. Beaumont seems not to have been employed regularly.

**Beaumont, Mrs** ₁*fl. 1769–1773?*₁, *singer.*

A Mrs Beaumont sang the part of Mary in *Love and Resolution,* a musical dialogue composed by Dr Arne, at the Haymarket Theatre on 8 December 1770. The performance was out-of-season and appears to have been specially licensed for the performers' benefit.

This Mrs Beaumont is likely the one who sang occasionally at Sadler's Wells in 1769 and on 21 May 1771. In 1769 her address was No 7, Bull-Head Court, Newgate Street. (The Mr [Henry?] Beaumont who was in the band at Sadler's Wells that year does not appear to have been her husband. At any rate his address was different: No 10, Turnagain Lane.) In 1773 a Mrs Beaumont played at Bristol in some capacity, but there is no proof of a connection with the London singer.

**Beaumont, Mrs, stage name of Mrs Ixon** ₁*fl. 1800–1802*₁, *actress.*

A Mrs Beaumont, billed only as "A Young Lady," was Nell in *The Devil to Pay* at Covent Garden Theatre on 17 March 1800. She was identified by the *London Chronicle* the next day as Mrs Beaumont, whose real name was Ixon.

On 17 March Thomas Dutton wrote:

A performer, of the assumed name of Beaumont, made her debut at this Theatre in the character of Nell. The bills announced her appearance as a maiden effort . . . but we understand she has been drilled to the service in the preparatory school in Tottenham-court Road [a private theatre].

Dutton added that she modelled herself on the great comedian Dora Jordan, was not altogether unqualified for low comedy, and was favorably received. But she did not appear again.

Mrs Beaumont received £2 13*s*. 4*d*. per week to begin the 1801–2 season, but a notation in the accounts dated 28 October 1801 says that she was then paid £30 in "lieu of her engagement."

**Beaumont, Henry** *d. 1791, violinist?*

A Mr Beaumont was on the pay lists for musicians at Covent Garden Theatre, earning 5*s*. per day in 1766–67 and 1767–68. He was probably the Mr Beaumont who was at Sadler's Wells in 1769 and whose address at that time was No 10, Turnagain

Lane, Fleet Market. Though we lose track of him for some time, it appears that he was the musician Henry Beaumont who on 10 February 1777 took as his apprentice Thomas, the son of John Gwillim (himself a musician) of Ratcliff Cross. For when Thomas was released from seven years' articles and became free of the Worshipful Company of Musicians in 1784, he gave as his address No 12, Turnagain Lane.

We learn nᵒ more of a Beaumont until 1790 and 1791, in which years the Minute Books of the Royal Society of Musicians list one of that name among the violins sent by the Governors of the Society to play the annual benefit concerts at St Paul's Cathedral.

Henry Beaumont died in December 1791, for on 1 January 1792 a petition to the Society from his relict, Sally Beaumont, advised the Governors that she was left in great distress, with three children—William Hawkes (born 25 January 1782), Henry Barnes Thornton (born 18 June 1784), and James Harris (born in April 1788). She was allowed £4 17s. 6d. per month and £8 for funeral expenses for her husband. (Strangely, Doane's *Musical Directory* of 1794 listed a Henry Beaumont, horn player and member of the Royal Society, who was said to have played in the Handel Memorial performances at Westminster Abbey. It is probable that Doane in this case was not current.)

On 3 August 1794, the three sons of Mrs Henry Beaumont were ordered properly clothed and sent to the tutelage of the Reverend Mr Addison's School at Thirsk in Yorkshire. From that date until 6 April 1806, when James the younger son was commended for honorably serving out his apprenticeship with Joseph Caulfield, music printer of Camden Town, and given £10, the Minute Books of the Society are replete with detail about the apprenticeships of the sons to various hot pressers and watch makers; but none seem to have been apprenticed to musicians.

Mrs Beaumont was "above 60" years of age in 1822. She died on 6 August 1826, and one of her sons was granted £8 for her funeral expenses.

**Beaupins, Mons** (*fl. 1672–1675*), *singer*.

A French opera singer who made his debut under Lully in 1672, Monsieur Beaupins (or Bopins, Beaupuis) appeared in London in 1675, probably specially engaged, and sang on 15 February 1675 in the court masque, *Calisto*.

**Beaupré, Mons** (*fl. 1788–1789*), *dancer*.

Gallini, the acting manager of the King's Theatre in the Haymarket, contracted with Monsieur Beaupré to dance during the 1788–89 season for £270 and a free benefit. The first notice of Beaupré appeared on 10 January 1789 when he danced in a divertissement; on 31 January he participated in the premiere of Noverre's *Les Fêtes provençales*, about which the *World* of 2 February had a most unfavorable comment: "The Dance, if such it can be called, was like the movements of heavy Cavalry. It was hissed very abundantly. Gallini has the excuse of not having been able to get better dancers." During the rest of the season Beaupré danced in most of the ballet offerings at the opera house, including three more Noverre pieces: *Les Jalousies du sérail* on 17 March, *Admète* on 31 March, and *Annette et Lubin* on 28 April. On 17 June the King's Theatre burned and, with the rest of the company, Beaupré completed the season at Covent Garden. Though he had been promised a benefit, none is listed for him in the bills—perhaps because of the disastrous fire.

**Beaupuis.** *See* **BEAUPINS**.

**Beaw, Mr** (*fl. 1730–1735*), *box-keeper*.

Mr Beaw (or Beau, Beeaw)—a man with a name so odd that it may be a scribal error—was a boxkeeper at Drury Lane from 1730 to 1735; during these years of service he was given regular shared benefits.

"Beck." *See* MARSHALL, REBECCA.

Beck, James. *See* BICK, JAMES.

Beckett, Phillip  [*fl. 1660–1674*], *instrumentalist.*

Phillip Beckett was a versatile member of the King's musical establishment, playing both in the band of 24 violins, to which he was appointed on 16 June 1660 replacing Thomas Lupo, and in the wind instruments, which he joined on 1 January 1661, replacing Christopher Bell. His salary as violinist was £46 12s. 8d. annually, and as a wind player he received £40 yearly plus £16 2s. 6d. for livery, the latter stipend being seldom paid on schedule. On 2 September 1661 he was paid £18 for a violin and a cornet, purchased for the royal service. During the 1660's he frequently went with Charles II on trips to Windsor, Portsmouth, Dover, and elsewhere, a fact which testifies to his high standing among the musicians.

His *forte* appears to have been the violin, for on 31 October 1666 a warrant was issued ordering nine of the royal violinists to meet and practice with Beckett "his Lessons," and he served in a special group of 12 violinists formed by John Banister and later led by Louis Grabu. He was not listed among the performers on 15 February 1675 when the great masque *Calisto* was given, for on 27 August 1674 he had surrendered his position as violinist to Henry Dove. He retained his place in the wind instruments until 17 May 1678 when he resigned it to Richard Robinson, but he appears not to have been very active in the years following 1674.

Beckham. *See also* BICKHAM.

Beckham, Mr  [*fl. 1731–1749*], *actor, prompter.*

A Mr "Peckman," possibly an error for Beckham, acted Sir Wilful in *The Banish'd General* at the Mills-Miller-Oates booth at Southwark Fair on 8 September 1731. The first certain mention of Beckham is at Goodman's Fields the following season when he played at least three roles: the second carrier in *1 Henry IV* on 1 November 1731, Porter in *The Footman* on 7 March 1732, and the servant to Yeoman in *Harlequin's Contrivance* on 10 May. The bills for the next season cite him only once: on 24 January 1733 he played the Beggar in *The Beggar's Opera*, though the Bickham who had a benefit at the Haymarket 20 August 1733 may also have been Beckham. During the 1733–34 season he was not a member of any of the main London companies, but on 27 June 1734 he acted Westmoreland in *1 Henry IV* at Richmond.

In 1734–35 he joined the Drury Lane troupe, but his only notice in the bills was on 22 January 1735 when he was one of several ruffians in *The Plot.* A Mrs Beckham, probably his wife, was at Lincoln's Inn Fields this season, but she, too, was only a minor member of the company. In 1735–36 Beckham was Porter in *The Harlot's Progress* on 15 November 1735 and —unless this is an error for Mrs Beckham —Kate Sutler in *Harlequin Restor'd* on 12 January 1736.

Mr Beckham was with Giffard's company at Lincoln's Inn Fields in 1736–37, his only recorded role being Slango in *The Honest Yorkshireman* on 15 June 1737. He returned to Drury Lane the next fall and received his first certain benefit on record, shared with two others, on 18 May 1738. No performances are recorded for him during the season, nor for the next three years, yet he was at Drury Lane and received yearly shared benefits through the 1740–41 season. He was very likely playing small parts and, in view of his later activity, assisting the prompter Chetwood. After concluding the 1740–41 season at Drury Lane, Beckham acted Sir Trusty in *Fair Rosamond* at Hallam's booth at Bartholomew Fair on 22 August 1741, and then, once again, he changed his company affiliation.

In the fall of 1741 Beckham joined Giffard's troupe at Goodman's Fields as prompter, and on 22 April 1742 he was given a solo benefit; the bill noted that tickets could be had of him at his toy shop in Cornhill. He stayed with Giffard through the memorable 1741–42 season when Garrick made his first London appearance, and he moved with the troupe to Lincoln's Inn Fields in 1742–43. In 1745–46 he joined Hallam's venture at Goodman's Fields, but when the company discontinued straight plays after Easter 1746, Beckham completed the season at Covent Garden as a minor actor. During the summer of this year he was a member of the company that played at Twickenham and Richmond. It appears that after Easter 1746 he gave up prompting.

For the 1746–47 season he and Mrs Beckham joined Hallam's company at the Lemon Street theatre in Goodman's Fields; though his wife played a considerable number of fairly significant roles, he is known to have acted only two parts: Manuel in *The Revenge* on 27 October 1746 and his old bit part of the second carrier in *1 Henry IV* on 29 October. What happened to him the next two seasons is not clear, but, with Mrs Beckham, he was at Cushing's booth at Bartholomew Fair on 23 August 1749, playing Tom Rash in *The Adventures of Sir Lubberly Lackbrains*, his last recorded appearance.

**Beckham, Mrs** *(fl. 1735–1749)*, actress.

Mrs Beckham was first noticed in the playbills on 12 June 1735 when she acted Altea in *Rule a Wife and Have a Wife* at Lincoln's Inn Fields. At this time a Mr Beckham, probably her husband, was a minor actor in the Drury Lane company, and though he remained active throughout most of the 1730's and 1740's, his wife seems not to have appeared on the stage again until 1746—unless the role of Kate Sutler in *Harlequin Restor'd* at Drury Lane on 12 January, assigned to Mr Beckham, was hers and not his.

In 1746–47 at the Lemon Street theatre in Goodman's Fields, Mrs Beckham suddenly began acting again, and in roles of some importance. She played Lucy in *The Recruiting Officer* on 28 October 1746, the Hostess in *1 Henry IV* on 29 October, Lady Bountiful in *The Stratagem* on 31 October, Mrs Foresight in *Love for Love* on 6 November, Betty in *A Bold Stroke for a Wife* on 7 November, the Doctor's Wife in *The Anatomist* on 13 November, Lady Wronghead in *The Provoked Husband* on 18 November (though on 25 February 1747 she played Mrs Motherly, and Mrs Bainbridge acted Lady Wronghead), Mrs Coaxer in *The Beggar's Opera* on 5 December, the Duchess of York in *Richard III* on 17 December, Isabella in *The Conscious Lovers* on 18 December, and the Gentlewoman in *Macbeth* on 5 January 1747. She shared a benefit with four others on 26 March 1747 when *Richard III* was performed. It is difficult to imagine how Mrs Beckham could have exploded into such activity unless, prior to this season, she had been learning her trade elsewhere, perhaps in the provinces; it is equally strange that after this burst of activity more should not have been heard of her. During this 1746–47 season her husband was also in the company, but he was infrequently noticed in the bills.

Mrs Beckham was not affiliated with one of the regular London companies in 1747–48, but on 4 April 1748 she made a single appearance as Lucy in *The Recruiting Officer* at the New Wells, Clerkenwell. With her husband on 23 August 1749 she was at Cushing's booth at Bartholomew Fair; she acted Moll in *The Adventures of*

*Sir Lubberly Lackbrains*—the last mention in the bills for either of them. Perhaps they retired to the toy shop Mr Beckham ran in Cornhill.

**Beckham, Mrs** ₁*fl. 1776–1777*₁, *candle woman.*

A Mrs Beckham was the candle woman at Drury Lane at a weekly salary of 12*s*. during the 1776–77 season, and it is likely she worked for the company both before and after this period.

**Beckington, Miss** ₁*fl. 1734*₁, *actress.*

Miss Beckington was first mentioned in theatrical records on 29 May 1734 when she played Harriet in *The Miser* at the James Street Theatre; she acted Ramilie in the same play on 31 May. On 21 June she appeared at the Haymarket Theatre as Molly in *The Beggar's Opera, Tragediz'd*, and she concluded her brief career by going back to her role of Harriet again, this time playing it at the Haymarket on 14 August 1734.

**"Becky."** *See* Wells, Mrs Ezra.

**Bedford, Edward** ₁*fl. 1667–1671*₁, *manager.*

In the spring of 1667 Thomas Killigrew, in cooperation with his rival manager Sir William Davenant, set up a training theatre for young actors in Hatton Garden called the Nursery, putting Captain Edward Bedford in charge. To this "school" came such neophyte actors as John Coysh and Joe Haines, both of whom had notable careers in later years. During 1667–68 Bedford seems to have operated the Nursery by himself, and one of Joe Haines's early biographers spoke later of the Hatton Garden playhouse as having been built by Bedford, though this may merely have meant "established." Audiences were small, and when Pepys went to see *The Spanish Tragedy* there on 24 February 1668, he received small pleasure from the actors; he said "the

house is better and the musique better than we looked for, and the acting not much worse, because I expected as bad as could be: and I was not much mistaken, for it was so." Ever courageous, Pepys went back the next day to see the learners do *The Faithful Shepherd*, but again he found "the meanest manner" of performance. Poor Bedford was in the awkward position of having to relinquish any really talented players to his masters at the two patent houses, so a fine comedian like Haines, whom Pepys saw at the Bridges Street Theatre on 7 March 1668 ("only lately come thither from the Nursery"), could benefit Bedford only a few months before he would be snatched away by the major theatres.

Bedford had other problems as well. Rival manager George Jolly, who had been trying regularly to break into the London theatrical monopoly, was refused permission to set up a third company in London and he was naturally incensed when the authorities allowed Killigrew and Davenant to do just that. Jolly posed enough of a threat to the two patentees that they apparently felt the best way to deal with the matter was to take the upstart on as the Nursery manager when its second season started. During 1668–69, then, Bedford either shared the management with Jolly or served under him; during this season, too, the troupe moved from Hatton Garden to the old Vere Street playhouse which the King's Company had abandoned in 1663.

It is not surprising that Bedford, in November 1669, left the Nursery to join the Duke of Monmouth's company—or, according to some sources, to organize that strolling troupe. A license was issued on 25 November 1669 permitting the company to play anywhere except London, so off to the provinces went Bedford, leaving John Perin in his place at the Nursery. Bedford's wanderings during the next four years are only occasionally documented. In late 1669 both Jolly and Bedford were apparently at Norwich, either in competition or in partnership; on 13 April 1671 Bedford was back in London, involved in a court case over a debt owed by John Perin to Bedford; and in December 1673 Perin purchased the Duke of Monmouth's license when the troupe was in Norwich and took over the management from Bedford. It is not known what happened to Bedford after this or why he was called Captain.

**Bedini.** *See also* **BADINI.**

**Bedini, Signora** [*fl.* 1787–1788], *dancer.*

Signora Bedini was a dancing member of the opera company at the King's Theatre in the Haymarket during the 1787–88 season; the librettist Carlo Francesco Badini was in London at this time and was associated with the King's both before and after this season, and if the records contain a misspelling, perhaps the two were husband and wife. Signora Bedini first appeared in a new divertissement on 8 December 1787, though her part was so small that it was omitted at the 3 January 1788 performance. On 12 January she participated in a military dance, and her next two assignments were in premieres of Noverre ballets: *L'Amour et Psiché* on 29 January and *Euthyme et Eucharis* on 13 March. Though she apparently continued dancing with the company until the end of June, her name was not mentioned in the bills of other ballets done in April and May.

The Mademoiselle Bedini who danced at the King's Theatre in 1793 was possibly her daughter; but if the "Mlle" in the records was an error, this may have been Signora Bedini herself. The female singer Badini, mentioned by Haydn in 1792, may also have been a relative.

**Bedini, Mlle** [*fl.* 1793], *dancer. See* **BEDINI, SIGNORA.**

**Bedotti.** *See* **BIDOTTI.**

**Bedwell, Mr** [*fl.* 1726–1727], *house servant?*

A Mr Bedwell was on the free list at the Lincoln's Inn Fields Theatre during the 1726–27 season, but his function in the company, if any, is not clear.

**Bee, la.** *See* **L'ABBÉ.**

**Beeland, Ambrose** [*fl.* 1624–1672], *violinist.*

On 27 December 1624 Ambrose Beeland was one of the musical members of the old King's Company exempted from arrest by Master of the Revels Sir Henry Herbert, though four years later, on 14 December 1628, this did not prevent Mr Hemmings from getting a warrant for Beeland's apprehension. Beeland was probably quite young in the 1620's, but he must have been a fairly accomplished musician by the time he was sworn a violinist in ordinary in the King's Musick 11–13 February 1640, replacing the deceased James Johnson. Since his name is found as Beland and Biland as well as Beeland, perhaps he was the Ambrose Balam or Balem "Musitioner" whose wife, unnamed, was buried at St Andrew, Holborn, on 19 September 1654. Beeland was reinstated as a violinist under Charles II and played at the King's coronation, the musician's official restoration being dated 3 August 1661. On 30 July 1662 he and Thomas Blagrave were paid £14 for two tenor violins — an instrument between a viola and a violoncello which went out of fashion in the eighteenth century. His salary in 1668 was £45 10s. 10d., but on 19 March 1672 he surrendered his position to Edmund Flower, probably because of his age.

**Beesley, Mr** [*fl.* 1780], *actor.*

Mr Beesley, from the Theatre Royal, Norwich, acted Alderman Increase in *The Detection* and Captain Constant in *The City Association* at the Haymarket Theatre on 13 November 1780.

**Beeson.** *See also* **BEESTON.**

**Beeson, Mr** *[fl. 1729–1731]*, *house servant?*

One Beeson shared benefits at Goodman's Fields on 19 June 1730 and 14 May 1731, but his function in the theatre was not mentioned in the bills.

**Beestian.** *See* BEESTON.

**Beeston, Mr** *[fl. 1708–1712]*, *violinist.*

Mr Beeston played violin at a benefit for himself at Epsom on 26 July 1708, again on 7 October 1711 at Wax Chandlers' Hall (his first recorded London appearance), and again on 28 November 1712 at Orlibeer's School. At this last benefit one of his students also performed, and Beeston's main career may have been as a teacher.

**Beeston, Mr** *[fl. 1782–1784]*, *house servant?*

The Covent Garden Theatre accounts show Mr Beeston, position not stated, earning a constant salary of 15s. daily from 21 December 1782 through 3 June 1784; he shared benefits with three others on 4 June 1783 and 29 May 1784. Beeston may have been one of the house servants.

**Beeston, George** *[fl. 1660?–1675]*, *actor.*

George Beeston's date of birth is not certain. His father William, the actor-manager, married on 15 July 1642, and 10 years later Francis Kirkman published his *The Loves and Adventures of Clerico and Logis*, speaking in the dedication to William of his son "Mr George Beeston (whom knowing men conclude, [is] a hopeful inheritor of his Fathers rare ingenuity)." Unless George was born out of wedlock or of an earlier wife of William, he would not have been more than about nine in 1652. Unfortunately, the parish registers of St Giles in the Fields, where William lived at the time, contain no mention of George.

The younger Beeston may have been a member of the troupe organized by his father in early 1660 at the Salisbury Court Theatre, but most references to him date from the late 1660's and early 1670's. *The London Stage* is in error in giving all of the roles allotted Mr Beeston in this period to a William Beeston Junior, for there was no such person; William's father was named Christopher, though William in his youth was sometimes called Beeston Junior, and William is not known to have had a son named after him. Some of the Restoration roles for a Beeston, then, probably belong to George, especially those appropriate to a younger actor, and others should be assigned to his father.

George Beeston may have played Lodovico in *Flora's Vagaries* on 14 February 1667 at court; he was certainly the page in *The Black Prince* on 19 October 1667 at Bridges Street; and a promptbook for a 1668–69 production of *The Sisters* clearly assigns him the part of Farnese. Though George was obviously a member of the King's Company before 21 August 1669, not until that date do the Lord Chamberlain's accounts confirm that "George Beestian" was a player in the troupe.

William Beeston spent a great deal of time involved with legal problems, but there seems to be only one notice of his son George having difficulties with the authorities. On 28 February 1671 he and several other comedians were arrested for unspecified misdemeanors.

Four roles in the 1670's should probably be assigned to George: Young Ozmyn in the two parts of *The Conquest of Granada* in December 1670 and January 1671 at the Bridges Street playhouse, Van Herring in *Amboyna* in May 1673 at Lincoln's Inn Fields (where the King's Company played temporarily after the Bridges Street Theatre burned down), Amante in *The Amorous Old Woman* in March 1674 at the same playhouse or possibly at the new Drury Lane, and Roderigo in *Othello* on 25 January 1675 at Drury Lane. Though his father had a splendid reputation for training young actors, he apparently was unable to make a star of his son, and Francis Kirkman's prophecy went unfulfilled.

### Beeston, William  *c. 1606–1682, actor, manager.*

Born about 1606, William Beeston, sometimes called William Hutchinson, was the son of the pre-Restoration theatre manager Christopher Beeston. From about 1604 to 1610 Christopher and his (first?) wife Jane lived in the parish of St Leonard, Shoreditch, where their children—Augustine, Christopher, Jane, and Robert—were baptized and buried; though no record of William Beeston's birth has been found, he was presumably a child of this union. The *alias* Hutchinson was also applied to the elder Beeston, so it cannot be supposed that William might have been a son of Jane by a previous marriage.

In later years William Beeston claimed to have been "bred up in the art of stage playing," so it is probable that he began acting as a boy, and though he was not named after his father, he became known as Beeston Junior. At about 18, he may have been the William Bee who was a member of Lady Elizabeth's troupe performing at Norwich, for his father was also a company member; on 26 May 1624 "Bee" was discharged from Norwich prison where he had been held on some unspecified charge. It is unlikely that, being a minor, he was the William Beeston who was mentioned on 29 June 1624 in a case involving lands and debts of Sir Edward Raleigh in Farnborough, Warwickshire. He may have been the William Beeston who, on 14 February 1627, was given permission to sue Sir John Wentworth, but there are too few details of the case to be certain.

It was certainly William Beeston the actor who petitioned with deputy Master of the Revels and theatre manager William Blagrave on 12 November 1632 for the return of a boy named Stephen Hamerton

who had been taken from them by Christopher Babham and employed at the Blackfriars Theatre. At this time Beeston was probably co-managing the Salisbury Court playhouse and the King's Revels Company with Blagrave, operating in competition with his father's group at the Cockpit. But father and son were not estranged, for on 7 November 1634 William and Christopher helped pay for the engraving of a plate of "The Powers" in *Hierarchie of the Blessed Angels* by Thomas Heywood, Christopher Beeston's lifelong friend. William joined his father's company (nicknamed "Beeston's Boys") by 1637, for on 12 May that year both of them, along with Theophilus Bird, Ezechiel Fenn, and Michael Mohun, were called before the Privy Council for acting at the Cockpit during a plague quarantine.

Christopher Beeston died in early October 1638, and by his will dated 4 October he left William a half share in his company, freehold land and houses in the parish of St Leonard, Shoreditch, and land in Lincoln's Inn Fields. William may have inherited the land on which the Curtain playhouse once stood, for his father's holdings included a ten-acre plot known as the Curtain. The younger Beeston's half share in the acting company was not a controlling interest, for the company held four shares and Christopher Beeston's widow Elizabeth (his second wife?) held one and a half; but on 5 April 1639 William was officially made "Gouuernor & Instructer of the Kings & Queens young Company of Actors." His position was powerful enough that on 10 August, at Beeston's complaint, other troupes were denied the privilege of acting any plays listed as his company's property.

His group overstepped its bounds on 3 May 1640 by acting an unlicensed play which made uncomplimentary references to the King's journey to Scotland, and the next day Beeston was committed to the Marshalsea. On 7 May the company was allowed to act again, and its governor was presumably released on that date. When the troupe abused their privileges again on 27 (or 28?) June 1640, Sir William Davenant was installed as manager; Beeston apparently remained with the company, serving as acting coach. Not until Davenant fled to the Continent in May 1641 was William reinstalled as the group's leader.

Beeston's ability was highly praised by playwright Richard Brome in his epilogue to *The Court Beggar* (published in 1653 but referring to Beeston's activities about 1640). Brome lauded William,

by whose care and directions this Stage is govern'd, who has for many yeares both in his fathers dayes, and since directed Poets to write & Players to speak till he traind up these youths here to what they are now. I some of 'em from before they were able to say a grace of two lines long to have more parts in their pates then would fill so many Dry-fats[vats]. And to be serious with you, if after all this, by the venemous practise of some, who study nothing more then his destruction, he should faile us, both Poets and Players would be at losse in Reputation.

Francis Kirkman also honored Beeston in his translation of *The Loves and Adventures of Clerico and Logis* (1652), which he dedicated to the manager:

Divers times (in my hearing) to the admiration of the whol Company, you have most judiciously discoursed of Poësie: which is the cause J presume to chuse you for my Patron and Protector; who are the happiest interpreter and judg of our English Stage-Playes this Nation ever produced; which the Poets and Actors of these times, cannot (without ingratitude) deny; for I have heard the chief, and most ingenious of them acknowledg their Fames & Profits essentially sprung from your instructions, judgment and fancy.

Richard Flecknoe in a postscript to his *Love's Dominion* (1654) added to these early testimonials:

That this Piece may receive no disadvantage (as I hope it will no prejudice) by the publishing it, I let thee understand (Gentile Reader) if ever it be acted, I intitle to my right in it, (not departing in the mean time with my right of altering my mind) Mr. Will. Beeston, who by Reason of his long Practice and Experience in this way, as also for having brought up most of the Actors extant [such as Burt, Shatterell and Mohun], I think the fittest Man for this Charge and Imployment.

By 1642 Beeston was leader of one of the most popular companies in London, an acknowledged authority on things theatrical, and a man of means. He was in his midthirties now and decided it was time to marry and raise a family. His bride was Alice Bowen, widow of Thomas Bowen, a mercer; they were married at St Giles in the Fields on 15 July 1642. The parish registers there show that a daughter Jane was christened on 1 April 1644, and from a reference in Kirkman's *The Loves and Adventures of Clerico and Logis* of 1652 we know that William (and Alice, presumably) had a son George: "I doubt not though [poets and actors] fail to receive incouragement from you, your son, M<sup>r</sup> George Beeston (whom knowing men conclude, a hopeful inheritor of his Fathers rare ingenuity) may receive them with a gracious allowance." Kirkman's reference to William's son seems inappropriate to a lad born less than 10 years before, so possibly George was born before William's 1642 marriage; but perhaps Kirkman was just engaging in the flattery typical of dedications.

After the closing of the theatres Beeston's theatrical activities diminished but did not cease. In 1648 an indenture was drawn up assigning Beeston the residue of a lease for 61 years on the Salisbury Court playhouse; John Herne of Lincoln's Inn, with the consent of the Earl of Dorset, made the assignment for a total of £700, of which Beeston gave £100 as a down payment. Before further payment was made, soldiers, on 24

March 1649, demolished the inside of the theatre. John Herne died, leaving the theatre to his son John, who began negotiations with a Mr Lightmaker, a brewer, to turn the playhouse into a brewery and give Beeston back his £100. The Earl of Dorset and his son, Lord Buckhurst, did not think a brewery would enhance their property, so they supported Beeston in his effort to get the theatre building from young Herne and Lightmaker. Their support consisted of a promise to pay Beeston £700 which Dorset had owed to Thomas Bowen, whose widow Beeston had married in 1642.

A new agreement with Herne was drawn up, and, apparently on the word of the aging Dorset that the £700 would be forthcoming, Beeston paid Herne with his own money all but £80 of the total, selling or pawning most of his own goods to raise the money. Lacking the last £80, however, Beeston still did not have full possession of the theatre. The younger Dorset did not keep the bargain with Beeston that his father had made; Herne and Lightmaker drew up a new agreement that would shut Beeston out, and Beeston landed in debtor's prison. Exactly when these various events occurred is not clear, though they probably stretched over about four years, beginning in 1648. The tale had a happy ending though: by 25 March 1652 the new Earl of Dorset had sided with Beeston; Beeston had raised the necessary £80; and the playhouse was signed over to Beeston's agent and brother-in-law, Theophilus Bird.

While Beeston was busying himself with the complex negotiations for the Salisbury Court playhouse, he was also trying to buy the Cockpit in Drury Lane, which he had managed in earlier years. For this he had to treat with Robert Rolleston, who had obtained the lease on the Cockpit in 1644. In October 1650 Beeston agreed to purchase the Cockpit from Rolleston for £351, but with what seems to have been characteristic carelessness, he sealed the articles without reading them. The agreement turned out to

be harder than Beeston had bargained for, and by early March 1651 he was in Fleet prison for debt and unable to continue payments on the theatre and hence unable to gain possession of it.

By 24 March 1651 Beeston was out of prison and trying to reach a new agreement with Rolleston, but to no avail. Having paid Rolleston £150 already and also having spent money to repair the playhouse, Beeston now found that Rolleston's right to the property had not been clearly established in the first place. Beeston apparently lost his battle to gain control of the Cockpit, and his efforts to repair it and train a company to perform there came to nothing. Not until 1657 was the case between Rolleston and Beeston settled, apparently in Rolleston's favor.

Busy Beeston was not content to confine his theatrical activities during the interregnum to negotiations for playhouses. He was probably also involved in surreptitious performances at Gibbons' Tennis Court in Vere Street in 1653. By this time Beeston had arranged for the purchase of the Salisbury Court playhouse but, as will be seen later, was still not in possession of the lease; this theatre, then, was not ready for his use, and his hopes of buying the Cockpit were fading fast. He seems, therefore, to have temporarily joined a group of players who, in March 1653, illegally produced Killigrew's *Claricilla* at Gibbons' Court. The *Mercurius Democritus* of 2–9 March reported how the building was raided: "an ill Beest, or rather Bird (because the rest denyed him a share of their profits) bet his own nest, causing the poor Actors to be routed by the Souldiery, though he himself hath since the prohibition of Playes, had divers Tragedies and Comedies acted in his own house." If the "ill Beest" referred to Beeston (and the reference to "Bird" was to his brother-in-law actor Theophilus Bird), then during the decade since 1642 Beeston had been producing plays at the Cockpit. Now, in 1653, he was in some way connected with the tennis court incident, and the implication is clearly that he informed on his colleagues when they refused him a share in the undertaking.

The *Claricilla* affair, however, was merely an interlude in Beeston's interregnum melodrama. The next major episode had to do, once again, with his efforts to gain possession of the Salisbury Court playhouse. On 25 March 1652 the theatre had been signed over to Beeston's agent Bird, but the new Earl of Dorset did not give Beeston the promised 80-year lease, even though Beeston had agreed to pay what for him was a prohibitive yearly fee of 40s. for it. He was determined to get the lease somehow and desperate enough to try anything. In 1654 his wife Alice bore him a son, and Beeston named him Sackville—the Earl's family name—hoping to win over Dorset by flattery. At one point in the negotiations the Earl happened to suggest that the theatre would look nice with a garden around it, and Beeston promptly planted one. Despite all, Dorset refused to grant the lease. In 1655 Beeston applied to his ex-enemy, the brewer Lightmaker, for a loan of £300 to make repairs to the old playhouse, hoping that Dorset would be pleased. The upshot of this was a complaint from the Earl about the plumbers who dug up the ground and broke a conduit conveying water to the theatre. Beeston finally turned to Dorset's financial manager, Sir Kenelm Digby, when the Earl was out of town; Digby was encouraging, so Beeston laid out more money on building repairs. This was premature, for in 1657 Dorset took the matter to court in hopes of evicting Beeston in favor of a Mr Wheeler; the case was still being contested in August 1658, and though the details are obscure, Beeston managed somehow to keep possession of the building, and, apparently, he finally got the lease he had so long sought.

During the 1650's when Beeston was trying to make his hold on Salisbury Court legal, he may have produced some plays

there, but the existing documents are ambiguous, and it may be that the playhouse stood idle after the soldiers ruined the interior in 1649. By 1659, however, the political situation had changed, and the determined manager renewed his efforts to fit up the theatre for productions. As might be expected, misfortune plagued him still. Toward the end of 1659, with the restoration of the monarchy imminent, Beeston hired carpenters Thomas Silver and Edward Fisher to do some repairs to the theatre for £120; they asked for security, and William made another typical Beestonian move: he mortgaged the theatre lease to them. When the carpenters finished their work Beeston was dissatisfied and had to have much of it redone. When the details came out in a court case in 1666, Beeston remembered having lost £2000 on the project—probably an exaggeration but indicative of his bad luck. The carpenters, in addition to having done a poor job, refused to give Beeston back his lease on the building, and in 1666 they claimed that the manager still owed them £299 2s. 6d. The final irony was that the theatre burned down in the great fire of 1666 before the case was settled. After the fire Silver and Fisher obtained rights to the land and planned, though did not build, a new theatre that would have cost £1000.

Beeston's expenditures on the Salisbury Court playhouse during the 1650's, though they involved the manager in exasperating court cases, made the building fit for productions by 1660. It is probable that Beeston had a troupe performing there by February or March of that year, just before the Restoration, and he may have produced, among other works, Tatham's *The Rump*. In the company were probably Beeston, his son George, his brother-in-law Theophilus Bird, John Lacy, George Jolly, Thomas Loveday, Richard Baxter, and possibly Henry Harris—though the makeup of the troupe is conjectural. By April 1660 Beeston had made further repairs to the play house, and, perhaps in June, he was issued a license by the Master of the Revels, Sir Henry Herbert:

. . . whereas Mister William Beeston hath desired Authority and Lycence from mee to Continue the house called Salsbury Court Play house In a Playhouse, which was formerly built and Erected into a Playhouse by the Permission and Lycence of the Master of the Revells.

These are therefore by vertue of a Grante vnder the Greate Seale of England, and of the Constant Practice thereof, to Continue and Constitute the said house called Salisbury Court Play house into a Play house, and to Authorize and Lycence the said Mister Beeston to Sett, Lett, or vse it for a Play house, wherein Comedies, tragedies, trage Comedies, Pastoralls, and Interludes, may bee Acted, Prouided that noe persons be admitted to Act in the said Play house but such as shall be allowed by the Master of his Majesties Office of the Revells.

(Unfortunately the document is a copy, not the original, and it is not dated.)

Beeston, with Rhodes and Mohun as rival managers at the Cockpit and Red Bull respectively, was apparently operating throughout the summer of 1660. On 14 August Herbert entered into an agreement with the Red Bull troupe which required them to pay him £4 weekly whenever they acted—a fee which Rhodes and Beeston were also paying. Later in August Sir William Davenant and Thomas Killigrew were negotiating for theatrical control, and by October the actors had started to regroup into what were to become the King's and Duke's companies. By 5 November 1660 Davenant's players (the Duke's Company) were acting at Salisbury Court, so Beeston's group had certainly dissolved by then, but it seems that Beeston still had control of the playhouse, if not of the performers. A year later, on 26 November 1661, he was still the lessee, for George Jolly paid him for use of the theatre.

Beeston's theatrical activities during the next few years are rather obscure, and some references to a Mr Beeston could be to his son George—though George's career seems to belong to the period from 1667 to 1675. Perhaps William toured, but he was certainly in London off and on. On 29 August 1663 and again on 7 September 1664 warrants were issued to apprehend Beeston, probably William, for acting illegally at the Salisbury Court Theatre. Though Downes reported that Beeston joined the King's Company shortly after they opened their new theatre in Bridges Street in May 1663, it is probable that he did not become a member until the 1664–65 season, just after his second attempt to perform at Salisbury Court. A manuscript cast for a performance of Ford's *Love's Sacrifice* in the early 1660's has a "Beeson" playing the servant Giacope; this was very likely William, and the performance was probably during the 1664–65 season.

*The London Stage* lists a William Beeston Junior and assigns him all the roles played by a Mr Beeston during the late 1660's and early 1670's, but there is no evidence that William Beeston had a son named after him, and the roles, at least the ones appropriate to a younger man, should probably be assigned to William's son George. Father and son were both members of the King's troupe for a time, but on the basis of the age of the characters and the elder Beeston's more extensive experience, the parts can be conjecturally distributed. On 15 September 1668 *Damoiselles à la mode* was performed at the Bridges Street Theatre; Pepys saw it and reported that the play was "so mean a thing as, when they come to say it would be acted again to-morrow, both he that said it, Beeson, and the pit fell a-laughing, there being this day not a quarter of the pit full." This was probably William Beeston, an old timer at making announcements to audiences. It was perhaps he who played Emanuel in *The Island Princess* on 6 November 1668, a role in *Catiline* on 18 December of the same year, and Kynaston's role in *The Heiress* on 2 February 1669. Pepys was again on hand to report on *The Heiress*; Kynaston having suffered a beating that made it impossible for him to perform,

his part is done by Beeston, who is fain to read it out of a book all the while, and thereby spoils the part, and almost the play, it being one of the best parts in it. . . . But it was pleasant to see Beeston come in with others, supposing it to be dark, and yet he is forced to read his part by the light of the candles: and this I observing to a gentleman that sat by me, he was mightily pleased therewith, and spread it up and down.

What role this was is not known, and if Kynaston, then a young man, was to have played it, the elder Beeston might not have been as appropriate for the part as his son, but the role was apparently a big one, William Beeston was an experienced theatre man, and so perhaps this was he, playing with script in hand. Two other roles were probably taken by William: Nigrinus in *Tyrannic Love* on 24 June 1669 and Macrinus in *The Roman Empress* in August 1670. He certainly must have acted other parts before and after these few that are in the records, but documents are scanty for the Restoration period, and Beeston was perhaps relegated to small parts much of the time. He was in his late fifties by now and probably not as useful to the troupe as the somewhat younger men he had helped to train. He remained a member of The King's Company until his death in 1682, but after August 1670 there would appear to have been no roles that could logically be assigned to him.

There are other references to Beeston during the 1670's, but they tell us precious little. Though his court cases were all settled in the previous decade, Beeston still managed to get himself into occasional trouble. On 5 July 1671 a Robert Smyth was permitted to take action against Beeston for a debt; on 20 August 1673 Jeremiah

Stillgore petitioned against William "Beestian" for another debt; and, as though the records wanted to explain all of poor William's troubles, on 10 March he was listed as not having attended his church, St Leonard, Shoreditch, for a month.

In 1681, when the King's Company was floundering, Beeston may have gone into at least semi-retirement, though he was still on the company's roster. In that year John Aubrey picked up from William some theatrical gossip, and in 1682 he wrote that "old Mr. Beeston, whom Mr. Dreyden calles 'the chronicle of the stage,' died at his house in Bishopsgate street without, about Bartholomew-tyde [the last week in August], 1682." Beeston's will, describing him as of St Leonard, Shoreditch, gentleman, was proved by his widow Alice on 7 September 1682; unfortunately, the will books for this year have been lost, as well as an inventory Beeston made on 7 May 1682 which might have provided valuable information about this important link between the old theatre and the new.

**Beeton, Mr** *[fl. 1794–1803]*, *house servant.*

Mr Beeton seems to have been a Drury Lane carpenter or watchman or both. On 2 September 1794 the Drury Lane chief carpenter, Richard Jacobs, was paid £10 10s. for Beeton and Jenu for five weeks' work; Jenu seems certainly to have been a carpenter—though a "Jennu" was a trombonist in the company a few years later—so the assumption is that Beeton was one of Jacobs's assistants. On 5 March 1803 Beeton was paid £5 8s. for nine weeks' watching, from 10 July to 11 September. It may be that the 1794 payment to Beeton was for duty as a watchman, too, since both payments were for the summer periods when Drury Lane was closed.

**Beezon.** *See* BEESTON.

**Begard.** *See* BEJARD.

**Beilby, Mr** (fl. 1784–1794), *violinist, violoncellist.*

Though Mr Beilby (or Bielby) was primarily a violinist, he played violoncello at the Handel Memorial Concerts at Westminster Abbey and the Pantheon on 26, 27, 29 May and 3, 5 June 1784. By 22 January 1793 he was a member of the Drury Lane band, for on that date Kemble advanced him £50 on his salary. According to Doane's *Musical Directory* of 1794, Mr Beilby was living in Castle Street, Leicester Square, that year. He may have been related to Sophia Westerly Beilby who married William Rowe Whitlock at St Paul, Covent Garden, on 25 February 1771.

**Bejard, Mons** (fl. 1675), *violinist, oboist.*

Monsieur Bejard (or Begard) played the French violin and oboe in the production of the court masque *Calisto* on 15 February 1675.

**Beland.** *See* BEELAND.

**Belenger, Mr** (fl. 1794–1795), *scene designer.*

Mr Belenger was one of the three staff scene designers at the King's Theatre in the Haymarket during the 1794–95 season; he provided new scenery for the ballet *Paul et Virginie* when it was done on 26 March 1795.

**Belfield, Mrs.** *See* BARRETT, MRS GILES LINNETT.

**Belfille, Mrs, stage name of Mrs Arnold, née Burdett** d. 1789, *actress.*

Most of what is known of the parentage and early life of the actress Ann Belfille (sometime Belville or Belsill) is found in a two-part "sketch" of her life published in the *Town and Country Magazine* in May and June 1788. The account is full of pathos and no doubt highly fictional. She was born probably in the late 1750's, the daughter of a Mr Burdett, who was an apothecary and surgeon at Lutterworth, in Leicestershire. Mr Burdett was said to be a well-known member of the community, a generous and liberal man, who had inherited a "handsome paternal estate" and by his own marriage had received a fortune of £3000. The Burdetts had five children (two sons and three daughters) including Anne, all of whom were well-educated. The elder son practiced medicine in Ireland and the other son was an army officer. Both died at the age of 37.

In September 1779, Ann Burdett married "privately" a young wastrel named Arnold who though but 23 years old had already squandered a handsome fortune. To make the match, she had rejected the hand of a Mr Rann, a sturdy clergyman, and her miseries became great—"the affected sympathy of friends bestowed upon her the title of the *Mourning Bride.*" The couple's distress was only temporarily relieved when they went to live with her mother-in-law at Coventry, but after a month of advice and no financial assistance from this old lady, they set off for London in January 1780. After more misery there, where Mr Arnold continued to indulge his bad habits, with "not the least turn for industry," and she was swindled by a fraudulent millinery partner, they left to set up a boarding school for girls near Coventry. In six months this venture failed, Arnold was carried off to debtor's prison, and Mrs Arnold's father died. (Although the latter had been a man of universal philanthropy, he left his family in poverty.) Arnold contrived to get his own debts paid by friends and then sailed off on a ship out of Bristol, but he died on the voyage six weeks after sailing, at the age of 25.

Mrs Arnold, now in London with her sister, experienced more misfortune, and just as the two women had determined to drown themselves in a pond in Green Park, they were befriended on the very scene by the poet Henry Lucas, son of the Irish patriot Dr Charles Lucas. His arguments "suddenly dissolved their resolutions," and he persuaded Mrs Arnold to go upon the stage instead. This she prepared to do under his tutelage, and Lucas procured her an engagement with Daly at Smock Alley. She assumed the stage name of Belfille "in respect to her husband's family," made her debut as Indiana in *The Conscious Lovers* and played for Daly in 1781–82. She was with Ryder at Crow Street in the next season, after which she returned to England.

By 1783–84, Mrs Belfille was engaged at the Norwich theatre, where she was on the bills for playing Sylvia in *The Recruiting Officer* on 31 January 1784. The Norwich proprietors, however, voted in April 1784 to give notice that her employment would end "with the summer engagement" if Barrett, the manager, could find a proper replacement. Perhaps she remained there for another two seasons, for when she made her debut at Covent Garden in 1786–87, she was announced as from Norwich. Newspaper puffs claimed she had been the favorite heroine of the Norwich company for several seasons and was also a pupil of old Macklin.

Mrs Belfille made her first appearance at Covent Garden on 13 November 1786 in the role of Belinda in *All in the Wrong*. She was apparently well-received, and her voice, beauty, and elegance were compared favorably by the press with those of Mrs Abington, whose characters she promised to be able to fill with "the aid of time and good instruction." Mrs Belville repeated Belinda on 20 November, but despite the favorable reception she had received, the theatre did not sign articles with her for the remainder of the season. The author of her "Memoir" in *Town and Country Magazine* insinuates that the manager—then Harris—"expected the completion of a preliminary article," which her honor forebade. On 6 December she was paid £21 10s. 6d. for a stage dress. Obliged to leave Covent Garden after two performances, she did appear in London one more time. On 20 June 1787 she played Rosalind in *As You Like It* in the opening performance at John Palmer's Royalty Theatre. The players acted that night without salary for the benefit of the London Hospital.

Mrs Belfille was in the Brighton theatre company for the summer season beginning on 18 July 1788 and also played at York. She was engaged to perform in principal roles at Edinburgh for the season of 1789, but she died at Glasgow, according to the *Scots Magazine*, on 23 January 1789. An obituary notice in the *Gentleman's Magazine* for February 1789 stated she "had ranked very high in her profession in the North of England for some time past."

In summing up her person and character the *Town and Country Magazine* described her:

Mrs. Belfille is above the middling size, and well made; her face is handsome, and her voice pleasing. She possesses a strong understanding, and has given a few instances of poetic genius. To her mother and sister her conduct has been truly exemplary; having liberally shared with them the earnings of her profession, and on every occasion evinced filial piety and affection.

Some writers have stated that Mrs Belfille later became Mrs Turner but retained her stage name. We find no evidence for this statement.

*Illustrations*

MAPS AND VIEWS OF LONDON
AND THEATRE SITES

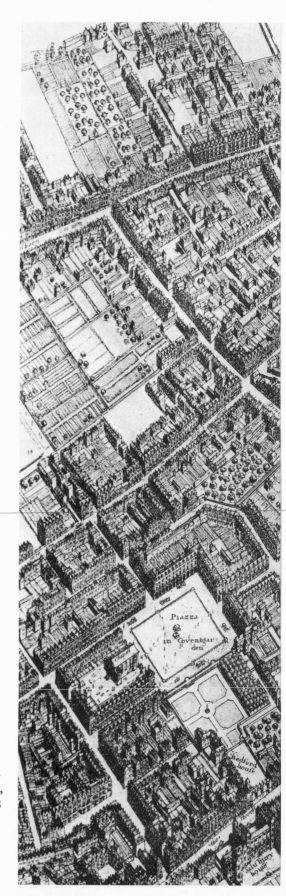

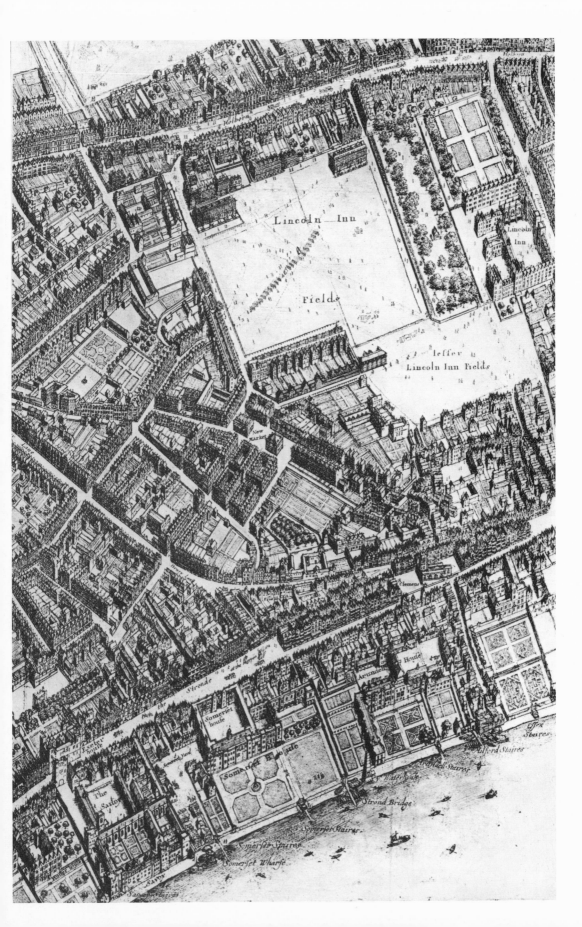

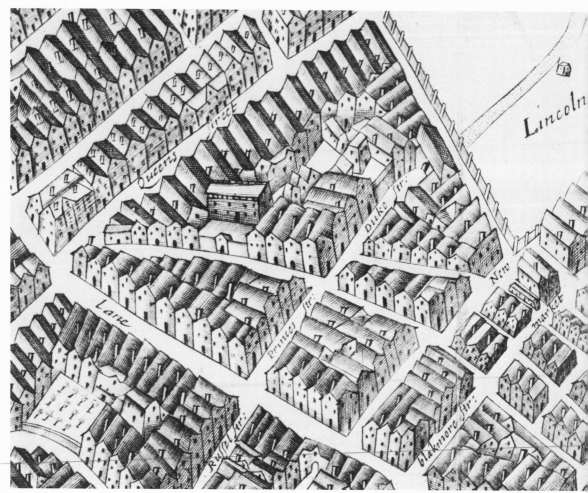

Gibbons's Tennis Court, Later the Vere Street Theatre, and Environs
from Newcourt's map of London, 1658

427

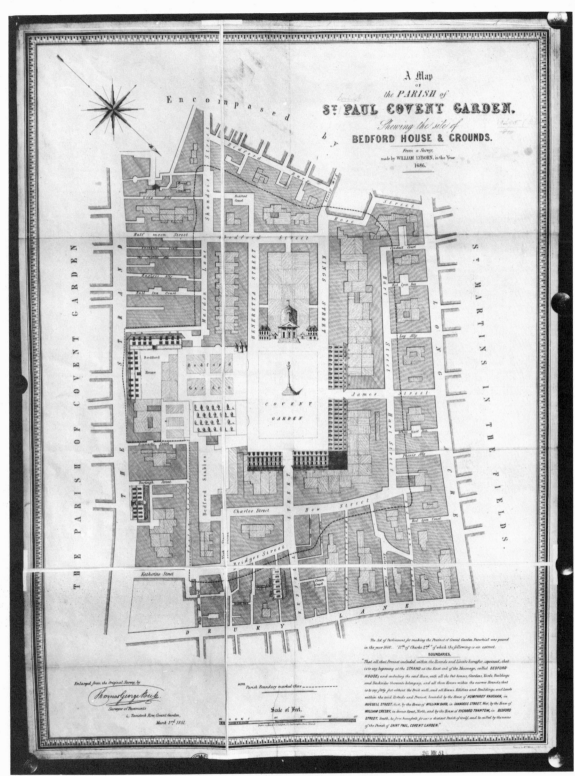

Covent Garden and Environs, Showing the Drury Lane Theatre
from Lyborn's map of Covent Garden, 1686

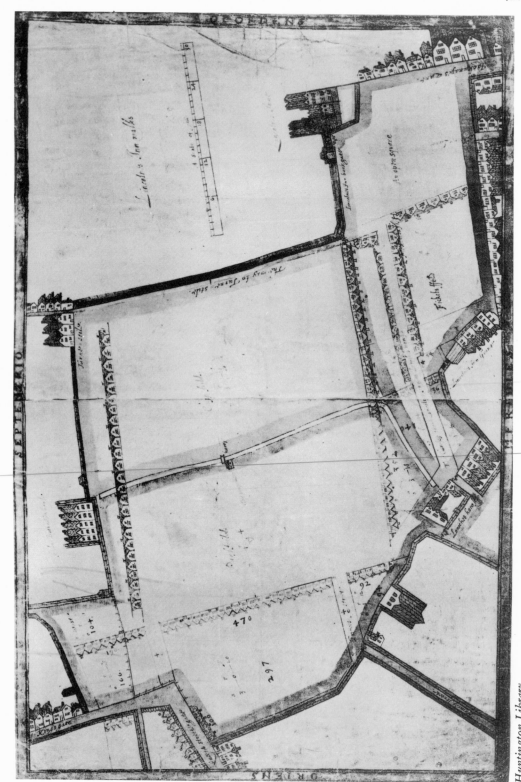

*Huntington Library*

Lincoln's Inn Fields and Environs, Showing Gibbons's Tennis Court,
c. 1657, Which Became the Vere Street Theatre in 1660
from Baildon's edition of *The Black Books of Lincoln's Inn*

North Bank of the Thames, Showing the Dorset Garden Theatre from Morgan and Ogilby's map of London, 1681–82

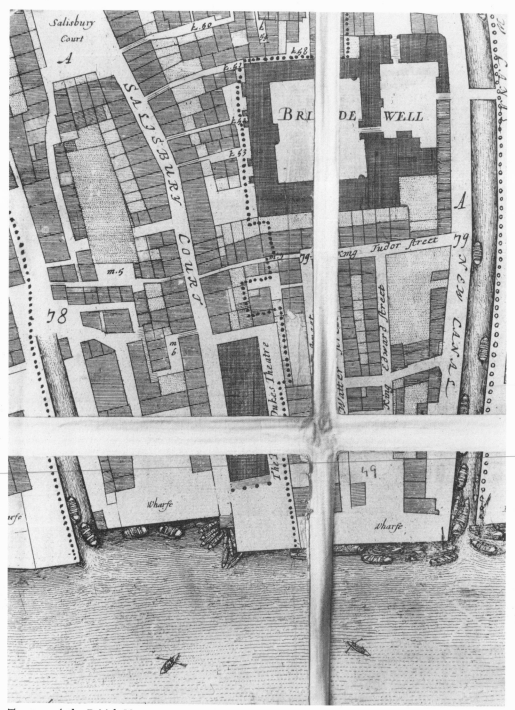

Dorset Garden Theatre Site and Environs
from Morgan and Ogilby's map of London, 1677

431

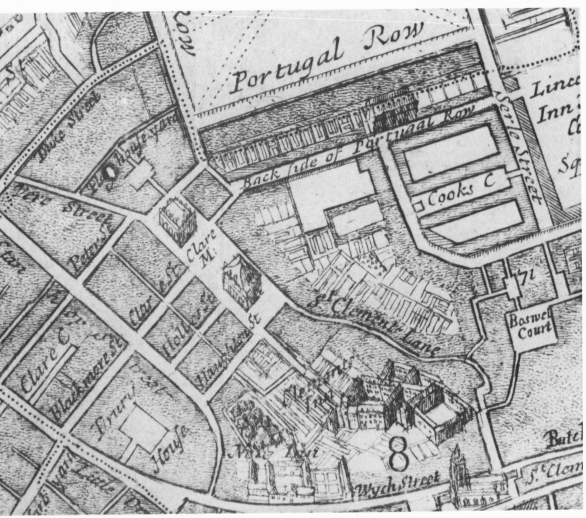

Lincoln's Inn Fields and Environs
from Lea and Glynne's map of London, 1706

London and Westminster from Roque's map of London, 1746

434

Covent Garden Piazza Seen from Russell Street
drawing by Maurer, 1744

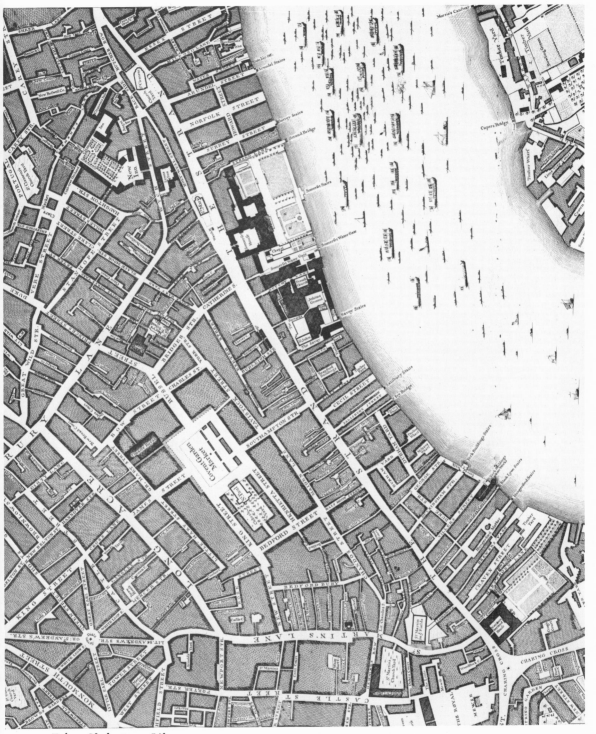

*Folger Shakespeare Library*
Covent Garden and Environs
from Roque's map of London, 1746

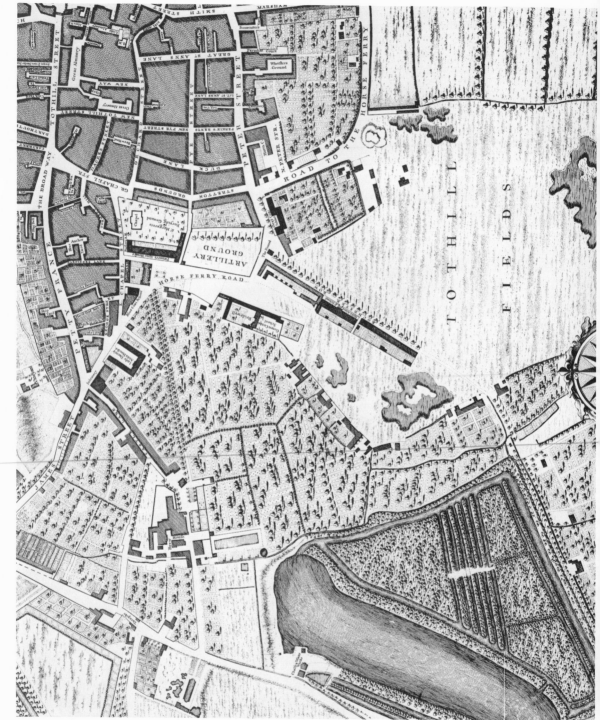

*Folger Shakespeare Library*
Tothill Fields and Environs
from Roque's map of London, 1746

436

437

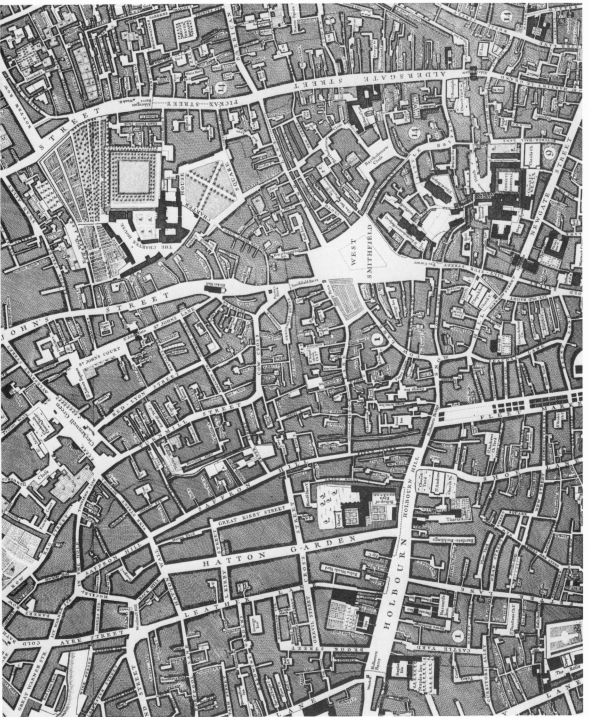

*Folger Shakespeare Library*
West Smithfield and Environs, the Site of Bartholomew Fair
from Roque's map of London, 1746

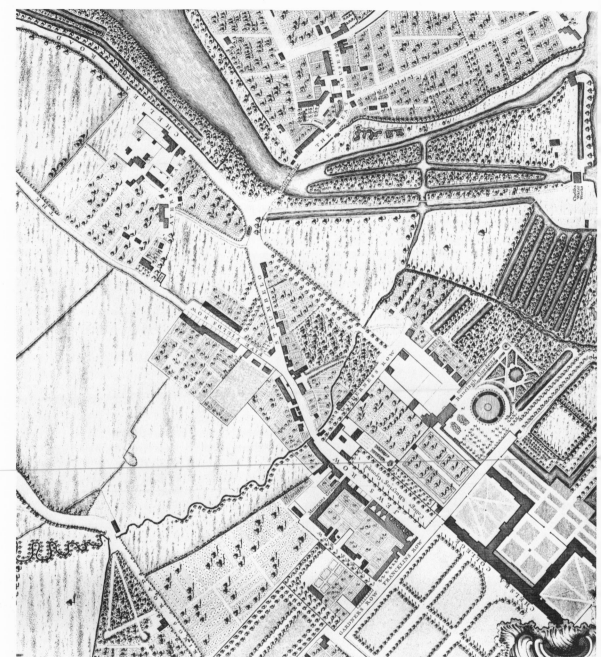

*Folger Shakespeare Library*
Ranelagh Gardens and Environs
from Roque's map of London, 1746

*Folger Shakespeare Library*
Rotherhithe and Environs on the South Bank of the Thames,
where William Bailey's China Hall Playhouse Was Located
from Roque's map of London, 1746

441

Opposite page:
*Folger Shakespeare Library*
Marylebone Gardens and Environs
from Roque's map of London, 1746

*Huntington Library*
Marylebone Gardens, 1761

*Folger Shakespeare Library*
Westminster Bridge and Environs, Showing the Site
of Astley's Amphitheatre South of the Bridge
from Horwood's map of London, 1794

*Folger Shakespeare Library*
Covent Garden and Environs
from Horwood's map of London, 1794